Lecture Notes in Computer Science   **9755**

Commenced Publication in 1973
Founding and Former Series Editors:
Gerhard Goos, Juris Hartmanis, and Jan van Leeuwen

Jia Zhou · Gavriel Salvendy (Eds.)

Human Aspects of IT for the Aged Population

Healthy and Active Aging

Second International Conference, ITAP 2016
Held as Part of HCI International 2016
Toronto, ON, Canada, July 17–22, 2016
Proceedings, Part II

 Springer

Editors
Jia Zhou
Chongqing University
Chongqing
China

Gavriel Salvendy
Purdue University
West Lafayette, IN
USA

ISSN 0302-9743   ISSN 1611-3349 (electronic)
Lecture Notes in Computer Science
ISBN 978-3-319-39948-5   ISBN 978-3-319-39949-2 (eBook)
DOI 10.1007/978-3-319-39949-2

Library of Congress Control Number: 2016940326

LNCS Sublibrary: SL3 – Information Systems and Applications, incl. Internet/Web, and HCI

Printed on acid-free paper

This Springer imprint is published by Springer Nature
The registered company is Springer International Publishing AG Switzerland

Foreword

The 18th International Conference on Human-Computer Interaction, HCI International 2016, was held in Toronto, Canada, during July 17–22, 2016. The event incorporated the 15 conferences/thematic areas listed on the following page.

A total of 4,354 individuals from academia, research institutes, industry, and governmental agencies from 74 countries submitted contributions, and 1,287 papers and 186 posters have been included in the proceedings. These papers address the latest research and development efforts and highlight the human aspects of the design and use of computing systems. The papers thoroughly cover the entire field of human-computer interaction, addressing major advances in knowledge and effective use of computers in a variety of application areas. The volumes constituting the full 27-volume set of the conference proceedings are listed on pages IX and X.

I would like to thank the program board chairs and the members of the program boards of all thematic areas and affiliated conferences for their contribution to the highest scientific quality and the overall success of the HCI International 2016 conference.

This conference would not have been possible without the continuous and unwavering support and advice of the founder, Conference General Chair Emeritus and Conference Scientific Advisor Prof. Gavriel Salvendy. For his outstanding efforts, I would like to express my appreciation to the communications chair and editor of *HCI International News*, Dr. Abbas Moallem.

April 2016   Constantine Stephanidis

HCI International 2016 Thematic Areas
and Affiliated Conferences

Thematic areas:

- Human-Computer Interaction (HCI 2016)
- Human Interface and the Management of Information (HIMI 2016)

Affiliated conferences:

- 13th International Conference on Engineering Psychology and Cognitive Ergonomics (EPCE 2016)
- 10th International Conference on Universal Access in Human-Computer Interaction (UAHCI 2016)
- 8th International Conference on Virtual, Augmented and Mixed Reality (VAMR 2016)
- 8th International Conference on Cross-Cultural Design (CCD 2016)
- 8th International Conference on Social Computing and Social Media (SCSM 2016)
- 10th International Conference on Augmented Cognition (AC 2016)
- 7th International Conference on Digital Human Modeling and Applications in Health, Safety, Ergonomics and Risk Management (DHM 2016)
- 5th International Conference on Design, User Experience and Usability (DUXU 2016)
- 4th International Conference on Distributed, Ambient and Pervasive Interactions (DAPI 2016)
- 4th International Conference on Human Aspects of Information Security, Privacy and Trust (HAS 2016)
- Third International Conference on HCI in Business, Government, and Organizations (HCIBGO 2016)
- Third International Conference on Learning and Collaboration Technologies (LCT 2016)
- Second International Conference on Human Aspects of IT for the Aged Population (ITAP 2016)

Conference Proceedings Volumes Full List

Human Aspects of IT for the Aged Population

Program Board Chairs: **Gavriel Salvendy, USA and P.R. China, and Jia Zhou, P.R. China**

- Ronald M. Baecker, Canada
- Marc-Eric Bobillier Chaumon, France
- Jeff K. Caird, Canada
- Alan H.S. Chan, Hong Kong, SAR China
- Judith Charlton, Australia
- Neil Charness, USA
- Fausto Colombo, Italy
- Sara Czaja, USA
- Richard Darin Ellis, USA
- Hua Dong, P.R. China
- Mireia Fernández-Ardèvol, Spain
- Mohammad Anwar Hossain, Saudi Arabia

- Jiunn-Woei (Allen) Lian, Taiwan
- Eugene Loos, The Netherlands
- Lisa J. Molnar, USA
- Richard Pak, USA
- Denice C. Park, USA
- Joseph Sharit, USA
- Marie Sjölinder, Sweden
- António Teixeira, Portugal
- Wang-Chin Tsai, Taiwan
- Gregg C. Vanderheiden, USA
- Brenda Vrkljan, Canada
- Jonathan Wallace, UK
- Martina Ziefle, Germany

The full list with the program board chairs and the members of the program boards of all thematic areas and affiliated conferences is available online at:

http://www.hci.international/2016/

HCI International 2017

The 19th International Conference on Human-Computer Interaction, HCI International 2017, will be held jointly with the affiliated conferences in Vancouver, Canada, at the Vancouver Convention Centre, July 9–14, 2017. It will cover a broad spectrum of themes related to human-computer interaction, including theoretical issues, methods, tools, processes, and case studies in HCI design, as well as novel interaction techniques, interfaces, and applications. The proceedings will be published by Springer. More information will be available on the conference website: http://2017. hci.international/.

General Chair
Prof. Constantine Stephanidis
University of Crete and ICS-FORTH
Heraklion, Crete, Greece
E-mail: general_chair@hcii2017.org

http://2017.hci.international/

Contents – Part II

Aging and Social Media

Aging, Mobility and Driving

Contents – Part I

Technology Use and Acceptance by Older Users

Psychological and Cognitive Aspects of Interaction and Aging

Mobile and Wearable Technologies for the Elderly

Smart and Assistive Environments

Design Research on Self-service Medical Apparatus and Instruments Aiming at Elderly Users

Jieqiong Huang[✉]

Huazhong University of Science and Technology,
Wuhan, People's Republic of China
jessica.8@me.com

Abstract. With the development of China's society, the aging population has become a more serious problem, and old drift family has come to a common phenomenon. These old parents who live in lonely big cities are away from their own home and are cut from the original social support system as they have to take care of their children's children, thus causing the loneliness of their mental life. And at the same time, they cannot travel conveniently like the young. What is even worse, some old parents are suffering from sugar (urine) disease, hypertension, heart disease and other chronic diseases, as a consequence, the high medical expense as well as their health condition cannot be monitored 24 h a day are causing headaches for them as they have no accessibility to local medical insurance. So, the research on the design of self help medical instrument products aim at the old is of great importance.

In this paper, the severe aging population is set as the background. Then first and foremost, this paper studies the mental state, physiological state and the present status of the products aiming at aged people in domestic market, and analyzes the existing problems of the products for aged people, including slack development of the market, simplicity of service and the randomness of industry's standard; second, based on theoretical knowledge, this paper analyzes the way old people studies, recognize the world and memorize things by referring to literature materials, also this paper analyzes the condition of using scientific and technological products of the old; at last, this paper analyzes the psychological and physical requirement of old people toward self help medical device based on survey and analysis, summarizing a more systematic design method which includes practicability, emotional, accessibility and security.

This paper starts from a people-oriented point, targets the seniors as the target group and studies the design orientation of self help medical devices from a variety of aspects, trying to integrate the special requirements of old people with design elements of this kind of product and combining them with the design of the products to optimize the design of our products. These idea aims at reducing the hidden danger caused by wrong operation and makes it danger-free, giving them care, improving their well-being, leading a more comfortable and heather lifestyle and realizing the care for old citizens. Also, this paper also aims at finding a design method of this kind of product, summarizing the principles of design, breaking the original design patterns of self help medical devices and providing an example for designers.

© Springer International Publishing Switzerland 2016
J. Zhou and G. Salvendy (Eds.): ITAP 2016, Part II, LNCS 9755, pp. 3–15, 2016.
DOI: 10.1007/978-3-319-39949-2_1

Keywords: The aged · Self-service medical apparatus · Physiological needs of aged people · Psychological needs of aged people · Design principles

1 The Development Status of Self-service Medical Equipment for Aged People

Currently, China is already one of the country that mostly affected by aging trends and has the largest population with aged people. With the improvement of life quality, people did enhance their consciousness on their health and the self-service simple medical measuring instrument and health recovery instrument are becoming the development trend for future. The US *Fortune* magazine has taken the self-service medical equipment as one of the industries that will have the fastest-growing business in coming 10 years. Even though the market related to self-service medical equipment in China is still in the embryonic stage, according to current situation in China, it shall inevitably be the emerging sunrise industry in China.

1.1 The Sluggish of Market Development

If we say that at present there's quite few R & D related to self-service medical equipment within China, then the self-service medical equipment designed for aged people shall be very little. Currently, the R & D made on such king of product depends on the influence of those important factors such as technology level etc., this shall be a procedure with long investment cycle, huge capital demand and higher risk, thus domestic enterprises did not pay attention on its R & D, and few investment has been made on the R & D accordingly, without enough enthusiasm, it's still in the stage that taking imitation as their main task.

1.2 Randomness of Industrial Standards

Currently there are many similar products in domestic market of China, they are mainly the products in middle/ low level and lack of independent R & D and innovative ability; this makes the design of such product is not reasonable, with quite little technology content and lower liability, weak practicability. Thus it also results in the non-standard state of the industry in R & D of such kind of product, and the whole industry is also in the chaos.

2 Living Conditions of Aged People

Through close observation to investigate the living conditions of some aged people in depth,the three representatives would be as investigation for total three units with fifteen people of each group.Such three cases that representing the living conditions and the common problems existed in most of aged people:

Case 1.

Observer	Author	Observing place	Daye city	Observing time	Nov. 2015
Observation subject	Grandma Yu	Age	70	Health condition	Old disease with leg ache

The old woman has both the visual and auditory degradation gradually and the old disease with leg ache, both her son and daughter is worked locally, and the old woman was living with her granddaughter separately, has not further trouble to take care of their basic life and daily life.

non-verbal behavior observation

1, Due to the old disease, grandma Yu cannot burden the walk for a long time and in a long distance, sometime the author did also ferry her granddaughter with the old woman together, and Grandma Yu often bent down to hold her knees with hands for rest, the author did want to help her, but Grandma Yu refused tenderly.

2, Occasionally in afternoon, Grandma Yu took some sewing work under sufficient sunshine wearing her presbyopic glasses, the author also helped the old woman to start the sewing work, and the old woman then gave some jokes like "I'm old enough and more disabled, even cannot put a thread through a needle".

3, While chatting with the old woman, the most concerned contents are the son and daughter of the old woman. She did also tell one thing that one day she come out of home for activities, when coming to the street, suddenly her mind was empty and even cannot find the way home.

4, Once the author came to the home of Grandma Yu for a visit, seeing that Grandma Yu was using the washer to clean the clothes, but trying too long a time without any progress.

target behavior analysis

1, Due to her old disease, the old women has the mobility trouble and may need the auxiliary products - by refusing the help provided by other people, it just reflects her strong mentality with self-reliance.

2, Because of the impaired vision, the old women has the trouble in self-care ability and her speech also shows some negative tendencies.

3, The largest thing the old woman wanted is the care from her children surrounding herself, and there's the brain degeneration symptoms with the old woman, it may also affect her daily life accordingly.

4, For the newly sprouted things, especially the usage of high-tech product, the old woman has the degradation on learning ability and with weakened operation ability.

Case 2.

Observer	Author	Observing place	Wuhan City	Observing time	Nov. 2015
Observation subject	Grandma Li	Age	72	Health condition	Old disease with waist ache

Grandma Li was widowed at her middle-age and cultivated his only son alone. Now she's lived with the couple of his son in metropolis and retired at home to help take care of her grandson in nursery school.

non-verbal behavior observation

1、Grandma Li has the old disease with waist ache, and the couple of his son was always busy for their job and only persuaded their mother to see the doctor in hospital alone for several times; but the old woman did think that it's not worthy to spend money in the hospital for such small pains and aches, and has been reluctant to go to a doctor.

2、Occasionally Grandma Li will go back to her home town for short term stay, the couple of her son has also bought an Apple mobile phone for communication, but Grandma Li did rarely use the mobile phone.

3、During the stay in her home town, she usually made the appointment with her old friends to play the flute in the small pavilion of the local park during spare time, when feeling tired she may talk with the old friends, once talking about the couple of his son, her speech was always fulfilled with praises and the expression with satisfaction.

target behavior analysis

1、The old woman has the old disease but was reluctant to go to see a doctor due to no correct consciousness of cure & treatment and not willing to spend money on the disease, thus delayed the treatment time.

2、The old woman has the lowered sensitivity on the high-tech products, and the degradation on the ability of learning, cognition and operation.

3、The old woman may also need her own social circle, so as to fulfill her psychological demand, at the same time, although the old woman was proud of her children, but eagerly want to be accompanied with her children.

Case 3.

Observer	Author	Observing place	Daye City	Observing time	Nov. 2015
Observation subject	Grand pa Xu	Age	75	Health condition	Myocardial infarction, cataract, hypertension

The old man was lived with his wife together, some of their children worked locally for business and some other worked in the field; they are quite busy to work at ordinary times and cannot take care of the aged couple accordingly.

non-verbal behavior observation

1、 The author has spent time to have the meal with the old man, seeing that his hand shaken terribly and can hardly clip the vegetables. The author has persuaded him for several times to change the chopsticks by spoon, but failed finally.

2、 The old man has the disease of hypertension, while the weather is good he may have the outdoor walk along the pedestrian, sometime due to his limited vision with the cataract, he even cannot help falling down in case of small pits or obstructions on the pavement, the author intended to support him, but he did refused.

3、 Occasionally his children did go back home to see the old couple, even in the cold weather the old man will wake up early to buy vegetable and meat from outside, urging his old wife to prepare the delicious meal for their children.

4、 The granddaughter has given a blood pressure gauge as the gift to Grandpa Xu and spent long time to teach her grandpa using it, and asked her grandpa to insist the daily measurement on his blood pressure; usually the old man readily promised but when his granddaughter left, the old man still pushed the blood pressure gauge aside again.

target behavior analysis

1、 The old man has the motor function degradation, cannot use the chopsticks more conveniently and flexibly but refuse to use the spoon with convenience, this shall be the psychological characteristics of the old man that being not satisfied with the old status.

2、 Due to his chronic disease such as the hypertension, the old man needs to be examined regularly, and his walk is also impacted according to the limited vision, but he still refuse to have support from the others, this can prove the psychological demand of self-reliance inside the mind of the old man again.

3、 While his children returned home, the old man was really happy and started to prepare the meal even earlier; being lack of the company of their children, the old man may form the empty and lonely psychological; the occasional return of his children may let the old man feeling extremely satisfactory.

4、 The granddaughter has given a blood pressure gauge as the gift to Grandpa Xu and spent long time to teach her grandpa using it, and asked her grandpa to insist the daily measurement on his blood pressure;finally the old man still pushed the blood pressure gauge aside again. This indicates that the old man shall have the degradation of cognition ability and learning ability, and cannot accept the complex operation methods easily, even form the rejection feeling.

2.1   The Physiological Characteristics of Aged People

Aging is the inevitably spontaneous process of the creature as time goes by, it's the unavoidable and irresistible natural law for each creature, being the complicate natural phenomenon, it shall represent as the degradation of the structure, recessed function, and the decline of adaptation and resistance.

While the human body entering in the aged stage, all the function of their body may generate the obvious recession, although the pace of such process shall vary with each individual, but it's really unavoidable for every one, it means the aged people shall have the degradation on the ability to adapt to the endogenous and exogenous environments.

Through the methods of reviewing the literature, investigating some of the survey targets and asking relative researchers etc., the author did summarize the physiological status change occurred in aged people as following:

Aging in the Form. While being the aged people, first of all the most obvious change is aging in the form, usually it represents as that the hair and beard becoming white and loosen, easy to break off; the skin losing its elasticity and the smooth lustre, and easy to generate the blemishes and wrinkles; the gum tissue becoming in atrophy, and the teeth becoming loosen even falling out; even the aspect characteristics in some aged people such as hunching over, etc.

The Function Decline of Sensory System. Human body's sensory organ system mainly include the sense of vision, hearing, smelling, touch and taste, etc. The physical function of aged people is fickle, with the increase of age, especially on the sensory organs, it shall represent the obvious degradation phenomenon relatively, and impact the life-independent of the aged people to varying degrees. Such as the degradation of the adjustment function in the sense of vision and hearing shall bring great confusion on the life of aged people. According to the newest statistical data, more and more aged people have the eye disease, thereinto, so many aged people have the so-called hyperopia on medicine, that is the commonly referred presbyopia; and some other aged people were deeply influenced by the cataract disease accordingly. The decrease of hearing function shall also be the common problem existed among most of the aged people, so that the aged people usually gave the speech loudly, or hear the voice in closer distance or the higher decibels to complement their deficiency in hearing. The degradation of sensory ability enabled the aged people being not adapted to the environment, meanwhile the chronic degenerative diseases are also easily occurred.

Function Decline in Motor System. Along with the increased age, the aged people may act even slower with uncoordinated movement and bad balance performance; and the aged people may also have the lower speed on learning the new things gradually, their operation ability and reaction speed shall be decreased accordingly, all these are caused by the tissue cell aging and declining of the aged people. So during the common daily life, the aged people may always need supporting tools to relieve such kind of physiological defect.

Decline in Brain Function and Forgetfulness. One of the most common dysfunction along with the aged stage is the decline in brain function and the decreased memory and cognition ability. These shall be the most common symptoms occurred in aged people and they can easily make the aged people with the feeling of "lack of strength to do what they really want". Usually it represents as the increased memory, preoccupied and pointless thinking contents, inattention, fatigue and amnesia, being good at remote memory and weak at the recent memory etc. These are caused by the reasons such as the decrease in the number of brain cells, brain atrophy etc.

Decline in Adaptability. With the loss of functional metabolism, the aged people may have even poor adaptability for the change of internal/ external environments, it usually represents as the decreased immunity of aged people and the declined sensory ability to the external environment and higher occurrence of any kinds of diseases in both small or large scale. Thus, the supervision made on the body of aged people in all kinds of healthy indicators shall be very important accordingly.

2.2   The Psychological States of Aged People

Being in the aged time, there shall be various problems coming with human body, such as the obvious decline in the variety of body function, the troubles of all kinds of diseases in both small and large scale, these enables their adaptability to the external environment being decreased accordingly, and irresistibly accepting the problems such as the transform of their identify and social status shall bring changed in the psychological states of the aged people to the different degree. Through viewing literature and investigating the survey targets, the author concluded the psychological states of aged people in following two categories:

The Changes of Psychological States Induced by the Physiological Dysfunction of Aged People. Being limited by physical function, the aged people can easily have the bigger psychological gap, so as to cause the emotional instability and poor self-control ability and the depression influenced by negative emotion, being prick, anxious and depressed, with inferiority autistic and often with negative speech and behavior, etc.

The Changes of Psychological States Induced by the Changes in Life Style of Aged People. The aged people usually have had the rich life experiences and formed the inherent model and habits; and all those models and habits have been reinforced among the social practice for so many years. The ritualized concept of aged people enables them hardly accepting the new things, so that hardly adapt to the changes of their living conditions.

Therefore, most of aged people usually refused to admit that they're old, some of them still have the confidence on themselves due to their own inherent models and concepts, some other aged people are worried to be their children's burden because of their old age and the declined physical function, then they even are eager to excel others especially.

3 Demand of Aged People

Relative functional characteristics	Behavior characteristic analysis	Matching demand information
Aging in the form	Wrinkle emerging, white hair and beard, loosen teeth and loss of teeth	To adjust own mood; with more communication and exchange.
Decline in visual function	Obvious degradation in vision; with limited vision, the self-independence ability is impacted, resulting in the loss of security feeling.	To see the doctor in time, by using the supporting tools to fulfill the visual demand.
Decline in hearing function	Sharp decrease in hearing, having trouble to communicate with the others, resulting in the character trait such as introversion, less speech, autism etc.	By using the auxiliary tools to fulfill the hearing demand, having more communication with the others, adjusting own attitude.
Decline in motor function	Slower movement, uncoordinated movement, the lowered reaction speed	By using auxiliary tools to ensure their own movement.
Brain function degradation	Forgetfulness, amnesia, decline in cognition ability, the severe in dementia, the decreased ability to accept the new things, seriously impact daily life.	More communication, more contact with the new things, to relieve the amnesia symptoms accordingly.
The lowered adaptability	Cannot adapt or hard to adapt to the changes of internal and external environment, ill at ease	To adjust the attitude, to see the doctor in time.

3.1 Physiological Needs of Aged People

From the abstraction of above tables, it can be seen directly that, due to body's aging and declines in all kinds of system function, aged people shall have the weakened self-independence ability, even with the chronic diseases, and their children couldn't be with them for necessary care, the security potential has been already the important problem among the life of aged people. Thus, the product design for aged people shall take the users of aged people as the starting point, to fulfill the demand that complement the physiological defects due ti aging and the inconvenience due to unattended aged people. Such as the magnified display, vocal operation method and simple operation interface etc.

3.2 Psychological Needs of Aged People

The psychological stages of aged people is both fickle and sensitive, the designed article aimed to take the aged people as the center shall enable them willing to use at first, so the design concept shall be determined according to the using and emotional psychological need of aged people.

The using psychological is to take that the designed article fulfilling the physiological need of aged people and complementing the physiological defect of aged people as the premise. For example, with the increased age, the hearing range of aged people may become smaller and they may take the hearing auxiliary products as reference, first of all the willing of aged people to use such auxiliary tool shall be ensured. According to survey, it shows that, being affected by negative emotion, most of aged people are unwilling to admit that they're old due to their degradation of physiological function, and they are also fear of that being commented as the old, thus some of aged people are not willing to use the auxiliary tools to complement their physiological defect; from this, in order to fulfill the using psychological need of the user, the Danish designer developed the micro hearing AIDS, due to its delicate and compact appearance, it can be easily wore in the ears to achieve the invisibility effect.

The emotional physiological need refers to that the majority of aged people shall be affected by the negative emotion and acted with negative thoughts and deeds and reject the medical equipment and products, and the aged people shall have stronger desire in the care on themselves as their age increased. Thus the emotionalized design shall be incorporated in the aspects such as interaction method, human-computer interface and appearance design etc., in order to fulfill the emotional need of aged people.

4 The Elderly Medical Equipment Product Research Analysis

The above-mentioned products as self-service medical machine are fit for the old and takes tracing pattern of big lead angle, mellow and rigorous geometrical morphology as the principle things from the appearance aspects. Big lead angle and mellow pattern with loveliness sense bring the appetency to buffer the mental pressure of users and improve the fear mood for the cold medical machine without rejection sense. Products appearances of geometric shape could bring sense of brief, rigorous, prudent and order but the appearances would be ordinary if the details are not dealt with very well (Figs. 1, 2, 3 and 4).

From color aspects, most of products could appear colorless serious –gray and white, and low-purity or high clarity color serious. Gray and white could give the peace and pure sense to reconcile with other colors without color bias. Low-purity or high clarity color serious could give soft visual sense as neutral color to be accepted by the old, for example, the light blue color serious as neutral color could be always used in the Siemens medical machine to butter the anxiety mood and give the soft sense.

From the materials aspects, the medical products used for the old are made of plastic materials to make feel softer and safer except the powerful plasticity.

From the operational interface aspects, the operational interface could be divided into display area, control area as the example of blood glucose meter. The display area focuses on the big screen and high contrast colors to meet the visual requirements for identification of the old. The control area focuses on the one-button operation to be learnt and used by the old, and the products creative parts of control area to make the form understand and identify for the user without mistaken or incorrect operation.

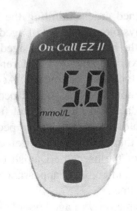

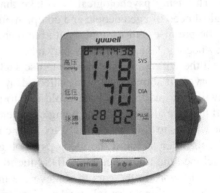

Fig. 1.　.   Fig. 2.　.

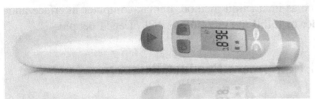

Fig. 3.　.

Fig. 4.　.

5   The Design Principles of the Self-service Medical Equipment and Product for Aged People

The Principle that Taking the User of Aged People as Center. First, the product R & D design for the self-service medical products aimed to the user group of aged people may require the industrial designer to set up the design concept that taking the user group of aged people as the center, insisting in the service & design principle of people first. As the healthy condition and aging status of aged people vary from each other, with the comprehensive knowledge of and understanding the characteristic for aged people- such a special group based on in-depth investigation, it shall abstract the demand information from the user of aged people and implement them into the R & D process of the product, such as the process of research, sorting, design, production and sales etc., thus it can only design the self-service medical product that really meet the demand of aged people.

The Principles of Learnability and Usability. The decline of the various physical function among aged people, such as slow response and movement due to motor function decline, the forgetfulness, these result in the decline of the cognition and learning ability of aged people, and it's even hard for aged people to accept the new

State	Brand	Product	Characteristic analysis
China	Sannuo		1. Mellow geometrical morphology appearance 2. Division for control area and display area by color parts. 3. The design of embossing touch key focuses on the products but is uncomfortable for the old owing to small key. 4. Grounding color and black for grey display area has lower font contrast that could not be identified by the old.
America	Johnson		1. Combined curved geometry appearance of tracing pattern shows its delicacy. 2. The display area with big screen and white background with black text could be easy to identify for the old. 3. One touch key is easier to be learnt and used, and embossing touch grain is more comfortable to be operated. 4. The technological process of rubber bounding the sides is avoided the slipping and falling.
Japan	Kyoto		1. Curved geometrical morphology appearance 2. Small screen could not be identified by the old. 3. It could be automatic controlled without touch key to decrease the mistaken operation.
Germany	Roche		1. Curved geometrical morphology appearance 2. Big screen could be identified by the old. 3. Division for control area and display area by color parts. 4. Touch key icon is used of the common icon to insure the operational information and feedback with meeting the users.

things. The principles of learnability and usability refer to that taking the user as the center, to fulfill the need of user's inherent thinking model and habitual actions etc. For example: the simple operation method; by enhancing the closer connection between production controller and the product functions, to get the match between controller and function more easier to understand; by guaranteeing the user to receive the feedback from production function and commonly-used information & concept even better, to enable the user spending minimum effort to achieve the maximum effect. Therefore, during the R & D process of such product, the principles of learnability and usability shall be necessary.

The Universality Principle. The universality principle for production design refers to that the design objects is all the people, to enable every one using the products fairly, flexibly and conveniently. The user of aged people shall be the vulnerable groups, the modern design initiates to insist on the universality principle, a good design can be used either by the vulnerable groups, or all of the people, thus it may require the designer to make the full consideration on the factors of product and environment and get user-oriented to the largest extent. Even during the using peak the barrier-free lavatory in high speed railway station is also rarely used by people, such design exists in name only, that is because that the design has separated the part of user from common people and cannot assure each user to be treated equally. Thus, for the aspects of human-computer interface design, visual information of the product and its size, they shall both fulfill the special need from the user of aged people, and consider of the using experience of common people.

The Emotional Principle. The emotion shall be human nature, it's in front of the consciousness and thinking and determines the first impression about the people. The communication between human and product is taking the product modeling, function and operating action as the carrier, during the usage of product, the user may generate the physiological and psychological reaction with different experiences and emotion, while the product fulfilling the demand of the user in daily life, it can also fulfill the spiritual demand in higher level. Relevant date show that the aged people mainly generate the negative emotion due to physiological function and life style, their need for esteem and respect, independence is increasing accordingly. While developing the new product, it shall relieve the negative emotion such as the sense of loneliness and frustration of aged people through the media like product modeling and operating action etc.

Principles of Safety and Reliability. With the decreased physiological function, the movement speed, memory, response ability, sense of vision, hearing and touch etc. of aged people may be declined in different levels respectively, while using the product, due to incorrect operation, the slow response speed etc., it may cause the potential safety hazard accordingly. Therefore, the factors for product's safety and reliability must be emphasized, thus it may require the designers to make the overall prediction on for the environmental status that may cause the safety potential during the development of product, and make the effort to eliminate unsafe factors through the design, such as the safety of product materials, the feasibility of product operation method, the reliability of product function, etc.

6 Conclusion

The self-service medical equipment for aged people shall be the development trend for future, the industrial designers shall pay attention to the independent R & D of product, to combine the special demand of aged people with the design elements of such kind of product and incorporate them into the product accordingly. During the R & D process of product, to insist and implement the principles of that taking aged people as center, the learnability and usability, universality and emotional principle and the principles of safety and reliability, to enable the product fulfilling the demand of user for daily use meanwhile fulfilling the emotional demand of user, to enable the user feeling the humanity care during using the product, and expect the barrier-free use of the product for each user, guiding them to the comfortable and healthy living conditions.

References

1. Norman, D.: The Emotional Design. Electronic Industry Press, Beijing (2015)
2. Norman, D.: Design Psychology. Citic Publishing House, Beijing (2006)
3. Sol, R.L.: The College, the Cognitive Psychology. Education Science Press, Beijing (1990)
4. GuanZhong, L.: Walk the Road of Chinese Contemporary Industrial Design. Hunan Science and Technology Press, China (2004)
5. Youyuan, S., Jie, T.: China home medical equipment present situation and prospects, vol. 17, no. 2, 28–29 July 2010

Gamification and Information Fusion for Rehabilitation: An Ambient Assisted Living Case Study

Javier Jiménez Alemán[1], Nayat Sanchez-Pi[2(✉)], Luis Martí[1],
José Manuel Molina[3], and Ana Cristina Bicharra García[1]

[1] Institute of Computing, Fluminense Federal University, Niterói, Brazil
{jjimenezaleman,lmarti,bicharra}@ic.uff.br
[2] Institute of Mathematics and Statistics,
Rio de Janeiro State University, Rio de Janeiro, Brazil
nayat@ime.uerj.br
[3] Computer Science Department, Carlos III University of Madrid, Madrid, Spain
molina@ia.uc3m.es

Abstract. Nowadays elders, often find it difficult to keep track of their cognitive and functional abilities required for remaining independent in their homes. Ambient Assisted Living (AAL) are the Ambient Intelligence based technologies for the support of daily activities to elders. Traditional rehabilitation is an example of a common activity elders may require and that usually implies they move to the rehabilitation clinics, which is the main reason for treatment discontinuation. Tele-rehabilitation is a solution that not only may help elders but also their family members and health professionals to monitor elder's treatment. The purpose of this paper is to present a tele-rehabilitation system that uses the motion-tracking sensor of the Kinect, to allow the elderly users natural interaction, combined with a set of external sensors as a form of input. Data fusion techniques are applied in order to integrate these data for detecting right movements and to monitor elder's treatment in the rehabilitation process.

Keywords: Gamification · Data fusion · Ambient assisted living · Human-computer interaction

1 Introduction

Ambient Assisted Living (AAL) are the Ambient Intelligence based technologies for the support of daily activities to elders. Nowadays elders, often find it difficult to keep track of their cognitive and functional abilities required for remaining independent in their homes. Traditional rehabilitation is an example of a common activity elders may require and that usually implies they move to the rehabilitation clinics, which is the main reason for treatment discontinuation. Tele-rehabilitation is a solution that not only may help elders but also their family members and health professionals to monitor elder's treatment [20].

© Springer International Publishing Switzerland 2016
J. Zhou and G. Salvendy (Eds.): ITAP 2016, Part II, LNCS 9755, pp. 16–25, 2016.
DOI: 10.1007/978-3-319-39949-2_2

Recently the domain of HCI began to grow rapidly with new forms of input (GPS, accelerometers, motion sensors, etc.) and new output devices (mobile phones, tablets, projectors, wearables, etc.) emerging in quick succession [1]. These has reveled a new paradigm of interaction which is "natural interaction", where the use of these ubiquitous sensors allow to interact with the user via gestures and pointing. An example of technology is the Kinect which has the capability to interpret three-dimensional human body movements in real-time and makes the human body the controller. These gaming technologies has been used and adapted by researchers and therapists to build assistive systems.

The purpose of this paper is to present a tele-rehabilitation system that uses the motion-tracking sensor of the Kinect, to allow the elderly users natural interaction, combined with a set of external sensors as a form of input. The elders interact with the system in a 3D environment, where they perform multiple movement combinations without the need of an attached device or a controller thanks to the Kinect. Information fusion techniques are applied to the data extracted to give a more precise feedback to the user regarding the rehabilitation exercises and a case study for AAL is presented. The paper is organized as follows: Sect. 2 presents the analysis of some studies and AAL applications for the elderly people. Section 3 describes the system model and design. Finally, in Sect. 4, a case study is presented and finally some conclusions are given and future improvements are proposed.

2   Related Work

Ambient Intelligence (AmI) refers to a vision in which people are empowered by an electronic environment that is sensitive and responsive to their needs, and is aware of their presence. Its target is improving quality of life by creating the desired atmosphere and functionality through intelligent and inter-connected systems and services. Inside AmI, Ambient Assisted Living (AAL) is an emergent area that provides useful mechanisms that allows tracking elders through sensoring, for example, using mobile devices, that not only work like communication devices, but also are equipped with several sensors like accelerometer, gyroscope, proximity sensors, microphones, GPS system and camera. Ambient Assisted Living (AAL) can be defined as the use of information and communication technologies (ICT) in a persons daily living and working environment to enable them to stay active longer, remain socially connected and live independently into old age [19].

Gamification dwells on established approaches like serious games and is defined as an "umbrella term for the use of video game elements to improve user experience and user engagement in non-game services and applications" [11]. We used gamification to motivate the patients, which means better adherence to the treatments and faster results.

Several other applied games have been proposed for rehabilitation activities. However, the problem with the sensors precision is still not solved by any of them and it has received less attention. The combination of observations from a number of different sensors provide a solid and complete description of the task, so information fusion techniques match perfectly in this solution.

Information fusion focused in sensors has become increasingly relevant during the last years due to its aim to combine observations from a number of different sensors to provide a solid and complete description of an environment or process of interest. The information fusion systems are characterized by its robustness, increased confidence, reduced ambiguity and uncertainty, and improved resolution.

The Data Fusion Model maintained by the JDL Data Fusion Group is the most widely used method for categorizing data fusion-related functions. They proposed a model of six levels, of which the first is related to information extraction, and the last with the extraction of knowledge. The JDL model was never intended to decide a concrete order on the data fusion levels. Levels are not alluded to be processed consecutively, and it can be executed concurrently [8]. Although the JD data fusion model has been criticized, still constitutes a reference to design and build systems to obtain information from the data in complex systems and generate knowledge from the extracted information.

After years of intensive research that is mainly focused on low-level information fusion (IF), the focus is currently shifting towards high-level information fusion [7]. Compared to the increasingly mature field of low-level IF, theoretical and practical challenges posed by high-level IF are more difficult to handle.

Some of the applications that involve high-level IF are:

- Defense [1,2,9,12,21]
- Computer and Information Security [10,13]
- Disaster Management [22–25]
- Fault Detection [3–5]
- Environment [15,16,18]

But these contributions lack of a well-defined spatio-temporal constraints on relevant evidence and suitable models for causality [6].

Our proposed model provides the big picture about risk analysis for that employee at that place in that moment in a real world environment. Our contribution is to build a causality model for accidents investigation by means of a well-defined spatio-temporal constraints on offshore oil industry domain. We use ontological constraints in the post-processing mining stage to prune resulting rules.

3   Model

In this section more details about the Knowledge Retrieval Model are provided. First a detailed description of the proposed architecture, domain ontology and reasoning process described by means of inductive learning process.

3.1 System Architecture

The architecture of our fusion framework is depicted in Fig. 1. This architecture was extended from our previous work [26–29]. Following we give some new details of the architecture.

The system developed has a hierarchical architecture with the following layers: Services layer, Context Acquisition layer, Context Representation layer, Context Information Fusion layer and Infrastructure layer. The hierarchical architecture reflects the complex functionality of the system as shown in the following brief description of the functionality of particular layers:

- Infrastructure Layer. The lowest level of the movement management architecture is the Sensor Layer which represents the variety of physical and logical sensor agents producing sensor-specific information. Kinect sensor and external arduino sensors used Fig. 5:
  1. Microcontroller ESP8266 HUZZAH
  2. Accelerometer and gyroscope MPU-6050
  3. Temperature sensor DS18B20
  4. Capacitive Touch
- Context Acquisition: The link between sensors (lowest layer) and the representation layer.
- Context Representation: This is where the low-level information fusion occurs by means of an ontology.
- Context Information Fusion layer: This layer takes the information of Kinect sensor and other contextual information related to the user as well as external sensors and transforms it into a standard format. This is where the high-level information fusion occurs. It is here where reasoning about context and trained neural network occurs. Extended description is given in next section.
- Service Layer. This layer interacts with the variety of users of the system (elders/health personnel/caregivers/ family members) and therefore needs to address several issues (who can access the information and to what degree of accuracy), privacy and security of interactions between users and the system.

3.2 Ontology

Normally, ontology represents a conceptualization of particular domains. In our case, we will use the ontology for representing the contextual information of the ambient assisted living environment. Ontologies are particularly suitable to project parts of the information describing and being used in our daily life onto a data structure usable by computers.

Using ontologies provides an uniform way for specifying the model's core concepts as well as an arbitrary amount of subconcepts and facts, altogether enabling contextual knowledge.

An ontology is defined as "an explicit specification of a conceptualization" [14]. An ontology created for a given domain includes a set of concepts as well as relationships connecting them within the domain. Collectively, the concepts and

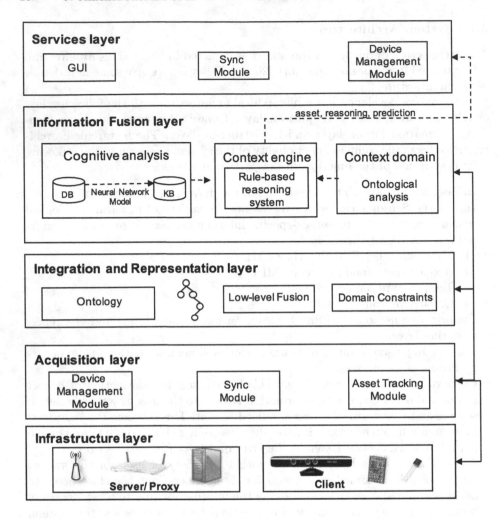

Fig. 1. Architecture.

the relationships form a foundation for reasoning about the domain. A comprehensive, well-populated ontology with classes and relationships closely modeling a specific domain represents a vast compendium of knowledge in the domain.

Furthermore, if the concepts in the ontology are organized into hierarchies of higher-level categories, it should be possible to identify the category (or a few categories) that best classify the context of the user. Within the area of computing, the ontological concepts are frequently regarded as classes that are organized into hierarchies. The classes define the types of attributes, or properties common to individual objects within the class. Moreover, classes are interconnected by relationships, indicating their semantic interdependence (relationships are also regarded as attributes).

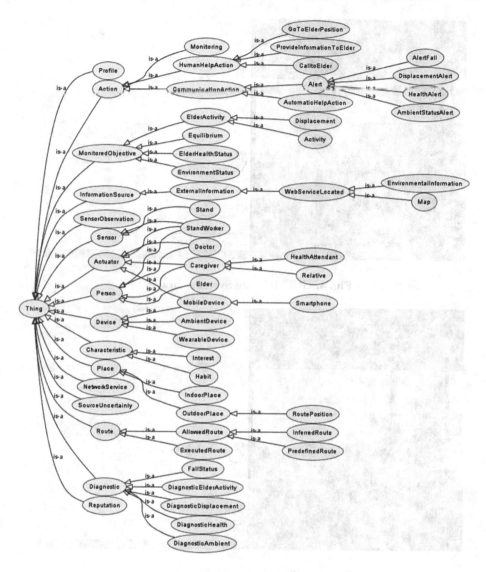

Fig. 2. Ontology hierarchical concepts.

We built a domain ontology for the Ambient Assisted Living environment (AAL) [17]. We also obtain the inferences that describe the dynamic side and finally we group the inferences sequentially to form tasks. Principal concepts of the ontology can be checked at Fig. 2.

3.3 Data Fusion Model

JDL model of six levels, of which the first is related to information extraction, and the last with the extraction of knowledge. These levels are characterize as:

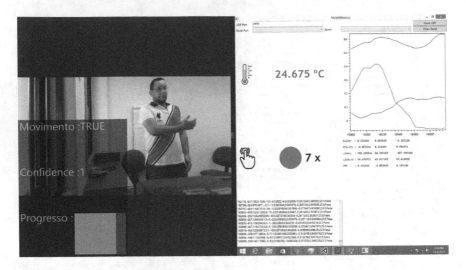

Fig. 3. GUI- Telecare System - in use

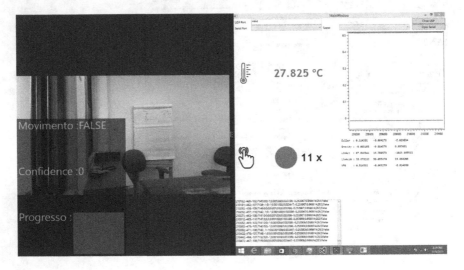

Fig. 4. GUI- Telecare System - no use

- Level 0 (Source Preprocessing/Subject Assessment): Estimation and prediction of observable states of the signal or object, based in the association and characterization of data at a signal level.
- Level 1 (Object Assessment): In this level, objects are identified and located. Hence, the object situation by fusing the attributes from diverse sources is reported.
- Level 2 (Situation Assessment): The goal of this level is construct a picture from incomplete information provided by level 1, that is, to relate the reconstructed entity with an observed event.

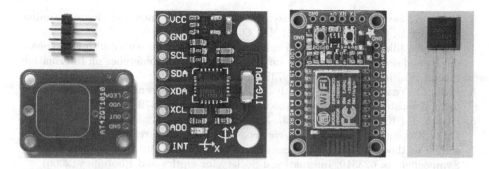

Fig. 5. Temperature sensor, micro-controller, accelerometer and gyroscope, temperature sensor and capacitive touch sensor

- Level 3 (Impact Assessment): Estimation and prediction of the effects that would have the actions provided by participants, taking into account the information extracted at lower levels.
- Level 4 (Process Refinement): Modification of data capture systems (sensors) and processing the same, to ensure the targets of the mission.
- Level 5 (User or Cognitive Refinement): Modification of the way that people react from the experience and knowledge gained.

There is a need of a fusion framework to combine data from multiples sources to achieve more specific inferences. A fusion system must satisfy the user's functional needs and extend their sensory capabilities (Fig. 3).

4   Final Remarks

Although we have introduced and presented the novel tele-rehabilitation solution, it must be pointed out that, this approach is currently deployed as part of a larger activity tracking system that includes also outdoor sensors. The first functional prototype of the system is currently developed (Fig. 4).

Acknowledgments. This work was partially funded by FAPERJ APQ1 Project 211.500/2015, FAPERJ APQ1 Project 211.451/2015, CNPq PVE Project 314017/2013-5 and by Projects MINECO TEC2012-37832-C02-01, CICYT TEC2011-28626-C02-02.

References

1. Ahlberg, S., Hörling, P., Johansson, K., Jöred, K., Kjellström, H., Mårtenson, C., Neider, G., Schubert, J., Svenson, P., Svensson, P., et al.: An information fusion demonstrator for tactical intelligence processing in network-based defense. Inf. Fusion 8(1), 84–107 (2007)
2. Aldinger, T., Kao, J.: Data fusion and theater undersea warfare-an oceanographer's perspective. In: OCEANS 2004. MTTS/IEEE TECHNO-OCEAN 2004, vol. 4, pp. 2008–2012. IEEE (2004)

3. Bashi, A.: Fault Detection for Systems with Multiple Unknown Modes and Similar Units. Ph.D. thesis, University of New Orleans (2010)
4. Bashi, A., Jilkov, V.P., Li, X.R.: Fault detection for systems with multiple unknown modes and similar units - Part I. In: 12th International Conference on Information Fusion (FUSION 2009), pp. 732–739. IEEE (2009)
5. Basir, O., Yuan, X.: Engine fault diagnosis based on multi-sensor information fusion using dempster-shafer evidence theory. Inf. Fusion 8(4), 379–386 (2007)
6. Blasch, E., Kadar, I., Salerno, J., Kokar, M.M., Das, S., Powell, G.M., Corkill, D.D., Ruspini, E.H.: Issues and challenges of knowledge representation and reasoning methods in situation assessment (level 2 fusion). In: Defense and Security Symposium, p. 623510. International Society for Optics and Photonics (2006)
7. Blasch, E., Llinas, J., Lambert, D., Valin, P., Das, S., Chong, C., Kokar, M., Shahbazian, E.: High level information fusion developments, issues, and grand challenges: fusion 2010 panel discussion. In: 2010 13th Conference on Information Fusion (FUSION), pp. 1–8. IEEE (2010)
8. Blázquez Gil, G., Berlanga, A., Molina, J.M.: Incontexto: multisensor architecture to obtain people context from smartphones. Int. J. Distrib. Sens. Netw. 2012 (2012)
9. Chong, C.Y., Liggins, M., et al.: Fusion technologies for drug interdiction. In: IEEE International Conference on Multisensor Fusion and Integration for Intelligent Systems (MFI 1994), pp. 435–441. IEEE (1994)
10. Corona, I., Giacinto, G., Mazzariello, C., Roli, F., Sansone, C.: Information fusion for computer security: state of the art and open issues. Inf. Fusion 10(4), 274–284 (2009)
11. Deterding, S., Sicart, M., Nacke, L., O'Hara, K., Dixon, D.: Gamification. using game-design elements in non-gaming contexts. In: CHI 2011 Extended Abstracts on Human Factors in Computing Systems, pp. 2425–2428. ACM (2011)
12. Gad, A., Farooq, M.: Data fusion architecture for maritime surveillance. In: Proceedings of the Fifth International Conference on Information Fusion (FUSION 2002), vol. 1, pp. 448–455. IEEE (2002)
13. Giacinto, G., Roli, F., Sansone, C.: Information fusion in computer security. Inf. Fusion 10(4), 272–273 (2009)
14. Gómez-Romero, J., Patricio, M.A., García, J., Molina, J.M.: Ontological representation of context knowledge for visual data fusion. In: 12th International Conference on Information Fusion (FUSION 2009), pp. 2136–2143. IEEE (2009)
15. Heiden, U., Segl, K., Roessner, S., Kaufmann, H.: Ecological evaluation of urban biotope types using airborne hyperspectral hymap data. In: 2nd GRSS/ISPRS Joint Workshop on Remote Sensing and Data Fusion over Urban Areas, pp. 18–22. IEEE (2003)
16. Hubert-Moy, L., Corgne, S., Mercier, G., Solaiman, B.: Land use and land cover change prediction with the theory of evidence: a case study in an intensive agricultural region of france. In: Proceedings of the Fifth International Conference on Information Fusion (FUSION 2002), vol. 1, pp. 114–121. IEEE (2002)
17. Jiménez Alemán, J., Sanchez-Pi, N., Bicharra Garcia, A.C.: Opportunistic sensoring using mobiles for tracking users in ambient intelligence. In: Mohamed, A., Novais, P., Pereira, A., Villarrubia-González, G., Fernández-Caballero, A. (eds.) Ambient Intelligence - Software and Applications - 6th International Symposium on Ambient Intelligence (ISAmI 2015). Advances in Intelligent Systems and Computing, vol. 376, pp. 115–123. Springer, Heidelberg (2015). http://dx.doi.org/10.1007/978-3-319-19695-4_12

18. Khalil, A., Gill, M.K., McKee, M.: New applications for information fusion and soil moisture forecasting. In: 8th International Conference on Information Fusion (FUSION 2005), vol. 2, p. 7. IEEE (2005)
19. Koch, S., Hägglund, M.: Health informatics and the delivery of care to older people. Maturitas **63**(3), 195–199 (2009)
20. Korn, O., Brach, M., Schmidt, A., Hörz, T., Konrad, R.: Context-sensitive user-centered scalability: an introduction focusing on exergames and assistive systems in work contexts. In: Göbel, S., Müller, W., Urban, B., Wiemeyer, J. (eds.) GameDays 2012 and Edutainment 2012. LNCS, vol. 7516, pp. 164–176. Springer, Heidelberg (2012)
21. Liggins, M.E., Bramson, A., et al.: Off-board augmented fusion for improved target detection and track. In: 1993 Conference Record of The Twenty-Seventh Asilomar Conference on Signals, Systems and Computers, pp. 295–299. IEEE (1993)
22. Little, E.G., Rogova, G.L.: Ontology meta-model for building a situational picture of catastrophic events. In: 8th International Conference on Information Fusion (FUSION 2005), vol. 1, pp. 1–8. IEEE (2005)
23. Llinas, J.: Information fusion for natural and man-made disasters. In: Proceedings of the Fifth International Conference on Information Fusion (FUSION 2002), vol. 1, pp. 570–576. IEEE (2002)
24. Llinas, J., Moskal, M., McMahon, T.: Information fusion for nuclear, chemical, biological & radiological (NCBR) battle management support/disaster response management support. Technical report, Center for MultiSource Information Fusion, School of Engineering and Applied Sciences, University of Buffalo, USA (2002)
25. Mattioli, J., Museux, N., Hemaissia, M., Laudy, C.: A crisis response situation model. In: 10th International Conference on Information Fusion (FUSION 2007), pp. 1–7. IEEE (2007)
26. Sanchez-Pi, N.: Intelligent techniques for context-aware systems. Ph.D. thesis, Departmento de Informática, Universidad Carlos III de Madrid, Colmenarejo, Spain (2011)
27. Sanchez-Pi, N., Martí, L., Molina, J.M., Garcia, A.C.B.: High-level information fusion for risk and accidents prevention in pervasive oil industry environments. In: Corchado, J.M., et al. (eds.) PAAMS 2014. CCIS, vol. 430, pp. 202–213. Springer, Heidelberg (2014)
28. Sanchez-Pi, N., Martí, L., Molina, J.M., Garcia, A.C.B.: An information fusion framework for context-based accidents prevention. In: 2014 Proceedings of the 17th International Conference on Information Fusion (FUSION), pp. 1–8. IEEE (2014)
29. Sánchez-Pi, N., Molina, J.M.: A centralized approach to an ambient assisted living application: an intelligent home. In: Omatu, S., Rocha, M.P., Bravo, J., Fernández, F., Corchado, E., Bustillo, A., Corchado, J.M. (eds.) IWANN 2009, Part II. LNCS, vol. 5518, pp. 706–709. Springer, Heidelberg (2009)

Dynamic Characteristics of the Transformation of Interpersonal Distance in Cooperation

Yosuke Kinoe[✉] and Nami Mizuno

Faculty of Intercultural Communication, Hosei University,
2-17-1, Fujimi, Chiyoda City, Tokyo 102-8160, Japan
`kinoe@hosei.ac.jp`

Abstract. This paper describes an empirical study that investigated how inter-personal distance under a cooperative situation varied in accordance with the differences of task, device, orientation of the body, and posture. Twenty young adults participated. The results revealed statistically significant effects of task (p < .01), device (p < .01), and orientation of the body (p < .01) on the transformation of inter-personal distance. In particular, there were statistically significant differences between "no particular task" > "holding a device" > "cooperative tasks"; between "face-to-face" > "side-by-side"; and between "notebook-PC" > "blackboard" or "smartphone". The results also suggested that not only a single cause but the complex of multiple factors of social interaction influenced the transformation of interpersonal distances. A new model of the measurement was also proposed.

Keywords: Personal space · Interpersonal distance · Measurement · Human services

1 Introduction

The *personal space* concept is a useful tool to investigate human spatial behavior in a relatively closer domain. It can be defined as "an area individuals actively maintain around themselves into which others cannot intrude without arousing some sort of discomfort" [13]. Research on human spatial behavior influenced various design issues not limited to the area of architecture and environmental design [4], but can be extended to the design of human services such as care-giving [12], and proxemics of social robots.

The present paper describes an experimental study that investigates dynamic characteristics of human spatial behavior in a cooperative situation.

1.1 Interpersonal Distance in a Cooperation

The dimensions of personal space are not fixed but vary according to internal states, culture, and context [14]. Research findings suggested that the influences upon inter-personal distance were caused by various factors including gender [5], attractiveness [5], personality traits [4], attitudes, culture, psychological disorders, approach angle [17], task [7], eye contact [1], and environmental factors including room size, lighting

© Springer International Publishing Switzerland 2016
J. Zhou and G. Salvendy (Eds.): ITAP 2016, Part II, LNCS 9755, pp. 26–34, 2016.
DOI: 10.1007/978-3-319-39949-2_3

conditions and outdoor/indoor [3]. Also, some conventional literature reported other factors such as race, age, cortical arousal seemed to play a minor role [16].

On the other hand, a cooperation occupies an important dimension of everyday life, however, few studies of the personal space were concerned with a cooperative situation (*e.g.* [15]). Note that unique and interesting movements of the body often appear in human spatial behavior of a cooperative situation. The present study shed light on the dynamic characteristics of human spatial behavior in a cooperation.

1.2 Re-Examining the Measurement of Interpersonal Distance

The stop-distance method had been widely used as a feasible and reliable technique for measuring an interpersonal distance [6]. In this method, the distance is usually measured by a foot position. It well works especially when participants stand in upright posture in a sufficient distance. However, a considerable error possibly occurs under a sort of situation such as a cooperative task. For example, collaborators sometimes move their upper bodies and lean back or bend their heads toward a partner, without moving their feet positions. Kinoe et al. [7] re-examined the measurement of interpersonal distance through their empirical study. In addition to a foot position, they focused on several landmarks on human body, which included Acromion, Thelion, Scapula, Vertex, and the tip of the nose (Fig. 1-a). Based on their previous study, we propose three different concepts of modeling an interpersonal distance: (i) *the "surface" model* which employed the distance between body surfaces, (ii) *the "center-center" model* which employed the distance between the centers of the bodies, and (iii) *the "center-to-surface" model*. As we focused on a cooperative situation, we adopted the "center-center" model (Fig. 1-b).

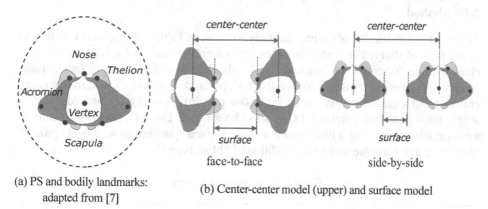

(a) PS and bodily landmarks: adapted from [7]

(b) Center-center model (upper) and surface model

Fig. 1. Landmarks of human body and models for measuring interpersonal distance

1.3 Our Approach

Our approach to the present study is threefold: (a) to shed light on the dynamic characteristics of the transformation of interpersonal distance with the emphasis on a cooperative situation, (b) to focus on the influences of four factors including task, device, orientation of the body, and posture, based on the framework by Kinoe and Hama [8], and (c) to employ a new model of the measurement effective for capturing the transformation of interpersonal distance in a cooperative situation. Based on the study, we also discuss the enhancement of a measurement technology, and the necessity as well as the difficulty of an empirical study of elderly persons on interpersonal space needs in a cooperation.

2   Empirical Study

The present study aimed to investigate the dynamic characteristics of the transformation of interpersonal distance between individuals in a cooperative situation (Fig. 2).

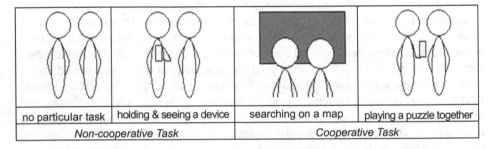

no particular task	holding & seeing a device	searching on a map	playing a puzzle together
Non-cooperative Task		*Cooperative Task*	

Fig. 2. Spacing behavior in non-cooperative and cooperative situations

2.1   Method

The experimental design of the present study is shown in Table 1. There were four factors in the present study. The within-subject factors were "posture" (2 levels: standing vs. chair-sitting), "orientation of the body" (2 levels: side-by-side vs. face-to-face), "task" {6 levels: (no task vs. before a cooperative task (= holding a device) vs. during a cooperative task) x (searching on a map vs. jigsaw puzzle)} (see Fig. 2), and "device" (3 levels: smartphone vs. notebook-PC vs. blackboard) (see Table 1). Due to the nature of a cooperative task using a blackboard, a "face-to-face" position as well as a "puzzle" task, were not available under the condition of "blackboard".

Table 1. Experimental Design

Factor		Level		
Within subject	Posture	2	standing, chair-sitting	
	Body orientation	2	side-by-side, face-to-face	
	Device	3	smartphone, notebook-PC, blackboard	
	Task	6	map	no task - before task (holding a device) - during task (using a device)
			puzzle	no task - before task (holding a device) - during task (using a device)

Participants. Twenty healthy university students (6 males, 14 females, age range: 18–23 years, who were educated between 13–16 years) participated. The participants were recruited individually and were informed that the study dealt with spatial preferences.

Materials and Apparatus. The materials consisted of combinations of three devices and two types of applications. The devices were a smartphone (iPhone; H: 123.8 × W: 58.6 × D: 7.6 mm, 112 g), a notebook-PC (Macbook Pro; H: 247.1 × W: 358.9 × D: 18 mm, 2.04 kg), and a blackboard (H: 1.50 × W: 3.40 m). The applications were puzzles (Jigty Jigsaw Puzzles ver.3.0) and maps which included Google Maps and a printed map (H: 375 × W: 295 mm) put up on a blackboard.

Procedure. The data collection was performed by ten different pairs of participants (A and B) who were not acquaintances. At first, one of participants (A) took a role of an evaluator and the other participant (B) took a role of an assistant experimenter (approacher). The data collection was performed in order of "no task", "holding a device", and cooperative tasks including "searching on a map" and "jigsaw puzzle". According to the experimental design, a set of 42 data of the interpersonal distances under different conditions were obtained per each participant. After all the data was obtained from a participant A, the participants exchanged their roles.

The stop-distance method was employed to measure interpersonal distances. At first, an assistant experimenter initially stood three meters from an evaluator and then approached an evaluator, in small steps (approx. 25 cm per step) at a constant slow velocity (approx. one step per two sec.) until an evaluator began to feel uncomfortable about the closeness. By saying stop, an assistant experimenter's approach halted. In order to minimize a measurement error, an evaluator was allowed to make fine re-adjustment of their positions. A foot position was used under non-cooperative task conditions (i.e. "no task" and "holding a device"). On the other hand, in a cooperative task condition, the experimenter asked an evaluator and an assistant experimenter to freeze their movements when they performed a cooperative task for approximately one minute in a distance comfortable to an evaluator. The remaining distance between the centers of their bodies was measured (see Fig. 1-b).

The data collection was carried out during daytime, in an empty and quiet class room (approx. 6.5 m × 6.3 m with a ceiling height of 3.0 m) of a university located in Tokyo metropolitan area. The brightness was appropriately maintained with an indoor lighting instead of natural light from outside. It took approximately one hour per participant. The data were collected in January 2015.

Data Analysis. A multiple comparison test was performed. We applied Bonferrroni-Dunn's procedure by using SPSS (ver. 22). It is not necessary to test the null omnibus hypothesis using an ANOVA prior to tD statistic [9]. In a case of using a foot position for measuring the distance, data correction was made with the center-center model, by using the anthropometric database [10] available from Digital Human R.C. of AIST.

2.2 Results

Means and standard deviations of all the interpersonal distances obtained under the condition of standing posture are given in Table 2. The observed data of standing posture ranged between 11.0 (face-to-face, searching on a map, smartphone) and 186.7 (face-to-face, no task) (mean = 50.36, SD = 24.89) cm. According to Hall's zone system, the observed data widely ranged from the intimate distance (0−18 in.), to the close phase of social distance (4−7 ft.).

Table 2. Means and standard deviations of interpersonal distances (center-center model)

Factors			Task													
			no particular task			before MAP task (holding a device)			during MAP task			before PUZZLE task (holding a device)			during PUZZLE task		
Posture	Orientation of the body	Device	n	Mean (cm)	SD	n	Mean (cm)	SD	n	Mean (cm)	SD	n	Mean (cm)	SD	n	Mean (cm)	SD
standing	side-by-side	smartphone	20	61.07	18.36	20	49.02	8.06	20	23.50	5.67	20	46.07	8.60	20	20.03	4.89
		notebook-PC	20	*61.07	18.36	20	47.65	8.80	20	34.78	7.00	20	43.85	8.09	20	32.78	7.03
		blackboard	20	62.24	18.90	20	48.30	6.77	20	30.28	4.40		n/a			n/a	
	face-to-face	smartphone	20	81.26	29.2	20	58.87	9.59	20	20.78	7.03	20	58.40	9.96	20	18.35	6.35
		notebook-PC	20	*81.26	29.2	20	59.90	10.34	20	33.23	8.25	20	56.82	10.96	20	35.35	11.55

Note *: The data under the "no task" condition of a smartphone was the same as that of a notebook-PC.

The result revealed that there were statistically significant simple main effects of the "task" (p < .01), the "device" (p < .01), and the "orientation of the body" (p < .01). On the other hand, neither a simple main effect of the "posture" nor an interaction related to the "posture" was statistically significant. In the present paper, the scope of analysis hereafter is narrowed down to the condition of posture "standing".

Task. The factor of "task" had six levels {(no task vs. before a cooperative task (= holding a device) vs. during a cooperative task) x (searching on a map vs. jigsaw puzzle)}. The simple main effect of the "task" was statistically significant (p < .01). In particular, under the condition of either cooperative task, there were statistically significant differences between "no particular task" > "holding a device" (p < .01) > "searching on a map" (p < .01), and between "no particular task" > "holding a

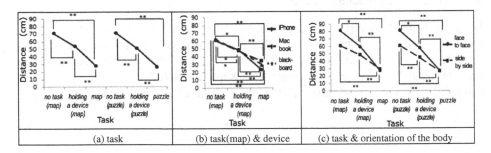

(a) task   (b) task(map) & device   (c) task & orientation of the body

Fig. 3. Mean of interpersonal distance

device" (p < .01) > "jigsaw puzzle" (p < .01) (Fig. 3-a). On the other hand, there was no statistically significant difference between "searching on a map" and "jigsaw puzzle".

Interaction of the Task and the Orientation of the Body. Under either condition of "side-by-side" or "face-to-face", there were statistically significant differences between "no particular task" > "searching on a map" (p < .01), between "no particular task" > "jigsaw puzzle" (p < .01), between "holding a device" > "searching on a map" (p < .01), and between "holding a device" > "jigsaw puzzle" (p < .01) (Fig. 3-c). Furthermore, statistically significant differences between "no particular task" > "holding a device" were found under the condition of "face-to-face" (p < .05), and under the combination of the conditions "side-by-side" and "jigsaw puzzle" (p < .01) (Fig. 3-c).

Interaction of the Task and the Device. Under each device condition of "smartphone", "notebook-PC", and "blackboard", there were statistically significant differences between "no particular task" > "holding a device" (p < .05) > "searching on a map" (p < .01). Also, under either device condition of "smartphone" and "notebook-PC", there were statistically significant differences between "no particular task" > "holding a device" (p < .05) > "jigsaw puzzle" (p < .01). (Fig. 3-b).

The above result indicated that interpersonal distances were reduced by initiating a cooperative task, under the condition of either cooperative task (map or puzzle), or either orientation of the body (face-to-face or side-by-side), or either device (smartphone, notebook PC or blackboard). Also interestingly, interpersonal distances were reduced when an evaluator held either portable device (a smartphone or a notebook PC).

Device. The factor of "device" had three levels (smartphone vs. notebook-PC vs. blackboard). The simple main effect of the "device" was statistically significant (p < .01). In particular, there were statistically significant differences between "notebook-PC" > "smartphone" (p < .01) and between "blackboard" > "smartphone" (p < .05) (Fig. 4-a). Under either condition of "side-by-side" or "face-to-face", there was a statistically significant difference between "notebook-PC" > "smartphone" (p < .01) (Fig. 4-b).

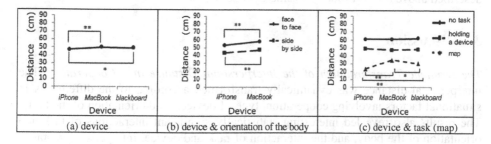

| (a) device | (b) device & orientation of the body | (c) device & task (map) |

Fig. 4. Mean of interpersonal distance

Interaction of the Device and the Task. Under the task condition of "searching on a map", there were statistically significant differences between the "notebook-PC" > the "smartphone" (p < .01), between the "blackboard" > "smartphone" (p < .01), and between "notebook-PC" > "blackboard" (p < .05) (Fig. 4-c). At least, under the condition of a certain cooperative task such as "searching on a map", the bigger size of a device did not always contribute to increase the interpersonal distance.

Orientation of the Body. The factor of "orientation of the body" had two levels (face-to-face vs. side-by-side). The simple main effect of the "orientation of the body" was statistically significant (p < .01). In particular, there was a statistically significant difference between "face-to-face" > "side-by-side" (p < .01) (Fig. 5-a). Also, under either condition of "smartphone" or "notebook-PC", there were significant differences between "face-to-face" > "side-by-side" (p < .01) (Fig. 5-c).

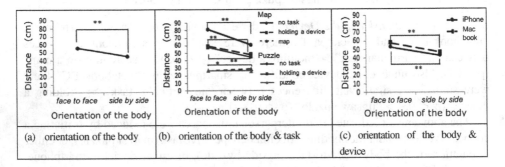

Fig. 5. Mean of interpersonal distance

Interaction of the Orientation of the Body and the Task. There were statistically significant differences between "face-to-face" > "side-by-side" under the condition of non-cooperative task (i.e. "no particular task" (p < .01) or "holding a device" task (p < .01)) (Fig. 5-b). Conversely, under the condition of the "searching on a map" task, there was a statistically significant difference between "face-to-face" < "side-by-side" (p < .05) (Fig. 5-b). At least, this result obtained under the condition of a certain cooperative task was different from the anisotropy observed under the condition of non-cooperative task described above ("face-to-face" > "side-by-side").

3   Discussion

The Dynamic Transformation of the Interpersonal Distance in a Cooperation. The interpersonal distance was dynamically transformed according to the differences in situational factors involving cooperation, type of devices, and orientation of the body. The results also revealed interesting statistically significant interactions of task and orientation of the body, and the interaction of task and device. Interpersonal distance varies with a complex of multiple causes rather than a single and identifiable cause such as device size. This results reflected not only the flexibility of individual personal space but the complexity of a cooperation. It is suggested that interpersonal space is actively co-constructed as a result of the cooperative process by two individuals who shared the same environment. The transformation can be facilitated by a kind of social interaction.

Technology for Capturing Dynamic Nature of Interpersonal Distance. The interpersonal distance frequently changes especially in a cooperative situation. The conventional stop-distance method has a methodological limitation, as it requires to freeze participants' physical movements for a moment. It is expected a new measurement approach using a sensor technology will provide a viable solution to capture its dynamic nature.

Multidisciplinary Study of Personal Space of Elderly Persons in a Cooperation. Personal space was considered as a meaningful element to be concerned by those giving care to or co-working with the elderly persons [11]. However, there was few study of personal space needs of elderly persons, especially, limited attention to an interactive situation.

In conventional studies on personal space of the decades, it had been considered the age factor played a minor role [16], except for their attentions to the developmental changes in childhood. For instance, it is known that the children tend to be happy to be physically close to each other but personal space gets bigger as they grow older. Developmental changes of personal space needs had been identified at least from infancy to adolescence [6].

On the other hand, recent neuro-cognitive literature [2] discussed the relationship between the neurological changes in older adults and the degradation of their peripersonal space representations compared with that of young adults. Those changes may influence their personal space needs and spatial behavior. However, surprisingly little is known about developmental changes of personal space needs in late adulthood [4]. Different age groups may have heterogeneous characteristics of personal space. Further multidisciplinary study is needed to address this issue appropriately from multiple related aspects, and to develop a viable technology for carefully understanding and harmonizing flexible needs of personal space in the advancement of aging society.

4 Conclusion

This paper presented an experimental study that investigated the dynamic characteristics of human spatial behavior in a cooperation. We focused on how interpersonal distance varied depending on the differences of tasks, devices, and orientation of the body.

The results revealed several unique dynamic characteristics of interpersonal distance in a cooperation. First, the results indicated statistically significant simple main effects of the "task", the "device", and the "orientation of the body". In particular, there were statistically significant differences between "no particular task" > "holding a device" > "cooperative tasks"; between "face-to-face" > "side-by-side"; and between "notebook-PC" > "blackboard" or "smartphone". Second, the results revealed that the interpersonal distance was reduced by initiating a cooperative task, under the condition of either cooperative task (map or puzzle), or either orientation of the body (face-to-face or side-by-side), or either device (smartphone or notebook-PC). Also interestingly, the interpersonal distance was reduced when an evaluator held a portable device such as a smartphone, even before initiating a cooperation. This suggested that the presence of a device facilitated some change on collaborators' interactive environment. Third, the results also revealed interesting statistically significant interactions of task and orientation of the body, and the interaction of task and device. This indicated that interpersonal distance varies with a complex of multiple causes rather than a single and identifiable cause. The dynamics of social interactions seemed to influence the transformation of interpersonal spaces. Other results also involved interesting findings, for instance, the anisotropy (face-to-face > side-by-side) observed under a non-cooperative situation was transformed into the opposite during a certain cooperation.

Different age groups may have heterogeneous needs of interpersonal space. The further empirical study is needed, in order to substantiate these findings, to address this vital issue in the environmental design of human services such as nursing and care-giving, and to find feasible solutions for harmonizing flexible needs for personal space in the advancement of aging society.

Acknowledgments. This work was supported in part by JSPS Grant-in-Aid for Scientific Research (23300263). We thank all the study participants and our laboratory members 2014-2015.

References

1. Argyle, M., Dean, J.: Eye-contact, distance, and affiliation. Sociometry **28**(3), 289–304 (1965)
2. Bloesch, E.K., Davoli, C.C., Abrams, R.A.: Age-related changes in attentional reference frame for peripersonal space. Psychol. Sci. **24**(4), 557–561 (2013)
3. Evans, G.W., Lepore, S.J., Schroeder, A.: The role of interior design elements in human responses to crowding. J. Pers. Soc. Psychol. **70**, 41–46 (1996)
4. Gifford, R.: Environmental Psychology, 5th edn. Optimal Books, Colville (2014)
5. Gifford, R.: Projected Interpersonal Distance and Orientation Choices: Personality, Sex, and Social Situation. Soc. Psychol. Q. **45**(3), 145–152 (1982)
6. Hayduk, L.A.: Personal space: where we now stand. Psychol. Bull. **94**(2), 293–335 (1983)
7. Kinoe, Y., Mizuno, N.: Situational transformation of personal space. In: Yamamoto, S., de Oliveira, N.P. (eds.) HIMI 2015. LNCS, vol. 9173, pp. 15–24. Springer, Heidelberg (2015). doi:10.1007/978-3-319-20618-9_2
8. Kinoe, Y., Hama, T.: A framework for understanding everyday situations through interactions. In: Proceedings of 16th World Congress of on Ergonomics, International Ergonomics Association. Elsevier (2006)
9. Kirk, R.E.: Experimental Design: Procedures for the Behavioral Sciences. Sage, Thousand Oaks (2013)
10. Kouchi, M., Mochimaru, M.: AIST Anthropometric database, H18PRO-503 (2006)
11. Louis, M.: Personal space boundary needs of elderly persons: an empirical study. J. Gerontological Nurs. **7**(7), 395–400 (1981)
12. Nord, C.: Individual care and personal space in assisted living in Sweden. Health Pract. **17**, 50–56 (2011)
13. Sommer, R.: Personal Space: The Behavioral Basis of Design. Updated. Bosko Books (2008)
14. Sommer, R.: Personal space in a digital age. In: Bechtel, R.B., Churchman, A. (eds.) Handbook of Environmental Psychology, pp. 385–504. Wiley, New York (2002)
15. Tedesco, J.F., Fromme, D.K.: Cooperation, competition, and personal space. Sociometry **37**, 116–121 (1974)
16. Winogrond, I.R.: A comparison of interpersonal distancing behavior in young and elderly adults. Int. J. Aging Hum. Dev. **13**(1), 53–60 (1981)
17. Wormith, J.S.: Personal space of incarcerated offenders. Clin. Psychol. **40**, 815–827 (1984)

Analysis of Elderly Users' Preferences and Expectations on Service Robot's Personality, Appearance and Interaction

Styliani Kleanthous[1(✉)], Christophoros Christophorou[1],
Christiana Tsiourti[2], Carina Dantas[3], Rachelle Wintjens[4],
George Samaras[5], and Eleni Christodoulou[1,2]

[1] CITARD Services Ltd, Nicosia, Cyprus
{stellak,christophoros,cseleni}@citard-serv.com
[2] University of Geneva, Geneva, Switzerland
christiana.tsiourti@unige.ch
[3] Caritas Diocesana, Coimbra, Portugal
carinadantas@caritascoimbra.pt
[4] ZUYDERLAND, Sittard-Geleen, Netherlands
r.wintjens@orbisconcern.nl
[5] Department of Computer Science, University of Cyprus, Nicosia, Cyprus
cssamara@cs.ucy.ac.cy

Abstract. Fortunately, improvements in welfare and medical care will allow life expectancy in Europe's population to increase by the year 2050. However, it is not always the case that living longer implies a healthier, more active and independent life. In this context, technologies and products that will act as assistive companions to elderly, who are living alone at their home, are attracting a growing interest from both a research and commercial perspective. Literature reports contradictory results on the preferences of elderly towards assistive technologies and more specifically, service robots. In this paper, we are called to present an empirical study, conducted in the scope of an EU – Horizon 2020 project, in order to explore people's perceptions, attitudes and requirements towards the idea of a future service robot for the home.

Keywords: Aging well · Service robots · User-centred requirements analysis

1 Motivation

During the last decade mainly due to the increase of life expectancy, researchers are looking into solutions that will improve elderly quality of life (QoL), keep elderly active for longer and help them socialise more. Robotic assistive partners are becoming the trend in elderly care, in an attempt to keep the elderly at home for longer and to reduce consumption of care resources. This move into the edge of the technological innovation called robotics, forced researchers in the academia but also in the care sectors to investigate the potentials and benefits that might arise from exploiting care provision through service robots.

© Springer International Publishing Switzerland 2016
J. Zhou and G. Salvendy (Eds.): ITAP 2016, PartII, LNCS 9755, pp. 35–44, 2016.
DOI: 10.1007/978-3-319-39949-2_4

A service robot can be defined as a special kind of robot that is specifically designed for personal use at home and is expected to communicate with its users in a natural and intuitive way. Service robots have been around in the care area for some time now and although many studies proven the positive impact of robots to older adults' everyday life and well-being [1], there are still unanswered questions [2] on what end-users really want from a robotic partner. More specifically, the infancy of this area [3], generates questions on, (i) how a service or social robot should look like on its outer appearance; (ii) what type of personality the robot is expected to demonstrate when interacting with the user and (iii) in what ways the user would like to interact with the robot?

In this paper, we are called to provide evidence to answer the abovementioned questions through an empirical study conducted in the scope of the GrowMeUp project, in order to explore people's perceptions, attitudes and requirements towards the idea of a future service robot for the home. A human-centered approach was adopted and a systematic human-centered methodology was developed using questionnaires to derive data from 16 older adults and 16 caregivers. In this paper priority is given to the replies provided by the elderly participants of the study who are, after all, the primary end-users of the technology under development.

In the coming sections a discussion is provided on similar studies and related literature report, followed by the methodology that guided us in conducting this study. A report on the answers we received from the elderly participants is given along with conclusions.

2 Related Work

Service robots studies usually end or have a stage where there is a trial with end users for evaluating, the technology developed and its effect and acceptance by, the end users. A great obstacle in the adoption of this kind of technology is its acceptance by the end users and integration into their everyday routine, which is actually the purpose for service robots development [3]. Broadbent et al., in their article, stress the importance of studies that will focus on the preferences of older persons related to the required features that a service robot might have (appearance) [3] and to the aspects of the personality [4] that should demonstrate and preferred interaction with end users. Currently, literature reports contradictory results in these areas, that usually occur due to the methodology selection for studies that investigate the adoption of technology by older adults [1, 5–8], or even due to the selection of user groups that is involved in the evaluation of the developed technology. For example in Roy et al. [5], a service robot that was developed particularly for elderly care, it was evaluated by a group of students whom, the needs, expectations and requirements differ greatly from those of elderly users. Similarly the service robot developed at [6], evaluated by a number of older adults at a serviced apartments for the duration of only 30 min. The results from such studies can create misunderstanding in the research community of ambient assisted living and misguide the development and design of relevant technologies. Thus a more active involvement of the end users is paramount and a user-centred methodology needs to be followed for understanding user needs and requirements and increase acceptance of service robots by elderly [9].

In this line, recent studies showed that the elderly are more willing to accept a robotic support partner that does not act as an "all knowing" superior being, especially when robots cannot achieve what is expected of them, due to technological limitations [3, 10, 11]. A robot in the elderly care might needs to demonstrate different roles and personalities, for example, to adopt the role of a friend, personal assistant, personal carer and should thus demonstrate a friendly or professional personality accordingly [12]. In addition, the interaction and support provided should demonstrate a non-invasive intervention of the robot to the older person's everyday life [2] and use a suitable and usable medium of input and output interaction (e.g., voice, touch, gesturing). Moreover, there are evidences [4] that support the argument that matching the personality of the end-user to the robot's behavior and personality can help the end user to accept the technology more easily.

3 Methodology

3.1 Trial Sites Involved

Two trial-sites, one in Portugal and one in the Netherlands, were involved in the overall process of extracting user needs and requirements for the GrowMeUp system. Each site has its own particular arrangements for providing services to the elderly in need and these are described below.

ZUYDERLAND: The target group members of ZUYDERLAND lives in two different care facilities in the Netherlands named Hoogstaete and Aldenhof. Both care facilities are part of the ZUYDERLAND care organization and are located on the north edge of Sittard and nearby a village called Born. Hoogstaete and Aldenhof are combined elderly houses with the following departments: (i) Small scale living for people with dementia (note: not in the scope for this study), (ii) Elderly home for people with dementia, mental and/or physical problems (the average size of these apartments is 30 m^2), and (iii) Care apartments for people with physical, mental and/or physical problems (these apartments are like normal apartments only adjusted for elderly like the presence of an alarm, adjusted bathroom, etc.). Elderly living in this department are (semi) independent but can make use of all the facilities from the attached care facility including care, meal service etc. All departments have a care staff consisted of Care Coordinators, Nurses with different education levels, Care Assistants and Activity Staff (occupational therapist).

CARITAS: The target group members of CARITAS live in three different home care services located in urban and suburban areas in Portugal. One of these services, Centro Rainha Santa Isabel, provides support mainly for the elderly that live in Coimbra city and that are still living in their own houses, many of which traditional houses in friendly neighbourhoods. The second is a social centre S. Pedro which is located in the outskirts of the city and congregates different types of elderly – either people retired from public services, with good cultural and economic conditions as well as beneficiaries of social housing, with some financial difficulties. The third service, Centro N.ª Sr-ª dos Milagres, is in a suburban area, about 11 km from Coimbra. All of these centres also have day care services and ensure to their clients a range of services including meals, house cleaning and laundry, leisure activities, transportation to the hairdresser, bank and doctor appointments, among others.

The elderly group that was selected to participate in the requirement gathering process is supported by these centres.

3.2 Participants' Selection Process

The target group of GrowMeUp is the big group of healthy older persons or with light physical or mental health problems who live alone at home and can find pleasure and relief in getting help or stimulation to carry out their daily activities.

Groups of elderly and caregivers (both formal and informal), from ZUYDELAND and CARITAS, were involved throughout the process of establishing and analysing the requirements in order to contribute their needs and ideas. During the requirement gathering process three different groups, with different target group members have been involved: Group 1: Elderly supported CARITAS; Group 2: Elderly Residents of ZUYDERLAND; Group 3: Formal and Informal Caregivers (from CARITAS and ZUYDERLAND).

The first group includes 8 elderly (4 men and 4 women) from CARITAS with ages between 69 and 85, the second group includes 8 elderly (5 women and 3 men) from ZUYDERLAND with ages between 65 and 85 and the third group includes 16 formal and Informal caregivers from both test beds. More specifically 13 formal (8 from ZUYDERLAND and 5 from CARITAS; including Care Coordinators, Nurses, Psychologists, Sociologists, Policy Advisors, Older Person Care Specialists, ADL Trainers, etc.) and 3 informal caregivers (1 from ZUYDERLAND and 2 from CARITAS; including family members, that is 2 Sons/Daughters and 1 Grandchild, of the elderly).

The selection of the elderly participants of ZUYDERLAND and CARITAS, was based on inclusion criteria considering profile variations within the target audience that the study aims to reach (gender, daily habits, capabilities, preferences, technological skills, social status, etc.). Other inclusion criteria take into account: expression of interest from elderly in the project and elderly at the age of 65 + with none or only light physical or mental health problems at the time of the study. Elderly that have severe physical or mental health problems at the beginning of the study or start showing signs of heavy degradation during the trials and elderly with no autonomy in their daily activities are excluded from participation in the study.

In ZUYDERLAND the elderly and the caregivers (both formal and informal) participants were invited in group sessions where they have been firstly informed about the overall scope of GrowMeUp. There were two sessions; one for the elderly and one for the caregivers. After understanding the main aim and objectives of the project, both the elderly and the caregiver were provided the questionnaire in a digital form (on-line) that they filled in and the data collected were analysed and processed. It is worth also indicating that during the time the elderly were filling in the questionnaires, caregivers were always there to provide them help and clarifications to the different questions included in the questionnaire.

For CARITAS, due to the delay in obtaining ethical clearance from national authorities to the implementation of the user requirements, the solution was to implement an anonymized questionnaire distributed online to all CARITAS elderly and caregivers. The online questionnaire included information about the overall objectives of the project.

3.3   Process of Understanding User Needs and Establishing Requirements

The general methodology for understanding user needs followed in GrowMeUp (see Fig. 1) is adapted from the Miraculous Life[1] project methodology presented and emphasised in continues user involvement in the whole process. In this paper we are focusing only in the process prior to the development of the prototype system.

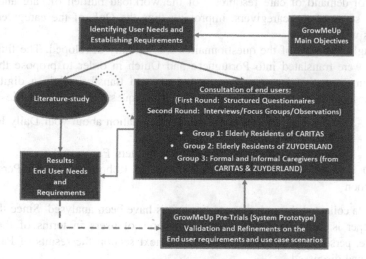

Fig. 1. End user needs and requirements extraction process flow-chart. The user is involved in the process at each stage.

More specifically, during the first round of the requirements gathering process, a literature study was performed that provided useful information from related research studies, particularly on the preferences of elderly users when interacting with robots and graphical interfaces. This information was considered as a starting and guiding point for discovering the link between the elderly and the use of ICT-based services and robotic technology. Furthermore, the results of this literature study provided understanding of the field and the theoretical background for the development of the

---

[1] Miraculous-Life project, funded by the European Commission under the 7th Framework Programme (Grant Agreement: 611421).

two extended requirement analysis questionnaires (the one distributed to the group of the elderly and the other one distributed to the formal and informal caregivers). Through these questionnaires end-users were requested to reflect on their daily life habits and patterns, their skills, their expectations and their ideas of being supported by a service robotic system. The data collected were considered for guiding the initial design of the overall GrowMeUp system.

The first questionnaire concerned the elderly and how they perceived certain issues and expectations when interacting with the GrowMeUp system. The second questionnaire was provided to the formal and informal caregivers in order to get their point of view of what the system should provide to the elderly and their perception of certain issues. Formal (i.e., Care Professionals) and informal (i.e., Family members of the elderly) caregivers, of the elders' care team were involved in the analysis as their point of view was essential for two reasons. Firstly for gathering more realistic requirements and secondly for identifying requirements that will assist in improving the efficiency and continuity of integrated care provision to the older person, leading thus in a reduction of demand of care resources, of the workload burden of care and of the associated stress of the caregivers, improving thus the QoL of the caregivers community, as well.

An English version of the questionnaires was initially developed. The final questionnaires were translated into Portuguese and Dutch in order to propose the questionnaire in the native language of respondents and transformed in a digital form (online questionnaires). The questionnaires included questions in 4 categories:

- Part A - Demographic, Social and General Information about your Daily Routines
- Part B - Health and Memory Status
- Part C - Questions related to the GrowMeUp System Functionality
- Part D - Questions related to the GrowMeUp Robot Appearance/Personality/ Interaction

The data collected through the questionnaires have been analysed. Since the focus of this paper is the preferences and requirements of users in terms of the Robot appearance, personality and interaction, in the next section the results of Part D are presented and discussed.

4   Analysis of Results and Establishing User Preferences

4.1   Demographics and General Information of Participants

In total the study involved 32 participants, 16 of which were elderly and 16 caregivers. As illustrated in Table 1, the majority of the elderly that participated in this study are female. The mean age of the elderly is 78.9 years while the mean age of the caregivers is 39 years old. The group of the thirteen (13) formal caregivers consisted of mostly Care Coordinators, Psychologists, Sociologists, Nurses and Policy Advisors. The three (3) informal caregivers were mainly family members of the elderly (Son/Daughter (or in-law) and a Grandchild). A summary is provided in Table 2.

Table 1. Summary of demographic information of elderly participants in the study

Elderly population	ZUYDERLAND	CARITAS	Total elderly
Amount of participants	8	8	16
Gender	3 male	4 male	7 male
	5 female	4 female	9 female
Average age	78.4	79.4	78.9
Range of age	65–85	69–85	65–85

Table 2. Information on caregivers that participated in the study

Caregivers population	ZUYDERLAND	CARITAS	Total caregivers
Amount of participants	9	7	16
Type of caregivers	8 formal	5 formal	13 formal
	1 informal	2 informal	3 informal
Profession of formal caregivers	1 Care coordinator	2 Care coordinators	3 Care coordinators
	1 Nurse	1 Nurse	2 Nurses
	2 Psychologist	1 Psychologist	3 Psychologists
	2 Policy advisors	1 Sociologist/SST	2 Policy advisors
	1 ADL trainer		1 Sociologist/SST
	1 Specialist older persons care		1 ADL trainer
			1 Specialist older persons care
Relationship of informal caregivers	1 Son/Daughter (or in-law)	1 Son/Daughter (or in-law)	2 Son/Daughter (or in-law)
		1 Grandchild (or in-laws)	1 Grandchild (or in-laws)

Although the goal of this paper is to highlight the needs and requirements of elderly and their caregivers when interacting with robotic technologies, it was interesting to understand also their familiarity with technologies during their everyday life. The results show that 62.5 % of the elderly of ZUYDERLAND use a tablet every day. The smart phone, laptop and the application Facebook are also used every day, by 37.5 % of the elderly. A desktop computer and the applications Skype and Viber are used the least by the elderly; the majority of the elderly participants never or rarely used these applications. As for CARITAS' elderly, only one of the elderly participants uses a smartphone on a daily basis and a laptop some times. All the other elderly don't use any of the technologies or applications specified.

The above information provides an insight on the potential users of the overall system under development. What follows will focus on the end users' preferences on (i) how a service or social robot should look like on its outer appearance; (ii) what type of personality the robot is expected to demonstrate when interacting with the user and (iii) in what ways the user would like to interact with the robot?

Prior to asking the elderly about their preferences, we asked CARITAS and ZUYDERLAND caregivers their opinion regarding the acceptance of this kind of technology by the elderly. CARITAS caregivers are convinced that the elderly would not have any issues having a Robot in their household. Most of the caregivers (13 out of 16) believe that the elderly would like to be with a robot on a daily basis. In ZUYDERLAND 2 caregivers replied negatively implying that the elderly will not accept the Robotic service provider in their daily life, mentioning also that *"elderly would prefer actual people delivering care, not a robot"*. Similarly in a question whether the elderly would feel comfortable with a robot inside their house 12 out of 16 caregivers replied positively while there was also a concern from ZUYDERLAND caregivers: *"I think they might be suspicious at the beginning (about the Robot), or maybe a bit ashamed. It might seem strange at the beginning."*

4.2   Users' Preferences on Robot's Appearance, Personality, Interaction

Appearance: One of the most important outer features of a device, hence a robot is the colour of its shell. In our study elderly participants provided mixed opinions on their preferences. Specifically, elderly in ZUYDERLAND equally (25 % of elderly respondents) selected pink, red, blue and grey. On the other hand CARITAS elderly in their majority (37.5 %) selected the red colour for the robot's shell. The results in this case show that possibly elderly are just concerned with the aesthetics and that colour will not affect their interaction with the robot.

The opinions about the height of the robot also vary between respondents. Some of them chose a small to a medium sized robot (smaller than 100 cm). However, according to the majority (50 % of the elderly at ZUYDERLAND and CARITAS) the preferable height for the robot is medium (between 100 cm and 120 cm).

Furthermore, the elderly in our study requested for an extra feature in the robot's shell that they can use to help them get up if needed. Specifically, 75 % of ZUY-DERLAND elderly would like to be helped getting up and sitting down and 37.5 % of the elderly from CARITAS believe they would appreciate this aid. These results show the elderlies' confidence and trust in using the robot for an important everyday activity that also devises a threat of injury. In addition, 87.50 % of all the elderly also think that it would be useful if the robot would be able to carry some products.

Personality: As mentioned above an important aspect of a companion robot is the personality that it demonstrates while interacting with humans [4]. It is proven that in the elderly assistive care it is important that the robot does not show behaviour of a superior being or to dictate the elderly on its every day needs and activities. In this respect the majority of the elderly participants mentioned that they would like the robot to adopt the role of a personal assistant (43.5 % of the respondents) rather than act as a friend or a caregiver. However, with respect to the robot's behaviour if they had to choose one, they want it to be friendly and informal (62.5 % of the elderly respondents), mentioning also that it would be good if they could choose between personalities of the robot according to their preferences. More than half (53.5 %) of the elderly in the two participating organisations would appreciate to have this feature available on their assistive robot.

Interestingly with respect to the voice of the robot, at ZUYDERLAND half of the elderly would prefer a female voice to talk to them and half would prefer a male's voice, while in Caritas 75 % would prefer a female voice.

Another aspect of the robot's personality is the behaviour of the Robot. Two options are examined: a guiding behaviour which means that the robot helps the elderly to decide what they should do by giving them advice and a directive behaviour which means that the robot "just tells them what they should do". For the elderly in ZUYDERLAND, 50 % would like a guiding robot, while the other half of the group would like a directive robot. In CARITAS, 73.33 % of the elderly selected the "guiding" answers.

The following extra suggestions about the personality of the robot were made by the elderly of ZUYDERLAND and CARITAS:

'The robot is like a friend. Personal bonding is important. It would be fun if the robot will take initiative to tell something from the news for example.'
'It must not be too directive and talk softly with the elderly.'

Interaction: With respect to the way (e.g. vocal, touch screen, etc.) the elderly prefer to interact with the robot, voice is preferred (87.5 % of the ZUYDERLAND elderly, all of CARITAS' elderly) and vocal calling using the robot's name is the most desirable option. Similarly, the elderly participants in the study (88 % of ZUYDERLAND elderly and 75 % of CARITAS elderly) prefer the robot to call them by their first name, consistently with the informal/friendly behaviour that they want the robot to demonstrate. Similarly, the majority of the elderly would like to have a proactive rather than a passive robot (75 % of CARITAS elderly and 50 % of ZUYDERLAND elderly); meaning that it will 'take the initiative' to remind them about certain events in their calendars, provide advice regarding current states or activities even if the elderly has not initiated a discussion. Having said that, when the elderly asked, they mentioned that the robot should be switched off if required and get activated accordingly: "Switch on-off as I choose" (37.50 %). It is not surprising that most of the elderly want to be in control of the activity level of the robot.

5 Conclusions

In conclusion, it is apparent that a service robot seems to be an appreciated technological solution for the home care services and the elderly that live alone at home. In order though for end-users to accept and integrate this technology in their everyday life and exploit the benefits of a service robot, the technology has to meet user requirements and preferences. One size does not fit all and thus, special design considerations need to be made while designing and developing robots that are meant to have specific purposes e.g. service robots for elderly care. According to the above results, a service robot needs to interact as a friendly assistant, with a pleasant and sensitive voice, allow the elderly to feel they can control its behaviour, so it doesn't intrude in their lives and preferences, and act in an informal and personal way. It is important to mention that this solution must always be integrated with human provided services, either formal or informal, and that it does not aim to replace human contact. However, robotic systems have the potential to get accepted by the elderly as long as they understand the benefits and their ability to improve the elderly QoL.

Acknowledgements. This work is supported by the GrowMeUp project, funded by the European Commission within the H2020-PHC-2014, (Grant Agreement: 643647).

References

1. Bemelmans, R., Gelderblom, G.J., Jonker, P., De Witte, L.: Socially assistive robots in elderly care: a systematic review into effects and effectiveness. J. Am. Med. Directors Assoc. **13**(2), 114–120 (2012)
2. Broekens, J., Marcel, H., Henk, R.: Assistive social robots in elderly care: a review. Gerontechnology **8**(2), 94–103 (2009)
3. Broadbent, E., Stafford, R., MacDonald, B.: Acceptance of healthcare robots for the older population: review and future directions. Int. J. Soc. Rob. **1**(4), 319–330 (2009)
4. Tapus, A., Țăpuș, C., Matarić, M.J.: User—robot personality matching and assistive robot behavior adaptation for post-stroke rehabilitation therapy. Int. Serv. Rob. **1**(2), 169–183 (2008)
5. Roy, N., Baltus, G., Fox, D., Gemperle, F., Goetz, J., Hirsch, T., Margaritis, D., Montemerlo, M., Pineau, J., Schulte, J., Thrun, S.: Towards personal service robots for the elderly. In: Workshop on Interactive Robots and Entertainment (WIRE 2000) vol. 25, p. 184 (2000)
6. Jayawardena, C., Kuo, I.H., Unger, U., Igic, A., Wong, R., Watson, C.I., Stafford, R.Q., Broadbent, E., Tiwari, P., Warren, J., Sohn, J.: Deployment of a service robot to help older people. In: IEEE/RSJ International Conference on Intelligent Robots and Systems, pp. 5990–5995. IEEE (2010)
7. Compagna, D., Kohlbacher, F.: The limits of participatory technology development: the case of service robots in care facilities for older people. Technol. Forecast. Soc. Chang. **93**, 19–31 (2015)
8. Andrade, A.O., Pereira, A.A., Walter, S., Almeida, R., Loureiro, R., Compagna, D., Kyberd, P.J.: Bridging the gap between robotic technology and health care. Biomed. Signal Process. Control **10**, 65–78 (2014)
9. Tapus, A., Mataric, M.J., Scasselati, B.: Socially assistive robotics [grand challenges of robotics]. IEEE Robot. Autom. Mag. **14**(1), 35–42 (2007)
10. Mori, M., MacDorman, K., Kageki, N.: The uncanny valley (from the field). IEEE Robot. Autom. Mag. **19**(2), 98–100 (2012). doi:10.1109/MRA.2012.2192811
11. Zawieska, K., Ben Moussa, M., Duffy, B.R., Magnenat-Thalmann, N.: The role of imagination in human-robot interaction. In: Proceedings of the Autonomous Social Robots and Virtual Humans workshop, 25th Annual Conference on Computer Animation and Social Agents (CASA 2012). Singapore (2012)
12. Dautenhahn, K., Woods, S., Kaouri, C., Walters, M.L., Werry, I.: What is a robot companion - friend, assistant or butler? In: Proceedings of the International Conference on Intelligent Robots and Systems, pp. 1192–1197 (2005)

Socio-Technical Challenges in Implementation of Monitoring Technologies in Elderly Care

Ella Kolkowska[1(✉)], Anneli Avatare Nöu[2], Marie Sjölinder[2], and Isabella Scandurra[1]

[1] Örebro University School of Business, Örebro, Sweden
{ella.kolkowska,isabella.scandurra}@oru.se
[2] SICS Swedish ICT, Kista, Sweden
{anneli,marie}@sics.se

Abstract. Although new monitoring technologies (MT) supporting aging in place are continuously developed and introduced on the market, attempts to implement these technologies as an integrated part of elderly care often fail. According to the literature, the reason for that may be the prevailing technical focus applied during development and implementation of monitoring technologies in real settings. The aim of this paper was to investigate the socio-technical challenges that arise during implementation of monitoring technologies in elderly care. We used a qualitative case study and semi-structured interviews to investigate socio-technical (S/T) challenges in implementation of monitoring technologies generally and social alarms especially. Based on our findings we suggest a framework for classification of S/T challenges arising during implementation of monitoring technologies in elderly care and in this way this paper contributes to a better understanding of these challenges.

Keywords: Monitoring technologies · Social alarms · Assistive technologies · Socio-technical aspects · Elderly · Security · Safety

1 Introduction

Utilizing monitoring technologies (MT) the caregivers can receive information about activities and the status of different entities in the home where an elderly person lives alone [1]. Continuous monitoring gives the caregivers the opportunity to quickly react in case of emergency and in this way increase their own and the elderly person's sense of safety and security [2]. The rapid development of MT and technologies generally supporting aging in place creates possibilities for new and more efficient solutions enhancing elderly people's quality of life through improved outcomes in safeguarding, living standards, social interaction and independence [1]. Such solutions also reduce workload for caregivers and decrease the costs for elderly care for the society [3]. Nevertheless, MT are not commonly adopted as a part of elderly care of today [4].

According to recent literature [4–7], the reason for that might be ignoring socio-technical (S/T) aspects in development and implementation of MT into everyday life. Various scholars [5–7] argue that MT, developed with a techno-centric perspective, are not able to address the needs that arise in complex social environments.

J. Zhou and G. Salvendy (Eds.): ITAP 2016, PartII, LNCS 9755, pp. 45–56, 2016.
DOI: 10.1007/978-3-319-39949-2_5

This is a common reason for the failure of many projects attempting to implement such technologies as a part of elderly care [6, 8]. Others [4, 5] argue that real-life implementations can be successful if we better understand potential S/T challenges in this context. Unfortunately, literature reporting on lessons learned regarding implementations of MT in real-life settings is still very scarse [4, 8, 9].

Against this backdrop, the aim of this study was to investigate the S/T challenges in implementation of MT in elderly care. By proposing a framework for categorizing S/T challenges that arise during implementation of MT in elderly care, this paper contributes to an increased understanding of S/T challenges in this context.

2 Related Research

Applying the S/T approach means that social and technical aspects are equally important in development and implementation of technology [10, 11]. Therefore, such development processes do not only focus on technical aspects, but also consider social, organizational and human needs [12]. In short, the S/T approach focuses on how individual and social requirements can be met by the design of technology.

In the paper "The Sociotechnical Challenge of Integrating Telehealth and Telecare into Health and Social Care for the Elderly", Eason et al. [5] investigated why common adaptation of telehealth has proven to be difficult and why, although having a great potential, the new technology does not contribute to improved healthcare in the community. The authors studied 25 health communities in England and found that most of the attempts to implement telehealth and telecare as an integrated part of elderly care failed. The authors concluded that the obstacles for a successful implementation of telehealth and telecare were not only of a technical nature, but equally important was the consideration of S/T aspects [5].

Other authors [1, 6, 8] also emphasize the importance of considering S/T aspects in implementation of technology in elderly care. McKenna et al. [1] investigated deployment of social alarms (Personal Emergency Response Systems) in elderly people daily lives and found that one of the major problems experienced by elderly was unclear decision-making around social alarms activation. Regarding the results, a technical focus in development and implementation of assistive technologies results in poorly designed solutions that do not address user needs, or are not suitable for the task they were meant to support [6]. Vichitvanichphong et al. [8] and Peek et al. [9] identified factors influencing adoption of technologies among elderly people through two separate literature reviews. Vichitvanichphong [8] found that some of the factors were related to technology, but there were also many social and individual factors such as *compatibility with seniors' values or compatibility with the life style* that affected adoption of technologies among the elderly. Peek et al. [9], identified 27 factors influencing adaptation of technologies supporting aging in place in the pre-implementation stage. The authors divided the factors into six themes: (1) concerns regarding technology (e.g., high cost, privacy implications and usability factors), (2) expected benefits of technology (e.g., increased safety and perceived usefulness), (3) need for technology (e.g. perceived need and subjective health status), (4) alternatives to technology (e.g., help by family or spouse), (5) social influence (e.g., influence of family, friends and professional caregivers) and (6) characteristics of older adults (e.g., desire to age in place). Additional factors identified by the authors in the post-implementation were for example satisfaction with technology and affect towards technology. As we can see most of the factors were of a S/T nature. Therefore, although literature on implementation of technology for aging in place is generally scarce [4, 8], we found some publications showing that the complexity of S/T relationships cannot be ignored in this context. In this study, we investigated S/T challenges in implementation of MT in elderly care in general and implementation of social alarms in particular.

3 Research Method

The empirical part of this study was conducted in two stages applying a mixed method approach [13]. Our ambition was to include a broad range of stakeholders to be able to study S/T challenges from different perspectives. The two stages and related empirical data methods are presented in Table 1.

Table 1. Empirical datasets

	Stage1	Stage2
Focus	To identify S/T challenges in implementation of MT in elderly care generally	To identify S/T challenges in implementation of indoor and outdoor social alarms
Method	Semi-structured interviews, focus group interviews	Case study, Open-ended interviews, focus group interviews
Subjects	Municipalities officers, home care personnel, relatives, users, IT department staff	Municipalities officers, IT-department, users, relatives, home care personnel, alarm operators
N	9 semi-structured interviews, 4 focus groups (approx. 10 in each group)	16 open-ended interviews, 3 focus group interviews (approx. 5 in each group)

3.1 Stage 1: Identifying Socio-Technical Challenges in Implementation of MT in Elderly Care

In the first stage, nine representatives of stakeholder groups that were involved or affected by implementation of MT were interviewed with focus on challenges related to implementation of such technologies in real settings. In this stage we also conducted four focus group interviews with potential users and their relatives. The focus group method allowed the respondents to build upon responses from other group members and in this way topics were discovered that otherwise may be missed [14]. According to literature, modern technology is often experienced as complex and abstract by elderly people [15]. To reduce this feeling, each focus group was invited to a Research and Innovation Apartment where some examples of MT were demonstrated. Individual interviews and focus group interviews were structured on similar themes. The informants were asked to describe their expectations, feelings, ideas about MT's role in elderly care, whether they see any benefits and/or problems related to use of such technologies. During the interviews, scenarios were sometimes used to aid the communication. Each individual interview lasted approximately one hour, focus group interviews lasted approximately two hours.

3.2   Stage 2: Identifying Socio-Technical Challenges in Implementation of In-Door and Outdoor Social Alarms

In the second stage, the work was conducted as a collaboration between SICS Swedish ICT and four municipalities in Sweden (see Table 2) [16]. The municipalities in the case study were selected to reflect the social alarm field from diverse needs and different circumstances. A traditional social alarm is an alarm device that is installed in a user's home and makes it possible for a user to call for help in urgent situations at home. In order to identify S/T challenges it was important to understand attitudes towards the alarm and how the entire alarm chain (it starts when an alarm holder presses the alarm button and ends when staff from home care visits the alarm holder) was working. We also investigated needs and attitudes among all relevant stakeholders and the interaction between stakeholders. Another thing that is important in this context is the process of procurement and requirements around social alarm. Open-ended interviews were conducted with managers in the municipalities, personnel at alarm centers, and alarm holders. Furthermore, alarm operators and other personnel were interviewed at alarm centers. Approximately 2–3 alarm holders, in each municipality, 1–2 managers, staff members, and alarm operators were interviewed. During all interviews, the researchers took notes.

In this stage, we also investigated needs among elderly users and their relatives regarding outdoor social alarms to identify S/T challenges. An outdoor alarm communicates typically via mobile networks and has a GPS receiver to locate a person. The material was gathered in two ways, through focus groups and open-ended interviews. Focus groups were used to gather new ideas from a broad perspective. The objective was to encourage the participants to evolve new ideas together with others. Interviews were chosen to detect phenomena, properties, and meanings of using outdoor social

Table 2. The case study in four municipalities

Municipality	Location	No of citizens	No of social alarms	Alarm centre
Botkyrka	Suburb to Stockholm	85 000	800	Connected to a large central alarm centre
Värmdö	Municipality in the archipelago (rural and urban)	38 000	275	Connected to a large central alarm centre
Örnskölds-vik	Small town and rural	57 000	1 300	Local alarm centre
Pajala	Rural area	6 000	144	Connected to a large central alarm centre

alarms with respect to safety. In the interviews, 15 participants from three user categories were included: elderly, middle-aged next of kin who took care of their elderly relatives, and younger people who assisted a grandfather or a grandmother. During the focus group and the interviews, the researchers took notes.

3.3 Data Analysis

Data collected during the two stages were analyzed in five steps. *Firstly*, we identified all S/T challenges highlighted by our respondents in relation to implementation of MT in elderly care (stage 1). *Secondly*, we read through all statements several times in order to identify the initial categories. We found that the S/T challenges were related to three levels: community level, organizational level and individual level (see Fig. 1). In step *three* we categorized the S/T challenges according to the three levels. In step *four* we identified S/T challenges concerning implementation and use of social alarms (stage 2) and categorized them in relation to the three levels. In step *five* we continued our categorization process utilizing content analysis [17] in order to find patterns and themes within each of these tree levels. The emerging categories were identified based on careful examination, interpretation and constant comparison. The identified categories were then labeled (see Sect. 5).

4 Challenges in Implementation of MT in Elderly Care – Empirical Investigations

We used the framework presented in Fig. 1 to classify the S/T challenges identified in our empirical studies. As defined in Sect. 2, S/T challenges consider both technical and social aspects. The social aspects in our study were divided in three levels: *community, organization* and *individual*, illustrated as three outer nodes in Fig. 1. Each of the nodes was related to the fourth node in the middle - technology. In our case the technology node illustrates MT implemented and used in elderly care generally and social alarms especially. The *community node* was related to norms, culture, laws, and roles as well as inter-organizational aspects that came up in implementation and use of MT. Many private and public organizations were involved in this context. Implementation of MT often meant that different organizations needed to interact with each other in new ways at various organizational levels. *Organization* is about organizational structures, processes, policies, regulations as well as human resources that are affected by implementation and use of MT. The last node, *individual,* represented the users: the elderly people and their relatives. This node dealt with aspects such as attitudes, beliefs, feelings, competence, and preferences, with regard to the implemented MT. In order to identify S/T challenges in implementation of MT in elderly care we needed to investigate the relationships between the three outer nodes and the technology node. Below, analysis of the empirical material structured according to the three levels as illustrated in Fig. 1.

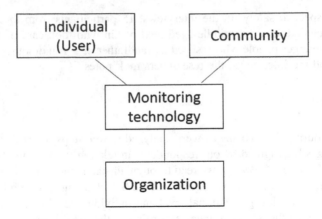

Fig. 1. Analytical model

4.1 Relationship: Community - Technology

In the relationship Community- Technology, the respondents highlighted the importance of including technology as a part of elderly care without decreasing its quality and with preserved freedom of choice for the elderly. *There must be alternative options for the elderly to choose from, the municipality must offer various possibilities. The technology can be one of them. No one should feel to be forced to choose technology if he/she does not want to.* One of the challenges highlighted in relation to this necessity was the need to change negative attitudes of technology existing among elderly and personnel who fear that implementation of technology will replace personnel and reduce possibility for human contact for the elderly. *It is important that technology is not solely seen as an efficiency measure but that technology might be a complement to existing care services and in this way it can increase the quality of the elderly care.* Municipality officers especially emphasized the significance of involving different stakeholders in the implementation of technology as a part of elderly care. *All the interested parties (organizations, individuals, representatives for unions and others) must be informed and aware about the new technical possibilities and involved in the process of implementation of these solutions in the real life!*

Other problems highlighted in relation to this category were lack of laws and regulations dealing with the issues arising in the new context as well as difficulty of applying existing laws and regulations in the new context, as one of our respondents explained: *Limiting measures are prohibited by law. However it is unclear how to deal with MT, whether it should be classified as limiting measure or not. Indeed, we need to interpret the law given the new technology.*

4.1.1 Examples from the Case Study "Social Alarm" in Relation to This Category

One challenge was to define responsibility structures when the analogue network is replaced with the digital infrastructure. Currently, the municipalities are responsible for social alarms and they are also responsible for providing a working solution for the users when the phone company 'turns off' the analogue telephone network. *The technology shift that occurs from analog to digital alarm solutions affects the municipality. There is not a total workable solution,* the respondents claimed. However it was unclear how the responsibility structures should look like in the digital infrastructure. Our respondents emphasized that responsibility for reliability in the digital infrastructure could not be the responsibility of the municipality only.

Another problem was that the municipalities had limited knowledge of products (social alarms) on the market and their functionality due to the complexity of social alarms. This lack of knowledge to procure the 'right' products for the users resulted in lower quality of elderly care. The solution to this problem could be cooperation across municipal boundaries, as one of the respondents argued: *It would be great if the municipalities could collaborate across municipal boundaries and work jointly in project to come up with better and more efficient solutions.*

Various stakeholders, such as homecare staff and operations managers in elderly care highlighted the need for outdoor alarms. According to them there were no concrete solutions regarding receiving and acting on alarms generated outdoors.

There were few municipalities that had the resources and procedures to deal with this type of alarm. New models for responsibility, for acting on alarm, for payment models etc., are needed to get this kind of complex structure to work. To find the right models for this challenge, the responsibility should be raised to a community level (not on a municipal level) where different organizations collaborate. An additional problem with current indoor and outdoor alarms is that they are based on different technologies and are not integrated into the same alarm solution. *"Cooperation among companies that develop social alarms, municipalities, home care, and end users are needed".*

4.2   Relationship: Organization - Technology

Challenges highlighted by stakeholders in relation to organization - technology consider homecare organizations, companies producing MT, municipalities and other organizations involved or affected of implementation of MT. Regarding homecare organizations, the stakeholders emphasized the importance of integrating technology as a natural part of business structures and processes. They found this very challenging because so far there is a lack of guidelines for how to do it. *The technical possibilities must comply with the procedures and processes existing in the organization. Technology must become an obvious part of the business and not something that exists outside!* Homecare personnel explained that introduction of technology, as a part of their work will probably change their way of working and thinking. They raised questions as: *Where should the collected data by MT be saved? Should it be a part of elderly's records or should it be saved somewhere else? For how long time should data be kept in the system and for what purpose?* They pointed out that these questions must be answered before MT can be implemented because otherwise there is a risk for the elderly's safety and a risk for violation of the elderly's privacy.

Homecare personnel were also concerned about how data collected by monitoring devices should be interpreted. They argued that elderly people are very different from each other and interpreting data on the basis of some standard might violate the elderly's dignity. *The risk is that we will interpret a specific situation based on general assumptions. What is common? What is a norm? People are so different. It's easy to make a general interpretation and upset a specific person.* Insufficient technical skills and uncertainty in using technology among homecare personnel was another challenge pointed out during the interviews. *The technology must be introduced in the right way, many of the staff are not familiar with the technology, they have not chosen the profession to manage technology, so they can become stressed if the technology is too difficult to handle or too complicated.*

Examples from the Case Study "Social Alarm" in Relation to This Category. An example showed that routines within homecare do not always work as desired. *You are working with other things even if you are responsible for receiving alarms and for going to the person who alerted. It can mean that you suddenly have to finish what you're doing, and even leave the person you are visiting.* It is important to integrate the technology with the workflows in elderly care. Today homecare staff cannot speak with the user on the speaker phone (integrated in the base unit of the social alarm), since it is only the staff at the alarm center who have this functionality, i.e., can talk to the user who activated the alarm. Our respondents argued: *It would be great, if it would be possible to call the speakerphone and talk to the user.*

Managers, which are responsibility for social alarms within the municipalities, need more knowledge about the technology and need to be able to offer current technology to its citizens. In the case study we observed that municipalities often do not have any methods in order to include the needs of users in the procurement process of social alarms. The challenges are to improve the dialogue with users and to develop methods to meet the needs to successfully introduce new types of alarms.

Results from the case study show that municipalities need to solve organizational processes in different ways. On islands and in rural areas in certain municipalities they have organized local alarm chains, meaning that each user must have his/her own alarm chain. Neighbors, relatives, etc. can be included in such alarm chain. If there is an incident, a person in the alarm chain can call health professionals, ambulance, etc.

4.3   Relationship: Individual - Technology

Challenges that different stakeholders highlighted in relation to this category were mostly related to the need of personalization and adjustment of technology to the users' specific and diversified needs, as well as to the need of ensuring the elderly people's privacy. This regarded both when the technology was implemented and when data collected by the monitoring systems was interpreted. As one of our respondents explained: *It is important to always take into account the individual's special needs. Every individual is different and must be treated in a special way when the technology is introduced.* This means that technology developed for elderly needs to be adjustable to the elderly's different needs and preferences. It was also pointed out that the elderly should be involved when the technology was implemented and that they always should have the right to decide about the implemented technology and services as well as about the time and extent of monitoring. *The users should decide by themselves where the sensors can be installed and which services can be implemented. Others should not be allowed to decide these things above the head of the elderly.* To be able to make such decisions, the elderly need to understand the consequences of the implemented services. Thus numerous respondents emphasized: *It is important to clearly explain to the elderly so they are able to understand the consequences of the implemented solution and specify their requirements.*

Examples from the Case Study "Social Alarm" in Relation to This Category. The social alarm was perceived as a security. *It is good both for my own part and for the family's sake to have a social alarm.* In interviews with managers in the municipalities it appeared that it was difficult for the municipality to identify and understand the user's needs. One important S/T challenge for the municipalities was to ensure that the quality of social alarms really addressed the users' needs, both with respect to alarm holders and personnel. One large problem was that the alarms had a very limited reach and were designed for indoor use only. *If I am too far away from the base unit, the alarm will not work.* In the analysis of the interviews a great need for an outdoor alarm was expressed. Currently, existing alarms cannot handle both traditional indoor alarm usage and outdoor alarm usage in the same solution. The problems of being unable to use the traditional alarm outdoors had the effect that some elderly people hesitated to leave their homes. One of our respondents argued: *It would be good with a longer reach between the alarm button and the alarm unit. It would also be great if there was GPS functionality, and that it was possible to talk via the alarm button.* Privacy regarding usage of social alarms was discussed with the participants in the focus group. The participants did not find the use of their geographical location as privacy invasive. The benefits were seen as far greater than the disadvantages to be located using GPS. The most important S/T challenge in this category seemed to be the possibility to offer outdoor alarms to everyone who wants it.

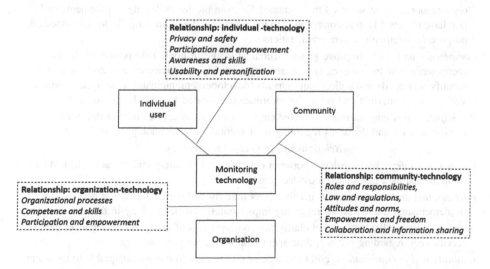

Fig. 2. Socio-technical challenges in implementation of MT in elderly care

5 A Framework for Classification of Socio-Technical Challenges

In Fig. 2, we present the framework for classification of S/T challenges arising during implementation of MT in elderly care. The framework is a refined version of our analytical model introduced in Fig. 1, Sect. 4. The technology node illustrates MT implemented in elderly care, the three outer nodes illustrate social aspects at community, organizational and individual level. The S/T challenges identified in this study

Table 3. Categories of socio-technical challenges

Relationship: community-technology
Roles and responsibilities: create clear responsibility structures and define new integrated care processes where different organizations and other parties are involved, define clear roles in these new care processes.
Laws and regulations: formulate new laws and regulations and adjust the existing ones so it is clear which rules should be applied when technology is an integrated part of elderly care.
Attitudes and norms: change users' and home care personnel's view of technology so they can see its potential to maintain or increase the quality in elderly care
Empowerment and freedom: ensure users' and homecare personnel's freedom to choose care services with technology or not. Involve users, citizens, homecare staff in decision regarding implementation of technology in elderly care
Collaboration and information-sharing: encourage, support cooperation and information sharing between private and public organizations and other parties regarding technical solutions that can improve quality of elderly care
Relationship: organisation-technology
Organizational processes: integrate technology as an integrated and natural part of care processes and organizational processes (in care organizations). In some cases new organizational processes need to be created for example for collecting requirements and purchase of new MT that corresponds to the users' need and are suitable for the specified purpose (municipalities, care organizations).
Competence and skills: improve general technical skills for home care personnel. Build competence how to compere, choose and purchase MT (municipality employees), how to identify user needs and collect requirements (developers, municipality employees, homecare staff), how to interpret and act to the information provided by MT (homecare staff)
Participation and empowerment: involve employees (e.g. homecare staff) in development, implementation and decisions regarding implementation of technology in their work.
Relationship: individual-technology
Privacy and safety: find a balance between elderly person's safety and privacy when MT is implemented as a part of the provided care services.
Participation and empowerment: involve users (elderly and their relatives) in development, implementation and decisions regarding implementation of technology in the care services.
Awareness and skills: explain and clarify the consequences of using MT as a part of care services e.g. regarding privacy, time spent with homecare personnel etc.
Usability and personification: build technology that is easy to use and adaptable to the users' diversified needs and preferences.

can be found in boxes connected to the relationships between the three outer nodes and the technology node.

The categories of S/T challenges illustrated in Fig. 2 are described in Table 3, below.

The framework and categories presented in this section were generated inductively from our empirical material and thus are not yet fully generalizable. However numerous of the S/T challenges identified in this study were also highlighted in literature (see Sect. 2, related research). For instance some of the factors identified by Vichitvanichphong et al. [8] and Peek et al. [9] as important for users' adaptation of technology, correspond to S/T challenges identified in this study in relation to the *individual –technology* category. Moreover, the S/T challenges identified during stage 1 and stage 2 in this study were similar even if the stages were conducted separately.

Nevertheless the framework and the categories need to be further verified and refined. The first step in our future research will be conducting systematic literature reviews focusing on S/T challenges in relation to the three levels identified in this study: community, organization and individual, aiming to refine and complement the categories identified and to assess the coherence with previous research.

6   Conclusion

Many of the existing projects aiming to provide a technology support to aging in place have a narrow technical focus ignoring the complex social and organizational context in which the technologies are implemented and used. In this paper we investigated the S/T challenges in implementation of MT in elderly care. *Based on qualitative inductive analysis of empirical data we suggest a framework for classification of the S/T challenges of MT in relation to the individual user, the organization and the community.* Our study shows that in order to be able to successfully implement monitoring technology one must to understand the social and organizational implications the technology implies for the different stakeholders, organizations and other areas of society. This paper contributes to a better understanding of S/T challenges in this context.

References

1. McKenna, A.C., Kloseck, M., Crilly, R., Polgar, J.: Purchasing and Using Personal Emergency Response Systems (PERS): how decisions are made by community-dwelling seniors in Canada. BMC Geriatr. **15**, 1 (2015)
2. Bowes, A., Dawson, A., Bell, D.: Implications of lifestyle monitoring data in ageing research. Inf. Commun. Soc. **15**, 5–22 (2012)
3. Koch, S., Marschollek, M., Wolf, K.H., Plischke, M., Haux, R.: On health-enabling and ambient-assistive technologies. What has been achieved and where do we have to go? Methods Inf. Med. **48**, 29–37 (2009)
4. Gruenerbl, A., Bahle, G., Weppner, J., Lukowicz, P.: Ubiquitous context aware monitoring systems in psychiatric and mental care: challenges and issues of real life deployments. In: 3rd International Conference on Context-Aware Systems and Applications, 15–16 October. ACM (2014)

5. Eason, K., Waterson, P., Davda, P.: The sociotechnical challenge of integrating telehealth and telecare into health and social care for the elderly. In: I.R.M.A. (ed.) Healthcare Administration: Concepts, Methodologies, Tools, and Applications, USA, pp. 1177–1190. IGI Global (2015)
6. Oishi, M.M.K., Mitchell, I.M., Van der Loos, H.F.M.: Design and Use of Assistive Technology Social, Technical, Ethical, and Economic Challenges. Springer, New York (2010)
7. Baxter, G., Sommerville, I.: Socio-technical systems: from design methods to systems engineering. Interact. Comput. 23, 4–17 (2011)
8. Vichitvanichphong, S., Talaei-Khoei, A., Kerr, D., Ghapanchi, A.: Adoption of assistive technologies for aged care: a realist review of recent studies. In: 47th Hawaii International Conference on System Sciences (HICSS), pp. 2706–2715 (2014)
9. Peek, S.T.M., Wouters, E.J.M., van Hoof, J., Luijkx, K.G., Boeije, H.R., Vrijhoef, H.J.M.: Factors influencing acceptance of technology for aging inplace: a systematic review. Int. J. Med. Inform. 8, 235–248 (2014)
10. Mumford, E.: Redesigning Human Systems. Information Science Publishing, Hershey (2003)
11. Ivari, J., Hirschheim, R.: Analyzing information systems development: a comparison and analysis of eight development approaches. Inf. Syst. J. 21, 551–575 (1996)
12. Mumford, E.: Systems design and human needs. In: Andersen, N.-B., Hedberg, B., Mercer, D., Mumford, E., Solé, A. (eds.) The Impact of Systems Change in Organisations. Results and Conclusions from a Multinational Study of Information Systems Development in Banks. Sijthoff & Noordhoff, Alphen aan den Rijn (1979)
13. Patton, M.Q.: Qualitative Research & Evaluation Methods. Sage Publications, Inc., Thousand Oaks (2002)
14. Stewart, D.W., Shamdasani, P.N., Rook, D.W.: Focus Groups: Theory and Practice. Sage Publications, Thousand Oaks (2007). 2 uppl
15. Zwijsen, S.A., Niemeijer, A.R., Hertogh, C.M.P.M.: Ethics of using assistive technology in the care for community-dwelling elderly people: An overview of the literature. Aging Ment. Health 15, 419–427 (2011)
16. Sjölinder, M., Avatare Nöu, A.: Indoor and outdoor social alarms: understanding users' perspectives. JMIR Mhealth Uhealth 2, e9 (2014)
17. Schreier, M.: Qualitative Content Analysis in Practice. SAGE, Los Angeles (2012)

Developing BIM-Enabled Facility Management Information System in Interior Design

Ju-Hung Lan[⊠]

Department of Interior Design, National Taichung University of Science
and Technology, Taichung 404, Taiwan, ROC
jhlan@nutc.edu.tw

Abstract. This study demonstrates how to integrate 2D and 3D information in the various design stages and provides an effective facility management solution from a life cycle point of view based on building information modeling (BIM) techniques. The research proposed a framework of design information structure by examining practical design projects. With the proposed information structure, the research applied Autodesk Revit Architecture and Solibri Model Viewer, which employs parametric modeling and visual design techniques, to develop a BIM-enabled facility management information system. The developed system provided consistent information service in various design stages. In addition, facility managers could make inquiries to acquire comprehensive information related with design components or installed facilities in the design project. The overall system provided an effective decision support mechanism to maintain the facility performance from a project's life cycle point of view.

Keywords: BIM · Facility management · FM · Interior design

1 Motivation and Purpose

In recent years, interior design industry has flourished concurrently with the advancement of information technology. The use of computer-aided design software to render the interior design efforts into three-dimensional and realistic drawings has become a popular trend. However, these computer-generated renderings can only portray efforts in the design stage. They cannot provide acceptable mechanisms for managing/maintaining subsequent indoor facilities. Building information modeling (BIM) can be used to collate and establish information concerning various stages of a building's lifecycle, thereby providing users with consistent project information throughout the entire lifecycle of the building. Under the concepts and technical application of BIM, design projects can not only be rendered into two-dimensional and three-dimensional design drawings, but also include water/power/ventilation pipelines, indoor facilities and systems, and equipment and machines, providing a comprehensive and effective project information communication and integration mechanism for developers in terms of planning and design, building and construction, and subsequent maintenance and management [1].

In this context, the present study aimed to develop a facility management information system (FMIS) for indoor projects based on BIM. By applying BIM techniques, the present study investigated the facility management (FM) of indoor projects to

© Springer International Publishing Switzerland 2016
J. Zhou and G. Salvendy (Eds.): ITAP 2016, PartII, LNCS 9755, pp. 57–69, 2016.
DOI: 10.1007/978-3-319-39949-2_6

elucidate how BIM can be utilized to reduce maintenance expenses and mitigate false information or resource wastage caused by inconsistent information at various stages, thereby improving the effectiveness of developing indoor projects and managing/maintaining subsequent facilities. The proposed system can be used to satisfy the FM requirements of users, providers, and designers/decision-makers at various stages.

2 BIM and FM

The American Institute of Architects (AIA) defined BIM as a type of "modeling technique for combining the information databases of engineering projects". This technique relies primarily on database technology. The structured file specifications of BIM are searchable and comply with local, national, and international standards [2]. Howell and Batcheler asserted that BIM encompasses geometry, spatial associations, geographic information, and data concerning the properties and quantities of various building components. The researcher also contended that BIM can effectively integrate the drawing and non-drawing data in architectural engineering into an information model [3]. Chien defined maintenance management as a frequent and uninterrupted process to ensure that equipment continues to operate at due performance, thereby improving equipment performance and competitiveness [4].

3 Methodology

Based on the life cycle of buildings, the present study aimed to develop a BIM-enabled FMIS for interior design. First, in-depth interviews were conducted to gain insight into the procedures of the building and interior design and renovation projects. Then, the BIM software development toolkit (SDK), was used to analyze the interior design and renovation element groups and FM functions. Finally, actual indoor projects were incorporated into the system to test system performance and determine overall research results. The research method and procedures are as follows:

1. Expert Interviews: Representative architects and interior designers were invited to participate in an in-depth interview survey to gain insight into the development procedures of the building and indoor projects and highlight various problems concerning the generation and collation of information in the various stages of project development. The interview data was collated and analyzed to clarify the challenges of developing an FMIS for indoor projects.
2. System Function Analysis: A collation and review of extant literature review were performed to analyze the hierarchical structures of group element modules for indoor spaces and the function demands of users. The data was then used to formulate the function modules, including the development of the BIM group elements, FM functions, and the design of the user interface.
3. System Development: The interview and system function analysis results were used to develop the system. The FMIS for interior design was constructed using the Revit software and the file exchange information format announced by the Industry

Foundation Classes (IFC). The proposed system provides users with relevant drawings, model information, usage conditions, and facility management and maintenance decisions.

4 Data Collection and Analysis

4.1 Collating Project Interview Data

To investigate the research topic, the present study first interviewed representative architects and interior designers that used computer-aided information technologies in managing projects in order to gain insight into the management procedures and information frameworks of design projects in relevant agencies. In addition, representative building and indoor project cases were collected for subsequent analysis. The interview content focused on the information management framework, document content and classifications, and illustration management required in the overall project execution process. Figure 1 illustrates the building project information framework collated from the interview data. The framework comprises seven items, namely planning stages, construction drawings, 3D computer drawings, valuation information, working drawings, completion drawings, and base images. Figure 2 illustrates the indoor project information framework collated from the interview data. The framework comprises six items, namely, planning stages, construction drawings, 3D computer drawings, valuation information, base images, and collection of papers.

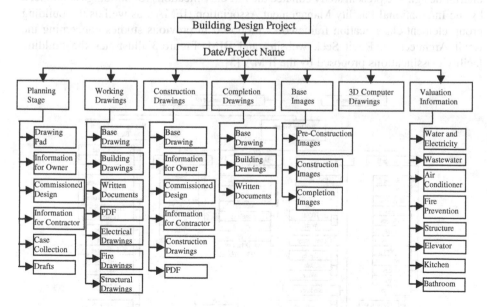

Fig. 1. Building design project information framework

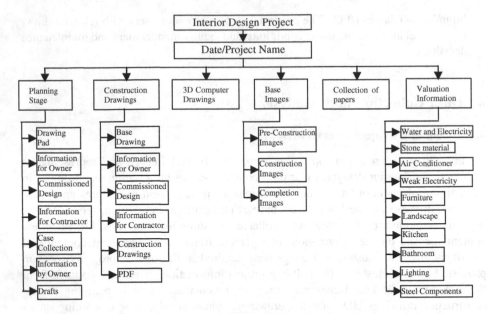

Fig. 2. Interior design project information framework

4.2 Analyzing the BIM-Enabled Group Classification Framework

To determine the feasibility and efficiency of developing a BIM-enabled FMIS for interior design, the present study collated the FM classifications for buildings announced by the International Facility Management Association (IFMA), as well as the building group element classification frameworks proposed in previous studies concerning the Revit Architecture, Revit Seek website, and BIM. Figure 3 illustrates the building facility classifications proposed by the IFMA [5].

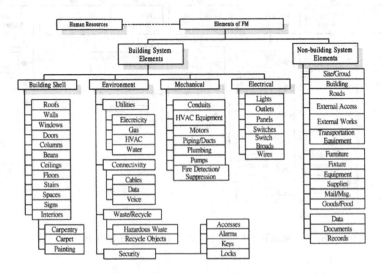

Fig. 3. IFMA group classifications

Table 1. Revit Group Classifications

Building	Indoor	Equipment	Landscape
Volume	Sofas	Ladders	Vehicles
Bases	Tables	Escalators	Plants
Columns	Chairs	Elevators	Sports Venues
Beams	Beds	Kitchen	Site components
Trusses	Cupboards	Bathroom	Views
Walls; Curtain Walls	Lighting	Cupboards	
Doors	Software accessories	Counters	
Windows	Appliances	Sports equipment	
Railings		Instruments	

Table 2. Revit Seek Group Classifications

Building	Indoor	Mechanics	Appliances	Pipes	Facilities
Beams	Beds	Air conditioners	Electricity cables	Water pipes	Benches
Columns	Tables	Air conditioner pipelines	Cooking equipment	Faucets	Parking
Ceilings	Chairs	Air regulators	Electricity boxes	Washing basins	Trees
Walls; curtain walls	Cupboards	Air processor	Lighting	Toilets	Streetlights
Doors	Lighting		Switches		
Windows			Refrigerators		
Stairs					
Trusses					
Gutter					

The group classifications included in the Revit software are tabulated in Table 1 [6]. The group classifications for Revit Seek are tabulated in Table 2 [7]. The group classifications proposed in previous BIM studies are tabulated in Table 3 [8].

4.3   The BIM-Enabled Group Classification Framework for Interior Design Projects

After summarizing the aforementioned figures and tables, the present study found that the groups in Revit were based on building design and lacked interior design group elements and classifications. This issue was improved in the database on the Revit Seek website by including interior design-related group elements. However, most of the elements were furniture group elements and lacked renovation ones. Therefore, the group database was relatively insufficient. A number of previous studies proposed classifications of BIM group elements based on building. However, certain classifications were different to

Table 3. Group Classifications Proposed in Previous BIM Studies

Structure	Door and window	Curtains	Decoration	Mechanics	Water and electricity	Air regulators
Columns	Doors	Curtain walls	Ceiling accessories	Elevators	Water intake/Discharge components	Regulator host
Beams	Windows	Curtain windows	Floor accessories	Mechanical parking	Sewage pipes	Ventilation system
Floors			Wall accessories		Rainwater pipes	Refrigerant pipe system
Walls					Water intake/Discharge systems	
Stairs					Hygiene equipment	
Roofs					Lighting	
					Weak electricity	
					Pipes	
					Ground	
					Switches	
					Fire prevention	
					Fire pipes	

those for interior design projects. Therefore, the present study collated the aforementioned classifications and independently classified interior design project groups into eight classifications, specifically, structure, doors and windows, building, renovation, water and electricity, ventilation, machines, and equipment. Associating elements were then allocated into these classifications, as shown in Table 4.

5 The Development of a BIM-Enabled FMIS for Interior Design

5.1 Incorporating Projects

To develop the system, the present study first incorporated the information of an actual interior design project. The information was then organized based on the framework illustrated in Table 4. The Revit Architecture was used to establish the relevant group elements for the interior design projects. At this stage, the group elements were established using the dimension style of two-dimensional construction drawings. Once the group elements were established, the object information within the project model was verified (e.g., size, specifications, and material properties).

5.2 Establishing Group Elements

The present study established group elements in the structure, doors and windows, building, and renovation classifications. The manufacturing method, material, and

Table 4. The Group Classification Framework for the BIM-Enabled Interior Design Project (Collocated in the Present Study).

Structure	Door and window	Building	Renovation/Decoration	Water and electricity	Air regulators	Mechanics	Equipment
Columns	Doors	Curtain walls	Ceiling renovation	Water intake/Discharge components	Regulator host	Elevators	Furnaces
Beams	Windows	Curtain windows	Floorboard renovation	Sewage pipes	Ventilation system	Mechanical parking	Lighting controller
Floors		Outer wall accessories	Floor renovation	Rainwater pipes	Refrigerant pipe system		Air conditioner controller
Walls		Umbrellas	Wall surface accessories	Water intake/Discharge systems			
Stairs		Fences; railings	Wall accessories	Hygiene equipment			
Roofs			Cupboard renovation	Lighting			
			Fixed partitions	Weak electricity			
			Arranged displays	Pipes			
				Ground			
				Switches			
				Fire Prevention			
				Fire pipes			

information of each element are presented in the description page. Once the classifications were established, the interference checking function was executed to check for erroneous information among the groups and elements in the project model and overlapping error dimensions. Establishing group elements were completed once no errors were confirmed.

1. Structure group:
   (a) Establishing the structural column: The structural column in the design project was a reinforce concrete (RC). Thus, the element was modified from the structural column group in Revit by changing the group type, element information, and properties, thereby completing the establishment of the structural column for the design project.
   (b) Establishing the floorboards: The floorboards in the design project were RC structures. Thus, the element was modified from the floorboard group in Revit. The floorboards in the design projects were paved with a terrazzo surface. Thus, the presents study modified the group type to RC material. The original floorboard group in Revit did not include a field for surface material properties. Therefore, the present study included a terrazzo surface layer to create a new structural floorboard.

(c) Establishing the walls: The wall group in Revit was modified. The wall was constructed with RC concrete with cement painted on the surface, hence RC concrete was chosen as the structural material in the edit wall type settings, and a layer of decorative cement paint layer was added to both the interior and exterior to create a new wall.

2. Door and window group:

(a) Establishing doors and windows: The door and window group available in Revit was modified. After selecting the type of door/window, its properties are edited according to the project and added as a new door or window.

3. Decoration group:

(a) Establishing elevated floorboards: The group elements in Revit are used as the components in the construction. Since there are no floorboard renovation components for interior design, this study must establish a set of group elements related to interior design. Hence the original floor components in Revit were used as a foundation for further modifications. The elevated floorboard consists of three layers, sequentially they are the elevated base layer, the shockproof structural layer and the surface layer. This is done by duplicating the original floorboard characteristics and using the component editor to insert the base layer and the shockproof structural layer into the internal structure. After modification according to the specified dimensions required in the project, the elevated floorboard component is added to the interior design, as shown in Fig. 4.

(b) Establishing Light partition wall: Light partition walls are created by modifying the walls that are originally available in Revit. Light partition walls can be constructed as single-sided or double-sided. Single-sided walls are used as decorative walls fixed on the original walls. Double-sided walls are used for dividing spaces. Single-sided light partition walls consist of three layers, sequentially they are: Type-C aggregate, the calcium silicate board, and surface paint; Double-sided light partition walls consist of five layers. From the interior to the exterior, sequentially they are: Type-C aggregate, calcium silicate boards on both sides, and surface paint on both sides. The original wall properties are duplicated as single and double-sided light partitioning walls, and their properties are modified with the component editor, and after inserting the layers into the internal structure and making modifications according to the specified dimensions required in the project, a new light steel frame partition wall component is added for interior design use, as shown in Fig. 5.

(c) Establishing waterproof brick partition wall: The waterproof brick wall was constructed using the brick wall originally available in Revit as a foundation. In the construction of the waterproof brick wall in the bathroom, the wall is divided into four layers. The sequence is: the brick layer, the cement layer, the waterproof layer, and the surface layer. However, an extra decorative board was added on top of the surface and so there are total of five layers. The component characteristics were edited on the original brick wall type to become a waterproof bathroom wall. After the internal structure of the layers is altered in sequence, modified and edited for the project, they are added as waterproof brick partition wall component, as shown in Fig. 6.

(d) Establishing movable glass partition: Partitions are created by modifying walls, doors or windows that are originally available in Revit. In our case, we used a movable glass partition, hence the window group was modified. The window component was imported and its properties modified according to the specified dimensions required in the project. The movable glass partition component is added for interior design use, as shown in Fig. 7.

(e) Establishing cabinet: The constructions of cabinets are carried out using the group elements that are already available in Revit. However, hollow bodies and countertops are separate components and require manual configuration. This study imported the cabinet and then the countertop component and modified their properties. The cabinet component is added for interior design use, as shown in Fig. 8.

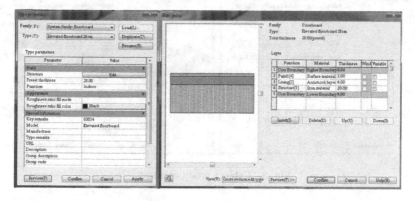

Fig. 4. Elevated floorboard group element

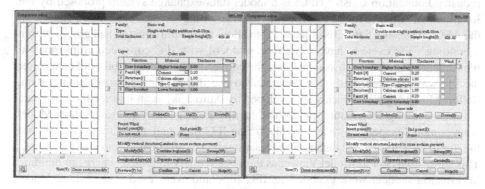

Fig. 5. Light partition wall group element

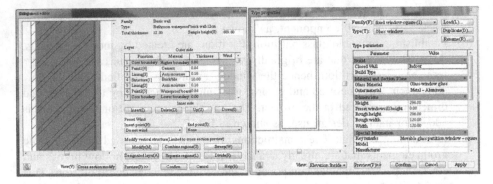

Fig. 6. Waterproof brick partition wall group element.

Fig. 7. Movable glass partition group element

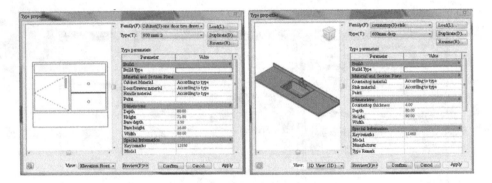

Fig. 8. Cabinet group element

5.3 The Facility Management System Interface

Industry Foundation Classes (IFC) is a model data exchange system proposed by the International Alliance for Interoperability (IAI) targeting the data exchange standards in the AEC/FM design fields. Its objective is to allow all the information and groups within a building's life cycle to have a common protocol with IFC construction information files that are convertible so as to increase the convertibility and reusability of data. After the file was exported, this study attempted to use the BIM model inspection system, Solibri Model Viewer, which was developed by Autodesk, as an intermediary software between building information model and facility management queries. Solibri Model Viewer model inspection system is able to read IFC files, and all the model data within the group elements can be displayed and is a stable and practical intermediary software. This study used Solibri Model Viewer as the system query interface, where our building information models were exported as IFC files and were used with Solibri Model Viewer. The system interface is shown as Fig. 9. Using this model inspection system's control interface to display all the data and illustrations from our building information

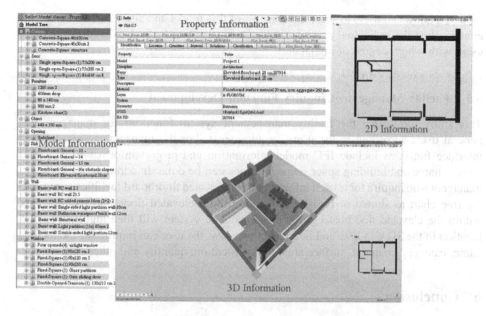

Fig. 9. The system interface

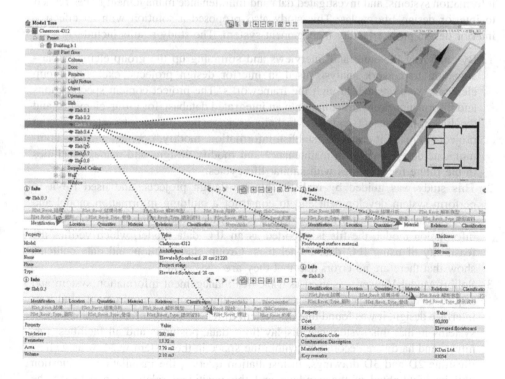

Fig. 10. Information windows for inquiry

model, it allows all users to share the contents of this model and also to select the model contents that the individual user would like to investigate further, as well as provides users with a high degree of interaction.

5.4 Facility Management Inquiry Function Development

This study formulated the facility management system functions for managers and general users according to the users' requirements. For the manager, system inquiry interface functions include IFC model information and project information contents. Project name and building space name inquiries can be done. In addition, for instance, managers who inquire for related information for elevated floorboard facilities can utilize the tree chart as shown in Fig. 10, to inquire about elevated floorboard components within the elevated floorboard group elements. The system will then highlight spatial location in the 3D window, and in the data window, the user can inquire for the facility name, category, material, surface area, floors, location, quantity and other data.

6 Conclusion

This study used BIM techniques to develop a set of interior design facility management information systems, and investigated data and maintenance management issues related to interior design life cycles. This study also proposed a solution with an effective interior design project facility management system. The study results include:

1. By analyzing literature and interviews and summing up the group elements classification framework analysis used in interior design projects, exclusive group elements were created through the frameworks. The project content specifications and information were structured into an integrated database for group elements, and the life cycle concept and BIM techniques were introduced into interior design projects to make it easier to establish information, modify, operate, analyze, communicate designs, perform maintenance and modify designs and manage facilities in the future for buildings with similar life cycles.
2. This study was guided by realistic interior design projects, and used Revit to perform system development and to construct a building information model and group element system for interior design use. After constructing the interior design information model, the file is exported as an IFC data model, which verifies the feasibility of using IFC data model files. Group classification and data contents show that there are no errors and that they are consistent.
3. Solibri Model Viewer was used as a facility management information system and inquiry interface. After function testing according to users' requirements and user interface design, it was found that the system differs from other facility management systems in that this system can display floor data, positions and all facilities, furniture, and hardware decorations within the space in the system window as well as illustrate 2D and 3D drawings. In installation queries, the installation in question will be highlighted in the window, and the positional relationship between the installation and space can be observed and the name, shape, dimensions, amount

and other properties of the installation will be shown. These are some of the differences with other facility management systems that contribute to user friendliness.

Acknowledgements. This study is supported by Ministry of Science and Technology, Taiwan, R.O.C., MOST 104-2221-E-025-013. The author is grateful to this support.

References

1. Eastman, C., Teicholz, P., Sacks, R., Liston, K.: BIM Handbook: A Guide to Building Information Modeling for Owners, Managers, Designers, Engineers, and Contractors. Wiley, New Jersey (2008)
2. AIA KnowledgeNet. http://network.aia.org/technologyinarchitecturalpractice/home/bimstandards
3. Howell, I., Batcheler, B.: Building Information Modeling Two Years Later – Huge Potential, Some Success and Several Limitations, The Laiserin Letter (2005)
4. Chien, S.K.: Use BIM to Construct Building Facility Management System (in Chinese), Master's Thesis, Department of Construction Management, Chung Hua University (2011)
5. International Facility Management Association. https://www.ifma.org/
6. Autodesk Revit Architecture User Guide (2014)
7. Autodesk Seek: BIM Content Catalogue. http://seek.autodesk.com/
8. Wang, C.S.: A Study to Develop Decoration Component based on BIM (in Chinese), Master's Thesis, Department of Civil Engineering, National Cheng Kung University (2009)

A Study on Re-usage of Historical Building - from the Aspect of Room Acoustic for Live House

Wei Lin[1(✉)], Hsuan Lin[2], Kung-Huang Huang[3], and Tin-Hang Lin[1]

[1] Department of Interior Design,
Hwa Hsia University of Technology, Taipei, Taiwan
weilin@cc.hwh.edu.tw, black3790@gmail.com
[2] Department of Product Design,
Tainan University of Technology, Tainan, Taiwan
te0038@mail.tut.edu.tw
[3] General Manager, Shang You Construction Co. Ltd., Kaohsiung, Taiwan
sf.land@msa.hinet.net

Abstract. Renovation of historical building not only by the performance of the new usage of space continues it life, but more importantly approaches through the musical performance can be activated. Re-use of buildings as a "Live house" which is performed for the musical show with sound reinforcement system is particularly welcome by young people in Taipei. It is important to foster the promotion of pop music platform since starting to focus on issues of re-use of the interior of historical space in the globe, even domestic and foreign literature on the study slightly is still insufficient, which is concentrated on the main function of music performances. Therefore, this study stationed at Red House Theater "Riverside Message Music Pavilion" to explore the subject through the perspective of redefine their spatial acoustic performance capability, and the issue of noise prevention, reinterpreting the historical space combined with industry existing development of live musical performances. Research method is verified by computer simulation which is to understand the optimization of the performance of room acoustic. The results of preliminary study may offer the on-site users and performers of questionnaire interviews which are corresponding on the future objective field measurement.

Keywords: Historical building · Room acoustics · Live house · Computer simulation

1 Introduction

Music Performance Space (Live house) is to provide independent band and singers small concert venue, in recent years, government departments in Taiwan and other public events, such as "International Gongliao Sea Music Season," "Kenting Spring Scream Music Festival" and other large activities, not only allows independent non-mainstream music band emerge in the big occasion, but also cooperates with promotion by international exchange of music season. Non-mainstream music belongs

© Springer International Publishing Switzerland 2016
J. Zhou and G. Salvendy (Eds.): ITAP 2016, PartII, LNCS 9755, pp. 70–78, 2016.
DOI: 10.1007/978-3-319-39949-2_7

creation, avant-garde with profound implications for the type of music, covering a wide range of music, like the "underground music", "independent music" and "minority music" are for instance, it is different from the pop music performances aesthetically. Performance hall for live music play an important promoter and concert performances can be divided into temporal and spatial factor [1]. Temporal factor tends to hold "festival-style", having temporal limit, short and dense. The space factor of performance hall in Taiwan is called music venue for performances (Live house), with respect to the temporal factor, long-term development in nature and continuity venue provide a culture trends with non-mainstream music in Taiwan [2]. The best-rated halls in the Niels Werner Adelman-Larsen's study have reverberation times that are approximately frequency independent from 0.6 to 1.2 s for hall volumes from 1000 to 6000 m3 [3]. Some researches presented suitable mid-frequency depending on musical style, room volume and seating capacity [3–6]. Through Live hall presence, creating another culture trend for the reuse of historical building, for its pop and independent music performers is encouraged by the formation of a kind of local arts and cultural characteristics to attract domestic and foreign musical performing arts groups have been pilgrimage. In addition to creating a good indoor acoustic space, the electronic sound system is another major focus of this study, the role and function of electro-acoustic system in hall, speakers deliver music to listeners by the PA sound system, known as PA (Public address = Public Broadcasting), however, it is not satisfied to meet various for live status, the system of sound reinforcement (SR) is also introduced in 1965, SR demands not simply transmit the sound, but also receive the brilliant sound from the source, high-quality of sound speaker lead to concert music clearly without distortion which could reach the ears of the listener's. In the Meanwhile, the musicians can also hear their own sound with the monitoring system, which can improve performance communication among musical band. This paper presents the acoustical simulation for the live house which is relocated at re-usage of historical space. A number of major acoustical features have been employed in order to provide a hall which meets the various criteria for a venue designed to accommodate a sound reinforcement repertoire of events [7]. The paper begins with the general absorption material for the interior elements. Following sections are dedicated to detailed studies concentrating on the major design components. The results presented here not only have been used to verify the design scheme concept, simple field verifications have also achieved in the future newly built in order to characterize information of room acoustic. Riverside Message Music Pavilion relocated at The Red House Theater is opened in September 2008 and has always been considered as the premier live music venue in Taipei city, giving people in Taiwan access to a wider range of music options. The concerts also offer performance groups worldwide opportunities to learn from one another and make improvements accordingly. The volume of the hall is 2420 m3, and equipped the hall with acoustical curtains by modifying its acoustical characteristics. A room form was developed as prototype that had overall proportion and volume similar to the 460 seats is a cross-shaped plane like a western cathedral.

2 Research Approaches

From its completion in 1908 to today, Red House has witnessed the Qing Dynasty, the Japanese occupation of Taiwan. Then in Taipei west door, the construction market and the first commodity trading market, as the major consumer markets of Japanese immigrants (See in Fig. 1). Coming under influences from Japan, Shanghai and Western cultures, it has served as a market for wealthy residents, a gathering site for various Chinese cultural industries, and a window to the ideological trends of Western civilizations. Riverside Message Music Pavilion is relocated east side of cross shape building, 460-seat concert hall will serve a variety of uses: Concert, amplified musicals, drama and speech events. The acoustic requirements for these usages are very different, in terms of reverberation time. There is especially a requirement for additional reverberation for concerts when compared to amplified events. Amplified usage requires a shorter reverberation time and additional acoustic volume for loudness control. The proposed design concept achieves the required variability with an additional variable acoustical absorption were hide behind the sides grillages of the hall. One row of the draperies which is surrounded the stage and projected to the main auditorium is also shown here.

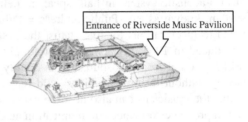

Fig. 1. Red House is used as Taipei Ximen Market (Taihoku Market, Formosa) inaugurated a century ago when the Victorian red and white appearance in period of Japanese government (Source of left photo: Taipics website, source of right Photo: drawing by Lee Chie Lan).

3 Survey and Raw for Study Field

The object of study is focused on Red House Theater _"Riverside Message Music Pavilion", although the body was established in a historic building, the interior floor plan and detailed configuration is not easy to obtain. The layers within a plane provided by the banks of a message APP configuration reference, scale control plane architecture body to re-draw, and to obtain the relative size of the building and interior configuration, the amount of space through complete three dimensional model of the body, as a follow-up to the performance of a computer simulation of room acoustics basis for assessment. Three dimensional modeling is mainly to carry out computer simulation for field and laboratory sound field performance analysis, including external build model structure cross building, interior beams distributed to the indoor compartment and floor openings, etc., thus rendering the entire system into a three dimensional model.

Exterior of the building components, including windows, sills, doors, roof, floor and other thick dimensions are in the field surveying (See in Fig. 2). As some information is also insufficient, we refer to the facade to match the size of the proportion of students drawn, the appearance of roof height model using by Google Earth is also referred. Get all of the above information, the three dimensional drawing of Riverside Message Music Pavilion began to be built into the model.

Fig. 2. Field surveying on exterior and interior of Red House Theater

From the observation the away from the stage at Riverside Message Music Pavilion, compared to outdoor concerts, sound and visual intimacy is an immersive experience. The main sound absorbing material are mostly black drapery which are installed in around the stage and vertical surface underneath balcony at second floor. Computer simulation does not require much space complex lines formed, this three dimensional model produced in a simplified manner. Due to the live house music is performed in the heritage building, so that the current much structural reinforcement beams are built as shown in Fig. 3 (Upper Left side photo). It will lead to computer simulation test system presents numerous calculation, but are still within the acceptable range. Three dimensional model showing the current status of the analog main draw (See in Fig. 3), according to the site to observe the pictures taken control position, the device comprising an line array sound system, stage lighting, draperies, furniture, and other equipment, in order to simulate the approaching sound performance of absorption the material authenticity.

4   Computer Simulation

When the musical perform, in addition to facing architectural space design, the tone, volume, reverberation may have a influence musical performance, may also have an impact on the live sound effects. To further confirm the performance hall planning

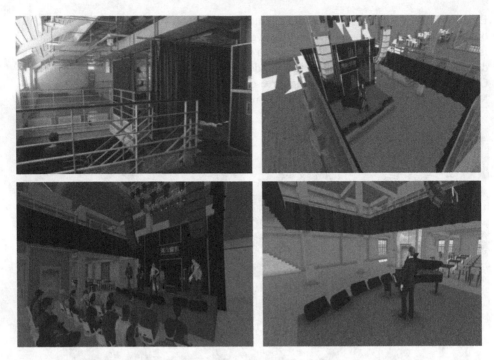

Fig. 3. Current much reinforcement beams were added for support building structure (Upper Left side photo). Three dimensional model drawing are also conducted for surveying

goals and acoustic parameters of the correlation between topography, assess technology includes the design stage through to computer simulation. Computer simulation technology in the 1960 s, Schroeder the basic principles of computer simulation into the room acoustics [8]. Asbjørn Krokstad the first published room acoustic of computer simulation papers, along with hardware and software technology continues to progress, the current auditorium acoustics computer simulation software has matured, widely used in research auditorium acoustics design and evaluation of sound field characteristics [9]. Computer simulation of room sound field by creating a mathematical model of the actual hall, according to the geometric method is for modeling acoustic sound wave propagation in the hall. Since the establishment of and modifications to establish a database of digital material model parameters through information operations, then check the status of the sound quality of the sound field. As shown in Fig. 4, the coverage of 1st order reflections can be evenly distributed to the stage and the frontal audience by only proposed upper reflectors.

The simulation was performed by using the upgraded Odeon software package that can handle energy parameters of ray tracing calculation and was used to validate the schematic concept of using the curve reflectors. The number of rays was set to 20000 and the truncation time of calculation was set to 2000 ms. The source was on the central axis and 3-m from the front edge of the platform. Initiate mode settings of Computer simulation of calculation are listed as shown in Table 1.

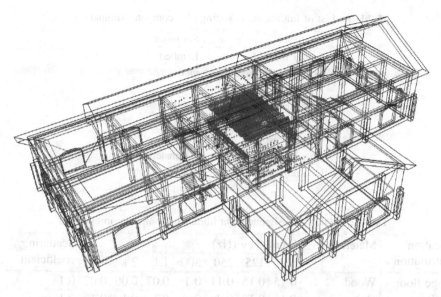

Fig. 4. Simulated 1st order reflection coverage from the upper reflectors.

A slot absorbing panels and a 0.4 scattering factor were assigned to the side and rear walls. Occupied seating with medium upholstery was used for the audience and a 0.7 scattering factor was assigned. 450 m2 absorptive draperies for reinforcement music with a 0.3 scattering factor were introduced. Furthermore, acoustics parameters were proposed design target values by computer simulation for the energy parameters RT, EDT and C80. Materials assignments in library of computer simulation are as shown in Table 2.

5 Preliminary Results

A omni-directivity sound source provided by the software package and was used occasionally as references. The source was on the central axis and 1.5-m from the front edge of the platform. Due to the cross-shaped hall-room space and symmetry, averaging 8 measuring points are chosen one side of seating which were symmetrically distributed. Sound source in front of stage is set and simulated perspective and distribution of sound energy particles of schematic model is shown in Fig. 5. Preliminary obtain mono sound parameter, reverberation time (RT), early decay time (EDT) and music clarity (Clarity, C80) are discussed. Acoustical indices, such as RT30, C80, D50, Ts and EDT, are derived from the impulse response which is based on the International Standard ISO 3382 (Bradley 2004) [10]. Preliminary results of acoustical parameters were calculated by computer simulation were summarized in Table 3 when all the acoustical draperies are taken on. The reverberation time at mid-frequency is resulted about 1.13 s.

Table 1. List of Initiate mode settings for computer simulation

Parameter	Set mode
Scatter method	Lambert
Decimate late rays	ON
Transition order	1
Number of rays	20000
Max. reflection order	2000
Impulse response length	2000 ms
Angular absorption	All materials
Late reflection density	600/ms

Table 2. Materials assignments in library of computer simulation

Location distribution	Materials	Frequency (Hz)							Scattering coefficient
		63	125	250	500	1 k	2 k	4 k	
Stage floor	Wood	0.15	0.15	0.11	0.1	0.07	0.06	0.07	0.1
Audience floor	Carpet	0.15	0.15	0.2	0.1	0.1	0.1	0.1	0.1
Audience seat	Medium upholstered	0.62	0.62	0.72	0.80	0.83	0.84	0.85	0.7
Ceiling	48 k Glass fiber	0.1	0.1	0.17	0.63	0.75	0.82	0.93	0.5
Side wall/Rear wall	Slot absorbing panels	0.28	0.28	0.5	0.65	0.7	0.7	0.7	0.4
Stage opening	Drapery	0.03	0.03	0.16	0.46	0.71	0.75	0.7	0.3

When comparing the reverberation time (T30) and early decay time (EDT) of the live concert configuration in the pavilion difference usage with 450 m2 absorptive draperies. The reverberation times (T30) and early decay time (EDT) derived from the simulation for the concert configuration and live music configuration are shown in Fig. 6. Reverberation time averaged from 250 Hz through 4 kHz was decreased by approximately 77 % when the draperies were totally opened.

6 Discussion

Re-use of buildings as a "Live house" which is performed for the musical show with sound reinforcement system is particularly welcome by young people in Taipei. The paper begins with the general absorption material for the interior elements. Computer simulation of room sound field by creating a mathematical model of the actual hall,

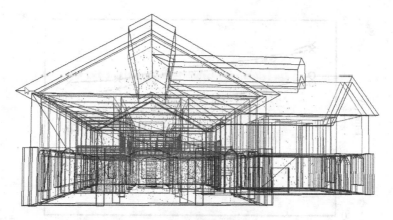

Fig. 5. Simulated perspective model and distribution of sound energy particles

Table 3. Acoustical parameters with live music performance were listed

Parameter \ Frequency	125 Hz	250 Hz	500 Hz	1000 Hz	2000 Hz	4000 Hz
T30(s)	1.43	1.27	1.21	1.15	0.98	0.91
EDT(s)	1.35	1.20	1.15	1.11	0.92	0.85
C80(dB)	2.01	2.45	3.54	3.28	2.52	3.31

according to the geometric method is for modeling acoustic sound wave propagation in the hall. Since the establishment of and modifications to establish a database of digital material model parameters through information operations, then check the status of the sound quality of the sound field. Following sections are dedicated to detailed studies concentrating on the major design components. The results presented here not only have been used to verify the design scheme concept, simple field verifications have also achieved in the future newly built in order to characterize information of room acoustic. Some preliminary results are abstracted as followed:

(1) Cross-shape room form distributed which is conective with heritage architecture, internal structure system are strengthened to against horizontal energy, interior partitions and related to openings are complete build to three dimensional models.
(2) The reverberation time at mid-frequency for live music performance is resulted about 1.13 s. derived from computer simulation.
(3) Reverberation time averaged from 250 Hz through 4 kHz was ideal decreased by approximately 77 % when the draperies were totally opened.
(4) Subjective assessment objective measurement in live house to investigate immediate hearing experiences, it will be the next phase of evaluation through questionnaires contribution which is corresponding to the physical room acoustics review of among the seats by differences on the property.

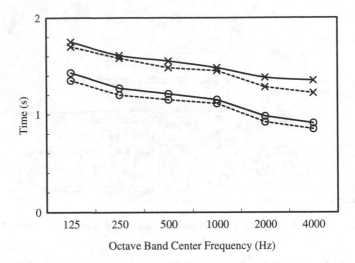

Fig. 6. Reverberation time (T30) (solid line) and early decay time (EDT) (dotted line) derived from computer simulation as a function of frequency band comparing the coupling configuration with curtains (X) to the configuration with all stage curtains (O).

Acknowledgments. The authors wish to thank Huang Kung Huang, Natural Acoustic for the helps of filed measurements, and Professor Wei-Hwa Chiang, Dep. of Architecture, National Taiwan University of Science and Technology the kindly assistances during the measurement phase.

References

1. Huang, S.-W.: The development of Taiwan's independent music and cultural policies. Master Thesis, Graduate Institute of Conservation of Cultural Relics and Museology, Tainan National University of the Arts' Tainan, Taiwan (2010)
2. Chen, C.I.: The development sttuation of live house in Taiwan: an example from river side. J. Art Collect. 233–253 (2012)
3. Siebein, G.W.: Project design phase analysis techniques for predicting the acoustical qualities of buildings. University of Florida (1986)
4. Adelman-Larsen, N.W., Thompson, E.R., Gade, A.C.: Suitable reverberation times for halls for rock and pop musica). J. Acoust. Soc. Am. **127**, 247–255 (2010)
5. Hoover, K.A., Ellison, S.: Electronically variable room acoustics-motivations and challenges. In: Proceedings of Meetings on Acoustics, Acoustical Society of America (2013)
6. Barron, M.: Auditorium acoustics and architectural design. Routledge (2009)
7. Chiang, W.-H., Lin, W., Chen, Y.-R., Hu, H.-Y.: Variable acoustics design of a small proscenium concert hall. J. Asian Archit. Build. Engineering **8**, 299–305 (2009)
8. Schroeder, M., Atal, B., Bird, C.: Digital computers in room acoustics. In: Proceedings of the 4th ICA, Copenhagen M 21 (1962)
9. Krokstad, A., Strom, S., Sørsdal, S.: Calculating the acoustical room response by the use of a ray tracing technique. J. Sound Vib. **8**, 118–125 (1968)
10. Bradley, J.S.: Using ISO3382 measures to evaluate acoustical conditions in concert halls (2004)

Identification of an Individual's Frustration in the Work Environment Through a Multi-sensor Computer Mouse

David Portugal[1], Marios Belk[1,2(✉)], João Quintas[3], Eleni Christodoulou[1], and George Samaras[1,2]

[1] CiTARD Services Ltd., 2064 Nicosia, Cyprus
{davidbsp,belk,cseleni,samaras}@citard-serv.com
[2] Department of Computer Science, University of Cyprus, 1678 Nicosia, Cyprus
{belk,cssamara}@cs.ucy.ac.cy
[3] Laboratory of Automatics and Systems,
Instituto Pedro Nunes, 3030-199 Coimbra, Portugal
jquintas@ipn.pt
http://citard-serv.com, http://dmac.cs.ucy.ac.cy, http://www.las.ipn.pt

Abstract. Older adults traditionally face major challenges at work when it comes to dealing with new technological tools. A sense of overwhelm and frustration can quickly arise under these circumstances. Continuous negative feelings in the work environment may lead to the increase of the risks for cognitive decline and threaten independence and quality of life. In this work, we focus on the seamless identification of frustration of older adults at work via physiological sensors embedded in an in-house developed computer mouse, denoted as CogniMouse. For the purpose of this research, we have developed a probabilistic classification algorithm that receives real-time signals and physiological measurement streams as input, and accordingly identifies frustration events. Ultimately, such classification can be leveraged to deliver user interventions and personalized solutions to help reduce user frustration.

Keywords: Active assisted living · Intelligent mouse · Physiological sensors · Cognitive support

1 Introduction

User modeling is a core area of research, which aims at endowing machines with intelligent mechanisms to understand and model human-like behavior. It finds vast applications in areas such as passive surveillance, health monitoring wearables, domotics, fitness applications, wireless sensor networks, and robotics to name a few [1].

In this work, we focus on a target group which consists of older adults (age 55+) that are still active in a computerized work environment. In general for this age group, virtual assistance systems [2] can play an important role in their

© Springer International Publishing Switzerland 2016
J. Zhou and G. Salvendy (Eds.): ITAP 2016, Part II, LNCS 9755, pp. 79–88, 2016.
DOI: 10.1007/978-3-319-39949-2_8

expectations for an active professional future, since typically they find it difficult to adapt their capabilities so as to cope with the most recent software changes, interface layouts, and computer work paradigms used in their work institutions. The CogniWin EU AAL project [3] aims at providing a personalization framework for motivating older adults to stay for longer active in the workplace. Thus, a virtual assistance system with learning and adaptation skills according to the user specificities is proposed, which also provides well-being guidance. Assistance to the older adults is delivered by analyzing multi-sensorial behavioral data provided at the low-level by an eye tracking system, and an intelligent computer mouse.

In this article, we will turn our attention to the intelligent computer mouse component of CogniWin[1], denoted as CogniMouse. Just like any other computer mouse, this human interface device enables the user to navigate within the operating system, and more importantly trigger computer actions as a result of physically clicking the mouse buttons. However, unlike other commercial mice, it encompasses several sensors that are additionally used to perceive human actions while working on a computer. Early detection of patterns and deviations from standard behavior is the main motivation of our work, as it enables to prevent further cognitive degradation in older adults by designing proper user intervention when abnormal episodes occur.

Besides developing the appropriate software drivers to extract the low-level sensor data, we propose a multi-sensor fusion process to detect whether the user is feeling frustrated while working on a computer with CogniMouse. Understanding that a user is frustrated is of key importance, as it enables a virtual assistance system to act accordingly to safeguard the user, *e.g.* by suggesting to take a break, or assisting the user in a computer task that he/she cannot complete by him/herself. Having this in mind, we not only provide a **definition of user frustration**, but also formulate a probabilistic algorithm that is based on a **multivariate Bayesian Classifier** [4], which takes processed sensor measurements and historical data as inputs, and continuously provides the likeliness of a user to feel frustrated.

In addition to describing the method to implicitly identify user frustration while using CogniMouse to interact with a software application, we plan a future validation study of the approach with a large group of active older adults in an end-user organization. Furthermore, we present a use case scenario to highlight the practical advantages to the user when running the proposed approach.

The article is organized as follows: in Sect. 2 we overview seminal work on frustration measuring and exploiting various inputs to examine user behavior. Afterwards we present CogniMouse, the multi-sensor computer mouse developed in the scope of the CogniWin project in Sect. 3, and describe how we identify frustrated behavior events while the user interacts with the system. We then reveal our planned method of study so as to validate the sensor fusion classifier and present a use case scenario in Sect. 4. Finally the article ends with conclusions and a discussion of future research directions in Sect. 5.

---

[1] http://cogniwin.eu.

2   Related Work

In the context of information technology and services, the literature reveals several works for detecting user frustration based on implicit user modeling approaches. Typically, frustration is detected and represented as a binary phenomenon (*e.g.*, frustrated vs. normal state) [7,10,11], while more recent works represent frustration in multiple levels [14] given that individuals might react differently (lower to higher levels) depending on the context of use (*e.g.*, an individual experiencing a slow internet connection while booking a flight ticket online *vs.* an individual browsing the Web over coffee). Popular examples of user frustration detection include approaches based on facial analysis [6], pressure sensors embedded in computer mice [7], behavioral observations and user system interaction analysis [8,9], speech patterns [10], and electrocardiograph data of individuals [11]. Other approaches include automated methods based on fusing multiple channels of affect-related information such as video camera, pressure sensing chair, pressure mouse and skin conductance measurement [12], and studies that compared frustration levels extracted through eye-tracking, mouse tracking tasks and electroencephalograph signals [13]. More recent works have focused on detecting user frustration in mobile contexts. Taylor et al. [14] developed models that predict multiple levels of user frustration through physiological signals retrieved from external devices (armband, wireless heart rate detector, finger clip skin conductivity sensor). A user study was conducted in a mobile setting aiming to evaluate the accuracy of the developed models by triggering user frustration through system response delays. Results revealed that the models of physiological responses classified five levels of frustration with over 80 % accuracy. Gao et al. [15] presented an alternative approach in the context of mobile devices, avoiding complications of external sensors, and instead leveraging how users touch and use mobile screen devices.

> **Frustration** is a negative emotional response to opposition and is viewed as a discrete or continuous state. Based on Rosenzweig, frustration is *"the occurrence of an obstacle that prevented the satisfaction of a need"* [5].

Considering the definition of Frustration presented above, in the next section we present an innovative probabilistic classification algorithm that receives real-time signals and physiological measurement streams given by an in-house instrumented computer mouse, named CogniMouse, so as to identify frustration events of older adults at work.

3   CogniMouse

CogniMouse is an advanced human interface device built around a standard computer mouse. Having the project's goals in mind [3], the sensors chosen when designing and assembling the device were: galvanic skin response sensor,

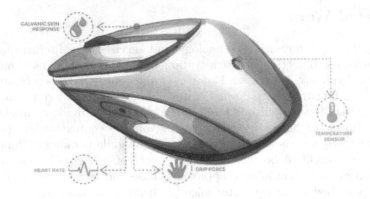

Fig. 1. Mouse sketch design.

temperature sensor, inertial measurement unit (IMU), grip/pressure sensor, and heart rate sensor.

The main innovative goal behind this smart device is to detect older adults' hesitation [16], emotional states (*e.g.*, anxiety) and frustration occurring whilst performing tasks in a personal computer. Hence, its user-friendly and familiar design illustrated in Fig. 1, has been selected to ensure the comfort of older adults, making them more likely to accept CogniMouse when carrying out their work. In fact, introductory interviews show that the design choice is particularly important, as users feel more comfortable with designs that are similar to the mice they normally work with. Furthermore, despite the suite of sensors included, the mouse has shown to be completely unobtrusive, and users frequently face it as a standard computer mouse.

Supporting Windows 7, 8 and 10, the software was developed in C# object-oriented programming language under the Sharp Develop integrated development environment (IDE). The C# language has been chosen for two main reasons: (*i*) it provides a good trade-off between efficiency, security and robustness and; (*ii*) it provides a number of libraries for communication with hardware components (*e.g.*, human-interface devices and sensors). Being able to run in the background without interfering with user actions, the software acquires multi-sensory information in real time. Besides this, the classification software leverages valuable information such as mouse motion and click streams through low-level Operating System (OS) calls, a priori knowledge of the user health profile and history of sensor data. From the combination of all these components, it is possible to assess the user's conditions. More particularly, we focus on the detection of symptoms associated to frustration episodes, such as: lack of control, agitation, general unhappiness, aggressiveness, etc. Furthermore, a Web-based graphical user interface has been designed and developed that illustrates in real-time the raw signals of the computer mouse, the user's current state (*e.g.*, increased frustration) and historical data about prior user states (Fig. 2).

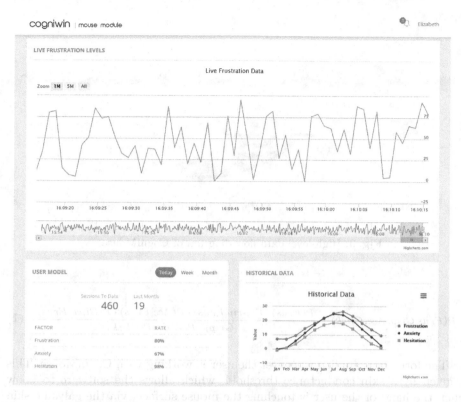

Fig. 2. Web-based graphical user interface of CogniMouse illustrating the raw signals of the mouse and the user's current and prior states.

A classification algorithm grounded on probabilistic theory is currently under testing. The algorithm continuously provides a level of certainty at which the user might be experiencing frustration. A probabilistic solution has been utilized due to the recognized results in the state of the art on classification algorithms from multiple sources with bounded levels of uncertainty [17].

In particular, we employ a Bayesian-based formalism inspired on conditional probability distributions to solve the problem due to its flexibility of incorporating new variables/inputs. The inputs used for the classification algorithm are: *(i)* grip force; *(ii)* acceleration vector and; *(iii)* click stream frequency. We use numerical series of past measurements of frustration with recursively decreasing weights to model the input prior distribution. Likelihood functions for each input have been derived heuristically by defining increasing influence to high deviations or abnormal input levels, considering the user typical health parameters. An independent frustration measurement is obtained by applying Bayes formula at each step considering prior and likelihood distributions, paired with a normalization factor that scales the result to a [0, 1] interval:

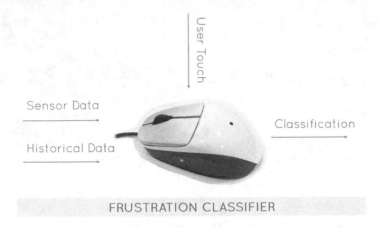

Fig. 3. High-level data flow diagram of CogniMouse.

$$P(Frus|Grip, Acc, Click) = \frac{P(Frus) \cdot P(Grip|Frus) \cdot P(Acc|Frus) \cdot P(Click|Frus)}{P(Grip) \cdot P(Acc) \cdot P(Click)} \quad (1)$$

The formula is applied whenever the user is working with CogniMouse. This is given by a skin conductance threshold, which allows the software to know when the hand of the user is touching the mouse surface, via the galvanic skin response sensor. The high-level classification approach is illustrated in Fig. 3.

In the next section, we reveal our plans to validate the method and present a use case scenario to highlight the importance of detecting user frustration.

4 Planned Evaluation and Use Case Scenario

Method of Study. A validation of the algorithm proposed is currently planned with a large group of active older adults in an end-user organization. The aim of the planned studies is threefold: *(i)* study the relation among user frustration and physiological signals extracted from the developed computer mouse; *(ii)* investigate the detection accuracy of triggering events of frustration; and *(iii)* adjust and improve the approach developed in an iterative mode.

The study's sample will consist of around 45 older adults (age 55+) that work in computerized environments. Following existing experimental approaches [13, 14,16], we planned several controlled laboratory sessions in which participants will perform a series of tasks (*e.g.*, change a setting on their desktop-based email client). While performing the tasks, the computer mouse will record the motion stream data and the users' physiological signals through the embedded sensors. We will follow the think-aloud protocol during the studies, utilizing screen capturing software and audio data for post-analysis by user experience experts. During user interactions, frustration events will be triggered by employing delays in the system's response [14] as well as providing tasks with different levels of difficulty (some tasks will be very hard, or impossible to complete). Frustration triggering events will be analyzed and cross-verified by annotations from psychologists and experts which will be witnessing the trials attentively. Finally, a post-study survey will be conducted based on the Rosenzweig Frustration Test (RFT) [18] to profile the users regarding their tolerance to frustration, and the NASA Task Load Index (NASA-TLX) [19] to assess the users' perceived workload and frustration aiming to triangulate the results.

Use Case Scenario. Susan is a 58 year old employee at Zuyderland Hoogstaete in Sittard, Holland. She is part of the entertainment staff of the extramural care department in the elderly home care facilities. She is an experienced worker who began her career 35 years ago in another regional elderly home institution. She has been working as a member of the entertainment staff for the last 6 years, and she is considered a very kind employee, being especially good in organizing activities for the elderly. In the last year, Susan has been experiencing some problems with her memory, which according to her doctor, is normal for her age. Besides that, she still feels young and active, and her intention is to stay for a few additional years working in the company in a paid mode.

Susan has basic computer knowledge and skills, and has been able to manage her computerized work at the institution so far. However, she feels that her younger colleagues can work more easily with the utilized software and sometimes she feels that she cannot handle new technological challenges that arise. At home, her children help her to do essential things *e.g.* online banking. At work, Susan often asks younger colleagues to help her with the computer tasks, such as writing the daily reports of the elderly.

The management of Zuyderland Hoogstaete recently decided to buy a new activity registration system called Citard Active. All seniors in Susan's department are going to use this application. The application, whose front-end is accessed on a tablet, smartphone or all-in-one PC make it possible for elderly to subscribe for activities, invite friends, has a notification reminder and provides accessory advice. All members of the entertainment staff have a key role in providing the system with relevant information about their elderly via an authentication and secure management system at the back-end.

With the arrival of Citard Active a few more responsibilities and work are expected from Susan. As a consequence, she is getting more and more insecure and nervous and she is even considering an early retirement. Susan experiences a lot of anxiety when working with Citard Active, because it makes her feel tired and she often gets frustrated from her non-productive way of using it and difficulty in the adaptation to the new system. She also finds it hard to read all the information on the screen and distinguish the different buttons. After 2 weeks working with the system, Susan hardly manages to login. Entering new activities for the elderly is very complex for Susan as well as other functionalities of the system. Therefore, she constantly needs help from a colleague.

Her director recognized her concerns and provides her with an innovative computer mouse called CogniMouse that will assist her to adapt her process' operations to accommodate the changes that the new software caused. She was told that the mouse will monitor her computer tasks' activities and adapt the new workload to her performance in order to avoid overloading her and all the frustration and performance loss that could be generated. One day, Susan was having a hard time in changing the properties of an activity that was previously created in the system. After a few failed attempts, she felt agitated and over-whelmed. CogniMouse detected her frustration by analyzing the data collected from the embedded sensors, and the contextual data from the operating system. Accordingly, the system presents a graphical help wizard of how to further pro-ceed by guiding Susan's mouse actions to the graphical system area that contains the next step of her process. Susan felt really happy for the assistance provided. Later on, in that same day when Susan was having a hard time creating a differ-ent activity type from the ones that she usually inserts, the system detected her frustration and advised her to stretch her legs and take a short break to clear her mind. Susan was very surprised to see that the system helps her as she feels that CogniMouse is refreshing her memory and assisting her to complete the tasks. Thus, she feels much more motivated at work. Moreover, when facing negative emotions she gets relieved by inspecting her health parameters on the screen so as to assess her own state. The quality of work and job satisfaction increases a lot and Susan can now manage to work for many years as an appreciated member of the entertainment staff.

5   Conclusion and Future Work

In this paper, building upon a classical definition of frustration, we have described a methodology to implicitly detect users' frustration in real-time while interacting with a computer mouse in the work environment. For this purpose, an existing off-the-shelf computer mouse was redesigned and developed, embedding physiological sensors for measuring in real-time the users' frustration levels. A user study is planned in the short-term future for the validation of the approach and a use case scenario has been designed to demonstrate the impact that our solution will potentially have in the effectiveness and motivation of older adults in the work environment.

In the future, we intend to combine information extracted from CogniMouse with additional sensors such as an eye tracker, and contextualize the mouse data so that the system provides adaptive support taking the user's task into account when frustration is identified. Moreover, this work also opens interesting prospects to similar classification methods for detection of user states in the future, such as stress and anxiety, tiredness or boredom while using the system.

Acknowledgments. This work was partially carried out in the frame of the CogniWin project (http://www.cogniwin.eu), funded by the EU Ambient Assisted Living Joint Program (AAL 2013-6-114).

References

1. Pantic, M., Pentland, A., Nijholt, A., Huang, T.S.: Human computing and machine understanding of human behavior: a survey. In: Huang, T.S., Nijholt, A., Pantic, M., Pentland, A. (eds.) ICMI/IJCAI Workshops 2007. LNCS (LNAI), vol. 4451, pp. 47–71. Springer, Heidelberg (2007)
2. Camarinha-Matos, L.M., Afsarmanesh, H.: Virtual communities and elderly support. In: Advances in Automation, Multimedia and Video Systems, and Modern Computer Science, pp. 279–284 (2001)
3. Hanke, S., et al.: CogniWin – a virtual assistance system for older adults at work. In: Zhou, J., Salvendy, G. (eds.) ITAP 2015. LNCS, vol. 9194, pp. 257–268. Springer, Heidelberg (2015)
4. Jansen, F., Nielsen, T.: Bayesian Networks and Decision Graphs. Springer, Heidelberg (2007)
5. Lawson, R.: Frustration: The Development of a Scientific Concept. Macmillan, New York (1965)
6. Grafsgaard, J.F., Wiggins, J.B., Boyer, K.E., Wiebe, E.N., Lester, J.C.: Automatically recognizing facial indicators of frustration: a learning-centric analysis. In: IEEE Humaine Association Conference on Affective Computing and Intelligent Interaction (ACII), pp. 159–165, Geneva, Switzerland, 2–5 September 2013
7. Qi, Y., Reynolds, C., Picard, R.W.: The bayes point machine for computer-user frustration detection via pressure mouse. In: Workshop on Perceptive user interfaces (PUI 2001). ACM, New York (2001)
8. Rodrigo, M.M., Baker, R.S.: Coarse-grained detection of student frustration in an introductory programming course. In: 5th International Workshop on Computing Education Research (ICER 2009), pp. 75–80, Berkeley, California, 10–11 August 2009
9. Harrison, L., Dou, W., Lu, A., Ribarsky, W., Wang, X.: Analysts aren't machines: inferring frustration through visualization interaction. In: IEEE Conference on Visual Analytics Science and Technology (VAST 2011), pp. 279–280 (2001)
10. Boril, H., Sadjadi, S.O., Kleinschmidt, T., Hansen, J.: Analysis and detection of cognitive load and frustration in drivers' speech. In: International Speech Communication Association (INTERSPEECH), pp. 502–505, Chiba, Makuhari, Japan (2010)
11. Belle, A., Ji, S.Y., Ansari, S., Hakimzadeh, R., Ward, K., Najarian, K.: Frustration detection with electrocardiograph signal using wavelet transform. In: IEEE International Conference on Biosciences (BIOSCIENCESWORLD), pp. 91–94, Cancun, Mexico, 7–13 March 2010
12. Kapoor, A., Burleson, W., Picard, R.W.: Automatic prediction of frustration. Int. J. Hum.-Comput. Stud. **65**(8), 724–736 (2007)
13. Noronha, H., Sol, R., Vourvopoulos, A.: Comparing the levels of frustration between an eye-tracker and a mouse: a pilot study. In: Holzinger, A., Ziefle, M., Hitz, M., Debevc, M. (eds.) SouthCHI 2013. LNCS, vol. 7946, pp. 107–121. Springer, Heidelberg (2013)
14. Taylor, B., Dey, A., Siewiorek, D., Smailagic, A.: Using physiological sensors to detect levels of user frustration induced by system delays. In: ACM International Joint Conference on Pervasive and Ubiquitous Computing (UbiComp 2015), pp. 517–528, Osaka, Japan, 7–11 September 2015
15. Gao, Y., Bianchi-Berthouze, N., Meng, H.: What does touch tell us about emotions in touchscreen-based gameplay? ACM Trans. Comput.-Hum. Interact. (TOCHI) **19**(4), 31 (2012)

16. Belk, M., Portugal, D., Christodoulou, E., Samaras, G.: Cognimouse: on detecting users' task completion difficulty through computer mouse interaction. In: Extended Abstracts on Human Factors in Computing Systems (CHI 2015), pp. 1019–1024, Seoul, South Korea, 18–23 April 2015

17. Aliakbarpour, H., Ferreira, J.F., Khoshhal, K., Dias, J.: A novel framework for data registration and data fusion in presence of multi-modal sensors. In: Camarinha-Matos, L.M., Pereira, P., Ribeiro, L. (eds.) DoCEIS 2010. IFIP AICT, vol. 314, pp. 308–315. Springer, Heidelberg (2010)

18. Rosenzweig, S.: The Rosenzweig Picture Frustration (P-F) Study. Rana House, St. Louis (1978)

19. Hart, S.G.: NASA-Task Load Index (NASA-TLX); 20 years later. In: Proceedings of the Human Factors and Ergonomics Society (HFES), vol. 50, no. 9, pp. 904–908. SAGE Publications, Santa Monica (2006)

Multi-sensory Cyber-Physical Therapy System for Elderly Monitoring

Md. Abdur Rahman[(✉)]

Computer Science Department, College of Computer and Information Systems,
Umm Al-Qura University, Makkah, Saudi Arabia
marahman@uqu.edu.sa

Abstract. This paper provides an overview of a multi-sensory cyber-physical therapy system suitable for old age people with physical impairments, which integrates entities in the physical as well as cyber world for therapy sensing, therapeutic data computation, interaction between cyber and physical world, and in-home therapy support through a cloud-based big data architecture. To provide appropriate therapeutic services and environment, the CPS uses a multi-modal multimedia sensory framework to support therapy recording and playback of a therapy session and visualization of effectiveness of an assigned therapy. The physical world interaction with the cyber world is stored as a rich gesture semantics with the help of multiple media streams, which is then uploaded to a tightly synchronized cyber physical cloud environment for deducing real-time and historical whole-body Range of Motion (ROM) kinematic data.

Keywords: Therapy CPS · Multimedia sensors · Gesture recognition · In-home therapy

1 Introduction

Therapy is prescribed to elderly population to move certain body joints and muscles through some targeted body motions. This helps in gaining enough muscle power to support daily life activities and keep one healthy. The status of muscle power is monitored by looking at the joint range of motion that is affected by the surrounding muscles [1]. Typical therapy modules targeting elderly people involve activities and gestures to monitor the whole body joint movements. In order to precisely find out the relative joint movement of the affected body, therapists either resort to very complex invasive skeletal devices that are impractical for elderly people or very much expensive to use it for general purpose in-home. For example, therapists use Goniometer to measure the angular displacement of an elbow joint manually during the elbow flexion/extension therapy, which is not scalable and/or practical for many elderly people. For example, in order to track 20 joints of a body, a therapist needs to attach 20 sensors or manual devices in each joint. Moreover, there are complex movements of the gestures that the therapists recommend to build and regain the affected joints and muscles that require high level therapist interventions. Examples of motions that are involved during existing therapies include Abduction/Adduction, Flexion/Extension, Pronation/Supination, Inversion/Eversion, Hyperextension, Dorsiflexion/Plantar flexion, Rotation/Circumduction,

© Springer International Publishing Switzerland 2016
J. Zhou and G. Salvendy (Eds.): ITAP 2016, Part II, LNCS 9755, pp. 89–100, 2016.
DOI: 10.1007/978-3-319-39949-2_9

Protraction/Retraction, and Elevation/Depression [2]. Existing invasive devices fail to dynamically track above motions of an elderly person and produce live kinematic data that can be used to gain deep knowledge about the status of each joint and associated muscle of affected region.

The non-invasive motion tracking capability could enhance the therapeutic diagnostics to the next level [3]. Therapists could assess the performance of the joints needing improvement. Hence, a therapist could provide feedback during or after a therapy session in a personalized fashion. Although sophisticated therapy facilities are available in medical institutions, in-home therapy is gaining popularity [4]. Therapy in the home is more flexible and convenient for an elderly person by allowing more frequent repetition of therapy exercises with the aid of caregiver family members. In order to keep the pace of improvement, therapists suggest that therapy modules be repeated the required number of times every day. While therapy sessions in front of a therapist are a necessary, a therapist cannot take care of a large number of elderly person, given the fact that our elderly population is very high [5]. Hence, a therapist cannot fulfill the required frequency of practice sessions necessary to increase the quality of improvement, making in-home exercises to complement this goal.

Although sophisticated therapy facilities are available in medical institutions, in-home therapy is gaining popularity [6]. Performing therapy in the home is more suitable for an old age person and their caregiver family members due to movement problems as well as it allows more frequent repetition of therapy exercises with the assistance of caregiver family members. To help during in-home therapy, various off the shelf gesture computing platform such as Microsoft Kinect, LEAP motion, MYO, have recently emerged that help in identifying physiological and gait parameters from a therapy session in real-time [7]. However, to the best of our knowledge, there is no gesture-based multi-sensory solution for cyber-physical therapy system, which supports in-home therapy. In this paper, we present a cyber-physical therapy system, which is based on client-server big data cloud architecture [8]. In the CPS framework, a user having old age motor disability can use multimedia gesture tracking sensors in the physical world and a middleware software as cyber world running on her PC/smartphone and in the cloud [9]. A therapist can suggest certain exercises to an elderly person, which she can perform at home [10]. The therapy CPS framework allows an exercise session to be captured, stored in Amazon Cloud Computing Cyber Environment and analyzed for deducing improvement factors. Moreover, a number of serious games have been designed to fully immerse a user in the cyber world while the multi-sensory physical world environment collects full body range of motion kinematic data [11].

The rest of the paper is organized as follows. Section 2 describes the CPS framework design. Section 3 outlines the implementation technologies while Sect. 4 concludes the paper.

2   Framework Design

The framework comprises of a physical world consisting of elderly people and gesture tracking sensors to support therapies at home, and a middleware interfacing the cloud environment acting as cyber world. The middleware has two main components, one residing at the client side and the other at the cloud environment. The client side is responsible to interact with the multi-sensory gesture data, process the gesture data, map with the therapeutic information, show live feedback and finally send the therapy data to the server side cloud environment for further processing and report generation. We now explain different framework components in details.

2.1 Motivating Scenario

Before we go into the framework design, let us assume a scenario where each elderly person having diversified in-home therapeutic needs has to be dealt separately. We assume a disability care hospital named PhysioPlus, which treats patients who have different levels of disability due to their old age. The hospital specializes in both intra-user and inter-user therapy management, both in-center and remote in-home care. In the former case, intra-user therapy is defined as follows: at the time of admission, an elderly person exhibits certain therapeutic needs in different joints of his/her body. After he/she is exposed to different therapies, the range of motion (ROM) [12] of the person is targeted to improve as close to normal. This development is said to be in-home intra-user therapy management. In the case of inter-user therapy management, it refers to how one elderly person's disability level is different from others. Since every elderly person has different physiological developments, we define a scenario for the in-home intra-user therapy management needs, which can be extended to inter-user scenarios as well.

We assume an elderly person named Alice suffers from sudden numbness in her left side. Her caregiver family members took her to the nearest hospital. After initial assessment, the doctors classified her sufferings as left Hemiplegic [11] and suggested her caregiver to take her to the Hemiplegia therapist at disability care hospital PhysioPlus to discover details about the type of Hemiplegia and make arrangements for needed therapy so that she can regain her physical strength in the affected body parts. At her first visit to the assigned therapist, the therapist requested Alice to make some gestures and motions, to see the current state of joints and muscles. Based on these initial physical movements, the therapist rates the severity level of Alice's Hemiplegia and chooses different therapy modules for Alice. The physical condition of Alice is such that she cannot wear complex gloves or wearable devices, rather a non-invasive way of tracking her movements is highly desirable. At her every visit to the therapist, Alice's kinematic data [13] needs to be recorded in her medical record so that the therapist can monitor the quality of improvement of the targeted muscles and joints that are affected.

Since most of the time Alice is at home due to her old age, her therapist wants that Alice carry on the therapy exercises, with the help of her caregiver family members. In order to assist Alice's caregiver family member, the therapist has defined some ideal therapy sessions and shared them with Alice such that she can do those exercises in a game-like environment with virtually guided. The therapist also wants that Alice conduct the required numbers of therapy sessions at home and that the results be available to him for review. The therapist wants to keep track of certain quality of improvement metrics that signifies that right therapy module is given to Alice and that she is improving at the desired pace. The therapist is interested to observe statistical data regarding quality of improvement in a weekly, monthly and yearly time period. While Alice is progressing, the therapist wants to increase the complexity and difficulty level to make Alice close to her normal counterpart. To be aligned with the distributed nature of the therapy scenario, the health and session data of Alice needs to be stored in an online repository. What's more, the therapist wants a visual feedback regarding the exercise sessions to make comments so that Alice can view those comments and act accordingly. Since Alice is old, the therapist wants to provide video and audio feedback on the actual therapy session so that Alice can play the multimedia feedback and make any necessary adjustments to her exercises.

From the above scenario and suggestion from other researchers [14], we can conclude that an elderly person such as Alice is recommended to be tracked by a multimedia gesture tracking in-home environment that can track the necessary joints, muscles, and actions and produce necessary Kinematic metrics that helps in decision making of a therapist. Next we present details about therapy and how it can be tracked by gesture tracking sensors.

2.2 Set Up of Therapy Sensing Environment at the In-Home Physical World

The physical world consists of elderly people and a set of surrounding movement tracking sensors. Figure 1 shows a person within an in-home therapy supported environment. The environment consists of three gesture tracking sensors, Kinect2, MYO armband and LEAP motion, each having different field of view. The physical world also consists of a visualization panel that will allow the therapy data available from the cyber world. Figure 2 shows each of the gesture tracking sensors and the types of joints that can be tracked by each of them.

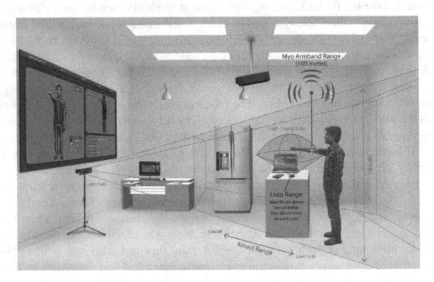

Fig. 1. In-home therapy management environmental setup at the physical world

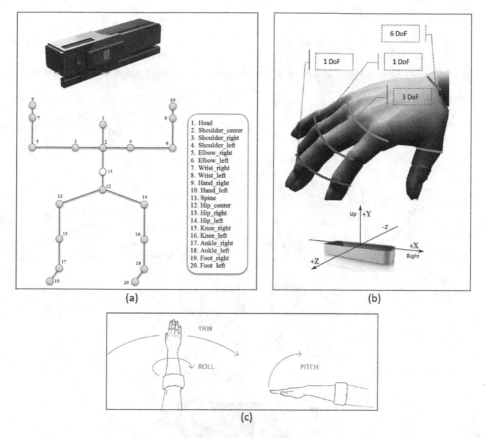

Fig. 2. Joint tracking capability of (a) Kinect, (b) LEAP, and (c) MYO armband

Kinect2 is specialized in tracking the whole body joints [15] (see Fig. 2(a)) while LEAP can only track hand joints [16]. Although Kinect2 can track whole body joints, including the hand joints, but it fails to provide sophisticated PIP, MCP and DIP joint range of motion, which can be obtained from LEAP sensor (see Fig. 2(b)). On the other hand, Kinect2 has greater range of spatial tracking capability while LEAP motion has less coverage (see Fig. 1). MYO has a unique feature such that it can be interfaced with a smartphone through Bluetooth Low Energy protocol, which makes its coverage greater than both Kinect2 and LEAP sensors. Another advantage of MYO is that it does not required line of sight contact with the joint, which allows avoiding occlusion. Once a MYO is worn by an elderly person, it can ubiquitously monitor the wearer's gestures. A great advantage of MYO and LEAP is that these not only support angular gestures such as flexion and extension (see Fig. 3), these also support rotational gestures such as pronation and supination (see Fig. 3(a)). Hence, combining these three within one framework gives a very rich source of gesture tracking capability. Moreover, all the three sensors can be bought off the shelf by anyone, which makes the in-home therapy monitoring a reality.

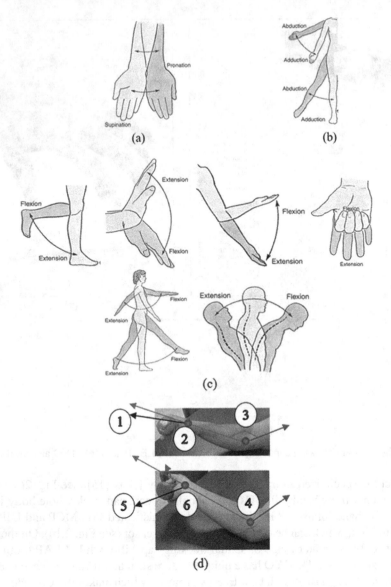

Fig. 3. (a–c) Primitive joint motions and (b) breakdown of a high-level therapy in terms of primitive joints and motions around wrist, elbow and forearm movements.

2.3 In-Home Therapy Monitoring

Each joint of a human body can produce a fixed subset of primitive motions as allowed by the human body anatomy. Figure 3 shows a number of primitive angular and rotational motions around different joints of human body. Each high-level therapy can be expressed as a set of primitive joint-motions. For example, the therapy "Medial Epicon-dylitis" can be broken down into the following primitive joint-actions (see Fig. 3(d)) performed in the following order:

1. Wrist FLEXED
2. Forearm PRONATED (palm surface facing downward)
3. Elbow at 90 DEGREE
4. Elbow EXTENDED
5. Wrist EXTENDED
6. Forearm SUPINATED (palm facing upward)

Hence, by individually tracking each of the above primitive joints and then ordering these temporally by the cyber system, the framework can infer the high level therapy. The framework can engage the right sensor for tracking the relevant joints needed to be tracked in a therapy monitoring process. For example, in case of the above therapy, the wrist joint motions can be tracked by LEAP sensor, the forearm motions can be tracked by MYO and the elbow can be tracked by the Kinect2 sensor. Similarly, any therapy can be broken down into a set of primitive gestures and each joint-motion can be assigned to be tracked by a unique gesture tracking sensor.

2.4 Guided Therapy Monitoring

Performing a therapy itself is a boring task, let alone doing at home and in the absence of a therapist. To address this concern, we have designed a model therapist as cyber world entity, which can act as a guide to an elderly person. The idea is that at the onset of the therapy, a virtual therapist will appear at the therapy recording window and guide an elderly person step by step. A scenario of model therapist is shown in Fig. 4. As shown in the top left figure, an elderly person has to first align him/herself with a virtual augmented reality stick diagram to start the therapy. Once the subject moves to the right position, the gesture tracking sensor Kinect2 senses the position and changes the state of the virtual therapist with right posture that needs to be followed by the elderly person. Once the subject's body posture matches with that of the avatar, the avatar shows the next step to follow. This process continues until the therapy is completed, as prescribed by the therapist. This guidance will help any elderly person to follow any prescribed therapy with right order and required number of frequencies. As shown in Fig. 4, while the subject follows the avatar movements, the kinematic therapeutic data is stored for live feedback as well as report generation.

2.5 Middleware Design as Cyber World

Framework Cyber World Architecture. We leverage our existing big data architecture detailed in [8]. As shown in the Fig. 5, API server handles the multimedia gesture data traffic which is available from various sensory media sources from the physical world as shown in Fig. 1. We have used the Amazon services as Infrastructure as a Service (IaaS). The Amazon EC2 instances allow quickly scaling capacity both up and down as the computing requirements changes, which is a fundamental case for our

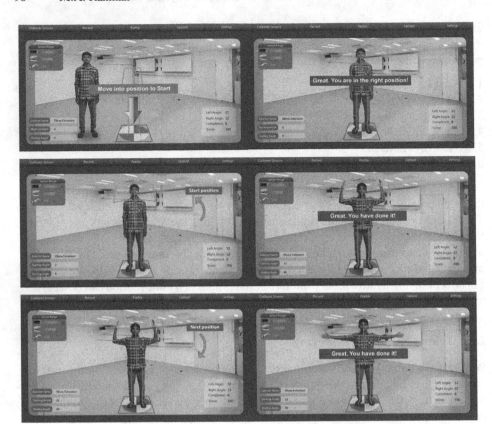

Fig. 4. A model therapist in the cyber world guides a subject in the physical world

application due to variable usage. The API server is deployed on the EC2 instances where scaling and load balancing is configured by creating AWS Auto scaling Group, which is monitored and triggered when the average utilization of EC2 is high or low. This is done using the Cloud Watch for scaling activities. Elastic Load Balancing is used to distribute traffic to instances within Auto scaling Group to get the optimum utilization of the resources and cost.

Any newly arrived therapy session file metadata is processed in the In-Memory Database and the complete payload is stored in DynamoDB after pre-processing. To handle the multiple media writes per second in DynamoDB, we use AWS SQS for live data that is directly stored in the queue and offline data is first uploaded to AWS S3 and then processed respectively using AWS Elastic Beanstalk with the support of AWS Auto scaling and AWS Cloud Watch. The Queries and Visualization components receive a therapist or a patient's request regarding quality of improvement metrics from the server side session data and accordingly interact with analytical layer which processes and returns the desired session statistics.

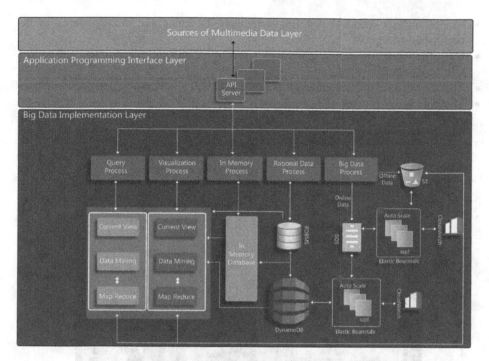

Fig. 5. Multimedia Big Data at the Cyber world

Serious Game as Therapy for Immersiveness. Serious games offer a way of alleviating the pain and uneasiness of performing therapies at home [17]. While a user plays therapy games, the framework tracks kinematic data and stores in the server for detailed analysis. A sample therapy game that is designed as part of this research framework is shown in Fig. 6. Ladder Man is a simple maze like game that consists of animated main character, the Ladder Man, with some visual goals. It also includes animated model therapy avatar or skeleton that will guide the elderly person step by step. The person's wrist flexion and extension makes the Ladder man run or walk to a goal based on the range of motion of flexion or extension. The game environment is illustrated in the following figure and illustrated as follows:

- Elderly person opens the game
- An introduction video will show how the game should be played
- The person will continue to next window
- Calibration screen will let patient know if the tracking sensor is calibrated and the target joint is in the optimal range for detection
- Person will continue to next window.
- A counter will count back to zero from 10, allowing the person to be ready.
- The game starts. Model therapy avatar/skeleton will indicate or guide the first gestures to be performed.
- The person performs the gestures

- Model therapy avatar/skeleton will indicate or guide the next gestures to be performed and so on.
- Once the therapy session requirement is met, the game will be complete and scores will be displayed
- The recorded session containing kinematic data will be saved and uploaded to server
- The person can preview the completed session or play the game again.

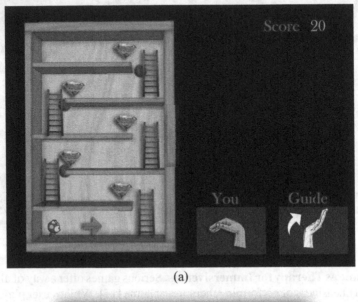

(a)

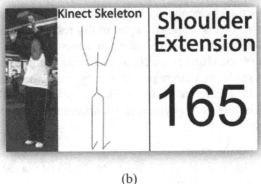

(b)

Fig. 6. Serious games to assist an elderly person in performing a prescribed therapy (a) ladder man game (b) shoulder movement game.

3   Implementation

The physical world gesture tracking sensors have been implemented using Kinect2, LEAP and MYO sensors. We have combined these sensors through our custom built websocket API. The sockets read frames from the sensors as they appear as stream. The web application server has been implemented using Laravel while the client side consists of HTML5 with AngularJS and three.js webGL libraries for rendering the gesture 2D/3D animations. We have implemented the cloud environment as shown in Fig. 5 using Amazon web services platform. The relational database has been implemented using PostGreSQL database environment. The framework has been tested with 25 different elderly subjects and found to be engaging themselves while providing in-home therapy data to the therapist online.

4   Conclusion

In this paper we have presented our ongoing research work targeting in-home therapy support for elderly persons. Since it is difficult to follow the prescribe therapies at home without the direct guidance of a therapist, the cyber physical system provides a model virtual therapist who will guide an elderly person while he/she performs a therapy at home. The game-like therapy environment will make sure that the therapy is performed in the correct manner and the required number of times per day. The CPS also records the kinematic data and other improvement metrics while the therapy session takes place at home. The cyber world embeds necessary analytics engine to produce reports showing different range of motion data containing improvement of an elderly person temporally.

Acknowledgements. This project was supported by the NSTIP strategic technologies program (11-INF1703-10) in the Kingdom of Saudi Arabia. The author would also like to thank Ahmad Qamar of UQU and Syed Abdullah, Delwar Hossain of NGMLab for helping in demo and usability testing.

References

1. Anderson, S.A., Blandine, C.-G.: Anatomy of Movement. Eastland Press, Chicago (1993). ISBN 0-939616-17-3
2. Zhou, H., Hu, H.: Human motion tracking for rehabilitation—A survey. Biomed. Sig. Process. Control **3**, 1–18 (2008)
3. Rahman, M.A.: i-Therapy: a non-invasive multimedia authoring framework for context-aware therapy design. Multimedia Tools Appl. **75**(4), 1843–1867 (2016). doi:10.1007/s11042-014-2376-5. Springer, USA
4. Baran, M., Lehrer, N., Siwiak, D., Chen, Y., Duff, M., Ingalls, T., Rikakis, T.: Design of a home-based adaptive mixed reality rehabilitation system for stroke survivors. In: 2011 Annual International Conference of the IEEE Engineering in Medicine and Biology Society, EMBC, pp. 7602–7605. IEEE (2011)
5. World Health Organization Annual Report 2015 on Ageing. Accessed 6 Mar 2016. http://apps.who.int/iris/bitstream/10665/186463/1/9789240694811_eng.pdf?ua=1
6. Rahman, M.A.: Gesture-based cyber-physical in-home therapy system in a big data environment. In: ACM/IEEE 7th International Conference on Cyber-Physical Systems (ICCPS), Vienna, Austria, 11–14 April 2016 (2016)

7. Qamar, A., Murad, A., Rahman, M.A., Ur Rehman, F., Ahmad, A., Sadiq, B., Basalamah, S.: A multi-sensory gesture-based login environment. In: ACM International Conference on Multimedia (ACM Multimedia 2015), Brisbane, Australia, 26–30 October 2015 (2015)
8. Qamar, A.M., Rahman, M.A., Hussain, S.O., Sadiq, B., Khan, A.R., Basalamah, S.: A multimedia big data e-therapy framework. In: IEEE International Conference on Multimedia Big Data (BigMM 2015), Beijing, China, 20–22 April 2015 (2015)
9. Don, S., Dugki, M.: Medical cyber physical systems and bigdata platforms. In: Proceedings of the Medical Cyber Physical Systems Workshop, Philadelphia, PA, USA (2013)
10. Hossain, M.A., Ahmed, D.T.: Virtual caregiver: an ambient-aware elderly monitoring system. IEEE Trans. Inf. Technol. Biomed. **16**(6), 1024–1031 (2012)
11. Rahman, M.A.: Multi-sensor serious game-based therapy environment for Hemiplegic patients. Int. J. Distrib. Sens. Netw. **2014,** Article 910482 (2014). Advances in Multimedia Sensor Networks for Health-Care and Related Applications (AMS), Hindawi Publishing Corporation
12. Lakany, H.: Extracting a diagnostic gait signature. J. Pattern Recogn. **41**, 1627–1637 (2008)
13. Rahman, M.A.: Multimedia environment toward analyzing and visualizing live kinematic data for children with Hemiplegia. Multimedia Tools Appl., 1–25 (2014). Springer, USA. doi:10.1007/s11042-014-1864-y
14. Huber, M., Rabin, B., Docan, C., Burdea, G.C., AbdelBaky, M., Golomb, M.R.: Feasibility of modified remotely monitored in-home gaming technology for improving hand function in adolescents with cerebral palsy. IEEE Trans. Info. Tech. Biomed. **14**(2), 526–534 (2010)
15. Chang, C., Lange, B., Zhang, M., Koenig, S., Requejo, P., Somboon, N., Sawchuk, A.A., Rizzo, A.A.: Towards pervasive physical rehabilitation using microsoft kinect. In: International Conference on Pervasive Computing Technologies for Healthcare (PervasiveHealth), San Diego, California, USA (2012)
16. Rahman, M.A.: Multimedia non-invasive hand therapy monitoring system. In: IEEE International Symposium on Medical Measurements and Applications (IEEE MeMeA 2014), Lisbon, Portugal, 11–12 June 2014 (2014)
17. Rahman, M.A., Hossain, D., Qamar, A.M., Ur Rehman, F., Toonsi, A.H., Ahmed, M., El Saddik, A., Basalamah, S.: A low-cost serious game therapy environment with inverse kinematic feedback for children having physical disability. In: ACM International Conference on Multimedia Retrieval (ACM ICMR 2014), Glasgow, UK, 1–4 April 2014 (2014)

A Virtual Testbed for Studying Trust in Ambient Intelligence Environments

Azin Semsar, Morteza Malek Makan, Ali Asghar Nazari Shirehjini$^{(\boxtimes)}$,
and Zahra Malek Mohammadi

Department of Computer Engineering, Sharif University of Technology, Tehran, Iran
{semsar,mmalekmakan,malekmohammadi}@ce.sharif.edu, shirehjini@sharif.edu

Abstract. Ambient Intelligence is a new paradigm in information technology that creates environments able to detect and respond to users' needs, actions, behaviors and feelings. User trust plays an important role in accepting Ambient Intelligence environments. In this paper we describe the design and implementation of a virtual reality based testbed for studying trust in Ambient Intelligence Environments.

Keywords: Trust · Ambient intelligence · Interactive realistic virtual reality

1 Introduction

Ambient Intelligence environments (AmIE) are responsive systems designed and implemented to support everyday living and working activities [1]. As with any other technology, trust plays a vital role in the wide adoption of Ambient Intelligence environments. Its role has been acknowledged for almost all application domains [3,4,15,18–20]. Therefore, to ensure the acceptance of Ambient Intelligence and support its wide adoption, it is critical to take into account the trust factor.

The major scientific problem is the lack of instruments for a runtime trust measurement. While some questionnaire-based instruments for empirical measurement of trust exist (cf. [5,10,11]), to the best of our knowledge, there is no computerized system that can directly measure users' trust in a system at runtime.

As we discussed in our previous publication [13], although we cannot directly measure trust, some of its determinants can be measured at runtime, which allows us to estimate the levels of trust with sufficient certainty. Examples of such determinants are usability, context information quality, system decision-making uncertainty, and interaction conflicts.

A. Semsar—Please note that the LNCS Editorial assumes that all authors have used the western naming convention, with given names preceding surnames. This determines the structure of the names in the running heads and the author index.

© Springer International Publishing Switzerland 2016
J. Zhou and G. Salvendy (Eds.): ITAP 2016, Part II, LNCS 9755, pp. 101–111, 2016.
DOI: 10.1007/978-3-319-39949-2_10

Theoretically, such data could be produced within large-scale real-life experiments. However, conducting real world experiments requires the full scale development and maintenance of sensors and actuators networks. This makes data collection from real deployments scarce, expensive and time consuming [8]. A solution would be conducting online experiments to collect the necessary data to produce trust estimation models.

However, a problem with conducting online experiments for this purpose is that AmI environments are relatively new for end users. As a result, most of the users do not have any experience with such systems, thus lack the necessary mental models to correctly assess the systems under study. To overcome this problem, interactive virtual environments of AmIE can be created to help develop the appropriate mental model for users, which is expected to improve their realization of AmI environments [12]. In our previous work, we have analyzed to which extent short-term experience with virtual reality based simulation of intelligent environments supports the development of novice users mental models [16]. Our results indicated a positive correlation between virtually experiencing intelligent environments and enhancements in mental models.

We have conducted mentioned virtual experiment and reported in [13]. In this paper, we describe more in detail the testbeds technical aspects. To make this paper more self-contained, we summarize literature in Sect. 2. As our major contribution, we describe the design and development of a virtual testbed for studying trust in AmIE. To overcome the above-explained problem of incomplete or missing mental models, we used 3D Virtual Simulator (3DVSim) of AmI. This is because 3DVSim of AmI will provide users with initial experience supporting the development of mental models. Improving subjects' mental models will decrease subject bias [7], i.e., through the extended interaction with the 3DVSim, users will better understand the system under assessment, which allows for low biased answers.

The remainder of this paper is organized as follows. In Sect. 2 we discuss research on measuring trust in automation systems and web-based surveys as an instrument in psychometric measurements. Section 3 presents our proposed method for virtual testbed development and an example experiment we conducted using the proposed 3DVSim.

2   Literature Study

To date, trust in automated systems has been under explored. However, some significant research exist.

In [17] the effect of automation error on system trust in the domain of route planning was studied. Participants experienced both manual and automatic mode of route planning. The number of errors was the independent variable of this study. Participants were recruited and assigned to 4 experimental condition. The experiment was done on the computers at laboratory. After completion, participants were asked to rate their trust in automatic system by a score between 1 to 7.

In another study [2] the effect of displaying system confidence on the user trust in context-aware mobile phone was investigated. The experiment showed that displaying confidence information increased users trust.

In another study [4] an experiment conducted to investigate the effect of dynamic adjustment of the level of automation on users trust in ambient-aware environments. The experiment was conducted on an experimental smart home environment.

All the above experiments were conducted in physical laboratories with 14–90 students and at most with 4 experimental conditions. One limitation of such experiments is the number of participants. Besides physical experiments are very time consuming and expensive. These challenges led us to seek for other experimental testbeds.

Online surveys help researchers to recruit large number of participants at a relatively low cost, with fewer physical resources. Factors such as costs of acquiring observers, participants, equipments and time consumption led to collect data from users by online survey tools (e.g., survey monkey.com) [6].

Behrend et al. (2011) collected both traditional university pool samples and Mechanical Turk samples to conduct a survey. The online sample were more diverse in demographic characteristics and showed higher internal consistency. They concluded that the reliability of data from online sample is as good as or even better than the university sample.

However, a challenge of online surveys when applied to AmI environments is that subjects may not have developed adequate mental models that are necessary to understand the system under study and deliver proper answers to the post experiment questions. Simulators or virtual environments were used to conduct human-computer interaction studies before. An instance is [14] that proposes an approach for user-user conflict resolution in smart environments.

Several challenges such as expensive appliances, collecting information from sensors, reasoning from knowledge base and the time and monetary cost make it difficult for researchers to study in a real smart home. To overcome mentioned challenges, we propose a virtual testbed for studying trust in AmIE. To overcome the problem of incomplete or missing mental models, we used 3DVSim of AmI. This is because 3DVSim of AmI will provide users with initial experience supporting the development of mental models.

3   The Proposed Virtual Testbed

There are nine main steps that are required for the development of the virtual testbed that we propose in this paper. These steps are shown in Fig. 1. It describes both the technical preparations and necessary steps of the proposed research method. Based on an example, we describe how to use the virtual testbed for studying trust in intelligent environments. Suppose that we aim to measure the relation between trust and interaction conflicts. Our main hypothesis is that higher conflict density results in higher loss of trust. In the next sections, we describe how to go through the mentioned steps to prepare the testbed that will allow to study the above hypothesis.

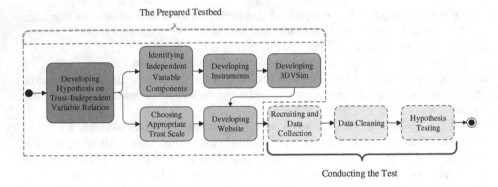

Fig. 1. The proposed method

3.1 Developing Instruments

In this step, we designed experimental conditions in which conflicts of various intensity and frequency were expected to occur at different stages (beginning, middle, or end) of the experiment. We name each of the designed experimental condition a test scenario. Each test scenario is clearly distinguishable within the prepared interactive 3D virtual environment.

In each scenario, subjects are expected to conduct five typical tasks of the analyzed study domain (e.g., smart home). Examples were turning on lights, opening a door or window, etc. Based on the interaction conflict components identified in the previous step and our hypothesis, we designed 3 types of scenarios: scenarios with low conflict densities, which contain no conflict or one conflict; scenarios with medium conflict densities, which contain 2 or 3 conflicts; and scenarios with high conflict density, which contain more than 3 conflicts. Figure 2 describes the formulation of the scenarios.

3.2 Developing 3DVSim

This step concerns with the development of the 3D simulation. Based on the scenarios sketched in the previous step, we have developed a 3DVSim, a virtual environment that supports interaction in the virtual/simulated smart home. It simulates the experimental scenarios. It provides users simulated smart devices such as smart TVs, connected lights, air conditioners, and so on. In addition, a virtual user interface is embedded into the 3DVSim that allows users to control the virtual smart devices involved in the virtual test. This component empowers users by allowing explicit command and control of their virtual intelligent environment. However, in order to induce conflicting scenarios, the 3D simulation also undertakes automated actions. Firstly, this simulates the intelligent behavior of the smart home system under study. Secondly, it triggers interaction conflicts. Through this nearly realistic experience, users are expected to (further) develop their mental models of the concepts under study (e.g., conflicts in Ambient

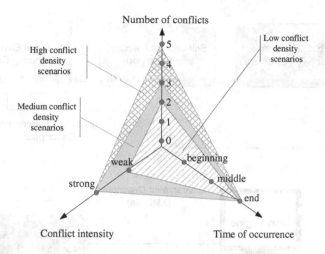

Fig. 2. Scenario formulation

Intelligence environments). As explained in section one, this will help improve the validity of users responses to trust measurement questionnaires (trust scales).

3DVSim allows to validate and test the dynamic behavior of strategy components, reactive agents, device composition platforms and adaptive user interfaces. It becomes possible by manipulating ambient settings, environmental conditions or device states, as these are the most relevant input parameters determining the behavior of mentioned components.

The process shown in Fig. 3 generates the 3DVSim dynamically. At the beginning of the process, the Environment Manager retrieves a complete environment overview in order to acquire the required data of the physical room, such as list of discovered devices, the 3D representation of each device, as well as the device profile, which is needed to retrieve the corresponding Device Control Interface (DCI). These DCI are usual controls, e.g. radio buttons or context menus. The overview defines by researchers in an editing tool which creates an abstract description of the experiment.

The Environment Monitoring component is responsible for device discovery and monitoring. This part of AmIE observes the whole environment and provides information about important changes to the other components such as the Interaction Appliance and automation agents (implicit interaction), e.g., changing in a device property like the on/off state of a lamp, or a change in room properties like the lighting. This component is necessary for both physical and virtual environment, because we need to detect and analyze changes in AmIE components.

After defining overview, we must select devices and behavior of each device in order to model virtual environment. Each device represented within the 3D-view has a unique ID. This ID allows the user interface to link the 3D object with a physical device which is usually controlled by our system. Then we need the

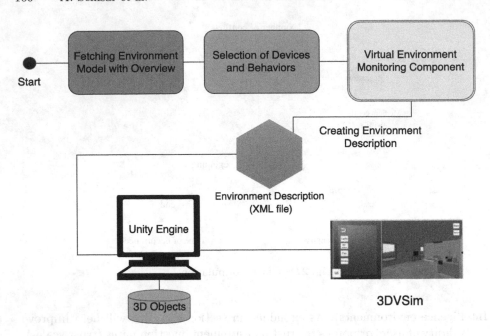

Fig. 3. Dynamic 3DVSim generation process

position and orientation information for each object, which is possible with XML description files. Each file can contain name, device ID, position of the object, orientation, affordances and behaviors of the object. An XML-file describing an example room is shown below:

```
<lamp>
<param name="guid" value="L1"
<param name="deviceName" value="LAMP1"/>
<param name="xvalue" value="10"/>
<param name="yvalue" value="25"/>
<param name="zvalue" value="44"/>
<param name="rotateAroundXAxis" value="2"/>
<param name="rotateAroundYAxis" value="75"/>
<param name="rotateAroundZAxis" value="20"/>
<param name="propertyentries">
<lighting>8</lighting>
</param>
</lamp>
```

At the end of the process, the Environment Monitor writes all the information needed to create the user interface into an XML file which is then sent to the Interaction Appliance.

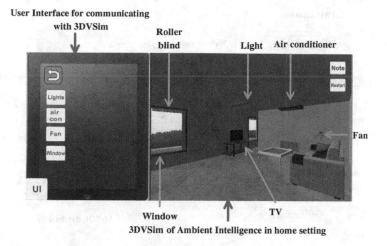

Fig. 4. Screenshot of 3DVSim developed by Unity game engine (Color figure online)

```
<device>
<param name="guid" value="L1cb3"/>
<param name="devicetype" value="LAMP1"/>
<param name="xvalue" value="10"/>
<param name="yvalue" value="25"/>
<param name="zvalue" value="44"/>
<param name="rotateAroundXAxis" value="2"/>
<param name="rotateAroundYAxis" value="75"/>
<param name="rotateAroundZAxis" value="20"/>
<param name="URLBase" value="11.11.120.13/deviceModel"/>
<param name="capabilityentries">
<lamp_ON>
<devicestatus/>
</Lamp_ON>
<Lamp_OFF>
<devicestatus/>
</Lamp_OFF>
</param>
<param name="propertyentries">
<lightlevel>50</lightlevel>
<devicestatus>1</devicestatus>
</param>
</device>
```

Using the output XML file and a database containing 3D objects, the 3DVSim generated using the Unity game engine. The output is WebGL. The Unity game engine (version 5) supports WebGL and can transfer the content directly to a web server. WebGL is a powerful API that is incorporated into Firefox, Chrome, etc. and can render 3D content within the browser [9] without requiring application installation or additional components. Figure 4 shows screenshots of the developed testbed. Controllable devices are signaled with red arrows.

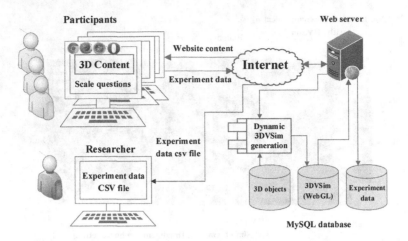

Fig. 5. Website IT architecture

3.3   Choosing Appropriate Trust Scale

Along with previous steps, appropriate trust scale must be chosen. Users evaluate the trust in the system with a proper scale. The questionnaire presented by Jian et al. (2000) presents a scale for human-automation trust measurement. Their proposed scale can be utilized in all automatic systems, such as AmI environments. It proposes several components for trust. It contains 12 items, each one evaluating a proposed component of trust such as familiarity, honesty and so on. All the items aggregately represent the user trust. This scale is the only empirically developed human-automation trust scale. We decided to use this scale because of its generality and usage in similar research studies [4]. For more detailed information on this scale, readers are referred to [5].

3.4   Developing Website and Recruiting

In this step the prepared virtual experiment needs to be extended to run within a web-page. This will allow a large-scale and wide area participation. Additionally, website contains the questionnaire. Users will be requested to read and complete the questionnaire (trust scale) After they have interacted with and experienced the simulated environment. Please note that through this short term experience, users are expected to have developed the necessary mental models. The experiment is conducted over an Internet connection, and it is hosted at shexperiment.hcilab.ir/en. The website uses a PHP server-side scripting language and a MySQL database to store 3D contents and participant responses. The online survey form is written in PHP/HTML. The experimental data are processed by a PHP script and stored in MYSQL database.

The experiment can be accessed from any system with an Internet connection and Firefox version 5 or newer, Chrome version 12 or newer, Safari version 5.1 or newer or Opera version 11 or newer. At least 256 MB of graphic memory

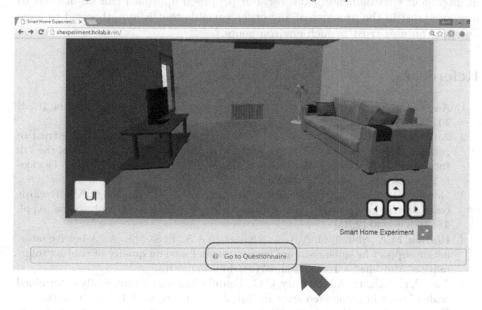

Below is a list of statement for evaluating trust between you and the Smart Home you explored. There are several scales for you to rate intensity of your feeling of trust, or your impression of the system.

(Note: not at all=1; extremely=7)

	1	2	3	4	5	6	7
This home is deceptive	○	○	○	○	○	○	○
This home behaves in an underhanded manner	○	○	○	○	○	○	○
I am suspicious of this home's intent, action, or outputs	○	○	○	○	○	○	○
I am wary of this home	○	○	○	○	○	○	○
The home's action will have a harmful or injurious outcome	○	○	○	○	○	○	○
I am confident in the home	○	○	○	○	○	○	○
This home provides security	○	○	○	○	○	○	○
This home has integrity	○	○	○	○	○	○	○

Fig. 6. Screenshot of the webform containing the questionnaire

Fig. 7. Screenshot of the experiment website - users are redirected to the webform through "Go to Questionnaire" button

is required. Figure 5 shows the IT architecture of the experiment website. The experiment link was shared on our social networks in Facebook, LinkedIn, and ResearchGate. Participants should be randomly assigned to an experimental 3D scenario.

Again, after experiencing the smart home and the related scenario through the 3DVSim, participants should be redirected to the questionnaire, where they are asked to answer the questions. At the end, the responses will be saved in a csv file for statistical analysis. Figure 6 shows the questionnaire. Figure 7 shows how users are redirected to the webform after having completed the 3D-based virtual experiment.

4 Conclusion

In this paper, we proposed a virtual testbed and its development process for measuring trust in Ambient Intelligence environments using online surveys. We described a web-based experiment to gather data from a large number of online participants. Within the presented testbed, subjects experience an intelligent environment through an 3D Virtual Simulator before attempting to complete a well-known trust questionnaire. Using our proposed method, we are able to conduct an experiment to analyze the effect of interaction conflicts on users trust in intelligent environments. However, our proposed approach can be utilized to measure trust in the presence of any other variable that is hypothesized to have an effect on user trust in such environments.

References

1. Aarts, E.: Ambient intelligence: a multimedia perspective. MultiMedia IEEE **11**(1), 12–19 (2004)
2. Antifakos, S., Kern, N., Schiele, B., Schwaninger, A.: Towards improving trust in context-aware systems by displaying system confidence. In: Proceedings of the 7th International Conference on Human Computer Interaction with Mobile Devices & Services, pp. 9–14. ACM (2005)
3. Gordon, D., Hanne, J.H., Berchtold, M., Shirehjini, A.A.N., Beigl, M.: Towards collaborative group activity recognition using mobile devices. Mob. Netw. Appl. **18**(3), 326–340 (2013)
4. Hossain, M.A., Shirehjini, A.A.N., Alghamdi, A.S., El Saddik, A.: Adaptive interaction support in ambient-aware environments based on quality of context information. Multimedia Tools Appl. **67**(2), 409–432 (2013)
5. Jian, J.Y., Bisantz, A.M., Drury, C.G.: Foundations for an empirically determined scale of trust in automated systems. Int. J. Cogn. Ergon. **4**(1), 53–71 (2000)
6. Kittur, A., Chi, E.H., Suh, B.: Crowdsourcing user studies with mechanical turk. In: Proceedings of the SIGCHI Conference on Human Factors in Computing Systems, pp. 453–456. ACM (2008)
7. Lazar, J., Feng, J.H., Hochheiser, H.: Research methods in human-computer interaction. Wiley, Chichester (2010)
8. Lee, J.W., Cho, S., Liu, S., Cho, K., Helal, S.: Persim 3d: context-driven simulation and modeling of human activities in smart spaces. IEEE Trans. Autom. Sci. Eng. **12**, 1243–1256 (2015)
9. Leung, C., Salga, A.: Enabling webgl. In: Proceedings of the 19th International Conference on World Wide Web, pp. 1369–1370. ACM (2010)

10. Madsen, M., Gregor, S.: Measuring human-computer trust. In: Proceedings of Eleventh Australian Conference on Information Systems, pp. 6–8. Citeseer (2000)
11. Merritt, S.M., Ilgen, D.R.: Not all trust is created equal: dispositional and history-based trust in human-automation interactions. Hum. Factors J. Hum. Factors Ergon. Soc. 50(2), 194–210 (2008)
12. Nazari Shirehjini, A.A., Klar, F.: 3DSim: rapid prototyping ambient intelligence. In: Proceedings of the 2005 Joint Conference on Smart Objects and Ambient Intelligence: Innovative Context-Aware Services: Usages and Technologies, pp. 303–307. ACM (2005)
13. Semsar, A., Nazari Shirehjini, A.A.: Multimedia supported virtual experiment for online user-system trust studies (2016). Submitted to Multimedia Systems
14. Shin, C., Dey, A.K., Woo, W.: Mixed-initiative conflict resolution for context-aware applications. In: Proceedings of the 10th International Conference on Ubiquitous Computing, pp. 262–271. ACM (2008)
15. Shirehjini, A.A.N., Hellenschmidt, M., Kirste, T.: An integrated user interface providing unified access to intelligent environments and personal media. In: Proceedings of the 2nd European Union Symposium on Ambient intelligence, pp. 65–68. ACM (2004)
16. Soltaninejad, F., Shirehjini, A.A.N., Saniee, G., Semsar, A.: Mental model development support using collaborative 3d virtual environments (2015). doi:10. 13140/RG.2.1.4616.1360. https://www.researchgate.net/publication/283854432_ Mental_Model_Development_Support_Using_Collaborative_3D_Virtual_ Environments
17. de Vries, P., Midden, C., Bouwhuis, D.: The effects of errors on system trust, self-confidence, and the allocation of control in route planning. Int. J. Hum. Comput. Stud. 58(6), 719–735 (2003)
18. Yassine, A., Shirehjini, A.A.N., Shirmohammadi, S., Tran, T.T.: An intelligent agent-based model for future personal information markets. In: 2010 IEEE/WIC/ACM International Conference on Web Intelligence and Intelligent Agent Technology (WI-IAT), vol. 2, pp. 457–460. IEEE (2010)
19. Yassine, A., Shirmohammadi, S.: Privacy and the market for private data: a negotiation model to capitalize on private data. In: IEEE/ACS International Conference on Computer Systems and Applications, 2008, AICCSA 2008, pp. 669–678. IEEE (2008)
20. Yassine, A., Shirmohammadi, S.: Measuring users' privacy payoff using intelligent agents. In: IEEE International Conference on Computational Intelligence for Measurement Systems and Applications, 2009, CIMSA 2009, pp. 169–174. IEEE (2009)

Smart Living for Elderly: Design and Human-Computer Interaction Considerations

Ranjana Sharma[1], Fiona Fui-Hoon Nah[1(✉)], Kavya Sharma[1],
Teja Satya Sai Santosh Katta[1], Natalie Pang[2], and Alvin Yong[3]

[1] Missouri University of Science and Technology, Rolla, MO, USA
{rsy6b,nahf,ks5x3,tkgk9}@mst.edu
[2] Nanyang Technological University, Singapore, Singapore
NLSPANG@ntu.edu.sg
[3] essentiallyMERIDIAN and ScentalWorld, Singapore, Singapore
alvin@scentalworld.com

Abstract. To address aging challenges, we examine the concept of smart living and its applications for the elderly. Smart living refers to improving quality of life by transforming environments to become more intelligent and adaptable to users. In this paper, we discuss how smart living applications can help to address the needs of the elderly, as well as the design and human-computer interaction considerations for such applications.

Keywords: Smart living · Elderly · Design · Human-computer interaction

1 Introduction

Smart living refers to improving quality of life by transforming environments, such as home, workplace, and transportation, to become more intelligent and adaptable to users [1]. Smart living has important implications for the elderly because of the increased needs and demands in their daily lives. In this paper, we will examine cognitive problems faced by the elderly, how these problems affect their daily living activities and appropriation of technology from the design and human-computer interaction (HCI) perspective, and the role of smart living for the elderly.

Over the last century, high healthcare standards and high birth rates have contributed positively toward the world population [2]. Access to high standards of healthcare has increased the average life expectancy, giving rise to a relatively larger elderly world population. According to a report by United Nations [3], people who were 60 year old and above constituted 11.7 % of the world population, which was an increase of 2.5 % from 1990 to 2013. The percentage of elderly people in the world is expected to continue to increase [3]. Given the global aging population trend, providing daily living assistance and support to the elderly to maintain or improve their quality of life is critical.

Daily living activities of the elderly can be categorized into: (i) activities of daily living (ADL), (ii) instrumental activities of daily living (IADL), and (iii) enhanced activities of daily living (EADL) [4]. ADL are personal activities of daily living with focus on self-care tasks such as bathing, dressing, eating/cooking, transfer, and hygiene [5]. Functional

© Springer International Publishing Switzerland 2016
J. Zhou and G. Salvendy (Eds.): ITAP 2016, Part II, LNCS 9755, pp. 112–122, 2016.
DOI: 10.1007/978-3-319-39949-2_11

mobility and physical strength are prime requirements for ADL [4, 6]. IADL are activities that enable an individual to live independently within a community [7]. These activities involve cognitive and physical activities such as shopping, laundry, managing finances, and monitoring health related activities [8]. Active elders also carry out EADL to adapt to the ever changing environment that requires them to be willing to accept challenges and engage in learning experiences [8]. Examples of such activities are leisure activities, learning new technologies, and communicating with family and friends [8]. EADL are primarily cognitive oriented, and they contribute to quality of life [4].

Technologies facilitating smart living have the potential to address issues of the elderly by assisting them with their daily life activities [9]. Chen et al. [10] defined the pursuit of smart living technologies in terms of increasing efficiency, affordability, and sustainability in everyday lives. Devices of smart living technologies can help the elderly to achieve greater independence while enhancing safety, health, and social interaction [11]. In terms of user driven concepts, these technologies aim to palliate day-to-day activities such as mobility, communication, medication, and environmental controls [9, 12].

Performing specific activities of daily living can be difficult for the elderly, as their cognitive and physical abilities deteriorate due to the aging process. The aging process also affects their social life by limiting their social activities and interactions [13] and increases their need for a safe and secure living environment [14]. Furthermore, most elderly people prefer to live independently at their home rather than in institutional care [14], and they face various issues due to the aging process.

The next section will discuss the needs of the elderly and provide examples of smart living applications that can assist them with their needs.

2   Smart Living for Elderly

Dohr et al. [15] have identified six needs of elderly people: health, safety/security, peace of mind, independence, mobility, and social contact. In this section, we offer perspectives on how technology interventions can support the daily needs of the elderly in these areas. These needs are not mutually exclusive but are overlapping; for example, it is possible for an application to offer mobility as well as reduce dependency on others.

2.1   Health

The aging population has posed a challenge to the healthcare industry in providing better care aiding facilities to the elderly at a viable cost that could fit their budget [16]. One way to address this challenge is to develop applications of ubiquitous healthcare solutions by creating an intelligent environment in the homes of the elderly [16]. Such ideas and applications have been termed a smart home, which refers to a living environment that is well equipped with technology to complement its occupants by predicting their activities and responding accordingly [17]. There are benefits of offering telemedicine services to elderly people in their homes, where the elderly can consult remote doctors through such services [18]. The concept of HomeADL (i.e., home activities of daily living) highlights the application of adaptive monitoring of ADL within smart homes based on the confluence of sensor technologies and wearable devices [19]. Under the umbrella of smart health, sensor embedded fitness trackers (e.g., Fitbit One, Vivo), and smartphone apps that monitor and maintain a log of daily activities such as walking, jogging, and sitting are also gaining popularity [20].

Le et al. [21] noted six categories of health-related smart home technologies identified by Demiris and Hensel [22]: (i) physiological monitoring (e.g., measurements of blood pressure, respiration, and pulse rates); (ii) functional monitoring (e.g., measurements of various daily activities and meal intakes); (iii) safety monitoring and assistance (e.g., automatic lighting, accident prevention, hazard detection and warnings, and personal alarms); (iv) security monitoring (e.g., identification of intruders versus familiar people in one's social network); (v) social interaction monitoring and assistance (e.g., phone and conference calls); (vi) cognitive/sensory assistance (e.g., medication reminders).

2.2 Safety/Security

Availability, accessibility, and affordability of in-home monitoring technologies have provided friends, family members, and caregivers with the convenience of tracking the activities of older people [23]. Monitoring of ADL of the elderly is also important to measure safety conditions of the elderly [24]. Smart homes are equipped with devices that allow monitoring of the elderly people and communication of real-time data/information to the stakeholders [25]. The combination of smart homes and in-home monitoring applications can not only provide the elderly with greater control of their home environment but also enhance the elderly's safety and security of being cared for [12, 23]. Besides safety, interrelated functionalities of in-home monitoring systems cover health care needs, security, and social connectedness [23]. Applications of smart technologies, such as motion and position detection, sensor based wearable systems, and automated monitoring, offer safety precautions to the elderly while performing their daily activities [26, 27].

2.3 Peace of Mind

Advancements of technology have allowed family, friends, and caregivers to take care of the elderly who live at a distance by facilitating face-to-face interaction, which in turn gives them peace of mind [23]. Mynatt et al. [28] have identified the following prime contributing factors to peace of mind: health related information, environment inside the house, social interaction, physical activity, and planned as well as unplanned events. Monitoring of these activities, events, and information, and alerting stakeholders to any deviations from expectations can contribute to peace of mind.

2.4 Independence and Mobility

One of the best ways to support the elderly is by maintaining and maximizing their independence with the support of applications related to the social, personal, and health dimensions [29]. Applications of smart living that support physical and cognitive issues related to the elderly and allow them to live independently include assistive robotics such as the Wheelchair Mounted Robotic Arm, feeding robots, and robotic workstations [30], as well as handheld computers such as smartphones [31] and wearable devices such as ECG monitoring systems [32]. Likewise, assistive technology (e.g., voice/activation commands), telemedicine applications that connect the elderly to their caregivers via television and the Internet, and medication adherence applications (e.g., a reminder system for medication) assist the elderly in performing ADL and IADL without compromising their independence [11].

Smart wheelchairs and smart walkers, along with navigation systems, are helpful to the elderly suffering from visual impairment and mobility restrictions [12]. For those who are not able to operate conventional powered wheelchairs, the smart wheelchair is a feasible alternative [33]. Smart wheelchairs can be equipped with sensors, software, and hardware which could be fitted aesthetically to avoid unnecessary attention [33]. Manipulation aids offered by the Wheelchair Mounted Robotic Arm can provide independence to the elderly in performing ADL such as moving objects, eating, drinking, and controlling devices in the environment [12].

2.5 Social Contact

Smart homes are typically equipped with communication technologies that allow the elderly to stay in touch with family and friends [12]. Communication applications and technologies, such as Skype and telepresence, also play a key role in this regard. The need for sociability and accessibility goes hand in hand in enabling the elderly to utilize technologies for social networking. Advanced technologies such as the 3D virtual worlds and Microsoft HoloLens also show promise in creating more options and flexibility for extending the elderly's social networks. Availability of elderly friendly communication devices, such as cell phones, video phones, e-mail, and the Web, has helped to reduce the virtual distance between the elderly and their friends/family as these applications facilitate daily audio and video communications [11]. Active social interaction offers positive fulfillment of EADL for the elderly.

3 Design and HCI Challenges of Smart Living for Elderly

Technology is ubiquitous and can help to overcome motor and cognitive barriers [34]. Elderly people face more challenges in utilizing technology, and hence, it is important to design and develop usable and accessible interfaces for them [35]. We discuss key considerations in interface design, adaptive design, complexity, affect, aesthetics, and privacy.

The elderly's cognitive and sensory capabilities, as well as motor skills, decline over time due to the aging process which affects their sensitivity toward defective design and their need for elderly friendly interfaces [31]. There are unique challenges in designing for the elderly. Elderly users are less able to block out distractions or irrelevant stimuli on the interface [36] and they tend to focus their attention on the center of the interface due to their reduced width of visual field [37]. They need bigger text on their screen, greater spacing between keys and buttons/icons, more color contrast, loud ringtones, prolonged backlight, and strong feedback (i.e., low frequency if it is an audio feedback) [37]. Kurniawan and Zaphiris [38] provided a list of research-derived web design guidelines for the elderly and it covers 11 categories ranging from navigation and use of graphics to use of color/background and text design. These guidelines include avoiding a deep menu structure, providing a site map, avoiding moving text, providing the location of the current page, avoiding scroll bars, and maintaining consistency in screen layout.

Although smart technologies have been in use by the elderly, their full potential has not been realized [10]. The lack of adaptable design for people with impairments is one of the reasons that has prohibited them from adopting wireless devices in their daily life [39, 40]. Research and development efforts in mobility-based smart devices for the elderly are striving to deliver a localized, context-dependent, and user adaptable design that will suit every user given their characteristics and conditions [33]. Adaptive design is an important aspect of smart living applications.

There are challenges in using restricted screen space of mobile devices for enhanced data access, particularly for elderly people. Moreover, the increased diversity of functions on these gadgets are creating huge psychological burdens for the elderly. Interfaces of systems and applications that are designed for the elderly should be simple, clear, consistent and straight-forward. In order to exploit the capability of mobile and wireless innovations, research needs to consider the effect of visual density and cognitive capacity of the users to avoid confusion and information overload [41]. Managing complexity is an important aspect of design for the elderly.

Design of technology should consider the emotional or affective aspects in terms of feel, value, sensitivity, and appeal [13]. Smart technologies allow the elderly to be self-reliant and can enhance their self-efficacy and confidence to live on their own with personal freedom and individuality [42]. However, the utilization of assistive technologies may intimidate individuality of the users because of concerns associated with how others might view them and their associations with others. Perceived disgrace and awkwardness might discourage elderly people from utilizing certain assistive technology systems [43].

Though numerous systems could be helpful to the elderly, acceptance might be hindered if they look awkward or unpleasant despite the benefits that can be gained from them [42]. If a wheelchair resembles a tank, we cannot expect the elderly to accept it with enthusiasm despite the fact that it could be helpful to them [44]. Sometimes, even wearable devices are not acceptable to the elderly due to their appearance [42]. Elderly people like to use assistive systems that not only provide support for practical necessities, but are also aesthetically pleasing [42]. Hence, aesthetic is an important design consideration for the elderly.

The safeguarding of users' identities, personal information, and information about their daily activities is another important design consideration in autonomous living.

A trade-off between privacy risk and utility needs to be made, and the users should be able to determine the desired trade-offs. Based on privacy calculus theory [45], users are expected to be willing to give up some degree of privacy (e.g., personal information) for the benefits received (e.g., personalization of services). In order to safeguard the privacy of the elderly (some of whom might be living alone), the Privacy by Design (PbD) approach is recommended in order to embed privacy preferences into the design of technologies and business practices for the elderly [46].

4 Future of Smart Living for Elderly

Frisardi and Imbimbo [47] described a smart home as a living arrangement outfitted with technology that enables the occupants to enhance their living standard, increase their physical freedom, and reduce their dependence on caregivers. Demiris [48] character-ized smart home innovation as an evolving multidisciplinary arena that expands on the utilization of innovation to bolster aging. Le et al. [21] have examined innovative ways to design a smart home to augment the autonomy, security, and personal satisfaction of elderly people. According to them, smart homes should have the following five basic features: automation, multi-functionality, adaptability, interactivity, and efficiency [21]. Automation can help to overcome cognitive limitations and assist with motor limitations of the elderly. Multi-functionality of the smart homes can help with various aspects of their daily living activities. Adaptability, or the ability to adjust to the needs of the user, is essential for meeting the diverse needs of the elderly. Interactivity refers to the ability to communicate or interact with smart devices and other users, and efficiency refers to the ability to deliver convenient services or help users to save time or money.

Artificial intelligence (AI) can be used to augment the living standard of elderly people [44]. For example, a remote robot such as Sony Qrio can perceive people by their countenances and discourse, interact with them, and recollect particular people and past discussions. Qrio has a lot to offer in terms of emotional and practical necessities [44]. Such autonomous remote robots can be utilized to enhance the living standards of the elderly by contributing towards EADL. Other AI techniques such as neural networks can be used to learn or recognize the behaviors of the elderly and identify any abnor-malities that may need attention.

As robots become more economical, adaptable and common, they can be used to accomplish a variety of tasks. Robots may soon be a regular face all over the globe. For example, telepresence robots [49] can offer mobility to the elderly, whereas Care-O-bot [50] can be an assistant to the elderly for accomplishing daily activities. The mobility of the elderly can be extended through the use of smart wheelchairs [42] such as those that can self navigate and avoid obstacles [51]. Toyota introduced a concept vehicle 'i-unit' that might help in enhancing the mobility of elderly people. The vehicle is very compact and is incorporated with an intelligent technology for avoiding mishaps [52]. If a voice-enabled intelligent navigation device is integrated into the vehicle, it can offer further extensions to the vehicle's capabilities in transporting elderly people to desti-nations of their choice. Robotic solutions, however, are still in development and much research is still needed to understand their effectiveness for the elderly, especially with regard to their social and unintended consequences. Usability and user acceptance are important for success. Various evaluation studies questioned the efficiency, effectiveness, user satisfaction, and level of autonomy of these robots, and the results are not satisfactory, which is a clear indication that there is a lot of scope for improvement.

An important aspect of smart living is Internet of Things (IoT), where objects interact with one another through the networks that interconnect them to provide adaptable and intelligent applications to users. Three important concepts related to IoT are: Ubiquitous Communications, Pervasive Computing, and Ambient Intelligence. Ubiquitous Communications refer to the interaction among the objects whereas Pervasive Computing refers to incorporating these objects with processing power. Ambient Intelligence is the capability of these objects to recognize and record the physical changes around them. Integration of these concepts leads to dynamic networks termed IoT [15].

Based on IoT, Ambience Assisted Living (AAL) refers to "technical systems that support elderly people and people with special needs in their daily routine" [15, p. 805]. The goal of AAL is to offer autonomy to the elderly and increase the safety of their lifestyle and environments. AAL can be helpful in fulfilling the needs of the elderly from the perspective of health, safety/security, peace of mind, independence, mobility and social contact.

IoT can incorporate various technologies such as sensors, robotics, and brain-computer interaction (BCI). Recent advances in sensor technologies give rise to the emergence of the smart home concept. Sensor technologies are used for mobility assistance and disease prevention, and they can be deployed to reduce manual labor and potentially eliminate the problem of social isolation that elderly face [53]. These sensor technologies, integrated with monitoring technologies, are useful for detecting the daily activities of elderly people in their homes. Five types of monitoring technologies have been identified [54]: Passive infrared motion sensors, body worn sensors, pressure sensors, video monitoring, and sound recognition. A combination of these technologies can be used in smart homes to monitor the activities of the elderly.

BCI is a new communication method that replaces existing augmentative and alternative communication methods. It involves analyzing physiological data with considerable accuracy. Invasive techniques are more efficient than non-invasive techniques, but they may not be the right option for the elderly unless the problem is severe. Electroencephalography (EEG) is one of the non-invasive techniques to collect data and it includes processes such as signal acquisition, signal preprocessing, signal classification, and computer interaction. BCI technologies are being used immensely in medicine, especially for people with disabilities. They can provide users with basic communication capabilities such as express wishes to caregivers, operate devices, and manipulate objects independently. In a smart home context, BCI can be implemented by arranging alphabets and/or numbers in a matrix form where users can then be asked to concentrate on a specific character in order to perform a specific task. The associations between characters and tasks can be coded and integrated with robotic technologies to accomplish specific tasks. However, elderly people may require extensive training to operate these technologies successfully.

5 Conclusions

Technology facilitating smart living applications should be marketed and distributed through appropriate channels such as health magazines, video display/demonstrations in hospitals or elder care, or recommendations by doctors. Appropriate distribution channels such as home delivery, e-commerce websites, or dedicated areas in frequently visited stores like Costco and Walmart can be used to reach targeted audiences such as the elderly and their family and friends. Moreover, a smart living application should be affordable and sensitive toward economic conditions of the elderly. Subsidized rate or insurance policy coverage for a wide range of smart living applications may motivate the older generation to adopt these products to support their day to day activities.

The aforementioned criteria are easier to achieve through policy intervention and strategies; however, adaptable smart living applications for the elderly are still at a very nascent stage. A standard design may not suit the requirements of all elderly alike. In dearth of literature, we would recommend relevant institutes to pursue research projects to develop prototypes of smart living applications tailored to the elderly needs and requirements. The prototype should be flexible and be subjected to improvisations and adjustments based on the geographical area, localized needs, cultural dimensions, and privacy protocols.

A smart living application should be able to sense its environment and respond effectively. It should be aesthetically pleasing and utilize modern technologies to offer the best value to its users. Elderly users should feel the betterment in quality of life and ease of performing daily activities by utilizing or interacting with the smart application. In conclusion, a smart living application for the elderly should be (S)ensible, (M)odern, (A)daptable, (R)esponsive, and (T)angible in delivering value to the elderly users through careful design and HCI considerations.

References

1. Missouri University of Science and Technology's smart living signature area. http://research.mst.edu/signatureareas/smartliving/
2. Izekenova, A.K., Kumar, A.B., Abikulova, A.K., Izekenova, A.K.: Trends in ageing of the population and the life expectancy after retirement: a comparative country-based analysis. J. Res. Med. Sci.: Official J. Isfahan Univ. Med. Sci. **20**(3), 250–252 (2015)
3. United Nations. World population ageing: United Nations Publication (2013). http://www.un.org/en/development/desa/population/publications/pdf/ageing/WorldPopulationAgeing2013.pdf
4. Rogers, W.A., Fisk, A.D.: Cognitive support for elders through technology. Generations **30**(2), 38–43 (2006)
5. Pendleton, H.M., Schultz-Krohn, W.: Pedretti's occupational therapy: practice skills for physical dysfunction. Elsevier, St. Louis (2013)
6. Wallace, M., Shelkey, M.: How to try this: monitoring functional status in hospitalized older adults. Am. J. Nurs. **108**(4), 64–72 (2008)
7. Lee, S.B., Park, J.R., Yoo, J.H., Park, J.H., Lee, J.J., Yoon, J.C., Jhoo, J.H., Lee, D.Y., Woo, J.I., Han, J.W., Huh, Y., Kim, T.H., Kim, K.W.: Validation of the dementia care assessment packet-instrumental activities of daily living. Psychiatry Invest. **10**(3), 238–245 (2013)

8. Rogers, W.A., Meyer, B., Walker, N., Fisk, A.D.: Functional limitations to daily living tasks in the aged: a focus group analysis. Hum. Factors: J. Hum. Factors Ergon. Soc. 40(1), 111–125 (1998)
9. Shieh, L., Yeh, C., Lai, M.: Evaluating smart living technology strategies using the analytic network process. J. Test. Eval. 41(6), 1–13 (2013)
10. Chen, M., Lughofer, E., Sakamura, K.: Information fusion in smart living technology innovations. Inf. Fusion 21, 1–2 (2015)
11. Daniel, K., Cason, C.L., Ferrell, S.: Assistive technologies for use in the home to prolong independence. In: 2nd International Conference on Pervasive Technologies Related to Assistive Environments. ACM, New York (2009)
12. Karmarkar, A.M., Chavez, E., Cooper, R.A.: Technology for successful aging and disabilities. In: Helal, A., Mokhtari, M., Abdulrazak, B. (eds.) The Engineering Handbook of Smart Technology for Aging, Disability, and Independence, pp. 27–48. Wiley, Hoboken (2008)
13. Lee, C., Coughlin, J.F.: PERSPECTIVE: older adults' adoption of technology: an integrated approach to identifying determinants and barriers. J. Prod. Innov. Manag. 32(5), 747–759 (2015)
14. Cheek, P., Nikpour, L., Nowlin, H.D.: Aging well with smart technology. Nurs. Adm. Q. 29(4), 329–338 (2005)
15. Dohr, A., Modre-Opsrian, R., Drobics, M., Hayn, D., Schreier, G.: The internet of things for ambient assisted living. In: Seventh International Conference on Information Technology: New Generations, pp. 804–809. IEEE Computer Society Washington, DC, USA (2010)
16. Deen, M.J.: Information and communications technologies for elderly ubiquitous healthcare in a smart home. Pers. Ubiquitous Comput. 19(3–4), 573–599 (2015)
17. Madhusudanan, J., Hariharan, S., Selvan, M.A., Venkatesan, V.P.: A generic middleware model for smart home. Int. J. Comput. Netw. Inf. Secur. 6(8), 19–25 (2014)
18. Rialle, V., Duchene, F., Noury, N., Bajolle, L., Demongeot, J.: Health "Smart" home: information technology for patients at home. Telemedicine J. E-Health 8(4), 395–409 (2002)
19. Hong, X., Nugent, C.D., Finlay, D.D., Mulvenna, M.: HomeADL for adaptive ADL monitoring within smart homes. In: 30th Annual International Conference of the IEEE Engineering in Medicine and Biology Society, pp. 3324–3327. IEEE (2008)
20. Su, X., Tong, H., Ji, P.: Activity recognition with smartphone sensors. Tsinghua Sci. Technol. 19(3), 235–249 (2014)
21. Le, Q., Nguyen, H.B., Barnett, T.: Smart homes for older people: positive aging in a digital world. Future Internet 4(2), 607–617 (2012)
22. Demiris, G., Hensel, B.K.: Technologies for an aging society: a systematic review of "smart home" applications. Yearb. Med. Inf. 3, 33–40 (2008)
23. Huber, L.L., Shankar, K., Caine, K., Connelly, K., Camp, L.J., Walker, B.A., Borrero, L.: How in-home technologies mediate caregiving relationships in later life. Int. J. Hum.-Comput. Interact. 29(7), 441–455 (2013)
24. Chen, Y.H., Tsai, M.J., Fu, L.C., Chen, C.H., Wu, C.L., Zeng, Y.C.: Monitoring elder's living activity using ambient and body sensor network in smart home. In: IEEE International Conference on Systems, Man, and Cybernetics, pp. 2962–2967. IEEE (2015)
25. Hossain, M.S., Muhammad, G.: Cloud-assisted speech and face recognition framework for health monitoring. Mob. Netw. Appl. 20(3), 391–399 (2015)
26. Lin, Z., Hanson, A.R., Osterweil, L.J., Wise, A.: Precise process definitions for activities of daily living: a basis for real-time monitoring and hazard detection. In: 3rd Workshop on Software Engineering in Health Care, pp. 13–16. ACM, New York (2011)

27. Pirapinthan, M., Moulton, B., Lal, S.: Trends in home-based safety and health alert support systems for older people. In: 6th International Conference on Broadband and Biomedical Communications, pp. 206–212. IEEE (2011)
28. Mynatt, E.D., Rowan, J., Craighill, S., Jacobs, A.: Digital family portraits: supporting peace of mind for extended family members. In: SIGCHI Conference on Human Factors in Computing Systems, pp. 333–340. ACM, New York (2001)
29. Erickson, J., Johnson, G.M.: Internet use and psychological wellness during late adulthood. Can. J. Aging 30(2), 197–209 (2011)
30. Abdulrazak, B., Mokhtari, M.: Assistive robotics for independent living. In: Helal, A., Mokhtari, M., Abdulrazak, B. (eds.) The Engineering Handbook of Smart Technology for Aging, Disability, and Independence, pp. 355–378. Wiley, Hoboken (2008)
31. Zhou, J., Rau, P.P., Salvendy, G.: Use and design of handheld computers for older adults: a review and appraisal. Int. J. Hum.-Comput. Interact. 28(12), 799–826 (2012)
32. Baig, M.M., Gholamhosseini, H., Connolly, M.J.: A comprehensive survey of wearable and wireless ECG monitoring systems for older adults. Med. Biol. Eng. Comput. 51(5), 485–495 (2013)
33. Belic, D., Kunica, Z.: A concept of smart wheelchair. Ann. Fac. Eng. Hunedoara 13(1), 37–40 (2015)
34. Holzinger, A., Ziefle, M., Röcker, C.: Human-computer interaction and usability engineering for elderly (HCI4AGING): introduction to the special thematic session. In: Miesenberger, K., Klaus, J., Zagler, W., Karshmer, A. (eds.) ICCHP 2010, Part II. LNCS, vol. 6180, pp. 556–559. Springer, Heidelberg (2010)
35. Arning, K., Ziefle, M.: Effects of cognitive and personal factors on PDA menu navigation performance. Behav. Inf. Technol. 28(3), 251–268 (2009)
36. Jia, P., Lu, Y., Wajda, B.: Designing for technology acceptance in an ageing society through multi-stakeholder collaboration. Procedia Manufact. 3, 3535–3542 (2015)
37. Hawthorn, D.: Possible implications of aging for interface designers. Interact. Comput. 12(5), 507–528 (2000)
38. Kurniawan, S., Zaphiris, P.: Research-oriented web design guidelines for older people. In: Proceedings of the 7th International ACM SIGACCESS Conference on Computers and Accessibility, pp. 129–135. ACM, New York (2005)
39. Henderson, V., Grinter, R.E., Starner, T.: Electronic communication by deaf teenagers. Technical report, Georgia Institute of Technology, College of Computing, GVU Center (2005)
40. Gandy, M., Westeyn, T., Brashear, H., Starner, T.: Wearable systems design issues for aging or disabled users. In: Helal, A., Mokhtari, M., Abdulrazak, B. (eds.) The Engineering Handbook of Smart Technology for Aging, Disability, and Independence, pp. 317–338. Wiley, Hoboken (2008)
41. Ziefle, M.: Information presentation in small screen devices: the trade-off between visual density and menu foresight. Appl. Ergonomics 41(6), 719–730 (2010)
42. Forlizzi, J., DiSalvo, C., Gemperle, F.: Assistive robotics and an ecology of elders living independently in their homes. Hum.-Comput. Interact. 19(1), 25–59 (2004)
43. Heinemann, A.W., Pape, T.L.: Coping and adjustment. In: Scherer, M.J. (ed.) Assistive Technology: Matching Device and Consumer for Successful Rehabilitation, pp. 123–141. American Psychological Association, Washington, DC, USA (2001)
44. Burgess, A.M., Burgess, C.G.: Aging-in-place: present realities and future directions. Forum Public Policy J. Oxford Round Table 1, 1–17 (2007). http://forumonpublicpolicy.com/archive07/burgess.pdf

45. Dinev, T., Hart, P.: An extended privacy calculus model for e-commerce transactions. Inf. Syst. Res. **17**(1), 61–80 (2006)
46. Cavoukian, A.: Privacy by design. IEEE Technol. Soc. Mag. **31**(4), 18–19 (2012)
47. Frisardi, V., Imbimbo, B.P.: Gerontechnology for demented patients: smart homes for smart aging. J. Alzheimer's Dis. **23**(1), 143–146 (2011)
48. Demiris, G.: Interdisciplinary innovations in biomedical and health informatics graduate education. Methods Inf. Med. **46**(1), 63–66 (2007)
49. Double robotics. http://www.doublerobotics.com/
50. Care-O-bot 4. http://www.care-o-bot-4.de
51. Jones, W.D.: Keeping cars from crashing. IEEE Spectr. **38**(9), 40–45 (2001)
52. Toyota I-unit overview. www.toyota.co.jp/en/news/04/1203_1e.html
53. Chan, M., Esteve, D., Escriba, C., Campo, E.: A review of smart homes—Present state and future challenges. Comput. Methods Programs Biomed. **91**(1), 55–81 (2008)
54. Peetoom, K.K., Lexis, M.A., Joore, M., Dirksen, C.D., De Witte, L.P.: Literature review on monitoring technologies and their outcomes in independently living elderly people. Disabil. Rehabil.: Assistive Technol. **10**(4), 271–294 (2015)

Usability Assessment of a Virtual Fitness Platform on Smart TV for Elderly Health Promotion

Chao-Hua Wang[✉]

Department of Multimedia Design, National Taichung University of Science and Technology, No. 129, Sec. 3, Sanmin Rd., North Dist., Taichung 404, Taiwan, ROC
chwang2nd@gmail.com

Abstract. The elderly maintain healthy by exercise and friendships connection which not only can reduce the cost of social care but also can contribute their knowledge and experiences to help the younger generation. This study is aimed to investigate the usability and functionalities of the fitness platform with multi-user virtual situations on smart TV service content, which was developed by the author. The main modules of the platform include limb movements driven by motion sensing interaction with Kinect, contactless graphical user interface, alternative 3D avatars and situational environments, synchronous interaction of distributed multi-users, and interface of unified computing health data. Group interview and a questionnaire were designed to evaluate the feasibility and usability associated with using the virtual fitness platform. A total of 40 elderly users assess this set of content service. The results of this study showed that most of the users are satisfied by the system functionality and usability. Furthermore, the platform also offers the interface for data connecting the wearable devices which assist in increasing the effectiveness of the real time elderly health maintenance.

Keywords: Elderly health promotion · Virtual fitness platform · Motion sensing · Smart TV · Usability assessment

1 Introduction

Adherence to exercise regiments and attending social activities can enable elderly population, in particular those residing in apartment based housing situated in urban setting, to improve their quality of home life, to allow these people to maintain fitness and health even in an environment where resources for mild exercise, such as playgrounds or parks are limited [1]. In addition, to provide equivalent beneficial effects to society with cost effectiveness of providing sustainable older people care enable this population to contribute their knowledge, wisdom and arsenal of experience to the younger generation. However, with regards to the maintenance of fitness, this is often affected by level of exercise intensity and frequency, both of technology and enhancement of urban dwelling older people's health which are often altered as a result of perseverance, peer motivation, weather, and environmental conditions [2, 3].

© Springer International Publishing Switzerland 2016
J. Zhou and G. Salvendy (Eds.): ITAP 2016, Part II, LNCS 9755, pp. 123–132, 2016.
DOI: 10.1007/978-3-319-39949-2_12

Therefore, a smart TV based multi-user virtual system was developed by author, which is pertinent in providing this population with interactive healthy activity and social network functionality, whilst being easily manipulable by the distributed elderly at home. The main modules of the system include limb movements driven by motion sensing interaction with Microsoft Kinect, contactless graphical user interface (GUI), alternative 3D avatars and situational environments, synchronous interaction of distributed multi-users, and interface of unified computing health data. Furthermore, the platform also offers the interface for data connecting the wearable devices which assist in increasing the effectiveness of the real time elderly health maintenance.

This study aimed to verify the functionality and usability of the fitness platform with multi-user virtual situations on smart TV (FMVSTV) service contents. Group interview and a questionnaire were designed to evaluate the feasibility and usability associated with using the virtual fitness platform. A total of 40 elderly users, who were investigated at home individually or gathered in a community, assess this set of content services. The results of this study are hoped to be efficacious to improve existing FMVSTV to meet the practical needs of further enhanced effectiveness elderly being able to maintain their fitness and health.

2   Related Work

2.1   The System Framework of FMVSTV

Smart TV for the elderly at home is just the same as smart phone for the young people to go out. However, smart TV is more like smart phone applications shown on a big screen and is more suitable for the elderly to use interactive applications [4]. The first generation of web TVs are only enable the users to browse the internet and thus are called Web TV or internet TV. The second generation of web TVs which realize diverse online application functions by means of such software as widgets are called connected TV and the new generation of connected TVs which have not only web browsing & diverse online functions but also additional functions such as internet information search engines as well as application store are named smart TVs. The smart televisions now have capability up to the internet and there are various benefits, including [5, 6]:

- Web browsing: Smart TV has built-in web browsers allowing user to surf the internet and view web pages, photos and videos. However, some are much easier to use than on personal computers.
- Apps: Apps on smart TVs either come pre-loaded, or are available to download from an app store. Most smart TVs offer TV and film streaming on services and social networking on Facebook and Twitter.
- Additional services: Cable service providers offer additional services such as online gaming on Smart TV to differentiate from the competitors, as well customisable home screens and recommendations of things to watch based on users' personal tastes.

In order to implement the functionalities of FMVSTV, the system goals are formulated as following: (1) developing the fitness treatment for elderly at home, (2) conducting distributed elderly users to their interaction by the implementation of avatars driven by motion sensing technology, (3) implementing the virtual reality application by Unity 3D program on protocol of Apps for Android TV to construct the real time feedback mechanism and data management of the system, (4) integrating all of the requirements that were elicited from the subjects of elderly and care staff to develop the UI-UX and communication feedback modules.

Accordingly, the analysis approach of service experience engineering was manipulated to establish the system framework of fitness service with motion sensing technology on smart TV [7, 8]. It was integrated and implemented with 2D/3D computer graphics technology, contactless and intuitive user interface design, multimedia database, motion sensing interaction by Microsoft Kinect sensor, synchronous/asynchronous fitness treatments, virtual reality app for smart TV by Unity 3D, and protocol of Apps for Android TV. Figure 1 illustrates the modular architecture of FMVSTV. There are six modules namely: System manipulation module for content editor to manage the service elements and materials; Alternative virtual situations module for presenting the immersive multiple scenes; Avatars and interactive objects module for users to choice the alternative avatar in fitness and social communication; Natural body language driven module for processing joints coordinates data from Microsoft Kinect sensor immediately; Virtual reality interface module for users to control and manipulate the service contents in intuition; and Physiological data management module for user and medical staff to maintain the detected data.

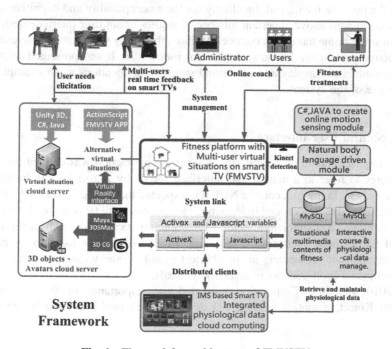

Fig. 1. The modular architecture of FMVSTV

2.2 User Interface Design for Elderly

By the year 2025, one in five of the Taiwanese population will be aged over 65, and meanwhile Asian countries will have most elderly population and will be the fastest growing in the world [9]. Nowadays, the population imbalance between the elderly who require daily care and caregivers is being one of global social issues since the population aging advances. In order to avoid the negative effects of population aging, people believe that the information and communication technology can support the daily lives of the elderly persons at the early stage for increasing active aging [10]. Accordingly, designer must develop handy interface for use by elderly to enable them to educate or entertain themselves, interact with the society, challenge themselves by completing task achievements and increase their changes of doing productive jobs such as writing, using emails, network communications and other computer manipulation.

There are three major barriers encountered by the elderly in their using of computer technologies which include the eyesight degeneration, memory degradation and cognition. Eyesight problems, such as prone to feel tired, are one of the major factors causing physiological burden of the elderly. Memory degradation causes them to become unable to quicken the paces at which they learn new things, resulting in their efficiency in handling difficult tasks being lower than those of groups of younger age. These frustrating and negative emotions will further affect their cognition and become the psychological factors preventing them from learning computer knowledge as they feel old and unfit for high-tech products or fear they are going to cause damage to such products during their learning process [11]. It is fortunate that the restrictions caused by degradation in eyesight and memory can be ameliorated by user interface design to enhance the positive feelings of the elderly for their acceptability and cognitive ability [12]. As mentioned above, a certain number of studies about user interface design for elderly in smart home have been conducted. Thus, this study was issued at the usability of interactive content service on smart TV for indoor use. It was presented with GUI based on contactless display and 3D virtual situation applications as an example of a practical use of the system.

2.3 A Natural User Interface

The first implementation of natural human-machine interaction was defined on voices and gestures to refer to a natural user interface (NUI) by Massachusetts Institute of Technology [13]. In the concept of a NUI, it is expected that the adjective "natural" will shorten the time that users spend in learning. This purpose will be achieved by the most natural, intuitive, and simulative method for obtaining experience such as the movements of human body, gestures, or language, which enables the users to understand how to interact with computers in the shortest possible time without resorting to the traditional media tools such as mice and keyboards.

In 2010 Microsoft Corporation reiterated the importance of the NUI within Microsoft Kinect, a motion sensing I/O device, which could be used in the future potential of contactless interface design. Kinect can detect user limb movements and signal the device that an interaction is occurring in motion sensing mode [14]. It can let users to perform three-dimensional interaction including manipulation displayed virtual objects and communication with each other by driven individual avatar in the virtual environment. Consequently, implemented for assuming Kinect functions, the interface of FMVSTV provides users to manipulate the contactless GUI displayed on the screen and to move interactive virtual objects to the expected destinations by their gestures in virtual situation.

3 Methods

3.1 Function and Content Characteristics of FMVSTV

Exercise is crucial to the health of body and brain for the elderly, but that doesn't mean they have to work out in parks or at gym. FMVSTV is designed to apply the skeletal tracking function of Kinect sensor, and to combine with the home based exercise for the elderly healthy living. There are 10 sets of moves in the virtual reality interface module, which were developed by professional medical staffs and hoped to help the elderly to boost metabolism, combat stress, improve memory and slim waistline. The design characteristics of functions and contents are described and shown in Table 1.

3.2 Experimental Tasks and Measurements

In order to confirm whether the comprehensive design of FMVSTV is feasible used at home and in facilities that the experimental tasks carried out by 40 subjects in the age range of 60–80 (6 elders at home and 34 elders in three daycare facilities) in the two experiments were as follows.

For Experiment I, each subject was invited to experience the functions of registration, tutorial, selections of avatar, virtual situation and aerobics, and processed health data; meanwhile, they completed three sets of aerobics with smart wrist band. After the tasks each elder finished the questionnaire of usability evaluation. For Experiment II, the same previous 5 subjects at home affiliated with 7 elders who were recruited from the original 34 subjects in one daycare facility to participate the investigation. A total of 12 subjects were invited to actual use the FMVSTV 8 times in 8 weeks, scheduled at 30-minute per time, including 2 times of 3 elders in a group online synchronization. During the field study period, qualitative methods such as observation and depth interview were executed to explore meaning and perceptions to gain a better understanding which encourages the interviewees to share rich descriptions of phenomena and to propose their suggestions.

A questionnaire used in Experiment I, which was adapted from the standard usability evaluation of virtual reality application [15]. This questionnaire contains two parts: (1) the basic subjects information, and (2) the usability evaluation included six major variables, such as Recognizability, Interface/Usability, Contactless/gesture control, Presence, Attitude to use, and Enjoyment. Each item were listed on a 7-point Likert scale with 1 signifying "strongly disagree" and 7 being "strongly agree". In addition, Experiment II focused on the observation accuracy of the user interface manipulation and to encourage users to propose specific improvement opinions for the FMVSTV. Either the implementation of Experiment I or Experiment II, each time of usability survey has two research assistants who help the elderly to complete all of the tasks.

Table 1. The design characteristics of functions and contents in FMVSTV

In order to maintain elderly cognitive functionality, the registration interface was developed as the pattern verification. Registered users enter selected pattern sequence initially by gesture control to pass validation.	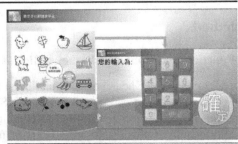
Interactive user guide was edited the actual use of skimming videos and the feature descriptions of the platform as tutorial.	
There are different genders, ages and styles of avatars for users choose to implement role-playing and to enhance the pleasure of use.	
Image based and model based of virtual reality techniques were applied to create the multiple situations for users to choice and simulate the scenes of outdoor exercises what they want.	

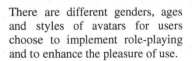

(*Continued*)

Table 1. *(Continued)*

There are 10 sets of moves in the virtual reality interface module, which will auto-demo moves content after chosen and are hoped to help the elderly to boost metabolism, combat stress, improve memory and slim waistline.	
System presents a virtual coach at the center of the screen and shows the briefing of the aerobics at the upper right corner. The lower right corner is the user's avatar where five corresponding points will make green/red feedback to show results of the user's joints coordinates which match or not with coach's synchronously.	
The avatars and interactive objects module offers visual and vocal social interaction functions and series the built-in Facebook and Twitter of smart TV. The social networking function also presents the percentage of correct moves done by each player in real time.	
Users health data, heart rate and body temperature, are collected by the smart wristband, such as blood pressure can be keyed in by gesture control. Data will be sent to cloud server and shown in various statistical graphs for user to catch real-time status.	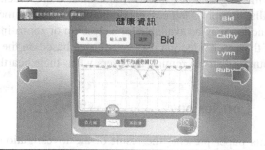

4 Data Analysis and Results

The SPSS statistical software was used to analyze the collected and processed data. For each question on the questionnaire, the mean and standard deviation were computed with respect to the statistical results. A report was proposed to the major findings of this study with regards to the visual recognizability, interface usability, contactless and gesture control, presence, attitude to use, and enjoyment.

A total of 40 elders were recruited and assessed the FMVSTV, 11 males and 29 females, with an average age of 68.9 years (SD: 8.4). 94 % of elders reported that using the set of fitness activity can increase their frequency of exercise at home (mean 5.9). 82 % of them showed that the interaction with others by motion sensing features can enhance their exercise motivation (mean 5.7). They also agreed that the FMVSTV is feasible and acceptable (mean 5.8). 61 % of elders considered that the graphic registration interface as the pattern verification is recognizable (mean 5). 73 % of elders indicated that the manipulation of interfaces by motion sensing is easy to learn and operate (mean 5.5). 86 % elders considered the feedback information such as pulse rate and actions completeness that provided help them to understand themselves performance in each section of fitness activity (mean 5.9). 76 % of them indicated the social interaction module was useful and interesting but it was missing some of the entertainment features (mean 5.7). 77 % of elders reported this content service on smart TV which was conducive to the activation of everyday life (mean 5.9). 88 % of elders indicated that the virtual fitness platform is enjoyment and satisfaction with it for activation of life, and are willing to continue to use (mean 5.7).

For Experiment II, the interviews were semi-directive (open questions) and held at elder's home or in co-discovery where the participants were in one daycare facility.

In co-discovery the functionalities of the system to assess were presented to the participants one after another and each participant had time to use them before being questioned or in the period of synchronous distributed interaction. The most understanding comments and suggestions were summarized as follows: (1) Adding some information regarding daily life, such as health-care knowledge. (2) The icon colors could be a little more vibrant and rejuvenating and shading effects could be added to the words. (3) The avatars of the fitness coaches may be a muscleman and famous figures. (4) Vocal teaching and voice interface, such as Taiwanese driver, may be useful for the elderly. (5) The social interaction function is useful and interesting but it is missing some of the entertainment features such as KALAOK, blowing ping pong balls, jumping lattices or digital gambling games. (6) When selecting avatars, a function may be available for a close-up or zoom-in of their faces. (7) The performance of the coach selection may be adjusted based on the preference of the users. (8) Provide sound effects to remind the users when their heartbeat reaches a certain rate.

5   Conclusion

This paper presents the result of the investigation that aimed at assessing the functionality and usability of the fitness platform with multi-user virtual situations on smart TV. In the beginning, it appeared that the elders' weak skills of ICT experiences and functional limitations of user interface had an impact on elders' confidence in playing FMVSTV. But the elderly quickly learn to use the platform by the help of research assistants and finally give the overall contents of positive reaction. They also believe that continued use of the service will help maintain healthy. Obviously, the FMVSTV offers elderly users with new and exciting ways such as contactless and gesture control, motion sensing interaction, driving avatar in virtual situation on smart TV and emerging social network to maintain their fitness and health at home. It has been found during the experimental process that most of the elders show their greatest interest in the contactless and gesture interface manipulation not only by giving it positive remarks but also taking great pleasure in trying it. Therefore some subsequent modifications will be made to enhance the usability of FMVSTV on the basis of the suggestions which obtained from the interview with the assessment subjects as mentioned in the end of preceding paragraph. In addition, one of the aspects that need improvement is how to reduce the extra cognitive load for learning to manipulate the platform and add more helpful feedback.

In the future smart TV will be the center of Digital Convergence to smart home devices. However, this study has argued that in addition to ensuring usability of interactive service content on smart TV for elders, makers need to make sure that there are substantial perceived benefits for elderly users so that they are willing to invest their valuable time and energy in what could potentially be a rich and rewarding experience. In other words, who can explore and understand the needs and motivations of elderly users of smart TV, will build useful programs by setting mutually satisfying goals between organization and elders, and producing positive feelings in all of daily service contents for the elderly.

Acknowledgment. This study is supported by the Ministry of Science and Technology, Taiwan with grant No: MOST 130-2218-E-025-001.

References

1. Larson, E.B., Wang, L., Bowen, J.D., McCormick, W.C., Teri, L., Crane, P.: Exercise is associated with reduced risk for incident dementia among persons 65 years of age and older. Ann. Intern. Med. **144**(2), 73–81 (2006)
2. Al Mahmud, A., Mubin, O., Shahid, S., Martens, J.B.: Designing and evaluating the tabletop game experience for senior citizens. In: Proceedings of the 5th Nordic Conference on Human-Computer Interaction: Building Bridges, pp. 403–406. ACM (2008)
3. Beswick, A.D., Rees, K., Dieppe, P., Ayis, S., Gooberman-Hill, R., Horwood, J., Ebrahim, S.: Complex interventions to improve physical function and maintain independent living in elderly people: a systematic review and meta-analysis. Lancet **371**(9614), 725–735 (2008)
4. Ingrosso, A., Volpi, V., Opromolla, A., Sciarretta, E., Medaglia, C.M.: UX and usability on smart TV: a case study on a T-commerce application. In: Fui-Hoon Nah, F., Tan, C.-H. (eds.) HCIB 2015. LNCS, vol. 9191, pp. 312–323. Springer, Heidelberg (2015)
5. Shin, D.H., Hwang, Y., Choo, H.: Smart TV: are they really smart in interacting with people? understanding the interactivity of Korean smart TV. Behav. Inf. Technol. **32**(2), 156–172 (2013)
6. Laughlin, A.: What is smart TV? http://www.which.co.uk/reviews/televisions/article/what-is-smart-tv
7. Hsiao, S.L., Yang, H.L.: A service experience engineering (SEE) method for developing new services. Int. J. Manag. **27**(3), 437–447 (2010)
8. Wang, K.J., Widagdo, J., Lin, Y.S., Yang, H.L., Hsiao, S.L.: A service innovation framework for start-up firms by integrating service experience engineering approach and capability maturity model. Serv. Bus. **2015**, 1–50 (2015)

9. United Nations.: Ageing in Asia and the Pacific: Emerging issues and successful practices/Economic and Social Commission for Asia and the Pacific, New York, United Nations (2002)
10. Yamamoto, G., Hyry, J., Krichenbauer, M., Taketomi, T., Sandor, C., Kato, H., Pulli, P.: A user interface design for the elderly using a projection tabletop system. In: 2015 3rd IEEE VR International Workshop on Virtual and Augmented Assistive Technology (VAAT), pp. 29–32. IEEE (2015)
11. Barnard, Y., Bradley, M.D., Hodgson, F., Lloyd, A.D.: Learning to use new technologies by older adults: perceived difficulties, experimentation behaviour and usability. Comput. Hum. Behav. **29**(4), 1715–1724 (2013)
12. Portet, F., Vacher, M., Golanski, C., Roux, C., Meillon, B.: Design and evaluation of a smart home voice interface for the elderly: acceptability and objection aspects. Pers. Ubiquit. Comput. **17**(1), 127–144 (2013)
13. Bolt, R.A.: "Put-that-there" voice and gesture at the graphics interface. In: Proceedings of the 7th Annual Conference on Computer Graphics and Interactive Techniques, SIGGRAPH 1980, pp. 262–270 (1980)
14. Microsoft.: Meet Kinect for Windows. https://dev.windows.com/en-us/kinect
15. Bowman, D.A., et al.: A survey of usability evaluation in virtual environments: classification and comparison of methods. Presence: Teleoperators Virtual Environ. **11**(4), 404–424 (2002)

Introduction of Telecare Mediated Home Care Services Pushes Forward a Re-Delegation of the Cooperative Care Work

Anita Woll[✉]

Department of Informatics, University of Oslo,
Ole Johan Dahls Hus, Gaustadallèen 23 B, 0373 Oslo, Norway
anitwo@ifi.uio.no

Abstract. In this paper, we apply activity theory as a theoretical framework to study conventional home care service practice versus telecare as a means for delivery of home care services. In doing so, we translate home care services into work activities to explore the cooperative nature between the nurses and the elderly care receivers. Findings indicate changes in how the cooperative care work are distributed when moving from conventional home care services to telecare mediated home care services. In our work, we conclude that introduction of new work practice results in increased delegation of responsibility and practical self-care activities to the elderly care receivers. Thus, telecare such as video consultation in the home is not appropriate for all elders. Nevertheless are those who mastery these responsibilities, rewarded with increased flexibility in their daily life activities since the delivery of services is more predictable and timely.

Keywords: Home care · Elders · Telecare · Work practice · Self-care

1 Introduction

The growth of the elderly population challenges the current organization of elderly care services in order to support sustainable development and efficient use of scare health care resources [1]. Housing – oriented elderly care services have become an international trend [2], but are still viewed as controversial in Norway. Housing – oriented care services are described as upscaling of sheltered housing together with extensive and robust home care services, and downscaling of nursing homes – but with maintained services for short – term stays for temporary in-patient care [2]. The housing - oriented care services are also motivating for a stronger involvement of the resident's family and local community. Additionally is incorporation of welfare technology valued as a key enabler for the re-organization of public health care services [3]. Welfare technology is the Nordic term for assistive technology and includes a wide range of technologies intended to support various users' need. The Nordic term is often classified into four main categories in relation to the technical assistance it seeks to support [3]: (1) safety and security technology (2) compensation- and wellbeing technology (3) technology for social contact (4) technology for care and treatment.

J. Zhou and G. Salvendy (Eds.): ITAP 2016, Part II, LNCS 9755, pp. 133–144, 2016.
DOI: 10.1007/978-3-319-39949-2_13

In this research setting, we are studying introduction of telecare as a means for delivery of selected home care services [4]. Our reference to telecare is restricted to the use of video consultation to provide remote home care services to home dwellers who are formal health care receivers. The introduction of telecare as a part of the home care service organization is not a new invention; however there are few studies of telecare that have touch upon cooperative care work within the research field of HCI. This paper aims to add to the existing HCI literature by comparing work arrangements of conventional home care setting with telecare mediated home care services. The paper is organized as follows. Section 2 presents background of this paper. Section 3 is about related work. Section 4 describes the empirical setting. Section 5 presents the analysis based on applied activity theory in order to explore the conventional versus telecare mediated care service as a new way of delivery home care services. Section 6 lists findings. Finally, we discuss findings in relation to related work as well as we make some design considerations for telecare as a means for delivery of home care services, before we conclude the paper.

2 Background

The effort of incorporating welfare technology in the home care service organization is an initiative to develop home care services that are more efficient. Thus, the objective of technology mediated home care services are to hopefully serve more care receivers by less use of resources. Additionally, the introduction of technology can offload the nurses with routine tasks and enable them to allocate time on their core activities such as personal care and grooming [3, 5, 6]. The municipal home care services are provided to those home dwellers that have special need for assistance in order to live as independent. The delivery of services is related to activities that elderly home dwellers cannot do themselves, as well as the nurses motivate the elderly care receivers to carry on with self-care activities as long as they master doing these. This aspect of caring requires the nurses to evaluated the care receivers' physical and cognitive capabilities to make formal decisions on which tasks the elders need support in doing, and which tasks they master to do themselves. Thus, the care service is encounter in the relationship between the home care service's nurses and their care receivers. However, the home care organization is challenged in their daily work of providing services to an increasing group of care receivers, as well as care receivers have experienced problems with conventional home care service's practice as the nurses have an unpredictable work flow and restricted time per visit. Each home visit is estimated in time according to the formal agreement on which tasks the user should be supported with. However, unexpected incidents during visits can prolong the nurses time spent in the home. Thus, it is difficult to arrange a fixed time for each visit, so often the users have to wait for the nurses to come along before they can carry on with their daily life activities. The user can expect the visit to take place within a set time interval, e.g. the nurses inform a user that they will arrive between 9 to 12 o'clock. Thus, the user has to be at home within this time range. Many users have severe health care issues and seldom leave their homes without accompany. While others, especially active aging users can find it troublesome to be stuck at home waiting for the nurse. Introduction of remote care services such as telecare has a greater flexibility for both the care giver and the care receiver as the service can be provided at a set time from a remote location. However, the conventional relationship between home care service staff and their care receivers will change when the caring is mediated by incorporation of technology as a part of the care work. Hence, the cooperative work processes will be different when the nurses and home dwellers are located at different places. We acknowledge that the cooperative work arrangements of the home care service organization is highly interdependent as the object of the care service depends on shared effort in order to receive the most optimal outcome of the service. In example, if the care receiver does not follow instructions given by the nurses for self-care activities such as for example fasting ahead of morning blood glucose monitoring; this can affect the outcome of the long term management of treatment. Similarly, if the nurses forget to bring forward essential information or instructions required for the maintenance of self-care activities (such as which symptoms to report if experienced); the care receivers are not able to have awareness of symptoms that may be critical to their health situation.

In this present paper, we study how the cooperative work arrangements between the home care service nurses and care receivers are changed by the introduction of home telecare. We are doing so under the assumptions that the care work that takes place in the home is interdependent and distributed cooperative work. Thus, we explore the care service duality by exploring how the object of the care service are mediated by the subject as the activities unfold in practice both in conventional home care services and in telecare mediated home care services. Particularly, we seek to explore interruptions or break-downs that are experienced during the cooperative work arrangements to inform further design of telecare mediated home care services.

3   Related Work

Fitzpatrick and Ellingsen [7] recognize the move of technology into the home as a *"movement towards technology - enabled care at home with a greater focus on self-care."* [p. 637]. The authors [7] further state that the exploration of telecare, telehealth, and other monitoring- and/or self-care technologies can indicate a drift towards increased remote care services, and a reduction of local care resources in the home, as well as the services are more user-centered with focus on the users well-being.

Bratteteig and Wagner [8] also discuss the move of home care technologies into the home in order *"to understand the work to make home care work"* (p. 145). The authors [8] explore how the introduction of technologies change the caretaking in the home in relation to the care receiver, informal caregivers (family members, friends and neigh-bors) and the larger network of professional caregivers (practical support, professional home care services and care centers with more). Procter et al. [9] explore user experi-ences of elderly people who are "aging in place"[1] with support of assistive technologies

---

[1] Aging in place is defined as *"having the mental and physical capability of living in one's own home in old age; not having to move from one's present residence to receive care or services in old age"*, retrieved 21.02.2016 from Dictionary.com.

and care services. Proctor et al. [9] state that "successful aging"[2] is feasible by daily effort of older people and their care network. Procter et al. [9] argue for the ease of customization of the technology in order to support individual needs, and the importance of mutual awareness within the care network to reduce response time when the care receiver has experienced adverse events or accidents.

Aaløkke et al. [10] argue that *"technology needs to evolve together with the elders as their needs and abilities change over time"* (p. 376). The authors present their findings by reflecting on the role of technology in assisted living housing [10]. They argue that assistive technologies often are introduced too late in the elderly care pathway, e.g. in acute phases of the old age [10]. Thus, the authors' stress the importance of introducing assistive technologies before extensive health care services are needed, as well as the technology should be more understandable for the elderly users in order for them to better succeed in adopting the technology [10].

Ballegaard et al. [11] explore use of supportive healthcare technology for elderly home dwellers (from age 60–77 years old). The authors [11] recognized that use of supportive technology is only one of several activities that elderly people are doing during a day. Hence, they argue for a design of technologies that can be integrated as a natural part of the home environment. They further state that this can be done if building services or products on familiar and/or existing technology in the home to maintain the *"continuity in the citizen's life"* (p. 1813). Thus, the authors further argue that elderly people can view modern technology as disruptions in their daily life activities.

4   Methods

4.1   The Empirical Setting – A Collaborative Change Experiment

The empirical setting is based on field work carried out in a sheltered housing located in the old town of Oslo, Norway. This sheltered housing contains 87 apartments for elderly residents as from 67 years of age. The homes are municipal rental flats, and the residents have applied for these through the municipal housing office. The office evaluates each application based on formal criteria for the allocation of sheltered housing. In this setting, we initiated a collaborative change experiment together with the district's municipal home care service organization. Home care services are complex in character by its multidisciplinary teams that performs a wide range of mobile and fluctuating care work. Thus, we chose to focus solely on the home care nurses work. The nurses provide their services to residents of the sheltered housing that have got formal decisions of receiving home based care services. We shadowed the nurses as part of our fieldwork whereas they were doing mobile home care work, thus in this manner we were given access to the homes of the elderly home dwellers. Thus, we were able to capture both the nurses and the elderly care receivers own user perspectives on the home based services. Several of the care receivers expressed a wish for more timely delivery of services

---

[2] Rowe and Kahn defined in 1997 three central components of successful aging as follows *"... low probability of disease and disease-related disability, high cognitive and physical functional capacity, and active engagement with life."*.

in order to get started with their day – thus we addressed this problem by introducing telecare as an alternative delivery of selected services for those who had minor care needs. We chose to build on existing and familiar technology in the home, by using the television as the platform for telecare mediated home care services. The change experiment consisted of five steps as follows: (1) Preliminary field studies (2) Task elicitation (3) Usability testing in controlled environment (demo - apartment) (4) Diagnostic evaluation in real environment (private homes) (5) Post – experiment workshop. For more detailed information of the change experiment and its various steps, see [4].

4.2 Participants

We recruited eight elderly participants who were existing home care receivers and who all lived in the sheltered housing. The participants expressed a motivation for participation based on own experience of delays of delivery of services, which resulting in them sitting home waiting for the nurses to come along. Additionally did one of the participants express concerns of having "strangers" from the home care service staff into the home several times during a day. The participants had various health issues, as well as different levels of user experiences with technologies. However, they all knew how to operate the television interface, and they quickly learned how to operate the TV- camera controller in order to operate the Skyping service. The average age of the residents in the sheltered housing was of 83 years of age, and the participants were represented by 6 women and 2 men.

The two participants from the home care service staff were home care service nurses. The staffs were especially selected by the home care service management as the study required them to get time off from some of the traditional work tasks in order to have time to participate in the study. The participating nurses had past experiences of using the Skype service.

5 Activity Theory as the Framework for Analysis

5.1 Activity Theory

Activity theory is based on the assumption that all human activity, from a historical standpoint, is mediated by use of cultural tools [12]. Thus, activity theory emphasizes that it is the activity itself that is the unit of analysis [13]. And it is the motivation behind the activity that separates one activity from another [14]. Cultural tools used in motivated activities can vary in shape and be from the material or ideal world [14].

Our initial analysis is based on Leont'ev's approach of activity theory [12] by the given assumption that a motivated human activity is carried out within a collective context. Leont'ev [12, 15] understands activities as *"units of life, which is organized in three hierarchical layers"* [16], see Fig. 1 below.

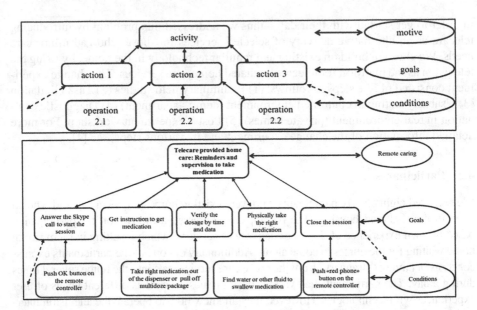

Fig. 1. Illustration of Leont'ev hierarchical structure of activity [16] above and the activity of remote caring below illustrates a simplified mapping of actions and operations.

Leont'ev argues that human activity is mediated by use of tools that need to be learned by repeated training [12]. Leont'ev further states that only after repeated training is humans able to become experienced practitioners [12, 17]. During the initial training of new practice, the practitioners are planning carefully the incremental actions needed to be carried out in order to reach the object of an activity. Thus, first over time, when these consciously goal-oriented actions are sufficient enough repeated; new practice is learned, and the users become experienced practitioners. Thus, the users are able to implement learned actions as familiar operations of routine work. Leont'ev [12, 15] states that experienced operations may be disrupted and changed during the course of an unfolding activity. Such disturbances are forcing operations to revert back to the level of action, where practitioners again have to raise awareness on their actions as new practice needs to be revised and learned [12]. The shifting mechanism between conscious actions and unconscious routine operations are as a whole the driving force behind all human activity, where human mediation of cultural tools are developed by recurring experience over time.

In this study, we also want to explicitly explore the relationships of the cooperative care activities by focusing on interruptions or breakdowns that occurred during the different work arrangements. Especially in situations where the activity is forced to take a different development than originally planned in order to adjust the mediating relationships within the activity system. We are doing so by applying Engeström's activity system model [18] that gives us an overall view of the activity system consisting of the relationship between the subject and object, object and community, subject and community. These relationships are mediated respectively by tools, division of labor, and laws. By applying Engeström's model we are able to highlight more explicit who are the subject of the activity, and we can map experienced interference that occurs as the activity unfolds. Thus, we consider Engeström's development of activity theory as a particularly suitable for bird's-eye view of a collective activity.

5.2 Conventional Home Care Practice

Conventional home care services are provided by the nurses in the homes of elderly care receivers. Thus, the cooperative work of home caring includes the nurses and care receivers. The nurses provide services such as personal care and grooming, supervision of medications, wound care, supervision of the general condition, dressing/undressing, motivate healthy nutrition and fluid intake, and preparation of simple meals. The home care services are shift based and divided into three shifts; day, evening and night. The nurses are working in teams that are covering services for users who are located in a fixed area within the district to reduce the time and distance when traveling on visit from one user's home to another. The head nurse divides an equal amount of users to each of the team members with considerations of providing them an evenly distributed workload throughout a work shift. The team members can adjust their workflow as they prefer to a certain degree. However, the health care needs of the users are essential to what extent the users are visited once or several times during a day. Their care needs and location of residence are central when the nurses are planning their work flow in regard to the visiting order of their assigned users. Users who need assistance to personal care and grooming, or those who have to get ready for the day care center are prioritized first during a day shift. While users with minor care needs, e.g. supervision of medication, are taken later after the prioritized morning visits are done. However, there are exceptions of the workflow order, e.g. if users with extensive and minor care needs live close to each other; the nurses may decide to put them in the following order if it is more efficient in regard to time consumptions. The prioritization of visits is to some degree opposite during the evening, as users with minor care needs are taken first during the shift, e.g. to prepare dinner or supervise the intake of medication. Thus, users with extensive care needs are taken in the end of the evening shift, e.g. for assistance to get into bed.

Users who get visits during the night shifts have often extensive care needs such as need for support in the home that includes support from two nurses. For example, this could be users who have physical disabilities and need support to be turned over in bed to prevent bedsores or who need personal care and grooming as a result of incontinence. However, night visits can also apply to care tasks that only require supervision from a nurse.

Figure 2 displays a simplified activity system of the nurse (subject) who by use of the medicine dispenser can provide the users with accurate medication dosage, and supervise that the elderly care receiver take the prescribed medication and drink water or other fluid to help passing the medication from the mouth to the stomach. The model has restriction as it does not explicitly illustrate the time aspect, but merely focusing on the object of conventional caring within its context. A number of elderly care receivers were complaining that the nurses came on delayed visits, and this interference the division of labor mediated relationship of the object and the community that is marked by the bold broken arrow, see Fig. 2. In order to develop more efficient and timely home care services to active elders; we chose to introduce and test telecare mediated home care services as part of the change experiment [4].

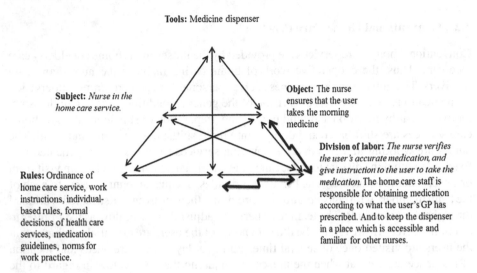

Tools: Medicine dispenser

Subject: *Nurse in the home care service.*

Object: The nurse ensures that the user takes the morning medicine

Division of labor: *The nurse verifies the user's accurate medication, and give instruction to the user to take the medication.* The home care staff is responsible for obtaining medication according to what the user's GP has prescribed. And to keep the dispenser in a place which is accessible and familiar for other nurses.

Rules: Ordinance of home care service, work instructions, individual-based rules, formal decisions of health care services, medication guidelines, norms for work practice.

Fig. 2. The illustration displays conventional home care service where the nurse ensures that the user takes the morning medication

5.3   Telecare as a Means for Delivery of Home Care Services

Telecare mediated home care services are carried out by the home care service nurses and users through the television interface by use of TV Cam HD for Skype calls (hdmi connection). Thus, the cooperative work of home caring is provided by the same participants, but the work is delegated differently and the participants are not located at the same place. The nurses provide selected services that are found appropriate for remote delivery of caring including supervision of medication intake, provide instructions for self – care of wound care, provide instructions for prevention and everyday rehabilitation activities, supervise the general condition, stimulate to proper nutrition with others. The users care needs are essential to the amount of telecare sessions per day, or if the telecare sessions are mixed together with conventional home care visits. However, the users are able to receive services timely and according to a time that is preferable for them. The work flow and the time of visits are less affected by other users' care needs or location of residence. However, this setting of care work requires that the users are prepared and ready to take the call when the nurse is calling.

Figure 3 displays a simplified activity system of the elderly care receiver (as the subject) who by use of the medicine dispenser and telecare technology is reminded of taking the accurate medicine dosage under supervision from the nurse. The remote delivery of services put the user as the subject of the activity, as the user is the one who is actually performing the practical work tasks. Thus, the user is assigned with increased responsibility and self-care activities. The assumptions for this delivery of services are that the user master the telecare session and that the dispenser is filled and accessible, as well as water or other fluid. In cases where the nurse is unable to perform supervision from remote as the user is not responding or there are technical issues, the nurse has to visit the user in addition to the telecare call. There is less flexibility in the remote setup of caring as every assumption behind the object of the activity has to be present in order for the work to be accomplished. Thus, the practical care work is done by the user and not the nurse in this setup of caring. Moreover, if the medicine dispenser is empty or absent, the user may not be able to perform the fixed work tasks; and managing work-arounds from remote location can be troublesome. However, telecare mediated home care services transform conventional home care service by the re-delegation of labor. Additionally we see a need for developing the law mediated relationship of the subject and the community. Especially concerning who are appropriate for remote delivery of services, is local and remote caring counted as equal home visits, should the deductible be adjusted when the user is doing more work and gets increased responsibility. More-over, we see a requirement for developing instructions for the new work routine, e.g. can users have a say about receiving remote versus local caring, or is it the application office for health care services that gets to decide, furthermore what actions should be taken if the user does not responds to the call etc.

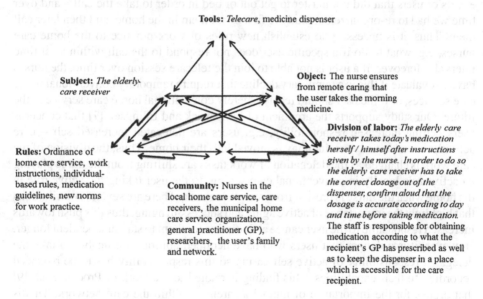

Tools: *Telecare*, medicine dispenser

Subject: *The elderly care receiver*

Object: The nurse ensures from remote caring that the user takes the morning medicine.

Division of labor: *The elderly care receiver takes today's medication herself / himself after instructions given by the nurse. In order to do so the elderly care receiver has to take the correct dosage out of the dispenser, confirm aloud that the dosage is accurate according to day and time before taking medication.* The staff is responsible for obtaining medication according to what the recipient's GP has prescribed as well as to keep the dispenser in a place which is accessible for the care recipient.

Rules: Ordinance of home care service, work instructions, individual-based rules, medication guidelines, new norms for work practice.

Community: Nurses in the local home care service, care receivers, the municipal home care service organization, general practitioner (GP), researchers, the user's family and network.

Fig. 3. The illustration displays the re-delegation of work when telecare is introduced in order for the nurse to supervise that the user takes prescribed morning medication.

6   Findings and Discussion

The introduction of telecare as the means to deliver home care services transforms the current cooperative work of conventional home care services since new delivery of service is forcing forward a redistribution of the practical work by delegating more work to the care receivers. We also experienced that telecare mediated home care services resulted in increased responsibility to the users because of the increased self-care activities. However, the users who mastered the telecare solution to its full potential were rewarded with increased flexibility in their daily life activities since the delivery of services was more predictable and timely. Though, we experienced during our fieldwork that some of the recruited participants got increased decline of physical or cognitive abilities, so over time they did not master to either respond to the telecare sessions or they needed care services that were not suitable for remote delivery, e.g. support with personal care and grooming. Thus, in the last period of our experiment; two participants received both telecare m home care services and conventional home care services.

To succeed in making the home care services more efficient by use of telecare, the telecare session should replace one or several conventional home care visits. It is therefore necessary to establish new work routines at the home care service office. For example in regard to the selection process of users that would be suitable candidates for remote delivery of home care services. The users should ideally have minor health care issues in order to supervise them from remote location. It is also important to implement mechanisms that capture signs of reduced abilities of self-care activities – since elderly people often have fluctuating general conditions. In our study, we experienced repeated events of users that did not master to get out of bed in order to take the call – and over time we had to re-organize our study to first assist them in the home, and then later call them. Thus, it is necessary to establish new rules of work practice to the home care nurses, e.g. what to do if a specific user does not respond to the call within a set time interval. Moreover, if a user is not able to join the telecare session over time, the nurses have to evaluate if this is a temporary decline that require temporary conventional home care services, or if the user should receive merely conventional home care service in the future. Our study supports the argument of Fitzpatrick and Ellingsen [7] that concerns users getting increased responsibility, e.g. users are delegated increased self – care activities when assistive technology is moved into their home. Thus, the division of the care work is changed as the delegation of work tasks are shifting from the nurse playing an active role locally in conventional care setting, to the user taking the active role in the home when the nurse is present from remote location. There are several contributions that highlight the importance of active aging and successful aging, thus this push towards increased responsible to the user can be an initiative for them to stay independent longer. However, it is a danger that users who have declined abilities are unable to take the delegated responsibility of active self-caring so this responsibility has to be balanced according to their capabilities. This finding is related to the work of Procter et al. [9] that argues for the importance of mutual awareness within the care network. This is especially critical in user situations where the user experiences sudden decline in the general conditions. Thus, the care network has to establish mechanisms that capture sudden changes in the current health situation. Aaløkke et al. [10] emphasize that technology has to develop according to the shifting need of users. This is a relevant argument in relation to telecare sessions, as telecare is valued as appropriate for users that have minor care needs, so telecare could be introduced in early onset of old age. Moreover, as users are experiencing declining health, they should be supported with additional technologies such as sensors to support their safety and security, e.g. fall sensors or door controllers for wanderers. The use of sensors requires none or less awareness from the user side since the technology is automated to alert in predefined situations. Future studies are required in order to fully capture the limitations and potentials of telecare mediated health care services for active elders.

7 Conclusion

In this present paper, we apply activity theory as a theoretical framework to study the cooperative care work in the home of elderly people. We are doing so by comparing conventional home care services with telecare mediated home care services. Especially we are concerned about the transformation of care work and how this affects the cooperative care work of the care providers and care receivers. We conclude that introduction of telecare mediated home care services results in increased delegation of practical self-care activities and responsibility to the elderly care receivers. Thus, telecare such as video consultation in the home is not appropriate for all elders. Nevertheless are those who mastery these responsibilities, rewarded with increased flexibility in their daily life activities since the delivery of services is more predictable and timely.

Acknowledgments. We thank all the participants who made it possible to carry out this study. We also thank the reviewers that gave constructive feedback for improvement of this paper. The authors also acknowledge the grant from Norwegian Research Council (NRC), project number 22201.

References

1. Ministry of Social services, NOU 1992:1 - Safety - Dignity – Care, Oslo (1992)
2. Daatland, S.O. og Otnes, B.: Housing oriented care: Trends, in S.O. Daatland(red.), Housing oriented elderly care. NOVA, Oslo (2014)
3. Ministry of Education and Research, NOU 2011:11 – Innovation in care. Ministry of Health and Care Services, Oslo (2011)
4. Joshi, S.G., Woll, A.: A collaborative change experiment: diagnostic evaluation of telecare for elderly home dwellers. In: Duffy, V.G. (ed.) DHM 2015. LNCS, vol. 9185, pp. 423–434. Springer, Heidelberg (2015). doi:10.1007/978-3-319-21070-4_42
5. Directorate of Health, Welfare technology. Technical report on the implementation of welfare technology in the municipal health - care systems 2013-2020. 5. Directorate of Health, Oslo (2012)
6. Ministry of Health and Care Services, Meld. St. 29 (2012-2013) - Tomorrow's care, Oslo (2013)
7. Fitzpatrick, G., Ellingsen, G.: A review of 25 years of CSCW research in healthcare: contributions, challenges and future agendas. Comput. Support. Coop. Work **22**, 609–665 (2013)
8. Bratteteig, T., Wagner, I.: Moving healthcare to the home: the work to make homecare work. In: Bertelsen, O.W., Ciolfi, L., Grasso, M.A., Papadopoulos, G.A. (eds.) ECSCW 2013: Proceedings of the 13th European Conference on Computer Supported Cooperative Work, Paphos, Cyprus, 21–25 September 2013, pp. 143–162. Springer, London (2013)

9. Procter, R., Greenhalgh, T., Wherton, J., Sugarhood, P., Rouncefield, M., Hinder, S.: The day-to-day co-production of ageing in place. Comput. Support. Coop. Work **23**, 245–267 (2014)
10. Aaløkke, S., Bunde-Pedersen, J., Bardram, J.E.: Where to Roberta? Reflecting on the role of technology in assisted living. In: Proceedings of NordiChi, pp. 373–376 (2006)
11. Ballegaard, S., Hansen, T., Kyng, M.: Healthcare in everyday life: designing healthcare services for daily life. In: CHI 2008, Proceeding of the Twenty-Sixth Annual SIGCHI Conference on Human Factors in Computing Systems, pp. 1807–1816 (2008)
12. Leont'ev, A.N.: Activity, Consciousness, and Personality. Prentice-Hall, Englewood Cliffs (1978)
13. Kaptelinin, V.: Activity theory. In: Soegaard, M., Dam, R.F. (eds.) The Encyclopedia of Human Computer Interaction, 2nd edn. The Interaction 89 Design Foundation, Aarhus (2013)
14. Kuutti, K.: The concept of activity as a basic unit of analysis. In: Bannon, L., Robinson, M., Schmidt, K. (eds.) Proceedings of the Second European Conference on Computer-Supported Cooperative Work, Amsterdam, The Netherlands, 25–27 September 1991 (1991)
15. Leont'ev, A.: The problem of activity in psychology. Sov. Psychol. **13**(2), 4–33 (1974)
16. Kaptelinin, V., Nardi, B.: Activity Theory in HCI: Fundamentals and Reflections. Synthesis Lectures on Human-Centered Informatics. Morgan & Claypool, San Francisco (2012)
17. Koschmann, K.H.: The concept of breakdown in Heidegger, Leont'ev, and Dewey and its implications for educations. Mind Cult. Act. **5**(1), 25–42 (1998)
18. Engeström, Y.: Expansive learning at work: toward an activity theoretical reconceptualization. J. Educ. Work **14**(1), 133–156 (2001). Rutledge

Interaction Design of Products for the Elderly in Smart Home Under the Mode of Medical Care and Pension

Minggang Yang[✉], He Huang, Haozhou Yuan, and Qichao Sun

School of Art, Design and Media,
East China University of Science and Technology,
M. BOX 286, No. 130, Meilong Road, Xuhui District, Shanghai 200237, China
{yangminggang,1983222hh}@163.com, dfyhz@vip.qq.com,
871778027@qq.com

Abstract. The problem of aging population in the world is increasing. Elderly health, daily life and other aspects of the problem with modern information technology, intelligent service facilities or product do not match the contradiction is increasingly prominent. At the same time, sensory function and action ability of the elderly are in the continuous degradation. Their cognitive and learning level is limited, which leads to experiencing smart home hardily. Therefore, it is imperative to study and improve the interaction design of smart home products for the elderly. In this paper, the contradiction between the design of smart home products and the demands of the elderly in daily life is studied under the mode of medical care and pension, as well as case analysis of smart home products for the elderly. The purpose of the paper is to study the type and interaction design of smart home products for the aged. The main method is through the investigation and user analysis of smart home, finding the principles and characteristics of interaction design from the products. Research shows that intelligent products can be divided into three types under the mode of medical and pension: smart home appliances, smart home management system and call monitoring system. Through the mobile Internet, intelligent terminal and touch screen control, smart home can meet the needs of the elderly users seamless, which will be a trend in the design of smart home products.

Keywords: Mode of medical and pension · The elderly · Smart home products · Interactive design · User experience

1 Introduction

The global economy and industry are in the development as well as the rapidly changing modern life. People's material life is enriched more and more while a series of problems brought by aging are still uncovered. In the contemporary social life products and the information product innovation, the elders cannot easily enjoy the life changes brought by the reform of science and technology. The life class medical supplies close to the daily needs of the elderly are simplex to function, lack of designing factors and quality is poor. Such as the elderly hearing aids, cane and bath products. The purpose of assisting

© Springer International Publishing Switzerland 2016
J. Zhou and G. Salvendy (Eds.): ITAP 2016, Part II, LNCS 9755, pp. 145–156, 2016.
DOI: 10.1007/978-3-319-39949-2_14

the elderly life is not really realized. Meanwhile, the smart home products for elderly have entered the public view and are in the continuous research and development stage. However, it needs some time and inspection for these products to really enter the daily life of the elderly. The elderly physiological and cognitive learning level is unceasingly in the recession, their physical decline and memory is poor. Based on these problems, concern and care should be highlighted in the interactive smart home products experience.

In November, 2015 the government launched China medical support combined with new pension model, which is to promote the health and pension services combination. Take pension as the main aim and medical service as auxiliary to drive the transformation of the whole social pension system upgrade and to maximize the use of social resources, in order to better serve the health of the elderly life. The demand of the elderly smart home products under this policy will be growing. On one hand, application of the smart home products can offer the convenience of the elderly living environment, strengthen communication with outside world, at the same time, the smart home system service to the elderly can reduce the cost of human resources and alleviate the pressure on the family and social old-age pension. On the other hand, the safe and convenient smart home furnishing life could help old people to improve their independence and quality of life and enhance the recognition and their sense of happiness in old age psychological downturn. In addition to the technical, economic, ecological construction and improvement, smart home product development and popularization should be constructed between the smart home and the elderly, and the smart home system with interaction design is particularly important.

This paper explored the Smart Home Furnishing products elderly interaction design. The work of this paper and the main results are summarized as follows: 1. Define the concept and characteristics of smart home furnishing products interaction design for elderly under the mode of raising and medicine combination on the basis of literature review. 2. Research the existing elderly smart home products by case analysis method, and carry out user interviews and questionnaire survey through the analysis to obtain the factors affecting the interaction design of elderly smart home products, and summarize the principles of interaction design from description of three aspects: sensory identification, cognitive function and associated behavior. Finally, discuss the improvement strategies and suggestions of interaction design of smart home furnishing products for elderly.

2   Research Background

The "2015 the global retirement index" published by Natixis Global Asset Management (Contains the 20 performance indexes including retirees financial status, health, safety and comfort of life, world economic environment etc.) indicates that Switzerland is the world's best national endowment. The 10 countries with the highest score of the pension, there are as many as 8 from Europe. Norway rank second, Australia rank third. The Fourth to tenth are Iceland, Holland, Sweden, Denmark, Austria, Germany and New Zealand. As to the Asian countries, South Korea ranked the highest as fourteenth.

In addition, Japan rank seventeenth, Singapore is thirtieth and the United States rank nineteenth.

At present, there are 4 main kinds of typical international pension service system, particularly represented by the United States, Japan, Sweden and Hong Kong, see sheet1. Foreign pension industry started early and developed rapidly, thus they have formed a relatively complete industrial chain and achieved a certain scale of the industry. The pension industry of the United States has become vitality and cannot be ignored is the aging society. It supports economic and social growth. The pension industry in Japan takes the aged care industry as the main line, covering a wide range from the welfare services to the value of life.

China National Bureau of statistics data show that by the end of 2014, Chinese people over the age of 60 has accounted for 15.5 % of the total population, reaching 212 million. It is predicted that by 2050, the elderly population in the world will reach 2 billion 20 million. The Chinese elderly population will reach 440 million, accounting for almost 1/4 of the world's elderly population. According to "China Aging Industry Development Report (2014)", during 2014 to 2050, the consumption potential of China's elderly population will grow from 4 trillion CNY to 106 trillion CNY accounting proportion of GDP will increase from 8 % to about 33 %. China will also become the country with the most potential in global aging industry. In general, China pension services are still in the early stages of development. Pension services and product supply shortage problems are serious. At present, the development of the urgent needs of the elderly life care, long-term care, spiritual comfort, culture and entertainment services are relatively slow. In December 2011, the Ministry of civil affairs of China promulgated the social old-age service system construction of "Twelfth Five Year" plan. It clearly put forward that by 2015, China will realize a social old-age service system with perfect system, perfect organization, moderate scale, good operation, excellent service, supervision in place and sustainable development. In July 2015, China's State Council promote the smart health care industry development and smart combination of medical care will be the future direction of development of health service system in actively promoting "Internet + action guidance".

With the popularization of the Internet technology, smart home furnishing products have entered the era of rapid development. The application of RFID technology, wireless sensor network, network cameras and other technology will change traditional old-age home in the future. Smart home such as smart medicine box, remote nursing system, smart food procurement system applications will also gradually mature in the future. The old man can complete a certain degree of self-care through their own activities, and their children can also observe the living conditions of the elderly through the remote monitoring. In general, with the increasing popularity of technology and progress, smart home system of the old in the home care, medical health monitoring, the elderly at risk prevention field elderly smart home plays an irreplaceable role in future pension field (Table 1).

Currently the Chinese market for the elderly design of intelligent home is not enough. Part of the smart home furnishing is independent of the individual like an information isolated island. There is no full interconnection, intercommunication and interoperation. It doesn't blend into the overall home design. The smart home for the elderly in the interaction design field did not fully realize mutual integration of person,

Table 1. Sheet 1 comparing of four typical pension service systems worldwide

Mode	Characteristics
The new liberalism service system (USA)	Introduce market mechanisms to reduce the responsibility of the government; take the civil service agencies as the center and emphasize the care and help among each other
Diversified service system (Japan)	The common participation of government, family, community, work units, non-governmental organizations, service units and main body diversification; stress the role of the family while the state investment in welfare is ignored
Uniform service system (Sweden)	The state makes the standards for all the national welfare service to provide unified services to all citizens through public welfare institutions, which leads to increased financial burden
The government based integrated service system (Hong Kong)	Emphasize the responsibility of the government and strengthen the community care

Origins: Juan [5]

matter and environment. Old people's increasing age will also have many problems. On one hand, aging of the physical function causes movement coordination and sensory ability weaker and weaker. Their prevalence of risk and number are in increase, and some of the diseases are difficult to cure. On the other hand, due to the age increases, psychological problems are more prominent. Elderly people are lack of awareness of the outside world, prone to loneliness and anxiety, not willing to accept and learn new things. Because of these physiological and psychological problems, there constitute a barrier for older people to use the smart Home Furnishing. According to the survey, more than 50 % of the problems the elderly encounter in daily life are potentially associated with product design. Only 53 % of them are well trained to use good products to meet their needs. From this aspect, the application of smart home can indeed bring a lot of convenience to old people in the future, but in which should pay attention to and study are the elderly user experience and interactive behavior. To overcome the elderly physiological and psychological obstacle, we must consider the common features of the elderly users group. Start from the interactive mode and apply the user experience design idea to the interaction design of smart home to truly enable older people to benefit.

3 Literature Review

Elderly people smart home has been constantly under test and development stage in the world. Mature products invested in market are not much. Some products are lack of system and are single in function. In the moral point of view, some monitoring equipment will be related to the elderly people's privacy. And at the same time, the relevant research on interaction design documents is little. But with the physical network technology unceasing popularization, improving of the interaction design and user experience perfecting, the elderly intelligent Home Furnishing will usher a rapid development.

Research in the field of user experience in foreign countries in the elderly intelligent Home Furnishing interaction design are mainly focus on the testing of new technology, the elderly acceptance and privacy issues. For example, EM Tapia, SS Intille, K Larson (2004) introduces the application of sensor can realize the omnipresent at home. Those simple and small sensor facilities can give people life convenience. Karen l Courtney and George Demirisa (2008) studies elders' privacy situation and acceptance in the smart home using sensor and finds that older people are willing to accept the change of smart home life, they have a high degree of participation and the development of new technology can eliminate privacy problems to a certain extent. Parisa Rashidi (2013) introduced the "auxiliary environmental life" (ambient-assisted living) and the possible application of the AAL system. They think that can better serve the health of the elderly life through the system. Francois Portet and Michel vacher (2014) study in-depth of the intelligent home in the elderly based on speech recognition system and conclude that older people could communicate more conveniently by speech remote control and communication, and home smart degree can also be improved and bring more convenience to the lives of the elderly.

China's elderly smart home is still in the starting stage. Most of the literatures are just based on the theoretical discussion of applied feasibility. Research papers are less on health care and pension services based on technology and interaction design and user experience. Zhang Jin (2014) thinks that through reasonable functional classification, reality enhanced technical assistance and the system security enhance can enhance the smart home system affinity for the elderly and make high-tech effective better serve the elderly. Li Yangfeng, Chenglong (2015) think that smart pension is to combine the medical support pattern in the "Internet + background", a modernized medical support using modern computer technology, network technology and artificial intelligence. It encourages the use of cloud computing, data and third-party service forces and provide long-time follow-up, forecasting warning individuation service management to achieve elderly timely information sharing in order to ensure the safety and health of the elderly. Liu Shulao (2015) divides elderly smart home furnishing into interaction property and support attributes. Attribute interaction is divided into six categories: easy operation, intuitive and representative, context awareness, spatial interaction and social interaction. Support property contains blow: mathematical degree, barrier free convenience, sensory support, safety and security, self-control and function of promoting.

Above all, the foreign research of smart home is much advanced compared to domestic. At present foreign elderly smart home research is forwarding to diversified development point of view, mainly emphasizing on the implementation and practical application of new technologies. But theory and research related to interaction design on the user experience is not rich. There is still some room for improvement.

4   Research Methods

The main research methods of this paper are:

Multidisciplinary Research Method: The content frame of the research uses inter-disciplinary knowledge system in interaction design construction of smart home furnishing products for the elderly. From intelligent home product technical means of combined with knowledge of the structure of the Internet of things, use the factors of psychology analysis of user demand levels. Applications need to try to accommodate users with higher levels of the hierarchy of needs. Analyze older users' interest points and viscosity category of smart home products. Then try to use psychology, aesthetics and design idea in the elderly people of smart home products interaction design.

Literature Research Method: This article translates and studies a collection of smart home product interaction design, the elderly related design and design aesthetics, psychology related books and materials. Methods and characteristics of research were combing and analysis for elderly people smart home product interaction design contents. At the same time, through comparative analysis of the literature, the article draws a conclusion to the user interface design strategy that we should be closely combined with the analysis of market environment and competitive factors. Choose the design approaches and methods more suitable for the elderly smart home product interaction.

Case Analysis Method: Compare and analyze the typical products in smart home furnishing, summarize and conclude features of different kinds of elderly intelligent home products application from the point of view of interaction design and user experience, summarize the elements that should be noted in the direction of the interaction of the elderly smart home system.

Model Research Method: Through the analysis of elderly users demand hierarchy induction in the field of intelligent home, study put forward the user cognition, emotion and behavior model. Through the user model construction and induction, put forward corresponding matching requirements to the smart home products elderly experience.

5   Results

5.1   Definition of the Concepts of Interactively Designed Smart Home Products for the Elderly

Broadly speaking, an intelligent home product that satisfies medical care and maintenance is a complete system that comprises of smart household electrical appliances, smart household management system and call supervisor system. A perfect solution to the smart household aimed at old people is supposed to have a combination of all the functions of the three aspects above. Its interactive design consists of two main aspects: the interactive design for the elderly and home products, and the smart home systemic design based on old users, which includes management system and call supervisor system.

The interactive design of elderly and home products refers to the human-computer interactive design which begins from perspectives including sensory organ, cognition and acts, and facilitates the elderly in using smart home products and gain active information or physical feedback from products so as to assist with the old people's demand and provide them with good experience.

The interactive design of smart home system at the basis of old users, and which realizes mainly through sensors and RFID technology, can be seen as an interactive systemic design constructed upon users, acts, circumstances and products, with Smart home, children, community and hospitals as informative communication terminals to realize the convenient communication among all terminals as well as timely medical care and maintenance feedback.

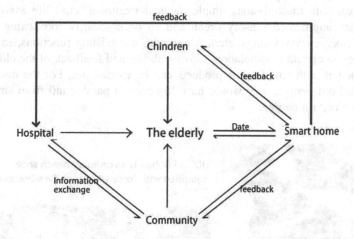

Fig. 1. Sketch map of smart home furnishing interaction system

It can be seen from the picture that smart home system for the elderly is pretty excellent, with the old users as center, and send their real-time conditions to their children, community center and hospital via the informative shift of smart home system. Children are informed of old people's daily life and health through Smart home system, instant communication with the elderly is also doable. Community center takes charge of storing up old people's health data and routine health care, and establishing uninterrupted informative communication with the hospital, feeding back physical change and medical information of the old people without delay. Hospitals can carry out timely cure for the elderly in emergency via Smart home system. The whole interactive system is a complete service close loop, actualizing informative and intelligent nurse for the elderly with the help of the Smart home system (Fig. 1).

Smart household system designed by the German team of engineers. It can send alarming information to old people's kinsfolk when they fall. The Safe home smart household system is virtually a group of sensor boxes placed in every room in the house. It can perceive movements, voices and locations of the family members via optical and acoustical sensors. It would at first await and judge whether the person stumbled down can get up by himself if perceive someone falls, and if not, then it will go to the second stage, during which the Safe home would firstly ask the person whether he needs to call. And if there's no response, it will immediately get through emergency service and inform other family members that the old people had fallen. Safe home system actualizes automatically domestic alarming for the elderly at home, offering an essential safety guarantee for them.

5.2   Influence Factors of Interactive Design of the Smart Home Products for the Elderly

According to the former surveys on smart home products, smart home products that serve the elderly are supposed to have three functions as medical aid and monitoring (physiological data transmission, simple medical treatment, etc.) life assists (sports exercise, diet, augmented sensory organ and so on.), security forecasting (forestall stumbling, emergency warnings, etc.). Along with the existing functions, smart home products require certain manipulation, moving ability and feedback of the elderly, thus basic interaction with smart home products can be carried out. For the disabled and semi-disabled old people, they would have to accept a passive aid from smart home products to a certain degree.

UD' s PDShoe is an ordinary beach shoe equipped with force sensors and a vibration system.

A UD doctoral student, conducts tests of the PDShoe at the Newark Senior Center in Delaware.

Fig. 2. Robotic shoe helps patients with Parkinson's walk smooth and steady

Researchers in University of Delaware contrive a kind of shoe with vibrating insole, whose vibration frequency is controlled by a micro-computer, to help improve the walking disorder of patients with Parkinson, reduce rigidity of pace, improve walking speed while keep in balance. This kind of shoe is provided with three functions in simple medical treatment, acts assistance and forestalling stumbles (Fig. 2).

Elder users, compared to youngsters, have problems below that affect the interactive experience when use smart home products:

Physiological functions decline: For instance, cardiovascular decline, osteoporosis, decline on moving ability and easy to stumble, etc. According to reports from the WHO, 20 % to 30 % American elderly got slight or severe wounded after fall. Falls mostly cause traumatic injuries, hip fracture and head traumas. Part of the reasons that bring about the risk may be the aging of body, sensory organ and cognition and the environment's failure to meet the needs of the aging of population.

Cognitive Decline: Like auditory and visual fade, serious memory fade, which also causes deficiency in learning and cognitive ability, so as to affect directly the experience in human—computer interaction, like the elderly people's frequent misrecognition of functional buttons when use smart home products.

Mental Change: Since some old people live in solitude, and due to their physical and mental changes, they tend to feel lonely and nervous, repelling strange surroundings and are reluctant to receiving and learning new things, owning contradictory emotions toward high—tech products such as smart home products and so alike.

Chart 2 carries out qualitative analysis on different kinds of smart home products based on the smart home products at service of medical treatments for elderly and its classification, summarizing how deeply different kinds of smart home products are affected by the elderly people's self—condition, which also indicates smart home products' demand level on the elderly people's self—condition. H, M and L represent high, medium and low impact level respectively (Table 2).

Table 2. Chart 2 Influence factors and relationships between smart home products and the elderly.

Influence factors / Smart home products		Sensory organs			Body		Learning & Memorizing
		Auditory sense & tongue	Vision	Tactile sensation	Hands	Limbs	
Medical aid	Physiological sensors	L	L	H	M	M	L
	Domestic medical treatment	L	M	M	M	M	M
Life assistance	Sports exercise	M	M	M	H	H	H
	Diets	L	M	M	H	M	H
	Sensory intensifier	M	M	M	M	L	M
	Independent auxiliary	L	M	M	H	H	M
Security alarming	Walker	L	L	M	M	H	M
	Alarming system	L	L	L	L	L	L

(H: High M: Middle L: Low)

Analysis shows that present smart home products require relatively high of old people's physical health and memory in most cases. And in the matter of sensory organ, vision and tactile sensations are at higher requirement while auditory sense and tongue less required on the elderly.

5.3   Construction Principle and Upgrade Strategy for the Interactive Design of Smart Home Products for the Elderly

Principles of design for the smart home products for the elderly proposed due to the poor physical condition in combination with the function of medical hygiene and pension services:

Principle of Accessibility of the Human-Computer Interaction: Accessibility consists of establishing accessible human-computer interactive interface, efficient and user-friendly feedback mechanism and reducing the elderly people's movement, cognitive, psychological and memory burden. Such as the elderly intelligent wearable device Tempo, which is equipped with a 9 axis MEMS sensor (including a 3 axis accelerator, a 3 axis gyroscope and a 3 axis magnetometer), enabling it to track acts like strolling and lying down. Battery-driven pointer points to where the home or the center of the sensor is. The system can locate where acts take place, like in the bathroom, bedroom or kitchen. Tempo reduces the burden to the minimum for the elderly when use intelligent products, and is designed in a way aimed at integrating into daily life in interactive form, which realizes indiscriminating communication between man and products (Fig. 3).

Fig. 3. Pic 5.1 Smart equipment "Tempo"

Principle of Security: The principle of security comprises of two aspects. One is the safety of old people that lives alone when use smart home products. The design of indoor smart home products is supposed to have certain fault tolerance. Considering first about all kinds of possible conditions when old people use them when design products, lowering the danger coefficient to the minimum. The other one is data safety of smart home products. In the overall environment of smart home products interaction, individual privacy and residential information safety shall be put under protection in time, since their capability to resist the external interference is relatively weak.

Principle of Practicability: Part of the old people deem products with high-tech as white elephants, cutting redundant interactively designed functions, and remain those succinct, central interactive design, establishing benign user experience with practicability as premise.

The interactive design of smart home products suggest that apart from satisfying basic functions and interactive communication among old people, further additional strategies are wanted on products and systems of smart home products to improve the experience of care and emotional solicitude toward old users.

Multi Sensory Interactive Design: Most of the elderly-served intelligent home products such as smart phones and domestic medical apparatuses are interactive products based mainly on tactile sensation and auxiliary with vision and auditory sense. Functional design in sensory organs should be augmented, like augmenting home furnishing experiences with audio-based orders, enabling the elderly to actualize interactions with the intelligent home products in least self-burden, and synchronizing the feedback from intelligent home products with the elderly sensory level. For example, measures like regulating intensity of light through acoustic control in the lighting system of the intelligent household can be adopted in accordance with varied regions or occasions.

Modularized and Standardized Design: Modularized interactive designs are in the light of different conditions of the elderly. The elderly have varied demand toward medical treatment and recuperation, thus modularized functional joint should be adopted to save resources and costs. Standardized designs are based upon the whole intelligent home products system. Close-related screen interaction enables the elderly to reduce their burden as they memorize and learn. At the same time, the intelligent home products have yet developed a unified standard in home-area network and technology layout, and lack of compatibility, putting some burden on the users.

Joyfully and Emotionally Interactive Designing: The elderly are psychologically fragile, lacking care and enjoyment of life. According to a survey, over 80 % of the elderly are pressed for care from their children, and don't get enough communication with the outside. For instance, traditional medical apparatuses are kind of cold, so warm color design in appearance can be carried out in related products, and meanwhile employ some approachable material design like acrylic, polycarbonate and rubber paint spray, improving affinity of the products, lessening the elders' indisposition towards technology products.

6 Conclusions and Discussions

To improve the interactively designed products for the elders under the mode of medical care and pension is to improve the interactive experience of the elderly in using the smart home products that are aimed at the elders' physical and mental features at the base of big data and technology advantages in information intelligence. The designer of the smart home products should design with a user-friendly, secure and practical interactive designing principle, along with experienced designing increments that are emotional and joyful, in addition to considering over the elderly interactive mode that is multi sensory and multi aspect, as well as designing methods which is standardized and modularized. Meshing the elderly and products design, and pay heed to what they need, understand their senses so that man-machine distance narrowed, and interactive products of more distinctive and more humanized quality can be designed in support of technology.

All in all, products that are seamlessly matched to the demand of the elderly users through mobile Internet, intelligent terminals and touch-screen control will be the trend in which the smart home products design will follow.

References

1. Guiding opinions of China State Council on promoting "Internet plus". http://www.gov.cn/zhengce/content/2015-07/04/content_10002.html
2. Yushao, W., Junwu, D.: The Report of Chinese Aging Industry Development (2014). Social Sciences Literature (CHINA), Beijing (2015)
3. China Ministry of Civil Affair Social Service Development Statistics in 2014, bulletin. http://www.mca.gov.cn/article/zwgk/mzyw/201506/20150600832371.shtml
4. Fact sheet N°344 of World Health Organization. http://www.who.int/mediacentre/factsheets/fs344/zh/
5. Juan, S.: Thoughts on constructing social pension service system in Shanghai. Sci. Dev. **11**, 61–70 (2014)
6. Tapia, E.M., Intille, S.S., Larson, K.: Activity recognition in the home using simple and ubiquitous sensors. In: Ferscha, A., Mattern, F. (eds.) PERVASIVE 2004. LNCS, vol. 3001, pp. 158–175. Springer, Heidelberg (2004)
7. Courtney, K.L., Demiris, G., Rantz, M., et al.: Needing smart home technologies: the perspectives of older adults in continuing care retirement communities. J. Innovations Healh Inform. **16**(3), 195–201 (2008)
8. Rashidi, P., Mihailidis, A.: A survey on ambient-assisted living tools for older adults. J. Biomed. Healh Inform. **17**(3), 579–590 (2013)
9. Portet, F., Vacher, M., Golanski, C., et al.: Design and evaluation of a smart home voice interface for the elderly: acceptability and objection aspects. Pers. Ubiquit. Comput. **17**(1), 127–144 (2013)
10. Jin, Z., Yue, Q.: Smart home design for the elderly. Des **9**, 31–32 (2014)
11. Yangfeng, L., Long, C.: A preliminary study on the innovation mode of Chinese wisdom medical support. Mod. Hosp. Manag. 6, (2015)
12. Shulao, L., Yijing, C.: The interactive design of intelligent appliances for the elderly. Furniture Inter. Des. 6 (2015)
13. Taking steps to fight Parkinson's disease. http://www.udel.edu/researchmagazine/issue/vol4_no1/taking_steps.html
14. Intelligent device "Tempo". http://36kr.com/p/214620.html

Aging and Social Media

Ageism and IT: Social Representations, Exclusion and Citizenship in the Digital Age

Ines Amaral[1,2,3(✉)] and Fernanda Daniel[3,4]

[1] Communication and Society Research Centre, University of Minho, Braga, Portugal
inesamaral@gmail.com
[2] Autonomous University of Lisbon, Lisbon, Portugal
[3] Instituto Superior Miguel Torga, Coimbra, Portugal
fernanda.b.daniel@gmail.com
[4] Center for Studies and Research in Health, University of Coimbra, Coimbra, Portugal

Abstract. The benefits of the introduction of technology in human life may be puzzled with the world evolution. Although the use of technology is limited by geographic, cultural and economic parameters, the benefits for mankind are proved every. However, the movement of globalization promoted by technology also produces new economical and social exclusions. Therefore, an idea of injustice arises. The aim of this paper is to discuss the condition of second-class citizenship of the elderly as a consequence of globalization.

Keywords: Ageism · ITC · Social exclusion

1 Introduction

In the recent years, the emergence of Internet enhances a new and dynamic model of communication. Network technologies present to man a new challenge: to rethink the reality and rework the image of himself and his environment. Therefore, it is impossible to think technology as an isolated element of society. Technology has proved to be an unequivocal benefit for mankind in public and private life. Different technological devices like mobile phones, computers or Internet have changed mankind all over the world in several spheres and areas. For instance, Health, Education, Economics, Communication and even Politics have improved significantly with technology. Although the use of technology is limited by geographic, cultural and economic parameters, the benefits for mankind are proved every day in simple things like connecting people geographic distant with a mobile phone or take a radiograph to help in a medical diagnosis. However, the movement of globalization promoted by technology also produces new economical and social exclusions. As Castells e Catterall argued, «this information age has never been a technological matter. It has always been a matter of social transformation, a process of social change in which technology is an element that is inseparable from social, economic, cultural and political trends» (2001: 3). The theoretical framework of this paper fits in the new digital scenario and in an urgent update of concepts to the reality that tend to establish itself as dominant in Western societies: the info inclusion. This paper discusses social representations, exclusion and digital

© Springer International Publishing Switzerland 2016
J. Zhou and G. Salvendy (Eds.): ITAP 2016, Part II, LNCS 9755, pp. 159–166, 2016.
DOI: 10.1007/978-3-319-39949-2_15

exclusion as a consequence of globalization and as a condition of second-class citizenship for those who do not have access to digital capital.

Internet may represent an opportunity for inclusion and improve quality of life of citizens, especially for senior individuals. However, demographic and socio-cultural changes push the elderly towards digital and social exclusion. Increased age is also associated with decreased levels of Internet access, limited modes of use and patterns of connecting. Age differences are especially pronounced in those individuals aged 60 years and over. The behavior of elderly people in the context of the Internet may depend on the their country, socio-economic status, education, family structure, race, gender, geography location, as well as cultural and social participation.

2   Social Representations of Ageism

Social representations arise from the socialization process and are directly associated with collective identity. Social facts can be understood as modes of action and the representations that are external to the individual. According to Durkheim (1964), society and the collective conscience are moral entities. Hence what people feel, think or do is independent of his individual will, which means that the behavior is established by society. From this perspective, social facts exert a coercive power. Therefore, it is something that exists and remains beyond the individual. In this sense, the construction of symbolic representations shared by members of social systems inhabits a universe of particular socialization.

In contemporary times there are multiple records that demonstrate that the present highlights major changes that affect both our lifestyles and the way we represent the others and ourselves. Several authors who reflect these societal transformations denominate the current period of 'reflexive modernity' (Beck et al. 1997), 'postmodernity' (Hall 1998), 'late modernity' (Chouliaraki and Fairclough 1999; Giddens 1997) or 'liquid modernity' (Bauman 2000). These perspectives open a new historical period, which emphasize the uncertainty, fluidity, individualism and insecurity. Despite the heterogeneous terms used in the characterization of the current socio-historical moment is consensual accept that stagiest linearity associated with the life cycle no longer reflects changes toward individualization and pluralisation that currently occur.

Ageing as a 'social problem' has emerged recently as one of the main challenges facing contemporary societies. The dimensions of ageing and its social importance have elevated it to a national and international political discourse and brought it into the domain of public opinion. Evidence of the socially constructed nature of the ageing phenomenon (Debert 1999) can be seen in the recent efforts in discursive 'requalification' of ageing, as it emerges linked to a terminological plurality of which the adjectives 'productive', 'healthy', 'successful', 'positive' and 'active' are the best illustration. The purpose of these new public terminologies has been, since the 1980s in the USA (AARP 2010) and the 1990s in Europe, to remove the negative image and social representation with which the concept of ageing is burdened. Affirming this revaluation of ageing, since the 1980s and 90s respectively organizations such as the WHO and the EU have launched the challenge nowadays known as 'active ageing'. A different view of the phenomenon is advocated, together with new approaches and political solutions in societies that value productiveness, youth and autonomy. These are, however, some of the factors that produce a negative image of old age, and the concept of active ageing itself therefore aims to combat the stereotyped production of negative ageism or, in other words, discrimination based on preconceptions directed towards one particular age group.

Ageing has emerged recently as one of the main challenges to present-day societies. Its dimensions and social importance have elevated it to a national and international political discourse and brought it into the domain of public opinion. The recent attempt at a discursive 'requalification' of ageing is evidence of the socially constructed nature of the phenomenon, associated with a plurality of terms of which the adjectives 'productive', 'healthy', 'successful', 'positive' and 'active' are the clearest examples.

Along with the impact of ageist stereotyping, the effects of institutionalizing the elderly have aggravated the representational image, since institutionalization signifies not only change, but also a break with the lifestyle, identities and social roles of the elderly. This leads to a determination of new forms of recognition and relationship (Daniel 2006). Several authors think that the negative stereotypes of 'old age' are still prevalent today (Palmore 2005). This prevalence will determine types of discrimination, studied by Alves and Novo (2006), who concluded that there is a strong awareness of ageist discrimination in Portugal.

As an academic concept, the term 'active ageing', the successor to concepts such as 'healthy ageing' or 'successful ageing', is far from consensual. In fact it was produced and has been conveyed essentially through political discourse. In 1997 the World Health Organization, inspired by the United Nations Principles for Older Persons, presented the concept of active ageing, defined as "the process of optimizing opportunities for health, participation and security in order to enhance quality of life as people age" (2002: 12).

An important body of scientific literature examines the evolution of political ideas on ageing on an international level in the world agenda since the Vienna World Assembly on Ageing in 1982 (Kildal 2009; Kildal and Nilssen 2010; Marin and Zaidi 2008; Nilssen 2009; Walker 2002; Walker 2008; Zelenev 2008). In this context we would highlight the critical analyses of policies and discourses on ageing, contrasting the EU's linking of the concept (from the 1990s onwards) to the economic and productivist discourse of the sustainability of states of well-being, with the broader concept centered on quality of life and rights contained in the WHO proposal (Kildal 2009; Nilssen 2009). The latter seeks to distance itself from the negative social representation influencing the concept of ageing, as the product of ageist stereotyping that emphasizes economic importance, dependency and lack of autonomy, and also from the idea of 'productive ageing' (Walker 2008). The 2002 Madrid International Plan of Action on Ageing was another sign of this paradigm shift, envisaging the need to change the social image of elderly people, old age and ageing. It also revealed the existence of gender differences and the implications of gendering ageing.

One of the most interesting works on the European discourse on ageing is by Alan Walker (2002, 2008). Since the Treaty of Lisbon, according to Walker (2008), two perspectives have defined the EU discourse on ageing: a more productivist discourse centered on employment, and a more 'comprehensive' discourse centered on diversity, heterogeneity, well-being and health throughout life, which he terms the "deserving or compassionate mode".

The need to pay attention to the heterogeneous nature of the situation and experiences of elderly people and the way in which (age, gender and socio-economic) differences make experiences of ageing very specific is one of the main warnings to political agents found in critical scientific literature (Walker 2008). This paper assumes that there is a tension and even a certain public dyslexia with regard to the phenomenon of ageing and old age. As evidence, we can mention the prevalence of negative ageist stereotypes that associate old age with dependency, lack of autonomy, illness, institutionalization and a lack of consideration for its heterogeneity (with reference to gender, for example). We also note a national and international public discourse that fosters positive stereotyping, molded by a concept of Active Ageing that aims to keep the elderly involved in civic, political and economic life as much as possible. However, the increasing technological changes of contemporary society refer the digitally excluded for a under citizenship condition. Due to different socio-cultural and economic factors, the elderly population is not equally endowed with the same digital knowledge of others. It follows that their citizen condition is substantially weakened.

3   Ageism and IT: Social Exclusion in the Digital Age

Digital divide refers to the gap that exists between those who can access and use (digital) technologies and information/content effectively, and those who cannot. Nevertheless it would be misleading to think of this divide as two separate fields instead of a gradation or continuum. As Selwyn puts it, digital divide «can be seen as a practical embodiment of the wider theme of social inclusion» (2004: 343). At the same time, effective access and use are dependent not only on economic conditions but also on social and cultural resources, considering individual and community levels. This means that digital divide must no more be understood as merely a 'technical' issue but also as a social one, involving dimensions like «skills, informed choice, content and community» (Selwyn and Facer 2007). Or, as Sorj (2008: 62) puts it, «[t]here is a strong correlation between the digital divides and other forms of social inequality». Because of the dualistic logic implied in this concept (haves and have-nots), this concept is increasingly less used.

The increasing technological changes of contemporary society refer the digitally excluded for a second-class citizenship condition. Due to different socio-cultural and economic factors, the elderly population is not equally endowed with the same digital knowledge of others. It follows that their citizen condition is substantially weakened.

Social exclusion, as a consequence of digital illiteracy, is a reality for millions of people around the world. This social phenomenon can lead to a global sense of injustice as it enhances info-exclusion as a contributing factor to the categorization of 'disadvantaged groups'.

The dimensions of social exclusion - assuming that these are not synonymous with poverty – can be defined as multidimensional, dynamic, relational, contextual and active. In this perspective and in the context of digital illiteracy, the 'disadvantaged groups' can be characterized in a multidimensional scale, which includes indicators of the absence of social rights and micro levels of social exclusion, and delimit the groups cut off from the digital information society by these reasons. Empowerment is the keyword of the several recommendations documents that are focused on teaching, good practices, induction of cultural shift and public-private partnerships at regional and national levels through different approaches. 'Disadvantaged groups' include elderly, even though the policies and political discourses.

A study from Pew Research Center states that 59 % of American adults over 65 years of age use the Internet. The data was collected in September 2013 and reveals that 71 % of the senior citizens with access to the Internet go online every day. Internet use differs by age, education and household income. The report shows that 87 % of seniors with a college degree go online as well as 74 % of seniors among 65–69 years old. 90 % of the higher-income seniors use the Internet. There is a direct correlation between well-educated seniors and higher levels of income. The study discloses that 90 % of older adults with an annual household income of $75,000 or more go online and 82 % have broadband at home. Seniors receiving less than $30,000 annually, 39 % go online and 25 % have broadband at home. 87 % of seniors with a college degree go online and 76 % are broadband adopters. Among older adults who have not attended college, 40 % go online and only 27 % have broadband at home. The report stresses that a significant majority of seniors state that they need assistance in order to use new digital devices. 77 % of American older adults indicate they would need help to access the Internet, while only 18 % states that feel comfortable to learn how to use a new technology device. Among the seniors who go online, 56 % state that need help to use social networking sites to connect and to interact with family members and friends.

Among the Internet-using elderly in United States, 46 % use social networking sites and 88 % use regularly email services. The top motivations for getting online are pointed to be communication with others and family, shopping and access to health information. 47 % of the older adults have a high-speed broadband connection at home 77 % have a cell phone.

In 2012 the population of the European Union reaches 500 million people. The reduction in birth rates over the past decades has contributed to a gradual aging of the population and a significant change in the 'age pyramid'. According to a study from Eurostat, 75 % of individuals in the European Union use the Internet in 2013 and 72 % on a regular basis. Digital divides in European Union persist as regards to age group, formal education and by country. The highest percentage of non-use of Internet is registered in Romania (42 %), Bulgaria (41 %) and Greece (36 %). In all countries, 55–74 age group registered a 46 percentage. Nearly 90 % of the European seniors online use the email and 60 % read online news and search for information about health. However, only 27 % participate in social networking sites. The share of senior users making telephone and video calls through internet-based applications is 25 %. In the 55–74 age group, one in ten users posted on civic or political issues in sites, blogs and e-government or other websites. Nearly 60 % of Internet users aged 55–74 read online news and searched for information about health. 50 % of the users consulted wikis. Among the European seniors, only 14 % use mobile devices to connect to the Internet. Within this age group it is more likely to have used a portable computer for Internet connections.

4 Conclusions

The 'individualization' stands in the mainstream of political agendas to value the individual as a builder of his career in the life course. Active ageing exemplifies this logic in the new guidelines that encourage the creation of opportunities for individuals to map their courses to life in this way, achieving live with greater quality of life. The Declaration of Alma-Ata (1978) appeals to health for all and the need for health promotion models no top-down (WHO 2002). It is the recognition of people's participation in promoting their citizenship as «the right and duty of the people to participate individually and collectively in the planning and delivery of health care». Giving digital competence to the protagonists is a way to empower them as this concept is assumed as «a transversal key competence, enabling the acquisition of other key competences» and has been broadly defined by the European Commission as «the confident, critical and creative use of ICT to achieve goals related to work, employability, learning, leisure, inclusion and/or participation in society».

During the World Assembly on Ageing Human, Kofi Annan quoted the African saying «when an ancient dies, a library disappears». However, today we are far from the models of learning based on the oral transmission of memories. The new learning models require training throughout life, oriented knowledge in permanent mutation and transformation in a world where information flows at a speed impossible to reach.

Contemporary society is founded on the permanent technological changes. In this regard, empowerment through knowledge is the only option that seems valid in today's world. The info inclusion as the dominant reality tends to turn elderly into citizens with fewer rights. Considering the Internet as a social and participatory space, it is imperative that active ageing would be promoted within the ICT context. The change in social and communicative paradigm, participatory culture and collective intelligence, reinvention of the concept of community, redefinition of the public sphere, the metamorphosis of the territory notion, interactions and digital communications, new forms of sociability and social dynamics based in technology are elements of an ongoing structural change that has implications for the entire population.

The label of 'retirement age' directly linked to the use of technical difficulty produces not only info excluded as considerably accentuates the gap between citizens and between age groups. It follows that we consider essential to develop synergies between different entities with responsibilities in society, in order to implement intervention projects for a digital citizenship in the context of active ageing. Promoting digital literacy is an effective approach to avoid digital divides and integrate the elderly in the context of new technologies.

In a civic camping in Barcelona, in May 2011, Manuel Castells stated that «communication for all of society is a fundamental right: free communication, autonomous and worldwide is a right as fundamental as health and education». In the words of the author, «this right is realized today through the Internet and by mobile networks as a fundamental human right». Against the condition second-class citizenship that the digital divide bans elderly citizens, we fully endorse the arguments of Castells.

References

AARP: Active, Productive and Healthy Aging in Germany and the United States (2010)

Alves, J.F., Novo, R.F.: Avaliação da discriminação social de pessoas idosas em Portugal. Int. J. Clin. Health Psychol. 6(1), 65–77 (2006)

Bauman, Z.: Em busca da política. Zahar (2000). Portuguese language

Beck, U., Lash, S., Giddens, A.: Modernización reflexiva: política, tradición y estética en el orden social moderno. Alianza Editorial (1997). Spanish language

Castells, M.: A era da informação: economia, sociedade e cultura. A sociedade em rede, vol. 1, Lisboa: Fundação Calouste Gulbenkian (2003). Portuguese language

Castells, M., Catterall, B.: The Making of the Network Society. Institute of Contemporary Arts, London (2001)

Chouliaraki, L., Fairclough, N.: Discourse in Late Modernity, vol. 2. Edinburgh University Press, Edinburgh (1999)

Daniel, F.: O Conceito de Velhice em Transformação. Revista Interacções 10, 113–122 (2006). Portuguese language

Debert, G.: A Reinvenção da velhice: socialização e processos de reprivatização do envelhecimento. São Paulo, USP (1999). Portuguese language

Durkheim, É.: Las reglas del método sociológico. Dédalo (1964). Spanhish language

Escobar, A.: Welcome to Cyberia: notes on the anthropology of cyberculture. Curr. Antropology 35(3), 211–231 (1994)

Giddens, A.: Política, sociologia e teoria social. Unesp (1997). Portuguese language

Hall, S.: The great moving nowhere show. Marxism Today 1, 9–14 (1998)

Jodelet, D.: Représentations sociales: un domaine en expansion. In: Jodelet, D. (dir.) Les représentations sociales, pp. 36–57. Presses Universitaires de France (Sociologie d'Aujourd'hui), Paris (1994). French language

Kildal, N.: Comparing social policy ideas within the EU and the OECD. In: Ervik, R., Kildal, N., Nilssen, E. (eds.) The Role of International Organizations in Social Policy. Edward Elgar Publishing, Cheltenham (2009)

Kildal, N., Nilssen, E.: Demographic crises and ageing policy ideas in the fields of health and long-term care. comparing the EU the WHO and the OECD. In: ESPAnet Annual Conference Social Policy and the Global Crisis: Consequences and Responses, Budapest, Hungary, pp. 2–4, September 2010

Marin, B., Zaidi, A.: Ageing trends and policies in the European region. In: Regional Dimension of the Ageing Situation, United Nations, Department of Economic and Social Affairs, New York, pp. 118–140 (2008)

Martin, A.: DigEuLit – a European framework for digital literacy: a progress report. J. eLiteracy 2, 130–136 (2005)

Nilssen, E.: Combating social exclusion in the European union. In: Ervik, R.; Kildal, N., Nilssen, E. (org.) The Role of International Organizations in Social Policy. Edward Elgar Publishing (2009)

Palmore, E.: Three decades of research on ageism. Generations 29(3), 87–90 (2005)

Selwyn, N.: Reconsidering political and popular understandings of the digital divide. New Media Soc. 6(3), 341–362 (2004)

Selwyn, N., Facer, K.: Beyond the digital divide: Rethinking digital inclusion for the 21st century (2007)

Sorj, B.: Information Societies and Digital Divides. Polimetrica, Milano (2008)

Walker, A.: A strategy for active ageing. Int. Soc. Secur. Rev. 55(1), 121–139 (2002)

Walker, A.: Commentary: the emergence and application of active aging in Europe. J. Aging Soc. Policy 21(1), 75–93 (2008)

WHO: Active Ageing: A Policy Framework. World Health Organization, Geneva (2002)

Zelenev, S.: The madrid plan: a comprehensive agenda for an ageing world. In: Regional Dimensions of the Ageing Situation, United Nations, Department of Economic and Social Affairs, New York, pp. 1–18 (2008)

Elder Adults Utilizing Social Networking Sites on Mobile Platforms

Jessica Arfaa$^{(\boxtimes)}$ and Yuanqiong (Kathy) Wang

Department of Computer and Information Sciences,
Towson University, Towson, MD 21252, USA
jessicaarfaa@gmail.com, ywangtu@gmail.com

Abstract. Although social media and mobile technologies are trending topics, only a small amount of elder adults utilizes these Web 2.0 technologies on portable platforms. To gain a better understanding of the current state of elder adults utilizing social media on mobile devices, a literature review regarding mobile interface design guidelines is presented. To further investigate the lack of mobile social media users, a usability study addressing social media interfaces for elders is proposed. The goal of this research is to have elder adults more comfortable using social media on mobile devices so that they can reap the benefits of these types of sites.

Keywords: Social media · Social networking · Elder adults · Usability study mobile · Tablets · Smart phones

1 Introduction

The use of smartphones and tablets for daily tasks have grown; and for some internet activities, surpassed the usage of desktop computer platforms. For example, Google [14] reported that in the US, more searches were conducted on mobile devices than on computers. This reflects today's user's expectations of having readily available information, as they do not perceive timing and logistics as a barrier in its delivery. Although mobile device usage has grown, usability and accessibly research on this type of platform is limited. Previously, desktop computer user experience was the main focus for standards and guidelines—with little accounting for mobile platforms, and an even smaller amount addressing the user experience for elderly users. Many elder adults did not have technology exposure in their youth and this lack of experience in their formative years can be seen as a contributing factor in their low technology acceptance rates. Of the approximately 44 million (14 %) elder adults in the United States [2], only a small amount uses smart phones, with only 18 % of elders owning these types of devices [17]. And not surprisingly, less than half (43 %) of online elders utilize social networking sites [7, 8].

The low number of elders engaged in social media needs to be addressed because this group is forgoing a number of its benefits [12, 19] [26]. Social media usage can promote learning through resource sharing, such as viewing news stories or commenting on current events. It can also build meaningful relationships with family,

© Springer International Publishing Switzerland 2016
J. Zhou and G. Salvendy (Eds.): ITAP 2016, Part II, LNCS 9755, pp. 167–175, 2016.
DOI: 10.1007/978-3-319-39949-2_16

friends, and people of similar interests. Most importantly, technology can promote independence and build self-esteem for elders impacted by health and mobility issues.

Previous studies from the authors suggested ways to improve interface design for elder adults using web-based social media access [6]. To expand this research, further investigation of elder adults utilizing social networking site applications on mobile devices is proposed. The objectives of this study are to: (1) understand if elder adults find value in utilizing mobile devices, (2) identify the common usability and accessibility issues experience when utilizing social media on a mobile device, and (3) establish ways to improve social media mobile/app interfaces for elder adults on a portable device.

To achieve this, the following paper summarizes the status of social media on mobile devices and suggests potential research directions. First, a discussion of available guidelines for desktop computers and mobile devices (responsive and apps-based) is presented. Next, the mobile version of a social media site is examined. Then, a proposal of future study involving elder adults utilizing social media on mobile devices is briefly presented. Finally, the limitations, conclusion, and future work of this study are discussed.

2   Literature Review

2.1   Existing Mandates and Guidelines

Numerous usability and accessibly guidelines were first developed to be applied to desktop interfaces. Although these best practices are intended to be readily available, easily implemented, and in some cases, easily tested, many websites do not incorporate these guidelines into their interface design. For example, an evaluation conducted by Arfaa & Wang [5] showed that out of the 19 social media websites tested on desktop computer platforms, all had some type of Section 508 Compliance, WCAG 1.0, and WCAG 2.0 violation. These violations could potentially hinder the use/access of a website for a disabled or elder user. As the mobile trend has become more mainstream, many of these popular guidelines have developed additional best practices to be applied to mobile devices, such as Section 508 Compliance, WCAG 1.0, WCAG 2.0, and Usability.gov. In addition, mobile device makers (e.g. Apple) and UI designers have also presented their "best practices" on how the apps should be developed for mobile devices in order to make them more accessible and usable. Although there are no specific guidelines established in terms of designs for the elderly from those manufactures, it is still worth noting the extra UI design guidelines presented.

2.1.1   Section 508 Compliance

Section 508 Compliance [1] is a government-mandated set of guidelines geared towards making all federal/government sites accessible for all types of users. Currently, there is a proposal to update the guidelines to address voice, text, and video capabilities found with smart phones and other mobile devices; however, no specific criteria have been developed. Although there are no formal constraints or amendments, Access-Board.gov [1] suggests referencing WCAG 2.0 guidelines for optional recommendations.

2.1.2   WCAG 2.0
Similar to Section 508 compliance, the Web Content Accessibility Guideline's [20] has drafted best practices for mobile interface design, however they have not formally added to the WCAG 2.0 guidelines. They identified the following overlap between desktop and mobile devices:

- Text-based alternatives should be applied to any non-text content. An example of this is using html alt tags on images.
- Time-based media should have an alternative option, such as having a transcript accompanying a video.
- Content should not lose its structure or presentation when adapting to different layouts or platforms.
- Content should be easily distinguishable. For example, an interface should use contrasting background and text colors to increase visibility.
- All content should be accessible utilizing a keyboard.
- Users should have ample time to read and use content, as well as complete tasks. For example, a user should have enough time to complete a form without being timed-out.
- An interface should be mindful of users who suffer from seizures.
- A site should be navigable so that the user can find and utilize the content.
- The formatting of a site should be readable to users.
- The site should be intuitive and predictable.
- The site should assist users when completing tasks, such as identifying required fields on a form.
- The site should be compatible with user agents and assistive technologies.

2.1.3   Usability.gov
Usability.gov [18] is a content-heavy site that provides non-mandated usability and accessibility guidelines for website design. However, there is no proposed initiative to update the guidelines to address mobile devices and simply suggests incorporating a responsive design site to accommodate screens of different shapes and sizes. However, a number of sections should be reviewed when accommodating mobile design, such as those sections pertaining to user experience, accessibility, page layout and navigation, and formatting and multimedia suggestions.

2.1.4   Mobile UI Design Patterns and Guidelines
Although limited, there is steady research regarding guidelines and design patterns for mobile devices; including considerations for early mobile devices such as Personal Digital Assistants (PDAs) to today's smart phones.

Gong and Tarasewich [13] reviewed guidelines for desktop applications and discussed how they could be applied or modified for mobile device interface design. They summarized some best practices, such as "enabling frequent users to use shortcuts", "offer informative feedback", "design dialogs to yield closure", "support internal locus of control". In addition, they extended the concept of "consistency" to call for the uniformity across multiple platforms and devices for the same applications. Moreover, they proposed that design considerations should include multiple and dynamic contexts, such as single or no-handed operation and other limitations of small devices. Although these were proposed over ten years ago, they still apply to the smart devices nowadays.

Nilsson [16] presented design patterns for mobile application user interfaces. He also addressed screen space and layout as main problem areas. He emphasized that horizontal scrolling should be avoided while limiting vertical. In addition, considerations for the keyboard as part of layout and finger friendly menu choices were also suggested.

Many practitioners have also presented their set of guidelines and best practices in the mobile interface design [e.g. 9, 21]. They all agree when it comes to the interface design for mobile devices, the inherent nature of a pocket-sized touchscreens requires extra considerations on the design for "thumb" interaction. They noted that even though it has been suggested to use 44 pixels for thumb friendly UI elements, exceptions should also be considered when a user has a "fat" finger to interact with the app. When the elderly are the target users, this should be a key consideration because of the difficulty in controlling the movements. Moreover, putting controls at the bottom of the screen (as opposed to the top navigation bars in traditional web or desktop software), the scrolling avoidance, and the need to leverage the touch UI by minimizing interface chrome, such as buttons, tab bars, checkboxes, sliders, etc. are also presented. This echoed the suggestions from previous researchers.

Major mobile manufacturers such as Apple has also presented some design principles for mobile apps. For example, in IOS Human Interface Guidelines [3, 10] suggested (1) keeping decorative elements subtle and unobtrusive and by using standard controls and predictable behaviors; (2) keeping consistent among different apps to make the transition from one app to another easy which can be achieved by using the existing standard/system provided controls; (3) provide approaches to allow direct manipulation (e.g. gestures) rather than using separate controls; (4) providing feedback (with potential to have multi-model, such as perceptible feedback and animation) to acknowledge people's actions; (5) using a metaphor to suggest a usage; and (6) having users, rather than the apps, initiate the control actions. Although some suggestions are more focused on the capability of the IOS itself, it can also be applied to the design for other mobile devices.

2.1.5   Additional Considerations

The review of existing guidelines and mobile research shows that there is still a lack of formalized comprehensive guidelines and evaluation methods. Mandated guidelines are in place to provide users a good experience when utilizing federal sites in all platforms, therefore government mobile sites should address the multiple mobile and wearable technologies that are in the market. Additionally, there are only a few simple mobile site evaluation tools available; however, a more robust, objective site/app evaluation tool is needed to test mobile interfaces.

The authors' second suggestion is for sites to offer custom calibration for input and output methods. Unlike desktop computers where monitors are in a static position, mobile users can experience many perspectives based on where the device is set (i.e. on a table versus holding the device in lap). Additionally, the input device experience should be customizable, depending on how a user holds and the way they interact with a device. For example, an elder adult might 'tap' on a screen using their entire finger pad, versus tapping from the top of their finger.

The final suggestion is to have icons accompanied by text. Many mobile versions of sites offer just an image of an icon. This can hinder a user's experience for an elder adult who is not as familiar with the site and its icons. If the design of the site cannot accommodate text to a mobile site, it is suggested to have the icon expand with more options, but not redirect when tapped. This behavior can then provide more room for text explaining each icon.

2.2 Current Mobile Version of Social Media Site

In the following example, the mobile and app versions of "Facebook" [11] are used as a basis for evaluating the 'mobile experience'. At first glance, both the app and mobile versions of the site follow some of the WCAG 2.0 guidelines, such as 1.3.1 and 1.3.2, using an appropriate amount of white space. In addition, the sidebar navigation meets a few WCAG 2.0 criteria, such as being predictable, having an intuitive navigation, and applying text-based alternatives alongside each icon (Fig. 1). In Fig. 2, the timeline on the app version appears clear, with each post separated into formatted sections (WCAG 2.0; success criterion 3.2.4).

Fig. 1. Main navigation on mobile version

Fig. 2. Timeline on app version

However, creating a simpler and less cluttered interface requires minimizing textual clues. For example, a closer look at the top navigation icons on the Facebook mobile version provides little insight into the icon's purpose, potentially violating WCAG 1.1.1 (Fig. 3). A user would need to tap the icons to decipher their functionality. In addition, the lack of contrast of the black icons against the dark blue background (violating WCAG 2.0 1.4.3) could impact users with poor vision, which a lot of elderly experience due to the natural aging process. When viewing the app version of the site, users have a different experience compared to the mobile version. For example, the main navigation icons are found at the bottom of the site, rather than at the top of the screen. Although each icon has a label explaining its purpose, the text is very small and there is little contrast of the gray icons behind a white background (Fig. 4).

Fig. 3. Main navigation on mobile version (Top)

Fig. 4. Main navigation on app version (Bottom)

As in Fig. 5, the layout and unnecessarily large images seen in the mobile versions of the site can distort the layout, causing the user to unnecessarily scroll to see more information (violating WCAG 2.0 2.2.2).

Fig. 5. Profile page (Mobile Version)

Fig. 6. Example of tagging (App Version)

Social media sites should also consider the different user experience levels by providing guidance and information for novice users. This could be very beneficial to elder adults with little exposure to Web 2.0 concepts such as "tagging" (a way to associate a person, place, or thing with media, such as an image, video, etc.) and "sharing" (a way to distribute links, images, videos, etc. to connections). As seen in Fig. 6, to tag an image, a user would need to (1) understand what tagging is and (2) how to complete the multi-step process. A person unfamiliar with this terminology might not understand the functionality or take full advantage of its usage.

3 Proposed Usability Study

To expand previous research completed by Arfaa & Wang (4,5,6), a three-phase usability study involving an in-group quasi-experiment design is proposed, focusing on elder adults utilizing social media on mobile platforms. The first phase will involve elder adults utilizing a simulation of a current social media site on a mobile device. Using the results found during the literature review and phase one, the development of an improved prototype will begin. During the final phase, elder adults will be asked to utilize the newly designed prototype on a mobile device. The results from both phases will be compared to evaluate the effectiveness of the proposed design.

3.1 Methodology

Elder adults aged 65 years and older will be invited to participate in this study. Although there are no additional prerequisites to participating in the study, elder adults will be asked to identify their computer experience as either "none-to-basic" or "intermediate-to-advanced". For this study, we suggest that at least two groups of eight elders participate in this study; however, future iterations of this study should aim for a larger amount of participants.

After the consent and pre-survey, the study will require the participants to complete typical tasks found on social media sites and apps, including activities such as: searching for friends, understanding a profile, and viewing and tagging photos. Participants will first interact with a simulation of an existing social media app interface on a mobile device. Then, based on previous literature and the feedback received from the first phase of the usability study, the same participants will be invited to utilize the redesigned social media app. During each phase, the completion rate and speed of task completion will be evaluated and compared against each of the phases. Additional comparisons may be completed comparing Arfaa & Wang's [6] social media results via desktop computer applications.

The usability study should incorporate common activities found on social media sites, such as (1) understanding and navigating through the site; (2) understanding the timeline; (3) interpreting your profile and other's profiles; and (4) utilizing Web 2.0 functionalities. These activities will be defined into major task categories and then divided into sub-task activities, similar to previous research conducted by Arfaa & Wang (2014).

This research is also limited by its scope. Mobile devices mentioned in this study refer to mainstream smart phones and tablets and do not include wearable technologies. The design of the site is also limited to "mobile versions" of sites, responsive sites, and custom apps. It does not include the 'desktop' version of a site viewed from a mobile device.

4   Conclusion and Future Work

To conclude, a summary and future research suggestions are discussed. Today, computers, the internet, and social media are utilized daily for multiple activities and tasks, with its usage increased due to mobile platform accessibility. Although there are benefits to technology usage, there are many barriers that keep elders from using a computer or smart device. One such issue is their limited computer exposure compared to younger demographics. This lack of computer knowledge makes new computer concepts, such as Web 2.0 technologies, hard to visualize and comprehend for those born in an analog time. Lack of computer experience also perpetuates negative perceptions of technology, such as privacy and trust issues.

Elders also face a number of usability and accessibility issues due to poorly designed desktop computer and mobile device interfaces that do not account for disabilities common in the natural aging process. In addition, there are many formatting considerations for mobile websites, such as the screen size, the ability to increase/decrease text, page orientation, and input devices such as keyboards and touch screens. As the use of mobile technologies increase, there is a need to expand best practices and guidelines so that the pages are accessible to all types of users.

To investigate these issues, a literature review and a proposed research study were presented. Future research should answer the research questions (1) do elder adults have an interest in learning how to use social media on a mobile platform; and after verifying the research has value, refine the findings by completing an evaluation to determine (2) if current social networking sites on mobile devices and/or mobile app follow available mobile standards and guidelines. With the lack of clear guidelines on mobile interface design, the findings from the proposed research should also shed lights on how the mobile design guidelines should be addressed to incorporate the requirements to best suit elderly users. The hope is that future research will incorporate these results to create, verify, and refine best practices for mobile interface design for elders.

References

1. Access-Board.gov. https://www.access-board.gov/guidelines-and-standards/communications-and-it/about-the-ict-refresh/proposed-rule/ii-executive-summary
2. AOA.gov. Aging Statistics. http://www.aoa.acl.gov/Aging_Statistics/index.aspx
3. Apple.com. https://developer.apple.com/library/ios/documentation/UserExperience/Conceptual/MobileHIG/
4. Arfaa, J., Wang, Y.: An improved website design for elders utilizing social media. J. Technol. Persons Disabil. (2015). San Diego, CA

5. Arfaa, J., Wang, Y.: An accessibility evaluation of social media websites for elder adults. In: Meiselwitz, G. (ed.) SCSM 2014. LNCS, vol. 8531, pp. 13–24. Springer, Heidelberg (2014a)
6. Arfaa, J., Wang, Y.: A usability study on elder adults utilizing social networking sites. In: Marcus, A. (ed.) DUXU 2014, Part II. LNCS, vol. 8518, pp. 50–61. Springer, Heidelberg (2014b)
7. Brenner, J., Smith, A.: 72 % of Online Adults are Social Networking Site Users (2013). http://www.pewinternet.org/2013/08/05/72-of-online-adults-are-social-networking-site-users/
8. Brenner, J.: http://pewinternet.org/Commentary/2012/March/Pew-Internet-Social-Networking-full-detail.aspx
9. CreativeBlog. The 10 principles of mobile interface design (2012). Accessed http://www.creativebloq.com/mobile/10-principles-mobile-interface-design-4122910
10. Ebner, M., Stickel, C., Kolbitsch, J.: iPhone/iPad human interface design. In: Leitner, G., Hitz, M., Holzinger, A. (eds.) USAB 2010. LNCS, vol. 6389, pp. 489–492. Springer, Heidelberg (2010)
11. Facebook. https://www.facebook.com/
12. Gatto, S., Tak, S.: Computer, internet, and e-mail use among older adults: benefits and barriers. Educ. Gerontol. **34**(9), 800–811 (2008)
13. Gong, J., Tarasewich, P.: Guidelines for handheld mobile device interface design. In: Proceedings of the 2004 DSI Annual Meeting (2004)
14. Google.com. Building for the next moment (2015). http://adwords.blogspot.com/2015/05/building-for-next-moment.html
15. Melenhorst, A., Rogers, W., Caylor, E.: The use of communication technologies by older adults: exploring the benefits from the user's perspective. In: Proceedings from the Human Factors and Ergonomics Society Annual Meeting (2015)
16. Nilsson, E.G.: Design patterns for user interface for mobile applications. Adv. Eng. Softw. **40**, 1318–1328 (2009)
17. Smith, A.: Older adults and technology use. Pew Research Internet Project (2014). Accessed http://www.pewinternet.org/2014/04/03/older-adults-and-technology-use/
18. Usability.gov. http://www.usability.gov/guidelines/index.html
19. Wagner, N., Hassanein, K.: Computer use by older adults: a multi-disciplinary review. Comput. Human Behav. **26**(5), 870–882 (2010)
20. WCAG 2.0. https://www.w3.org/TR/WCAG20/
21. Weeve, I.: Seven Guidelines For Designing High-Performance Mobile User Experiences. Smashing Magazine (2011). Accessed https://www.smashingmagazine.com/2011/07/seven-guidelines-for-designing-high-performance-mobile-user-experiences/

The Elderly, IT and the Public Discourse. Representations of Exclusion and Inclusion

Piermarco Aroldi[✉] and Fausto Colombo

Università Cattolica del Sacro Cuore, Largo Gemelli 1, 20123 Milan, Italy
{piermarco.aroldi,fausto.colombo}@unicatt.it

Abstract. The paper focuses on the political and institutional trends that foster digital literacy among seniors, and the forms it takes in both the public discourses and the concrete practices of teaching seniors how to use information technologies (IT). IT often recur as an essential element in the discourses that stress the importance of an active, healthy and independent aging, as well as the need for mechanisms that reduce potential isolation and exclusion of seniors. Nonetheless, the inconsistency of these different discourses makes it hard to represent the older people using IT in a clear, convincing and believable way.

Keywords: Aging · Information technology · Digital literacy · Training the elderly in the use of IT · Digital agenda

1   Introduction

Old age, as it exists today in countries with high rates of aging, is not just a biological fact (the increase in individuals' life expectancy, the development of a fourth phase of life between maturity and true old age), or a statistical one (the increased percentage of elderly individuals both in the population as a whole and compared to the total number of young individuals); it is also a social fact (the representation of the problem, for example in the media, the birth of shared narratives of it, as in the cinema or fiction, the construction of socially 'acceptable' forms of longevity, as in welfare policies). If we consider this last point, which we might call the 'social construction of the senior', it naturally becomes important to understand the functioning of public discourses and especially their normative function, capable of shaping the self-perceptions of individuals and consequently their individual and collective behaviour, and how effectively they match the concrete practices of promoting active and socially involved aging, for instance in the use of digital resources.

In this paper we firstly address the problem of the institutional discourse, which in almost all countries with a high rate of aging has the aim of ensuring that seniors are 'healthy, active and independent'. In particular we compare the forms, objectives and reasons for this discourse with those of other public discourses, such as film and literary narrative and advertising practices, so as to better understand its status and possible repercussions. Secondly, we analyze examples of the 'governmental' discourse on Information Technology (IT) literacy among seniors, highlighting points of contact with some empirical evidence arising from research into the use of IT by the elderly

J. Zhou and G. Salvendy (Eds.): ITAP 2016, Part II, LNCS 9755, pp. 176–185, 2016.
DOI: 10.1007/978-3-319-39949-2_17

population. Finally, we study some documents used for encouraging IT literacy among the elderly within social solidarity projects.

2 Aging and Public Discourse

The general aging of societies (especially some, but potentially the majority of societies worldwide) entails a general reorganization of welfare policies, which are central to advanced democracies, and is a problem for all societies [1, 2]. Furthermore, the emergence of a new age, caused by increased life expectancy, is generating new subjective sensibilities, so that we can say that the current generation of young seniors (people in the 60/65 to 75/80 age group) is living through a personal experience (a degree of wellness, generally satisfactory health conditions, and a complex network of generational relationships that comprise children and grandchildren on the one hand and in some cases very elderly parents on the other) that is largely unparalleled in earlier periods among people of the same age [3, 4, 5].

The two situations (private and public) have naturally become the subject of public discourse on various levels that reveal a significant breakthrough in recent years [6, 7]. Here we point out three, which we believe are helpful to understanding the collective adaptation to the aging society. First, the literary and cinematic narrative, which customarily has the task of representing potential problems by relating them to the experiences of exemplary protagonists; secondly, advertising campaigns, which are aimed at certain target groups and represent their patterns of life and consumption; finally, the political/institutional discourse, through which lawmakers and administrators justify and implement policies for the citizens directly or indirectly affected by them and the citizenry in general.

The literary and cinematic narrative insists increasingly on old age as a new opportunity; this is the case with films like *The Bucket List* (2007), *Up* (2009), *Youth* (2014), *The Hundred-Year-Old Man Who Climbed Out the Window and Disappeared* (2013). If these examples are compared with other earlier forms, one immediately realises that the elderly whose functions were largely narrative (and not active), being mainly oriented to the past (of which they were the guardians), and often described as being weakened or withdrawn, have been replaced by the images of seniors who decide to start over and have new experiences. Advertising targeting old age also reveals significant changes. While it is clear to advertisers and their clients that their target requires specific attention (for example, the adoption of traditional media rather than the new digital media, the use of clearly visible print and so forth), making allowance for the elderly consumers' real infirmities, the representation of seniors has changed in at least two ways: first their image is increasingly youthful (through endorsements by celebrities or actors who are actually youthful-looking or in fact younger than the characters they play); secondly through the use of paradoxical narratives that describe seniors as still intent on forms of consumption and pastimes (such as sports) that attest to their good physical and mental shape. The two types of public discourse presented above – although showing significant changes in their ways of representing the new Seniors – does not yet significantly incorporate the use of IT by seniors, at least in Europe. This can be seen as a minor contradiction, because in public discourse IT is the quintessential symbol of inclusion and integration, and therefore it calls for an explanation why, while we tend to represent seniors in their gradual integration into social life, they are not yet represented as actively using IT. There may be two reasons for this lack of representation: first, the relatively small percentage of seniors who are currently computer literate out of the total target of the elderly; the other is the social stereotype that presents seniors as digital immigrants, not entirely at ease with the new technologies [8].

So, even though the research suggests a growing tendency among seniors to use IT [9], in the narrative and advertising that targets them, they still do not appear as IT users.

The governmental discourse is different, since it includes legislation and administrative practices that foster the use of IT by Seniors. Here we find general discussions that stress on the one hand the importance of an 'active, healthy and independent' image of seniors, while on the other it insists on the need for mechanisms that reduce their potential isolation, and overall exclusion (in this sense the discrimination against older people is comparable to that based on gender, ethnicity or status). In this case, as will be seen, IT often recurs as an essential element in the inclusion of seniors, together with the significant outlines of policies to promote the use of IT by the elderly.

The next two points will seek to show respectively some key points of government policies that envisage digital inclusion and the actual practices of inclusion, carried out as part of lifelong learning.

3 Policy Discourse, Digital Skills and Their Indicators

Our first examples of representation of the 'digital elderly' come from the area of the European policy documents. Such documents, both as a general framework and specific recommendations, contribute to the social construction of the old people facing the IT in a very effective way, since they are the premises for the – more or less consistent – government projects addressed to the elderly. Research on this topic [10] has already shown the presence of a new 'digital divide rhetoric' focused on a deterministic view of both aging and IT. While the old age is often represented as a period associated with risks of exclusion, isolation, retirement, disability and cognitive deficits, IT seems to offer the possibility to reduce older age related problems, fostering a more autonomous life and cutting public costs for welfare.

We are here referring to some documents from different international institutional sources in two relevant frameworks: 'active aging' and 'digital agenda'. In the first case, IT access and use are seen as tools for fostering e-health and healthy aging; in the second one, they are seen just as preconditions enabling consumption of goods and services of the 'single digital market' that is the horizon of the European Digital Agenda.

In both the frameworks, there are two major concepts: 'digital literacy' and 'digital skills. They are, at the same time, a criterion by which the digital divide of the elderly can be measured and the goals of the policies can be addressed to them. Since only the 'digitally literate' older people would have the competences to benefit from digital technologies for active and healthy aging (as well as to access the digital market), the criteria to evaluate digital literacy and skills tend to become normative.

Our aim is to account for the plurality of the criteria used to assess digital literacy and skills among the elderly, in order to show how they are socially constructed; behind the adopted indicator is thus possible to see some implicit considerations about IT and aging.

A first example is the Active Aging Index (AAI), 'a tool to measure the untapped potential of older people for active and healthy aging across countries. It measures the level to which older people live independent lives, participate in paid employment and social activities as well as their capacity to actively age' [11]. Adopted by the United Nations Economic Commission for Europe (UNECE) and the European Commission's DG for Employment, Social Affairs and Inclusion (DG EMPL) in the policy framework of 'Social investment' designed to strengthen people's skills and capacities and support them to participate fully in employment and social life, with a peculiar focus on the elderly in order to give them more opportunities for an active participation in society and the economy, the AAI consists of twenty indicators in four different areas: Employment, Participation in society, Independent, healthy and secure living and Capacity and enabling environment for active aging. The last one includes the use of IT as an indicator taken from the Eurostat ICT Survey. As reported in the official website of UNECE, 'This indicator aims to measure the degree to which older people's environments enable them to connect with others with the help of information and communication technologies, thus reflecting one aspect of their capacity for active aging [...] The question refers to internet use at least once a week (i.e. every day or almost every day or at least once a week but not every day) on average within the last 3 months before the survey. Use includes all locations and methods of access and any purpose (private or work/business related)' [11].

Irrespective of the actual online practices, their goals or motivations and social context, the pure and simple frequency of use is thus considered as predictive of social inclusion and active aging. As stated in an explanatory note, 'larger number of older people using the internet points to a higher ability to communicate with others, and engage actively in society. While excessive use of the internet can be detrimental to one's health, such phenomena have been observed mainly for younger people thus far. It is therefore reasonable to associate the use of internet among older people positively with their capacity for active aging' [12].

A very different example comes from Europe 2020 Strategy and its Digital Agenda, whose main objective is to develop a 'digital single market' in order to better exploit the potential of IT, to foster innovation and to generate smart, sustainable and inclusive growth in Europe. It is made up of seven pillars, and two of them are interesting for our analysis: Pillar VI (Enhancing digital literacy, skills and inclusion) and Pillar VII (ICT-enabled benefits for EU society). While Pillar VII mentions e-health and IT for aging well as a strategy to provide European citizens with better and cheaper services towards a new 'silver economy', Pillar VI aims to tackle the digital divide.

As far as the digital literacy is concerned, the Digital Agenda of the European Commission (EC) acknowledges the need for every citizen – elderly included – to have at least basic digital skills in order to live, work, learn and participate in the modern society. But what does 'basic digital skills' actually mean? How to assess them, in order to develop them?

In the Digital Agenda Scoreboard – a tool used to measure the progress of the European digital economy – some of the Digital Economy and Society (DESI) Index indicators [13] concern individual digital skills on the basis of the following areas:

- Information skills area: Copying and pasting files or folders. Getting information from public authorities/services' websites. Finding information about goods or services. Reading online news/newspapers/news magazines.
- Communication skills area: Sending/receiving emails. Using social networks. Audio/video calling in the internet. Uploading self-created content to any website to be shared.
- Problem solving skills area: Transferring files between computers or devices. Connecting and installing devices. Installing a new or replacing an old operating system. Online shopping and banking. Making an appointment with a practitioner via a website.
- Content creation skills area: Using Word Processing Software. Using spreadsheet software. Creating presentations or documents integrating text, pictures, tables or charts. Creating websites or blogs. Writing a code in a programming language.

It is noteworthy that these indicators merge computer skills and internet skills, taking for granted that the PC is the main device to access internet (irrespective of the amount of internet users accessing through smartphone or tablets); the indicators also refer to some age-specific activities, but mix different ages (e.g. 'using social networks' and 'making an appointment with a practitioner'). Together with other DESI Index indicators – such as 'Persons employed using computers at work' or 'Individuals who have obtained ICT skills through formal educational institutions' – the individual digital skills assessed by the Digital Agenda Scoreboard turn out to be consistent with the horizon of the 'digital single market', but somewhat indifferent to 'social inclusion' or 'active aging' of the digital elderly.

While the Active Aging Index assumes that having an internet access enables – by itself – the elderly to participate in the network society, the DESI Index indicators describe the 'basic digital skills' assuming, in a normative way, that some online activities have to be equally performed by different age groups. In the first case, indicators do not take in consideration the actual use of internet; in the other one, they take in consideration some not age-specific uses. In both cases, the indicators seem to be inadequate, and contribute to construct a non-realistic social representation of the elderly, as either automatically included, or irremediably meant to be excluded from the digital environments. Thus, it is probably no coincidence that the number of actions addressed to the older people encompassed by the Digital Agenda framework is very low; for example, in the Italian section of the Grand Coalition for Digital Job – a multi-stakeholder partnership led by the EC to tackle the lack of digital skills in Europe – only 4 out of 68 action projects involving citizens are focused on the elderly, even if Seniors, together with people in the southern regions, are considered as the most disadvantaged national targets [14].

In the next point we are going to analyze an example of such projects.

4   Writing in the Education of Seniors: IT as a Cultural Object

In Italy, as in other European countries, digital literacy courses for seniors took off in the Eighties, in the context of voluntary activities aimed at reducing the digital divide. The objects used in these courses have gradually changed: first standalone computers and the use of their software (mainly the MS Office package), then gradually Internet and today the Web and services. Then their teaching methods have also varied. What we want to analyze here is a rather widespread occurrence, which could be called the 'grandparents and grandchildren' model, namely the involvement of children and youngsters in assisting the elderly in their digital learning.

In particular, we analyze a program coordinated by Fondazione Mondo Digitale (FMD) that is called Grandparents on Internet (GOI) [15]. It has been running since 2002, involving government institutions and schools, and in 13 years has completed courses for 25,700 seniors (those over 60, of whom about 65 % are women), conducted by 18,600 students tutors and 1,800 teacher coordinators.

To analyze the type of program conducted, here we will examine the three manuals used in the course, including one for older course members, one for student tutors and one for teachers.

The three manuals are part of the documentation that reflects the many years' experience of training. Hence they are not just practical guides but excellent material for understanding the results and achievements of the program, including feedback from participants.

In particular we will focus on the following points:

1. the purpose of the program;
2. the content and structure of the courses;
3. the method: identifying of the strengths and weaknesses of the elderly in learning to use IT.

4.1   The Purpose of the GOI Program

The documents analyzed here clearly reveal that the objectives of the program are twofold. On the one hand they are intended to make the elderly digitally competent. On the other (and this seems the true aim), they seek to reduce the risk of the elderly suffering from exclusion.

The teachers' manual accompanying the courses states: 'Digital literacy among those sectors of the population at risk of exclusion from the benefits of the knowledge society is essential for the dream of an inclusive knowledge society.' Hence digital literacy is crucial principally as creating 'a knowledge society', which will reward those with access to knowledge and exclude those without it. In illustrating the programme's objectives, the manual states that computer usage is increasingly essential 'in order to participate effectively in the social life of the community (neighbourhood, city, country, world), to communicate more fully and better with all and to use important services online.' On the basis of these aims the program provides for the active involvement of children and young 'digital natives', who are invited to become 'knowledge volunteers':

'Being a knowledge volunteer means exactly this: I put myself at the service of others. I fill my backpack with things I can do or that I like to do and I pour them out for other people, explaining what I do to them. We young people are a generation highly skilled in using the new technologies. Those of us with younger siblings realise they are even more advanced in their ease of understanding technology than we were at their age. […] The invitation is very real: go to your neighbour and show them how to log on to Internet. Go to your grandparents and explain how they can keep in touch with you on Facebook. Help your parents find their classmates by using the social networks. […] In short, get cracking. Today, now, at once. There is a huge need to spread digital culture in Italy. A culture that goes beyond simply being glued to Facebook and similar sites. A culture that doesn't just say "Learn to use the computer because otherwise you're not worth anything".'

4.2 Contents, Objectives and Structure of the GOI Courses

The courses last 30 h, divided into lessons of two hours each held once or twice a week. Classes are held in a multimedia classroom, equipped with computers and other hardware (printer, scanner, projector etc.). The skills to be attained in the various courses cover mainly computing (there is no mention of literacy in the use of tablets or smartphones) and include: using a word processor (e.g. Word); using Internet and email; doing calculations (e.g. with Excel); computer drawing (e.g. with Paint); downloading and processing digital photos (e.g. with Picture Manager); writing presentations (e.g. with Power Point); speaking on Skype.

In practical terms, the seniors sign up for a course that interests them, or that they think might be useful. In this course they will have a teacher who explains the content and a child or youngster who concretely helps them carry out the necessary operations using the various programs on the computer.

The presence of the child-tutor is a typical feature of this type of program. It is based on a kind of new generational contract in which it is no longer only the elderly who teach young people, but in some areas, especially technological ones, it is rather the young who have more experience and expertise than the elderly. Moreover, a practice of this type is also educational for children and adolescents, because it shows they can play a publicly useful part in society. Finally, programs of this kind also perform a social function, as they tend to create links across generations which reduce the isolation of individuals and expand the network of relationships. This, as various studies have shown, is particularly useful for improving the general quality of life of the elderly.

4.3 GOI Method: The Elderly's Strengths and Weaknesses in Acquiring Computing Skills

The method these courses adopt lies essentially in integrating the teaching provided by the teacher in the classroom equipped with computers and the tutorship function performed by the young 'knowledge volunteers' who act as 'personal teachers' of seniors.

The manuals, from this point of view, constitute a highly interesting material for understanding the concrete difficulties involved and the strategies gradually developed to overcome them. They contain clear indications of both, developed for the three types of readers of the manuals: teacher-technicians, very young tutors and senior learners.

Teachers, for example, are recommended to adopt a combination of rigid and flexible programmes. Rigid, because of the plurality of learning situations (a single class may include seniors with different digital backgrounds). Flexible, because the differences in starting levels may require the objectives to be organised for different subjects.

The manual for the young tutors, however, contains some advice about behaviour that always starts from real situations, observed during extensive experience of the courses:

'Seniors [...] might be irritated if a tutor strikes them as rude. Don't expect to get on close terms at once with seniors, but wait for them to trust you and recognise your role. For this reason, you should always be courteous'.

In the manual addressed to the elderly, finally, we find an interesting way to illustrate the skills that will be taught. They are exemplified by possible objectives, so relating to the non-technological needs of the elderly in their everyday lives: 'writing documents (letters to the administrator of the condominium, requests for services from the council, etc.). quickly and with a pleasant layout, without having to rewrite everything all over again in the case of changes or corrections (as was the case before with typewriters); keeping household accounts automatically and tidily;... writing original and personalised greetings cards (with drawings, images, colourful speech bubbles) for birthdays, festivities or just as a surprise for your grandchildren.'

These strike us as good examples of the promotion of digital learning based not on technological performativity, but concrete needs, very close to the public in question, and bringing out the practical uses of computing, both to improve their ability to achieve something and to take advantage of the new services.

The advice includes further suggestions for coping with potentially difficult situations during the course:

'The tutor, trying to explain something more clearly, takes over the mouse and keyboard and takes your place, leaving you to look on and feel discouraged. You ask for an explanation and the tutor explains, you ask for a further explanation of certain points and the tutor explains them in much the same way as before... Hence it is essential for you seniors to understand the difficulties and the effort that tutors make in carrying out their important and delicate function. So try to be patient and understanding with them'.

In summing up this analysis of the concrete experience of teaching computing to seniors, we can say that

- though based on assumptions rather typical of the emphasis placed on computing as a favoured instrument for inclusion, it mediates these assumptions with the need for social rather than technological inclusion, based on intergenerational interaction and the teaching-learning role of young tutors;
- while setting technical objectives, the GOI program takes into account the basic difficulties of seniors and their age-related attitudes and habits;

- the computer remains at the core of the literacy process, with little interest being shown in smartphones and tablets.

5 Conclusions

In this paper we have shown some examples of normative social discourses about aging and IT. On the one hand, fiction and advertising represent the 'new' elderly as a subject still active, socially integrated and open to life. Addressing to the older people as their target, this kind of discourses contribute to the social construction of an idealized representation of aging; nevertheless, they usually avoid to represent the elderly as IT users.

On the other hand, policy documents take on board the matter of IT diffusion amongst the elderly as a resource for their social integration. Two kinds of discourses have been analyzed: firstly, the normative representation implicitly or explicitly embedded in the indicators adopted to assess digital literacy and skills; secondly, the discourse of a project aimed at achieving the goal of digitally literate seniors.

Our analysis of such discourses highlights several problems. First of all, the inconsistency of these different discourses makes it hard to represent the older people using IT in a clear, convincing and believable way. A further analysis of the most common stereotypes would probably be very useful in order to produce a more efficient public discourse.

There is also some ambiguity about the reasons why the elderly should be digitally literate, due to different frameworks; while the Digital Agenda fosters the participation in the 'single digital market', either or welfare costs cutting, active aging and e-health policies focus on social inclusion and wellbeing. As a consequence, different digital capacities and skills are requested, assessed and proposed.

Another critical point is a 'technocentric' approach, with the consequence of stressing the central role of the personal computer and its technical features instead of the need, interests and social practices of the users. On the one side, this approach understimates such devices as tablets and smartphones, becoming ever more common among the elderly; on the other side, it results in the disregard of subjective elements of the 'age digital divide', such as personal motivations [16].

Finally, in a more general perspective, public discourses aimed at social inclusion of the older people through digitalization should better balance the fostering of technical solutions with the offering of a more integrated plurality of services, both online and offline.

References

1. Rossi, G., Boccacin, L., Bramanti, D., Meda, S.: Active Aging: Intergenerational Relationships and Social Generativity, Active Aging and Healthy Living: A Human Centered Approach in Research and Innovation as Source of Quality of Life. IOS Press, Amsterdam (2014)
2. Nussbaum, J., Coupland, J. (eds.): Handbook of Communication and Aging Research. Lawrence Erlbaum Associates, Mahwah (2004)

3. Schmid, W.: Gelassenheit. Was wir gewinnen, wenn wir älter warden. Insel Verlag, Berlin (2014)
4. Augé, M.: Une ethnologie de soi. Le temps sans âge. Seuil, Paris (2014)
5. Bodei, R.: Generazioni. Età della vita, età delle cose. Laterza, Bari (2014)
6. Gullette, M.M · Aged by Culture. University of Chicago Press, Chicago (2000)
7. Colombo, F.: Aging, media and communication. In: Nussbaum, J.F. (ed.) Communication Across the Lifespan: ICA theme book. Peter Lang, Berlin (2016)
8. Loos, E.F.: Generational use of new media and the (ir)relevance of age. In: Colombo, F., Fortunati, L. (eds.) Broadband Society and Generational Changes, pp. 259–273. Peter Lang, Berlin (2011)
9. Colombo, F., Aroldi, P., Carlo, S.: New elders, old divides: ICTs, inequalities and wellbeing amongst young elderly Italians. Comunicar 23(45), 47–55 (2015)
10. Sourbati, M., Carlo S: The mutuality of age and technology in digital divide policy. In: International Conference Partnership for Progress on the Digital Divide, Scottsdale (Phoenix), Arizona, USA, 21–22 October (2015)
11. UNECE: AAI in brief. http://www1.unece.org/stat/platform/display/AAI/I.+AAI+in+brief
12. UNECE: Annex A.4: information on indicators for the 4th domain: capacity for active aging. http://www1.unece.org/stat/platform/display/AAI/Annex+A.4%3A+Information+on +indicators+for+the+4th+domain%3A+Capacity+for+active+aging
13. EC: digital agenda for europe: digital economy and society index. http://digital-agenda-data.eu/datasets/desi/indicators
14. Coalizione per le Competenze Digitali. http://competenzedigitali.agid.gov.it/progetti/cittadini
15. FMD: Nonni su Internet. http://www.mondodigitale.org/it/risorse/materiali-didattici/nonni-su-internet
16. Van Dijk, J.: The Network Society: Social Aspects of New Media. Sage, Thousand Oaks (1999)

Elderly and IT: Brand Discourses on the Go

Karine Berthelot-Guiet[✉]

CELSA-Paris-Sorbonne, Sorbonne Universités, Paris, France
karine.berthelot-guiet@celsa.paris-sorbonne.fr

Abstract. In countries where IT products have been an everyday commodity for some time and mass consumption a major social feature for a long time, very different kind of economic and social players picture elderly as the «new frontier». That is to say that elderly appear as the new generation that have to be converted to IT in order to benefit from these devices and become consumers. The challenge is, from a marketing point of view as expressed by professionals, huge since elderly are supposed to be, by nature, deeply attached to traditions and at least suspicious or at most resistant to change, especially when it comes to technological change. We intend here to question and analyze in which respect advertising discourse should, theoretically, be a huge help and drive regarding the acculturation of elderly to the use of IT products. As a matter of fact, commercials and brand content, being brand discourses, should have a major part to play in this process.

Keywords: Advertising · Elderly · IT · Stereotype

1 Elderly as a «New Frontier» for IT Products

In countries where IT products have been an everyday commodity for some time and mass consumption a major social feature for a long time, as in North America and the western part of Europe, very different kinds of economic and social players picture elderly as the «new frontier». That is to say that elderly appear, especially in Europe with the demographic weight of «baby boomers» born during the post-World-War-2 period, as the new generation that have to be converted to IT in order to benefit from these devices and become consumers. The challenge is, from a marketing point of view as expressed by professionals, huge since elderly are supposed to be, by nature, deeply attached to traditions and at least suspicious or at most resistant to change, especially when it comes to technological change.

We intend here to question and analyze in which respect advertising discourse should, theoretically, be a huge help and drive regarding the acculturation of elderly to the use of IT products. As a matter of fact, commercials and brand content, being brand discourses, should have a major part to play in this process. This results from a particular conjuncture of factors as: the traditional educational role of advertising since the nineteenth century, the targeting work made by marketing specialists about the differentiation of subcategories among the big group of people over 50 that is traditional and questionable borderline for «old-age», the assumed attachment to brands of this group of population.

© Springer International Publishing Switzerland 2016
J. Zhou and G. Salvendy (Eds.): ITAP 2016, Part II, LNCS 9755, pp. 186–193, 2016.
DOI: 10.1007/978-3-319-39949-2_18

2   Advertising: A User's Manual for Life[1]

2.1   Brands and Advertising: An Education to Commodity

Brands and advertising are both the result, along with packaging, of the evolution of consumption during the nineteenth century first in USA, then in Europe. They were the result of the new relations manufacturers and growers wanted to create directly between them through their products and the consumers. At that time people were buying goods from grocers. The latter were the ones making the choice between products, buying them from producers and displaying them in their shops, counseling people about their qualities. The producers had to deal with the retailers who had the upper hand in market relations and transactions. Grocers were dealing with clients[2].

When manufacturers decided to take the lead in this system, they invented three elements to transform store clients into consumers of specific goods, in a process of commodification of the market. This is precisely when and why brands were invented. Manufacturers wanted people to go to the grocery store asking for a certain brand of wheat, sugar or oat, compelling the seller to add these specific brands to his stock. Then the link and the trust began to switch from grocers to brands. In a rather quick lapse of time, buyers who believed in their grocer's skills in the process of choice and his ability to undertake responsibility began to believe that a symbolic element, the brand attached to a product, had the same kind of power. This transition could not have occurred only with brands. Because they needed to be written on something, the packaging was developed and because people were to be informed of the brand and motivated to ask for them, advertising appeared too.

At the same time, brands needed to explain a whole set of commodities to consumers and to educate them to new ways of life in order to have them buy their products. It is well known that toothpaste and soap brands were leading actors in the explanation and the installation in everyday life of new habits such as brushing teeth, soaping oneself more than once in a while, giving good care to infants and toddlers, etc. More recently brand and advertising do the same with more specific points regarding life and food hygiene: they insist on the use of deodorant, shampoo against dandruff, health food as fruit and vegetable, etc.

2.2   Brands and Advertising: Education Through Stereotype[3]

Education can be seen as a paradoxical effect of brands and advertising. They achieve this in a very specific way that is linked to the advertising discourse system. Advertising is a highly particular type of discourse since it is submitted to a very complex set of constraints. Regardless of the country where it occurs, it happens to deal with external restrictions such as the ones coming from different sets of laws and self-regulation, the sociological and organizational operation of the inter-profession dedicated to the buying

---

[1]   This title refers to the title of Georges Perec novel: Life, A User's Manual.
[2]   All the elements about the birth of brands in USA and France are coming from [1].
[3]   On these aspects see [2, 3].

and selling of advertising, and the fact that only a few words, a few seconds or a little space is needed to achieve persuasion.

All of these aspects, and others, put under pressure this plurisemiotic system. It ends in the production of highly condensed and oversized semiotic forms. The advertising discourse has to find a balance between all these strains and its first function to show off the brand. It needs a particular work on signs, a semiotic densification that explain some characteristics of advertising discourse: firstly, advertising is dedicated to selling, all is done in order to sell; secondly, advertising is a discourse that needs to exist, because people are not so willing to look at it; thirdly, advertising has to serve the brand and it always conveys the same message: my brand is the best [4].

At the same time a huge semiotic work is done to turn this ever the same message into something apparently different and naturalized. To achieve this, advertising discourse deals with collective imagination and uses very well known symbols and ready-made sentences. Both Roland Barthes and Umberto Eco have the hypothesis, and we'll go in the same way, that people receive the complex system of advertising as a whole, something someone already knows because of intertextuality and/or stereotypy. As Eco puts it, it is a discourse that uses. Whatever will be the brand, the tone, spectacular, educational or informative, advertising is obliged to use stereotypes and sometimes to help to establish some of them.

3 Elderly: Apparition of a Class of Consumers

3.1 Where there Is as a Market, there Comes a Target: Teenagers and Senior Persons

The brand managers have, since the second half of the twentieth century, started to work on new markets to sell their products. First of all they have looked inside their own country towards new segment of population and sometimes they helped trough their «targeting» work to enhance the place of a type of people. For example, when teenagers began to appear as a specific age of life, soon enough, marketing people realized what it meant in terms of money reserve. Almost as they were recognized in society, first in USA, then in Europe, teenagers became a marketing target through a process of selection, construction and reduction that can change an executive young woman into an «under-50 housewife».

The whole society of consumption has evolved in the past sixty years scouting new segments of population with enough money to spend in all kinds of branded products. Advertising people have adapted their activity, collecting different stereotypes to speak to new people.

Regarding teenagers, a swelling literature from management psycho-sociological sciences is dedicated to the role of first children, then teenagers and young adults regarding consumption. For example, in France, teenagers appear as a marketing target worth the work at the beginning of the 90's. Since then marketing people are going towards an ever better refinement and creating new «fictions» as «adulescents», «X generation», «Y generation», «Millenials». All these targets are supposed to be a potential source of money because they are able to buy or to have influence [5]. But this is not enough, these young people are supposed to build a specific link with brands during this highly complex time of life that is supposed to last for the rest of their life as consumers.

This is why brands take so much time, energy and care to try to understand how teenagers choose what they buy and what they want, even if the buyer is a parent or a grand-parent. This ever-changing generation is also thought as particularly at ease with IT products. They are even frequently surnamed «digital natives» as if they knew from the start how to «speak» the IT language. We can make fun of this, but this categorization is interesting because it induces that the rest of population, especially elderly, are in a second language situation. Taking for granted that young people can master any new IT products, the brands that advertise towards them tend to choose a specific way of doing it, going towards spectacular and aestheticized forms of advertising.

Advertising as an aesthetic mediation is due to E.Morin [6]. According to his analysis, the incentive aspects of advertising are based on a work about aesthetic, ludic and erotic springs that entice the public because it gives them a kind of pleasure. In this respect we can say that Nike brand, highly appreciated by teenagers works on an aesthetical mediation of sport. Everybody is able to reach as personal achievement. The Nike Fuel Band, a connected wristband, is also giving a view to even small but aesthetic personal performances.

Advertising is also a spectacular mediation and works on the show side. This is not dedicated to young targets but we can say that some brands have chosen to work the show on IT devices that give access to social media. Brands are ubiquitous in social media for the few last years. This presence is linked to different aims and accompanied by a string of commentaries. Mainly, the professional point of view has been focused on the idea that social medias enable a conversation supposedly based on transparency, equality of places and proximity. They depict a new Eldorado of pacified and non-hierarchical communication.

A content and discourse analysis of this exchanges show instead a one-way messaging system, comparable to stimulus/response. The brand initiates something and people are reacting, individually, without any brand feed back. It is a one-way system. At the same time this does not mean that nothing happens, communication happens even if it is not conversation. People tend to react to the brand proposal considering that this is an advertising show. We can say that, first, because most of the posts are in fact the written equivalents of cheers, claps, and laughs in other words, what people usually do when they enjoy a show in order to express their positive appreciation. Secondly, we can state that this show is acknowledged as advertising because they consider that (they write it openly) the discourse produced by these brands on their Facebook pages is fathered by advertisers and marketers.

Here lie several interesting points:

- The followers of these specific Facebook brand pages register in order to receive on an almost daily basis an advertising product they enjoy. This point is quite remarkable when we know that people are supposed to be repelled by marketing and advertising. This is one of the main arguments of conversation. Here some participants are freely asking and enjoying the show of advertising.

- Whenever they register, they freely accept to enter a state of "willing suspension of disbelief" (Coleridge) that prove they fully consider advertising as fiction putting an end to the idea of the manipulation of consciousness. Advertising cannot lure people whenever they qualify it as fiction.
- These very same people commonly give their opinion about the value of this show, on its aesthetic aspects, its cohesion with the brand discourse and what they are waiting/wanting from these brands in terms of advertising quality.

But who knows how old they are?

3.2   Brands and Advertising, Converting Elderly to IT Products: Using Stereotype to Change Stereotype

What happened when the young ones, becoming a marketing target multiplied in a constellation of sub-targets, finally touched to the other end of the generational scale around the beginning of the twenty first century? Once Elderly were no target at all. Older people where supposed, even when mass consumption started fully first in North America during the Interwar period and in Western Europe in the 60's, not to enter consumption, especially for new products related new technology. They were thought too stuck to old ways and habits and difficult to convince because of a great suspicion towards advertising. Consumption was not the only field to think about older people in this way; many pieces of popular culture such as songs used to stress the fact[4]that old people had no curiosity, no dreams left.

But people born around World War 2 started to change this stereotype. They appear to stay «younger later» and most of all they still had money to spend after retirement. This opened a new field of expectation for marketing people who developed first a single new target named "senior". A bunch of specific products were launched: magazines, radios, TV broadcasts and programs, specific food etc. They appeared in more and more commercials for cars, insurance, banking, and rather expensive goods[5]. On this matter, advertising began the work of stereotypy, choosing carefully nice looking not so old people, very dynamic, beautifully tanned, hair brand white, doing with great joy and smile physically demanding activities. The senior target was a very acceptable socio-marketing construct artifact using a stereotype to replace the previous one. The new representation spread by commercials depicting people looking forward future with confidence and buying power. As Alyette Defrance put it, instead of becoming old these "seniors" appeared as "still young" (Fig. 1).

Along with this new era representing elderly in advertising, the commercial discourse chose a very old way to ensure an optimal communication with this huger and huger part of occidental countries population: communication tending towards education. Dedicated and general media are now commonly containing advertorials on topics linked to various health issues such as cholesterol, osteoporosis, and digestive wellness.

---

[4] This is underlined by Alyette Defrance with the analysis of the differences between a Jacques Brel song and songs from 2000 [7].
[5] These elements of analysis [7].

Fig. 1. Advertisings including «young» elderly and advertising for Funeral Planning Insurance

As once sugar was presented as a healthy food for kids and hard-working people and chocolate as well, nowadays specific brands of margarine enriched with omega-3 or 6 fatty acid, yogurt with vitamin D or bifidus lactobacillus take time and space to present the dietary problems due to aging, their source in body metabolism and how the manufactured products launched on market food can help balancing the problems if not cure them. Whenever one takes time to read these advertorials, they appear to be truly informative, achieving a work of popularization about these topics along with TV and radio programs or magazine articles. They give elements related to scientific knowledge and appear or look like pages torn apart from a popular encyclopedia.

Then came the time, at the end of the twentieth century for sub-targeting in the elderly kingdom. Thus appeared, in the first instance the "very old people" or "fourth age" or "oldest old", their markets and advertising messages, less euphoric than the one dedicated to senior, dealing with retirement homes, life insurances, enuresis, funerals, etc. Even in this case, stereotypes are present. If we analyze the very common TV commercials about what French call «convention obsèques», that is to say funeral planning insurances, we can see that they deal with the announced death of the subscriber through the use of other themes that make it work: death is dodged or understated. These advertising messages show not so old people, still in shape, training in sport, gardening, participating in cultural activities who are caring to avoid imposing further worry to their loved ones. But, at the same time, they stay consumers, even after death, choosing for themselves the proper standard. They can master the whole process regarding rituals, materials, and the location of the grave. Consumption and customization stay distinctive signs even for a deceased.

But stereotype is still there. Taken as a whole, these TV commercials are based on a few variations: the subscriber is still a "young senior", sometimes with no white hair; whenever their children are speaking instead of them, they don't seem, physically, so different from the previous ones. Discourses are using some linguistic cliché like "with the loss of a loved one", and so on. On this very theme IT products and productions appear with the online condolences. Something must have changed about IT and elderly.

IT products, being the most quickly changing part of technological latest innovation, were supposed to be prohibitive for elderly. They were meant not to be able to cope with

Fig. 2. Advertorial about cholesterol in French magazine Pleine Vie, mars 2016

these new devices such as cellular phones, laptop and tablet computers. But, in this respect, marketing people have lagged behind the new kind of elderly they contributed to put into the light. Apart from the intergenerational link between grandparents and their grandchildren, TV commercials tend to deal, even now, with elderly people still in the old stereotype of technophobia. They don't want to use these devices, they are suspicious about the service offer that comes with them and are supposed, even young as they look, to need the help of a young one or a teenager to use IT products, with reluctance and as a little time as possible.

Brand managers and advertisers have partly missed the point about how people become old and most of all how they dealt, all their lifelong, with IT change, from radio to TV to tape-recorder, CD's, streaming, from video-recorder, to DVD and blue-ray players and then router boxes. At work, they swung to everyday use of computers and web services and kept on using it after retirement coping with new devices as was necessary (Fig. 2).

4   Elderly, the New Frontier for Advertisers

It seems that the future challenge for marketing and advertising professionals is to understand fully the elderly they still too much categorize as a whole, especially when it comes to IT products. The newcomers in the class of age are totally users of IT devices and will go on like this for a while, inventing new uses, and new sociabilities. It is a challenge to be able to keep these very well trained, experienced consumers that do not stick to international brands as oldest old people do.

The question is to know how to deal between educational, spectacular and aesthetical advertising discourses.

References

1. Cochoy, F.: Une Histoire du Marketing. Discipliner l'Économie de Marché. La Découverte, Paris (1999)
2. Berthelot-Guiet, K.: Paroles de Pub. La vie Triviale de la Publicité. Éditions Non Standard, Le Havre (2013)
3. Berthelot-Guiet, K.: Analyser les Discours Publicitaires. Armand Colin, Paris (2015)
4. Barthes, R.: Le message publicities. Les cahiers de la publicité 7, 243–247 (1963)
5. Berthelot-Guiet, K.: La marque médiation marchande ou mythologie adolescente. In: Lachance, J., Saint-Germain, P., Mathiot, L., Marques cultes et culte des marques chez les jeunes: Penser l'adolescence avec la consommation, Presses Universitaires de Laval, Laval (2016)
6. Morin, E.: Préface-*Publicité et société*. In: Cathelat, B., Paris, Payot (1968)
7. Defrance, A.: Penser, classer, communiquer. Publicité et catégories sociales. Hermès 38 (2004)

Using Information and Communication Technologies to Promote Healthy Aging in Costa Rica: Challenges and Opportunities

María Dolores Castro Rojas[1(✉)],
Ann Bygholm[1], and Tia G.B. Hansen[2]

[1] E-LearningLab, Department of Communication and Psychology,
Center for User Driven Innovation, Learning and Design, Aalborg University,
Aalborg, Denmark
mariacastro@hum.aau.dk
[2] Department of Communication and Psychology, Center for Developmental
and Applied Psychological Research, Aalborg University, Aalborg, Denmark

Abstract. Several authors have suggested that ICTs have the potential to promote healthy ageing by supporting social inclusion, access to products and services and learning. However, older people often do not use ICT and information about patterns of usage is scarce. Data from the Costa Rica Census 2011 and two questionnaires showed that older people between 65 and 74 years old, living in urban areas, with more education and higher socioeconomic status are the most active ICT users. They presented a tendency to mobility and connectivity when using ICTs, reported positive perceptions of technology and were favorably disposed to learning about and using ICT. Based on the analysis of data we conclude that opportunities to promote healthy aging through use of ICT include use of public infrastructure and community-based learning services to increase the number of ICT users and facilitate progression from social networking activities to activities supporting the maximization of functional status such as instrumental activities and learning for personal development.

Keywords: Older adults · ICT literacy · Healthy/Active aging · ICT and active aging

1 Introduction

This paper is part of a project about using Information and Communication Technology (ICT) to promote healthy aging among older Costa Ricans in order to prevent cognitive impairment. This is the first analysis of data relating to how older Costa Ricans are currently using ICT.

Models of active and successful ageing suggest that it is possible to remain functional, independent, and autonomous and have good quality of life during old age [1–4]. According to the WHO [3], active aging is a multifactorial process which is dependent on population and individual factors. At population level active aging requires that individuals have opportunities to realize their potential for physical, social and mental wellbeing throughout their lifespan, and that they are able to participate in society

© Springer International Publishing Switzerland 2016
J. Zhou and G. Salvendy (Eds.): ITAP 2016, PartII, LNCS 9755, pp. 194–206, 2016.
DOI: 10.1007/978-3-319-39949-2_19

irrespective of illness and disabilities. At individual level the most important factors in successful ageing include the maintenance of autonomy and independence.

Powerful individual-level predictors of active ageing include psychological factors such as intelligence and cognitive ability, e.g. capacity for solving problems and adapting to changes and losses produced by aging, and social engagement, defined as productive interaction with society, with one's community and with a social network [1, 2, 4, 5].

Technology can play an important role in work, leisure and healthcare provision. Specifically, ICT can increase opportunities for social learning and create new ways to access information and services [6]. ICTs have the potential to promote healthy aging by supporting social inclusion, increasing access to products and services, supporting learning for pleasure and fulfillment as well as being used for specific cognitive training [6–10].

Despite the potential of ICT to improve many aspects of daily life including learning processes and cognitive activities, older people often do not use ICT. In 2014 just 29 % of people aged between 65 and 74 years living in the 28 countries of the European Union were using the Internet frequently (every day or almost every day); this produces an age-based digital divide [11]. In 2011 just 14 % of people in this age group in Costa Rica were using the Internet according to the National Census [12].

There is some information available about ICT usage among older people living in European countries and in the United States of America [9–12], but there is not much detailed information about when and how are they using ICT. In general, information about this topic tends to be even scarcer in developing countries.

In the light of the aging of the population, the low usage of ICT by older people and the lack of information about this topic in Latin American developing countries, we decided to investigate patterns of ICT usage, interest in ICT and motivation to use ICT among older Costa Ricans. Knowing how older people are using ICT, what obstacles and barriers they face, and what their needs and expectations are would enable the development of tailored interventions using ICT to promote successful or healthy aging.

2 Methodology

We analyzed data from the last National Census 2011 to enable us to describe the patterns of ICT access and usage among older Costa Rican people and how ICT usage was related to socio-demographic characteristics. We also administered two questionnaires to 59 older Costa Ricans participating in educational programs offered by governmental and non-governmental institutions. Recruitment was a two-stage process. First we put out a general call through governmental and non-governmental organizations and then we screened potential participants for cognitive impairments using the Mini Mental State Examination (MMSE) [13]. All participants were older than 60 years. We used this criterion as it is the criterion used by the United Nations to define "older" people [3].

One of the questionnaires included socio-demographic questions so that we could compare our participants to the general population; the questionnaire also included questions about access to, and experiences with technologies, as well as questions about interest in ICT, expectations of ICT and barriers to learning about and using ICT.

Participants also completed the Survey of Technology Use (SOTU), which explores experiences with technologies and socio-personal characteristics [14]. Descriptive statistics were calculated using SPSS 22.

Because there was little variance in MMSE scores it was not possible to calculate reliability measures. Nevertheless it is important to note that we used the MMSE as a screening tool and not as a diagnosis tool. The SOTU was translated and adapted using the back-translation procedure and two cognitive interviews. On the basis of the cognitive interviews we made some final modifications to the translated versions of the instrument.

3   Results

3.1   Description of Older People in the General Population and the Study Participants

Table 1 describes the general population and participants in the research project. Women made up just over half the general population (53.4 %) and 78 % of study participants, the average age of study participants was 67.46 years (SD = 5.31) and the mean score in the MMSE was 28.63 (SD = 1.29).

About half the study participants (48.8 %) had university level education and 20.3 % were high school graduates, whereas the most frequent educational level among

Table 1. Demographics

	National census N = 311,712	Participants n = 59
Age group (%)		
60–64	–	32,2
65–74	58	61
75–84	21	5,1
85 and more	11	1,7
Marital status (%)		
Married/civil union	53,4	57,6
Separated/divorced	9,8	20,3
Widowed	24,6	11,9
Single/never married	12,2	10,2
Education level (%)		
Without any degree	13,6	0
Some primary school	36,7	3,4
Primary school	23,8	10,2
Some high school	7,4	15,3
High school	4,8	20,3
Technical high school	0,9	1,7
1–3 years of college	1,5	3,4
University	11,2	45,8

the general population was some primary school education (36.7 %) followed by completed primary school (23.8 %). Most study participants (71.2 %) received a pension from some kind of public institution, which indicates that they had a medium or high income. In contrast just over a quarter of the general population (27 %) did not have health insurance or had state-provided social health insurance, which is an indicator of low income. These data indicate that study participants were of medium or high socioeconomic status; later we report our analysis of the impact of socio-demographic variables on the ICT usage patterns among older Costa Ricans.

3.2   ICT Access and Usage Among Costa Rican Older Adults

According to the 2011 Census 24 % of older Costa Ricans had a desktop computer at home, 19 % had a laptop, 25 % had Internet access and 69.3 % had a mobile phone. The majority (56.1 %) of study participants had a desktop computer, 76.3 % had a laptop, 91.5 % had Internet access at home and 100 % had a mobile phone. This shows that our sample had better access to ICT devices than the general population, and that the ICT device most commonly available to older people is the mobile phone.

Of the 24 % of the general population who had a computer at home, just 11.3 % were using it, a similar pattern was observed with respect to availability and use of the Internet and mobile phones; just 50 % of 69,3 % of people with access were using them. (See Table 2).

Table 2. Older people using computer, internet and mobile phone

Have you used (item) in the last three months?	National census N = 311,712		Study participants n = 59	
	Yes (%)	No (%)	Yes (%)	No (%)
Computer	11.3	88.5	78	22
Internet	10.5	89.5	83,1	16,9
Mobile phone	32	68	100	0

A larger proportion of study participants were using the devices and services to which they had access. In both groups the most commonly used ICT device was the mobile phone.

Analysis of the relationship between socio-demographic characteristics and ICT usage showed that people living in urban areas were more likely to have access to ICT than people living in rural area (30 % and 8 % respectively). Analysis of ICT usage by sex, showed that more men than women were using ICT, but the difference was non-significant. The majority of users were from the 65–74 years age group. In the population as a whole the number of users decreases by around 50 % for each extra decade of age e.g. 42 % of people in the 65–74 years age group were using a mobile phone; but this figure decrease to 22 % in the 75–84 years group and to 10 % in the 85 years and older group. As most of the study participants were in the 65–74 years age group we could not detect this pattern in our sample.

ICT usage varied with educational level. Most ICT users had some university education, whereas most of the people who were not educated above primary school level were non-users (See Fig. 1).

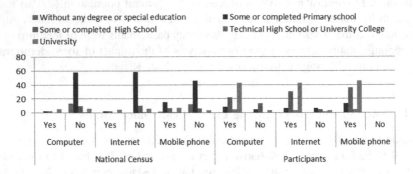

Fig. 1. ICT usage by educational level

The majority of the study participants, who had some university education or had graduated from high school, were active users.

The relationships between ICT usage and employment and disabilities were also investigated. The 39 % of users in the general population and 71.2 % of users in the study participants) were pensioners, employees or independent workers, and thus had a medium or high income. ICT users in the general population (14 % of computers users, 7 % of Internet users and 38 % of mobile phone users) reported no disability, whereas around 90 % of people reporting a disability were non-users. In comparison around 30 % of study participants reporting a disability were non-users. Mobile phones were used by 23 % of people in the general population with a sensory impairment, 19 % of people with a motor impairment and 9 % with an intellectual impairment. All the study participants with some kind of impairment were using a mobile phone.

To summarize, at national level only around 11 % of older people were using computers and the Internet, although 32 % were using a mobile phone. People from urban areas have better access to ICT than those in rural areas. ICT usage is most common in the 65–74 years age group. Although the most frequent educational level categories for the general population were some primary school education and completed primary school, most ICT users had some university education; they also tended to have a medium or high income level and to be without disability. This information suggests that as well as being age-based, the digital divide is also related to socioeconomic status. The majority of our participants represented the active users from the national level. The composition of our sample allowed us to gain a better understanding of usage patterns among older Costa Ricans users.

3.3   ICT Access and Usage Among Study Participants

In an attempt to explain the gap between access and usage we asked our participants what ICT devices were available to them personally. The majority (76.9 %) had access to, and were using, a smartphone, 59.3 % were using the Internet and 54.2 % were

Table 3. Devices for personal use and knowledge of public spaces with free access to computers and internet

Devices	n (%)	Places	n (%)
Smartphone	45 (76,3)	Cafe internet	28 (47,5)
Internet	35 (59,3)	Public universities	16 (27,1)
Laptop	32 (54,2)	Libraries	9 (15,3)
Mobile phone	31 (52,5)	Municipalities	7 (11,9)
Desktop	21 (35,6)	NGO	7 (11,9)
Tablet	21 (35,6)	None of the above	16 (27,1)

using a laptop. The least commonly used ICT devices (35.6 %) were the desktop computer and the tablets (See Table 3).

We wanted to distinguish between mobile phones with basic functionality only (voice calls and SMS) and smartphones (touchscreen interface, operating system and Internet access). Although we explained the difference to participants some were confused and the answers in this item about mobile phone could not be very accurate, in another item we clarified this issue when asked about the type of mobile phone they were using, results are presented in the section about mobile phone and internet usage.

Mobile devices and the Internet were the devices that participants most willingly use. Although tablets are a relatively new category of mobile device a significant number of participants were using them, reinforcing the idea of that older people are interested and willing to adopt new mobile devices and take advantage of their connectivity. We also asked participants if they knew of any public institutions and organizations offering access to computers and the Internet. Internet cafés were the most frequently mentioned public-access option, only 27.1 % knew that public universities offered this service and fewer than 20 % mentioned other options; 27.1 % did not have information about public options.

Mobile Phone and Internet Usage Among Study Participants. Most study participants were using smartphones. The most frequent use for mobile phones and smartphones was voice calling, followed by texting and instant messaging; Internet searching was less common (See Table 4).

The most commonly used applications were those related to social interaction (mobile messaging, social networking and email) followed by leisure application (video sharing and online games) and finally functional applications (reminders, weather, Internet browsers and banking). Smartphones were used for social interaction and, to a certain extent, in support of instrumental activities of daily life. Increasing knowledge and use of such applications for instrumental tasks represents an opportunity to use ICT to support independence and autonomy in daily life.

The majority of participants (47) were using the Internet on several devices, most (61 %) were going online several times a day and spent four or more hours a week using the Internet (See Table 5).

We asked participants if the number of hours they had spent online in the last week was typical; 67.8 % confirmed that it was whilst 10.2 % reported that it had been an atypical week.

Table 4. Type of mobile phone, uses and applications

Mobile phone	N (%)	Mobile phone applications	Count [a]
Type:		Mobile messaging (Whatsapp, Messenger, Line, Viber)	56
Smartphone	48 (81,4)	Social networking (Facebook Twitter)	27
Mobile phone	11 (18,6)	Email	16
Uses:		Video-sharing website (Youtube)	9
Voice calling	58 (98,3)	Video chat and voice call (Skype, Line, Viber)/Reminders (notes, agendas, reminders)	7
Texting (SMS)	48 (81,4)	Online games/Picture editing	6
Mobile messaging	42 (71,2)	Weather/Traffic and navigation/Mapping	4
Internet searching	35 (59,3)	Bowsers (Chrome, Safari, Firefox)/Internet banking	3

[a] n = 48, but the answer reflects how many applications participants were using e.g. if a participant was using messenger and line then both applications were counted.

Table 5. Start Internet use, frequency and hours per week using Internet

Starting	n (%)	Frequency	n = 47 (%)	Hours per week	n = 47 (%)
More than 1 year	39 (66,1)	More than once a day	36 (61,0)	More than 5	20 (33,9)
1 year	7 (11,9)	Once or twice a week	5 (8,5)	4 or 5	11 (18,6)
6 months	4 (6,8)	Once a day	4 (6,8)	2 or 3	9 (15,3)
N/A	9 (15,3)	Twice monthly	2 (3,4)	1 or less	7 (11,9)
		N/A	12 (20,3)	N/A	12 (20,3)

We found that eight of the Internet non-users in our sample had some primary school education or some high school education. Internet non-users also reported low monthly incomes (between 370 and 750 USD). Five of them did not have access to the Internet at home and had mobile phones with basic functionality; only two knew about public spaces offering free access to the Internet. This profile corresponds to that of non-users in the general population. It highlights the fact that people with limited access to ICT have little information about opportunities to use ICT devices free of charge. Finally, we found that four of the non-users were people who had a technical or university education; these non-users did have access to the Internet at home.

We asked Internet users about their performance of 26 ICT-based activities and ranked these activities according to percentage of participants who reported performing them (see Table 6).

Between 50–83 % of participants reported performing the top ten activities. Most participants sent or read emails. The next most common activities were related to social interaction (staying in touch with distant friends, using social networking and instant messaging, in that order). The second most important category of the top activities was accessing health and wellness information. The middle positions in the top ten were occupied by other activities related to social interaction and the lower top ten positions were occupied by activities related to leisure and instrumental activities. Turning to the ten least commonly performed activities, the bottom positions were occupied by social

Table 6. Most and least commonly performed ICT-based activities (n = 47)

Top performed ICT based activities	n (%)	Lowest performed ICT based activities	n (%)
Send or read e-mail	39 (83,0)	Do any banking online	13 (27,7)
Staying in touch with distant friends	36 (76,6)	Participate in informal educational processes	12 (25,5)
Using social networking sites	34 (72,3)	Buy or make a reservation for a travel service, like an airline ticket, hotel room	11 (23,4)
Send "instant messages" to someone who's online at the same time	32 (68,1)	Play a game online	11 (23,4)
Look for health and wellness information	32(68,1)	Buy a product online, such as books, music, toys or clothing	9 (19,1)
Staying in touch with local friends	31 (66,0)	Exchange personal stories	6 (12,8)
Make a phone call online, using the internet	27 (57,4)	Participate in formal educational processes	6 (12,8)
Look for information about movies, music, books	26 (55,3)	Reading or participating in blogs	3 (6,4)
Look for products and services	25 (53,2)	Participating in forums	0
Explore personal educational needs or interests	24 (51,1)	Participating in an online virtual world	0

participation activities such as having a personal say, taking an active role in producing or exchanging information and participating in formal learning. Playing online games occupied a middle position; whilst this is a leisure activity it requires players to take an active role. The highest positions were occupied by instrumental activities (online banking; online shopping) and informal educational activities. It is important to note that although ICT has the potential to facilitate learning few older people were using ICT for formal or informal learning. Internet users took advantage of ICT to enhance their social interaction, but they tended to be passive consumers of information from the Internet and did not take advantage of its interactivity to produce and share information; this reduces its potential to promote social inclusion.

3.4   Older People's Needs, Motivations and Barriers to Using ICT

The two most frequently cited motivations for using ICT did not correspond with the most commonly performed activities; they were in fact related to instrumental activities: "I realize that they are useful in daily life" and "I think it is important to be up to date and know about new technologies (both cited by 50.8 %). The third most frequently given reason was "To communicate with family members" (33.9 %). Less frequently cited motivations were "Job/working motivations" (18.6 %) and "I knew about ICT courses for older people" (8.55 %).

Table 7. Barriers to learning about and using ICT (n = 50)

Barrier	n	%
Memory problems, or difficulty to understand the information	20	40
It is not easy to understand information in different devices (amount, size and disposition on information in different software)	17	34
The teaching and learning processes are not adequate for older people	17	34
There are not enough opportunities to learn how to use ICT	11	22
Access to devices and applications	7	14
Psychomotor disabilities (problems with specific movements on hands)	3	6
Disabilities in vision or hearing	2	4
Other	19	38

The most common method of learning to use ICT among our 54 users was by participating in special courses for older people (42.6 %), followed by with the help of a young person (37 %) and by oneself (20.4 %). Participants reported that their biggest difficulties in learning and using ICT related to their cognitive performance (declining memory and attention), followed by courses are not appropriate/suitable courses for older people and lack of learning opportunities. Sensory and psychomotor impairments were not important barriers for them (see Table 7).

Most of the barriers in mentioned in the "Other" category were individual factors such as "fear" or "shame". Participants reported that memory or attention problems meant that during tuition they frequently forgot the instructions and information; they felt that the people who were teaching them did not have enough patience and such situations made them feel ashamed and anxious. They also reported being afraid of making a mistake that would damage equipment or result in loss of information. Other barriers to learning about and using ICT were lack of practice at learning things and that devices and software display information in a language in which participants are not fluent (sometimes most of the available information is in English).

The overwhelming majority of participants (93.2 %) reported that they had the capacity to use ICT devices and applications without discomfort, stress, or fatigue, so physical factors were not a barrier to usage. Only 2 participants responded negatively to this question about physical capacity. To gain more insight into the relationship between ICT usage and psychophysical factors we analyzed associations between ICT usage in the last three months and items in the Experiences with current technology subscale from the SOTU (See Table 8).

The majority of users described their current experiences with technologies in positive terms (being satisfying, adding to their creativity, encouraging and bringing them closer to people). However some users were neutral to negative in their responses. More specifically, some participants reported that although ICT brought them closer to distant family or friends, it sometimes separated them from people in the interactions of daily life.

When emotions related to technology at different stage of life were evaluated in the SOTU "use and perspective subscale" user's responses were positive. But, most participants had not had access to technology at school (95 %) or during childhood

Table 8. People using ICT in the last three months by use and experience with current technologies from SOTU

	Frustrating	Neutral	Satisfying
Computer users [a]	3	1	42
Internet users [b]	2	1	46
Mobile phone users[c]	4	2	53
	Interferes with creativity	Neutral	Help creativity
Computer users	0	4	42
Internet users	0	4	45
Mobile phone users	0	5	54
	Separates me from people	Neutral	Brings me together with people
Computer users	6	5	34
Internet users	6	5	37
Mobile phone users	8	7	43
	Discouraging	Neutral	Encouraging
Computer users	1	3	42
Internet users	0	3	46
Mobile phone users	2	3	54
	Lowers my opinion of self	Neutral	Raises my opinion of self
Computer users	2	5	39
Internet users	1	5	43
Mobile phone users	2	6	51

[a] n = 46 computers users.
[b] n = 49 Internet users.
[c] n = 59 mobile phone users.

(86 %). Users were favorably disposed to using technology, and in the "personal and social characteristics" subscale the majority of users described themselves in positive terms, reporting characteristics such as being calm, positive, persevering, physically and emotionally independent.

4 Discussion and Conclusions

We found that few older people were using ICT in the general population (11 % were using computers and the Internet; 32 % were using mobile phones). Most of the active ICT users were between 64 and 75 years old, living in urban areas, and were high school graduates or had some university education; they also tended to have a medium or high income and to be without disability. In contrast most of the non-users were people who had not been educated beyond primary school and had a low income; this indicates that the digital divide is not just age-based but is also related to socio-economic factors. There is an association between socio-economic factors and the social and cultural background which is necessary to a willingness to learn and use technology and this factor would help to account for the gap between access and usage. Most participants were active ICT users and fitted the profile of ICT users in the population; non-users in our sample also shared the same profile as non-users in the general population.

The most commonly used ICTs were mobile devices and the Internet, indicating that mobility and connectivity were important drivers of usage. In the population and in our sample the mobile phone was the most commonly used ICT, suggesting that it has potential as a gateway device for promoting ICT literacy. Examining use of smartphone applications and online activities we found that the most frequently performed activities were related to social interaction and leisure, whilst the least frequently performed were related to learning, social participation and instrumental activities.

Online activities reflect ICT usage to maintain a social "engaged life" one of the most powerful predictor of successful aging [4]. But increasing the use of ICT for instrumental activities, social participation and learning would promote better functional status and more independence and autonomy among older people. Use of ICT for learning should be promoted, as learning activities and other forms of cognitive stimulation may counteract cognitive decline [2, 15–19]. Despite the potential of ICT to facilitate the development of flexible learning models, combining self-managed and organized education, which would give older people the additional time they sometimes need for processing and reflection on new information [6], the analyses suggest that the low usage of ICT for learning were due to perceived non-availability of relevant learning options and programs.

Users in our sample had positive perceptions of technology, and they were favorably disposed towards using it and self-reported positive personal and social characteristics; a similar user profile was reported by Vroman et al. [10]. The most frequently cited barriers to learning about and using ICT were external barriers such as lack of learning opportunities and inadequate learning environments.

According to the Information and Communication Technology Social Networking Motivational model proposed for older adults by Vroman et al. [10], our participants were in the first level of ICT adoption, i.e. they used ICT mainly to support personal relationships and for social networking with family and friends. They were also using ICT to access information, an activity associated with the second level of the model; the other component of this second level is "performing instrumental tasks online". The final level is "sharing through online groups and communities".

In conclusion the main challenges in the promotion of healthy aging among older Costa Ricans are: ensuring that most older people benefit from ICT, promoting the "higher" levels of ICT adoption [10] and promoting learning as an activity, which includes learning for personal development [6]. Nevertheless, older people largely have positive perceptions of ICT and are favorably disposed towards using it, thus, the existence of a public ICT infrastructure and the creation of community-based learning services present opportunities to overcome the digital divide and promote healthy aging. However services must be tailored to the needs and characteristics of older people and it is important to ensure that information about services reaches the target audience.

Limitations. Since the call for participants was made in institutions providing educational opportunities and social activities for older adults, our sample contained a high proportion of older adults who were already using ICT and were interested in improving their knowledge and skills. These sample characteristics limit the conclusions we can draw from our data and the generalizability of the findings. There is a need to reach older adults who are non-users of ICT, particularly older adults with disabilities and those living in rural areas.

References

1. Baltes, P.B., Baltes, M.M.: Successful Aging: Perspective from the Behavioral Sciences. Cambridge University Press, Canada (1993)
2. Fernández-Ballesteros, R., Molina, M.A., Schettini, R., Del Rey, A.L.: Promoting active aging through university programs for older adults an evaluation study. GeroPsych **25**(3), 145–154 (2012)
3. World Health Organization: Active Aging: A Policy Framework. http://whqlibdoc.who.int/hq/2002/WHO_NMH_NPH_02.8.pdf?ua=1
4. Rowe, J.W., Kahn, R.L.: Successful aging. Gerontologist **37**, 433–440 (1997)
5. Fernández-Ballesteros, R., Caprara, M., García, C.: Vivir con vitalidad-M: a european multimedia programme. Psychol. Spain **9**(1), 1–12 (2005)
6. Ala-Mutka, K., Malanowsky, N., Punie, Y., Cabrera, M.: Active Ageing and the Potential of ICT for Learning. [Version Adobe Digital editions] (2008). doi:10.2791/33182
7. Charness, N., Boot, W.: Aging and information technology use. Curr. Dir. Psychol. Sci. **18**(5), 253–258 (2009)
8. Czaja, S.J., Charness, N., Fisk, A.D., Hertzog, C., Nair, S.N., Rogers, W.A., Sharit, J.: Factors predicting the use of technology: findings from the center for research and education on aging and technology enhancement (CREATE). Psychol. Aging **21**(2), 333–352 (2006). doi:10.1037/0882-7974.21.2.333
9. Sagayo, S., Forbes, P., Blat, J.: Older people becoming successful ICT learners over time: challenges and strategies through an ethnographical lens. Educ. Gerontol. **39**, 527–544 (2013)
10. Vroman, K.G., Arthanat, S., Lysack, C.: "Who over 65 is online?" Older adults' dispositions toward information communication technology. Comput. Human Behav. **43**, 156–166 (2015)
11. European Commission: Eurostats. Individuals frequently using the internet. http://ec.europa.eu/eurostat/tgm/refreshTableAction.do;jsessionid=Zyj7xgvEHH3XdLb1YPDJM-Rua4b5Cn7AlqlDZArOsdKKkEs0Yk9j!-1797539252?tab=table&plugin=0&pcode=tin00092&language=en
12. Instituto Nacional de Estadística y Censos (INEC): Censo 2011 (2012). http://www.inec.go.cr/Web/Home/GeneradorPagina.aspx
13. Folstein, M.F., Folstein, S.E., McHugh, P.R.: "Mini-mental state": a practical method for grading the cognitive state of patients for the clinician. J. Psychiatr. Res. **12**(3), 189–198 (1975)

14. Scherer, M.J., Craddock, G.: Matching Person & Technology (MPT) assessment process. Technol. Disabil. Spec. Issue Assess. Assistive Technol. Outcomes Eff. Costs **14**, 125–131 (2002)
15. Fernández-Ballesteros, R.: Active Aging: The Contribution of Psychology. Hogrefe & Huber, Göttingen (2008)
16. Schaie, K.W.: Developmental Influences on Adult Intelligence: The Seattle Longitudinal Study. Oxford University Press, New York (2005)
17. Schaie, K.W.: What can we learn from longitudinal studies of adult development? Res. Hum. Dev. **2**, 133–158 (2005)
18. Willis, S., Tennstedt, S., Marsiske, M., Ball, K., Elias, J., Koepke, K., Wright, E.: Long-term effects of cognitive training on everyday functional outcomes in older adults. J. Am. Med. Assoc. **296**(23), 2805–2814 (2006)
19. Baltes, P.B., Staudinger, U.M., Lindenberger, U.: Lifespan psychology: theory and application to intellectual functioning. Annu. Rev. Psychol. **50**, 471–507 (1999)

The Mediations of the Identity of Seniors on IT.
The Case of Grand Parenthood

Élodie Llobet-Vachias and Yves Jeanneret(✉)

GRIPIC, CELSA, Paris Sorbonne University, Paris, France
yves.jeanneret@celsa.paris-sorbonne.fr

Abstract. This paper studies a particular way to categorize people as "grand parents" instead of considering them simply as "seniors". It describes several communicational approaches and questions the consequences of such a choice on the relation of people with IT, and especially computer mediated communication. The empirical basis of this research is constituted by the observation of several associative, political and economic organizations devoted to the defense and institutionalization of grand parenthood as a social form in France.

Keywords: Computer mediated communication · Generation · Grand parenthood · Mediation · Senior · Social categorization · Stereotype

This paper aims to contribute to the analysis of the social uses of IT by aged people in a particular perspective: (1) to study the way people assume the familial role of grand parents, instead of assigning them to an aged-based category as "seniors"; (2) to address the problem, not by opposing stereotypes and practices, rather by analysing how they become interdependent, when actors, institutions, firms pursue the objective to invent a social form, which is called in French *"grand parentalité"* (we can approximately translate as *grand parenthood*)[1] to structure it and to legitimate it; (3) to consider IT in the wide sense of various info-communicational devices by which this mediation [7, 23] can be embodied, including computer mediated communication (from now on CMC) as other media practices.

Our inquiry is grounded in the tradition of analysis of media practices, but also in the works about the social mediation of knowledge and culture [12]. The concrete basis of our research is an inquiry into several organisations (associative, editorial, industrial ones) the main activity of which is to take part in the recognition of grand parenthood. We plan to determine the place they attribute to the appropriation of media and especially CMC by grand parents, on symbolic, imaginary and practical levels.

After having discussed the process of construction of the category itself, we propose to identify major issues of this interaction between representations and computer

---

[1] The French « grand parentalité », which is of common use for the organizations we study, is much more abstract and symbolic than english equivalents as « grand parenting » or « grand parenthood ». In different texts as « Rhétorique de l'image » and *Mythologies* [4, 5], Roland Barthes uses words as « italianité » (for Italy) or « sinité » (for China) to stress the imaginary dimension of categories. It sounds like "parentality".

© Springer International Publishing Switzerland 2016
J. Zhou and G. Salvendy (Eds.): ITAP 2016, Part II, LNCS 9755, pp. 207–216, 2016.
DOI: 10.1007/978-3-319-39949-2_20

mediated communication, then to comment on some examples of organisational projects in their own history and specificity.

1   Some Social Constructions of the Idea of Generation

Everybody can observe the words we use about aged people to be all but natural. They are social constructs linked to precise stakes and projects. They change with time (for instance the way kids call their grand parents: in France "*mamie*" looked very modern in the 60's when "*mémé*" became obsolete, but it sounds now very dated); but also with social censure (we say rather "third age" than "elderly", as we say "hearing-impaired" instead of "deaf"). Categorization plays a role in the construction of our means of thinking because it is dependent on different interests of knowledge [13]: it has many consequences on the questions we can or cannot ask. For instance, the French nomenclatures about life ages were elaborated, first by State offices for surveys, and then by marketing techniques in order to target groups of consumers. The category of "seniors" must be considered that way. It is a compromise between the pragmatic aim to identify a profitable target and the social necessity to offer a positive representation of an age which is currently associated with negative connotations. It is also a means to shift the boundaries between the groups. For instance, as says advertising expert Alyette Defrance, "The category of seniors works better as long as the 4th age exists. The discourse on the dynamism and eternal youth of Seniors stresses implicitly the distance with the 4th age by opposing 'privileges' to 'handicaps'" [11, 158][2]. We have no room here to develop this analysis, but we can recall three major milestones for our subject. First, it is a dynamic process and, in a society in which youth is a value, aged people can be qualified as young; second, any categorization serves certain interests, which can be political, economic, scientific ones; third, the dominant actor of this process, marketing, privileges the "core meaning" of life styles defined by the social value of certain practices and objects. Now we can note it is very important for the question we are studying, because, both in the representation of aged people and in the way CMC is considered, the strength of this process of categorization is considerable.

On the one hand, the discourse about generations is engaged in the success of the industry of computers and networks, which has gradually developed a real "generational storytelling" [1]. The idea of youth is at the heart of the promotion of technical revolutions, which take their strength from their capacity to be in line with a society that gives value to novelty and health and dynamism. This powerful rhetoric lines up a set of notions which are related by metonymic relations: young, new, futurist vs. old, obsolete, backward-looking. It is not rare, from the times "digital era" opened, that the succession of human generations should be defined in reference to that process of innovation in technologies, like calling adolescents "Internet generation" or "F[acebook] generation". Moreover, the constant innovation, which makes this industry profitable, is frequently formulated in terms of successive *generations*, a word easily used both to qualify persons and machines. One of the major French associations about CMC in France is called

---

[2] Strategic planning manager of the leading French advertising agency, *Publicis*.

"Internet New Generation Federation"[3], playing with the ambiguity between technical innovation and life ages.

On the other hand, the dynamic evolution of the representations hinges widely on the fact of denying ageing and so to speak of rejuvenating the elderly. This, in relation with real evolutions in life expectancy, familial relations and consumption – the average age to become a grand parent in France is 54 for women and 56 for men [6] and most grand parents are professionally active –; but also with the affirmation of youth, health, novelty, future. A new definition of aged populations asserts itself, combatting and reinforcing at the same time the stereotyped representation of "old" grand parents as conservative, tired, old-fashioned people in advertising and entertainment [20]. The phrase "New grand parents" sums up this new way to depict the social group with features usually attributed to young generations. Logically, the reference to uses of IT plays a major role in that kind of relooking of previous generations.

2   Categorization and Relation to Technology

In front of this omnipresent discourse, some actors contribute in a very different way to building social categories: they first consider people, not by their age, but by their familial role as grand parents. As we shall see below, it is not sufficient to emancipate those projects from the imaginary of ages; but it leads to a different way to theorize the relation between generations and media. We shall try first to figure the main difference between categorizations in terms of seniors and grand parents, and see then the interactions between the two points of view.

We observe here the process of institutionalization of a social form. The consideration of the role of grand parents is not new – even if the category moved a lot a century along – but the claim for a specific identity, is. We can observe it through the creation of associations, the publishing of guidebooks, the creation of platforms devoted to such a community, the setting of training programs and even, in France, of a school, the "School of European Grand parents" (École des grands parents européens, from now on EGPE).

There are two main differences between those two ways to categorize people. First, if you define people by the means of age difference, you privilege "factors of differentiation", to use marketing vocabulary, in order to singularize groups: so are digital natives, so are active adults, so are seniors, so is 4th age. On the contrary, the category of grand parents cannot be defined without referring to the relation it forms with other generations, not only with grand-children but with the intermediate generation [2].

Such a difference is important for the way we problematize the relation between people and technologies. In an approach grounded on age targets, the succession of human generations is usually defined in reference to that process of innovation in technologies. From that viewpoint, aged people are usually associated with the idea of "digital immigrants", people who enter CMC as strangers, coming from an ancient world. In contrast, the young audience appears as the representative of the future in our

---

[3] http://fing.org/. Visited on feb. 4th, 2016.

world and, in an industrial strategy, the promise of success in the uncertainty of present[4]. Aged people are facing a test they can pass or fail, entering "information society". On the contrary, grand parents can be apprehended through the nature, the sense and finality of their role as social actors.

Symmetrically, instead of being an objective in itself, CMC can help or handicap this social role. In an approach focused on the role of grand parents, what is decisive is the way familial and social relations develop, not the ability of individuals to cope with technical skills. To quote a famous phrase, the question is to consider attentively *"what people do with media"* instead of focusing on *"what media do to people"* [17, 3]. The aim of the enquiry is not to evaluate the acceptability of the media, but to explore the sense of meeting, information retrieving, dialoguing. In this perspective, CMC appears as a new means to actualize practices, commitments and relations that have developed for years through previous communication devices. For instance the EGPE has a rich expertise in the media creativity, as the creation of phone service for care, or the diversion of holidays notebooks or comics for popular education purposes, and the creation of *kits* in order to equip interveners in situations [21]. With a very important methodological consequence: people are not by principle classified according to their ability, but by the aims they share. So we can find, in the same field of practices, both people who are very fond of CMC and people who never use it.

3   Building an Intergenerational Perspective

Nevertheless, even if this approach in terms of familial roles modifies significantly the means to address the uses of media, it is impossible to strictly distinguish between those two ways to categorize people, as actors of intergenerational relations, and as individuals of the same age – as grand parents and as seniors. Such representations constantly interfere. So, as soon as *IT, the Net, Digital* come to be mentioned, this idea mainly refers to social stereotypes and is part of what Roger Silverstone calls "Media morality": the implication of media innovations in our conception of identity and otherness [22].

Such a reality lies on four interdependent processes that have been pointed out for a long time by socio-semiotic studies on communicational practices: (a) the fact that the stereotypes are not only deceptive conceptions that could be simply corrected, but rather major ingredients of culture and identity; (b) the link between the perceptions of ages and the imaginaries of time; (c) the reality of the generational experience in which each of us in different historical contexts builds different relations to the media; (d) the fact that media practices do not operate as pure technical abilities, but refer to collective memories and to forms of life. For instance, the EGPE mentioned above (a) uses the imagery of grandmothers knitting pull-overs for kids which is the symbol *par excellence* of an epoch, in order to organize one of its successful activities; (b) argues the duty of transmission from past to future to convince people to intervene voluntarily in schools;

---

[4] Debate at the Celsa « Le public jeune : promesse ou mirage ? », may 16th, 2011, (*Young audience: a promise or a mirage?*). Streaming online: https://www.youtube.com/watch? v=zkQzYZnQrnY. With a thematic note: http://www.celsa.fr/pub/lesentretiens/LePublic-Jeune.pdf. Visited on feb. 3th 2016.

(c) is facing the fact the association was created in a very different media environment than ours; (d) has much debate about what signifies using for instance social networks instead of books.

The weight of stereotypical representations of each generation is particularly impressive in advertising and branding. One of the leading brands in the food industry is named "Mamie Nova", a common friendly name for grandmothers. Far from any intergenerational signification, it operates as a metonymy of age, which is not less present in the Internet. In this way we can find *Mamie regale* (www.mamieregale.fr, *Mummy is treating*), a platform that puts in touch amateur cooks with customers, or "le gang de grand-mères (http://gangdegrandmeres.fr/fr/, *Racket of grand-mothers*), a factory of fashion commodities paying 10 % of their incomes to an association of leisure for seniors.

But what is more central for our inquiry is the way the two perspectives collide in particular communicational devices. We have an interesting example with the guide-books devoted to this mediation. Editing a guide is a way to define a social form, not only by practices, rather by knowledge and know-how. The guidebook tells us we can identify ourselves as grand parents, but we have to learn how to be completely so. The titles of the books are interesting in that respect. One of them [18] is entitled "Les nouveaux grands-parents" (*The new Grand parents*) and another one [19] entitled "Grands-parents et malins" (*Grand parents and cunning*) includes a subtitle that evokes "les grands-parents *nouvelle generation*" (*the* New generation *Grand parents*"). The stereotype of *seniors* is implied in the definition of the intergenerational project: grand parents are young and their generation is new. They are not 4th age people.

Even more interesting is the way the reference to new media works in the guidebook itself. The ability to use IT is not a central topic of these books, which are published by authors who belong to traditional media industries, i.e. editing in one case, TV in the other[5]. The use of contemporary communication tools does not occupy a wide space in those books; it intervenes in the middle of the books, and it is not regarded in itself but as a means to develop specific relations with grand-children. Nevertheless, the need to introduce grand parents to a world they are supposed to ignore is evident, because those chapters include a methodical popularization, not only of technical tools, but also of young people uses. In a chapter entitled "Remain connected", we read: "You can not only speak to them by video conference or follow their holiday achievements by photo sharing, but also enter their life (without interfering except in dangerous situations) by seeing who are their friends and interests" [18, 110]. Which is rather astonishing if we remember it is devoted to "new grand parents". Moreover, it acts in a paradoxical way: far from rejuvenating, it makes grand parents older. In one book, CMC (illustrated by a couple in front of a laptop) is introduced by the title "Quel coup de vieux!" (a familiar expression stressing a brutal aging); in the other, it is approached in relation to the last years of life ("Les petits-enfants grandissent et les grands-parents vieillissent": *Grand-children are growing and grand parents are ageing*).

---

[5] *Les nouveaux grands parents* is a derived product from a program broadcasted on the TV channel France 5, ("Les maternelles").

Nevertheless, the content of those chapters does not stress the performance of mastering digital tools, rather the role they can play in the development of new and original relations between generations. The opposition between "digital natives" and "digital immigrants" is at stake to the extent using network technology is presented as a strict condition to enter the world of kids. But different examples illustrate what Austin [3] calls "felicity" in communication, because they describe the family enjoying the presence and wisdom of grand parents. Considering seriously the role of grand parents softens the brutality of stereotypes in the use of digital media. When seniors are approached via the category of grand parenthood, they are no more digital immigrants, but rather *digital guests*.

4 'Grandparent Generation' as a Metaphor

We propose now to move to a more accurate observation of the way "*grand parenta-lité*" affects the manner media practices are involved in different projects.

For this purpose, we must briefly go back over some major conclusions of the research developed on the question of generations in social sciences. We can sum up three interdependent definitions of the concept of generation. Of course it refers to different stages of life; but it depends also on historical periods and, especially, of different stages of development and innovation of media techniques and culture; at last, people do not completely belong to a generation if they do not think themselves to belong to it, both because they use this designation and they are assigned to it by the social and vernacular discourse [1]. For instance, many grand parents belong to the generation called "*baby boomers*" and were represented as "*teen-agers*" in the beginning of the 60's; but many "new grand parents" are people "who did not do 68" [8], being too young then, and even some of them were called "generation X" [10] in the early 90's. All those people did not share the same dominant values nor the same experience of media inno-vation and in their life the arrival of colour TV, "pirate" radio stations and the Macintosh played different roles.

So, when approaching the media culture of several organizations which are acting for *grand parentalité*, we have to consider altogether the building of the category, the historical experience of actors, and the way media are invested for the goals of each organisation. But one process seems to be common to all the organizations we studied: the mutation of the category of grand parents to a social and political form. It is a kind of metaphor: grand parenting, which is a biological and familial process, becomes the icon of a kind of social commitment. In the programmatic discourses of many organi-zations we find the phrase "grand parent generation". In rational terms, the population of grand parents do not constitute a generation: it does gather several generations, as we just saw. But to invent a "grand parent generation" conveys to that heterogeneous community a universal dimension and draws a simple biological condition to become a stance, a role in front of the world. Gradually, it allows to attach to the category people who have no relation to real grand-children, but are considered as *potential grand parents*, and even people who are invited to consider themselves as "grand parents de cœur" (grandparents at heart): people having affective relations with the generation of children without any familial link. This metaphoric role of grand parenthood includes by principle any person of the third or fourth age in the same mission, because they embody the attention paid to intergenerational relations. It is a kind of mission: a specific duty of grand parents in the society. So, each time somebody commits to a cause explicitly as a grand parent, this act conveys a particular added value and brings a specific strength to the project.

5 Organizational Stories

The two actors who first defined their identity by the category of *grand parentalité* in France emerged from the frame of associative life in the 90's: the School of European Grand parents (EGPE) yet mentioned (1994), and the *Grands parrains* (*Grand godparents* 1998). Such organizations were joining the associative tradition by grounding on voluntary work and physical meetings, and at the same time by drawing their values and models from the bookish culture of their founders, who were then young grand mothers[6]. Digital communication was not an issue for them in a time innovation reached mainly "early adopters", who were very few here[7]. Those two initiatives had the effect to legitimate the idea grand parents to have a social role beyond the strict frame of the family. In that respect, the approach developed by *Grands parrains* is especially interesting. Its purpose is really to create the category of "grandparents at heart". It releases the grand parental link from biology by giving the media the role of matching "potential grand parents" with "adoptive grand children", what is impossible without resorting to communicational devices, even if very classical ones. Thanks to organizational and communicational means, people are supposed no more to put up with grand parenting, but to choose it.

The landscape or the actors of *grand parentalité* took a new turn in the 2000's with the creation of the firm *Super-grand parents*, which professed the same goal as *Grand-godparents*, i.e. to create "grandparents at heart", but in a doubly original way. First, it was initiated by the "middle generation", the one of parents[8]. Second, instead of grounding on a traditional associative format, it created an original type of mediation, so to make the program of "grand parentalité" enter an economically viable model. And it is the innovation in the media structure itself and in the exploitation of digital media specific properties that was fostering the circulation between associative and economic relations, which is indispensable to this business model. Beyond the punctual use of the image of grand parents with the sole end of advertising and merchandising, *grand parentalité* becomes the core of both business and intergenerational links which is characteristic of the "industry of passages" [15]. So this economic actor is a forerunner in the re-categorization of seniors on a grand parental angle, even if on the basis of an

---

[6] Marie-Françoise Fuchs for the EGPE and Annick Glorieux for Grand-Godparents.

[7] The Internet, which is then 30 years old as a scientific device, becomes a common tool in France in the late 90's.

[8] http://www.super-grandparents.fr/fr/why_grandparents.awp. Visited on feb. 5th 2016. Founder: Christelle Levasseur.

opportunist operation linked to its activity, rather than as a real marketing analysis of the perspective the shift from seniors to grand parents opens on strategic possibilities.

After those two steps of associative and economic conceptions of grand parents, a third stage is reached with the creation in Norway of "Bestefoeldreaksionen", translated as "Grand parent climate campaign". An example of the way "grand parent generation" can use digital communication, as a basis and support for ideological and political action. Indeed, from their creation on, Grand parents for climate have been using digital tools as the real skeleton of the organization: through them they could recruit members and make their actions visible, and even make the cause to fertilize other European countries. It is a very different relation to media in regard of other organizations evoked above. For a deeper examination of the relation between the organizational structure and the media practices, we shall focus here on two examples: the EGPE and Grand parents for climate.

Even if it developed in a bookish and associative universe, EGPE has managed to conquer the world of mass media by positioning itself as the expert of "grand parentalité" and qualifying their members as spokespersons of grand parenthood. Such a strategy for recognition was not initially grounded on digital tools, rather on interpersonal relations and reputation. They choose now to put forward on the Internet a rhetoric of doing – showing the achievements of the organization in its workshops – instead of demonstrating knowledge and expertise. It is a particular positioning in the public sphere (which can be accepted and "excused" by the fact itself they are grand parents and it fits the representation of that category by the media); but it is also relevant with the fact associative life having structured itself widely on the consideration paid to experience compared with academic diplomas. The approach of Grand parents for the climate is totally different: as we just saw, CMC is structurally implied in the creation itself of the organization; so its active use expresses the will to lean on it in order to defend a cause which is presented as clearly surpassing grand parenthood.

6 Trivial Philosophies of Time

If we take a distance regarding the making of the mediation process as it was just described, we can understand media strategies contributing to a redefinition of important cultural categories. One of them is the way our society represents the relation between different scales of time, from immediate *hic et nunc* situations to anthropological perspectives, via historical changes. As said above, the usual way to articulate them is to associate youth with future and elderly with past. And we cannot deny this representation to be at stake in the mediation of *grand parentalité,* especially with the necessity to picture seniors as dynamic people facing the weight of the memories of the past.

In contrast, the affirmation of the abstract category of *grand parentalité* and the metaphoric role attributed to the "grand parent generation" permit a process of refashioning this complex of representations and practices. This, as a result of multiple recourses to media: popularizing the imagery of the category; embodying it in community platforms; mobilizing it in collective manifestations. The fact to institute the "grand parent generation" as the guarantor of the care of future generations offers the opportunity to inverse those temporal perspectives. In such a narrative, older generations – represented both by their wisdom as aged people and their "natural" role as "grandparents at heart" – become the representatives of the future destiny of nature and humanity. Young people are not thrown back to past, as "digital immigrants" are in the mainstream stereotype, but rather to "*presentism*" which is stigmatized as the ideology of our time [14], i.e. the legitimate but short-sighted moral of *carpe diem* which was powerfully glorified by cultural industries in the years of formation of these actors (*Dead Poets Society* 1989). Such assimilations, via the media, between a generation and a representation of times, is a kind of trivial philosophy of History. One the one hand, it reinterprets the destiny of the generation of "baby boomers", who were strongly committed in the cult of technical development and so took a responsibility in neglecting the environmental issues, in a rather euphoric way. On the other hand, it comes back strangely to the first roots of sustainable development in the 80's – forgetting the evolution this political cause has experienced in the following decades to a conciliation between the economy, society and environment [16]. Indeed, in the so-called *Bruntland Report* which is the real "bible" of this movement, the reference to the responsibility of generations is the core idea of a new political cause: "Humanity has the ability to make development sustainable to ensure that it meets the needs of the present without compromising the ability of future generations to meet their own needs" [8]. We could say the two main mythic narratives of our society, information society and sustainable development, collide here inside the process of categorizing generations media experience.

Finally, beyond the wide diversity of the actions that can be undertaken under the banner of grand parenthood, we can draw three general conclusions; first, it is impossible to understand the role played by IT innovations and uses without introducing them into the wider question of media and mediations; second, even if all the practices are displayed in front of us as contemporary ones – what they are really – they belong to temporal perspectives which are not separable from different epochs; third, the idea of generation is very a complex one, melting in an indissoluble way stereotypes and practices, and social creativity about the intergenerational process with rather fossilized and dividing figures of ages.

References

1. Aroldi, P., Colombo, F.: Questionning 'digital global generations'. Crit. Approach Northern Lights **11**, 175–190 (2013)
2. Attias-Donfut, C., Sagalen, M.: Grands-parents. La famille à travers les générations. Odile Jacob, Paris (2007)
3. Austin, J.L.: How to do Things with Words. Urmson, Oxford (1962)
4. Barthes, R.: Rhétorique de l'image. Communication **4–1**, 40–51 (1964)
5. Barthes, R.: Mythologies. Paladin, London (1962)
6. Blanpain, N., Lincot, L.: 15 millions de grands-parents. Insee Première, 1469 (2013)
7. Bolter, J.-D., Grusin, R.: Remediation. Understanding New Media. The MIT Press, Cambridge (1999)
8. Bruntland, G.-H. (ed.).: Our Common Future. From One Earth to One World. UNO, New-York (1987). http://www.un-documents.net/wced-ocf.htm
9. Colombo, F.: Boom. Storia di quelli che non hanno fatto il 68. Rizzoli, Milano (2008)

10. Coupland, D.: Generation X. Tales for an Accelerated Culture. St Martin's Press, New-York (1991)
11. Defrance, A.: Penser, classer, communiquer. Publicité et catégories sociales, Hermès **38**, 155–162 (2004)
12. Gellereau, M., Jeanneret, Y., Le Marec, J.: Social sciences and the communication of science and technology in France. Implications, experimentation and critique. In: Schiele, B., Claessens, M., Shunke, S. (eds.) Science Communication in the World. Practices, Theories and Trends, pp. 109–123. Springer, Dortrecht (2012)
13. Habermas, J.: Knowledge and Human Interests. Beacon Press, Boston (1972)
14. Hartog, F.: Regimes of Historicity. Presentism and Experiences of Time. Columbia U.P, New-York (2015)
15. Jeanneret, Y.: Critique de la trivialité. Les mediations de la communication, enjeu de pouvoir. Éditions non standard, Le Havre (2014)
16. Jeanneret, Y.: The epistemic jumble of sustainable development. In: Cheng, D., et al. (eds.) Communicating Science in Social Contexts. New models, New Practices, pp. 243–257. Springer, Dortrecht (2008)
17. Katz, E.: Mass communication research and the study of popular culture. Editorial Note Possible Future J. Stud. Public Commun. **2**, 1–6 (1951)
18. Lebreton, N., Vernin, M.: Les nouveaux grands-parents. La Martinière, Paris (2012)
19. Le Bras, F.: Grands-parents et malins. Le meilleur guide pour les grands-parents nouvelle génération. Quotidien-malin éditions, Paris (2014)
20. Llobet-Vachias, E.: Les grands-parents. Des seniors mais pas que... Étude des enjeux liés à l'évolution de la grand parentalité dans la société contemporaine et des représentations associées dans les médias. MS Dissertation. Paris Sorbonne University (Celsa) (2015)
21. Seurrat, A.: Les médias en kits pour promouvoir 'la diversité'. Les enjeux de l'information et de la communication (2010). http://w3.u-grenoble3.fr/les_enjeux/2010/Seurrat/home.html
22. Silverstone, R.: Media and Morality. On the Wide of the Mediapolis. Polity Press, Cambridge (UK) (2007)
23. Thonon. M. (ed.).: « Médiation et médiateurs ». Médiation & Information, 19 (2004)

Senior Citizens, Digital Information Seeking and Use of Social Media for Healthy Lifestyle

Ágústa Pálsdóttir(✉)

Faculty of Social and Human Sciences, University of Iceland,
Gimli v/Sæmundargötu, 101 Reykjavík, Iceland
agustap@hi.is

Abstract. The study investigated how Icelanders who are 60 years and older seek and communicate about digital health and lifestyle information of health and lifestyle information. Random samples were used and participants categorized into two groups, 60 to 67 years old and 68 years or older. The development of information seeking on the Internet in the years 2002, 2007 and 2012 was examined, as well as the use of social media in 2012. Data analysis was performed with ANOVA (one-way). The study revealed that the pattern of seeking and communicating about information was very similar for the age groups. The frequency for information seeking on the Internet was low for both groups, although it had increased since 2002. Results about social media revealed that both age groups chose to receive information rather than share it or communicate with others. The results further revealed that the frequency of using social media was low for both groups. The findings of the study indicate that senior citizens have not yet adapted to the digitalization of health and lifestyle information.

Keywords: Health information · Information seeking · Internet · Senior citizens · Social media

1 Introduction

The growing proportion of older people in the world's population is an established trend. The progress is expected to continue in the coming years, from 2013 to 2050 it is predicted that the number of people aged 60 years and older will more than double [1]. This poses challenges for the nations that need to prepare for the increasing number of senior citizens and ensure their quality of life. It involves promoting their possibilities to manage their everyday life affairs, as well as their prospects to participate in society and continue to contribute to it.

An important factor at enhancing the wellbeing and independence of older people is to encourage them to be actively involved in health promotional interventions, through life-long learning. To be able to obtain the necessary knowledge about healthy lifestyles people need to have an easy access to adequate information that satisfy their needs and can be obtained in a way that suit them.

The increasing digitalization of health related information provides opportunities for an easy access to it. Although it is well known that elderly citizens have adopted

© Springer International Publishing Switzerland 2016
J. Zhou and G. Salvendy (Eds.): ITAP 2016, Part II, LNCS 9755, pp. 217–226, 2016.
DOI: 10.1007/978-3-319-39949-2_21

information technology at a slower rate than those who are younger [2, 3], it has been suggested that, because those who are younger are more accustomed to using the internet in their work or private life, older people will gradually become more active users of the internet [4, 5].

Online access is a prerequisite for accessing information on the internet but other aspects should also be considered. Various factors have been identified that may have an impact on senior citizens use of information technology and act as barriers. This includes for example weak physical condition and health problems which can cause challenges for a certain group of elderly people [2]. Communication barriers, such as problems with the visual and auditory presentation of information [6], and changes in the motor ability which people can experience as they grow older [7], have also been recognized and can affect the ability to use digital devices. The group of seniors who is affected by this is probably in the greatest need for health related information. Therefore, it is every reason to focus on their abilities and make an effort to enable them to access the information. By taking the needs of elderly people into account when information technology is designed, for example with suitable interface design and touch screen solutions [8], some of the obstacles that they are faced with might be minimised.

Other essential matter which may have a bearing on the use of digital information is attitudinal issues. This includes for example aspects such as the perceived reliability of the information [9], or mistrust in it [10], as well as beliefs about the benefit of the information [9, 11]. In fact, if senior citizens consider the relevance of digital information to be high they are prone to make more effort at seeking it [5]. Attention has also been drawn to how important it is that senior citizens are health literate [12]. More recently, the significance of media and information literacy, or the ability to "…access, retrieve, understand, evaluate and use, create, as well as share information and media content in all formats…" has been recognized [13].

Social media (e.g. Facebook, Twitter, Wikipedia, and YouTube) has become increasingly important in peoples everyday lives and in the past few years and the use of it among senior citizens has been growing considerably [14–16]. Social media has proved to be influential in improving access to health related information [17, 18]. Contrary to traditional internet sources, such as webpages, newspapers or journals on the web, social media is characterized by a dialog where a number of people can communicate, exchange information and get feedback from each other [19]. It offers the possibility for groups, either broad and diverse groups consisting of strangers or more narrow and intimate, to connect and discuss shared health interests. Thus, by providing opinions and advice through social media, people may have impact on the health behaviour of others [20], as well as offer emotional support [21–23]. In addition, health specialists have the opportunity to employ it to disseminate quality information about healthy lifestyles.

The aim of the study is to investigate how Icelanders 60 years and older have adopted to the digitalization of health information. The paper will seek answers to the following research questions:

1. How has the frequency of digital information seeking about health and lifestyle developed, among Icelanders who are 60 years and older, in the period 2002, 2007 and 2012?
2. Do Icelanders who are 60 to 67 years old seek digital information about health and lifestyle more frequently than those who are 68 years and older?

It has been implied that senior citizens problems at using information technology will disappear, as those who are younger move up the age scale. Although the age limits for retirement varies widely across countries, it has been traditional in western countries to use the retirement age to define senior citizens [24]. Therefore it was decided to compare people at the age 60 to 67 years old, a group who is approaching retirement, with those who are 68 years or older, who in Iceland are defined by law as elderly [25]. The paper will present findings about how the health and lifestyle information seeking of these two age groups, in various sources on the internet, has developed in the years 2002, 2007 and 2012. In addition, results from the year 2012, about how they use social media in relation to health and lifestyle information, will be presented.

2 Methods

2.1 Data Collection

Data were gathered as postal surveys in 2002 and 2007. For both data sets random samples consisting of 1,000 people aged 18 to 80, from the whole country, was used. The response rate was 51 percent in 2002 and 47 percent in 2007. In 2012 data was gathered using an internet and a telephone survey from two random samples of 600 people each, aged 18 years and older from the whole country (oldest respondent was 92). The datasets were merged allowing answers from all individuals belonging to each set of data. Total response rate was 58 percent.

The current study involves participants in the age groups 60 to 67 years old and 68 years or older. The number of participants in each group is presented in Table 1.

Table 1. Number of participants by age group, in 2002, 2007 and 2012

Participants	2002	2007	2012
60–67	32	55	90
68+	44	61	90
Total	76	116	180

2.2 Measurements and Data Analysis

3. Socio-demographic information included traditional background variables. In the current analysis the variable age is used and participants 60 years and older were divided into two groups, those who are aged 60 to 67 years and those who are 68 years and older.

4. Information seeking on the internet was measured by asking 'Have you sought information about health and lifestyle in any of the following sources'? A five-point response scale was used (5: Very often – 1: Never). A list of over 20 information sources was presented but in this paper the focus is on sources on the internet. This includes five items: Discussion groups or news groups; Magazines or newspapers; Websites by the health authorities; Websites by others; Advertisements. Over the years, the questionnaire used in the surveys has developed in line with advances in technology and includes more digital sources in 2012 than in 2002. However, for comparison reasons it is important to use the same sets of measurements for the data from 2002, 2007 and 2012. Factor analysis (Principal Component) was used to produce scales from the list of all sources presented at the question. The criteria for factor loadings were set above 0.4, and oblique rotation (Oblimin) was adopted. Multiple criteria, based on eigenvalue >1.00 and a scree test suggested the extraction of three scales. The scales were checked for internal reliability and Cronbach's alpha for the Internet scale was 0.88 in 2002, 0.87 in 2007 and 0.90 in 2012.

5. Social media use was measured by asking 'Have you used social media (e.g. Facebook, Twitter, Wikipedia, YouTube, blog, etc.) in the following ways'? Subsequently seven questions about different ways to use social media in relation to health and lifestyle information were asked. This included for example questions about if the participants had provided information about health and lifestyle to social media, if they had received information from others, as well as commenting, forwarding or "liking" information in social media. A five-point response scale was used (5: Very often – 1: Never). It was decided to use factor analysis (Principal Component) to extract latent factors on the seven questions. The criteria for factor loadings were set above 0.4 and oblique rotation (Oblimin) was adopted. Multiple criteria, based on eigenvalue >1.00 and a scree test suggested that extracting one factor would be adequate. The factor which was named Social media explained 72 % of the total variance in the data. The scale was checked for internal reliability and Cronbach's alpha was 0.93.

ANOVA (one-way) was performed to examine difference across the age groups for the frequency of information seeking on the internet, as well as for each of the seven questions about the use of social media. To analyse the relationship between the age groups and the variable Social media, chi-squared and ANOVA (one-way) was used.

3   Results

The chapter starts by presenting results about how health and lifestyle information seeking on the Internet, by participants in the two age groups, has developed in the period 2002, 2007 and 2012. This will be followed by results about the relationship between the two age groups and the variable Social media. Finally, results about the participants various ways of using social media for information seeking and communicating about health and lifestyle, will be introduced.

3.1   Seeking Information About Health and Lifestyle on the Internet

Results about how the use of the internet for seeking information about health and lifestyle has developed in the period 2002, 2007 and 2012, on the scale 1 to 5, are presented in Fig. 1.

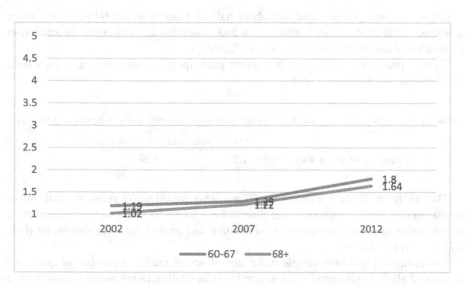

Fig. 1. Information seeking on the internet. Development in the period 2002, 2007 and 2012 (Color figure online)

Figure 1 shows that, both participants who are at the age 60 to 67 years old and those who are 68 years or older, sought information about health and lifestyle on the internet infrequently in 2012. Nevertheless, in the period 2002, 2007 and 2012, the frequency for information seeking on the internet increased for both age groups. This happened mainly between 2007 and 2012. Although the younger age group sought information slightly more often than the older group, the difference across the age groups is very small. Nevertheless, the results show that there was a significant difference across the age groups in 2002 ($p = 0,05$). In 2007 ($F(1, 110) = 5,82$; $p = 0,447$) and in 2012 ($F(1, 180) = 1,74$; $p = 0,189$), however, no significant difference was revealed.

3.2   Social Media

In recent years, social media has increased the opportunities for people to access health related information. For comparison reasons, the analysis of information seeking on the Internet did not include the use of social media, which was examined separately.

Results about the relationship between the variables age and Social media (factor analysis) are presented in Tables 2 and 3.

Table 2. Use of social media for health and lifestyle information. Participants 60 years and older

	Have used social media	Never used social media
60 years and older	49,6 %	50,4 %

Chi-square analysis revealed that about half of those who are 60 years and older have used social media to seek information and communicate with others in relation to information about health and lifestyle (see Table 2).

Table 3 presents results about how often participants in the two age groups used Social media, on the scale 1 to 5.

Table 3. Frequency of using social media for seeking information about health and lifestyle

	60–67 years old	68 years and older
Frequency of using social media	1,56	1,37

The results in Table 3 revealed that those who are 60 to 67 years old seek information slightly more often more often than those who are 68 years and older. However, the difference across the age groups is very small and proved not to be significant ($F(1, 167) = 3,13$; $p = 0,079$).

To further explore how people make use of social media, a number of questions were asked about the different ways to employ it in relation to information about health and lifestyle. The results are presented in Fig. 2.

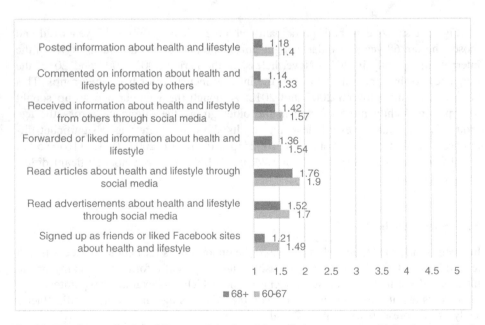

Fig. 2. Frequency of using different action of social media by age groups (Color figure online)

As can be seen in Fig. 2, the frequency for using the different actions is low for both age groups. Nevertheless, a comparison of the various functions that can be employed, shows that the groups choose to use some of them more often than others. The most favoured action by both of the age groups is to use social media to read articles about health and lifestyle. After that, both groups preferred to read advertisements about this topic. The functions that were employed least often, by both age groups, were making comments on information that others had posted, post information themselves and sign up as friends or like sites on health and lifestyle on Facebook.

A significant difference was found for two of the questions. Those who belong to the younger age group posted information more often than those are in the older age group (p = 0,05). Likewise, the younger age group signed more often up as friends, or liked Facebook sites, than those in the older age group (p = 0,05).

4 Discussion

The study investigated how Icelanders who are 60 years and older seek and communicate about digital health and lifestyle information. Senior citizens form the fastest growing group of citizens in western societies, as in many other parts of the world [1]. Concerns have been raised that, due to the complexity of using information technology for health communication, senior citizens may not benefit as much from digital health information as others [26]. By comparing results about two age groups, people who are 60 to 67 years old and those who are 68 years and older, the study gives evidence about how their digital information seeking in has developed in the years 2002, 2007 and 2012. Furthermore, the use of social media in the year 2012 was explored.

The internet has become an increasingly important channel of health related information [27] but it is contingent on people having online access. In the past years the prevalence of Icelanders with internet access has increased steadily. A total of 78 % of the population had online access in 2002 [28], the figure had gone up to 84 % in 2007 [29] and 95 % had internet access in 2012 [14]. Although figures for senior citizens are not available, these statistics indicate that their prospects for accessing the internet are good. The availability of online information may also be of consequence, and it is fair to assume the amount of it has increased since 2002. Information that used to appear only in print was often also available in digitalised form already in 2007, for example newspapers or magazines offering websites. Furthermore, the amount of information on websites of health authorities and public health institutes has grown steadily in the period 2002 to 2012, with brochures, articles and news about research findings, being published in both print and digital form. Hence, the possibilities that senior citizens have to access digital information have improved.

In the past few years, the use of social media among senior citizens has been growing [14–16]. Social media has the potential of supporting and influencing information behaviour in several ways. About half of the participants who were 60 years and older were found to have used social media in relation to health and lifestyle information. The results further revealed that the frequency was low for both age groups. However, there was some variation in how often the different actions that social media offers were employed. Both age groups, chose to receive information rather than share it or communicate with others. Using social media to open links and read articles, and after that advertisements, were the most favoured actions. Through this health professionals may have an opportunity to disseminate quality information and advocate healthy living for senior citizens. Functions such as posting information, commenting on what others have posted, or signing up as friends or liking Facebook sites about health and lifestyle, where least preferred. Furthermore, the only significant difference across the age groups was for posting information and signing up or liking Facebook sites, which the younger group employed more often than the older group. Thus, the study demonstrates that although the frequency of use was slightly higher for those who are 60 to 67 years old than those who are 68 years and older, the use of social media was very similar for the groups.

An examination of information seeking on the internet revealed that it has increased since 2002. Despite of this, digital information were still sought infrequently in 2012, a finding which is further supported by the result about the low use of social media. A comparison of the age groups shows that, although the younger group sought digital information and used social media for health communication slightly more often than the older group, the difference across them was very small and not statistically significant. Thus, those who are at the age 60 to 67 use information technology for health and lifestyle information in a similar way as those who are 68 years or older.

This is interesting in the light of the idea that has been so persistent [4, 5], that the problems which senior citizens deal with at using information technology will gradually dissolve, and as a result they will become more active users of digital information. The findings of the study indicate that changes in using information technology for seeking and communicating about health related information, by senior citizens, may happen at a slower rate than anticipated.

The study is limited by a response rate of 51 percent in 2002, 47 percent in 2007 and 58 percent in 2012. Although this may be considered satisfactory in a survey it raises the question whether or not those who answered the survey are giving a biased picture of those who did not respond. Nevertheless, the findings provide valuable information about the development in digital information seeking since 2002.

Information about healthy lifestyles is increasingly being disseminated digitally. It is important to realize that people may not always change their information seeking behaviour in line with the new opportunities that technology offers. Particularly senior citizens who have formed their habits during a lifetime. Senior citizens did not grow up with computers or the internet, and not all of them have had an opportunity to grow accustomed to using it while they were still active on the labour market. In addition, information technology develops rapidly, so even though it can be assumed that the coming generation of senior citizens will be more used to seeking information digitally, the skills that they possess today may be irrelevant in the future. The society has a duty to ensure all senior citizens access to information in a way that suits their needs and capabilities. A question remains whether senior citizens will be able to adapt and learn how to use new technology. Or, if they should be ensured an access to information through the means that they themselves prefer.

Acknowledgements. The study was funded by the University of Iceland Research Fund.

References

1. United Nations: World Population Aging (2013). http://www.un.org/en/development/desa/population/publications/pdf/ageing/WorldPopulationAgeing2013.pdf
2. Pew Research Centre: Older Adults and Technology Use (2014). http://www.pewinternet.org/2014/04/03/older-adults-and-technology-use/?utm_expid=53098246-2.Lly4CFSVQG2lphsg-KopIg.0
3. Pálsdóttir, Á.: Seeking information about health and lifestyle on the internet. Inf. Res. **14**(1), 389 (2009). http://InformationR.net/ir/14-1/paper389.html
4. Bromley, C.: Can Britain close the digital divide? In: Park, A., Curtice, J., Thomson, K., Bromley, C., Phillips, M. (eds.) British Social Attitudes: The 21st Report, pp. 73–97. National Centre for Social Research, London (2004)
5. Loos, E.: Senior citizens: digital imigrants in their own country? Observatorio **6**(1), 1–23 (2012)
6. World Health Organization: Global Age Friendly Cities: A Guide. WHO, Geneva (2007). http://www.who.int/ageing/publications/Global_age_friendly_cities_Guide_English.pdf
7. Hoogendam, Y.Y., van der Lijn, F., Vernooij, M.W., Hofman, A., Niessen, W.J., van der Lugt, A., Ikram, M.A., van der Geest, J.N.: Older age relates to worsening of fine motor skills: a population-based study of middle-aged and elderly persons. Front. Aging Neurosci. **6**, 259 (2014). http://www.ncbi.nlm.nih.gov/pmc/articles/PMC4174769/
8. Piper, A.M., Campbell, R., Hollan, J.D.: Exploring the accessibility and appeal of surface computing for older adult health care support. In: Elizabeth Mynatt, E., Don Schoner, D., Fitzpatrick, G., Hudson, S., Edwards, K., Rodden, T. (eds.) CHI 2010: Proceedings of the 28th International Conference on Human Factors in Computing Systems, Atlanta, GA, USA, 10–15 April 2010, pp. 907–916. ACM, New York (2010)
9. Pálsdóttir, Á.: Senior citizens, media and information literacy and health information. In: Kurbanoglu, S., et al. (eds.) ECIL 2015. CCIS, vol. 552, pp. 233–240. Springer, Heidelberg (2015). doi:10.1007/978-3-319-28197-1_24
10. Fischera, S.H., Davida, D., Bradley, H., Crottya, B.H., Dierksa, M., Safrana, C.: Acceptance and use of health information technology by community-dwelling elders. Int. J. Med. Inf. **83**, 624–635 (2014)
11. Jimison, H., Gorman, P., Woods, S., Nygren, P., Walker, M., Norris, S., Hersh, W.: Barriers and drivers of health information technology use for the elderly, chronically ill, and underserved. Evidence Report/Technology Assessment No. 175. AHRQ Publication No. 09-E004. Rockville, MD: Agency for Healthcare Research and Quality (2008)
12. Eriksson-Backa, K., Ek, S., Niemelä, R., Huotari, M.-L.: Health information literacy in everyday life: a study of finns aged 65–79 years. Health Inf. J. **18**(2), 83–94 (2012)
13. UNESCO: Media and Information Literacy (2014). http://www.uis.unesco.org/Communication/Pages/information-literacy.aspx
14. Statistics Iceland: Computer and Internet Usage by Individuals 2012. Statistical Series: Tourism, Transport and IT 97(33) (2012). https://hagstofa.is/lisalib/getfile.aspx?ItemID=14251
15. Statistics Iceland: Computer and Internet Usage in Iceland and Other European Countries 2013. Statistical Series: Tourism, Transport and IT 99(1) (2014). https://hagstofa.is/lisalib/getfile.aspx?ItemID=14251
16. Zickuhr, K., Madden, M.: Older Adults and Internet Use: For the First Time, Half of Adults Ages 65 and Older are Online, Washington, D.C.: Pew Research Center's Internet & American Life Project (2012). http://pewinternet.org/Reports/2012/Older-adults-and-internet-use.aspx

17. Freyne, J., Berkovsky, S., Kimani, S., Baghaei, N.: Improving health information access through social networking. In: Dillon, T.S., Rubin, D.L., Gallagher, W., Sidhu, A.S., Tsymbal, A. (eds.) IEEE 23rd International Symposium on Computer-Based Medical Systems, 12–15 October 2010, Perth, Australia, pp. 334–339. IEEE, Piscataway (2010)
18. Zhang, Y., He, D., Sang, Y.: Facebook as a platform for health information and communication: a case study of a diabetes group. J. Med. Syst. **37**(3), 9942 (2013)
19. Boyd, D.M., Ellison, N.B.: Social network sites: definition, history, and scholarship. J. Comput.-Mediated Commun. **13**(1), 210–230 (2007)
20. Scanfeld, D., Scanfeld, V., Larson, E.L.: Dissemination of health information through social networks: twitter and antibiotics. Am. J. Infect. Control **38**(3), 182–188 (2010)
21. Moen, A., Smørdal, O., Sem, I.: Web-based resources for peer support: opportunities and challenges. Stud. Health Technol. Inf. **150**, 302–306 (2009)
22. Oha, H.J., Lauckner, C., Boehmer, J., Fewins-Bliss, R., Li, K.: Facebooking for health: an examination into the solicitation and effects of health-related social support on social networking sites. Comput. Hum. Behav. **29**(5), 2072–2080 (2013)
23. Savolainen, R.: Dietary blogs as sites of informational and emotional support. Inf. Res. **15**(4), 438 (2010). http://InformationR.net/ir/15-4/paper438.html
24. Thane, P.: History and the sociology of ageing. Soc. Hist. Med. **2**(1), 93–96 (1989)
25. Lög um málefni aldraðra nr. 125/1999
26. Wang, M.P., Viswanath, K., Lam, T.H., Wang, X., Chan, S.S.: Social determinants of health information seeking among chinese adults in Hong Kong. PLoS ONE **8**(8), e73049 (2013). doi:10.1371/journal.pone.0073049
27. Harris, R.M., Wathen, C.N., Fear, J.M.: Searching for health information in rural Canada: where do residents look for health information and what do they do when they find it? Inf. Res. **12**(1), 274 (2006)
28. Statistics Iceland: Use of ICT and Internet by Households and Individuals 2002 and 2003. Statistical Series: Information Technology 89(12) (2004). http://www.statice.is/publications/publication-detail?id=54347
29. Statistics Iceland: Use of ICT and Internet by Households and Individuals 2007. Statistical Series: Information Technology 92(39) (2007). http://www.statice.is/publications/publication-detail?id=54558

Concepts, Terms, and Mental Models: Everyday Challenges to Older Adult Social Media Adoption

Kelly Quinn[✉], Renae Smith-Ray, and Kristin Boulter

University of Illinois at Chicago, Chicago, IL, USA
{kquinn8,rsmith27,kboult2}@uic.edu

Abstract. Social connection and social support are strong predictors of well-being, but maintaining social relations often becomes more difficult at older ages. Because social media enhance feelings of connectedness and reduce feelings of loneliness, they may present accessible and relatively low cost mechanisms to enhance life quality at older ages. Using data gathered from two focus groups of potential older adult social media learners, we explored the physical and cognitive challenges to social media use, perceptions of social media benefits, and conceptual barriers to use. Findings support earlier studies that identify perceived benefit as important to social media adoption at older ages, and extend these by identifying that a lack in conceptual knowledge of these technologies is an additional barrier to use. We then discuss the cognitive implications of gaining this knowledge.

Keywords: Older adults · Social media · Social connection · Social support · Perception of benefit

1 Introduction

Social connection and social support are strong predictors of well-being at all ages: individuals with larger and stronger networks are healthier and experience greater social support and reduced levels of cognitive decline [1] than those with lower levels of social connection. Yet, maintaining social relationships often becomes more difficult at older ages due to retirement, bereavement, mobility limitations, and chronic disease. Retirement and the death of spouses and friends make older adults more vulnerable to loneliness and social isolation, factors that are linked to depression and mortality [2, 3].

Newer communication technologies, including social media platforms like Facebook and Twitter, have rapidly gained prominence because they enhance social connection. Preliminary studies indicate that communication through social media enhances feelings of social connectedness [4] and reduces feelings of loneliness [5]. Social media platforms, therefore, may present accessible and relatively low cost mechanisms to enhance social well-being and life quality at older ages.

While popular images in the media portray youth and young adults as the most active users of social media, recent studies indicate that older adults are rapidly adopting these technologies to communicate with friends and family [6]. However, as with other forms of new technology, training support is often necessary to reduce perceived barriers and

© Springer International Publishing Switzerland 2016
J. Zhou and G. Salvendy (Eds.): ITAP 2016, Part II, LNCS 9755, pp. 227–238, 2016.
DOI: 10.1007/978-3-319-39949-2_22

stimulate technology use at older ages [7]. Therefore an important first step is to explore training needs and potential obstacles for social media's use. What are prevalent attitudes regarding the use of social media for social connection? What perceived benefits are attributed to social media use? What potential barriers inhibit using these media?

This study represents the initial phase of a larger study that examines how social media technologies might be employed to offset health risk factors and improve health outcomes in an aging population. As an initial step, we address the question, "What are the perceived challenges and benefits of social media use among older adults?" Two focus groups were conducted with potential older adult social media learners to explore the physical and cognitive challenges to social media use, perceptions of social media benefits, and conceptual barriers to use. This paper presents findings from these focus groups. We discuss potential obstacles to social media use and potential cognitive implications that may result from social media skills training.

2   Older Adults and Social Media

The internet is increasingly part of everyday life, and it has spawned new communication technologies that have diffused rapidly throughout society [8]. Social media, especially, have become a near universal means of interacting, with platforms such as Facebook and Twitter enabling users to easily share information and maintain connection. These "networked communication platforms" enable users to construct a unique profile that contains identity information, maintain visible lists of connections to other users, and view streams of news, information and comments, along with system-generated content such as birthday reminders and sponsored advertising [9]. In addition, the platforms feature "one-to-many" broadcast capabilities which facilitate the dissemination of information between users. Although social media are most commonly characterized as social network sites such as Facebook and Twitter, social media also include online communities, like SeniorNet and GreyPath, content-sharing sites such as YouTube, and discussion boards such as those on AARP.org.

Today, approximately 60 % of US and UK adults over the age of 65 years report using the internet to look for information and communicate with others [10, 11], a substantial increase from a decade ago. The use of social media is growing rapidly as well; in 2014, for example, more than 56 % of US adults over the age of 65 and more than 30 % of UK adults over the age of 65 reported using these media [12, 13]. However, despite these increasing levels in social media use, levels of engagement lag that of youth and young adults by a considerable degree.

Because of social media's significance to other societal age groups, researchers have attempted to identify reasons for these slower adoption rates and high levels of non-use at older ages, and studies have highlighted two dimensions that may be contribute to the disparity: the physical and cognitive changes associated with aging, and attitudinal factors such as concerns about privacy and/or a lack of perceived benefit resulting from technology's use. In addition, deficiencies in digital skills at older ages may play a role, and therefore several studies have highlighted the importance of basic technological training for increasing usage rates.

2.1 Physical and Cognitive Challenges

As individuals age, they encounter physical and cognitive changes that impede the ability to interact with technology. Declines in motor response time, coordination, and the ability to maintain continuous movements make using an input device like a keyboard or mouse more challenging [14]. Difficulty with fine motor control impacts the ability to click, drag and locate position on a screen [15], and becomes especially inhibiting as devices become smaller and more tactile. Visual acuity, color perception, and contrast discrimination tend to decrease with age [16] and this impacts how screen-based materials are interpreted. Hearing deficiencies also increase at older ages [31], and impedes the recognition of synthetic speech and reduces sensitivity to pure tones [17]; while a lesser concern in the visually-oriented web environment, hearing deficiencies are increasingly relevant with the proliferation of multimedia content.

Cognitive functioning also plays an instrumental role in social media use. Most adults experience age-related declines in cognitive functioning that are not clinically recognized. Typically, cognitive functioning improves until approximately the mid- to upper-20s, followed by a steady decline throughout adulthood, with the greatest declines occurring around age 80 [18]. This holds true for most critical aspects of cognition including processing speed, reasoning, visuospatial skills, and memory [18], with the exception of crystallized intelligence—that is, learned or acculturated knowledge—which remains relatively stable until late life [18, 19]. Certain behaviors including social engagement and cognitive engagement (i.e., learning) are capable of enhancing or preserving cognitive functioning in late life [20]. What is unknown, however, is whether engagement in social media positively impacts cognitive functioning in late life.

2.2 Attitudinal Factors: Privacy and Perception of Benefit

Concerns about privacy and personal security, often fueled by media reports, prompt older adults to be cautious about providing personal information to social media platforms [21]. In addition, concern that individual privacy may be breached leads some older adults to avoid online interactions with other users [21, 22]. The privacy controls embedded within social media platforms, intended to offer users control over privacy management, are often difficult to implement [23], leading some older adults to lack confidence in their own ability to protect themselves during use. As a result, older adults may perceive that social media technologies have more risks than benefits, and therefore are less likely to use them.

Lower levels of social media engagement may also result from a lack of relevance to everyday living. Perceived benefit is a strong motivator for technology adoption at older ages [24], so a failure to understand social media's potential benefits may inhibit its uptake [22, 25]. Social media are often considered a lesser form of interaction than more traditional communication forms [22, 26], so older adults may opt to engage in richer media, such as a telephone, to communicate with others. In addition, social media are sometimes viewed as a forum that is oriented toward youth [23], which potentially deters older users.

Older adults who perceive higher benefits from social media participation are more likely to use it [25]. Connection with family members is an important reason to consider using social media [26]. Social media adoption is dependent on a 'critical mass' of one's friends and acquaintances also using the specific platform [27], which may suggest that having fewer peers with which to connect diminishes the relevance of the medium [22].

2.3   Training and Support

Finally, older users often cite a lack of skills, or lack of confidence in their own skills, as reason to not engage in social media [22, 26]. Instructional support engenders social media participation [26], and specifically can address issues related to a perceived lack of benefit of their use [7] and concerns about privacy [21].

Few studies address the learning processes and strategies which older adults utilize to gain technology skills and master technology concepts, despite their importance to technology adoption. One ethnographic study of the learning strategies used to master technologies such as word processing and email found that older learners prefer learning collaboratively and informally. They also place a priority on taking their own notes over reading books or magazines, perhaps to compensate for perceived challenges such as age-related declines in fluid intelligence and memory [24]. Older adults also tend to orient their learning activities toward addressing real-life needs [24], underscoring the importance of perceived benefit in technology use.

In summary, research on the challenges facing older adults in their social media adoption has focused on three primary dimensions: age-related declines physical and cognitive abilities; privacy and perceived benefit of the technologies involved; and the need for user training to address a lack of skills or confidence. However, limited attention has been placed on practical dimensions of social media skills acquisition.

To further explore the everyday challenges and obstacles related to the acquisition of social media skills in a workshop setting, and ultimately to the everyday use of social media, this study attempts to address the question of, "What are the perceived challenges and benefits of social media use among older adults?" Using data gathered from two focus groups, we examine baseline awareness of social media platforms and perceived barriers and motivations for their use.

3   Method

Two focus groups were conducted to understand the practical challenges in facilitating social media skills. A moderator guide was developed and administered by the study investigators, covering topics of social media use; sources of social connection and support; loneliness; and barriers to and motivations for social media use. Three popular social media platforms were used as context for the discussion—Facebook, LinkedIn and Twitter. The focus groups were conducted as part of a larger study which explored the cognitive and social effects of social media use by older adults; this paper specifically highlights findings related to the everyday challenges to skills acquisition for using these technologies.

3.1 Participants and Recruitment

Two sponsor independent living facilities (ILCs) in the Midwestern United States provided access to a pool of potential participants; these included both residents of the ILCs and older adults living in nearby communities. ILC residents were recruited through newsletter announcements as well as in-person presentations made by the principal investigators. Community-dwelling adults were recruited using a quarterly newsletter announcement which was mailed to older adults living within a 5-mile radius of the facilities.

Participants were screened for inclusion criteria, which included a minimum age of 65 years and being cognitively intact, as determined by the Short Portable Mental Status Questionnaire [28]. The final group consisted of 16 adults, ranging in age from 65 to 72 years. Seven participants were male and four participants were ILC residents, with the remainder residing in nearby communities.

3.2 Procedures

Two focus groups were conducted. Each began with a brief description of the three social media platforms of interest, followed by questions involving baseline familiarity, accessibility, and perceptions of each platform. The sessions lasted for approximately 90 min each, and were audio recorded and transcribed for further analysis; transcriptions were verified by research assistants who had attended the sessions.

Focus group data were then analyzed by the investigators to identify themes related to perceptions of social media, challenges inherent in acquiring social media skills, and social isolation. Once these analyses were complete, themes were compared and negotiated until agreement of the findings was reached. These themes were then clustered into an explanatory framework consistent with the focus group texts.

4 Findings

Several themes emerged through the analysis of data as significant to the acquisition of social media skills and subsequent use of social media platforms: physical and cognitive factors affecting use; perceptions of social media benefit; and a lack of conceptual knowledge of social media generally, which included the concepts and terminology related to the platforms. The first two of these themes support prior studies of older adult perceptions of social media [7, 25], however the third theme extends previous work by detailing the ways in which gaps in conceptual knowledge of social media may also inhibit the ability to utilize these media. The following subsections will review these findings, and will discuss how conceptual knowledge of social media may enhance the potential cognitive and social benefits of using these technologies.

4.1 Physical and Cognitive Challenges to Social Media Use

As previously noted, past studies have highlighted age-related cognitive and physical factors that challenge internet use [29]. Perhaps unsurprisingly then, participants highlighted similar factors when discussing these platforms, and especially when accessing through mobile technologies. Consistent with prior studies [14], they described decrements in fine motor skills which interfered with the ability to use screen-based technologies: *"I may be old fashioned [but], I still have a laptop. And I have to have a mouse, because I cannot move my finger around. I can't do it. It won't work. It doesn't cooperate."*

Similarly, cognitive changes due to aging often involve slower information processing [30], which impacts the ability to learn and comprehend new technologies quickly. Participants noted that it took longer to 'catch on' to new technologies than their younger family members: *"Um, the kids have tried to teach me to text. I've done a little bit of it, but I say I'm still confused. I'm no genius with this technology."* The challenges in acquiring new skills may impact the willingness to attempt the process [29].

Not owning a smartphone device was also seen as an impediment to social media use, as participants observed that family members gain access through such devices. Moreover, several participants indicated a strongly functional approach to their mobile devices, emphasizing voice communication capabilities over other uses; they did not envision mobile devices as access points to social media use. One participant summarized: *"That's what cell phones are for, to make telephone calls. You know, I've got a cell phone that you can take pictures and you can do all kinds of other things, and all I want to do is make a telephone call with my cell phone, to people that I want to talk to."*

4.2 Perception of Benefit

Perception of benefit is a major factor in the decision by older adults to adopt technology [25, 31], and social media, particularly, are seen as spaces for unacceptable or irrelevant social behaviors [22]. Some participants questioned the relevance of social media, noting that these platforms *"wasted time,"* were *"senseless,"* or *"unnecessary."* One participant contextualized the use of social media as information overload, noting *"I get inundated with so much stuff, so many people, that I could care less that Joe Smith went to this affair."*

Yet, these sentiments were countered by others who noted that mundane details were exactly the information they sought about younger family members. One woman described how she would like to know about her granddaughter's wedding plans: *"We're going to have the first wedding next summer. I think it'd be nice to, because they're all over the country, to connect with [younger family members]... But I would like to see pictures. I'd like to see her dress that she picks out."*

Another noted that he would like to connect with his grandsons by using the technologies they used: *"I think I would like to connect with them the way that they do. And that's something I suppose I would have to ask. Because and I'd like to be knowledgeable about that and be funny too, you know."* It was evident that the ability to connect with younger family members is a clear and powerful benefit of using social media technologies.

Another benefit recognized by these participants is the ability to overcome age-related deficits, such as reduced mobility. One woman noted that social media might preserve her ability to socialize with more distant friends: *"We used to be quite active in different groups… And so we used to socialize quite a bit by going out, traveling often to [major city] or you know, even [another district], quite a ways up. And that way we would connect. As we've gotten older, we are not that eager to drive to [nearby town] at night and then come back late, so we have cut back on some of the wonderful things that we used to do. And because that comes with age. And that is one of the reasons why I would like to get interested in possibly now reaching out to some of those people through the media, because I like to keep in touch with people."*

Though sociality is a potential benefit sought by participants, some were also quick to note potential cognitive benefits that learning something new might hold. A desire to maintain cognitive health was expressed by several, and one participant noted that change, as in adopting new ways of doing something, may be an important benefit to using technology: *"That's why I think even though the, you know, older adults sort of take some time to change. But change is a must. Because, well, I think you're younger when you change. You know, it's just 'go past the fear and jump into it.'"*

As previous research has noted, educational strategies can alter perceptions of the benefits that social media provide and reduce concerns about using these technologies [7]. The participants in this study reinforced these findings, by indicating that a training workshop is a way for them to understand social media's benefits. As one participant noted: *"I think we need to know about Facebook, before we, before we can tell you how it's going to help us."*

4.3   Conceptual Understanding of Social Media

Throughout the sessions, questions and comments of participants seemed to indicate an interest in gaining a conceptual understanding of social media more generally. Participants indicated they had very broad questions regarding social media, such as: *"Okay, since I know nothing about this, could you explain all three of them [Facebook, Twitter, LinkedIn]? What's the purpose of each one?"* and *"Twitter, I have no idea what Twitter does."* One participant, who had some limited experience with a social network site, expressed confusion about platform interoperability and how different information providers might work in tandem to deliver content: *"And a new thing that I've been getting now on Facebook. And I don't know how I got this, something News Link… And it's a news story if I want to click on it I can read it."*

Distinctions among social media technologies and their differences from other, more familiar, technologies were often unclear to participants. One individual asked, *"How is it [Twitter] really different than from Facebook?"* Another asked, *"Why can't you just use e-mail? Because to me it's the same thing."*

One person described his attempts at using the internet as: *"I just don't have the sense of how to, you know, how to describe what I'm even trying to do. Yeah, I can plug along a little bit. But as I say it's, I find it difficult because they use a different language."*

Often, acquiring a new vocabulary goes along with gaining new skills. Unfamiliarity with social media terminology hindered participant's understanding of how various platforms worked. As one participant noted: *"I think one of the biggest problems is the words they use in all this stuff are not in the dictionary yet. So if you go into Facebook, you know, and it says you have notification. How is that different from a message? And unless you understand what the language is you can't function."*

Social media platforms each have their own terminology associated with different concepts and functions, and frequently the same concept is referred to by different terms within and among platforms. For example, the concept of a content stream differs depending on whether it is generated by the user (a "timeline" in Facebook) or aggregated by the platform (a "newsfeed" in Facebook or a "timeline" in Twitter). Learning each platform's associated language can be a challenge to older adults who may have limited exposure to the internet. It demands conscious cognitive processing, requiring learners to process at the semantic and conceptual levels and pay attention to the form-meaning connection [32]. Learning and integrating the language of social media may be one way that social media engagement can facilitate maintenance or improvement of cognitive functioning in later life [20].

These questions also highlight the importance of helping older adults to establish mental models when developing social media skills. Mental models are cognitive representations that form the basis for an individual's reasoning, decision making, and behavior [33]; they facilitate learning by helping individuals to simplify and visualize various phenomena [34]. Mastery of internet skills involves the construction of mental models which enables learners to reason about problems, predict probable events, and discover solutions [35]. When learning to use a new technology, mental models of previous versions of such technology are important to understanding and adaption [36]. Because social media differ functionally from predecessor technologies such as email and telephone, it is important to assist older learners in bridging differences and developing new mental models for their use.

5 Discussion and Conclusion

What are the everyday challenges to older adult social media adoption? Several strong themes emerged from the two focus groups that are relevant to the everyday challenges facing older adults as they contemplate engaging with social media.

First, physical and cognitive factors impact older adults' willingness to engage in social media use. Many participants indicated that their lack of general knowledge of social media platforms held them back from experimenting with their use and, importantly, they expressed a desire for adequate training and support as they initiated use. They were aware that it may take them longer to gain social media skills than their younger counterparts, perhaps due to declines associated with cognitive aging, and there was agreement that staying current with these rapidly changing technologies presents a continuing challenge. It was evident that participants not only require skills training, but also some form of ongoing support to stay abreast of new developments and answer questions that arise as they expand use of these media. This ongoing support may be critical to maintaining continued social media participation.

Second, while many participants acknowledged that use of social media technologies might be a good way to keep in touch with younger relatives, several indicated that they did not see a clear benefit to using these media. In particular, participants had difficulty understanding the benefit of maintaining connection with weaker social relationships. For most of this generation's existence, maintenance of weaker connections was done through more traditional communication technologies such as personal letters and telephone; this process was resource intensive, requiring time, effort, and attention and held little discernible benefit. Over time, the value of these weak relationships may have been discounted due to their high maintenance cost. Yet, weak connections hold considerable value for individuals, providing distinct functions for social support: extending access to information, good and services; promoting social comparison with dissimilar others; facilitating low-risk discussions of high-risk topics; and fostering a sense of community [37]. Weak connections are maintained at a much lower cost through social media; yet, a lack of familiarity with these technologies made the reduced costs in maintaining these ties less perceptible to participants. Additional concerns about privacy made participants doubt whether weak ties could be maintained without undue disclosures. It is important to communicate the benefits of weaker connections when training older adults to use social media, along with guidelines on appropriate privacy controls and disclosure levels. This additional information might encourage continued use.

Third, developing adequate mental models may help older adults understand social media more readily. An important conceptual distinction in learning and development lies in procedural and conceptual knowledge: procedural knowledge refers to an ability to execute steps in a process, while conceptual knowledge is an understanding of the governing principles and interrelationships between concepts [38]. Both forms of knowledge are critical to understanding. Successful everyday navigation of the internet and social media requires conceptual understanding as well as procedural knowledge [39].

While procedural knowledge is important to physically navigating through social media platforms, the process of acquiring the new language of social media engages conceptual learning. Prior studies emphasized the value of procedural knowledge when training older adults to use the internet [40], favoring simplistic instruction over more cognitively-taxing conceptual learning. Yet this approach does not adequately equip older adults to navigate in 'real world' settings. Although acquisition of new concepts and terminology, such as "wall" and "timeline" may be cognitively taxing, it is precisely this process of learning that may be one of the greatest benefits of social media use at older ages. Future studies should examine whether the implicit process of conceptual and procedural learning, coupled with expanded social connectedness obtained from social media use, improves cognitive functioning among older adult users, noting that reducing barriers to learning should in turn enhance utilization and adherence rates.

In conclusion, the everyday challenges of social media use at older ages extend beyond more commonly understood age-related declines in physical and cognitive functioning. A lack in perceived benefit of social media use is a real obstacle at older ages, but one that potentially could be addressed by providing evidence of the value of maintaining weaker ties through these media. Learning social media concepts and terminology may be cognitively taxing at older ages, yet this process of learning may hold the greatest benefit for social media use in later life.

6 Limitations

The voluntary nature of focus group research precludes generalizability of these results to other populations and data is potentially prone to bias resulting from its self-reported nature. Despite these limitations, the results are salient for social media researchers and site designers alike, as they provide a more nuanced view of challenges to social media adoption facing adults at older ages.

Acknowledgement. The project described was supported by Grant Number P30AG022849 from the National Institute on Aging. The content is solely the responsibility of the authors and does not necessarily represent the official views of the National Institute on Aging or the National Institutes of Health.

References

1. Cherry, K.E., Walker, E.J., Brown, J.S., Volaufova, J., Lamotte, L.R., Welsh, D.A., Su, L.J., Jazwinski, S.M., Ellis, R., Wood, R.H., Frisard, M.I.: Social engagement and health in younger, older, and oldest-old adults in the Louisiana Healthy Aging Study (LHAS). J. Appl. Gerontol. **32**, 51–75 (2013)
2. Luo, Y., Hawkley, L.C., Waite, L.J., Cacioppo, J.T.: Loneliness, health, and mortality in old age: a national longitudinal study. Soc. Sci. Med. **74**, 907–914 (2012)
3. Pantell, M., Rehkopf, D., Jutte, D., Syme, S.L., Balmes, J., Adler, N.: Social isolation: a predictor of mortality comparable to traditional clinical risk factors. Am. J. Public Health **103**, 2056–2062 (2013)
4. Ballantyne, A., Trenwith, L., Zubrinich, S., Corlis, M.: "I feel less lonely": what older people say about participating in a social networking website. Qual. Ageing Older Adults **11**, 25–35 (2010)
5. Lee, K.-T., Noh, M.-J., Koo, D.-M.: Lonely people are no longer lonely on social networking sites: the mediating role of self-disclosure and social support. Cyberpsychol. Behav. Soc. Netw. **16**, 413–418 (2013)
6. Smith, A.: Older Adults and Technology Use, Washington, DC (2014)
7. Xie, B., Watkins, I., Golbeck, J., Huang, M.: Understanding and changing older adults' perceptions and learning of social media. Educ. Gerontol. **38**, 282–296 (2012)
8. Loos, E.F., Haddon, H., Mante-Meijer, E.A.: The Social Dynamics of Information and Communication Technology. Ashgate, Aldershot (2008)
9. Ellison, N.B., Boyd, D.: Sociality through social network sites. In: Dutton, W.H. (ed.) The Oxford Handbook of Internet Studies, pp. 151–172. Oxford University Press, Oxford (2013)
10. Office for National Statistics: Internet Users, 2015 [dataset], Newport, South Wales (2015)
11. Pew Research Center: Libraries and technology use [dataset], Washington, DC (2015)
12. Duggan, M., Ellison, N.B., Lampe, C., Lenhart, A., Madden, M.: Social Media Update 2014, Washington, DC (2014)
13. Ofcom: Adults' Media Use and Attitudes Report, London (2014)

14. Rogers, W.A., Fisk, A.D., McLaughlin, A.C., Pak, R.: Touch a screen or turn a knob: choosing the best device for the job. Hum. Factors J. Hum. Factors Ergon. Soc. **47**, 271–288 (2005)
15. Czaja, S.J., Lee, C.C.: Information technology and older adults. In: Sears, A., Jacko, J.A. (eds.) The Human-Computer Interaction Handbook: Fundamentals, Evolving Technologies, and Emerging Applications, pp. 778–792. Lawrence Erlbaum, New York (2008)
16. Rubin, G.S., West, S.K., Muñoz, B., Bandeen-Roche, K., Zeger, S., Schein, O., Fried, L.P.: A comprehensive assessment of visual impairment in a population of older Americans: the SEE study. Invest. Ophthalmol. Vis. Sci. **38**, 557–568 (1997)
17. Chien, W., Lin, F.R.: Prevalence of hearing aid use among older adults in the United States. Arch. Intern. Med. **172**, 292–293 (2012)
18. Salthouse, T.A.: Selective review of cognitive aging. J. Int. Neuropsychol. Soc. **16**, 754–760 (2010)
19. Loos, E.F., Romano Bergstrom, J.C.: Older adults. In: Romano Bergstrom, J.C., Schall, J.S. (eds.) Eye Tracking in User Experience Design, pp. 313–329. Elsevier, Amsterdam (2014)
20. Institute of Medicine: Cognitive Aging. National Academies Press, Washington (2015)
21. Dumbrell, D., Steele, R.: Privacy Perceptions of Older Adults When Using Social Media Technologies. IGI Global, Hershey (2015)
22. Lehtinen, V., Näsänen, J., Sarvas, R.: "A little silly and empty-headed": older adults' understandings of social networking sites. In: Proceedings of the 23rd British HCI Group Annual Conference on People and Computers, pp. 45–54. British Computer Society, Swinton, UK (2009)
23. Hope, A., Schwaba, T., Piper, A.M.: Understanding digital and material social communications for older adults. In: Proceedings of the 32nd Annual ACM Conference on Human Factors in Computing Systems - CHI 2014, pp. 3903–3912 (2014)
24. Sayago, S., Forbes, P., Blat, J.: Older people becoming successful ICT learners over time: challenges and strategies through an ethnographical lens. Educ. Gerontol. **39**, 527–544 (2013)
25. Braun, M.T.: Obstacles to social networking website use among older adults. Comput. Human Behav. **29**, 673–680 (2013)
26. Luders, M., Brandtzæg, P.B.: "My children tell me it's so simple": a mixed-methods approach to understand older non-users' perceptions of Social Networking Sites. New Media Soc. (2014). doi:10.1177/1461444814554064. Accessed at http://nms.sagepub.com/content/early/2014/10/09/1461444814554064.abstract
27. Hargittai, E.: Whose space? Differences among users and non-users of social network sites. J. Comput. Commun. **13**, 276–297 (2008)
28. Pfeiffer, E.: A short portable mental status questionnaire for the assessment of organic brain deficit in elderly patients†. J. Am. Geriatr. Soc. **23**, 433–441 (1975)
29. Charness, N., Boot, W.R.: Aging and information technology use: potential and barriers. Curr. Dir. Psychol. Sci. **18**, 253–258 (2009)
30. Czaja, S.J., Lee, C.C.: Older adults and information technology: opportunities and challenges. In: Jacko, J.A. (ed.) The Human-Computer Interaction Handbook: Fundamentals, Evolving Technologies, and Emerging Applications, pp. 825–840. CRC Press, Boca Raton (2012)
31. Melenhorst, A.-S., Rogers, W.A., Bouwhuis, D.G.: Older adults' motivated choice for technological innovation: evidence for benefit-driven selectivity. Psychol. Aging **21**, 190–195 (2006)
32. Laufer, B., Hulstijn, J.H.: Incidental vocabulary acquisition in a second language: the construct of task-induced involvement. Appl. Linguist. **22**, 1–26 (2001)
33. Jones, N.A., Ross, H., Lynam, T., Perez, P., Leitch, A.: Mental model an interdisciplinary synthesis of theory and methods. Ecol. Soc. **16**, 46–58 (2011)

34. Seel, N.M.: Mental models in learning situations. In: Held, C., Knauff, M., Vosgerau, G. (eds.) Mental Models and the Mind: Current Developments in Cognitive Psychology, Neuroscience and Philosophy of Mind, vol. 138, pp. 85–107. Elsevier, Amsterdam (2006)
35. Brandt, D.S.: Constructivism: teaching for understanding of the Internet. Commun. ACM **40**, 112–117 (1997)
36. Laux, L.F.: Aging, communication, and interface design. In: Charness, N., Park, D.C., Sabel, B.A. (eds.) Communication, Technology and Aging: Opportunities and Challenges for the Future, pp. 153–168. Springer Publishing Company, New York (2000)
37. Adelman, M.B., Parks, M.R., Albrecht, T.L.: Beyond close relationships: support in weak ties. In: Albrecht, T.L., Adelman, M.B. (eds.) Communicating Social Support, pp. 126–147. Sage Publications, Thousand Oaks (1987)
38. Rittle-Johnson, B., Siegler, R.S., Alibali, M.W.: Developing conceptual understanding and procedural skill in mathematics: an iterative process. J. Educ. Psychol. **93**, 346–362 (2001)
39. Cahoon, B.: Teaching and learning Internet skills. New Dir. Adult Contin. Educ. **1998**(78), 5–13 (1998)
40. Morrell, R.W., Park, D.C., Mayhorn, C.B., Kelley, C.L.: Effects of age and instructions on teaching older adults to use Eldercomm, an electronic bulletin board system. Educ. Gerontol. **26**, 221–235 (2000)

Older People's Use and Learning of New Media: A Case Study on Remote Rural Villages in Finnish Lapland

Päivi Rasi[1(✉)] and Arja Kilpeläinen[2]

[1] Centre for Media Pedagogy, Faculty of Education, University of Lapland,
Rovaniemi, Finland
paivi.rasi@ulapland.fi
[2] Faculty of Social Sciences, University of Lapland, Rovaniemi, Finland
arja.kilpelainen@lapinensijaturvakoti.fi

Abstract. People aged 65+ generally use new media technologies less, in less mobile ways, and for less versatile purposes than younger age groups do. This has raised concerns about older people's potential exclusion from the digital society. In this paper we present a case study on how older people, who were living in small rural villages in Finnish Lapland, use new media in their everyday lives. According to the participants, how do they use new media in their everyday lives? How do they learn to use new media? Our results point to the diversity in terms of the participants' self-reported Internet use and related skills. The results also indicate that the participants' social networks, especially grandchildren, play a more important role in their use of and learning about new media technologies than formal instruction does. Therefore, it is important to recognize that older people who lack social networks are most vulnerable in terms of being excluded from the digital society.

Keywords: Older people · Internet use · Internet non-use · Rural areas · New media technologies

1 Introduction

People aged 65+ generally use the Internet and social media less, in less mobile ways, and for less versatile purposes than younger age groups do [1–3]. This has raised concerns about older people's potential exclusion from the digital society; thus, public authorities and international organizations have launched a number of media literacy initiatives aimed at older people in recent years [4].

The use of the Internet is also related to the area in which older people live such that urban and suburban areas have slightly more Internet users than rural areas do [5]. However, previous research on young and older people's use of new media technologies has tended to focus more on urban dwellers [6].

The aim of this paper is to gain a better understanding of how older people living in remote rural areas use and learn new media technologies in their everyday lives. The site of this case study is Lapland, the most northern and most sparsely populated area of Finland, with some areas having very few residents. Finland is one of the most "rural"

© Springer International Publishing Switzerland 2016
J. Zhou and G. Salvendy (Eds.): ITAP 2016, PartII, LNCS 9755, pp. 239–247, 2016.
DOI: 10.1007/978-3-319-39949-2_23

countries within the Organization for Economic Cooperation and Development (OECD), with its northern and eastern regions having greater dispersion [7].

Older People's Use of New Media. According to previous research, older people most often use the Internet to keep in contact with their family and friends, to manage their banking, to research health-related issues, and to read up on hobbies [8–11].

In the national context of this study, Finland, people aged from 65 to 89 years old use the Internet substantially less than those in younger age groups do [3]. Ninety-seven percent of people in the 45–54 age group were reported to have used the Internet in the last three months of spring 2015, whereas the percentages for the 55–64, 65–74, and 75–89 age groups were 90 %, 69 %, and 31 %, respectively. Furthermore, 25 % of people in the 65–74 age group reported having never used the Internet, and the percentage for the 75–89 age group was even higher at 65 %.

The existing research indicates a need to support older people's skills and competences related to new media. For example, the Office of Communications (Ofcom) [1] recently investigated media use (TV, radio, mobile phones, games, the Internet), attitudes, and understanding among UK adults aged 16+. The study focused on participants' media literacy, which was defined as "the ability to use, understand and create media and communications in a variety of contexts" [1, p. 19]. According to the results, narrow users of the Internet were predominantly aged 65+. Narrow users differed from the younger age groups in several respects: (1) their self-reported confidence in using the Internet was lower, (2) their understanding about how search engines operate was more restricted, (3) their competence in critically assessing the accuracy of search engine results was lower, and (4) their awareness and use of security measures was lower.

Older People's Use of New Media in Remote Rural Areas. An individual's use or non-use of the Internet is also related to the area in which he or she lives. In Finland, in 2015 [3], out of people aged 16–89 years old, 93 % of people living in the Finnish Capital (i.e. Helsinki) Region reported having used the Internet within the previous three months. The percentage for people living in other big cities in Finland was 87 %, for people living in urban municipalities, it was 87 %, and for people living in densely populated or rural municipalities, it was 82 %. These statistics are in line with, for example, Internet use in America, where urban and suburban dwellers have nearly a 15 % and 14 % lead over rural residents, respectively [5].

Research has identified the following demographic explanations for rural dwellers' lower usage of the Internet: older age, lower education level, and lower occupational status [5]. Furthermore, low use and non-use can be explained by social, cultural, and local factors [12, 13]. For example, Hakkarainen [14, 15], studied Finnish people aged 60+ living in eastern and northern Finland's non-urban environments who deliberately refused to use the Internet. She found that the participants viewed the computer and the Internet as useless and risky "tools and things" that threatened their freedom, nature-oriented lifestyle, health, and security, as well as creating differences between users and non-users. The study concluded that some older people's distinct identities, interests, history, and culture might shape their motivation and capacity to welcome and use computers.

Internet infrastructure continues to be a limiting factor for Internet use in rural areas [10, 16]. However, information and communication technologies (ICTs) have been shown to ease the difficulties involved in everyday living in sparsely populated remote areas. Kilpeläinen and Seppänen [10] studied how people aged 17–98 living in remote villages in Finnish Lapland used ICTs and what that use meant in terms of social communality. Their results are in line with previous research, in that the most popular reasons behind computer use were searching for information and online banking, and that the use of computers was strongly connected to age. Keeping in contact with family, friends, and relatives was important for the participants. Kilpeläinen and Seppänen concluded that the use of ICTs offers an important means through which to create and maintain communality in remote rural areas.

Research on older people's use of new media has been criticized for neglecting gerontological knowledge about *diversity in ageing*, and accordingly, treating older people as a homogenous group [17]. However, several researchers have underlined the diversity of older people's media use and competencies [11, 18], as well as the diversity of older rural dwellers' everyday lives [19].

New Media Learning Strategies for Older People. Previous research indicates that older people's personal interests and needs are the most important factors explaining their motivation to learn and use ICTs [11, 20, 21]. Accordingly, Vroman and colleagues [11] suggest a *person-focused approach* when designing instruction and learning for older people, meaning that the design should always be based on their individual, subjective interests and needs.

Older people's *self-efficacy as technology users* is positively related to the development of their ability to use, understand, and create new media content [22]. Pedagogical interventions that rely on *peer support* and *collaborative* problem solving are therefore promising. A case study performed in rural northern Finland [23] showed that through a person-focused, collaborative, and problem-solving oriented pedagogical approach resorting to peer support, it was possible to support older people in learning to use a tablet computer for their individual needs.

Social support networks are crucial for older people to learn about new media, which is also the case for younger age groups. Older people often learn to use the Internet under the guidance of their *friends* and *family* members [4, 22]. Within the field of intergenerational studies, encouraging results have been attained from technology-oriented *intergenerational learning programs*. In these programs, young technology-savvy people have acted as technology tutors for older people [24].

2   Method

In this paper, we will answer the following research questions: According to the participants, how do they use new media in their everyday lives? How do they learn to use new media? To answer the research questions, we collaboratively conducted three focus groups with 16 older people, aged from 62–86, who were living in three small rural villages in Finnish Lapland (see Table 1) during the spring of 2015. The names of the villages are not provided for privacy reasons. The focus groups were audio recorded with the participants' informed consent and were later transcribed verbatim by a trainee in the second author's faculty.

Table 1. Description of focus groups

Focus group (FG)	Number of participants (female/male)	Age (years)	Internet user/non-user	Duration
FG 1	3/3	62–86	4/2	1 h 31 min
FG 2	3/2	64–85	3/2	1 h 2 min
FG 3	5/0	67–84	4/1	1 h 39 min

In our previous analysis of these data [25, 26], we read, analyzed, and coded the transcripts to identify and mark focus group passages in which the participants talked about their Internet use and digital competences in terms of modalities of agency, as defined by Jyrkämä [27]. Jyrkämä argues that human behavior is the result of the dynamic interaction of the modalities of agency: *knowing how to, being able to, having to, having the opportunity to,* and *wanting to and feeling.* In this paper, we take a closer analytical look at the coding categories of "Internet use" and "knowing how to," which we have only briefly touched upon in our previous publications.

3   Results

Diversity in New Media Use. Our participants constituted a *diverse* group in terms of their self-reported Internet use and related skills. The group included five Internet non-users and eleven users whose usage varied in terms of breadth and frequency. The Internet non-users justified their non-use with reasons that were familiar from previous research: lack of need and interest, as well as a lack of confidence in their ability to learn due to weakened memory [14]. As one of the participants in focus group 3 explains: "Well, I would like to learn, but this head of mine starts to be pretty thin and all information falls out of it."

In our data analysis, we identified the following purposes that the participants used the Internet for: searching for information (e.g. health, hobbies, travelling); managing their banking and taxation; providing customer feedback; updating their blogs; signing up for courses; storing and sharing digital photographs; keeping in contact with friends and family (e-mail, Facebook, Skype); playing digital games; making doctors' appointments; buying train tickets; reading newspapers; watching TV; and shopping.

For example, one of the active Internet users (aged 67) reported that she considered the Internet as "a necessity" and that she used her laptop for banking, making doctors' appointments, signing up for courses, purchasing tickets, searching for information, and for updating a blog about her dog. Another respondent (aged 64) told us he was planning to buy a smart phone for the local moose-hunting activities. With the phone, he would then be able follow the real-time movements of the hunting dogs equipped with GPS collars and the moose that they were running after in the woods.

The rural and remote living areas of the participants and the associated *long distances* to public and private service providers affected some participants' choice in terms of using new media to handle their business. One of the participants in focus group 3 told us that she had recently filled in her tax refunds online because she "would have to drive all the way to [name of the place deleted], almost a hundred kilometers, to get the printed form that you would then fill out."

Another respondent in the same focus group told us that she had purchased clothes for her grandchildren online, because "it is convenient here, since we don't have shops nearby." For one respondent in focus group 1, reading the local newspaper with a tablet had resolved an old problem of getting one's newspaper in the early afternoon instead of in the morning. In some of the remote rural villages of Finland, newspapers are not delivered in the morning as they are in the cities, but later on in the day.

In our previous paper on this research data [25], we also argued that digital competences (i.e. a complex set of knowledge, skills, and attitudes that is required to participate in digital societies [28]) are very much *distributed competences* of older dyads (couples living together), families consisting of three generations, and informal networks of villagers. This was evident in the research data: The participants reported that their spouses, children, grandchildren, or fellow villagers did Internet tasks (e.g. searching for recipes and paying bills) for them, and helped and supported them in their Internet use. In this way, the village community was an important social asset for some participants, which is evident in the following excerpt from the second focus group (R = researcher, P = participant):

R: How about you [name omitted] then?
P1:   Well, I often have to call [name of the other participant] for help.
R: Will he then come to help?
P1:   Yeah, he always comes.
R: That's great.

Learning About New Media. Participants' children, and especially their grandchildren, had a role to play, first, in the development of the participants' understanding regarding the *opportunities* afforded by the Internet technologies [25]. For example, one respondent (aged 85) told us in the second focus group, somewhat amazed, about how her grandson had found information about a nearby car accident from the Internet:

Yesterday my grandson [name omitted] came, opened his laptop, and started to look for where the car accident had happened. He was saying, "Oh, it was right there."

Even if the participants' family supported their Internet use by, for example, paying bills for them online, the issue of *family members teaching* them computer skills was sometimes complicated. In the following excerpt, a respondent (aged 78) from the third focus group talks about her daughter being fast and busy:

But my daughter [name omitted] is so fast that [...] she just gets in and out fast and when I think about something and try to tell that to her, she's gone already. She has already closed the windbox door behind her and no longer hears anything.

Furthermore, in the second focus group, some of the participants expressed how they were not comfortable with asking for help too often from their family:

P1:   And then it annoys me, that how can I do this. My husband [name omitted] can do things [with the computer] better than me, but I don't want to bother him too much.

P2:   Yes, it would be so good to always be able to manage by oneself.

Grandchildren seemed to be more available as *technical tutors* in the case of several participants. One respondent (aged 68) from the second focus group had learned that grandchildren's technical support is best realized via phone calls, instead of through face-to-face encounters:

> That's why getting advice on the phone is easy, because if they [grandchildren] stand by you, they will show things so fast. [...] But if they give advice on the phone, they can't show things so fast, because they have terribly fast fingers [demonstrates how grandchildren type extremely fast with their fingers].

The participants reported various other ways in which they had learned to use new media. In the second focus group, participants told us that they had recently managed to set up *a computer club* at their village school where they received instruction, and in which five aged villagers took part. One respondent (aged 78) from the first focus group told us about how she had started *a computer class* with her husband and how she had experienced difficulties [25]:

> My husband [name omitted] and I, we went to that computer class together, and I thought that, for sure, I will learn these things. [...] But that didn't work out, because my husband [name omitted], who, at that time, already had pretty poor hearing, and the instructor teaching the course, he was talking behind our backs, and for a man, he had such a quiet voice that even I couldn't hear. So, I didn't want to bother. I dropped out of the course.

Our research data indicate that at times, the villagers are left with *no options*: they just have to manage by themselves and try to learn to, for example, fix things. One respondent from the third focus group talked about an incident with her printer:

P1:   But I think this is so characteristic of modern times, that when we had problems with our printer, it didn't intake paper from the trail ...

P2:   Umm ...

P3:   Exactly!

P1:   ... I found out who fixes these [printers] and sent an e-mail to them asking where's the service, where could I take this. And they sent me back instructions on how to fix the machine. Do this and do that!

P3:   Did you start fixing it?

P1:   Well, I had to. There was no other option. [...] I was cursing to my husband that ... if my car breaks down, then I don't call somewhere and get a list of instructions on how to fix it, like "grab your tools and ..."

P3:   ... start fixing.

R: Did you manage to fix it?

P1:   No, it still doesn't intake paper.

4 Conclusion and Discussion

Our results clearly confirm previous findings about the *diversity* in terms of the self-reported Internet use and related skills of older people [22] living in remote rural areas. The results also indicate that the participants' *social networks* play a more important role in their use of and learning about new media technologies than formal instruction does, which can be difficult to realize in a remote area with very few older residents. However, as we tried to describe in the results section, support and instruction from children and grandchildren can sometimes be a complicated issue.

Some of our participants clearly expressed an interest in and a need to learn about and use new media technologies for their *personal interests* [15, 24, 25], such as moose hunting or *needs* related to overcoming the long distances to public and private service providers. Some of the participants talked in a very positive manner about their relationships with their *grandchildren,* who also acted as their technology tutors. Therefore, we see promise in technology-oriented *intergenerational learning programs* [24].

However, it is important to recognize that older people who lack social networks are most vulnerable in terms of being excluded from the digital society. Designing support and instruction for older rural dwellers with non-existing or limited social networks requires creative thinking and good existing professional networks. These services should be designed and implemented for those individuals who are keen to learn. For example, in Finland, at the site of this case study, several non-governmental organizations (NGOs) presently provide older people with personalized support and tutoring in the use of new media technologies. In all of the service provider sectors (private, public, NGO) there is a growing need to think of new, creative ways through which to *integrate* personalized new media support and tutoring services into already existing social, health, cultural, and educational services. In remote rural areas, the special challenge is how to bring the support services as close to the people as possible and even directly into their homes.

References

1. Ofcom. Office of Communications: Adults' Media Use and Attitudes. Report 2015 (2015). http://stakeholders.ofcom.org.uk/binaries/research/media-literacy/media-lit-10years/2015_Adults_media_use_and_attitudes_report.pdf
2. Quinn, K.: Learning new tricks: the use of social media in later life. In: Harrington, C.L., Bielby, D.D., Bardo, A.R. (eds.) Aging, Media, and Culture, pp. 183–192. Lexington Books, Lanham (2014)
3. Tilastokeskus: Väestön tieto- ja viestintätekniikan käyttö 2015 [Use of Information and Communication Technology by individuals] (2015). http://www.stat.fi/til/sutivi/2015/sutivi_2015_2015-11-26_fi.pdf
4. Abad, L.: Media literacy for older people facing the digital divide: the e-inclusion programmes design. Comunicar Media Educ. Res. J. **21**, 173–180 (2014)
5. Boase, J.: The consequences of personal networks for internet use in rural areas. Am. Behav. Sci. **9**, 1257–1267 (2010)

6. Awan, F., Gauntlett, D.: Remote living: exploring online (and offline) experiences of young people living in rural areas. Eur. J. Cult. Stud. **16**, 3–23 (2012)
7. OECD: OECD Rural Policy Reviews: Finland (2008). http://www.oecd.org/document/46/0,3343,en_2649_33735_40462382_1_1_1_1,00.html
8. Buse, C.E.: When you retire, does everything become leisure? Information and communication technology use and the work/leisure boundary in retirement. New Media Soc. **11**, 1143–1161 (2009)
9. Wagner, N., Hassanein, K., Head, M.: Computer use by older adults: a multi-disciplinary review. Comput. Hum. Behav. **26**, 870–882 (2010)
10. Kilpeläinen, A., Seppänen, M.: Information technology and everyday life in ageing rural villages. J. Rural Stud. **33**, 1–8 (2014)
11. Vroman, K.G., Arthanat, S., Lysack, C.: "Who over 65 is online?" Older adults' dispositions toward information communication technology. Comput. Hum. Behav. **43**, 156–166 (2015)
12. Chamberlain, K., Hodgetts, D.: Social psychology and media: critical considerations. Soc. Pers. Psychol. Compass **2**, 1109–1125 (2008)
13. Talsi, N.: Kodin koneet: Teknologioiden kotouttaminen, käyttö ja vastustus [Mundane Machines: Domesticating, Using and Opposing Technologies]. Publications of the University of Eastern Finland. Dissertations in Social Sciences and Business Studies, No. 75 (2014)
14. Hakkarainen, P.: "No good for shovelling snow and carrying firewood": social representations of computers and the internet by elderly Finnish non-users. New Media Soc. **14**, 1198–1215 (2012)
15. Rasi, P., O'Neil, C.: Dinosaurs and fossils living without dangerous tools: social representations of computers and the internet by elderly Finnish and American non-users. Seminar.net: Int. J. Media Technol. Lifelong Learn. **10**, 56–72 (2014)
16. Milbourne, P., Kitchen, L.: Rural mobilities: connecting movement and fixity in rural places. J. Rural Stud. **34**, 326–336 (2014)
17. Harrington, C.L., Bielby, D.D., Bardo, A.R.: New areas of inquiry in aging, media, and culture. In: Harrington, C.L., Bielby, D.D., Bardo, A.R. (eds.) Aging, Media, and Culture, pp. 1–9. Lexington Books, Lanham (2014)
18. Ofcom. Office of Communications: Media Literacy Audit: Report on Media Literacy Amongst Older People (2006). http://stakeholders.ofcom.org.uk/binaries/research/media-literacy/older.pdf
19. Davies, A.: On constructing ageing rural populations: "capturing" the grey nomad. J. Rural Stud. **27**, 191–199 (2011)
20. Xie, B., Watkins, I., Golbeck, J., Huang, M.: Understanding and changing older adults' perceptions and learning of social media. Educ. Gerontol. **38**, 282–296 (2012)
21. González, C., Fanjul, C., Cabezuelo, F.: Consumption and knowledge of new technologies by elderly people in France, United Kingdom and Spain. Comunicar Media Educ. Res. J. **23**, 19–27 (2015)
22. Livingstone, S., Van Couvering, E., Thumim, N.: Adult Media Literacy: A Review of the Research Literature on Behalf of Ofcom. Department of Media and Communications, London School of Economics and Political Science, London (2005). http://core.ac.uk/download/pdf/4155054.pdf
23. Hyvönen, P., Romero, M., Hakkarainen, P., Impiö, N.: Creative collaboration for enhancing older adult's ICT use. In: Presentation at the EARLI Biennial Conference, 27–31 August, Munchen, Germany (2013)
24. Sánchez, M., Kapland, M.S., Bradley, L.: Using technology to connect generations: some considerations of form and function. Comunicar Media Educ. Res. J. **45**, 95–103 (2015)

25. Rasi, P., Kilpeläinen, A.: The digital competences and agency of older people living in rural villages in Finnish Lapland. Seminar.net. Int. J. Media Technol. Lifelong Learn. **11**, 149–160 (2015)
26. Kilpeläinen, A., Rasi, P.: Paikallisuuden paradokseja digiajassa: Lappilaisissa sivukylissä asuvien ikäihmisten digitaaliset kompetenssit paikallisuuden valossa. In: Luoto, I., Kattilakoski, M., Backa, P. (eds.) Paikkaperustainen aluekehittäminen [Place-Based Regional Development]. Publications of the Ministry of Employment and the Economy, Helsinki, Finland (in press)
27. Jyrkämä, J.: Toimijuus, ikääntyminen ja arkielämä – hahmottelua teoreettis-metodologiseksi viitekehykseksi [Agency, aging and everyday life: an outline for a theoretical-methodological framework]. Gerontologia **4**, 190–203 (2008)
28. Ferrari, A.: Digcomp: a framework for developing and understanding digital competence in Europe. In: European Commission, Joint Research Centre–Institute for Prospective Technological Studies. Publications Office of the European Union, Luxembourg (2013)

Improving User Experience and Engagement for Older Adults: A Case Study

Krysta Hedia Salera[1], Pejman Salehi[1]([⊠]), Neel Desai[2],
Lia E. Tsotsos[3], and Kathryn Warren-Norton[3]

[1] School of Applied Computing, Sheridan Institute of Technology
and Advanced Learning, Oakville, Canada
{salerak,pejman.salehi}@sheridancollege.ca
[2] Chumbuggy.com, Toronto, Canada
neel@chumbuggy.com
[3] Centre for Elder Research, Sheridan Institute of Technology
and Advanced Learning, Oakville, Canada
{lia.tsotsos,kathryn.warrennortonl}@sheridancollege.ca

Abstract. Our work focuses on user engagement and the impact of UI design on older users' level of engagement when using web-based applications. For the purpose of this research we are using Chumbuggy.com, an online service which allows people over 50 to engage in small group discussions about topics that are important and interesting to them. Due to the nature of the service provided by Chumbuggy and its target audience, we needed to design its UI to meet the high level of usability required to maximize the engagement of older adults. To this end, we created an iterative and incremental process of designing and testing Chumbuggy's UI components. This paper presents our design and testing process, our findings, and a set of guidelines for increasing the online engagement of older adults through effective UI design.

Keywords: Aging and social media · Aging and technology acceptance · Elderly-specific web design

1 Introduction

The adoption of older adults' technology has increased in recent years, [1] but current websites have not been designed with the needs of older adults in mind; resulting in the challenges that older adults are facing. Recent studies show that older adults are facing challenges when using new technologies, and in particular, online services which often stem from how they are presented to older adults [2]. As a result, in recent years a field of research has emerged within the HCI community to explore HCI and aging [3].

This paper will focus on technically proficient adults ages 50 to 70, and the impact of UI design and user engagement when using web-based applications. Chumbuggy.com will be used for this study, as its services allow users 50 and over to take part in small group discussions and to meet new people. Due to the site's nature, the UI needed to be designed so as to maximize older adults' engagement and to address the

© Springer International Publishing Switzerland 2016
J. Zhou and G. Salvendy (Eds.): ITAP 2016, PartII, LNCS 9755, pp. 248–255, 2016.
DOI: 10.1007/978-3-319-39949-2_24

challenges that they are facing when using new technology. And so, an iterative and incremental process was created to test Chumbuggy's UI components.

It will also present our design and testing process, our findings, and a set of compiled guidelines from both research literature and user feedback; targeted for increasing the online engagement of technically proficient older adults ages 50 to 70 through effective UI design.

2   Aging Challenges and the Web

We start by examining literature covering multiple impairments that effect older adults as they age. Such impairments can affect their ability to see [4–7] and adapt to rapidly changing visual stimuli [8, 9], to hear the correct tone, intensity and pitch [10], to remember and process information correctly [9, 11] and to move with stability, strength and flexibility [12, 13].

Ultimately when it comes to using computers, older adults have different needs and concerns due to the physical and cognitive changes associated with aging, which become evident around 45 years of age [14]. To meet the needs of older users experiencing these common conditions, all of these changes need to be reflected in computers. As such, these challenges along with the compiled guidelines were included throughout the iterative design process; to ensure that the website factored the changes associated with aging.

3   Methodology

In order to determine what UI designs would be most effective and engaging to technologically literate users' ages 50 to 70; two user tests were designed which will be presented below (Fig. 1).

Fig. 1. Process to determine user interface and design effects on users 50 to 70 years old

3.1 Outline

The process began with the development of Chumbuggy.com via paper prototyping; with significant consideration for colour contrast, white space, simplistic design, and minimum required font size. During development we also obtained the help of The Sheridan Centre for Elder Research to provide their expertise on the design and implementation of the test framework.

A survey via Survey Monkey was used to collect and measure the test subjects' technical knowledge and abilities as well potential psychological and socio-economic factors.

After obtaining test users, designing the test framework in which the users would carry out the main activities came next. Once user feedback from the first test was obtained, further research on usability and engagement was done; and changes were then made within the site and were once again tested a second time by a different set of users in an iterative and incremental process.

3.2 Test Users

In order to accurately obtain the correct sample type representing the desired demographic the survey included their age, sex, location, highest level of education and tech savviness. The survey results were then categorized by age and sorted to determine if they met our desired profile of testers that consisted of being comfortable in using technology and desired meeting new people.

A minimum of 6 users were used to test the 2 versions of the website. The first was a formal testing, while the second was an informal testing workshop where users would be observed while testing the website and verbally asked about their feedback. In the first version there were 6 users with a median age of 70 and an average of 68.3 who were all women and in the second version there were a varying number of users who were a mix between men and women.

3.3 Testing Framework

Chumbuggy.com's end to end experience consists of four main activities and thus, there were four components to the test. First, users would create a profile by providing their name, age, address, email address, password, hobbies and interest (Fig. 2).

Second, users would create a discussion based on a pre-defined topic by writing a short description of the elements of the topic they wanted to discuss, the date, time and number of users they wanted in the discussion (Fig. 3).

Third, users would take part in the audio/video or chat-only discussion and in the fourth step, they would test payment for membership by using test credit card

Fig. 2. Screen shot of the step 1 of user profile process

Fig. 3. Screen shot of the discussion topic creation

Fig. 4. Screen shot of users participating in a group discussion

information (Fig. 4). During each activity, specific feedback would be obtained from the users and after completing all the activities additional feedback would be obtained from a focus-group style discussion.

3.4   Testing Process

Prior to the start of the first test, users were informed of what they could expect to see throughout the test. After receiving this explanation, users could decide if they still wanted to continue with the test. Each individual was then seated in front of a test computer, and provided with a set of written tasks to complete and space to document their experience on performing each task. After completing all the tasks, they were then invited to a focus-group style discussion to provide additional qualitative feedback.

Prior to the start of the second test, users were given a brief introduction to the website and were invited to test the site without strict parameters; to emulate a true user experience. While testing the site their feedback was recorded. Users were also provided with verbal guidance if they had any questions.

4   Findings

Users' feedback in both tests was primarily on UI design, starting with and in descending order of focus: navigation, content and organization, readability, and accessibility. It was also learned that web pages that more closely followed usability guidelines resulted in a more positive user experience. It is interesting to note that users were very selective in terms of the type of words or media used and the tone that it conveyed, and as such there were multiple revisions of diction and sentence structure. Users also expressed a desire in having the ability to change font size and to have a printer friendly version of the site and group discussions in order to think about and revisit at a later time.

5   Guidelines

Included below is a subset of a compiled list of guidelines obtained from research literature and user feedback from testing, for application developers aimed at increasing engagement for technically proficient users 50 to 70 [8, 15–24] (Table 1).

Table 1. Compiled guidelines for increasing engagement for older adults 50 to 70

	Guidelines	Used?	Effect on 50 to 70 year olds		Guidelines	Used?	Effect on 50 to 70 year olds
Navigation	Breadcrumbs and site map			Content and Organization	Form labels and hint outside of form field	✓	Minimize form input submission
	Flat navigational layout	✓	Minimize motor difficulty with mouse navigation		Form fields do not auto correct for names, home and email addresses	✓	Minimize typing errors and form submission
	Consistent navigation	✓	Minimize navigation confusion		Active and positive tone used	✓	Higher engagement
Content and Organization	Enough spacing for form input and area	✓	Higher visibility and minimize input selection errors	Readability	Printer friendly version		
	Visual and/or audio notice for correct user data submission	✓			Information focused on center	✓	Better readability
	Avoid deeply nested info, cascading and pull down menu /input	✓	Increase user access and minimize motor difficulty with mouse navigation		Customer focus language	✓	Higher engagement
	Group similar information together	✓	Better understanding		Able to change font size and contrast		Better readability
	Avoid moving text and unnecessary info	✓	Better understanding		Shortest steps possible to complete actions	✓	Minimize mental workload
	Simple displays	✓	Minimize mental workload		Confirmation prompts		
	Visible search functionality				Event based reminders with unique tones	✓	Minimize mental workload
	Search accepts spelling errors and provide suggestions			Accessibility	Simple instructions that are context based	✓	Minimize mental workload
	Online help available	✓	Higher engagement		Plenty of time to read information	✓	Minimize mental workload and better readability
	Graphic is simple and meaningful	✓	Minimize mental workload		Develop with a focus on recognition rather than recall	✓	Minimize mental workload
	Information on graphic available on text				High contrast between foreground and background	✓	Minimize mental workload and better readability
	Audio follows linguistic structure and pauses	✓	Minimize mental workload and higher engagement				

6 Conclusion

In conclusion, this paper aims to serve as a starting point to compile a subset of multiple guidelines for desktop sites on what UI designs provide higher engagement for technically proficient adults ages 50 to 70.

Based on the findings, it was learned that overall a higher compliance to usability guidelines for older adults lead to a more positive user experience, and that certain UIs have more impact on technically proficient users than others. And so, it would be interesting in the future to observe technically proficient older adults' interactions with the site when other guidelines that they did not focus on or were not initially used, are included or removed. Would user engagement decrease, increase or stay neutral?

As for the limitations of the study, it was learned that a limited number of sample size and test cases were present which may skew the study validity.

Overall, further investigation into using advanced equipment, such as eye tracking or muscle tracking technologies, could provide more insight into usability and engagement. Moreover, as Chumbuggy.com's client base grows, more information could be gathered to verify if the findings would also apply to other technologies, such as tablets, TV, and wearable technologies. As the population of older adult increases, so increases the need for investigation into the older adult-specific HCI and the multiplicity of possible future research streams which spring from this area of study.

References

1. Hart, T., Chaparro, B., Halcomb, C.: Evaluating websites for older adults: adherence to senior-friendly guidelines and end-user performance. Behav. Inf. Technol. **27**, 191–199 (2008)
2. Sayago, S., Blat, J.: About the relevance of accessibility barriers in the everyday interactions of older people with the web, pp. 104–113. ACM Press (2009)
3. Silva, S., Braga, D., Teixeira, A.: AgeCI: HCI and age diversity. In: Stephanidis, C., Antona, M. (eds.) UAHCI 2014, Part III. LNCS, vol. 8515, pp. 179–190. Springer, Heidelberg (2014)
4. Pirkl, J.J.: Transgenerational Design: Products for an Aging Population. Wiley, New York (1994)
5. Weale, R.A.: Retinal illumination and age. Trans. Illum. Eng. Soc. **26**(2), 95–100 (1961)
6. Elliot, D., Whitaker, D., Macveigh, D.: Neural contribution to spatiotemporal contrast sensitivity decline in healthy ageing eyes. Vis. Res. **30**, 541–547 (1990)
7. Scialfa, C.T., Garvey, P.M., Tyrell, R.A., Leibowitz, H.W.: Age differences in dynamic contrast thresholds. J. Gerontol. **47**, P172–P175 (1992)
8. Lynch, K.R., Schwerha, D.J., Johanson, G.A.: Development of a weighted heuristic for website evaluation for older adults. Int. J. Hum. Comput. Interact. **29**, 404–418 (2013)
9. Wirtz, S., Jakobs, E.-M., Ziefle, M.: Age-specific usability issues of software interfaces. In: Proceedings of the IEA 2009 – 17th World Congress on Ergonomics (2009)
10. Davis, A.C., Ostri, B., Parving, A.: Longitudinal study of hearing. Acta Otolaryngol. **111**, 12–22 (1991)
11. Beni, R.D., Palladino, P.: Decline in working memory updating through ageing: intrusion error analyses. Memory **12**, 75–89 (2004)
12. Edström, E., Altun, M., Bergman, E., Johnson, H., Kullberg, S., Ramírez-León, V., Ulfhake, B.: Factors contributing to neuromuscular impairment and sarcopenia during aging. Physiol. Behav. **92**, 129–135 (2007)
13. Cheong, Y., Shehab, R.L., Ling, C.: Effects of age and psychomotor ability on kinematics of mouse-mediated aiming movement. Ergonomics **56**, 1006–1020 (2013)

14. Hawthorn, D.: Possible implications of aging for interface designers. Interact. Comput. **12**, 507–528 (2000). Elsevier
15. Wagner, N., Hassanein, K., Head, M.: Computer use by older adults: a multi-disciplinary review. Comput. Hum. Behav. **26**, 870–882 (2010). Elsevier
16. Sherwin, K.: Placeholders in Form Fields Are Harmful. Nielsen Norman Group, 11 May 2014. https://www.nngroup.com/articles/form-design-placeholders/. Accessed 09 Sept 2015
17. Farage, M.A., Miller, K.W., Ajayi, F., Hutchins, D.: Design principles to accommodate older adults. Glob. J. Health Sci. **4**, 2 (2012)
18. Kurniawan, S., Zaphiris, P.: Research-derived web design guidelines for older people, pp. 129–135. ACM Press (2005)
19. Czaja, S.J.: The impact of aging on access to technology, pp. 7–11. ACM Press (2005)
20. Johnson, R., Kent, S.: Designing universal access: web-applications for the elderly and disabled. Cogn. Technol. Work **9**, 209–218 (2007). Springer
21. Chadwick-Dias, A., Mcnulty, M., Tullis, T.: Web usability and age. ACM Press (2003)
22. Bergstrom, J.C., Olmsted-Hawala, E.L., Jan, M.E.: Age-related differences in eye tracking and usability performance: website usability for older adults. Int. J. Hum. Comput. Interact. **29**, 541–548 (2013)
23. National Institute on Aging: Making Your Website Senior Friendly. National Institute on Aging and the National Library of Medicine, September 2002. https://www.nlm.nih.gov/pubs/checklist.pdf. Accessed 11 Sept 2015
24. Pernice, K., Nielsen, J.: Usability Guidelines for Accessible Web Design: A Report by NN/g. Nielsen Norman Group (2001). http://www.nngroup.com/reports/usability-guidelines-accessible-web-design/. Accessed 11 Sept 2015

Understanding Mobile SNS Usage for Aging People in China: A Perspective from Motivations, Trust and Attitude

Zhongping Zeng[✉], Liu Liu, Ye Han, and Zhaoyin Liu

College of Public Administration, Huazhong University of Science and Technology,
Wuhan 430074, Hubei, People's Republic of China
zpzeng@hust.edu.cn

Abstract. The aim of this research is to investigate the determinants of Chinese older adults in the use of the social network service (SNS). Qualitative and semi-structure analysis were applied to understand what factors encourage or discourage older adults use WeChat, a most frequently used SNS in China. Our findings show a digital divide: the number of the older people used WeChat is far less than that of teenagers and young generation. Even those who used WeChat, they tend to use a small part of functions within WeChat. The survey demonstrated that psychological motivations such as sociality need, information exchange and entertainment had positive effects on older adults' attitudes. The level of WeChat usage in the context of aging is influenced by the following major themes: usage purpose and motivation, social influence, physical fitness requirements and self-efficacy. For those users who have experienced WeChat, most have positive attitude toward WeChat. Security concerns and perceived cost are not strong negative factors impeding on the older adult using the WeChat but how they use the functions provided by WeChat.

Keywords: Aging people · Mobile SNS usage · Technology usage and adoption

1 Introduction

Population aging is taking place in nearly all the countries of the world, including the most population in the world - China. According to China National People's Congress statistics predicting, the number of aging people 60 years and older was 212 million in 2014 and is supposed to arrive 243 million by the end of this decade. It is estimated that the percentage of people over 65 years in China will surpass that of Japan in 2030, and the percentage of people aged 60 or older is expected to increase to 30 % of the Chinese population in 2040. Thus, with the rapid aging process in the world, the development of China is facing the rapid population aging challenges. With the largest older population, China will probably experience heavy economic and social development pressure in the next several decades. How to sustain an autonomous and active lifestyle for the aging by optimizing opportunities for health to enhance quality of life has raised much concerns.

© Springer International Publishing Switzerland 2016
J. Zhou and G. Salvendy (Eds.): ITAP 2016, Part II, LNCS 9755, pp. 256–265, 2016.
DOI: 10.1007/978-3-319-39949-2_25

There are several approaches to cope with the problems of aging from a variety of advanced technologies and national policies. Among them one is that the sustainable development of information industry which the developing countries can benefits from its advantages to economic growth. In many countries, economic reform and techno-logical innovations are encouraged to promote the aging society development. An example is that the European Union's Ambient Assisted Living Joint Program has invested significantly as part of a social inclusion agenda to improve access and uptake of ICT-based products and services by disadvantaged groups, such as older people, and to exploit the opportunities this brings for European industry [1]. Similarly, facing with the coming of aging society, China government also proposes the promotion of the aged industry from the technology besides social, economic, and policy response to alleviate the negative influence of the aging. Thus, the aging people may have accommodated to more technological changes than any previous generation for their medical services, social mobility and compatible interpersonal relations, etc.

Previous studies demonstrated that ICTs can be a possible support to help the older adults lead active and participatory life. For example, information technology such as Internet can decrease vulnerability resulting from social isolation and loneliness [2]. The older adults who use it in their personal life for activities such as reading news, trading stocks, and viewing videos will naturally find it convenient to use for personal purposes after they retire. Advanced technology is also frequently postulated as a means of supporting aging in place. Theoretically, ICTs have a huge potential to improve the quality of life for the older people, however, in practice, information technology are often found used by young generation, older adults face a number of hurdles to adopt new technologies. Thus, there is a need to explore the determinants influencing the older people accept and use the new ICTs.

In our study, we attempt to provide a research on understanding older adults' social media usage by collecting both qualitative data to analysis the determinants of using WeChat, one of the most widely used social networking service in China. And also to articulate some of the key challenges that will need to be addressed if the full potential of WeChat is to be exploited. To the best of our knowledge, this is one of the first studies to investigate information communication and sharing in social media in the context of the older generation in China.

2   Social Media and WeChat

Social Network Sites (SNS) is a new emerging technologies and applications that utilize the Internet and Web 2.0 technologies and allow users to create and participate genre of community-based websites. According to [3], SNS can be characterized as web-based services that allow individuals to construct the presence usually including a photo and descriptors like location, study concentration and interests, publicly display a list of other users with whom they share a connection, and to traverse those list of connections to view the profiles of others within the system. As a digital platform, SNS provides convenience for sharing the interests and social interaction amongst various ethnic groups having common thoughts on a particular topic or theme. Through functions such as communicating, sharing, collaborating, publishing, managing, one in SNS can imitate a dialogue amongst the community members.

There are hundreds of SNSs available in the market, with various technological affordances, supporting a wide range of interests and practices. In China, the most commonly used mobile SNS products is WeChat [4, 5]. Integrating a variety of functions in traditional medium and communication technology such as text, instant messaging, hold-to-talk voice messaging, broadcast (one-to-many) messaging, etc. WeChat provides a medium of interaction that allow people to create, generate and exchange media content between users. Users can share their photographs and videos, and location, organize offline meetings and group work, etc. As a means of effective and efficient communication, WeChat has gained its popularity of 650 million active users in 2015 according to the users reports.

In general, available, effective and affordable communication facilities are important for maintaining a good quality of life. Through engagement with WeChat, older people can have more active later life. Unfortunately, despite WeChat have been increasingly popular and widely used in China [6], most users focus young generation between 13 and 35 years old [7]. The number of the older adults using WeChat is also far lower that most developed Western countries. SNS in China are still a young person's game and the elderly population have been found less familiar with IT, which implies that issues pertaining to their acceptance of WeChat deserve special attention.

3   Methods

3.1   Sampling

The study was carried out in 2015. Participants were recruited in Wuhan City, a megacity in the center of China. Criteria for inclusion were: (1) community-dwelling, (2) individuals aged 50 or older, and (3) not cognitively impaired. Most interviewee lived near campus. There were nine college students participated in our survey and these students were divided into three groups for survey and interview. The questionnaires form were assisted by students according to their answers due to their weak eyesight and reading difficulties. The older adults who did not heard about SNS/WeChat before were ignored in our survey. Therefore, most respondents knew WeChat more or less and some are using WeChat.

Two types of questionnaires, online and offline were designed for data collection. For online survey, older adults who were likely to meet those criteria were selected and given the website linkage to the questionnaires if they expressed interest in participating our survey (n = 12). We also made an appointment with local community and scheduled the interview with senior citizen association (n = 53). In addition, some interviewee, very small part in our samples, were approached in person near the supermarket and the kindergarten (n = 5). That is, although we developed the questionnaires online version, most questionnaires (84.5 %) were completed by interview offline because it was difficult for older adults to continue the online questionnaires.

Finally, we got the samples consisted of 69 participants whose ages ranged from 50 to 70. WeChat use and adoption among them fall off notably starting at approximately age 70 due to the olds' physical conditions and operation ability. The average age was 57, and 64 % of the participants were female, seemingly indicated that female were more likely to use WeChat than male. Of the participants, most of our samples had attained high school education and above. The majority of the participants considered their health to be good or excellent, and easy to communicate. Our analysis is based on these samples.

3.2 Questionnaires and Interview Questions

We used semi-structured interview to collect the data. In order to ensure the interview can continue, we list the possible influencing factors derived from prior western litera-ture. For example, the widely used technology acceptance model (TAM) [8], Unified Theory of Acceptance and Use of Technology (UTAUT) [9], and previous studies on the technology acceptance pertaining to older adults [10]. The reason that we did not completely use the determinants and scale items in these two models as empirical vali-dation is that both models were primarily designed for the organizational context. The respondents we interviewed were all retired and we believed that their purpose and motivation might have distinct comparing to the organizational context. Additionally, there is no prior studies on the determinants pertaining to WeChat and there is a need to explore the possible determinants conducted with a fairly open framework which allow for focused, conversational, two-way communication.

The possible factors led to an interview guideline used for each group. This is a list of questions and topics that need to be covered during the conversation. Different inter-view tactics were guided to support the goal of creating a broad comprehensive under-standing. For instance, regarding to those used WeChat, the questions were guided to the reasons why and how they start their usage such as the factors pertaining to social influence, the benefits WeChat brought to them, etc. While for those not used, purposive attention was paid to capture their views on the barriers such as health status, education, and level of technology experience, the difficulties and the cost, security concerns, etc. In addition, participants were asked how frequently they used these devices and what they used these devices for. Other gathered background information included educa-tional level and previous vocation.

3.3 Data Collection

All the interviewer were required to record the new information which are not list on the guideline since the determinants cannot be all designed and phrased ahead of survey. Questions could be added during the interview, allowing both the interviewer and the person being interviewed the flexibility to probe for details or discuss issues. After the interview was completed, the interviewer were urged to list new insights to a report shared by all the members.

The determinants were discussed within the team and then combined into the list. As more data are collected, and as data are re-reviewed, determinants can be grouped into concepts, and then into categories. In this way, new and overarching categories of factors were formed, added and refined, and the findings was shaped. The entire process took 6 weeks, and in the last 1 weeks, few new information about determinants were added, indicating that data saturation was reached. These data and the data on background information of participants were entered in SPSS version 21 in order to produce descriptive statistics. All possible determinants are sorted by frequency, which have been extracted from the data. Finally, 10 critical determinants were built, based on the reports from each member and group.

4 Data Analysis

4.1 Usage Purposes and Motivation

The usage of technology depends on his purpose and motivation. Most respondents left the working environment, thus, extrinsic motivation such as salary, awards, job performance might not be but intrinsic desire or need might be the forces driving older adults to use WeChat. As a social human, older adults will have the need to communicate with others peoples, know about the information of his living environment and interact with the environment. Hence, a communication channel is important for them to exchange and share the information with other people, which can be transferred by text, symbolic, voice, pictures and video through network.

Our survey indicated that communicating with family members is one of motivations of using WeChat. Many older adults did not live with their children since their children work out-of-town or at other cities far away from their living place. Comparing to mobile call, WeChat is a better alternative to transfer richer information such as pictures and video besides voice and text. Additionally, some respondents especially retired Chinese women often support their children and grandchildren by taking after the younger households with child-care and house-work, they need WeChat to communicate with their children.

Another reason is that some attend the association and need WeChat for the club activity, or for health information and national news. WeChat provides the old with a way to share their life and opinions with others, allows the old to access a broad range of learning materials for personal use. Some often look through the Moments to know about others' life. Most think the information on WeChat is very useful, and many respondents say that they often show their life through Moments.

Not all respondents used WeChat. Some respondents said that WeChat was useless for them because his friends and relatives are always close to them, and they can contact with them using phone call or text. Whenever participants did not use WeChat, they stated that they did not see a need for it, particularly when mobile phones can meet the needs for communication. Additionally, they argued that their friend did not use WeChat and he did not know what they would do with WeChat. Thus, perceived need is one of the critical factors that the respondents use WeChat.

4.2 Mobile Smart Phone Devices Ownership and Use

WeChat primary runs on mobile smart phone with Android, windows phone and IOS system. This means it is not possible to get into the WeChat network if one do not possess a suitable smart phone with the app installed. Therefore, if the older adults have no smart devices, he has no opportunity to try and use WeChat. Unlike smart phone is popular in young generation, not all the old own smart devices. On average, around two thirds of older adults own smart phone in our survey. Some old adults use the geriatric mobiles with big pressing button and large fonts, which provides simple functions and ease of use.

There are several reasons contributing to the older adults' not having smart phone. Buying a new phone can be costly. Our survey indicated that one is that most popular smart phone are more expensive than geriatric mobiles, the other is those devices always developed with complex functions out of the older adult's capability. For some respondents, the functions of geriatric mobiles is enough for their communications. Thus, the price and complexity of smart phone could be two of the critical barriers using the WeChat. Only when the relative advantages of using WeChat are greater than these hindrance force, will older adults upgrade their phones.

4.3 Self-efficacy

In our research, most of the old people who use WeChat have received senior high school education and above, and their physical conditions are good, therefore, they don't think it hard for them to learn how to use WeChat. For most people in our survey, WeChat is easy to learn and the operation is simple. However, the older adult require a greater amount of assistance on WeChat usage. Most respondents start to install and use WeChat helped by their children and members in the club.

The age changes in perception and motor control may make it harder to see a mobile screen, type on a button, or knowledge leap. For example, several respondents replied that they could not recognize and use English alphabetic characters to input Chinese characteristics. In addition, there need more time it takes to learn a new technology.

4.4 Personal Interests and Individual Innovation Awareness

Not all the respondents are interested in WeChat. Some participants spoke they were 'non-technological' person and they were not interested in WeChat. Some old people have conservative opinions. They think WeChat is for the young and don't support old people to use WeChat. For example, some said that WeChat was trifles for young generation and kids. Some respondents said that they preferred their entertainment and games such as Chinese Chess, dancing in their age. Most WeChat functions are generally aimed the young that don't interested older people.

4.5 Perceived Benefit

When asked about the role that WeChat played in their social activities, most of those used WeChat agreed that WeChat could meet their social activity need and make the connections between them and their relatives/friends. WeChat enlarges their social network because they can keep touch with their friends and relatives. WeChat provides useful ways to contact with their friends. What's more, they can send SMS and voices through WeChat, which is more convenient than phones calls and messages. WeChat communication has been a emotion expression tool through many kinds of media such as speech, image, facial expression, red packet and so forth.

Older people might weigh benefits heavily when deciding whether to adopt new technology since they learn technology not for future but now. Therefore, relevance such as convenience, entertainment and pleasure is important for them to learn to use WeChat. Besides the obvious benefit in connecting to their friends and family, WeChat is an alternative of phone calls and messages. Many old people will run WeChat when WiFi is available, thereby they can save the phone calls and messages fee.

4.6   Enjoyment and Pleasure

For those used WeChat, especially for women, they agreed that it was pleasant to chat and interact with their friends through WeChat. WeChat always gather people with the same interests, or, people with common goals and aspirations. Thus, WeChat provided news or issues personal interests in common, hobbies, sports, etc. Sharing on how to take care their grandchildren is a major topic. Also the old are very happy to get to know about their relatives' especially their children's life. They agreed the interesting things in the Moments bring them a lot fun.

4.7   Influence of the Social Network

Members of the social network of the participant can act as an alternative to the participant's personal technology use, and participants were concerned how their technology use affected other people in their social network. As others talk about "WeChat" from time to time, they also start to use WeChat to catch up with the fashion. As a result, the social network plays more direct, roles in influencing the participants' use WeChat and their technology-related attitudes and beliefs. People who were in close contact with the participant could recommend or against certain technologies. An example is this dialogue between a participant and her daughter: "… And then she said to me: "Mum, I installed WeChat in your cell phone and you have to learn to use WeChat. If I added you as a friend of mine then you can see my photos and moments every day. …you can see me and your grandson by WeChat.""

4.8   Perceived Cost-Data Access Charge

Cell phone expenses can be a significant part of old people's budget. Most old people care about cost resulting from data access. There are many different carriers for text, calling and data access. They will find one plan that meets his needs. Most respondents are light users who only use WeChat for text and message browse. Some respondents won't use WeChat unless Wifi is available. Another case is that the carriers is sufficient for them. Anyway, most don't think using WeChat will really kill their savings and they can afford it, so data access charge is not a critical barrier for the older adults using the WeChat but it has impact on when and how to use WeChat.

4.9   Security Concerns

Most respondents in our research concerned about WeChat security. They don't believed they have enough knowledge and experience about WeChat. They worried about possible loss in using WeChat, so they didn't use the functions such as e-pay, financial assistant and charge service in WeChat. They are also concerned about the leak of their personal privacy and doing something wrong. Thus, due to security concerns, many old people only used a small part of functions such as message, chat, news reading and browse the others' Moments. Compared to the young, most functions in WeChat were not used by old adults.

WeChat allows people to add friends by a variety of methods, including searching by username or phone number, adding from phone or email contacts, or viewing nearby people who are also using the same service. However, most of respondents will not add stranger as his friends in WeChat.

4.10   Other Barriers

Education, physical conditions and previous career are important factors influencing the WeChat usage of the older adults. If the old people is low educated and his physical conditions is not very good, for example, weak eyesight problems. Some old people are very busy with their own things and don't have time for social media. Some old people don't have a person who can teach them to use WeChat. Otherwise, some old people think phone calls and SMS can totally satisfy their need because they have small social circles and children are around them.

5   Discussion

Sociality interaction need is the primary purpose for the old people to use the WeChat. Our survey indicated that the daily life and interpersonal relationship had a lot influence on the old adults' SNS usage. SNS is a reflection of his/her real life, increases the connection to family and friends, feelings of relevance and an interactive outlet to the real world. Our result indicated that there were two resources from which they start to use WeChat, one is from their Children's persuasion, the other is showed and recommended by their friends. Thus, sociality need in his daily life, social influence, such as from his children and his friends in later life have a great influence on his intention and usage in WeChat. If in social life many of their relatives and friends use WeChat, the older adults will have more willingness to use WeChat. If their daughter and son lived far away, WeChat can provide the relative advantage such as remote video call. This suggests that the older adults will change their WeChat usage behavior according to their social surroundings. In addition, research found that WeChat provides a tool for older adults to stay connected with loosely their children and friends, to expand one's social network by linking like-minded people. Thus, it is important to note that older adults may be aware of technological solutions that could benefit them.

Besides perceived need and social influence, WeChat usage links to individual interests. If the older adults have hobbies together with his friends such as Chinese Chess and Ping Pong they can spare time, they might not have interests in WeChat. Although the relationship between active later life and WeChat remains unclear, it is found that those who use WeChat have more assertive personality, more active in our interview, and usually participate in group activities. They are more willing to spend time to know about his friends moments and his environment from WeChat.

Among individual factors, age, gender, prior career and education seem to be the most important factors having a direct or indirect impact on the use of WeChat by active older Internet users. In our survey, the younger the seniors are, the more willingness they have to use WeChat. Most respondents who used WeChat are blessed with higher education and rich knowledge. Regarding to the influence by age, the number of the female users is more than male users, the female participants are more familiar with the term 'online social network' and are also more frequent users, compared to male participants. The results are in line with the existing body of research on technology acceptance by community-dwelling older adults [11]. The possible reason is that females' needs of information acquisition and emotional experience such as anecdotal and entertaining were more gratified compared with males' needs. While for old man, they are more concern about the utility functions.

Our findings indicate that participants face several challenges in acceptance of WeChat, e.g. self-efficacy, physical and psychological conditions, etc. For example, the older adults preferred to using phone call if they need to communicate with their daughters, sons and friends when they have something important to communicate. The older adults need invest more effort in using technology. Most respondents were helped by others people, if his children and most of his friends are not using WeChat, they are unlikely to use WeChat. Hence, lack of social support is an important factors hinder the older adults to develop their skills to use WeChat.

Although it is important to take into account older adults' attitudes and opinions regarding technology, more studies need to take into consideration why older adults hold such attitudes and opinions of technology. Our survey indicated that behavior-related consequences form one's attitude toward the behavior, that is, more positive attitudes toward WeChat tend to outweigh negative viewpoints, especially the older adults had used and experienced WeChat. In addition, supporters also believed that WeChat was overall safe for chatting, message and information browse. Although the income of the older adults is not high, data access cost is not a critical factor impeding their using the WeChat. Thus, such attitudes of older adults toward WeChat can be successfully manipulated through training and social support that provides direct and positive experience. The older people are capable of learning SNS albeit they might take more effort. The future SNS development for the older adults is to provide more appropriate services that reflect older peoples' interests and their needs, make the service run on geriatric mobiles.

6   Limitations

This study fills existing research gap by empirically explaining the factors impacting the adoption of social media of the older adults in China. However, this study has some limitations. Firstly, most samples are from campus with higher education. Seniors, like any other demographic group, are not monolithic, and there are important distinctions in their WeChat adoption patterns, therefore, the number of the samples should be expanded. Secondly, this study only based on qualitative analysis, future studies are encouraged to use quantitative analysis to specify and expand the implications of the findings.

Acknowledgements. This research is supported by National Natural Science Foundation of China (No. 71173084).

References

1. Leist, A.K.: Social media use of older adults: a mini-review. Gerontology **59**, 378–384 (2013)
2. White, J., Weatherall, A.: A grounded theory analysis of older adults and information technology. Educ. Gerontol. **26**, 371–386 (2000)
3. Boyd, D.M., Ellison, N.B.: Social network sites: definition, history, and scholarship. J. Comput. Mediat. Commun. **13**, 210–230 (2007)
4. Zhou, T., Li, H.: Understanding mobile SNS continuance usage in China from the perspectives of social influence and privacy concern. Comput. Hum. Behav. **37**, 283–289 (2014)
5. Xu, J., Kang, Q., Song, Z., Clarke, C.P.: Applications of mobile social media: WeChat among academic libraries in China. J. Acad. Librariansh. **41**, 21–30 (2015)
6. Lien, C.H., Cao, Y.: Examining WeChat users' motivations, trust, attitudes, and positive word-of-mouth: evidence from China. Comput. Hum. Behav. **41**, 104–111 (2014)
7. Guo, C., Shim, J.P., Otondo, R.: Social network services in China: an integrated model of centrality, trust, and technology acceptance. J. Glob. Inf. Technol. Manag. **13**, 76–99 (2010)
8. Davis, F.D.: Perceived usefulness, perceived ease of use, and user acceptance of information technology. MIS Q. **13**, 318–339 (1989)
9. Venkatesh, V., Morris, M.G., Davis, G.B., Davis, F.D.: User acceptance of information technology: toward a unified view. MIS Q. **27**, 425–478 (2003)
10. Lian, J., Yen, D.C.: Online shopping drivers and barriers for older adults: age and gender differences. Comput. Hum. Behav. **37**, 133–143 (2014)
11. Vošner, H.B., Bobek, S., Kokol, P., Krečič, M.J.: Attitudes of active older Internet users towards online social networking. Comput. Hum. Behav. **55**, 230–241 (2016)

Aging, Learning, Training and Games

Operational Assistance for Elderly People
Using a Rhythm System

Hiroko Akatsu[1]([✉]) and Akinori Komatsubara[2]

[1] Oki Electric Ind. Co., Ltd, 1-16-8 Chuou, Warabi-Shi, Saitama 335-8510, Japan
akatsu232@oki.com
[2] Waseda University, Tokyo, Japan

Abstract. Information Technology machines as MFPs (Multiple Function Printers) and ATMs (Automatic Teller Machines) with complicated functions require better user assistance, particularly for elderly people. It is necessary to reduce psychological loads such as a sense of insecurity or impatience in operation, as well as the cognitive load.

This study focuses on enhanced operational rhythm to reduce psychological load on the elderly when using MFPs, which require the user to navigate between quite a few settings. Evaluation was carried out by observing elderly subjects and middle-aged subjects using MFP interfaces whilst hearing an audio rhythm at a Tempo of 40, 60 and 120 bpm (beats per minute).

The number of operational errors and overall time taken to complete the task were recorded, along with subjective evaluation via interviews with the subjects. The results showed that elderly subjects tended to operate in accordance with the operational rhythm. On the other hand, middle-aged subjects tended to operate at their own rhythm.

Keywords: Elderly people · Operational assistance · MFP interface design · Usability

1 Introduction

These days, many people are required to use multifunction machines such as ATMs (Automatic Teller Machines) and MFPs (Multiple Function Printers). Since they are becoming more and more complex with many services and functions, the elderly especially have difficulties in using such equipment.

Since elderly users have expressed their concerns and requests for improved usability, IT equipment should provide better assistance and usability for elderly people.

In order to achieve this objective, it is necessary not only to reduce cognitive load, but also to reduce psychological load, such as a sense of insecurity or anxiety, because these factors trigger operational errors.

Voice guidance is often used as a method for providing operational assistance; however, the guidance speed used can cause negative psychological impacts on users when it is too fast or too slow, depending on how fast users can process the voice guidance [1]. Moreover, when the time taken for the display to respond to an input is faster

J. Zhou and G. Salvendy (Eds.): ITAP 2016, Part II, LNCS 9755, pp. 269–276, 2016.
DOI: 10.1007/978-3-319-39949-2_26

or slower than user expectations or physiological and cognitive speed, it can cause negative psychological impacts [2]. This impact, it is believed, occurs because of a disrupted operational rhythm. For instance, in the operation of an ATM that requires a lot of input, such as the bank and branch name in a step-by-step process, it has been observed that users operate the system at a certain rhythm during normal smooth operation [3]. Therefore, Akatsu et al. propose a hypothesis for simple assistance that aims to provide step-by-step interface and operational rhythms in order to reduce user psychological load and to allow users to conduct operations at their own pace without presenting information such as voice or visual guidance [4]. Their study focuses on operational rhythms to reduce user psychological load when using an MFP which requires many operation settings. The operational rhythm was created with a metronome, and the effects of the rhythm on elderly subjects were measured.

2   Previous Study and Hypotheses

2.1   ATM Interface with Voice Guidance

In this previous study, we (Akatsu et al.) designed the new ATM interface for elderly users based on cognitive aging [5]. This ATM provides a step-by-step interface and voice guidance. Thanks to this new interface design, elderly users were able to operate them more successfully, and the number of time-outs (system reset due to lack of user response) following operation errors decreased.

When developing this ATM interface, we conducted usability testing. We found that in ATM processes which require a lot of user input, for example bank and branch names, when a user completes them smoothly, they tend to follow their own individual rhythm. Figure 1 shows the remittance amount input screen. When the ATMs voice message says "The amount is 65,000 yen, is it OK?", the elderly users would reply "Yes, it is Ok" as they push the button. It was just like they were responding to a real person. The voice message created an operational rhythm which elderly users could easily identify and follow.

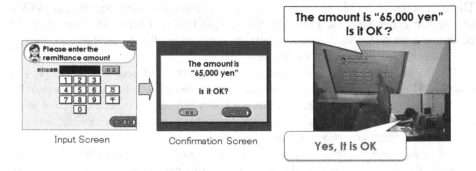

Fig. 1. ATM interface with voice messages

Rhythm is important in assisting elderly users, and this led us to experiment using an actual rhythm or beat instead of a voice message. We aimed to study the effects of simple assistance combing a step-by-step interface with operational rhythms.

2.2 MFP Interface with Using Metronome Rhythms

Our previous study focused on "operation rhythm" as a method for reducing user psychological load when operating an MFP, which requires selection of many copy functions. Operation rhythms were created and the effects of these rhythms on elderly users' MFP operation were examined [4].

Most Conventional MFP interface designs are similar to that shown in Fig. 2. As shown in Fig. 2, when the "One Side/Two side" button is pressed, secondary options appear in a pop-up window, from which the user chooses exact settings.

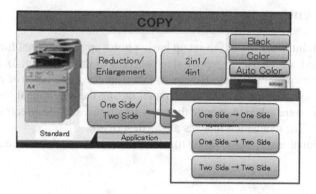

Fig. 2. MFP interface design-conventional interface

In our previous study, an interface system to set up basic photocopy functions for an MFP was created, which uses a step-by-step procedure instead (shown in Fig. 3). We changed to a step-by-step interface structure as this type of interface is easy for novice users. A rhythm was then played during the operational period.

Three rhythms created by a metronome were used, at the standard speed of Tempo 60, double-speed Tempo 120, and Tempo 40. The metronome was set by the side of the touch panel display.

Results showed that when a rhythm was provided for the elderly, they displayed a tendency to synchronize their operation with the rhythm. However, it was also indicated that a rhythm which is too fast can have a negative impact on the elderly's operational ability. We also focused on psychological aspects via a questionnaire evaluation and interview, which suggested that better familiarity with the operation had a stronger effect than the metronome rhythm.

Therefore, in our new study, we ensured the elderly subjects were completely familiarized with operation, enabling us to accurately examine the impact of rhythm on their performance. For comparison, we used a group of subjects in their 30 s and 40 s who work in offices and are familiar with MFPs.

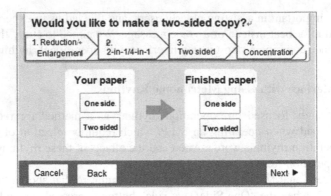

Fig. 3. MFP interface design-new interface

3   Experiment

In this study, an interface system to set up basic photocopy operational functions for an MFP was created, which uses a step-by-step procedure (shown in Fig. 3). It is the same interface as in the previous study. However, this time the three types of rhythms were played through speakers next to the touch panel during the operational period.

The subjects were asked to operate the copy functions, and the effects of the rhythm were evaluated. The evaluation indexes are as described:

(1) Operational error, (2) Overall time taken, (3) Subjective evaluations from a survey.

3.1   Experimental System

Figure 4 shows the experimental system. In this study, an experimental simulator where users sequentially set up MFP basic copy functions was prepared, as shown in Fig. 3. The subjects were asked to operate the simulator using a 15-inch display on a personal computer. Three rhythms were used at the standard speed of Tempo 60, double-speed Tempo 120, and Tempo 40. Rhythms were output from the speakers next the touch panel display.

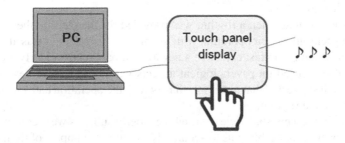

Fig. 4. Experimental system

3.2   Evaluation Method

(1) Experiment Subjects. The subjects consisted of 4 elderly people (2 males and 2 females between the ages of 63 and 73) and 4 middle-aged subjects (4 males between the age 32 and 40). The subjects had made simple copies using a copy machine previously, but they had no experience using the two-sided or 2-in-1/4-in-1 copy functions.

(2) Experiment Procedures. First, the purpose of the experiment was explained to the subjects, and a pre-test survey on MFP use was conducted. Then, the subjects were asked to participate in the experiment tasks. As indicated in Table 1, the subjects learnt how to set up the functions as they participated in the practice tasks in order to make them fully familiar with the operation. Task 1 (Two-sided and 4-in-1 copy) was conducted without any rhythm as the control group. This was compared to the next three tasks which were conducted to rhythm of Temp 40, 60 and 120 respectively. Upon completion of the four experiment tasks, an evaluation survey and an interview with each subject was conducted.

Table 1. Experiment task list

	Practice Task	Condition			Task	Condition
1	Black and White	NO TEMPO		Task1	4-in-1 & Two-sided Copy	NO TEMPO
2	Color	NO TEMPO	→	Task2	4-in-1 & Two-sided Copy	TEMPO 40
3	Enlarged	NO TEMPO		Task3	2-in-1 & Two-sided Copy	TEMPO 60
4	2-in-1/4-in-1	NO TEMPO		Task4	4-in-1 & Two-sided Copy	TEMPO 120
5	Two-sided copy	NO TEMPO				

4   Results and Consideration

4.1   Errors

All subjects were able to complete the tasks without any errors by the end of the practice period. They were all fully accustomed to operation. For this reason, there were no errors during the evaluated tasks.

However, as the subjective evaluation described later shows, the subjects felt some ambivalence at Tempo 120 when participating in a task they could accomplish under the other rhythm conditions, although they did not commit significantly more errors.

Even if the elderly and the middle-aged subjects were familiar with the operation, too fast a rhythm was shown to have a negative impact on the subject's psychological state.

4.2   Task Achievement Time

Figure 5 shows the results for overall time taken. The number of subjects is small but Statistical analysis was performed for reference. The Analysis of Variance (ANOVA) for Age (2) × Tempo (4), the results indicate a significant difference (F $(1, 24)$ = 39.10, p < 0.01) among the age groups. The middle-aged group was faster than the elderly group. The significant difference between the ages was observed, but difference between tempo conditions was not observed.

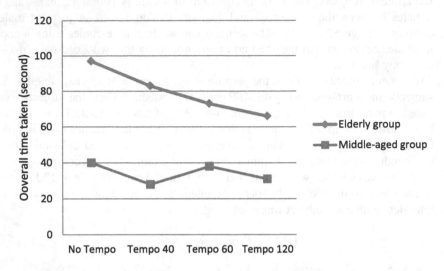

Fig. 5. Overall time taken (Color figure online)

Although a significant difference does not exist, as the tempo got faster, a tendency can be seen the overall time taken is shorter. In the previous study at Tempo 120, it was observed that the performance of most elderly subjects was disturbed, and the overall time taken increased [4]. However, when the elderly are familiar with the operation, the faster rhythm has less effect.

4.3 Psychological Evaluation on a Given Rhythm

After each tempo operation was completed, a survey was conducted for ten things; level of calmness, sense of security, ease in understanding the operation,, operational errors, etc., on a scale of one to six (e.g., Very calm: $6 \rightarrow$ Not calm at all: 1).

With the ANOVA for Age (2) × Tempo (4), the results indicate a significant difference ($F(1, 24) = 39.10$, $p < 0.01$) among the two-factor interaction effect, the age and the tempo in "level of calmness". Figure 6 shows the result of the calmness score.

Other factors (comfortable operation, operation at own pace) which significantly differed were mainly due to age, the elderly scores were higher than for the middle-aged.

In addition, in the interview after completion of the task, the elderly said that they felt the rhythm sound of Tempo 40 and 60 was not annoying and they could concentrate on operation of the screen. While they felt rushed by Tempo 120, they tried to match it, but could not. On the other hand, the middle-aged subjects that the rhythm was noisy and rushed them at any tempo. They operated the machine while ignoring the tempo.

So we can see, the elderly subjects were strongly affected by rhythm, but the opposite was true for the middle-aged subjects. It was considered that middle-aged are more familiar with the operation than the elderly and can complete the task more quickly. In

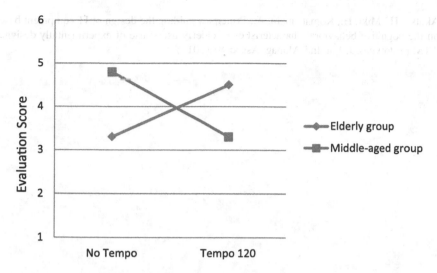

Fig. 6. Psychological evaluation (Color figure online)

fact, they avoid the influence of external factors, and they were controlled by their own temperament.

5   Results and Consideration

This study focused on "operation rhythm" as a method for reducing user psychological load when operating an MFP, which requires selection of many copy functions. Operation rhythms were created and the effects of these rhythms on elderly and the middle-aged people's MFP operation were examined. When a rhythm was provided for experiment subjects, the elderly displayed a tendency to synchronize their operation with the rhythm. On the other hand, the middle-aged tended to display more control and try to operate the machine at their own rhythm.

The results of our experiment indicated that too fast a rhythm has a negative impact on both elderly and middle-aged users. However, if the elderly are familiar with the operation, too fast a rhythm has less effect.

References

1. Akatsu, H., Miki, H., Komatsubara, A.: Dynamic guidance: synchronized auditory and visual guidance for elderly people. Jpn. J. Ergon. **47**, 96–102 (2011)
2. Komatsubara, A., Yokomizo, Y.: On the ergonomic limits of computer system response time. Jpn. J. Ergon. **4** (1988)
3. Akatsu, H., Harada, E., Miki, H., Komatsubara, A.: Design principles for IT equipment based on cognitive behavioral characteristics of elderly users; usability test applied to automatic teller machines (ATMs). J. Jpn. Ind. Manag. Assoc. **81** (2011)
4. Akatsu, H., Komatsubara, A.: Operational assistance for elderly people by using audio rhythms. In: AAATE 2015 (2015)

5. Akatsu, H., Miki, H., Komatsubara, A.: Principles guiding the design of IT equipment based on the cognitive behavioral characteristics of elderly users; use of experimentally designed ATM prototypes. J. Jpn. Ind. Manag. Assoc. **81** (2011)

You Can('t) Teach an Old Dog New Tricks: Analyzing the Learnability of Manufacturing Software Systems in Older Users

Katrin Arning[✉], Simon Himmel, and Martina Ziefle

Human-Computer-Interaction Center, RWTH Aachen University,
Campus Boulevard 57, 52074 Aachen, Germany
{arning,himmel,ziefle}@comm.rwth-aachen.de

Abstract. Modern manufacturing processes are based on complex computer-aided planning processes, which are provided by CAM (computer-aided manufacturing)-software systems. Due to increased functional capabilities of CAM software, the complexity of these systems and the demands on CAM users are rising. Facing the demographic change (cognitively aging users, retiring of experienced CAM experts who are succeeded by inexperienced users), not only general learnability issues but also user-specific requirements are becoming increasingly important. An online-survey focusing on the learnability of CAM-software, and existing learning environments and strategies in manufacturing practice was conducted (n = 76) and effects of age and CAM expertise were analyzed. Implications for CAM skill acquisition among users of different age and expertise groups were derived.

Keywords: Computer-aided manufacturing software · User diversity · Age · Expertise · Learnability · Training · Survey

1 Introduction

Todays' automated product manufacturing processes require complex computer-aided planning processes, which make use of CAx-software systems (computer-aided technologies). CAx-software systems integrate a broad range of components such as CAD (computer-aided design), CAM (computer-aided manufacturing), computer-aided process planning (CAPP), and several other simulation features like FEM (finite elements method), and CFD (computational fluid dynamics) [1]. The increasing number of machine tools and functions, simulation- and visualization features come at a price: CAx software systems have become highly complex. Even with standardized tools and functions, the complexity of CAD/CAM-software has already risen to a level where only highly trained experts are able to effectively use current CAx-software. The development of computer-integrated manufacturing (CIM) - the simulation of the entire production process and organization with fully integrated CAx-features - will boost complexity to an even higher but also inevitable level if manufacturers want to stay competitive [2]. Due to the enormous functional spectrum of CAx-software, we focused on only one part of the CAx process chain (Fig. 1): computer-aided manufacturing (CAM) and its software (CAM system).

© Springer International Publishing Switzerland 2016
J. Zhou and G. Salvendy (Eds.): ITAP 2016, PartII, LNCS 9755, pp. 277–288, 2016.
DOI: 10.1007/978-3-319-39949-2_27

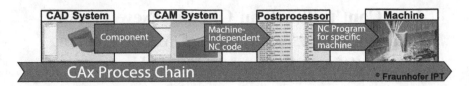

Fig. 1. CAx process chain

Since CAx/CAM-systems are too complex and demanding to be intuitively used, novel users usually receive extensive trainings. However, workplace practice shows that despite of this learning support most CAx/CAM novices are not able to successfully handle their software, which leads to longer training periods and frustration on the users' side and, as a consequence, to an inefficient allocation of resources, reduced product quality, and delivery delays on the business side. Hence, the learnability of CAx/CAM software systems is an important, but rather neglected issue so far.

According to the HCI community, the learnability of a system is a central aspect of its usability [3]. Learnability refers to the initial learning experience of a user until he/she is able to successfully interact with a technical system [e.g., 4]. However, most of the HCI learnability research since the 1980ies focused on desktop computing [e.g., 5] or the usage of (mobile) "everyday technology" [e.g., 6], but little is known about the learnability of CAx/CAM software systems. Facing the demographic change and its implications, i.e., cognitively aging users or the retiring of experienced CAx/CAM experts who are succeeded by inexperienced users, not only general CAx/CAM learnability issues but also user-specific requirements in software skill acquisition become increasingly important.

1.1 Software Skill Acquisition in Older Users

Research concordantly shows, that older users face greater difficulties in interacting with software systems and in acquiring computer skills. Training takes significantly more time for older adults, they commit more errors in post-training evaluations compared to younger learners and considerable age differences remain in computer performance after receiving instructional support [e.g., 7]. These age-related differences in technical skill acquisition are explained by declines in sensory, motor and cognitive abilities, lower levels of technical experience and inadequate mental models [8]. Domain expertise was found to reduce or fully compensate age differences in performance and learning [e.g., 9]. Hence, apart from users' age, the impact of user diversity factors such as CAM expertise should also be considered when investigating the learning conditions for a successful CAM-software skill acquisition. Although a lot of research was conducted on user interface interaction and technical skill acquisition in recent decades, most studies evaluated specific trainings formats (e.g., "training wheels" [10]) based on specific learning theory assumptions (e.g., "constructivism" [11], "active learning" [12]) or procedural instructional design schemes [13] without being connected to existing learning conditions or constraints in manufacturing practice. Therefore, the purpose of this study was to increase our knowledge about the learnability and learning conditions of CAM software systems in workplace reality. Our study focused on an evaluation of perceived learnability of CAM software systems, an assessment of formal learning environments and individual learning strategies, the availability of CAM support and CAM learning outcomes. In order to consider user diversity and user-specific demands, the factors age and expertise were integrated into the analysis to get insights into "tailored" optimal learning conditions for different CAM users.

2   Method

2.1   Questionnaire

The questionnaire started with a demographic section (age, gender, education, profession) and an assessment of CAM expertise (type of CAM system, usage experience in years, usage frequency, self-ratings of CAM system knowledge and problem-solving competency). The following items dealt with a learnability evaluation of the CAM system, an evaluation of formal and individual CAM learning environments and strategies, and an evaluation of the CAM support. Questionnaire items were answered on a six-level Likert-scale (totally disagree – totally agree).

2.2   The Sample

The study was run as online-questionnaire, which was distributed in several German manufacturing companies and in CAM-related online forums. A total of n = 119 participants volunteered to answer the questionnaire, but only n = 76 data sets were used for statistical analysis due to incomplete data.

Respondents' age range was between 23 and 62 (M = 41.1, SD = 10.5), the majority (97.4 %) of participants was male. Asked for the level of education, 36 % held a university degree, 30 % completed an apprenticeship, 17 % had a secondary school degree, and 14 % a technical diploma. Half of the participants (49 %) were software developers, 24 % were technical draftsmen, and 21 % were toolmakers. CAM usage experience was between 2 months and 39 years (M = 8.1 years, SD = 6.9). Respondents frequently used their CAM-software (73 % several times a day, 21 % several times a week). The majority (43 %) worked with Siemens NX, followed by Tebis (8 %), CATIA, and SolidCam (both 7 %). Since the study focused on a learnability evaluation, no comparisons between different CAM-software solutions were made.

2.3   Data Analysis

Data was analyzed by MANOVAs (level of significance = 5 %). Due to the higher heterogeneity of older samples, marginally significant findings (level of significance = 10 %) are also reported. The Likert-scale range was transformed to −2.5 (totally disagree) to 2.5 (totally agree) with ratings <0 indicating negative evaluations and ratings >0 indicating positive evaluations. To analyze effects of age and expertise, the sample was divided into subgroups according to age (young = 23–34 years, middle = 35–45 years, old = 46–62 years) and expertise (novices and experts). To quantify expertise, an expertise score was calculated based on the multiplication of "CAM knowledge"- and "problem-solving competency"-ratings (M = 1.94, SD = 2.18, min = −6.25, max = 6.25). Two expertise groups were derived: novices with an expertise score <0 and experts with an score >3.75. Novices had M = 6.2 years (SD = 5.4) and experts had M = 9.6 years (SD = 7.8) of CAM usage experience. A longer duration of CAM usage was related to higher expertise levels (r = .24; p < 0.05). Age and expertise were not correlated (r = .19; p > .1), i.e., age and CAM expertise were independent from each other.

3   Results

3.1   CAM Learnability Evaluation

CAM users evaluated the general learnability of CAM software as not very high (M = 0.2, SD = 1.6). The evaluation of the duration of the individual CAM learning process and the achieved CAM skill level was more positive: CAM users perceived the trainings process duration as "rather short" (M = 0.6, SD = 1.5) and rated their individual CAM skill level as "rather good" (M = 1.3, SD = 1.1).

A 2 × 3 (expertise × age) MANOVA revealed, that learnability ratings significantly differed between CAM experts and novices (F(3,23) = 63.0, p < 0.000) and between CAM users of different age- and expertise groups (F(6,66) = 1.9; p < 0.1). Novices evaluated the CAM learnability negatively, perceived the learning period as longer and estimated their CAM skills to be lower than experts (Fig. 2).

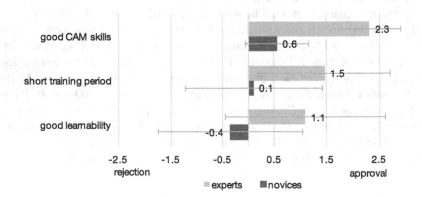

Fig. 2. CAM learnability ratings for experts and novices

A more detailed picture provided the differentiation of CAM learnability ratings in the age- and expertise-groups (Fig. 3). For younger CAM users, the learnability evaluations of novices and experts were similar and not very high. In the middle-aged group, differences in evaluations emerged with a more positive learnability evaluation of experts. In the group of older CAM users, the deviations even further increased: older CAM novices evaluated the learnability of CAM software negatively (M = −1.2), whereas older experts perceived a good learnability (M = 1.6) of their CAM software system.

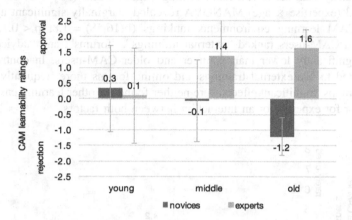

Fig. 3. CAM learnability ratings for the age- and expertise-groups

3.2   CAM Learning Environments and Strategies

3.2.1   Formal CAM Learning Environments

The preferred and best ranked environment for acquiring CAM knowledge was during university studies or in lectures (M = 1.29, SD = 2.4, Fig. 4).

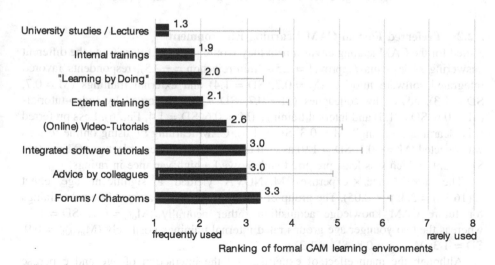

Fig. 4. Ranking of formal CAM learning environments

Further frequently used learning strategies were internal trainings (M = 1.9, SD = 1.9) or by "learning by doing" (M = 2, SD = 1.3), external trainings (M = 2.1, SD = 1.9), video-tutorials (e.g., "youtube", M = 2.6, SD = 2.5), software-integrated tutorials (M = 3.0, SD = 2.6), advice by colleagues (M = 3.0, SD = 1.9), and, as learning strategy with the lowest rank, visiting online-forums (M = 3.3, SD = 2.9).

A 2 × 3 (expertise × age) MANOVA revealed marginally significant age differences in CAM learning environments rankings (F(16,58) = 1.8; p < 0.1, Fig. 5). Middle-aged CAM-users ranked "external trainings", "forums", and "advice by colleagues" significantly lower than younger and older CAM-users. In contrast, older users reported to use external trainings and online forums more frequently than the other age groups. Significant effects were neither found for other learning environment rankings nor for expertise or an interaction between both factors.

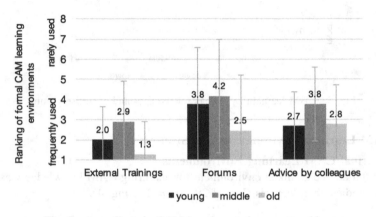

Fig. 5. Age effects in CAM learning environment rankings

3.2.2   Preferred Formal CAM Learning Environment

Asked for the CAM leaning environment they would prefer in future (note the different answering scale – max/approval = 2.5 – min/rejection = −2.5), respondents favored integrated software tutorials (M = 0.7, SD = 1.4) and external trainings (M = 0.7, SD = 1.3), advice by colleagues (M = 0.7, SD = 1.5), followed by video-tutorials (M = 0.6, SD = 1.5) and internal trainings (M = 0.6, SD = 1.4, Fig. 6). Less preferred was "learning by doing" (M = 0.3, SD = 1.3). CAM learning by using online forums was rejected (M = −0.1, SD = 1.9) as well as university studies or lectures (M = −0.8, SD = 2.9), which was least preferred and showed a high variance in ratings.

The 3 × 2 (age × expertise) MANOVA yielded a significant age effect (F(16,16) = 2.3; p < 0.05). The group of older CAM-users evaluated internal trainings for future CAM knowledge acquisition rather neutrally (M_{old} = 0.1, SD = 1.4), whereas the two younger age groups rated internal trainings positively (M_{middle} = 0.9, SD = 1.3; M_{young} = 0.8, SD = 1.3).

Although the main effect of expertise and the interaction of age and expertise missed statistical significance, the ratings of internal trainings in the different age × expertise groups can help to achieve a deeper understanding of the above

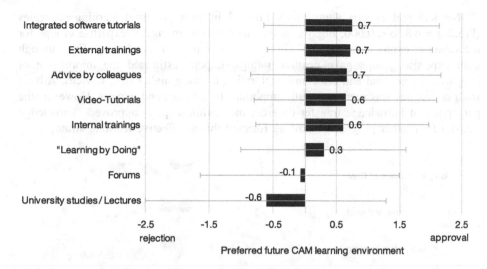

Fig. 6. Preferred formal CAM learning environment

reported age effect (Fig. 7). Especially the group of older CAM experts rejected internal trainings, whereas older novices and younger CAM users in general – independent from their CAM expertise – evaluated them positively as preferred future learning environment.

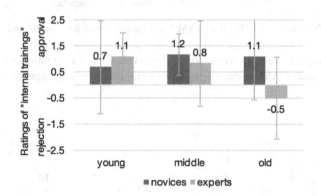

Fig. 7. Preferences for internal CAM trainings for the different age- and expertise-groups

3.2.3   Individual CAM Learning Strategies

Apart from an evaluation of formal CAM learning environments, respondents assessed different individual CAM learning strategies. Long-term usage was perceived as most effective learning strategy ($M = 1.9$, $SD = 0.9$), followed explorative learning ($M = 1.0$, $SD = 1.3$), by advice from colleagues ($M = 0.4$, $SD = 1.4$) and interacting with the CAM software in a "trial-and-error"-modus ($M = 0.1$, $SD = 1.3$). Transferring knowledge from other programs received the lowest ratings and was not perceived as effective individual learning strategy ($M = -0.1$, $SD = 1.6$).

Novices and experts significantly differed in their preferred learning strategies $(F_{(5,28)} = 6.8; p < 0.000$, Fig. 6), as well as the different age × expertise groups for the strategy "explorative learning" $(F_{(10,58)} = 1.8; p < 0.1$, see Fig. 8). Even though both expertise groups gave positive ratings, experts estimated the importance of long-term usage, trial and error and explorative learning higher than novices. Advice from colleagues was seen as equally important by novices and experts. However, the perception of knowledge transfer differed: meanwhile experts approved "knowledge transfer from other programs", novices rejected this as effective learning strategy.

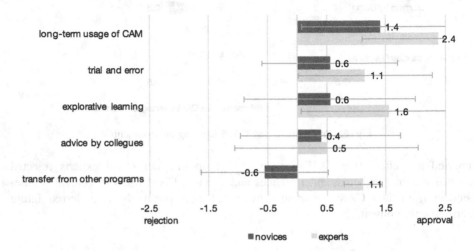

Fig. 8. Evaluation of individual CAM learning strategies for experts and novices

Further insights were derived from the evaluation of explorative learning as effective individual CAM learning strategy in the different age- and expertise-groups (Fig. 9).

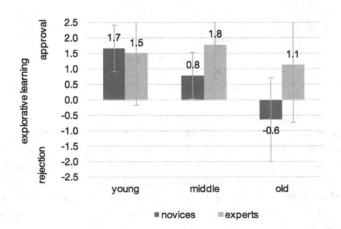

Fig. 9. Explorative learning ratings for the different age- and expertise-groups

Experts of different age groups positively rated "explorative learning" as effective learning strategy. This positive perception was also present in younger novices, but explorative learning was seen as less effective learning strategy – and even rejected – with increasing age by novices.

3.3   Evaluation of CAM Support

The evaluation of the CAM support in the company was comparably positive (Fig. 10). Respondents showed a high willingness to answer colleagues' CAM questions and also felt confident to ask colleagues for CAM advice vice versa. The risk of loosing the main contact for CAM-related questions in future due to fluctuation or retirement was perceived to be low. The availability of several contacts for CAM support was approved to a lesser degree, as well as a fast response time until the CAM support answers.

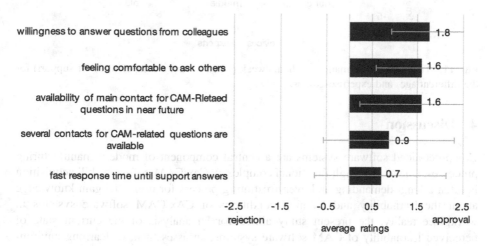

Fig. 10. Evaluation of CAM support

Respondents' estimations of savings in working time per week if an improved CAM support was available revealed an enormous potential for efficiency improvement (Fig. 11). CAM users estimated to save on average $M = 2.5$ h per week ($SD = 4.8$) if a competent CAM support for problems and questions was provided. The time saving estimations differed significantly between experts and novices ($F(1,19) = 5.8$; $p < 0.5$). Novices estimated to save $M_{novices} = 5.3$ h ($SD = 8.2$) with a competent CAM support in the background, while experts expected considerably lower time savings ($M_{experts} = 0.7$, $SD = 1.0$). Again, it was highly informative to differentiate between age- and expertise-groups. In the group of young CAM users, the time saving estimations of novices and experts did not deviate much ($M_{young\ novices} = 2.0$ vs. $M_{young\ experts} = 1.3$). In the middle-aged group, novices reported to have a higher benefit of a competent CAM support ($M_{middle-aged\ novices} = 3.2$ vs. $M_{middle-aged\ experts} = 0.7$). This gap enormously increased in the older CAM user group. Meanwhile older experts reported not to benefit at all from a competent CAM support ($M_{older\ novices} = 0.0$), the group of older novices expected the highest time savings ($M_{older\ experts} = 12.7$).

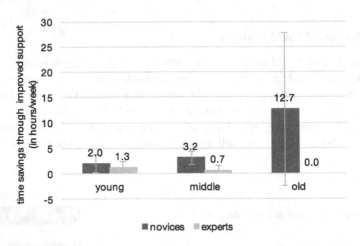

Fig. 11. Time savings estimations in hours/week (when having a competent CAM support) for the different age- and expertise-groups.

4 Discussion

Computer-aided software systems are a central component of modern manufacturing processes. Due to their high functional complexity Cax/CAM-software skill acquisition is often a long, demanding and even frustrating process for users. To gain knowledge about the learnability and learning conditions of CAx/CAM software systems in workplace reality, the present study aimed for an analysis of the current state of perceived learnability of CAM software systems, an assessment of learning environments and individual learning strategies on the workplace, the availability of CAM support and CAM learning outcomes by running an online-survey in German manufacturing companies. To account for effects of the demographic change on the workforce, user diversity factors such as age and CAM expertise where included into the analysis.

Learnability of CAM Software. At first sight, the learnability and learning conditions of CAM software systems in manufacturing companies receive positive evaluations. However, this finding needs to be revised, when a more detailed, user-group-specific perspective is taken. A high learnability evaluation of CAM software only applies for older and experienced CAM practitioners. We assume that the positive expert learnability evaluation of CAM interfaces is affected by a "hindsight bias", where the invested efforts in the personal CAM learning history are retrospectively blinded out. In contrast, the CAM learnability evaluation by unexperienced and younger CAM users is not satisfying at all, since these groups formulate an enormous need for an improved

CAM learning support. Inefficient working procedures are the economic consequence of the current state of CAM system learnability, as the time saving estimations (up to 12 working hours a week) if a competent support was provided, demonstrate.

Effects of User Factors on CAM Learnability. The CAM learnability analysis revealed, that one user group specifically needs improved CAM learning support: older novices. The older and less experienced CAM users are, the less they benefit from exploratory interaction experiences and the less he/she is able to transfer knowledge from other programs. This outcome fits well into the research body of age- and expertise research. Novices do not possess highly organized domain-specific knowledge structures. Hence, while learning to use CAM software or solving CAM interaction problems, novices cannot draw upon extensive domain-specific knowledge structures, which often leads to a superficial perception of problems and less flexible problem solutions [14]. Moreover, age effects in information processing abilities also contribute to problems in CAM skill acquisition. This especially refers to age-related declines in spatial abilities, processing speed, reasoning and memory abilities, which were identified as relevant cognitive abilities for a successful interaction with technical devices and the acquisition of computer skills [15, 16]. But not only cognitive or expertise-related factors should be considered in developing CAM learning support strategies, emotional and motivational factors also play a role. Due to a lower self-efficacy, the learning confidence in older learners is lower [17], which stresses the role of facilitating learning conditions during initial use [18].

Recommendations for CAM Learning Environments and Strategies. Future CAM learning environments should take the diversity of their users into account. For older and novice CAM learners a more structured and knowledge-structure-supporting learning support is recommended. Not only formal learning (in trainings), but also informal workplace learning should be strengthened [19], which stresses the role of older experts as "CAM mentors" in the CAM learning process. Considering the fact, that (older) CAM experts might retire or leave the company, the integration of social media into CAM learning environments is a promising way for 1:n-knowledge exchange and CAM learning support [20]. On the other side, when looking at expert users, HR practitioners should critically question their reliance on formal internal CAM-trainings, since especially older CAM experts reject this formal learning environment.

Limitations and Future Research. Future studies on this topic should aim for a larger sample size, even though it has to be noted, that the response rate in such specific user groups is usually low. The analysis of CAM system learnability should be widened, e.g. by including DIN evaluation criteria [21]. Since learnability and usability are closely connected, future studies should investigate usability improvements of CAM software interfaces and their effect on learnability outcomes. Finally, trainings formats, specifically designed for the needs of older and CAM-unexperienced users should be designed and evaluated.

Acknowledgments. We owe gratitude to Conrad Schnöckel and Sarah Völkel for research support.

References

1. Dankwort, C.W., Weidlich, R., Guenther, B., Blaurock, J.E.: Engineers' CAx education—it's not only CAD. Comput. Aided Des. **36**, 1439–1450 (2004)
2. Hunt, V.D.: Computer-Integrated Manufacturing Handbook. Springer Science & Business Media, Berlin (2012)
3. Nielsen, J.: Usability Engineering. Elsevier, Philadelphia (1994)
4. Shneiderman, B., Plaisant, C.: Designing the User Interface: Strategies for Effective Human-Computer Interaction. Addison-Wesley, Boston (2010)
5. Carroll, J.M., Mack, R.L., Lewis, C.H., Grischkowsky, N.L., Robertson, S.R.: Exploring exploring a word processor. Hum. Comput. Interact. **1**, 283–307 (1985)
6. Ziefle, M.: The influence of user expertise and phone complexity on performance, ease of use and learnability of different mobile phones. Behav. Inf. Technol. **21**, 303–311 (2002)
7. Kelley, C., Charness, N.: Issues in training older adults to use computers. Behav. Inf. Technol. **14**, 107–120 (1995)
8. Hawthorn, D.: Possible implications of aging for interface designers. Interact. Comput. **12**, 507–528 (2000)
9. Nunes, A., Kramer, A.F.: Experience-based mitigation of age-related performance declines: evidence from air traffic control. J. Exp. Psychol. Appl. **15**, 12–24 (2009)
10. Carroll, J.M., Carrithers, C.: Training wheels in a user interface. Commun. ACM **27**, 800–806 (1984)
11. Gold, S.: A constructivist approach to online training for online teachers. J. Asynchronous Learn. Netw. **5**, 35–57 (2001)
12. Arning, K., Ziefle, M.: Ask and you will receive: training novice adults to use a PDA in an active learning environment. Int. J. Mob. Hum. Comput. Interact. **2**, 21–47 (2010)
13. Mayhorn, C.B., Stronge, A.J., McLaughlin, A.C., Rogers, W.A.: Older adults, computer training, and the systems approach: a formula for success. Educ. Gerontol. **30**, 185–203 (2004)
14. Glaser, R., Chi, M.T., Farr, M.J.: The Nature of Expertise. Lawrence Erlbaum Associates, Abingdon (1988)
15. Czaja, S.J., Sharit, J.: Age differences in the performance of computer-based work. Psychol. Aging **8**, 59–67 (1993)
16. Arning, K., Ziefle, M.: Effects of age, cognitive, and personal factors on PDA menu navigation performance. Behav. Inf. Technol. **28**, 251–268 (2009)
17. Maurer, T.J.: Career-relevant learning and development, worker age, and beliefs about self-efficacy for development. J. Manag. **27**, 123–140 (2001)
18. Barnard, Y., Bradley, M.D., Hodgson, F., Lloyd, A.D.: Learning to use new technologies by older adults: perceived difficulties, experimentation behaviour and usability. Comput. Hum. Behav. **29**, 1715–1724 (2013)
19. Ellström, P.-E.: Informal learning at work: Conditions, processes and logics. In: Malloch, M., Cairns, L., Evans, K., O'Connor, B.N. (eds.) The SAGE Handbook Workplace Learning, pp. 105–119. SAGE Publication, London (2011)
20. García-Peñalvo, F.J., Colomo-Palacios, R., Lytras, M.D.: Informal learning in work environments: training with the social web in the workplace. Behav. Inf. Technol. **31**, 753–755 (2012)
21. IEC, I.: 9126-1: Software Engineering–Qualität von Softwareprodukten-Teil 1: Qualitätsmodell. Int. Stand. Organ. Berl. Beuth Verl. (2001)

Designing a Web-Based Application to Train Aging Adults to Successfully Use Technologies Important to Independent Living

Ronald W. Berkowsky[✉], Sara J. Czaja, and Philip D. Harvey

University of Miami Miller School of Medicine, Miami, FL, USA
{rxb285, sczaja, PHarvey}@med.miami.edu

Abstract. The purpose of this study was to develop and pilot-test a web-based application that could train a diverse group of aging adults to more successfully use technologies vital to functional tasks and independent, everyday living. The training application simulated the use of automatic teller machines (ATMs) and the use of a mobile phone to call and fill a prescription. Thirty-two adults (age range 28–71, 63 % aged 55+) were assessed at baseline on functional task performance by being given an ATM task and a prescription task assessment to complete. Participants then underwent 2 weeks of training before being given a follow-up assessment; informal evaluation interviews were also administered. Overall, participants found it easy to use the training interface and that the presentation of material was favorable, however some would have preferred less repetition in training tasks. Recommendations on application-development and design as well as training structure are discussed.

Keywords: Aging · Functional living · Independent living · Simulation training technologies

1 Introduction

In an increasingly technological society, more and more everyday activities are utilizing more advanced gadgets and devices with the purpose of making completion of these activities easier and more efficient. However, for groups who are at risk for decreased technology utilization or decreased tech-literacy and for those at risk for experiencing cognitive impairment (e.g., older adults) use of these advanced gadgets and devices may make completion of these activities more difficult. As an example, older adults who are used to filling a prescription by visiting a pharmacy and who have little experience with mobile phones (e.g., cellular phones or smartphones) may have difficulty with using these devices to refill a prescription. Previous research has shown that online-based training can increase the accuracy of successfully completing technology-based functional tasks. The purpose of this study was to develop and pilot-test a web-based application that could train a diverse group of adults, including middle-aged and older adults, to more successfully use technologies vital to functional tasks and independent, everyday living. The training application was developed with a touchscreen interface and designed to simulate technologies aging adults may need to use in their daily lives:

© Springer International Publishing Switzerland 2016
J. Zhou and G. Salvendy (Eds.): ITAP 2016, PartII, LNCS 9755, pp. 289–299, 2016.
DOI: 10.1007/978-3-319-39949-2_28

automated teller machines (ATMs) and mobile phones used to call a pharmacy and refill a prescription. We discuss the design of the application and the training procedure and discuss results taken from evaluation surveys given to participants at the completion of the training. We also make recommendations on application development and design as well as training structure based on participant responses.

1.1   Background

Technologies are evolving at a rapid pace, so much so that they have become unavoidable in everyday life [1]. While most new technologies introduced to the market are developed with the purpose of making the completion of everyday tasks easier and more efficient, use of these technologies typically requires a certain level of technical know-how to successfully use and are not always intuitive. As such, those with little to no experience with technology or those with decreased tech-literacy are at a risk for not being able to successfully use new and evolving technologies which, in turn, can inhibit daily functioning [2–4]. The challenges of this disadvantaged group can be exacerbated among those experiencing cognitive impairment as this can inhibit the learning process and make mastery of new technologies more difficult [5–13]. Despite difficulties with learning and mastering new technologies, many aging adults recognize that it is an important endeavor to pursue in an increasingly technological society [1, 14, 15], although many lack the resources (access to the technology, lack of sufficient training) or the motivation to do so [2, 10].

Advanced technologies such as information and communication technologies (e.g., Internet-connected computers or smartphones) can be especially useful to aging adults experiencing functional limitations, as the communication and information capabilities of these gadgets and devices can allow the user to transcend these limitations [16]. As an example, frail older adults with mobility concerns (e.g., inability to drive, needing assistance to walk) can use ICTs to accomplish daily tasks that would typically require them to leave their home, such as grocery shopping or banking. Despite the advantages of ICTs and other advanced technologies in enhancing the lives of aging adults, those experiencing functional limitations are also less likely to utilize these technologies [11, 17].

A major barrier to successful use of evolving technologies among aging adults experiencing functional limitations, aside from physical barriers such as poor vision preventing the user from being able to see screens or buttons [11], is that of literacy. With technologies becoming embedded into our daily routines, successful use requires knowledge across a variety of domains, increasing the complexity of certain tasks especially to those with little technology experience. As an example, studies examining aging adults' use of online personal health records shows that successful navigation and use of such sites requires not only technological expertise, but also a certain amount of health literacy and numeracy skills [18–20].

Catering technologies to differing users based on digital and technological literacy, health literacy, or numeracy skills is not always feasible or possible. In the absence of more catered technologies, training designed to enhance technology use and make gadgets and devices easier to use becomes a necessity. Previous work has found that when developing training protocols specifically for older adults and technology, online instructional programs that provide hands-on practice with task components (in contrast to instructional programs that provided written or visual information but do not allow for practice with the technologies or with simulations of the technologies) facilitated increased knowledge acquisition and transfer performance [4]. This study contributes to the previous literature by pilot-testing an online-based training application designed for aging adults to increase their technology skills, increase confidence in being able to use technologies associated with functional living, and allow them to perform daily tasks important to independent living.

2 Method

Data for this study come from a project titled "The Development and Validation of Computer Based Cognitive Assessment and Functional Skills Training Package" conducted at the University of Miami Center on Aging in the Summer of 2015. The purpose of the project was to develop a technology-based functional skills training application suite that could ultimately be integrated with cognitive assessment and cognitive training protocols; the final product would be able to assess the cognitive ability of the user based on functional task testing as well as train the user to gradually improve functional task skills. The sample consisted of 32 individuals: twenty identified as having severe mental illness or mild cognitive impairment and 12 identified as cognitively healthy. As this study was a pilot test of the training application, enrollment was open to adults aged 18+. Age ranged from 28–71, with 63 % of participants aged 55+.

The training application was designed to simulate the use of an ATM as well as the use of a mobile phone to call a pharmacy and refill a prescription. These tasks were deemed important to functional, independent living due to the prevalence of these technologies as well as their widespread use. The application was designed to be used with a touchscreen interface (e.g., touchscreen desktop computer, tablet) so as to more closely mirror the physical requirements of using ATMs and mobile phones (rather than using a mouse to click on the appropriate buttons). Our pilot-test was conducted using a touchscreen desktop computer. As shown in Figs. 1, 2 and 3, the visual appearance of the ATM and prescription training application emulated what one might see with these technologies in a real-world setting.

2.1 Training Procedure

The training sessions were designed based on previously tested guidelines regarding technology training for aging adults [21, 22]. Participants were asked to come in for 6 sessions: a baseline assessment, 4 training sessions, and a follow-up assessment. The first of the participants' 6 visits included acquiring informed consent, completing a baseline survey packet (more thoroughly detailed in the next section), and completing baseline assessment tasks. The baseline assessment tasks consisted of 1 ATM task and 1 prescription task wherein the participants were given instructions on completing an exercise related to using an ATM and filling a prescription using a mobile phone. Participants were allowed to complete the baseline assessment at their own pace.

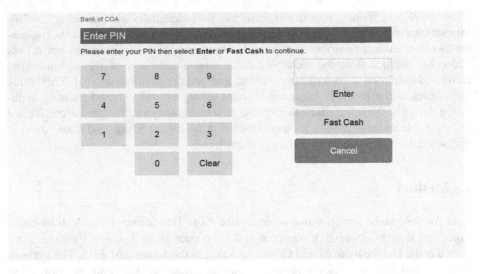

Fig. 1. Screenshot of "Enter PIN" screen from the ATM training application

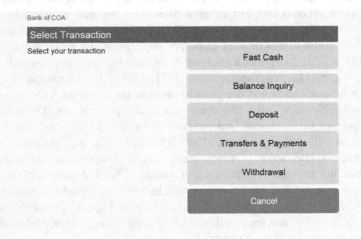

Fig. 2. Screenshot of "Select Transaction" screen from the ATM training application

After the baseline assessment, participants returned for 4 training sessions. The training sessions, when possible, were scheduled within a 2-week timeframe, however in some cases the timeframe was extended if there were conflicts with the participants' schedules. There were no time limits set for the training sessions (participants were given a certain number of tasks to complete and were thus free to complete them at their own pace); some were able to complete the trainings relatively quickly (approximately 30 min) while others took a great deal longer (90+ min).

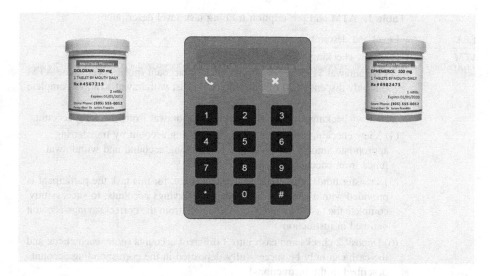

Fig. 3. Screenshot featuring mobile phone and two pill bottles from prescription training application; participants must successfully choose which prescription should be re-filled based on information provided on bottles.

Participants were given a series of tasks to complete during each training session: 6 tasks related to using an ATM and 4 tasks related to filling a prescription using a mobile phone. At the beginning of each task, the participants were given instructions on how to complete the task. The training sessions would begin with simpler tasks (e.g., for the ATM training the first task involved viewing the balance of a checking account, and for the prescription training the first task involved filling the prescription of one empty pill bottle). If the participant made a mistake while completing the task, a pop-up window would appear re-stating the instructions of the task. If the participant continued to make mistakes, pop-up windows would continue to appear with detailed tips on how to complete the task. If the participant made mistakes even after these tips were revealed, the training application would then reveal the step-by-step procedure of how to complete the task by highlighting the correct buttons to push.

The training started with simple tasks but increased in difficulty (i.e., "levels") as the participant progressed. For the ATM training, tasks that the participants were asked to complete included withdrawing cash, transferring funds from one account to another, and depositing checks/cash. For the prescription training, participants would be provided multiple prescription bottles and would need to assess, based on the information from the bottles, which prescriptions needed to be refilled and then go about refilling the correct prescription(s) (e.g., in one task the participant is provided with two prescription bottles but only one bottle has remaining valid refills, and so the participant can only refill the prescription of the bottle with the remaining refills). A more detailed description of the levels is provided in Table 1.

Upon completing a set of tasks, the participants would then be asked to repeat the tasks based on their success in the first set. During this second set of tasks, the participant would begin with "level" below the last in which they made a mistake.

Table 1. ATM and prescription training task level descriptions

Task	Level and description
ATM	(1) View checking account balance
	(2) Withdrawal $175 in cash from checking account (note: because the ATM can only dispense $20 bills, participant must withdrawal $180 to complete task)
	(3) View checking account and make a withdrawal from checking account
	(4) View checking account, replenish checking account by transferring appropriate amount from savings to checking account, and withdrawal funds from checking account
	(5) Transfer funds into checking account (note: for this task the participant is provided with a checking account and 2 savings accounts; to successfully complete the task they must transfer funds from the correct savings account outlined in instructions)
	(6) Deposit 2 checks and cash into 3 different accounts (note: each check and the cash can only be successfully deposited in the corresponding account described in the instructions)
Prescription	(1) Participant provided with 1 prescription bottle – must call pharmacy and follow audio instructions to refill prescription
	(2) Participant provided with 2 prescription bottles – must call pharmacy and follow audio instructions to refill both prescriptions
	(3) Participant provided with 2 prescription bottles – must call pharmacy and follow audio instructions to refill the prescription which has remaining refills (note: only 1 of the bottles had refills remaining, the other had 0)
	(4) Participant provided with 2 prescription bottles – must call pharmacy and follow audio instructions to refill the prescription which had not expired (note: only 1 of the bottles had prescriptions that did not expire)

As an example, let us imagine a participant who, during the first set of ATM tasks, was able to complete levels 1, 2, 3, and 5 without any mistakes but then made mistakes on levels 4 and 6 – in this instance, when the participant begins the second set of tasks, they would begin with level 3 (a level below 4, the task in which they made their first mistake). Upon completing the tasks a second time, the participants would then be instructed to complete the tasks a third time, once again beginning a level below their last mistake made. The training session would end upon the completion of the third set of tasks.

If the participant was able to complete a set of tasks without making any errors, in the next training set the participant would be asked to begin from the first level and repeat all tasks. If the participant was able to complete all the tasks again without errors, the training session was ended early. Upon completing the 4 training sessions over 2 weeks, participants returned for a follow-up assessment where they were given 1 ATM and 1 prescription task to complete.

2.2   Data and Analysis

At the baseline assessment, participants were administered a survey collecting information on demographic characteristics, prior computer and Internet experience, attitudes towards computers, and self-assessed proficiency of computer use. A series of tests measuring cognitive ability were also administered. Participants were also given a Computer Tasks Evaluation Questionnaire at the completion of the baseline assessment tasks so that they may give their opinions on the training application (e.g., legibility of the text, touchscreen easy to use). At the follow-up assessment, the tests measuring cognitive ability were administered again as well as the Computer Tasks Evaluation Questionnaire once the follow-up assessment tasks were completed.

An informal, qualitative evaluation interview was also conducted at the follow-up assessment so as to allow for participants to give more detailed feedback on the training application and the training procedures. These interviews provide the primary data for this investigation. Participants were asked open-ended questions about whether they found the training useful, whether they found the training enjoyable, if they thought the training would help them carry out the tasks on a day-to-day basis, and how the training could be improved. These evaluations were systematically reviewed by researchers with qualitative training for common themes and concepts regarding what the participants liked and did not like about the training.

Data was also collected during the training sessions themselves in the form of log data and task observations completed by study personnel; however this data is not used for this investigation.

3   Results

3.1   Descriptive Statistics

The mean age of participants was 53 (as previously reported, 63 % of the sample was aged 55+). Sixty-three percent of the sample identified as male with most participants indicating they had a high school degree or less (67 %). Approximately 59 % of the sample identified as Black/African and 22 % identified as White Hispanic/Latino, 4 % as White Non-Hispanic/Latino, and the remaining 15 % as multi-racial or other. All participants who revealed income information reported a yearly household income of less than $40,000; fifteen percent reported less than $5,000 per year, 33 % reported between $5,000–$9,999 per year, 26 % reported between $10,000–$14,999 per year, and the remaining respondents reported somewhere between $15,000–$39,999 (note: 1 participant chose not to report income while 1 was unsure of the total). Regarding occupational status, most categorized their employment as "other" and, when asked to elaborate, indicated that they were unemployed due to disability (30 %). Eleven percent indicated that they were working full- or part-time, 11 % indicated they were retired, 7 % indicated they primarily performed volunteer work, and 15 % indicated that they were unemployed due to being laid off/actively seeking employment. The remaining participants indicated they were unemployed but did not indicate they were actively seeking employment.

3.2   Training Evaluation

The informal evaluation interviews administered after the follow-up assessment showed that a majority of participants were pleased with the training. Ninety-four percent of participants indicated that they found the training useful, 91 % indicated that they found the training enjoyable, and 91 % indicated that they believed the training would help them carry out the ATM and prescription tasks on a daily basis.

When asked to elaborate on how they found the training useful, common themes mentioned were that the training taught the participants something new and potentially important to everyday life (22 %), that the training helped to increase overall task performance to the point that the participants felt comfortable in their ability to perform the tasks outside of a training setting (25 %), and that they felt the training helped to train their memory and increase their attention and awareness to detail (31 %). As noted in one interview:

> Was able to apply skills from the training classes to real-life. Indicated he actually filled a prescription via phone for the first time ever a week prior to follow-up, said "I wouldn't have been able to do it without this study. It was great."

When asked to elaborate on how they found the training enjoyable, two predominant themes emerged: that the challenge of completing the tasks in conjunction with new skill acquisition was appealing, and that the training itself was fun and almost game-like despite not being designed as a game. From the evaluation interviews:

> Tasks were challenging. "I like to challenge myself. I get enjoyment out of challenging myself." Liked how tasks made him "stop and think about things."

Forty-one percent of participants highlighted that they gained personal satisfaction from the training through the process of learning something new and challenging themselves. Twenty-two percent specifically highlighted how they found the training fun. Interestingly, while the training was not designed to be used as a game, a few participants treated it as such to make the experience more enjoyable and to challenge themselves. As one participant noted, during each training session he would attempt to do it "as fast as I can" and try to complete the tasks faster with each session.

While some participants indicated that they had previous experience with using an ATM or using a mobile phone, the majority still indicated that the training would help them in accomplishing tasks on a day-to-day basis. Twenty-eight percent indicated that the training either taught them something new about completing these tasks or helped to reinforce what they already knew. The theme of memory and paying attention to detail also re-emerged, with 4 participants discussing how the tasks highlighted things they would not usually think much about:

> The training helped to "reinforce what I already know." He felt he didn't learn anything new but the training made him more attentive. He brought up an example from the prescription tasks: "I pay attention to the writing on the prescription bottles more."

Participants were also asked to be critical of the training application and training sessions and provide recommendations on what they felt may improve the experience. When asked how the training could be improved, the most prominent theme was that of repetition. Eight of the participants (25 %) felt that the tasks were repeated too often with 6 others indicating that they would have preferred additional tasks that were more challenging and more diverse in the skills that were taught. Two participants also indicated that they would have liked to see more training programs that went beyond ATM and mobile phone/prescription tasks (e.g., training on the basics of using the Internet). Only one participant suggested tailoring the training sessions based on skill level, recommending that a survey be administered prior to the training measuring task knowledge and having the training sessions cater to the "problem areas" identified in the survey. Nine participants (28 %) indicated they wouldn't change anything about the training.

4 Conclusion

Research has shown that individuals with low levels of tech-literacy and experience and those experiencing cognitive declines may be less successful at utilizing technologies in everyday life [2–13]; this can pose as a significant issue for this group as technologies become more embedded in daily activities, potentially preventing these individuals from carrying out necessary tasks of daily functioning. This study pilot-tested an online training application suite designed to train aging adults in successful use of an ATM and use of a mobile phone to promote independent living. Results from informal interviews conducted after the training revealed that online-based programs simulating real-world technologies can benefit aging adults. However, a common criticism noted by participants was the repetition of tasks. While repetition is recommended in technology training [2] so that older adults can more easily absorb new material, many of our participants felt that this took away from the novelty and enjoyment of the experience, making some of the training sessions almost "boring." Participants also requested increased diversity in tasks as well as more challenging tasks.

As mentioned previously, the ATM and prescription training applications were the first of a proposed web-based application suite that would train aging adults to more successfully use gadgets and devices vital to functional tasks and independent, everyday living. In addition to modifying the design of the ATM and prescription applications as well as modifying the training procedures to better reflect the training needs and preferences of aging adults, our intent is to expand the number of training applications. Applications currently under development would train aging adults to more easily and successfully use ticketing kiosks, self-checkout counters (e.g., self-checkout kiosks found at a grocery store), and technologies used during a doctor's visit (e.g., a check-in kiosk). Such an application suite could assist aging adults with living independently in an increasingly technological society by training them to use technologies they may be unfamiliar with or training them to more successfully use technologies they may have little experience with or little understanding of.

Acknowledgements. The project described was supported by the Wallace H. Coulter Center for Translational Research at the University of Miami. The content is solely the responsibility of the authors and does not necessarily represent the official views of the Wallace H. Coulter Center for Translational Research.

References

1. Broady, T., Chan, A., Caputi, P.: Comparison of older and younger adults' attitudes towards and abilities with computers: implications for training and learning. Br. J. Educ. Technol. **41**, 473–485 (2010)
2. Berkowsky, R.W., Cotten, S.R., Yost, E.A., Winstead, V.P.: Attitudes towards and limitations to ict use in assisted and independent living communities: findings from a specially-designed technological intervention. Educ. Gerontol. **39**, 797–811 (2013)
3. Czaja, S.J., Charness, N., Fisk, A.D., Hertzog, C., Nair, S.N., Rogers, W.A.: Sharit, J: Factors predicting the use of technology: findings from the center for research and education on aging and technology enhancement (create). Psychol. Aging **21**, 333–352 (2006)
4. Rogers, W.A., Fisk, A.D., Mead, S.E., Walker, N., Cabrera, E.F.: Training older adults to use automatic teller machines. Hum. Factors **38**, 425–433 (1996)
5. Beier, M.E., Ackerman, P.L.: Age, ability, and the role of knowledge on the acquisition of new domain knowledge: promising results in a real-world learning environment. Psychol. Aging **20**, 341–355 (2005)
6. Charness, N., Kelley, C.L., Bosman, E.A., Mottram, M.: Word-processing training and retraining: effects of adult age, experience, and interface. Psychol. Aging **16**, 110–127 (2001)
7. Czaja, S.J., Sharit, J., Ownby, R., Roth, D., Nair, S.: Examining age differences in performance of a complex information search and retrieval task. Psychol. Aging **16**, 564–579 (2001)
8. Dickinson, A., Arnott, J., Prior, S.: Methods for human-computer interaction research with older people. Behav. Inf. Technol. **26**, 343–352 (2007)
9. Gatto, S.L., Tak, S.H.: Computer, internet, and e-mail use among older adults: benefits and barriers. Educ. Gerontol. **34**, 800–811 (2008)
10. Purdie, N., Boulton-Lewis, G.: The learning needs of older adults. Educ. Gerontol. **29**, 129–149 (2003)
11. Renaud, K., Ramsay, J.: Now what was that password again? a more flexible way of identifying and authenticating our seniors. Behav. Inf. Technol. **26**, 309–322 (2007)
12. Sharit, J., Czaja, S.J., Nair, S., Lee, C.C.: Effects of age, speech rate and environmental support in using telephone voice menu systems. Hum. Factors **45**, 234–251 (2003)
13. Umemuro, H.: Computer attitude, cognitive abilities, and technology use among older japanese adults. Gerontechnology **3**, 64–76 (2004)
14. Boulton-Lewis, G.M., Buys, L., Lovie-Kitchin, J., Barnett, K., David, L.N.: Ageing, learning, and computer technology in australia. Educ. Gerontol. **33**, 253–270 (2007)
15. Hanson, V.L.: Influencing technology adoption by older adults. Interact. Comput. **22**, 502–509 (2010)
16. Winstead, V., Anderson, W.A., Yost, E.A., Cotten, S.R., Warr, A., Berkowsky, R.W.: You can teach an old dog new tricks: a qualitative analysis of how residents of senior living communities may use the web to overcome spatial and social barriers. J. Appl. Gerontol. **32**, 540–560 (2013)
17. Greyson, S.R., Garcia, C.C., Sudore, R.L., Cenzer, I.S., Covinsky, K.E.: Functional impairment and internet use among older adults: implications for meaningful use of patient portals. JAMA Intern. Med. **174**, 1188–1190 (2014)
18. Rodríguez, V., Andrade, A.D., García-Retamero, R., Anam, R., Rodríguez, R., Lisigurski, M., Sharit, J., Ruiz, J.G.: Health literacy, numeracy, and graphical literacy among veterans in primary care and their effect on shared decision making and trust in physicians. J. Health Commun. **18**, 273–289 (2013)

19. Taha, J., Czaja, S.J., Sharit, J., Morrow, D.G.: Factors affecting usage of a personal health record (PHR) to manage health. Psychol. Aging **28**, 1124–1139 (2013)
20. Taha, J., Sharit, J., Czaja, S.J.: The impact of numeracy ability and technology skills on older adults' performance of health management tasks using a patient portal. J. Appl. Gerontol. **33**, 416–436 (2014)
21. Czaja, S.J., Sharit, J.: Designing Training and Instructional Programs for Older Adults. CRC Press, Boca Raton (2013)
22. Fisk, A.D., Rogers, W.A., Charness, N., Czaja, S.J., Sharit, J.: Designing for Older Adults: Principles and Creative Human Factors Approaches. CRC Press, Boca Raton (2009)

Exploring the Relationship Between Computer Proficiency and Computer Use Over Time in the PRISM Trial

Walter R. Boot[1(✉)], Joseph Sharit[2], Sara J. Czaja[3],
Neil Charness[1], and Wendy A. Rogers[4]

[1] Department of Psychology, Florida State University, Tallahassee, FL, USA
{boot,charness}@psy.fsu.edu
[2] Department of Industrial Engineering, University of Miami, Coral Gables, FL, USA
jsharit@miami.edu
[3] Department of Psychiatry and Behavioral Sciences,
University of Miami Miller School of Medicine, Miami, FL, USA
SCzaja@med.miami.edu
[4] School of Psychology, Georgia Institute of Technology, Atlanta, GA, USA
wendy@gatech.edu

Abstract. The aim of the PRISM trial was to examine the potential benefits of a Personal Reminder Information and Social Management (PRISM) computer system on the well-being and perceived social support of an older adult sample at risk for social isolation. Participants ($N = 300$) were randomly assigned to receive the PRISM system, which was designed to support social connections, information gathering, prospective memory, and access to local and national resources, or a binder that contained similar information. The intervention lasted one year, and the computer usage of the PRISM group was monitored. This trial represented a unique opportunity to explore potential barriers to the adoption and continued use of information and communications technologies. Specifically, this paper explored the relationship between computer proficiency and use of the PRISM system over time. Contrary to what one might predict, participants with initially low proficiency used the system more over the course of the trial ($r(123) = -.22, p < .05$). The fact that even those with the lowest levels or proficiency were able to become among the most active PRISM users may reflect that the system was designed well for older adult computer novices (the intended target of the intervention). Over the course of the trial, participants assigned to the PRISM condition improved substantially in their computer proficiency. Increased computer proficiency from baseline to 12 months was a much strong predictor of system use ($r(123) = .53, p < .001$), possibly reflecting increased proficiency as a result of greater use over time. Overall, data suggest a complex relationship between computer use, computer proficiency, and changes in computer proficiency over time worthy of additional exploration to further understand the effects of, and barriers to, the use of information and communications technologies.

Keywords: Older adults · Technology · Computer proficiency

© Springer International Publishing Switzerland 2016
J. Zhou and G. Salvendy (Eds.): ITAP 2016, Part II, LNCS 9755, pp. 300–307, 2016.
DOI: 10.1007/978-3-319-39949-2_29

1   Introduction

Information and communications technology (ICT) has the potential to assist older adults and help them maintain their independence in a variety of ways [1]. For example, ICT allows access to information about local and national resources and organizations that can assist older adults with important daily activities such as shopping, transportation, and meal preparation. The Internet has useful information related to maintaining mental and physical health and remaining safe (e.g., fall prevention strategies). Calendaring and reminder software applications can help support prospective memory by providing alerts related to upcoming appointments and when medications need to be taken. Social media and videoconferencing software can help older adults connect with friends and family. Finally, gaming and other leisure activities can be supported by ICT. Overall, there is a great deal of potential for ICT to enhance the well-being and quality of life of older adults, especially those who may be at risk for social isolation [2].

Unfortunately, there still exists a large digital divide, with older adults adopting ICT to a much lesser extent compared to their younger counterparts. For example, in the United States, fewer than one third of older adults (65+) owned a tablet computer in 2015, and fewer than one third owned a smartphone. This is striking compared to the 50 % tablet computer and 86 % smartphone ownership rates among adults 18 to 29 years of age [3]. While only 15 % of adults in the US. do not go online, 44 % of older adults do not [4]. Lower ICT adoption rates suggest that many older adults, especially those in the older cohorts or of lower economic or educational status, may not have access to the benefits that ICT offers.

Why is it that older adults are less likely to adopt ICT? Both cognitive and attitudinal barriers to technology adoption have been observed. For example, higher levels of fluid intelligence and lower levels of computer anxiety predict technology use and adoption [5]. Many adults not online feel that the Internet is not relevant to them, and others report or worry that the Internet is too difficult for them to use or learn to use [4]. These concerns are consistent with models of technology adoption that predict that perceived usefulness and perceived ease of use are among the most important factors influencing technology acceptance and adoption [6, 7]. It is also important for technology design and technology-training protocols to take into account the abilities, needs, and preferences of older adults [8, 9], as poor ICT design and training are also likely contributors to lower adoption rates.

The current paper explores how initial ICT proficiency, and changes in ICT proficiency, relate to long-term ICT use. Data were collected as part of the Personal Reminder Information and Social Management (PRISM) system trial (see [10] for a detailed description of the trial and procedures). The aim of the trial was to provide robust evidence for the benefits of access to the Internet and an easy-to-use computer system, with respect to reducing the isolation and improving the well-being of older adults at risk for social isolation. The PRISM system was designed for older adults with little or no previous computer experience, and featured components to connect older adults with friends and family members and provide access to important information about local and national resources. Digital games offered the opportunity for leisure activities and calendaring software was included to help support prospective memory. A classroom feature included text, links, and videos aimed at improving knowledge of various topics such as health and transportation.

The design of the PRISM system was based on an iterative, user-centered design process. PRISM prototypes were presented to older adults and the system was modified based on feedback. The modified system was then pilot tested with representative participants. Training procedures and materials were also pilot tested. Additional refinement to the system and training protocol and materials were made based on the pilot testing. With the attention given to the design of the PRISM system, training, and help system, one hypothesis explored here is whether there would be minimal correlation between initial ICT proficiency and PRISM usage over the year-long intervention. This would be a sign of success with respect to the design process and training protocol developed. Another hypothesis relates to whether access to an easy to use system and computer training might substantially improve ICT proficiency from the start of the trial to the end of the trial, and whether this improvement in proficiency might be an important predictor of system use.

2 Methods

All trial procedures have been described previously [10]. Briefly, 300 participants were recruited and randomly assigned to receive the PRISM computer system in their home, or a notebook containing much of the same information as the PRISM system (e.g., paper versions of classroom activities and resource guides, non-digital games). Participants were 65 years of age or older, lived alone, engaged in minimal work and volunteer activities, and used computers and the Internet minimally. Activity on the PRISM system was monitored (which system features were accessed and when). Our main measure of activity reported here is the number of days on which any activity on the PRISM system was observed (measure could range from 0 to 365 days). The reported analyses focus on participants in the PRISM condition who had computer proficiency data at the start of the trial and at the end of the 12-month trial period ($N = 125$). Computer proficiency [11] was measured using a validated survey (Computer Proficiency Questionnaire, or CPQ) that was administered prior to PRISM training, and once again approximately 12 months later. CPQ scores range from 6 (minimally proficient) to 30 (extremely proficient) with a higher score indicating higher proficiency. PRISM training was accomplished over the course of three home-based training sessions.

3 Results

Overall, participants used the PRISM system frequently, however there was substantial variability in system use. Over the year-long trial, on average, there was system activity on approximately 202 days ($SD = 106$). Prior to the start of the trial, PRISM participants had very low computer proficiency ($M = 10, SD = 4$). At the end of the trial, proficiency was substantially higher ($M = 18$, $SD = 5$). Note on this scale, floor is a score of 6, and ceiling is a score of 30.

First we explored whether system activity might be explained by initial levels of computer proficiency. Do participants who start with initially lower levels of proficiency use the system less? This would be evidence that the design of the PRISM system and associated training could not overcome a lack of previous computer experience and proficiency. Surprisingly, the opposite was true. Those with initially lower computer proficiency used the system more over the year-long intervention ($r(123) = -.22$, $p < .05$). Some of the most active PRISM users were those who started out with the lowest levels of computer proficiency (Fig. 1). It should be noted overall, through, that initial proficiency seemed to play a relatively minor role, accounting for only 4.8 % of the variance in system usage.

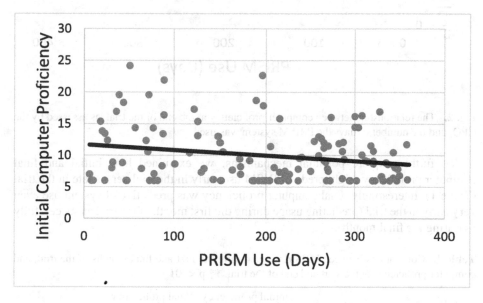

Fig. 1. The relationship between initial computer proficiency, as assessed by the CPQ at the start of the trial, and the number of days the PRISM system was used.

Final computer proficiency (assessed at the end of the trial) was a positive predictor of PRISM use ($r(123) = .38$, $p < .001$, Fig. 2), as was the increase in proficiency from baseline to 12 months ($r(123) = .53$, $p < .001$). Unlike initial proficiency, final proficiency and increases in proficiency were associated with increased PRISM use. A number of potential mechanisms might explain this relationship: (1) participants who were unable to acquire sufficient proficiency used the system less over the course of the trial, (2) participants who used the system more gained more proficiency through greater use, and (3) some third variable, such as computer anxiety, discouraged both use and the acquisition of proficiency.

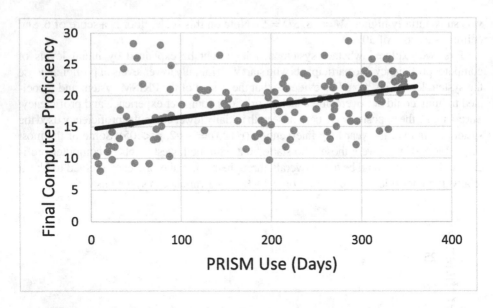

Fig. 2. The relationship between computer proficiency at the end of the trial, as assessed by the CPQ, and the number of days the PRISM system was used.

To further explore potential mechanisms, we examined how initial and final computer proficiency might predict PRISM use early in the trial versus late in the trial (Table 1). Interestingly, final computer proficiency was predictive of system use even very early in the trial (predicting usage during the first month of the trial as successfully as during the final month).

Table 1. Correlations between PRISM usage during the first and final months of the trial, and computer proficiency at the start and end of the trial. ** $p < .01$

	Initial proficiency	Final proficiency
Month 1 Use	−.07	.30**
Month 12 Use	−.13	.27**

This pattern suggests that whatever mechanism is at play in producing the observed relationship between PRISM usage and final proficiency had an influence very early in the trial. One possible explanation is that this relationship partially reflects individual differences in the success of learning during the PRISM training protocol. Some participants may have gained more from training than others, producing a long-lasting effect on subsequence use, starting during the very first month of usage.

4   Conclusion and Discussion

The PRISM trial was successful in that participants used the PRISM system frequently. However, individual differences were observed with some participants using PRISM substantially more than others. Encouragingly, even participants with minimal initial computer proficiency were able to learn and use the system. This may reflect success of the iterative design process and the careful development of training protocols and materials. Initially low levels of computer proficiency did not act as a barrier to the adoption and use of the PRISM system. This finding is consistent with the Unified Theory of Acceptance and Use of Technology (UTAUT) which proposes that a variety of facilitating conditions (in this case, the PRISM help system and PRISM training) can have a positive impact on use behavior [6].

Why might have participants with higher levels of proficiency used the system less over the year-long intervention? Participants were selected based on the fact that they did not own a computer and that they had minimal Internet/computer experience over the past three months. However, even among this sample previous computer and Internet experience may have varied (i.e., prior to the three months before recruitment into the study). If some participants had more experience using computers and the Internet over their lifetime, the system may not have been as novel and they may have used the system less as a result. The sample might also have included some participants who used computers in the more distant past, resulting in initial proficiency, but who may have ended up becoming non-computer users because of their lack of interest in or perceived value of computers. This could explain a relationship between initially high proficiency and a lack of use of the PRISM system. Participants who were initially low in terms of proficiency may have also been more motivated to practice using the system, contributing to the observed pattern. Although we observed a significant relationship between initially higher proficiency and lower PRISM use, this accounted for less than 5 % of the variance in total PRISM use.

Results suggest a dynamic relationship between proficiency and system use. While initially lower levels of proficiency predicted higher levels of PRISM use, at the end of the trial higher levels of proficiency predicted higher levels of PRISM use. One of the strongest predictors of PRISM use was the *change* in proficiency from baseline to 12 months. An interesting finding was that final computer proficiency predicted use during the first month of the trial. One explanation for this finding might be that, as previously stated, gains in proficiency partly reflect individual differences in learning during the three training sessions at the start of the trial. Another explanation is that PRISM use during the first month may have encouraged a habit of use in subsequent months. This habit of use then may have resulted in greater use overall, and increased proficiency as a result.

In explaining individuals differences in the adoption and use of ICT systems such as PRISM, other factors may play larger roles than initial ICT proficiency, especially when the system is well-designed for non-users and older adults. Related to use, a variety of individual difference characteristics appear to be related to older adults' attitudes toward the PRISM system [12]. These include factors such as self-efficacy, computer interest, demographic variables, and personality characteristics.

About Measuring ICT Proficiency. In this study we used the Computer Proficiency Questionnaire (CPQ) to assess computer proficiency [11]. Previously reported analyses have demonstrated the reliability and validity of this measure. Results reported here further speak to the validity of the CPQ. Here we have demonstrated that the CPQ is sensitive to change over time and that changes in CPQ correspond to different levels of PRISM use. However, it should be noted that more and more people are accessing the Internet and software through tablets and smartphones, necessitating the need for an analogous measure to the CPQ specific to mobile devices [13].

Future Directions. In this paper we present an initial analysis of one potential predictor of overall system use. Many other analyses are also possible such as examining how proficiency as measured by various CPQ subscales relate to use of the various individual features of the PRISM system (classroom, Internet, email, games, etc.). Future analyses will examine other possible predictors (e.g., proficiency, attitudes, demographics, personality attributes), to determine which are the best predictors of PRISM use, and continued use over time. Overall, the results will provide insight into factors that facilitate or act as barriers to the adoption of ICT among older adults.

Acknowledgments. We gratefully acknowledge support from the National Institute on Aging, NIA 3 PO1 AG017211, Project CREATE III– Center for Research and Education on Aging and Technology Enhancement (www.create-center.org). Data were collected as part of a larger trial examining the benefits of the PRISM system, with a focus on social isolation and social support [ClinicalTrials.gov Identifier: NCT0149761]. In support of the PRISM project we also acknowledge and appreciate the assistance of Tracy Mitzner, Chin Chin Lee, and Sankaran Nair.

References

1. Charness, N., Boot, W.R.: Aging and information technology use potential and barriers. Curr. Dir. Psychol. Sci. **18**(5), 253–258 (2009)
2. Choi, M., Kong, S., Jung, D.: Computer and internet interventions for loneliness and depression in older adults: a meta-analysis. Healthc. Inf. Res. **18**, 191–198 (2012)
3. Anderson, M.: Technology device ownership: *2015*. Pew Research Center. (2015). http://www.pewinternet.org/2015/10/29/technology-device-ownership-2015
4. Zickuhr, K.: Who's not online and why. Pew Research Center (2013). http://www.pewinternet.org/2013/09/25/whos-not-online-and-why/
5. Czaja, S.J., Charness, N., Fisk, A.D., Hertzog, C., Nair, S.N., Rogers, W.A., Sharit, J.: Factors predicting the use of technology: findings from the center for research and education on aging and technology enhancement (CREATE). Psychol. Aging **21**(2), 333–352 (2006)
6. Venkatesh, V., Morris, M.G., Davis, F.D., Davis, G.B.: User acceptance of information technology: toward a unified view. MIS Q. **27**, 425–478 (2003)
7. Davis, F.D., Bagozzi, R.P., Warshaw, P.R.: User acceptance of computer technology: a comparison of two theoretical models. Manag. Sci. **35**, 982–1003 (1989)
8. Fisk, A.D., Rogers, W.A., Charness, N., Czaja, S.J., Sharit, J.: Designing for Older Adults: Principles and Creative Human Factors Approaches, 2nd edn. CRC Press, Boca Raton, FL (2009)
9. Czaja, S.J., Sharit, J.: Designing Training and Instructional Programs for Older Adults. CRC Press, Boca Raton, FL (2012)
10. Czaja, S.J., Boot, W.R., Charness, N., Rogers, W.A., Sharit, J., Fisk, A.D., Nair, S.N.: The personalized reminder information and social management system (PRISM) trial: rationale, methods and baseline characteristics. Contemp. Clin. Trials **40**, 35–46 (2015)

11. Boot, W.R., Charness, N., Czaja, S.J., Sharit, J., Rogers, W.A., Fisk, A.D., Nair, S.: Computer proficiency questionnaire: assessing low and high computer proficient seniors. Gerontologist **55**(3), 404–411 (2015)
12. Mitzner, T.L., Rogers, W.A., Fisk, A.D., Boot, W.R., Charness, N., Czaja, S.J., Sharit, J.: Predicting older adults' perceptions about a computer system designed for seniors. Universal Access in Information Systems (in press)
13. Roque, N.A., Boot, W.R.: A new tool for assessing mobile device proficiency in older adults: the mobile device proficiency questionnaire. J. Appl. Gerontol. (in press)

Exploring the Next Generation of Older Gamers: Middle-Aged Gamers

Julie A. Brown[✉]

Ohio University, Athens, Ohio, USA
brownj14@ohio.edu

Abstract. In recent years, much attention has been drawn to the burgeoning market of older gamers. As such, a greater base of knowledge has been amassed from studies that assess the characteristics of this active gamer population. Yet, not much is known about today's Middle-Aged Gamers, the next generation of older gamers. Using grounded theory methodology and a life course perspective, the interview responses of 56 gamers – 30 Older Gamers (age 60 to 77) and 26 Middle-Aged Gamers (age 43 to 59) – were coded and examined with an eye for recognizing generational characteristics. This resulted in the identification of three distinct themes: game preferences, platform used, and anticipated future gameplay. The findings demonstrate that it cannot be assuming that the Middle-Aged Gamers will, in time, be like today's Older Gamers. Rather, they exhibit qualities that will reshape scholars' and game developers' notions of gameplay in old age.

Keywords: Middle-Aged Gamers · Older gamers · Audience study · Digital game design · Life course · Play

1 Introduction

Older persons playing digital games are not necessarily a new trend and the proportion of older populations comprising of the gaming market has been increasing over the past decade. The most recent publication of the Entertainment Software Association, Essential Facts About the Computer and Game Industry, provided a demographic overview of the gaming market and stated that 27 % of the market consisted of persons aged 50+ years [1]. Similarly, survey results from the Pew Research Center indicated the proportion of persons who play video games within respective age groups: age 30 to 49–58 %, age 50 to 64–40 %, and age 65+–25 % [2].

In comparison to other select countries (e.g., United Kingdom and Belgium), the United States hosts the largest percentage of persons between the age of 50 and 65 who actively gameplay (72 % male, 72 % female) [3]. In addition, it was identified that this age cohort plays more hours per week than their same-sex counterparts in the compared countries (4.9 h male, 7.5 h female). When reviewing market reports and surveys that focus on gamers within the United States and abroad, it is evident that digital gaming is a popular activity for older populations.

© Springer International Publishing Switzerland 2016
J. Zhou and G. Salvendy (Eds.): ITAP 2016, Part II, LNCS 9755, pp. 308–318, 2016.
DOI: 10.1007/978-3-319-39949-2_30

Although digital games have been commercially available for over 40 years, it has not been until the about the last ten years, that research on digital game engagement among older persons began to indicate signs of proliferation. This increased dramatically since 2009 and has become a source of serious scholarly inquiry [4]. This growth even spurred the formation of a special-interest organization that highlights and promotes the value of gameplay among older populations – the Gerontoludic Society (http://www.gerontoludicsociety.com/).

Consequently, knowledge pertaining to older adult engagement with digital games has increased with the growth of research in this area. A portion of this includes the exploration of characteristics of older adults who actively play games. Yet, despite these strides, there is still a dearth of information that provides rich insight of this heterogeneous population [5].

To compound this issue, such a need is more pronounced for game players who are middle-aged – the next generation of older gamers. It cannot and must not be assumed that the needs and preferences of today's older gamer will be reflected among tomorrow's. Indeed, that would be akin to comparing a 30-year-old in 1986 to a 30-year-old in 2016, or a 70-year-old in 2016 to a 70-year-old in 2036. From a temporal standpoint, these respective individuals would have been influenced by different life-shaping forces that mold aspects of their identity. For examples of the interplay between temporal influences and consecutive generations, see [6, 7].

This study proposes that it is critical to explore and compare the gaming characteristics of both demographics: Older Gamers and Middle-Aged Gamers. In doing so, insight is gained in the identification of select gameplay qualities of Middle-Aged Gamers. In turn, it is suggested that these characteristics may serve as indicators of their future play in old age. To initiate discourse, this study reports findings that targeted the following research question: *How do the digital gaming characteristics of Middle-Aged Gamers differ from Older Gamers?*

2   Review of the Literature

Game player demographics have broadened from the traditional view of a gamer (i.e., tech-savvy "core gamer") to include new audiences [8]. In fact, studies assessing Older Gamers began as early as 1983 [9] and since then, have widely ranged in scope – from using games to improve static and dynamic balance [10] to exploring the meaning of digital gameplay [11]. When assessing such studies collectively, i.e., research focusing on older adult engagement with digital games, they tend to fall into one of three categories: design studies (e.g., [12]), effect studies (e.g., [13]), and audience studies (e.g., [14]). For an overview, see [5].

Audience studies offer scholars and game developers insight into the gaming characteristics of older gamers *and* the characteristics of the respective gamer. Yet, having a thorough understanding of gamer demographics and user characteristics is not limited to the development and design of games. It also lends to understanding the significance and meaning of games as a valuable expression of the self. Nonetheless, there is an imbalance with respect to the foci of older gamer audience studies, as there is a dearth of research that examines the underlying precursors – often originating in youth – that foster gameplay in old age [15]. Rather, audience studies typically focus on the context of older gamers and their gameplay by examining game-related aspects, including game adoption and game preferences.

For example, it has been found that many of today's older gamers began playing digital games because a friend or family member introduced it - e.g., a spouse [16] or adult child [17, 18]. Others began playing because they became aware of a game(s) that was pre-installed on a platform that they interacted with regularly, such as a personal TV [19] or computer that was used for work [16–18]. Another circumstance identified within the literature relates to the health status of the older adult as a precursor. For example, persons who are homebound or immobile due to an illness may adopt the digital game as play activity [15, 17, 20].

Knowing how these gamers began playing is useful, but equally insightful is *why* they continued playing. In other words, what motivated the older gamer? Research indicates a wide range of motivating factor that include, but are not limited to: a sense of mastery [18], enjoyment of the game world [16], socialization [15], challenge [5], reminiscence [15], and the game being reflective of a prior, non-digital hobby [15, 16, 18].

Although these studies provide a sturdy framework to build upon in understanding the heterogeneous qualities of older gamers, there is minimal in-depth assessment of Middle-Aged Gamers. Pearce [16] first explored this age group by surveying persons age 40 to 65 (inclusion criteria) in 2006. Yet, those participants are now approximately age 50 to 75. Thus, insight gleaned from this study cannot be assumed of today's gamers in their 40s – the first generation that is comprised of members who were young children when first exposed to a digital game. In addition, little was found within the research about how digital games were adopted by Middle-Aged persons in their childhood and how this lifelong exposure may have influenced their current gameplay and has the potential to shape future gameplay.

3   Methods

Prior to this study, there was no gerontology-based theory to examine the life and gaming context of aging digital game players (i.e., middle to older age populations). Thus, grounded theory methodology was employed [21–23]. This qualitative approach is typically used in areas of inquiry that have minimal exploratory findings that provide a theoretical framework, as was the case here.

In addition, this study used a life course lens. This means that a temporal perspective was emphasized to examine the theme of "play" and "digital games" within the lives of the participants. In particular, this highlights how age-graded trajectories may be influenced by individual life experiences [24, 25]. Within this historical context, a participant's introduction to and engagement with digital games over time can be assessed and compared with others to identify themes.

3.1   Participants

This study was originally designed to assess one age group – persons age 60+ who currently play digital games. Yet, as the study proceeded, it was observed that some of the younger aged persons within this participant pool (i.e., those who were in their younger 60's) provided responses that varied notably from their older counterparts. To further explore this, measures were taken to recruit a second pool of participants – persons between the age of 40 and 59 who currently play digital games. This resulted in a total of 56 participants: 30 *Older Gamers*, Age 60 to 77 (19 females, 11 males) and 26 *Middle-Age Gamers*, Age 43 to 59 (16 females, 10 males). The participants were recruited from suburban towns Virginia, Kentucky, and Ohio. The vast majority of the participants identified as Caucasian and most attended college.

3.2   Inclusion Criteria and Recruitment

To be identified and recruited as an Older Gamer or Middle-Aged Gamer, the participant had to (1) meet the age requirement, (2) currently play at least one hour of digital games per week, and (3) self-report having at least a "fair" health status. To recruit participants, a variety of methods were employed: snowball sampling, fliers posted within the community, and ads placed within a local senior newsletter. Interested persons contacted the primary investigator via email or office phone and were informed of the general aim of the study, which was to be addressed via individual semi-structured interviews.

Once a candidate was screened and deemed eligible as a participant, a mutually agreed upon time and location was decided for the interview. Meeting locations had to afford privacy and were typically held at one of the following: a reserved room at the local library, the primary investigator's office, or the participant's home.

3.3   Interview Guide

An interview guide was constructed as a tool to explore how the interviewee recalled engaging in self-identified forms of play from early stages of life (i.e., childhood) to current day. Specifically, questions targeted age-related stages [26]: childhood (up to age 19), young adulthood (ages 20–39), middle adulthood (ages 40–59), and older adulthood (ages 60 and above). This included inquiring about preferred forms of play (including non-digital) at each stage, who he or she may have played with, circumstances that hindered or promoted play, and the extent to which play was engage in and valued at each stage of life.

To reduce bias, the participant was encouraged to construct and articulate their personal notions of and engagement in "play" throughout their life course. By doing so, an individual play timeline (or, play history) was created for each participant. If it did not come about organically by the time current day play was discussed, the participant was asked to describe how he or she was first introduced to digital games. This was followed-up by a variety of questions that probed the participant's individual gameplay history, such as factors/circumstances that encouraged or hindered gameplay. And, for the purpose of this manuscript, this also included preferred games and platforms (from a temporal perspective) and anticipated engagement with digital games in their future.

3.4 Analysis

Interviews were digitally recorded and transcribed verbatim. In addition, member checking was employed; each participant was provided a transcript of their interview as a means to verify accuracy and they were encouraged to express any additional information that may have come to mind. Following, transcripts were uploaded to a qualitative software program, NVivo 9 and later updated to NVivo 10, to identify, categorize, and compare emergent themes. Coding (i.e., open, axial, and selective) and the constant comparative method were employed in this process to accomplish this [21–23].

4   Findings

A rich source of qualitative data resulted from interviewing the 56 participants and although there were similarities among the participants, it was evident that there were distinct differences between the youngest interviewees and the oldest. Although the parameters of these two groups were age-based, there was no distinct age-based division when it came to participant responses. For example, it was not unusual for some of the participants in their early 60's to provide responses that reflected those given by some of participants in their late 50's. Nonetheless, three particular themes that emerged from an assessment of the two groups include digital game preferences, platforms used, anticipated future play.

4.1   Digital Game Preferences

The majority of the Older Gamers showed a preference for playing card-based, puzzle, and similar casual games. This was even more pronounced among the older participants within this group. Games typically included *Solitaire* (and alternate versions of this card game, e.g. *Spider Solitaire*), *Free Cell* (a card game), *Words with Friends* (a word game, similar to the board game, *Scrabble*), and *Bejeweled* (a match-three game). It is noteworthy that for many of the participants, their preferred game was reflective of a non-digital game that they played earlier in their life – i.e., childhood.

Rebecca, age 76 and averages 24.5 h of gameplay per week, shared that she regularly plays *Words with Friends* as a means to socialize with her adult children and female friends. Yet, it was discovered that she was first exposed to this type of game when she was a young girl and has fond memories of it.

> I remember growing up, that's what I did with my dad. He and I played a lot of word games, a lot of *Scrabble*. … My mother, she wasn't into that kind of stuff, but we played a lot of word, making words [games]. – Rebecca

Contrary, few of the Middle-Aged Gamers reported playing card-based and puzzle games. Instead, there was an overall preference for casual games (like those enjoyed by some of the Older Gamers), action/combat games (e.g., first-person shooter games), and narrative games. Randy, age 55 and averages 14 h of gameplay per week, expressed his preference for first-person shooter games, which was typical among the men (and some women) in his age group. Randy replied with the following when asked about his game preferences.

> First-person shooter games and any kind of strategies games. I still like them type of games. [I like] strategy [games] because it's competition against somebody else; first-person shooter because you're killing stuff. You're going back to your childhood, playing *Army* or *Cowboys and Indians*. – Randy

Again, this is an instance where current game preference seemed to originate in forms of play that were explored in childhood. This demonstrates the significance of using a life course perspective in game studies, as potential associations could be identified. Although such a link could not be deciphered for every game currently played by the adults, definite patterns or relationships were identified for most of the participants upon comparison of their preferred play activities in childhood and young adulthood.

4.2 Platforms Used

Participants were asked which platform(s) they typically used to play their digital game(s). The majority of the Older Gamers (18) responded that they primarily used a desktop computer or laptop. Yet, there were some (7) who enjoyed tablets as their primary platform, and most of these participants were in the younger range of this group (i.e., younger 60s). A common advantage reported among the tablet users is that the platform could be easily carried around the home and used while engaging in other activities, such as watching TV or lounging in bed. Also, there were those who used multiple platforms – typically a computer and tablet.

Only three of the Older Gamers (between age 63 and 65) reported using a smartphone as their primary platform for gameplay. When other participants within this cohort were asked why a smartphone was not used for gameplay, it was commonly expressed that either a smartphone was not owned, they had minimal knowledge or desire to do, or it interfered with the social use of their phone.

Todd, age 65 and averages 15 h of gameplay per week, enjoys playing *Sudoku* on his computer. When asked if he tried playing on his smartphone, he responded with the following.

> I did for a while. I had a *Sudoku* downloaded on the phone then I took it off. I thought that it was interfering with social interaction more than it should and I would tend to, I mean I'm bad enough as it is, looking up news or things like that on my phone and I thought having a game on phone would make that even worse. And so I deleted it. - Todd

Rodney, age 75 and averages 12.5 h of gameplay per week, indicated that he did not own a cell phone and typically played on his desktop computer or laptop. It is worth noting that he preferred playing on his desktop, as it afforded him to have better control and manipulation of the game elements via use of the mouse. However, it is inconvenient for him to access it because it is on the second floor of his home and, due to an old injury, it is challenging for him to navigate the stares. Thus, he resorted to connecting a mouse to his laptop so that he could continue playing without worrying about the sensitivity of the keypad. "Yeah, and it's much easier to use than the pad [on the laptop]."

In comparison, it was found that the Middle-Aged Gamers typically played either on a desktop computer or a smartphone. (All of the participants within this group indicated ownership of a smartphone.) There was a clear distinction between these two platforms and upon further questioning, it was oftentimes attributed to the type of game.

For example, Mike (age 47 and averages 30 h of gameplay per week) plays online first-person shooter games and told of how he occasionally updates his computer (e.g. processors, large monitors) to accommodate his gameplay needs. Mike first began playing *Pong* when he was 10 and was finally able to afford his own desktop computer when he was in grad school.

> …it was when I was in grad school that I finally bought my own PC for the first time ever. And that's when I got really serious in computer gaming. - Mike

Although Mike owns a smartphone, he continues to use his desktop computer because a smartphone would be able to accommodate to his gameplaying. On the other hand, smartphone use for gameplay was more common among the Middle-Aged Gamers who preferred casual games, such as those that could be played through Facebook. It was reported that the mobility of this platform was regarded as convenient, as the game could be played nearly anywhere. Katy, age 51 and averages 2.5 h of gameplay per week, shared that she once used to rely upon her computer for gameplay, but now uses her smartphone as a primary platform. When asked about whether or not she still uses the computer, she responded, "Not so much. Most of what I play now is either through Facebook or on my iPhone."

4.3 Anticipated Future Play

Overall, the Older Gamers did *not* express a notably strong desire that they *must* continue playing digital games as they get older; meaning, they did not believe it would be a priority in comparison to other matters, such as family. More so, some expressed concern that they would not have the functional ability to continue, especially when considering some of their current physical challenges. Suzanne, age 68 and averages 3 h a week, expressed, "I already have a lot of arthritis in my fingers… Maybe when those computers come out with the voice activated one, that might be a little easier for me in terms of the challenges with my dexterity."

Nonetheless, the majority of the Older Gamers shared that they wanted to continue playing, especially for those who rely upon it as a mode for socialization, but they recognized that their desire may wane at some point or they may become functionally unable to continue. Trish, age 65 and averages 10.5 h of gameplay per week, enjoys playing *Words with Friends* with her family members who live out of state and does not intend to stop. "Well, it keeps me connected with them, because otherwise, they're far away. And it keeps us more positive."

Contrary, the majority of the Middle-Aged adults shared that they anticipated playing in the future, including in old age. This sentiment was most prominent among those who have been playing since their youth, i.e., childhood and young adulthood. In this respect, gameplay is not perceived as a mere hobby, but a meaningful form of play that has been integrated into their life.

Thus, it is noteworthy that the Middle-Aged Gamers expressed greater concern pertaining to whether or not they would be able to continue gameplay in old age. This stemmed from reports of ability-related issues that have become more noticeable with age and have interfered to some extent with their gameplay. This was more common among those Middle-Aged Gamers who play games that require skills that may be influenced by age-related decline. Specifically, reports of declining visual acuity, dexterity, fine motor skills, and response time surfaced among these gamers and have even influenced some of them to alter their current form of play (e.g. make adjustments within the game) or find a new game that is more accommodating.

Jeff, age 50 and averages 7 h of gameplay per week, began first began playing games in arcades when he was a child and nowadays plays games on his computer. When asked if he has noticed any age-related changes that affect his gameplay and if it will influence his future play, he replied with the following.

> Oh sure, hell yeah. I can already tell my reflexes are crap compared to my nephew who… plays these games and he's much quicker. I guess that you can tweak those games to give one person a cheat or to compensate… but I don't think that the game designers worry too much about that.

It is worth noting that participants within this age group, like Jeff, were children when digital games became fixtures within many American homes (e.g., Atari). In addition, these games were popular among teens and young adults. Although not every young person at that time engaged in or continued to play digital games, it at least exposed many to this form of play.

5 Discussion

The participants of this study expressed an abundance of information pertaining to the history of their gameplay and aspects that allow one to glean insight into their intentions for continuing to gameplay with age. The participants of the two age groups shared some similarities, such as the influence of early childhood play on digital game preferences as an adult. Yet, when assessing game engagement characteristics between the two, there were differences that merit attention and further analysis and investigation.

In particular, findings from this study suggest that current game and platform preferences of the Middle-Aged Gamers will not likely change (i.e. be reflective of today's Older Gamer preferences) as they transition into older adulthood. For many of this group's members, this is bolstered by years of gameplay. In addition, participant responses suggested that there is resistance to abandoning gameplay once they transition into old age, but there is concern that game designers may not know how to accommodate to this need.

Also, when considering Middle-Aged Gamers, presumptions about "typical" games for this population merit examination. Based on the findings of this study, the game genre landscape for this population will become increasingly diverse. Yet, this also brings into question how games and platforms will change in the coming years as technology advances exponentially. Although it is impossible to examine future technologies, researchers and game designers can be prepared to meet the gaming needs for what may be one of the larger portions of the gaming market.

A clear distinction was also found between the older participants of the Older Gamers and those Middle-Aged Gamers who expressed a strong desire to continue playing into old age. One may hypothesize that Older Gamers, like Suzanne, may not anticipate playing into later adulthood due to age-related declines that inhibit gameplay. For example, it is likely to become too challenging for an adult with severe arthritis to manipulate a game controller. Contrary, participants in this category shared that the games they typically play are adequately compatible to their level of functional ability. In other words, the older adult continues to play their digital game not only because it may be reflective of a non-digital game that was enjoyed in their youth, but also because it is accommodating to (or is not overly challenging to) their physical and mental capability to engage in the game.

For example, it was previously stated that *Solitaire* is a popular digital card game among many of the Older Gamers. As compared to games that are more popular among the Middle-Aged Gamers (e.g. first-person shooters), *Solitaire* does not call upon a player's reaction time, fine motor control and acute accuracy – as was the case with participants like Jeff.

With this in mind, researchers must further examine how age-related aspects may hinder gameplay as the Middle-Aged Gamer transitions into older adulthood and become Older Gamers. Specifically, this gives way to implications for game design, as broader scale challenges are slated to arise when considering how player demographics will shift. For example, those gamers who currently gameplay, and have been game-playing for years, will likely want to continue playing their traditional games in light of a potential decline of age-related abilities. This means that the gaming industry will need to become more familiar with how normative age-related declines can influence game-play. More importantly, they will need to consider not just the accommodations that may need to be implemented, but how gaming in and of itself is valuable and meaningful to the older game.

6 Conclusion

This study examined the characteristics of 56 gamers, ranging from age 43 to 77. In particular, an assessment was provided of identified themes that highlighted differences between the two age groups – Older Gamers and Middle-Aged Gamers. Like all qualitative studies, it is subject to researcher bias even though measures were taken to reduce them (e.g., member checking). In addition, this study would have benefited from having participants that are more reflective of the demographic characteristics of the older adult market.

Aging is not stagnant, but occurs along a continuum and is multidimensional. With this in mind, it is critical for those who study or design for Older Gamers – including potential Older Gamers – to not confine their thinking to socially constructed notions of that generation alone. An adult gamer cannot, and should not, be characterized by his or her age. Indeed, there are older adults who enjoy playing fast-paced action oriented digital games. Furthermore, the findings of this study suggest that in light of identified age group differences, it cannot be assumed that the characteristics of the Middle-Aged Gamers will change over time simply as a virtue of age.

This next generation of older gamers will be the first age cohort to have been exposed to digital games throughout their entire life course, from childhood to older adulthood. As such, it is important for researchers to consider how, in the future, this particular age group has the potential to dramatically reshape current notions and understandings of older adult digital gaming.

References

1. Essential Facts about the Computer and Video Game Industry - 2015. http://www.theesa.com/wp-content/uploads/2015/04/ESA-Essential-Facts-2015.pdf
2. Duggan, M.: Gaming and Gamers. Pew Research Center. http://www.pewinternet.org/files/2015/12/PI_2015-12-15_gaming-and-gamers_FINAL.pdf
3. Hagoort, T., Hautvast, C.: National Gamers Survey. http://www.gamesindustry.com/company/542/service/1765
4. De Schutter, B., Gandy, M., Mosberg Iversen, S., Nap, H.-H., Hunicke, R.: Digital Games in Later Life: Challenges and Opportunities, Symposium, Foundations of Digital Games (2015)
5. De Schutter, B., Brown, J.A., Nap, H.: Digital games in the lives of older adults. In: Prendergast, D., Garattini, C. (eds.) Aging and the Digital Life Course, vol. 3, pp. 236–256. Berghahn Books, New York (2015)
6. Loos, E.F., Haddon, L., Mante-Meijer, E.A. (eds.): Generational Use of New Media. Ashgate, Farnham (2012)
7. Riley, M.W., Riley, J.W.: Structural lag: past and future. In: Riley, M.W., Kahn, L., Foner, A. (eds.) Age and Structural Lag, pp. 15–36. Wiley-Interscience, New York (1994)
8. Scharkow, M., Festl, R., Vogelgesang, J., Quandt, T.: Beyond the ''Core-Gamer'': genre preferences and gratifications in computer games. Comput. Hum. Behav. **44**, 293–298 (2015)
9. Weisman, S.: Computer games for the frail elderly. Gerontologist **23**(4), 361–363 (1983)
10. Gil-Gomez, J.A., Llorens, R., Alcaniz, M., Colomer, C.: Effectiveness of a Wii balance board-based system (eBaViR) for balance rehabilitation: a pilot randomized clinical trial in patients with acquired brain injury. J. Neuroeng. Rehabil. **8**, 30 (2011)
11. Schutter, B., De Vanden Abeele, V.: (2008). Meaningful Play in Elderly Life. Paper, International Communication Association
12. Gerling, K.M., Schulte, F.P., Masuch, M.: Designing and evaluating digital games for frail elderly persons. In: Romão, T., Correia, N., Inami, M., Kato, H., Prada, R., Terada, T., Dias, E., Chambel, T. (eds.) Proceedings of the 8th International Conference on Advances in Computer Entertainment Technology. ACM, New York (2011)
13. Basak, C., Boot, W.R., Voss, M.W., Kramer, A.F.: Can training in a real-time strategy videogame attenuate cognitive decline in older adults. Psychol. Aging **23**(4), 765–777 (2008)
14. Brown, J.A.: Let's play: understanding the role and meaning of digital games in the lives of older adults. In: Proceedings of the International Conference on the Foundations of Digital Games, pp. 273–275. AMC, New York (2012)
15. Skalsky Brown, J.: Let's Play: Understanding the Role and Significance of Digital Gaming in Old Age. http://uknowledge.uky.edu/gerontol_etds/6
16. Pearce, C.: The truth about baby boomer gamers: a study of over-forty computer game players. Games Cult. **3**(2), 142–147 (2008)

17. Quandt, T., Grueniger, H., Wimmer, J.: The gray haired gaming generation: findings from an explorative interview study on older computer gamers. Games Cult. **4**(1), 27–46 (2009)
18. Nap, H.H., de Kort, Y.A.W., IJsselsteijn, W.A.: Senior gamers: preferences, motivations and needs. Gerontechnology **8**(4), 247–262 (2009)
19. Haddon, L., Silverstone, R.: Information and Communication Technologies and the Young Elderly. University of Sussex, Falmer (1996)
20. De Schutter, B.: Never too old to play: the appeal of digital games to an older audience. Games Cult. **6**(2), 155–170 (2011)
21. Charmaz, K.: Constructing Grounded Theory: A Practical Guide Through Qualitative Analysis. Sage Publications Ltd., Thousand Oaks, CA (2006)
22. Corbin, J.M., Strauss, A.: Grounded theory research: procedures, canons, and evaluative criteria. Qual. Sociol. **13**(1), 3–21 (1990)
23. Glaser, B.G., Strauss, A.L.: The Discovery of Grounded Theory: Strategies for Qualitative Research. Aldine, New York (1967)
24. Elder Jr., G.H.: Perspectives on the Life Course. Life Course Dynamics 23–49 (1985)
25. Elder Jr, G.H.: Time, human agency, and social change: perspectives on the life course. Soc. Psychol. Q. **57**, 4–15 (1994)
26. L'Abate, L.: The Praeger Handbook of Play Across the Life Cycle: Fun from Infancy to Old Age. Praeger/ABC-CLIO, Santa Barbara (2009)

Mobile Learning Concepts for Older Adults: Results of a Pilot Study with Tablet Computers in France and Germany

Eline Leen-Thomele[(✉)], Sonia Hetzner, and Paul Held

Innovation in Learning Institute,
Friedrich Alexander-University Erlangen-Nuremberg, Fürth, Germany
{eline.leen, sonia.hetzner, paul.held}@ili.fau.de

Abstract. This paper sums up the evaluation results of a tablet computer course for older adults. As part of an European research project, the SenApp project, online course modules were developed to teach older adults the first steps on a tablet computer. After the course, a questionnaire was filled in Germany and France ($N = 26$). The evaluation focused on differences in satisfaction with support and course contents and in learning routines between age groups, education level, countries and pre-experience conditions. Main findings suggest that both courses were rated good, but that some support and content aspects were rated less good in France and by lower educated participants, by participants with less pre-experience in e-learning and by older age groups. This suggests that future course concepts should be created more flexible with different learning amounts for different experience levels and that especially support possibilities can be improved for some groups.

Keywords: Older adults · Tablet computer · ICT courses

1 Introduction

The heterogeneous group of older adults is a growing and promising target group for new learning concepts. As life expectancy increases and people stay healthy and fit for longer periods, more and more older adults are looking for useful leisure activities and are willing to learn something new. Nowadays in Western Europe, life expectancy at 60 years of age is 85 years for women and 81 years for men. This an increase of more than ten years for women and eight years for men compared to the life expectancy 100 years ago [1]. This gives more older adults the time to learn something new during retirement. As numbers of further non-occupational education institutions show, more and more older adults engage in further education and many of them in the area of ICT [2].

1.1 Learning in Older Age

As the group of adults older than 60 years of age is very diverse in cognitive, physical and learning abilities, creating learning programs that suit the entire target group is challenging. In general, many abilities decline in older age, e.g. fluid intelligence and

© Springer International Publishing Switzerland 2016
J. Zhou and G. Salvendy (Eds.): ITAP 2016, PartII, LNCS 9755, pp. 319–329, 2016.
DOI: 10.1007/978-3-319-39949-2_31

the speed of information processing and reaction times. This means that learning something new might take more time in older age, but is possible [3]. Also hearing and visual performance decline, which are also important senses for learning. This and other health problems can hinder potential participants in travelling to learning institutions. Although these problems are more or less relevant for all older adults, there are many older adults who have no problem with engaging in learning activities and others who have many problems. Pre-experiences with learning influence the perception of learning in general: people who engage in learning activities often, rate learning often as fun, whereas older adults without learning experience think that it is more exhausting than pleasant and are less willing to participate [4]. Also a minimum of self-organization, motivation and autonomy in learning is important for all further education offers for adults. People without many learning experiences in their adult life, often lack skills like self-organization and need a lot of structure and guidance in learning [5]. Also motivation for learning differs between older adults and motives change with age. Whereas competition, social comparison and instrumental motives are important for younger learners, motives like additional social contacts and intrinsic motivation and personal growth increase with age [6, 7]. E-Learning and blended learning concepts can be a solution at least to some of these points. E-Learning includes all forms of electronically learning and teaching; electronical media is used for presentation and/or distribution of learning material and/or is used for communication between learners and teachers [8]. Blended learning combines classical face-to-face learning with the flexible methods of e-learning [9]. These concepts enable many degrees of freedom regarding learning time, speed, material and place but also have possibilities for structure, guidance and communication [10].

1.2 ICT Use in Older Age

However, e-learning and blended learning require a minimum of ICT skills. Before e-learning and blended learning can take place, basic ICT skills are compulsory. This can also be done in a blended or completely online way, as long the new users have support for the first steps and good learning material that guides them step by step. Already since 2004, different e-learning courses for older adults were developed at the University of Erlangen-Nuremberg and its partner institutions and successfully integrated in an e-learning platform [10]. The platform enables learning, practicing and rehearsing in the participants' own speed, is enriched with different multimedia elements, suits to the daily living circumstances of the target group and shows added value for daily activities. Studies found, that these e-learning approaches can be very successful as long as individual support and feedback, communication, individual learning speed and the possibility to repeat everything at home and as often as it is needed, is given [10, 11]. Also age and pre-experience differences can be compensated by online learning approaches and it is therefore possible for different age groups and experience levels to learn in the same learning group [12]. At the moment, e-learning and blended learning approaches for older adults concentrate often on learning ICT skills, but of course, in the future also diverse learning topics are possible.

Of course, ICT users are growing, but many older adults still see themselves as computer novices and have no e-skills so far (e.g. 62 % of population 60 years old and over use a Computer on a regular basis in Germany. Yet, among those who are 70 years old and over, the percentage decreases to 29.4 %) [13]. This means that there are about 70 % of people above seventy years of age and also many younger adults, who might be interested and might profit from ICT learning. In the group of older adults, there are of course many in-group differences: Older women use the internet and ICT in general not as often as older men and also report more fears and negative attitudes against ICT [14]. Also low income, lower formal education and living in rural areas increase the possibility that an older adult is a non-user of online services [15]. The reasons for non-use are different, as a study in Germany has shown [16]: One group of older adults is interested in ICT in general, but gave up learning how to use it. Some report that the effort is too high and that it is too complicated. This was especially true for very old adults with some impairments e.g. sensory impairments with reading the screen, using the mouse or cognitive impairments with memorizing processes. Also frustrations with quite long learning processes and confusions e.g. with changing screens, pop-ups etc. lead to high drop-out rates in other studies [17]. The other group of non-users is not interested to learn how to use ICT, because they see no added value, they are satisfied with the existing mass media or because of time and/or financial constraints. Additionally, a big percentage of this group of non-users in general disapproves the internet and is afraid that it can be like an addiction or it can be dangerous to be online [16]. Although many of the convinced non-users will not be interested in learning how to use ICT, some of the non-users with false beliefs or with problems in their first learning attempts might profit from online or blended learning as this enables them to rehearse more often, use their own device and learn at home. Although, this seems promising, many older adults still feel overwhelmed by the many possibilities a desktop computer or a laptop have and/or have problems using a mouse or a keyboard. For this group, tablet computers can be an alternative.

In general, tablet computers are easy to use with limited technology experience, they have neither mouse nor keyboard but an intuitive touch screen, they are easy to bring to courses or use wherever the user wants and have easy and quick to use applications. First results of a study in Austria in 2012 show high acceptance and satisfaction rates [18]. Based on this findings, a comparison study in 2012 [19] took place in Germany. Two matched groups (n = 18 per group, mean age 71.5 years, range from 63 to 85 years) of older adults got the same training (a blended learning course) and used a tablet computer or a notebook to learn first steps on the internet. Results of this study showed that the perceived competence at the end of the course was similar in both groups, but that the tablet group needed less learning hours per week to reach the same competence. The tablet group also showed a higher commitment to the course and seemed to be more motivated at the end of the course. Nearly all participants found the tablet easy to use and information was very quickly found via different applications. Also the portability of the devices was rated very positively.

1.3 The SenApp Project: Learning with Tablet Computers: Project Description and Research Questions

Based on these positive findings, a project to develop online course material for tablets (android and IOS) to support older adults with learning how to use a tablet computer, started in 2014. This project, SenApp, is funded by the Erasmus plus program of the European Union and has the aim to develop and test course material for tablets in four countries (Germany, France, Romania and Spain). The content of this first mobile learning course for older adults are learning elements about ICT use like the use of e-mail, skype, photos and so on. In total, 12 short learning units were developed. Additionally, all courses offer support and communication possibilities via e-mail, phone and a forum with other participants and tutors, as this was found to be essential for learning success [12]. Also materials to train tutors are developed. The learning platform is created with the open source software ILIAS, version 5.0. In a first interview study in 2014 with 23 potential trainers and participants of these courses [20], it was found that all current older tablet computer users were very satisfied, rate the device as easy to use and very convenient. The trainers and more experienced users all mentioned that rehearsing, patience and explanations of added values are important. Also the reduction of fears play a role for many new users, this is an important topic teachers need to be aware of. To motivate new learners it is important to find suitable contents which are in line with interests and daily activities of the target group. Also good, up to date learning material is important for teachers and learners. Additional material on new topics like security questions, social networks, tablets and smartphones and so on can help to motivate new learners. Based on these findings, the modules of the SenApp course were adapted and additional material was added. Courses were guided by experienced older adult trainers. The course content for this pilot course was developed and tested in 2015 and between November 2015 and January 2016 the first pilot courses took place in all partner countries. Due to some translation delays, the courses in Romania and Spain did not start in November, but in December. Therefore, no data of these countries is available yet and for this paper only the data of the German and the French course is used. The evaluation results of these two pilot courses are described in this paper.

Based on previous findings [19] and our aim to offer a course that suits a very heterogeneous target group, we expect that not many differences will be found regarding satisfaction with the course based on age, education, previous experience and gender groups. As we try to offer courses with high support standards and train the tutors carefully, we also do not expect differences between countries as all should receive the same high standard course. But we expect differences on learning routines (hours of learning, learning methods) between participants with more ICT experience and a higher level of ICT confidence and participants with less experience and confidence.

2 Method

2.1 Participants

All respondents of our questionnaire participated in advance in the SenApp course in Germany or in France (basic pilot course) between beginning of November 2015 and end of January 2016. In total, 40 persons participated in the two courses, 20 persons per country. Course participants enrolled voluntarily. They were contacted via organizations for older adults. The final questionnaire was filled in by 26 persons. The missing persons were partly on holiday or ill during the time the evaluation took place and partly did not finish the course (per country 3 persons did not finish the whole course). Demographic data of the surveyed participants can be found in Table 1.

Table 1. Demographic data of the course participants ($N = 26$)

Country	Age group (M/SD)	Gender (female in %)	Years of formal education (M/SD)
Germany	4.77 (.59)	100 %	14.08 (4.15)
France	5.23 (.92)	85 %	12.85 (2.38)

Participants in both countries did not differ in age, gender and years of education. Age was measured in groups. All people belonged to age group 4, 5 and 6, this means they were between 61 and 69, between 70 and 79 or older than 80 years of age. In total, only two men participated in the courses. Therefore gender differences are not analyzed in this paper.

2.2 Procedure

After completing the last course module, the participants were asked to fill in an online questionnaire on the course platform. This was announced on the front page of the course and they were reminded to do so by their trainers. The questionnaire is divided in different parts. These are displayed in Table 2.

On the first page of the questionnaire, participants were informed that the questionnaire was filled in anonymously, that it was voluntary to fill in, but that it would be very important to the developers and researchers to get feedback. To fill in the questionnaire took approximately 20 min. At the end of the questionnaire, the participants were thanked for their help and had the possibility to leave additional comments.

3 Results

In this paper, only quantitative data will be analyzed. Answers about learning routines, course support and course content will be analyzed by group differences. Therefore t-tests will be used to analyze differences between countries and low and high education groups (group 1 between 6 and 12 years of education, group 2 more than 13 years of education). Age differences were analyzed with ANOVAS and with three age groups.

Table 2. Questionnaire details

Part	Method	Number of questions	Example item
Demographic data	Quantitative	4	How old are you?
Experiences with ICT	Quantitative	4	How confident do you feel when you use the internet?
Satisfaction and expectation	Qualitative	5	Which contents are the most useful one's for you?
Learning routines	Quantitative	5	How do you work through new learning modules?
Course support	Quantitative	13	My questions were answers professionally.
Course content	Quantitative	6	The length of the learning modules was too short for me.
Course platform	Quantitative	6	The layout of the platform suits well to the target group of older adults.
Exercises	Quantitative	5	Did you use the possibilities for exercises?

Also differences between participants with and without e-learning course experiences and people who feel more confident in using ICT and people who feel less confident in using ICT than average were analyzed. Answers about the course platform and exercises and some questions about learning routines were not analyzed, due to the length of this paper. Nearly all samples met requirements for normal distributions. However, based on the small sample size, normal distribution tests are very conservative. As t-tests stay very robust also under these conditions, t-tests were selected based on previous findings of Bortz and Schuster [21].

3.1 Group Differences in Learning Routines

First we analyzed how many hours our participants learn with the course material per week. In general, participants learn between one and 30 h per week ($M = 5.67$, $SD = 7.82$). These differences were found between groups: There was a big difference between countries, in Germany, people worked on average 8.85 ($SD = 9.81$) hours per week with the SenApp course, in France only 2.5 ($SD = 3.07$) hours per week. This might be due to the fact, that French participants needed more assistance, they did not learn much on their own, but usually only with the tutor or with other assistance. No differences in learning hours were found between people with higher and lower education. A difference was found between age groups: Participants of the oldest age group (older than 80 years) learned less hours per week than the other age groups ($F(2,23) = 3.94$, $p = .034$). The level of confidence using ICT and the level of experience with similar courses had no influence on the learning hours per week.

To find more answers about the flexibility our participants want and need, we asked them when they use the SenApp course (at different time slots or always at the same time, e.g. always in the morning) and if they work though the material step by step or prefer other learning methods. Most participants use the SenApp material at very different times, e.g. always when they have some free minutes (61.5 %), 23.1 % use the course material in the evening and the other 15.4 % gave different answers (usually in the morning, at the weekend).

53.8 % go through the material step by step, 19.2 % work though it at random, 11.5 % only use the parts, they are interested in and 15.5 % work first with the parts they are interested in and then they do the other parts. No differences were found between countries, age groups, education groups, experience and ICT confidence.

3.2 Group Differences in Course Support Ratings

In this part, we asked participants to rate different aspects of our support possibilities on a five point Likert scale (1 = "I totally agree", 5 = "I totally disagree"). It was also possible to answer with "no experience" as some services might not be used by all participants. Descriptive statistics of the questions about support rated on this scale are displayed in Table 3. The answer "no experiences" was excluded from analysis, therefore all questions have slightly different group sizes.

Table 3. Descriptive statistics for aspects of support ($N = 26$)

Question	Germany (M/SD)	France (M/SD)
My questions were answered professionally. ($n = 22$)	1.00 (0.00)	1.25 (0.45)
My questions were NOT answered fast enough. ($n = 21$)	4.67 (0.71)	3.83 (1.12)
My questions were answered friendly. ($n = 23$)	1.00 (0.00)	1.00 (0.00)
I was very satisfied with the support by my tutor. ($n = 23$)*	1.00 (0.00)	1.54 (0.66)
I was NOT satisfied with the support by the technical support team. ($n = 14$)	4.75 (0.50)	4.30 (1.25)
I was very satisfied with the support by the organizational team. ($n = 21$)*	1.00 (0.00)	1.46 (.52)
I was NOT satisfied with the availability of my tutor. ($n = 19$)	4.75 (0.46)	3.64 (1.75)
The support offers were absolutely sufficient for my needs. ($n = 23$)	1.50 (1.27)	2.00 (0.82)
The support offers were NOT very helpful for me. ($n = 21$)	4.75 (0.43)	3.54 (1.16)

*Group differences: $p < .05$

Additionally to differences between the two countries, possible group differences between educational groups, between high and low experience with e-learning courses and between high and low confidence levels in using ICT were analyzed. Also age differences for the three existing age groups were analyzed per question.

Differences were found for question four: in France people were less satisfied with the support of the tutors during the course ($t = -2.56$, $df = 21$, $p = .018$). Additionally people in Germany were more satisfied with the work of the organization team ($t = -2.49$ $df = 19$, $p = .022$) than in France (question six). For the question if the support was sufficient for the needs of the learner (question eight), an education difference was found: the lower education group ($M = 2.33$, $SD = 1.16$) rated the support as less sufficient than the high education group ($M = 1.18$, $SD = 0.41$) ($t = 3.13$, $df = 21$, $p = .005$). Additionally, people with some experience in course participation rated this question more positively ($M = 1.22$, $SD = 0.41$) than people without course experience ($M = 2.14$, $SD = 1.17$) ($t = -2.25$, $df = 21$, $p = .035$). For the last question, a difference was found between people with course experience ($M = 4.78$, $SD = 0.44$) and people with no experience ($M = 3.42$, $SD = 1.68$) ($t = 2.36$, $df = 19$, $p = .029$). People with e-learning experience rated the support as more helpful than persons without experience.

Moreover, participants rated these communication channels as the most useful to them: 34.6 % rated the forum as most helpful for support and questions, 27.9 % email and 42.3 % phone calls. Additionally in the French group, face-to-face meetings were conducted and were rated as very useful. As this was not foreseen in the first place, this aspect was not part of the evaluation. When participants had questions, 73.1 % asked their tutor, 23.1 % someone from their family, 0 % friends, 3.8 % someone else. 50 % said that their tutor helped them with motivational aspects, 50 % with technical questions, 30.8 % with organizational questions; 61.5 % with questions about the content, 15.4 % gave emotional support and 3.8 % that the tutor did not help with any of these aspects.

3.3 Group Differences in Course Content Ratings

Also the content aspects were rated on a five point Likert scale (1 = "I totally agree", 5 = "I totally disagree"). It was again possible to answer with "no experience" as some services might not be used by all participants. Also here, the answer "no experiences" was excluded from analysis; therefore all questions have slightly different group sizes. Descriptive statistics of the questions about the content rated on this scale are displayed in Table 4.

For the questions related to the course content, all questions were again analyzed by group differences between the two countries, educational level, experience with e-learning, confidence on ICT use, and age group. These differences were found: People with more e-learning experience rated the relatedness of the content to daily life examples as better ($M = 4.78$, $SD = 0.44$) than people with no course experiences ($M = 3.46$, $SD = 1.13$) ($t = 2.08$, $df = 21$, $p = .050$). Moreover, for question three, persons of the lower education group rated the amount significantly more often as too big ($M = 2.83$, $SD = 1.12$) compared to the higher education group ($M = 3.91$, $SD = 0.70$) ($t = -2.74$, $df = 21$, $p = .012$). Also the oldest age group rated the amount more often as too big for them ($M = 2.5$, $SD = 0.84$) compared to age group 4 ($M = 3.29$, $SD = 0.95$) and age group 5 ($M = 3.90$, $SD = 0.99$) ($F(2,20) = 4.14$, $p = .031$). In question four only a difference in age groups was found: The youngest

Table 4. Descriptive statistics for aspects of the content ($N = 26$)

Question	Germany (M/SD)	France (M/SD)
I was very satisfied with the up-to-datedness of the content. ($n = 22$)	1.30 (0.68)	1.75 (0.62)
I was NOT satisfied how related the content was to real life. ($n = 23$)	4.17 (0.84)	3.45 (1.13)
The amount of the learning units was too big for me. ($n = 23$)	3.50 (1.09)	3.18 (1.08)
The amount of the learning units was too short for me. ($n = 20$)	3.42 (1.08)	2.88 (1.46)
The theoretical explanations about the learning contents were completely sufficient. ($n = 24$)	2.25 (1.21)	1.75 (0.75)
The videos were very helpful as addition to the learning content. ($n = 23$)	1.27 (0.65)	1.33 (0.65)

age group rated the learning units more often as too short ($M = 2.29$, $SD = 1.11$) than the second oldest group ($M = 3.80$, $SD = 1.03$) ($F(2,17) = 4.10$, $p = .035$). The oldest group did not significantly differ from the other two ($M = 3.33$, $SD = 1.16$). Finally in question five, the theoretical explanations were rated as more sufficient by the group who feels quite or very confident on using ICT ($M = 1.55$, $SD = 0.52$) than by the group with insecure feelings on using ICT ($M = 2.38$, $SD = 1.19$) ($t = 2.16$, $df = 22$, $p = .042$). For the other questions, no group differences were found.

4 Conclusion and Discussion

In order to better understand learning needs of older adults who learn how to use a tablet computer, this paper addresses age, education, pre-experience, and country differences on course satisfaction and learning methods in an online learning course.

Main findings revealed some differences between the courses in Germany and in France. Participants in France learned less hours per week with the material, were less satisfied with the support by the teachers and less content with the organization of the course. Although we did not find differences on age, education and pre-experience between countries, we assume, based on the feedback of the French trainers that the participants were in less good health conditions than the German participants and that many lived in retirement homes. Furthermore, a lot of face-to-face support took place in France as some participants had problems to work with the course on their own. It needs to be further investigated how this can be improved as flexible and self-organized learning is important for the course concept. Also some age differences were found. Older participants used the learning material less often per week and for them the amount of material was too big. The same was true for people in the lower education group. Moreover, people in this group rated the support as less sufficient for them. Participants without experience on e-learning courses rated some aspects also a little more negative than the group with e-learning experience. Furthermore, people with high confidence on using ICT found the theoretical explanations more sufficient than the group with low confidence. However, the courses were evaluated positively, as many ratings are above average.

Although most of these findings are understandable, we did not expect age, gender and pre-experience differences on course content and support as previous research based on similar courses with desktop computers showed that ratings between groups were similar high [12]. This suggested a very well suited approach to a heterogeneous target group based on multiple degrees of freedom to choose material and support. As we want to create a flexible course about tablet use for all older adults with limited ICT skills, we need to further investigate were these differences come from. It might be due to the fact that learning units are much shorter for the tablet course and less flexible to use, e.g. there are less possibilities to skip parts of the units or use additional material. As communication was very important in other courses which were developed earlier, it might be negative for the tablet users to use a forum on regular basis as some participants seemed to have trouble to write longer text parts with the touch screen.

Several limitations should be noted for this study. Although we found some interesting results, these findings are still preliminary findings. We aim to evaluate all courses in all four countries and compare them carefully to find differences between these courses. As only the German and the French courses were finished before the deadline of this paper, a more detailed analysis with all partner countries will be conducted in spring 2016. Also the small number of participants is a big limitation of this study. For future evaluations, it seems to be useful to additionally ask some health and living condition questions as this might influence skills to use the course.

References

1. Statistisches Bundesamt: Bevölkerung und Erwerbstätigkeit 2010. Statistisches Bundesamt, Wiesbaden (2010). https://www.destatis.de/DE/Publikationen/Thematisch/Bevoelkerung/Bevoelkerungsbewegung/Bevoelkerungsbewegung2010110107004.pdf?__blob=publicationFile
2. Gatzke, N.: Lebenslanges Lernen in einer alternden Gesellschaft. Friedrich-Ebert-Stiftung, Berlin (2007)
3. Filipp, S.-H., Staudinger, U.M.: Entwicklungspsychologie des mittleren und höheren Erwachsenenalters, pp. 300–341. Hogrefe, Göttingen (2005)
4. Kolland, F., Ahmadi, P.: Bildung und aktives Altern. W. Bertelsmann Verlag, Bielefeld (2010)
5. Malwitz-Schütte, M.: Selbstgesteuerte Lernprozesse älterer Erwachsener. Deutsches Institut für Erwachsenenbildung, Bonn (2000)
6. Grube, A., Hertel, G.: Altersbedingte Unterschiede in Arbeitsmotivation, Arbeitszufriedenheit und emotionalem Erleben während der Arbeit. Wirtschaftspsychologie 3, 18–29 (2008)
7. Leen, E.A.E., Lang, F.R.: Motivation of computer based learning across adulthood. Comput. Hum. Behav. 3, 975–983 (2013)
8. Kerres, M.: Multimediale und telemediale Lernumgebungen. Konzeption und Entwicklung. Oldenburg Verlag, München (2001)

9. Sauter, W., Sauter, A., Bender, H.: Blended Learning: Effiziente Integration von E-Learning und Präsenztraining. Luchterhand Verlag, München (2004)
10. Hetzner, S., Held, P.: E-Learning for senior citizens. In: Bernath, U. (ed.) Distance and E-Learning in Transition, pp. 109–129. ISTE Wiley, London (2009)
11. Coroian, E., Held, P., Schüring, L.: Lern@Haus. Nie zu alt fürs Internet. Dokumentation and Evaluation. Bundesministerium für Familien, Senioren, Frauen und Jugend. http://www.programm-altersbilder.de/fileadmin/user_upload/dokumente/LernHaus-Bericht-final-120828.pdf (2012)
12. Hetzner, S., Leen, E.: Personalisation and tutoring in e-learning: the key for success in learning in later life. Eur. J. Open Distance E-Learn. Spec. Issue: Best EDEN 2012, 14–25 (2013)
13. Initiative D21: D21-Digital-Index 2014 (2014). http://www.initiatived21.de/wp-content/uploads/2014/11/141107_digitalindex_WEB_FINAL.pdf
14. Forschungsgruppe Wahlen, e.V.: Internet Strukturdaten. Repräsentative Umfrage – II. Quartal 2012 (2012). http://www.forschungsgruppe.de/Umfragen/Internet-Strukturdaten/web_II_12_1.pdf
15. Doh, M.: Ältere Onliner in Deutschland. Entwicklung und Determinanten der Internetdiffusion. In: Baier, E., Kimpeler, S. (eds.) IT-basierte Produkte und Dienste für ältere Menschen - Nutzeranforderungen und Techniktrends, pp. 43–64. Fraunhofer IRB-Verlag, Stuttgart (2006)
16. Schweiger, W., Ruppert, A.K.: Internetnutzung im höheren Lebensalter – Lebensglück, Alterserleben und die unerkannte Problemgruppe 'Männer'. In: Schab, B., Hartung, A., Reißmann, W. (eds.) Medien und höheres Lebensalter. Theorie - Forschung – Praxis, pp. 171–186. VS, Wiesbaden (2009)
17. Gatto, S.L., Tak, S.H.: Computer, internet and e-mail use among older adults: benefits and barriers. Educ. Gerontol. 34, 800–811 (2008)
18. Werner, F., Werner, K., Oberzaucher, J.: Tablets for seniors – an evaluation of a current model (iPad). In: Wichert, R., Eberhardt, B. (eds.) Ambient Assisted Living. ATSC, vol. 2, pp. 177–184. Springer, Heidelberg (2012)
19. Hetzner, S., Tenckhoff-Eckhardt, A., Held, P.: The joy of learning in later life: the ap(p)titude for tablets for seniors. In: Proceedings of the annual EDEN-Conference 2013, pp. 553–567 (2013)
20. Leen-Thomele, E., Hetzner, S., Held, P.: Mobile learning for older adults: new learning concepts for seniors without e-skills. In: ICERI2015 Proceedings, pp. 996–1001 (2015)
21. Bortz, J., Schuster, C.: Statistik für Human- und Sozialwissenschaftler. vollständig überarbeitete und erweiterte Auflage, Bd. 7. Springer, Heidelberg (2010)

Silver Gaming: Serious Fun for Seniors?

Eugène Loos[(⊠)] and Annemiek Zonneveld

University of Amsterdam, Nieuwe Achtergracht 166,
1018 WV Amsterdam, The Netherlands
e.f.loos@uva.nl, annemiekz@hotmail.com

Abstract. This exploratory qualitative study provides insight into the role that exergames play for seniors. 15 participants (aged 53–78) engaged in playing Your Shape Fitness Evolved 2 on the Xbox 360 Kinect, after which we conducted a semi-structured interview with each participant. We found that in all cases, the innate psychological needs of autonomy and competence (Self Determination Theory) were met. Playing the exergame served not only as a therapeutic instrument with a capability to exert a positive effect on physical and social wellbeing, it also brought entertainment, providing excitement and fun.

Keywords: Exergames · Digital games · Older adults · Seniors · Meaningful play · Self-Determination Theory (SDT) · Autonomy · Competence

1 Introduction

Aging and digitalization are important trends in the Netherlands. Moreover, the number of Dutch seniors who make use of digital media is growing swiftly [1]. As people age, their risk of developing health problems also increases. Exercise is one of the ways people can stay healthier longer. In recent years, silver games have emerged as an instrument to stimulate seniors to exercise regularly [2]. Exergames in particular are viewed as an effective means of doing so, as these games focus on physical exercise, with the players performing movements that they see on a screen, and thus being given direct digital feedback [3, 4].

According to Huizinga [5], games are a fundamental aspect of life. In 1938, he observed that, next to *homo faber* (man the maker), there is also the concept of *homo ludens* (man the player). Bogost [6] comments that these days, we have become as used to playing digital games in the living room as watching television (see also [7–10] on the role of ICT in our daily life and Juul [11] on the casualness of video games for our lives). An increasing number of people are familiar with digital games that are played "for fun". [12] However, there are also digital games that serve to convey a "serious" message to the player. These are known as serious games. Wiemeyer and Kliem [13] clarify this as follows: 'The idea of "serious games" is to integrate playing games, simulation and learning or training for serious purposes like education, exercising, health, prevention, rehabilitation and advertisement' (p. 41).

Research has shown that playing exergames can benefit the health of young people, and thus form a valuable therapeutic instrument [14–16]. Other studies show that seniors are extremely interested in traditional games that can be deployed as a

© Springer International Publishing Switzerland 2016
J. Zhou and G. Salvendy (Eds.): ITAP 2016, PartII, LNCS 9755, pp. 330–341, 2016.
DOI: 10.1007/978-3-319-39949-2_32

therapeutic instrument, and that their health appears to benefit also from playing digital games [4, 17–20]. But are games of this type so attractive to seniors that they actually want to play them? International research into the motivation of seniors for playing digital games reveals that physical and social well-being are important factors in this respect [21–23]. Far less is known about the way Dutch seniors give meaning to digital games. An exception is a study conducted by Nap et al. [24], which shows that fun and relaxation are the main reasons for seniors to engage in digital games, while according to the Dutch white paper Let's play [25], social interaction is the main motivation. Health considerations make it essential to gain more insight into the motivation for Dutch seniors to play, or not to play, exergames. To that end, we conducted an exploratory qualitative study with semi-structured interviews with fifteen Dutch seniors, who we recruited to play the Xbox 360 Kinect's exergame Your Shape Fitness Evolved 2.

2 Self-Determination Theory

We used Self-Determination Theory (SDT) [26–28] for our study into seniors' motivation for playing an exergame. Ryan and Deci define motivation as follows: 'To be motivated means to be moved to do something' (p. 54) [28]. SDT distinguishes between intrinsic motivation (doing something because it is inherently interesting and provides enjoyment) and extrinsic motivation (doing something because it leads to a specific result) (p 55) [27]. SDT addresses the three innate psychological needs of autonomy, competence and relatedness. These needs affect motivation and well-being within domains such as sports and health care [27]. Using SDT, insight can be gained into what moves seniors to play exergames.

From a study conducted among students, Peng et al. [29] concluded that an exergame incorporating gaming elements that support the innate psychological needs of autonomy and competence increase the motivation to play this game. They did not study the third basic need supported by SDT, i.e., relatedness, as this played no role in the exergame examined by Peng et al. [29]. Our research further elaborates this study and likewise focuses on the psychological basic needs of autonomy and competence. However, where students with an average age of 21 served as the target group for the exergame studied by Peng et al. [29], in our research [30], we opted to study seniors (aged 53–78) playing an exergame.

2.1 Autonomy

Ryan et al. [31] define autonomy as self-regulation – a person's ability to perform a particular task of his or her own volition. Related to the play of a digital game, the voluntary choice to play such as game, as well as by factors in the game (e.g., the extent of freedom in choosing the order in which to perform tasks, the freedom to choose specific goals), and the rewards provided for feedback purposes, or to control the player's behavior play an important role.

2.2   Competence

Competence, according to Ryan et al. [31] is reflected in the need of people to be able to act in such a way that a desired outcome is reached. Hence they state that competence is expressed in the need to seek out challenges and in the feeling of being able to act effectively. In digital games, it is important that players are able to master the game easily and intuitively, that the tasks in the game offer optimum challenges and provide opportunities for positive feedback.

3   Method

We have taken the measurement instrument 'Player Experience of Need Satisfaction' (PENS) developed by Ryan et al. [31] on the basis of the SDT and the results of Peng et al. [29] as the starting point for the topic list of our study (see also Sect. 3.3 and the Appendix), based on research conducted by Zonneveld for her Master thesis [30].

The results of the study conducted by Peng et al. [29] showed that the innate psychological needs of autonomy and competence influenced the following factors: (1) game enjoyment, (2) motivation for future play, (3) likelihood of game recommendation, (4) self-efficacy for exercise using the game, (5) game rating.

Our exploratory study is qualitative in nature. This means that we attempted to recognize trends on the basis of semi-structured interviews. Hence, the aim was not to look for significant generalizable results. This study could serve as a pilot for an eventual large-scale follow-up study, in which the trends emerging from this study can be tested in the light of hypotheses.

3.1   Participants

Fifteen Dutch seniors participated in the study, eight of whom were members of the ANBO, The Netherlands' largest organization representing the interests of seniors (four women and four men aged 55 to 78) and seven seniors from our personal network (three men and four women aged 53 to 74). The mean age of the participants was 65.3. Eight participants were research university graduates, five had attended a university of applied sciences, one participant had completed senior secondary vocational education and training and another participant had completed the Dutch MAVO general secondary education program. Of the fifteen participants, four worked and eleven had retired. Two participants in total already played exergames on a regular basis, while the other thirteen were as yet unfamiliar with these. A few participants indicated that at the most, they had seen their grandchildren playing exergames. Three of these thirteen participants indicated that they played digital games, such as solitaire and mahjong; the other ten participants had no experience at all with digital games.

To take part in the study, two criteria had to be met. First, the participants had to be aged 50 or more, the age limit for the Silver Generation used by Jäger and Weiniger in their study [2]. In the second place, the participants needed to have good balance and be able to engage in physical activity without the use of an assistive device. This criterion was explained during the telephone call or in the email in which the initial contact was made. Moreover, their balance was tested prior to playing the exergame by means of the Timed-Get-Up-and-Go-Test (TGUGT) used by physical therapists [32]. The participants had to stand up from a chair, walk three meters to the wall, turn around without touching the wall, walk back and sit down again. This was repeated three times; the participants were timed with a stopwatch and the average time was calculated from these three measurements. The TGUGT distinguishes three categories with regard to balance: normal, frail seniors and further evaluation required. To participate in our study, participants had to belong to the first category (normal), so that they would not be at risk of falling while playing the exergame. This meant that they had to complete the test with an average score of less than ten seconds. The exergame was required to be played while standing, which meant that it was important for these seniors to have good balance. Of the fifteen participants who participated in this study, the average score for performing the TGUGT was 6.5 s. The fastest average time was 4.8 s, achieved by a 53-year-old man, and the slowest (average) time was 8.5 s, scored by a 66-year-old woman. Next to performing the TGUGT, the participants also delivered background details, such personal data (male/female, age, highest level of education completed), use of PC/Laptop/IPad or other tablet/Smartphone, use of games, physical activity.

In total, an hour and a half was reserved per person for semi-structured interviews based on a topic list prior to the gaming session, the gaming session itself and the topics after the session (see also Sect. 3.3 and the Appendix).

3.2 Game Session

For this study, we used an Xbox 360 Kinect game computer to play the exergame Your Shape Fitness Evolved 2. The spoken language of the game in question is English, with subtitles in Dutch. The game was entirely controlled by the movements of the player. The Kinect cameras and sensors registered these movements, determined the location and position of the player, analyzed the movements, communicated this information to the game, and provided direct feedback to the player. Thus the player, standing a few meters from the screen, was able to control the game with hand movements (Fig. 1). Using hand movements, players could select menus on the screen or scroll through the main menu. The game offered familiar activities, such as walking, playing soccer, yoga and tai chi. In the main menu of this exergame, a distinction was made between various menus. As the participants were seniors, games were selected from the activities and classes menus. We deliberately decided not to choose any games from the workout menu, as the pace of these was too high and many of the exercises had to be performed standing on one leg, which could lead to balance problems.

3.3 Interviews After the Game Session Had Ended

After the game session, a semi-structured interview was conducted, which included topics relating to autonomy and competence.

Fig. 1. Senior playing the exergame

Autonomy was divided into internal and external autonomy. Internal autonomy referred to the participant's feeling of being able to make his or her own choices while playing an exergame. External autonomy dealt with the voluntary performance of tasks, without any feeling of pressure, in order to play the game.

Competence was divided into two aspects: playing the game and dealing with the game interface.

To reach our aim that the participants' answers concerning the two innate psychological needs of autonomy and competence might offer insight into the degree of motivation for playing an exergame we conducted our semi-structured interviews on the basis of the following clusters of topics (see also the start of Sect. 3):

(1) game enjoyment – based on the 'Enjoyment Scale' developed by Song et al. [33]
(2) motivation for future play – based on Ryan et al. [31]
(3) likelihood of game recommendation – by means of the question of how likely they were to recommend others to try playing the game, based on Peng et al. [29]
(4) self-efficacy for exercise using the game – derived from the General Exercise Self-Efficacy Scale developed by Shin et al. [34]
(5) game rating – the participants ranked their ultimate level of enjoyment derived from playing the game by assigning a number from 1 to 10, where 10 indicates the highest level of enjoyment.

4 Results

4.1 Autonomy

As explained in Sect. 2.1, Ryan et al. [31] define autonomy as self-regulation – a person's ability to perform a particular task (such as playing a digital game) of his or her own volition. Autonomy was divided into internal and external autonomy (see also Sect. 3.3).

The semi-structured interviews revealed that none of the fifteen participants experienced pressure from the game to play this in a certain way: there was a sense of internal autonomy. Six of the fifteen participants stated explicitly that they felt they had experienced ample freedom of choice because of the extensive range of games and the different levels available. Also, six participants mentioned that the game determined how it was to be played, but that they had not experienced this as pressure. These participants saw this as a positive aspect, as it contributed to achieving a particular goal: 'I experienced no pressure while playing, at the most a challenge because it's fun to play and because you're striving to achieve something and you see the scores rising, so that provides the challenge.' Participant 4.

The semi-structured interviews also showed that of the fifteen participants, eight expected to experience no external pressure at all to play the game. They have a sense of external autonomy: 'Well, other people don't come into it.' Participant 6.

4.2 Competence

As explained in Sect. 2.2, according to Ryan et al. [31], competence in digital games is expressed in the need to seek out challenges and in the feeling of being able to act effectively. In digital games, competence it is important that players are able to master the game easily and intuitively, that the tasks in the game offer optimum challenges and provide opportunities for positive feedback. Competence was divided into two aspects (see as also Sect. 3.3):

The first aspect focused on competence in playing the game. This study showed that fourteen participants felt satisfied about the way they had played the game: 'Well, I thought I managed it fairly well. Considering I'm still a bit stiff and out of shape right now, but it was actually not bad at all, it went fine.' Participant 11.

The sole participant who was not wholly satisfied did indicate that he improved as he was playing the game. In total, ten of the fifteen participants stated that the next time they played they expected to be better at playing the exergame.

The second aspect focused on competence in dealing with the game interface. All the participants felt quite a sense of competence when playing the game, in how they played it and how they controlled it. Seven of the participants even indicated that their feeling of competence in dealing with the game interface increased as they played: 'Better than expected. I thought beforehand that'll be a disaster. But as far as that goes, it's pretty simple. I call myself digitally challenged, and it was really very easy. But it's also about being calm, because you notice when you raise your finger and you wait a moment, because sometimes you have to wait for a pretty long time before it's really green, so then there's this wondering is it working or not [...]. But I am satisfied with how I controlled the game. Very much so.' Participant 2.

4.3   A Closer Look at the Motivation of Exergame Playing Seniors

The average rating (on a scale of 1 to 10) given by the participants for playing the exergame was 7.7. The lowest mark was 7.0, the highest was 9.0. Hence playing the game earned a (very) satisfactory from everyone.

Eleven of the fifteen participants expressed their appreciation of the new experience and the discovery of a new way to exercise. The four other participants had various reasons for the ratings they gave. Two of them, who were prior exergame players, motivated their rating by saying they had enjoyed playing a different game from the Nintendo Wii that they used themselves. Another participant cited as reason for her rating that she had not expected to enjoy it as she is not someone who likes games, but she hadn't been bored for a moment when playing the exergame and she was very pleased with the feedback the exergame provided.

Four of the eleven participants stated explicitly that they considered exergames to offer an attractive great alternative to a current exercise program, such as the home trainer of fitness. Three of these participants moreover commented that they thought it would be fun to play the exergames with the grandchildren when they came to visit. The same went for other family members and friends. The participants also indicated that when they played with the intention of working out, they preferred to play alone.

Five participants explicitly commented that they did not yet, at this point, consider exergames to be of value. Four of them indicated that they preferred other type of exercise to playing exergames. The other participant stated that the games should be better adapted to Dutch culture. She said that, instead of a virtual stroll through New York, she would like to walk around Amsterdam or Utrecht. She also noted that not only the text on the screen, but also the spoken language of the exergame should be Dutch. If these requirements were met, in her view exergames would then become a valuable instrument, because of the exercise aspect.

Other reasons for currently viewing exergames as not of value were the fact that traditional exercise programs (such as walking, playing tennis, bicycling, team sports) were considered more attractive; and that engaging in a sport in front of a screen was inferior to performing an outdoors sport.

There were also participants who emphasized that they would consider the exergames to be more valuable if the surroundings or the movements required by the game were more familiar and recognizable. This is in line with the outcomes of earlier studies, which showed that seniors appreciate playing digital games when these remind them of traditional games from their own childhood [24]. A number of participants also commented that it was fun to have the chance to take part in sports that they used to engage in, or perform sports movements again that they recognized from the past, with the help of the exergame.

4.4 Comparison with the Results of the Peng et al. Study

Just as in the case of the students in the Peng et al. study [29], the seniors in our study felt a sense of autonomy and competence. It should be noted, however, that despite the fulfillment of these two innate psychological needs, six of the fifteen participants indicated that they would not recommend the exergame to others. Their reasons for this were that they felt that other people should be free to decide for themselves what they should or should not do, or that they knew of no one in their vicinity to whom they could recommend playing exergames. Possibly the difference in life stage and educational background between these seniors and the students could explain the discrepancy with the Peng et al. study [29]; that study had demonstrated that game elements leading to the fulfillment of the innate psychological needs of autonomy and competence usually have a positive effect on recommending the game to other people.

5 Conclusions

The seniors professed to be motivated to play exergames. All rated playing the exergame as (very) satisfactory (between 7.0 and 9.0, average 7.7). They all claimed to be motivated to play exergames by the satisfaction they derived from the game itself and to have experienced no pressure from the game (internal autonomy). Eight participants stated that they expected no external pressure to play exergames (external autonomy). All the participants, save one who was not wholly satisfied, felt really competent to play the game.

Nine of the fifteen participants indicated that they would recommend playing exergames to other people. Next to exergaming for health reasons, the participants were also motivated to play exergames with family members (including grandchildren) and friends for fun.

A potential advantage of exergames for some seniors was the ease with which exercise could be taken indoors. The seniors also praised the choice of games and levels offered by the exergame. The same applied in respect of the way the exercise was to be performed when playing the game and the feedback provided by the game, as it were, to coach the player. The participants moreover commented that they would like to see themselves in a game environment that they were familiar with. Another remark was that it was fun to do sports they used to do again or perform sports movements they recognized from the past with the help of this exergame.

One minus point a female participant mentioned was the fact that the exergame was not tailored to the Dutch culture and that the surroundings therefore evoked less recognition. Adjusting this would boost her motivation to play exergames in the future.

A number of seniors experienced a different barrier towards exergaming. They indicated that they were motivated to play in the future, but stated that exergames were at present not of value to them. The reason for this was because traditional exercise programs currently presented a more attractive choice. They felt that working out in front of a screen was inferior to an outdoor activity. Another reason that was mentioned was that exergames could not replace team sports.

Just as in the case of the students in the Peng et al. study [29], our study also revealed that the innate psychological needs of autonomy and competence of most of these seniors were satisfied and that they were motivated to play exergames. The play element in the exergame played a role in the degree to which the participants consider exergames an attractive exercise program option. In 1938, Huizinga [5] mentioned as characteristics of play that, among other things, it is a voluntary activity, which is accompanied by a feeling of enjoyment and tension. In the case of the exergames played by seniors, this also applies, namely that they not only served as a therapeutic instrument with a capability to exert a positive effect on physical and social wellbeing, but also brought entertainment, providing excitement and fun.

6 Discussion

Large-scale quantitative follow-up research (including more higher educated seniors) is essential to determine whether the trends we describe are significant. Our approach, based on Deci and Ryan' Self-Determination Theory [26–28] Peng et al. [29], Song et al. [33] and Shin et al. [34], could serve as a framework for this.

As the results of our study show, seniors would like to play exergames with family members (including grandchildren) and friends, which indicates the importance that the role of relatedness, the third innate psychological need in SDT, may play. In view of the type of exergame, i.e., Your Shape Fitness Evolved 2, which was played on the Xbox 360 Kinect game computer, the focus of our study, like that of Peng et al. [29], was on the innate psychological needs of competence and autonomy. We recommend that relatedness be examined in a follow-up study, and that an exergame suitable for playing together with other people be studied.

Finally, the results reveal that seniors are motivated to play exergames when the game environment or games themselves summon up memories. Exergames designed for Dutch seniors can take this into account by integrating typical aspects of Dutch culture into the exergames. Instead of strolling through New York, the exergame could be adapted to allow players to walk around in Dutch cities, such as Amsterdam or Utrecht. Typically Dutch sports might also be added to exergames for Dutch seniors.

Acknowledgement. This paper is based on the translation of the Dutch paper published by A. Zonneveld and E.F. Loos (2015): Silver gaming: ter leering ende vermaeck? in *Tijdschrift voor Gerontologie en Geriatrie*, 152-159 (DOI:1007/s12439-015-0129-1). The authors thank this Dutch journal and the organisers of the 2nd International Conference on Human Aspects of IT for the Aged Population as part of HCI International 2016 for their permission to use this Dutch paper for its updated English version in this volume of the LNSC series.

Appendix Topic List [Abbreviated Version for This Article]

Topic List (Prior to the Game Session)

1. **Personal data** (male /female, age, highest level of education completed)

2. **Use of PC/Laptop/IPad or other tablet/Smartphone** (If never used: why?, if used: on average, how many days a week, on average, how many hours a day, what is it used for?)
3. **Use of games** (If games never played: why?, if games are played: why? on how many days a week, on average, how many hours spent playing games, on average, first game why play/never play?)
4. **Physical activity** (Physically active on how many days a week, if on average physically active on less than one day a week: why?, value sufficient physical activity? What is sufficient amount physical activity?)
   Administration of Timed Get Up and Go Test (http://www.fysiovragenlijst.nl/docs/pdf/Timed%20Get-Up-and-Go-Test%20_TGUGT_.pdf)

   Topic List (After the Game Session)

5. **Autonomy**
5.1 Internal autonomy (Pressure-Tension, Perceived choice: intrinsically motivated/not motivated to play the game)
5.2 External autonomy (Pressure-Tension Perceived choice: extrinsically motivated/not motivated to play the game)
6. **Competence**
6.1 **Competence in playing the game** (can/cannot play the game)
6.2 **Competence in dealing with the game/interface** (able/unable to understand and use the game interface)
7. **Game enjoyment** (exciting, entertaining/pleasurable, interesting, not fun, boring, not enjoyable)
8. **Motivation for future play** (willingness to continue playing)
9. **Likelihood of game recommendation** (advising others to play the game)
10. **Self-efficacy for exercise using the game** (willingness to play the game twice a week in certain situations, such as when tired or bad weather)
11. **Game rating** (If you had to give playing this game a school mark, what would that be?)

References

1. More older people active online, Dutch statistics (2013). http://www.cbs.nl/en-GB/menu/themas/vrije-tijd-cultuur/publicaties/artikelen/archief/2011/2011-3537-wm.htm? Languageswitch=on
2. Jäger, K.-W., Weiniger, R..: Silver Gaming – ein zukunftsträchtiger Baustein gegen altersbedingte Isolation. In Tagungsband 3. Deutscher AAL-Kongress, 26–27 January 2010, Beitrag 15.1. VDE Verlag, Berlin (2010)
3. Oh, Y., Yang S.: Defining exergames and exergaming. In: Proceedings of Meaningful Play, pp. 1–17 (2010)
4. Agmon, M., Perry, C.K., Phelan, E., Demiris, G., Nguyen, H.Q.: A pilot study of Wii Fit exergames to improve balance in older adults. J. Geriatr. Phys. Ther. **34**(4), 161–167 (2011)
5. Huizinga, J.: Homo ludens: Proeve eener bepaling van het spel-element der cultuur. Amsterdam University Press, Amsterdam (1938, 2008)

6. Bogost, I.: Persuasive Games: The Expressive Power of Video Games. MIT Press, Cambridge (2007)
7. Loos, E.F., Mante-Meijer, E.A., Haddon, L. (eds.): The Social Dynamics of Information and Communication Technology. Ashgate, Aldershot (2008)
8. Loos, E.F., Mante-Meijer, E.A.: Navigatie van ouderen en jongeren in beeld. Explorerend onderzoek naar de rol van leeftijd voor het informatiezoekgedrag van websitegebruikers [Older and younger users navigating at the internet. Exploring the role of age for internet information search behaviour]. Lemma, The Hague (2009)
9. Loos, E.F.: De oudere: een digitale immigrant in eigen land? Een terreinverkenning naar toegankelijke informatievoorziening [Senior citizens: Digital immigrants in their own country? An exploration of information accessibility]. Boom/Lemma, The Hague (2010)
10. Loos, E., Haddon, H., Mante-Meijer, E. (eds.): Generational Use of New Media. Ashgate, Farnham (2012)
11. Juul, J.: A Casual Revolution: Reinventing Video Games and Their Players. MIT Press, Cambridge (2012)
12. Markopoulos, P., et al. (ed.): Fun and games. In: Proceedings of the Second International Conference, Eindhoven, The Netherlands, 20–21 October 2008. Springer, Berlin (2008)
13. Wiemeyer, J., Kliem, A.: Serious games in prevention and rehabilitation – a new panacea for elderly people? Eur. Rev. Aging Phys. Act. **9**(1), 41–50 (2011)
14. Biddiss, E., Irwin, J.: Active video games to promote physical activity in children and youth: a systematic review. Arch. Pediatr. Adolesc. Med. **164**(7), 664–672 (2010)
15. Baranowski, T., et al. White paper: games for health for children – current status and needed research. Games Health J. Res. Dev. Clin. Appl. **5**(1), 1–12 (2015)
16. Papastergiou, M.: Exploring the potential of computer and video games for health and physical education: a literature review. Comput. Educ. **53**(3), 603–622 (2009)
17. Hoppes, S., Hally, C., Sewell, L.: An interest inventory of games for older adults. Phys. Occup. Ther. Geriat. **18**(2), 71–83 (2000)
18. Hoppes, S., Wilcox, T., Graham, G.: Meanings of play for older adults. Phys. Occup. Ther. Geriatr. **18**(3), 57–68 (2001)
19. Aarhus, R., Grönvall, E.: Turning training into play: embodied gaming, seniors, physical training and motivation. Gerontechnology **10**(21), 110–120 (2011)
20. Hall, A.K., Chavarria, E., Maneeratana, V., Chaney, B.H., Bernhardt, J.M.: Health benefits of digital videogames for older adults: a systematic review of the literature. Games Health J. **6**(1), 402–410 (2012)
21. Aison, C., Davis, G, Milder, J., Targum, E.: Appeal and interest of video game use among the elderly. Harvard Graduate School of Education (2002)
22. De Schutter, B.: Never too old to play: the appeal of digital games to an older audience. Games Cult. **6**(2), 155–170 (2011)
23. De Schutter, B, Vanden Abeele, V.: Designing meaningful play within the psycho-social context of older adults. In: Proceedings of the 3rd International Conference on Fun and Games, pp. 84–93. ACM (2010)
24. Nap, H.H., De Kort, Y.A.W., IJsselsteijn, W.A.: Senior gamers: preferences, motivations and needs. Gerontechnology **8**(4), 247–262 (2009)
25. Heuvelink, A., De Groot, J., Hofstede, C.: Let's play: Ouderen stimuleren tot bewegen met applied games [Let's play: The deployment of applied gaming to encourage the elderly to exercise]. TNO & Vita Valley (2014). http://www.vitavalley.nl/items/whitepaper-lets-play/
26. Deci, E.L., Ryan, R.M.: Intrinsic Motivation and Self-determination in Human Behaviour. Plenum, New York (1985)
27. Ryan, R.M., Deci, E.L.: Self-Determination Theory and the facilitation on intrinsic motivation, social development, and well-being. Am. Psychol. **55**, 68–78 (2000)

28. Ryan, R.M., Deci, E.L.: Intrinsic and extrinsic motivations: classic definitions and new directions. Contemp. Educ. Psychol. **25**, 54–67 (2000)
29. Peng, W., Lin, J.-H., Pfeiffer, K.A., Winn, B.: Need satisfaction supportive game features as motivational determinants: an experimental study of a Self-Determination Theory guided exergame. Media Psychol. **15**, 175–196 (2012)
30. Zonneveld, A.: Wat beweegt ouderen? Kwalitatief onderzoek naar het gebruik van exergames onder ouderen [What motivates older people to exercise? Exergaming older people: a qualitatief study]. [Unpublished Master thesis. Utrecht University School of Governance Departement Bestuurs-en Organisatiewetenschap] Utrecht (2013)
31. Ryan, R., Rigby, C., Przybylski, A.: The motivational pull of video games: a self-determination theory approach. Motiv. Emot. **30**(4), 344–360 (2006)
32. Fysiovragenlijst Timed Get-Up-and-Go-Test. Timed-Get-Up-and-Go-Test. http://www.fysiovragenlijst.nl/docs/pdf/Timed%20Get-Up-and-Go-Test%20_TGUGT_.pdf
33. Song, H., Peng, W., Lee, K.M.: Promoting exercise self-efficacy with an exergame. J. Health Commun. **16**, 148–162 (2011)
34. Shin, Y., Jang, H., Pender, N.J.: Psychometric evaluation of the exercise self-efficacy scale among Korean adults with chronic diseases. Res. Nurs. Health **24**, 68–76 (2001)

Teaching Older Adults with Multiple Chronic Conditions to Use a Tablet and Patient Application for Health Management

Rony Oosterom-Calo[1(✉)] and Benjamín López[2]

[1] Philips Research, Cambridge, MA, USA
rony.calo@philips.com
[2] Philips Design, Eindhoven, The Netherlands
benjamin.lopez@philips.com

Abstract. Within home telehealth programs, patients often receive devices and applications which they may need to learn how to use. A user feedback study with training materials on a tablet PC and patient application, designed for older chronic patients, was conducted with fifteen USA patients from the Philips Intensive Ambulatory Care home telehealth program. Two themes emerged from the findings, in relation to the training program: (1) Relevance, appreciation and user experience, and (2) patient preferences, which had two sub-themes (a) Manner of communication and (b) designing the interaction. Participants found training materials relevant, preferred materials that allow practicing and provide feedback, especially when worded in a manner that is encouraging but not patronizing. They preferred information in audio as well as text formats due to their abilities. Training materials introducing technologies to patients, appropriate for their abilities and preferences, need to be devised and provided to promote telehealth patient engagement.

Keywords: Older adults · Chronic disease · Home telehealth · Tablet computer · Tutorial · Training · User feedback

1 Introduction

Telehealth is defined as the provision of care to patients at a distance, using audio, video and/or other telecommunications technologies [1]. Home telehealth programs for patients with chronic conditions may include various monitoring, education, coaching, communication and support components that can improve clinical [2] and patient outcomes [3], support patients to manage their conditions [4, 5], and may reduce costs [6]. Often within home telehealth programs, communication with medical professionals, education and coaching are done digitally. For example, patients may be provided a device (e.g. a tablet computer) which may include applications providing allowing communication with the telehealth professionals, educational content, surveys, and other features to support patients to manage their health.

Engagement in the devices and applications that are provided within telehealth programs is of utmost importance for program effectiveness. However, often patients in

© Springer International Publishing Switzerland 2016
J. Zhou and G. Salvendy (Eds.): ITAP 2016, Part II, LNCS 9755, pp. 342–351, 2016.
DOI: 10.1007/978-3-319-39949-2_33

telehealth programs are older adults who may have limited knowledge about and experience with such forms of technology, which could affect their use and engagement levels. To promote engagement with the devices, it is therefore important to teach patients how to use, and support them in gaining experience with, the devices that are provided within a telehealth program. In addition, since it is known that older adults may experience computer anxiety leading them to refrain from using new technology [7], telehealth patients could become anxious about technology which is newly introduced to them within a telehealth program, leading to less engagement in it. In order to reduce the likelihood that patients feel anxious due to the new technology they receive after joining a telehealth program, it is imperative to introduce it to them in a non-threatening manner. One possibility is to introduce the technology with a training program consisting of appropriate and non-threatening learning materials. Although the technologies could potentially be taught to patients by a human (e.g. a healthcare provider), this could be less desirable for pragmatic reasons (such as high cost, less possibility for on-demand instruction and limited technology teaching skills).

To devise an appropriate training program and materials for this patient population, it is important to take into account their unique characteristics, needs and preferences. Besides the obvious physical disabilities due to having multiple chronic conditions, also cognitive decline which needs to be taken into account when designing user interfaces for older adults [8–10]. It is also important to understand this target populations' preferences regarding training materials since incorporating their preferences into the materials would make it more likely that they would use them [11].

The aim of the current work was to devise recommendations for training materials concerning how to use a tablet and patient application for health management, targeting older adults with chronic conditions within telehealth programs. The research question was, what should be included in a training program teaching how to use a tablet and health management application for older chronic disease telehealth patients, to ensure patient needs and preferences are addressed in the program? To address the aim and answer the research question, a user feedback study was conducted with patients from the Philips Intensive Ambulatory Care (IAC) home telehealth program at Banner Health in Arizona. The IAC program targets complex chronic patients with multiple conditions, and includes an interdisciplinary care team consisting of physicians, nurses, pharmacists and social workers providing care to patients remotely, as well as health coaches providing care at the patients' homes.

1.1 The Importance of User Research in the Design Process of Interfaces for Older Adults

Needs assessment is an integral part of the development of technology training programs for older adults [12]. It has been argued that researchers and developers typically find it easier to design for someone who is similar to them [13–15]. Younger people may find it difficult to understand the needs and preferences of older adults [8]. However, it is important to understand the specific needs and preferences of typical persons within the target user population when designing interfaces meant for that population of users.

There are a few reasons why it is was particularly important to include older chronic patients as the target users in the design process of the (digital) training materials related to tablets, and incorporate their needs and preferences in the resulting training program. First, technology acceptance is an important factor affecting older adults' technology use [16]. It is therefore necessary to increase user acceptance of the (digital) training program by incorporating users' preferences into the program design. Second, older adults may have specific needs, different than those of younger people when it comes to learning how to use technology. Older adults often have cognitive changes that may make it more difficult for them to interact with technology [17], such as interactive training materials. Physical (motoric and sensory) disabilities are central barriers to older adult learning as well [18]. Attitudes toward technology and learning how to use technology are also important to understand and address in training materials about technology, including perceived benefits of the technology, which may be low among older adults, reactions to making errors when using the technology, and perceptions of being too old to learn to use technology [19].

Previous research has demonstrated specific needs of older adults in relation to technology training, for example it has been found that older people may require more time than younger people to learn how to use computers [20]. Our target users were older adults who have joined a telehealth program that specifically targets complex chronic disease patients with multiple chronic conditions. This specific group may have additional needs when it comes to learning how to use technology.

1.2 Designing a Patient Training Tutorial for Tablet Use Within a Telehealth Program

In the context of the current work, we designed a prototype of a training tutorial which consisted of a click-through demo containing the main interaction flow, navigation and content relevant to evaluate the first-time user experience but did not contain a full set of working interactive elements. The demo was aimed at teaching older telehealth patients how to use a tablet and patient application, and took into account the learning needs of older adults. This tutorial was used in feedback sessions and new versions were created on an ongoing basis in the study, based on the feedback received.

Before designing the first version of the tutorial, we first considered the different methods of information delivery (storytelling, chucking information and tutorial) and different types of media (printed information, on-screen and a combination of those) that can be used when devising training materials. We selected one methodology, namely the tutorial, and two types of media – paper-based and interactive. The reason we selected the tutorial methodology was that a tutorial allows information provision but also practicing the tasks, which in the case of learning how to use the tablet was deemed most suitable. We opted to use a paper-based booklet to teach about the hardware components so that patients can, as a next step engage in the interactive part after turning on the tablet and logging as the booklet supports them to do. The paper-based element was necessary because patients need to operate the hardware components to be able to interact with the software components, and therefore the training program could not be entirely digital.

The resulting tutorial (Fig. 1) included two parts: In the first part, included the paper-based booklet. In this part the tablet was introduced and an explanation why patients receive a tablet as part of the telehealth program was provided, and then the hardware components were explained as well as how to log into the application once the tablet is turned on. Within this part, patients were requested to perform various activities which allow practicing the tasks that are being taught. When patients complete this first part they have the tablet turned on and are logged into the application. At the point the patient is logged into the tablet, the tutorial automatically begins. Within the interactive part of the tutorial, patients are guided through the different features of the application, using a voiceover as well as text, in addition to different visual cues. They are asked to click buttons themselves and are guided in practicing the application.

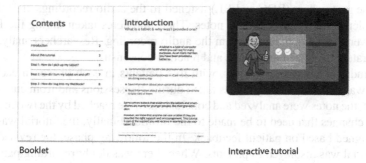

Booklet   Interactive tutorial

Fig. 1. Training materials for telehealth patients with paper-based (left) and digital (right) elements

2 Method

The tutorial demo which was displayed to participants in the feedback sessions was created by the researcher (BL) on Apple Keynote. The tablet (an Apple iPad) on which the tutorial demo was provided to participants was brought by the researchers to the feedback sessions at patients' homes (Fig. 2).

Fig. 2. Range of avatars presented to participants within the study.

All participants were enrolled in the IAC pilot program prior to their participation in the study and signed an informed consent during their recruitment to the program. During a regular scheduled visit with the health coach Potential participants were asked to participate in the feedback sessions. If they agreed, they were contacted by the researcher (ROC) who provided more information about the study and set a date for the feedback session. The researchers (ROC and BL) both conducted the feedback sessions at the patients' homes, which were planned to be an hour in length. Upon arrival, the researchers introduced themselves, explained the study procedure and asked to conduct the study at a place that would be comfortable for the patient to use a tablet and read a booklet.

Each feedback session included four parts: (1) Introduction and patient characteristics, (2) Questions about patients' prior experience with, and use of the tablet (i.e. the device and application), (3) Patients' interaction with the training materials, (4) Obtaining feedback regarding the materials, their perceived suitability and relevance, patients' preferences regarding its content and design, user experience and likelihood of use. User sessions were audio recorded and notes were taken relating to the context of use. The researchers (ROC and BL) listened to the audio recordings after the study was completed, and took extensive notes. Then, the notes taken during the feedback sessions were added to the notes from the audio recording. Researchers analyzed their note separately discussed the results and reached consensus.

The study included three phases, with five patients in each phase. In each phase, feedback was collected through notes taken during the sessions and from audio recordings. Next, the notes were analyzed and conclusions were reached by the two researchers about the changes that need to be made to the tutorial. Finally, the tutorial was revised and redesigned based on patient feedback. In the following phase, the revised version of the tutorial was displayed to patients. When there was doubt regarding patient preferences of a certain aspect of the tutorial, more than one version was displayed to patients who were asked to indicate which version they preferred and explain why. For example, one of the aspects explored was preferences relating to an avatar for provision of feedback on task completion. Participants were presented with a few avatars, including a range of characters from friendly and even cartoon styles, to serious and figurative styles (Fig. 3).

3   Results

The study included 15 participants (10 male patients, age range from 77 to 94; average age 82). Two themes emerged from the findings, in relation to the training program: (1) Relevance, appreciation and user experience and (2) Patient preferences, which had two sub-themes (a) manner of communication, and (b) designing the interaction. The results in relation to each of the themes are discussed in detail below.

3.1   Relevance, Appreciation and User Experience of the Training Materials

Results demonstrated that, in the context of a telehealth program, interviewed patients found it relevant and necessary to receive training materials about the tablet and patient application. They remarked that this type of materials could support them after joining the telehealth program, and could help them feel more confident in using the tablet

"You need to get confidence to do this thing. This material can help you to build up confidence" (IAC patient).

Many patients explained that if soon after joining the IAC program they would have been provided a training program similar to that which they completed during the current study, they would have used it. They recognized it would have supported them to learn how to use the tablet, which most did not know how to use before they joined the IAC program. Some of the patients expressed their preferences to still have a human (e.g. a formal or informal caregiver) support them in addition to the training program. However, it was observed that patients were able to complete the training program by themselves, with very minimal explanation necessary on behalf of the researchers.

Patient's user experience of the tutorial was favorable. However, their overall experience of the digital part of the tutorial was better than of the paper-based part of the tutorial. This was despite the fact that they remarked that the booklet format was more familiar to them, and they explained they have seen similar instruction booklets before (and even received such booklets as part of the telehealth program). Specifically, participants appreciated the interactivity in the digital part of the tutorial, and the ability to try the tasks themselves after receiving instructions for tasks. Moreover, information that was provided in audio as well as text formats was preferred by participants to text only. Patients explained that they prefer to be able to read and listen simultaneously, and that on different days they may primarily use one of the modalities (e.g. if they are tired they may only listen to the audio and not read the text).

Participants remarked that information regarding how to perform troubleshooting by themselves was necessary. They expressed their satisfaction with learning what they can do to troubleshoot issues which may arise with the tablet. Patients who have been in the program for a longer time remarked that they experienced such issues in the past and called the IAC center for help, and would have appreciated being able to solve the issues themselves.

3.2 Patient Preferences in Relation to Aspects of the Training Program

A few patient preferences emerged from the findings. These were specifically in relation to (a) the manner of communication within the training program, including the text, wording, and tone of voice of the materials, and (b) the interaction design of the program, including the interface design and the interactive activities within the training program.

3.2.1 Manner of Communication

In relation to how to communicate with patients within a training program, it was found that patients had preferences related to the manner of communicating feedback and to the length of text in the paper-based part of the tutorial. The responses of patients were mixed in relation to avatars that could potentially be provided as a communication tool within a training program.

Participants appreciated receiving feedback on their use of the tablet and application. They specifically preferred feedback that is worded in a manner that is encouraging but not patronizing. In the first study phase, the tutorial provided positive feedback on every task that was completed well by the user ("Well done!" or "Good job!"), but some participants did not appreciate this feedback and found it patronizing when it referred to smaller, more menial tasks. One participant, for example, explained that providing such encouragement for every simple task performed accentuates to her that she is older and less experienced with technology. Participants thus preferred to be provided positive feedback when they complete a significant task, while for smaller tasks would prefer only an indication that the task was completed.

As mentioned before, the paper-based part of the tutorial consisted of a booklet with text and diagrams. The observations of participants' interactions with the booklets demonstrated that many did not read the text carefully and in detail. Some of the participants also did not look at the booklet pages in the right order (i.e. starting with the first and ending with the last page). As we went through the study phases, we tried to shorten the text and make sure that it is explained at the very beginning of the booklet that it is important to read the whole text as well as read the pages in the right order. This change led to more patients reading the booklet as intended, but some patients still did not read all of the text and did not read the booklet in order.

When presented with the different avatars, patients had different preferences. Some of the interviewed patients preferred not having an avatar at all and had no preference from the avatars they were presented. Most of those that did have a preference, preferred the friendly and professional-looking avatars (Fig. 2) explaining those were more relevant in the telehealth program context, but also appeared more empathic. However, a minority of patients had other preferences (e.g. one patient preferred the puppy avatar).

3.2.2 Designing the Interaction

Participants appreciated the fact that the training materials allowed them to practice using the device and application in a stepwise manner, and provided feedback on the use. Specifically, patients particularly appreciated the possibility to practice the actions they would need to take when they engage with the tablet and application and remarked that it would have helped them to have practiced these actions soon after they joined the telehealth program. They appreciated being able to practice even simple tasks, such as clicking a button on a touchscreen.

A few aspects of the user interface design were confusing to patients and lead to errors or misunderstandings. These were redesigned in each phase until we observed patients were comfortable with the interaction and were not making errors. It was important to visually differentiate the tutorial user interface elements from the application user interface elements to avoid confusion. In order to direct the users' gaze to specific user interface (UI) elements on the screen, it was necessary to (1) use very a high contrast to highlight elements visually, (2) include a voice over and slow transitions to reinforce the image from different channels; and (3) sync multi-modal interactions while minding transition speed, including a timely voice over and a high-level of contrast.

4   Conclusion and Implications

Although telehealth is promising, there are various obstacles to telehealth implementation, including patients' knowledge and attitudes [21]. Designing and providing appropriate and accepted training materials relating to devices and applications used within the programs can facilitate optimal patient engagement in telehealth programs by increasing knowledge and experience levels and decrease fear and anxiety of the devices and application, which can thereby influence program efficacy. It has been found that some (potential) telehealth patients incorrectly assume that special skills are necessary to operate devices, leading them to reject telehealth programs [21]. Training programs that teach patients to use the devices in a stepwise manner and allow patients to practice using the devices, could help to eradicate such assumptions and increase patient acceptance of telehealth programs.

The need for technology training programs targeting older adults has been noted in literature [22]. Previous work has shown that older adults prefer receiving training before adopting a new technology [11]. Our findings are in line with previous work, demonstrating that a training program teaching telehealth patients how to use technology that is provided as part of the telehealth program and is new to them (a tablet computer and patient health management application) is regarded relevant and is appreciated by patients. Our results suggest that patients are willing to engage in such a training program, and that they would be able to do so on their own. Since some patients expressed a preference to have access to a human who can support them to navigate the training program if needed, it is advisable to have such an option available for patients. Since the results also suggest that patients are likely to be able to complete a training program designed to accommodate their needs without additional support, it is possible that the reason for the request for human support is for added confidence rather than inability to complete the program on their own.

The research question addressed in the current work was: What should be included in a training program teaching how to use a tablet and health management application for older chronic disease telehealth patients, to ensure patient needs and preferences are addressed in the program? Our findings suggest a number of preferences of older adults that should be taken into account when devising a training program about technology, related to the manner of communication and the interaction design of the training program. Although previous work has investigated among older adults the perceptions of, and preferences in relation to, a training program about a technology that is new to them (e.g. personal computers) [11], the current work is the first to investigate this in the context of a home telehealth program with older patients who have multiple chronic conditions. The results suggest that the manner in which feedback on technology use is worded is important to this user population. Based on some of the remarks provided by patients, it seems that some patients may feel that their age and limited experience with technology is accentuated, making the feedback feel patronizing to them. It is important to define user feedback provided within a training program about technology with this in mind. Interestingly the results also suggested patients prefer receiving interactive digital training materials than paper-based materials, despite their expressed greater familiarity with the latter. They appreciate the opportunity to practice the tasks and to receive feedback on their progress. Digital training programs should provide information in audio as well as text allowing patients the choice of modality based on their abilities or their state.

5 Limitations

The current work has a few strengths as well as a few limitations. First, the work included in-depth feedback sessions with patients who were presented a training program. The results lead to an understanding of their preferences and perspectives and allow researchers and designers who need to devise training programs for similar populations to use the results of the current work as a guideline. The feedback sessions were conducted with the target population in their natural setting and allowed observing them interact with the training materials as they would have interacted with them in "real life". This leads to results that are based on an understanding of the situation in which the training process would occur. On the other hand, the sample size in the current study was relatively small and the sample was not selected at random. We focused on patients within one specific telehealth program and one geographic location. The results cannot be generalized to the entire chronic disease population in different geographic locations.

Although our work demonstrates how training materials for use in a telehealth program could be designed to address preferences of older adults with multiple chronic conditions, the current work has not examined the timing within the telehealth program that such materials should ideally be provided to patients. Materials that teach patients how to use devices or services could be provided to patients immediately after joining a program, for example. However, it could be that patients who have just recently joined a telehealth program may experience an informational or emotional overload, especially if they have recently experienced an acute clinical episode and joined the program following a hospitalization. It is advised that future work establishes when is the best timing within a telehealth program to provide training materials to patients, and if multiple devices and services are provided with a program, how such materials should be ordered.

References

1. Paré, G., Mirou, J., Sicotte, C.: Systematic review of home telemonitoring for chronic diseases: the evidence base. J. Am. Med. Inform. Assoc. **14**, 269–277 (2007)
2. DelliFraine, J.L., Dansky, K.H.: Home-based telehealth: a review and meta-analysis. J. Telemed. Telecare **14**, 62–66 (2008)
3. Polisena, J., Tran, K., Cimon, K., Hutton, B., McGill, S., Palmer, K., Scott, R.E.: Home telehealth for chronic obstructive pulmonary disease: a systematic review and meta-analysis. J. Telemed. Telecare **16**, 120–127 (2010)
4. Radhakrishnan, K., Cynthia, J.: Impact of telehealth on patient self-management of heart failure: a review of literature. J. Cardiovasc. Nurs. **27**, 33–43 (2012)
5. Davis, R.M., et al.: TeleHealth improves diabetes self-management in an underserved community diabetes TeleCare. Diabetes Care **33**, 1712–1717 (2010)

6. Polisena, J., Coyle, D., Coyle, K., McGill, S.: Home telehealth for chronic disease management: a systematic review and an analysis of economic evaluations. Int. J. Technol. Assess. Health Care **25**, 339–349 (2009)
7. Czaja, S.J., Charness, N., Fisk, A.D., Hertzog, C., Nair, S.N., Rogers, W.A., Sharit, J.: Factors predicting the use of technology: findings from the Center for Research and Education on Aging and Technology Enhancement (CREATE). Psychol. Aging **21**, 333–352 (2006)
8. Eisma, R., Dickinson, A., Goodman, J., Syme, A., Tiwari, L., Newell, A.F.: Early user involvement in the development of information technology-related products for older people. Univ. Access Inf. Soc. **3**, 131–140 (2004)
9. Czaja, S.J., Lee, C.C.: The impact of aging on access to technology. Univ. Access Inf. Soc. **5**, 341–349 (2007)
10. Loos, E.F., Romano Bergstrom, J.: Older adults. In: Romano Bergstrom, J., Schall, A.J. (eds.) Eye Tracking in User Experience Design, pp. 313–329. Elsevier, Amsterdam (2014)
11. Mitzner, T.L., Fausset, C.B., Boron, J.B., Adams, A.E., Dijkstra, K., Lee, C.C., Rogers, W.A., Fisk, A.D.: Older adults' training preferences for learning to use technology. In: Proceedings of the Human Factors and Ergonomics Society Annual Meeting 52, pp. 2047–2051 (2008)
12. Mayhorn, C.B., Stronge, A.J., McLaughlin, A.C., Rogers, W.A.: Older adults, computer training, and the systems approach: a formula for success. Educ. Gerontol. **30**, 185–203 (2004)
13. Keates, S., Cherie L., Clarkson, P.J.: Investigating industry attitudes to universal design. In: Proceedings of the Rehabilitation Engineering Society of North America Annual Conference (RESNA 2000): Technology for the New Millennium, pp. 276–278. RESNA Press (2000)
14. Akrich, M.: User representations: practices, methods and sociology. Pinter, London (1996)
15. Oudshoorn, N., Rommes, E., Stienstra, M.: Configuring the user as everybody gender and design cultures in information and communication technologies. Sci. Tech. Hum. **29**(1), 30–63 (2004)
16. Or, C.K., Karsh, B.-T.: A systematic review of patient acceptance of consumer health information technology. J. Am. Med. Inform. Assoc. **16**, 550–560 (2009)
17. Charness, N., Boot, W.R.: Aging and information technology use potential and barriers. Curr. Dir. Psychol. Sci. **18**, 253–258 (2009)
18. Purdie, N., Boulton-Lewis, G.: The learning needs of older adults. Educ. Gerontol. **29**, 129–149 (2003)
19. Wagner, N., Hassanein, K., Head, M.: Computer use by older adults: a multi-disciplinary review. Compt. Hum. Behav. **26**, 870–882 (2010)
20. Kelley, C.L., Charness, N.: Issues in training older adults to use computers. Behav. Inf. Tech. **14**, 107–120 (1995)
21. Sanders, C., Rogers, A., Bowen, R., Bower, P., Hirani, S., Cartwright, M., Fitzpatrick, R., Knapp, M., Barlow, J., Hendy, J., Chrysanthaki, T., Bardsley, M., Newman, S.P.: Exploring barriers to participation and adoption of telehealth and telecare within the whole system demonstrator trial: a qualitative study. BMC Heal. Serv. Res. **12**, 220 (2012)
22. Heart, T., Kalderon, E.: Older adults: are they ready to adopt health-related ICT? Inter. J. Med. Infor. **82**, e209–e231 (2013)

Family Matters: The Role of Intergenerational Gameplay in Successful Aging

Sanela Osmanovic[✉] and Loretta Pecchioni

Department of Communication Studies, Louisiana State University, Baton Rouge, USA
{sosman3,lpecch1}@lsu.edu

Abstract. Successful aging in Western cultures is associated with remaining independent based on physical and mental health while also remaining engaged with others. Video game play has been found to enhance physical and mental health in older adults, however engagement with others has received less attention from scholars. This study examines the multiple reasons older adults provide for playing video games with family members, focusing on how this process maintains intergenerational relationships. While design issues and negative attitudes may prevent some older adults from playing video games, we offer solutions to overcome these barriers.

Keywords: Older adults · Successful aging · Video games · Intergenerational · Gaming · Interpersonal relationships

1 Introduction

Although the vast majority of older adults live independently and are financially secure, with advanced age they are at greater risk of isolation due to physical and financial limitations [1]. The consequences of becoming housebound include depression, lower quality of life, and shortened life expectancy [2]. New technologies, however, may reduce social isolation and its resulting negative consequences. As technologies become both more affordable and user-friendly, they are more easily adaptable to the needs of older adults. One aspect of technology that may be of particular benefit in fighting these negative consequences are social video games. In this study, we examine the experiences of intergenerational game-playing by older adults, the attitudes that create barriers to such play and conclude with recommendations for game design that might enhance their experiences and potential for more successful aging.

1.1 Successful Aging

Gerontologists Rowe and Kahn [3] identified the key components of successful aging in Western cultures as: (a) freedom from disease and disability, (b) high cognitive and physical functioning, and (c) social and productive engagement. In Eastern cultures, social belonging is ranked by older individuals as more important than independence [4]. Older adults identify maintaining interpersonal connections as crucial to the quality of their lives [5–7].

© Springer International Publishing Switzerland 2016
J. Zhou and G. Salvendy (Eds.): ITAP 2016, Part II, LNCS 9755, pp. 352–363, 2016.
DOI: 10.1007/978-3-319-39949-2_34

This sense of connection with valued others is often fostered through shared activities, such as playing games [8]. In previous generations, those games may have required physical proximity for the game players to gather around a table to play cards or a board game [9, 10]. With the advent of digital games and on-line game playing, physical proximity is no longer a requirement. As families become more geographically dispersed, being able to maintain emotional connections may rely on being able to share activities through mediated means [11].

1.2   Video Games and Older Adults

Video games are frequently perceived as an arena for young revelers [12]. However, considering that the population who were the focus of game developers in the late 1980s are now on the brink of their 50s and in large part continuing to play games, the gaming demographic is changing rapidly. Between 1999 and 2011, the percentage of gamers older than 50 has increased from nine to 27 percent [13, 14]. In Europe, 15 percent of those aged 45–55 and 11 percent of those aged 55–64 reported playing video games [15].

The number of older gamers may be growing, but the research on video games and the population above the age of 50 has largely focused on rehabilitation or prevention of physical and mental decline. Studies have shown that casual video games can enhance reaction time, processing speed, and general cognition in older population [16], help in stroke rehabilitation [17, 18], and improve interaction with caregivers [19].

While most of the research on older adults and gameplay has focused on the aspect of successful aging related to physical and cognitive abilities, a few studies have found that older adults play games to entertain themselves, to relax, to escape, and to socialize. Schultheiss [12] reported that older adults prefer accessible games that combine knowledge and entertainment, and their solvency and tendency to invest in high-end technologies makes them a perfect audience. Nap et al. [20] found that older adults stay faithful to the games they play, citing fun and relaxation as the main motivator for playing, closely followed by escape from reality and staying in touch with society. Pearce, however, reported that older adults enjoyed more demanding, intellectually challenging games with rich narratives, and large, involved communities in which they can take part – "in short… they just want to have fun" [21, p. 171].

One common theme threads through most of the above research – older adults enjoy the social side of gaming [12, 20, 21]. This aspect was corroborated by De Schutter and Vanden Abeele, whose research placed an emphasis on the connectedness that video gameplay offers even across great distances, providing a "means to spend time together apart… a means for requesting help and attention from sons, or something to structure the conversation with friends" [22, p. 90]. Not unexpectedly, Gajadhar et al. [23] found that older adults reported the highest levels of satisfaction in playing with another person, with physical presence taking precedence over mediated co-play. Participants reported more pleasure, fun, and challenge when playing side-by-side. These findings were supported by De Schutter [24], who found that social interaction was the most important predictor of length of gameplay for older adults. With social engagement being one of the core aspects of successful aging, we turn to social interaction in families and its perpetuation through gaming.

1.3   Social Intergenerational Gaming

Older adults are not alone in finding that playing video games with another person is more conducive to enjoyment and length of play [23, 24], younger generations also report that social interaction is one of the strongest motivators to play video games [25]. For example, co-playing video games has positive effects among adolescents: playing with family members decreases the level of internalizing and aggressive behavior, and increases prosocial behavior [26]; while playing with friends maintains and enhances their relationships [27]. Parents in the United States [14] and Europe [15] report playing games with their children because it is fun and gives them an opportunity to socialize with their children.

Very little research, however, has focused on whether older adults play video games with family members, nor how this co-play is performed and how it affects intergenerational family groups. Of the few studies available, Voida and Greenberg [28] identified more passive gameplay behavior by older players in the presence of children, suggesting some older adults are more likely to give gameplay priority to younger partners. Additionally, Gajadhar et al. [22] found that compared to younger players, older adults are less competitive and take on a more supportive role. In turn, younger adults doubt older adults' ability to successfully partake in the game, and take time to explain and help when their playing partner asks for aid [28, 29].

In spite of these apparent challenges, intergenerational gameplay proves to be satisfying, with participants enjoying social interactions with their partners (which was demonstrated during gameplay by shared laughter and remarks that is was fun to play) and being willing to play again [29]. Osmanovic and Pecchioni [30] found that older adults who regularly play video games with their families find the experience enjoyable, fun, and a source of bonding, providing opportunities to generate talk. Younger adults saw intergenerational gameplay as a means of maintaining or deepening the relationships with older family members, to spend time together, and to talk about simple and complex topics in a setting they find comfortable and comforting [30].

1.4   Purpose of the Study

Throughout history, as games have added enjoyment to everyday life, the perceived fun-factor was both the reason we engaged in them and rarely took them seriously. Goffman [31] emphasizes the necessity to treat fun seriously, underlining that games abide by formal regulations of societal engagement and are thus no different than other aspects of social life.

As noted above, previous research reveals that older adults enjoy both the serious and more leisurely aspects of video gaming; see also Loos and Zonneveld [32]. As a result, in this study we want to address the questions of the effect of intergenerational gaming within families on the experience of aging. Concretely, we seek to find whether playing games with family members provides a path towards successful aging. In other words, the goal is to begin to examine if and in what ways intergenerational family game playing may help stave off disease and disability, maintain high cognitive and physical functioning, and maintain meaningful social connections.

2 Method

In order to gather information on gameplay experiences and compare those experiences, participants were recruited from two sources: older adults who report playing video games with family members, and older adults who do not report such play.

The participants were recruited from three sources after receiving approval from the appropriate Institutional Review Board. Older adults who play video games were recruited through the research system at a large university in the southern United States, as well as through online gaming forums at King.com, Gamesdreams.com, and IGN.com. These websites were chosen as they cater to audiences of varying ages and gaming interests, including casual social games such as Facebook and phone games. Older adults who do not play video games with others were recruited locally from a southern United States community. The participants did not receive any compensation for taking part in the research.

Data collection from the participants who play video games was divided into two parts. In the first part, researchers held short 10 min interviews with participants, either face-to-face or through a mediated format. The participants were asked general questions about their gaming habits (e.g. "What games do you play most frequently?", "Who do you play with and why?"). The interviewees who reported regularly playing games with their family members were asked to fill out a questionnaire in which they were asked about outcomes of intergenerational gaming with family members (e.g. "What do you enjoy about playing video games with family members?").

Of the 38 older adults who were interviewed, 33 were asked to take part in the follow-up questionnaire. The participants in this group who chose to disclose their geographic location were from Western Europe and North America, and the group consisted of 19 females and 14 males, ages 55–70 ($M = 60.97$, $SD = 4.48$). The questionnaire was distributed online, together with the digital consent form. The questionnaire took approximately 30 min to fill out.

Participants who reported not playing video games were recruited through snowball sampling – one participant recruited her friends – and were not separately interviewed. All six participants took part in a focus group and all were female and ages 59 to 68 ($M = 65.17$, $SD = 3.19$). The participants in this group were from the U.S. Their discussion was video and audio recorded, and transcribed.

Focus group organization: The investigators greeted the participants, introduced themselves, and explained the purpose of the study. The participants read and signed the required consent forms. After these forms were collected, the investigators initiated the discussion, focusing on three main questions: what games do you play and with whom (or why not), what do you do while playing, and why do you play, i.e. what do you get out of playing.

The first author reviewed the responses, reading and re-reading to identify themes in the participants' answers, looking particularly for similarities and differences in those experiences. Exemplars for each theme were identified and placed in a draft file of findings. The second author then reviewed the draft findings and the two researchers discussed them at length. Agreement on the appropriateness of the themes and exemplars was 100 %. The researchers then discussed how these findings relate to previous research and agreed on their interpretations of motivations and behaviors which are reported in the next section.

3 Findings

Based on the responses from our participants, we answer our questions about if and in what ways intergenerational family game playing may help enhance experiences of successful aging. These older adults overwhelmingly reported positive outcomes from playing video games with family members – while enjoyment was an important aspect, maintaining connections with each other, and training cognitive and physical abilities were repeatedly emphasized. The concerns of the non-gamers highlight common negative attitudes toward video game play, but also point to ways in which these negative attitudes may be overcome.

3.1 Intergenerational Gameplay in Families

Whether active video game players or not, all of the participants reported that they enjoyed playing games, however, we should note that the members of the group that identified as not being active on-line gamers said they preferred playing card games, either playing with family members or having a regular group of people with whom they played in person. Even though they do not consider themselves to be active on-line, two of the older adults in this group reported that they do play video games on Facebook such as *Candy Crush*, *Bubble Witch*, and *Pet Rescue* and one participant reported playing a puzzle game – *Four Pic One Word* – on her phone. The older adults who identified as active gamers played a variety of casual games, from *Candy Crush* and *Trivia Crack* to Wii games and sports simulations such as *Madden* to complex and immersive games such as *Halo* and *World of Warcraft*. Therefore, these older adults have broad gaming interests and play a wide variety of video games of different levels of involvement and difficulty.

The active older gamers reported mainly playing video games with younger family members, typically children or grandchildren. When asked what drives their family gameplay, 13 participants (39.4 %) cited entertainment, connectedness, spending time together, and sharing in a joint activity. As one female participant, age 59, reported:

> I play because I want the opportunity to do something with my grandchildren, an activity that allows us to actively enjoy each other's company. It lets me spend time with them and have fun through some good friendly family competition.

While nearly three-fourths (72.7 %) of our participants reported preferring cooperative gameplay, over one-third (39.4 %) of the older gamers reported also enjoying the competition and showing that old age still carries knowledge and skill. For example, one female participant, age 63, said:

> They introduced me to the game, they taught me how to play it, and honestly I like showing them that their grandma can beat them every once in a while. It's funny when you beat your grandkids in something because they always think they are better than us old people.

Only four participants (12.1 %) reported playing with family members because they have not find anyone with gaming interests among their own age group. One male participant, age 63, reported playing with his grandson because "he plays back":

I play with him because he is the only person I know who plays these games.

These players were then asked what they get out of playing video games. Over two-thirds (69.7 %) of the participants listed that game play was fun and/or relaxing, while nearly one-fifth (18.2 %) identified a sense of accomplishment as the most prominent reasons for playing. As a male participant, age 59, explained:

It's like watching a really good movie while still being able to write it yourself. An interactive movie. You get to create and experience the thrill of the story, to have an impact on the story. I am never bored with video games around, I am sometimes frustrated, sometimes accomplished (usually in that order), scared, intrigued, intense…

One-third (33.3 %) also saw it as a way to escape day-to-day routine, but only four (12.1 %) identified escape as the primary reason for playing. As a female participant, age 57, said:

You can do it at your own pace, in your own free time, and you don't have to physically go somewhere. Sometimes I don't leave work for lunch but stay and play, and it makes me feel like I'm getting away even when I'm not physically leaving.

A male participant, age 60, added:

What I enjoy most about playing my game is that it gives me a release and seems to free my mind for a little while. It also keeps the gears turning in my mind, because some levels can be challenging and it really makes me think. It is different from the everyday tasks I perform at work, so it makes my brain operate in different ways.

While 14 participants (42.4 %) said that games keep challenging their cognitive abilities, only 7 (21.2 %) of them listed this as the primary reason for engaging in game play. A female participant, age 59, explained:

Since I am older, I feel like learning to play these games keeps me "up to speed" with technology. I also like playing it because it's entertaining yet challenging, something to keep me sharp.

A relatively small number (4, 12.1 %) reported the physical aspect of gaming as the most rewarding, enjoying both the competitiveness and the accompanying exercise. All of these participants report only playing games focused on physical activity. As a male participant, age 70, reported:

My grandson and I play Wii games frequently, and I must say it is my trying to compete with him that keeps me physically fit. We play several times a week and can get very competitive with each other, but we are also becoming closer through different conversations had throughout trying to complete the latest level. It gets very intense between the two of us.

The vast majority (27 participants, 81.8 %) focused on closeness and connectedness brought on by playing video games together, not only as a common activity for the participants, but a bonding factor, a shared experience. One female participant, age 65, wrote:

I don't really care about the game I play with my granddaughter, I just play to spend time with her. I feel like we are understanding each other better, I feel closer to her generation.

One male participant, age 59, wrote about the gameplay with his son:

I have really enjoyed being able to connect with my son through a different medium. Playing games together has allowed us to grow closer through fun competition. We talk and see each other more. When he comes home to visit for a weekend, we play, and when he calls and checks in on us, the game always comes up in discussion. We share some friendly trash talk to make it more fun, and he usually enjoys more success than I do. It has given us another subject that we can connect on, and I have really enjoyed it.

These findings are similar to previous research, finding that older adults prioritize being able to enjoy time together and maintain their connection with other family members [27, 30].

While the active gamer group reported very positive experiences gaming with family members, the group of older adults who do not play online games expressed concerns about the games their grandchildren regularly play – particularly interacting with strangers and engaging in violent games as well as the time and money devoted to such play.

The capacity of some games to provide a platform for communication with others outside the household raised an uproar of voices who unanimously agreed such access is dangerous. One female participant, age 67, stated:

And they can interact with other people all over the place! And that's scary to me. You don't know who these people are, you don't know their age, you don't know anything about them. And they could be asking questions and back and forth, and my 13-year-old grandson wouldn't realize that they are picking him for information.

They also expressed concerns about the violent nature of many games. The group unanimously agreed with the statement of one female participant, age 66:

My problem is, I don't like the games. There is just too much violence. To me, there is just too much violence, shooting and killing, blood and guts everywhere.

In addition to their concerns about violence, they thought that their grandchildren spend too much time playing video games, and their children spend too much money buying games and the latest consoles.

Their concerns about the negative consequences of digital game play reflect the findings from previous research [see 33, 34]. Unfortunately, the negative effects tend to receive more media attention than do the positive effects. This aspect may be particularly true for violence in games, which has been found in other studies to be of concern to older adults [21]. Helping older adults to understand the potential benefits may be one strategy to help overcome some of the barriers to game adoption.

In spite of these concerns, the participants discussed extensively the games their grandchildren play and time spent watching them play as well as their potential interest in being more actively involved. One female participant, age 66, reported:

My youngest grandson plays this little game where you build things, Minecraft. I would play that with him. I've sat with him, and we've talked about it, but I've never played with him. I do like that game, he plays that a lot. And when we sit together, he shows me and tells me what he is building. It's really kind of fun. But I've never played with him.

Although five of the six members of this focus group said they had never played with their grandchildren, they all reported that in spite of all their reservations, they would be willing to try playing games with their grandchildren. They are interested in spending time with them and sharing an activity, but they think the games should be more appropriate and accessible. One female participant, age 59, said:

I watch my grandchildren play but don't play with them. I probably would, but I have never been invited....Board games, I play with them.

This more passive role during game play is similar to the findings of Voida and Greenberg [28] who argued that older players may prioritize gameplay time for their younger partners.

Besides these concerns, the group members also expressed concerns about the speed of action in many games which might make it difficult for them to play with their grandchildren. One female participant, age 68, captured their sentiments when she said:

Some games are not violent, but it's so fast, it's wham wham wham wham. There is no way I can keep up with that. I'd break things.

Because of their resistance to playing, we asked what kind of games they would like to see. They proposed games with an educational undertone that contain puzzles, riddles, perhaps even some of their favorite card games in some form – anything but violence. As one female participant, age 66, said:

If they had games we enjoy, we would play with them for sure. It would be a good thing, grandparents playing with their grandchildren.

To summarize, older adults who regularly play video games with their families find the experience fun, relaxing, positively challenging, and a bonding experience. They credit their younger family members for driving them to start and continue playing video games, but rate highly the perceived cognitive and physical benefits of this joint activity, as well as the bridging of the generational gap in families. In contrast, older adults who do not play video games with family members perceive games as violent, and online gaming as dangerous. They take on the role of an audience to their younger family members during video game play, but do not join in because of the violence or the swift tempo of the games. Finally, they collectively identify playing video games with younger family members as a potential bonding experience, and are interested in taking part in this activity provided that the games are accessible, slower, and the content at least in some way educational or beneficial to the children. However, they are waiting to be asked to join in on the fun.

3.2   Recommendations for Game Design

Our participants reiterated many of the recommendations for game design that have been suggested elsewhere. These suggestions fall into two broad categories: the content of the game itself and the operation of the technology related to the game.

Games that are violent or highly competitive are less enjoyable for older adults. Our older participants who are not currently playing video games, not only disliked violence in their own gameplay, but preferred that younger family members not engage in violent games. While they might co-play or enjoy watching a grandchild play a game, they avoided doing so when the game was violent. Voida and Greenberg [28] also suggested that the design of games for older adults should entail aspects that encouraged players working together to accomplish goals. Marston [35] suggested that digital gaming should be designed to enhance social enjoyment, feeling connected, and enhancing kinship.

The pace of the games bridges the content and the technological interface. Games that are fast-paced create greater cognitive load that may become challenging as individuals reach advanced old age. Some of these pacing challenges, however, may have more to do with manipulating the physical interface. Rapid movements of buttons or arrow keys was problematic. Interfaces that draw on larger physical and intuitive movements may help even the playing field across generations [35–37].

As Östlund says, negative stereotypes of aging have inhibited game design that would be appealing to the current cohort of older individuals – "researchers often view older users as 'old' first and 'users' much further down the proverbial list – somewhere after 'physically impaired', 'socially bereft', 'technically illiterate' and 'struggling to use unmodified versions of mainstream technologies'" [38, p. 27]. These negative attitudes are apparent in the design of digital resources for older adults, which as a rule focus on encouraging physical and cognitive activities instead of maintaining them, revealing the underlying assumption that the ageing demographic is immobile, disinterested, and incapable of engaging in these activities without the aid of new technologies.

In previous research, young adults reported that the games they choose to play with older adults are selected for the simplicity of the controls and soft learning curve even if these are games they do not necessarily enjoy playing [30]. They suggested linear multiplayer games with clean yet immersive storylines, with quests that require solving word or picture puzzles, cooperative work, and a "handicap" option so all players could play at their skill level, thus getting greater enjoyment from the game, yet equally contribute to the common game goal. Older adults also expressed interest in playing games they observe their grandchildren playing, but are discouraged by the complexity of the controls and the speed of the gameplay.

4 Conclusion

In this study, we explored intergenerational video game playing - and lack of it - in the family setting, seeking to find whether playing games with family members provides a path towards successful aging. This qualitative approach allowed us to collect detailed accounts and explore the nuances of rich gaming experiences of both older adults who play with their family members, and older adults who are skeptical about gaming they witness.

The social aspect of gaming, the opportunity to stay connected through gameplay was the most prominent element in the involvement in and adherence to gaming for active older players. The time spent together, the bonding and conversations, the bridging of the intergenerational gap resulted in affirmative feelings such as joy, satisfaction, and happiness. In addition, there was a sense of accomplishment in mastering new technologies, as well as spending time on an activity that is perceived as beneficial in enhancing mental or physical capabilities. As high cognitive and physical functioning, as well as the maintenance of important interpersonal relationships are key to successful aging [3], intergenerational gaming has an enormous potential in improving the lives of the growing population of older adults.

Older adults who do not play video games with family members primarily act as an audience, and from the passive role and the stereotypical view on the games fostered by mass media, they see games as a violent waste of time. This perception likely extends to a large part of the population of older adults, precluding them from taking part in gaming activities that could have a positive effect on their physical, mental, and social wellbeing. Taking this in consideration, it is important to design video games not only with the players, but also with an audience in mind, and in a way that the spectators immerse into the games as well. Games used in increasingly popular esports show that such design is achievable.

5 Implications

With each year, the population of older gamers grows. If our goal is to enhance lives across generations, designing games that encourage involvement by and with older adults would be beneficial – to individuals and their families as well as the gaming industry. While researchers have long acknowledged the physical and cognitive benefits of particular design choices, the social aspects should receive more attention in the future. Given that the maintenance of important interpersonal relationships and social and productive engagement are imperative to successful aging, video games have the potential of improving the lives of millions.

6 Limitations

As with any research, this project has its limitations. The number of participants was relatively small, and mainly from the United States and Western Europe. As a consequence, we should not over-generalize our findings. In addition, social desirability may impact what was and was not shared during the focus group session. Future research should address the limitations to this study, as well as examine more specific aspects of rewards. Design that allows for greater interaction among the generations should also be studied. These additional motivations are important to developing a better grasp of what games should be developed and how they should be delivered.

References

1. Federal Interagency Forum on Aging-Related Statistics: Older Americans 2012: key indicators of well-being. Federal Interagency Forum on Aging-Related Statistics. Government Printing Office, Washington (2012)
2. Fisher, C.L., Canzona, M.R.: Health care interactions in older adulthood. In: Nussbaum, J.F. (ed.) The Handbook of Lifespan Communication, pp. 387–404. Peter Lang, New York (2014)
3. Rowe, J.W., Kahn, R.L.: Successful Aging. Pantheon, New York (1998)

4. Phelan, E.A., Anderson, L.A., Lacroix, A.Z., Larson, E.B.: Older adults' views of 'successful aging'—how do they compare with researchers' definitions? J. Am. Geriatr. Soc. **52**, 211–216 (2004)
5. Depp, C.A., Jeste, D.V.: Definitions and predictors of successful aging: a comprehensive review of larger quantitative studies. FOCUS **7**, 137–150 (2009)
6. Reichstadt, J., Sengupta, G., Depp, C.A., Palinkas, L.A., Jeste, D.V.: Older adults' perspectives on successful aging: qualitative interviews. Am. J. Geriatr. Psychiatry **18**, 567–575 (2010)
7. Montross, L.P., Depp, C., Daly, J., Reichstadt, J., Golshan, S., Moore, D., Sitzer, D., Jeste, D.V.: Correlates of self-rated successful aging among community-dwelling older adults. Am. J. Geriatr. Psychiatry **14**, 43–51 (2006)
8. Kennedy, G.E.: Shared activities of grandparents and grandchildren. Psychol. Rep. **70**(1), 211–227 (1992)
9. Hoppes, S., Hally, C., Sewell, L.: An interest inventory of games for older adults. Phys. Occup. Ther. Geriatr. **18**(2), 71–83 (2000)
10. Hoppes, S., Wilcox, T., Graham, G.: Meanings of play for older adults. Phys. Occup. Ther. Geriatr. **18**(3), 57–68 (2001)
11. Hiller, H.H., Franz, T.M.: New ties, old ties and lost ties: the use of the internet in diaspora. New Media Soc. **6**(6), 731–752 (2004)
12. Schultheiss, D.: Entertainment for retirement?: Silvergamers and the internet. Publ. Commun. Rev. **2**(3), 62 (2012)
13. ESA: 2004 essential facts about the computer and video game industry (2004). http://www.theesa.com/facts/pdfs/ESA_EF_2004.pdf
14. ESA: 2015 essential facts about the computer and video game industry (2015). http://www.theesa.com/facts/pdfs/ESA_EF_2015.pdf
15. European Summary Report: Videogames in Europe: consumer study (2012). http://www.isfe.eu/sites/isfe.eu/files/attachments/euro_summary_-_isfe_consumer_study.pdf
16. Kueider, A.M., Parisi, J.M., Gross, A.L., Rebok, G.W.: Computerized cognitive training with older adults: a systematic review. PLoS ONE **7**(7), 1–13 (2012)
17. Broeren, J., Claesson, L., Goude, D., Rydmark, M., Sunnerhagen, K.S.: Virtual rehabilitation in an activity centre for community-dwelling persons with stroke. Cerebrovasc. Dis. **26**(3), 289–296 (2008)
18. Cameirão, M.S., Bermúdez i Badia, S., Duarte, E., Verschure, P.J.: Virtual reality based rehabilitation speeds up functional recovery of the upper extremities after stroke: a randomized controlled pilot study in the acute phase of stroke using the rehabilitation gaming system. Restorative Neurol. Neurosci. **29**(5), 287–298 (2011)
19. Boulay, M., Benveniste, S., Boespflug, S., Jouvelot, P., Rigaud, A.: A pilot usability study of MINWii, a music therapy game for demented patients. Technol. Health Care **19**(4), 233–246 (2011)
20. Nap, H.H., de Kort, Y.A.W., IJsselsteijn, W.A.: Senior gamers preferences motivations and needs. Gerontechnol. **8**(4), 247–262 (2009)
21. Pearce, C.: The truth about baby boomer gamers: a study of over-forty computer game players. Games Cult.: J. Interact. Media **3**(2), 142–174 (2008)
22. De Schutter, B., Vanden Abeele, V.: Designing meaningful play within the psycho-social context of older adults. In: Proceedings of the 3rd International Conference on Fun and Games, pp. 84–93 (2010)
23. Gajadhar, B.J., Nap, H.H., de Kort, Y.A.W., IJsselsteijn, W.A.: Out of sight, out of mind: co-player effects on seniors' player experience. In: Proceedings of the Fun and Games Conference, Leuven, Belgium (2010)

24. De Schutter, B.: Never too old to play: the appeal of digital games to an older audience. Game Cult.: J. Interact. Media **6**(2), 155–170 (2011)
25. Sherry, J., Lucas, K., Greenberg, B.S., Lachlan, K.: Video game uses and gratifications as predictors of use and game preference. In: Vorderer, P., Bryant, J. (eds.) Playing Video Games: Motives, Responses, and Consequences, pp. 213–224. Erlbaum, Mahwah (2006)
26. Coyne, S.M., Padilla-Walker, L.M., Stockdale, L., Day, R.D.: Game on… girls: associations between co-playing video games and adolescent behavioral and family outcomes. J. Adolesc. Health **49**(2), 160–165 (2011)
27. Wohn, D.Y., Lampe, C., Ellison, N., Wash, R., Vitak, J.: The "S" in social network games: initiating, maintaining, and enhancing relationships. In: Proceedings of 44th Annual Hawaii International Conference on System Sciences, Kauai, HI (2011)
28. Voida, A., Greenberg, S.: Console gaming across generations: exploring intergenerational interactions in collocated console gaming. Inf. Soc. J. - JUAICS **11**(1), 45–56 (2012)
29. Rice, M., Yau, L., Ong, J., Wan, M., Ng, J.: Intergenerational gameplay: evaluating social interaction between younger and older players. In: CHI 2012 Extended Abstracts on Human Factors in Computing Systems, pp. 2333–2338 (2012)
30. Osmanovic, S., Pecchioni, L.: Beyond entertainment: motivations and outcomes of video game playing by older adults and their younger family members. Games Culture Spec. Ed.: Games Ageing (2015)
31. Goffman, E.: Encounters: Two Studies in the Sociology of Interaction. Bobbs-Merrill, Indianapolis (1961)
32. Loos, E.F., Zonneveld, A.: Silver gaming: serious fun for seniors. In: Human Aspects of IT for the Aged Population. Design for Aging. Second International Conference, ITAP 2016, Held as Part of HCI International 2015, Toronto, 17–22 July 2016. Proceedings. Springer, Berlin (accepted)
33. Anand, V.: A study of time management: the correlation between video game usage and academic performance markers. Cyberpsychol. Behav. **10**(4), 552–559 (2007)
34. Burgess, S.R., Stermer, S., Burgess, M.R.: Video game playing and academic performance in college students. Coll. Student J. **46**(2), 376–387 (2012)
35. Marston, H.R.: Design recommendations for digital game design within an ageing society. Educ. Gerontol. **39**(2), 103–118 (2013)
36. Bianchi-Berthouze, N., Kim, W.W., Patel, D.: Does body movement engage you more in digital game play? And why? In: Paiva, A.C., Prada, R., Picard, R.W. (eds.) ACII 2007. LNCS, vol. 4738, pp. 102–113. Springer, Heidelberg (2007)
37. Khoo, E.T., Cheok, A.D.: Age invaders: inter-generational mixed reality family entertainment. Int. J. Virtual Reality **5**(2), 45–50 (2006)
38. Östlund, B.: Design paradigms and misunderstood technology: the case of older users. In: Jæger, B. (ed.) Young Technologies in Old Hands: An International View on Senior Citizen's Utilization of ICT, pp. 25–39. DJØF Forlag, Copenhagen (2005)

Coping with Ageing Issues:
Adoption and Appropriation of Technology
by Older Adults in Singapore

Natalie Pang[1(⊠)], Xue Zhang[2], Pei Wen Law[2], and Schubert Foo[1]

[1] Wee Kim Wee School of Communication and Information,
Nanyang Technological University, 50 Nanyang Avenue,
Singapore 639798, Singapore
{nlspang, sfoo}@ntu.edu.sg
[2] Center of Social Media Innovations for Communities,
Nanyang Technological University, 14 Nanyang Drive, HSS-06-15,
Singapore 637332, Singapore
{zhangxue, pwlaw}@ntu.edu.sg

Abstract. Older adults are facing various challenges while using technology. With an ageing society, it is desirable to develop senior-friendly innovations to empower older adults to lead enjoyable and fulfilling lives. This study examines ageing issues of older adults in Singapore and their coping strategies through adoption and appropriation of technology in the form of smartphones and wearable devices. Data was collected through in-depth interviews (10 participants) and focus groups (26 participants in 4 groups). Health problems, financial difficulties, loneliness and security concerns were the major ageing –related issues emerged from our analysis. The current status of technology use, adoption barriers and desired functions are discussed.

Keywords: Ageing · Technology adoption · Older adults · Smartphones · Wearable devices

1 Introduction

Technology adoption is becoming imperative to function in today's society, as it is pervasive across all domains of daily life and societal contexts, such as work, communication, healthcare, education and entertainment [1]. Not having access to or inability to use technology may put older adults at a disadvantage in the society. Czaja and Lee [2] pointed out that although use of technology such as computer and the Internet was found to be increasing among older people, an age-based digital divide still exists. Older adults usually feel more anxious while less confident and willing to use technology [2].

Like many other societies in the world, the population in Singapore is ageing with low local birth rates and longer life expectancies. With an ageing society and shrinking workforce, there are increasing opportunities for information and communication technology (ICT) to empower older adults left out by technology to lead fulfilling lives, to play active roles in the society, and to develop or sustain relationships with other people.

© Springer International Publishing Switzerland 2016
J. Zhou and G. Salvendy (Eds.): ITAP 2016, Part II, LNCS 9755, pp. 364–374, 2016.
DOI: 10.1007/978-3-319-39949-2_35

It is critical to understand their needs, preferences and expectations, as well as the existing barriers for older adults' technology adoption.

This study explores ageing issues and coping strategies of older adults in Singapore through interviews and focus groups, especially those living alone. Smartphones, which is widely adopted by younger adults, and wearable devices, which is an emerging mobile technology, were used as examples for discovering the current status of technology usage, and identifying adoption barriers and desired functions.

2 Literature Review

2.1 What Ageing Brings

The ageing process has rarely been portrayed as a positive experience by both scientific and humanistic scholars [3]. It is often described as a constant state of decline, which may result in considerable fear and anxiety [3]. Lasher and Faulkender [4] defined ageing anxiety as "combined concern and anticipation of losses centered around the ageing process" (p. 247). Ageing anxiety is not only an important mediating factor in attitudes and behavior toward older adults, but also a mediating factor in adjustment to one's own ageing processes [4].

Functional Decline. Ageing is often described as a constant state of decline. Bodine [5] pointed out that around 80 % of older adults had certain type of functional impairment. For vision, the changes include color perception, visual acuity and susceptibility to glare; for hearing, older adults have greater interference from background noise and difficulty in perceiving high-pitched sounds; for mobility, the decline in motor skills due to disease like arthritis may change the way older adults physically interacting with technology, such as keyboard and a mouse device [6, 7]. Memory span [8] and spatial cognition [7] are also found to be declined with age. Reduced capacity in working memory may result in poor performance in reasoning and procedural tasks [9], and declines in spatial ability may lead to navigation related problems [10].

Loneliness. Loneliness is a depressing, pervasive and debilitating condition due to the discrepancy between a person's social and/or emotional needs and their social reality [11, 12]. Loneliness may occur in people of all ages, but it is often associated with ageing and regarded as a serious problem for older adults [13]. With loss of social contracts due to decreasing health and age-related losses, older adults are facing higher risk of loneliness [14]. Finding new mates may not be desirable or easy for those being widowed. Diggs [15] pointed out that ageing people may have limited ability to continue social activities due to lack of self-esteem or interpersonal skills, which results from their functional decline or disability. Moreover, they may not have the skills or financial resources to seek alternative activities in today's continuously changing, technology-driven society.

Financial Strain. Financial strain is one of the major issues for older adults, as incomes tend to decline in late life, while health-related expenses tend to rise [16, 17]. Despite partial subsidy of healthcare expenses they could receive from Medicare and private insurance, older adults have to spend more on health as compared to other age groups, with the greatest concern of managing costs associated with long-term care for chronic and life-threatening disease [18].

2.2   The Role of Technology in Ageing

The Positive and Negative Impacts. Older adults' inclusion in the digital era could positively impact their economic and social welfare and on their quality of life [19, 20]. Technology has been argued to enable older adults to live independently, and support their ageing in place [1]. For example, technology can make daily tasks, such as cleaning, cooking, shopping and banking, easily manageable for older people [2]. Technology also allows older adults to play a more active role in their own healthcare: reminding them to take medications on time and enabling them to have a better sense of control over their health conditions. There are also a number of new developments in assistive technology which have made an important contribution to the care of older people at home, e.g. video-monitoring, fall detectors, hip protectors, door alerts and pressure mats [21].

Technology also offers the potential for enhancing older adults' quality of life by augmenting their ability to access information, to communicate with family and friends, to participate in various social activities [22, 23], and even to enhance their educational and employment opportunities [2]. Older adults could also use Internet as a platform to access more specific health information, and engage in patient-to-patient or patient-doctor conversations [24].

However, Dickinson and Gregory [25] noted that technology may also have some negative effects on older adults' well-being. For example, some systems allowing autonomous use may make people isolated and feel more lonely and depressed. Usability studies of smartphones or tablets with touch-screen interface have just begun for older adults [26]. Given the unfriendly interface design, older people may feel frustrated and become more reluctant to use the systems. The increment of task complexity will place greater demand on user's working memory, and hence leads to lower task performance [27, 28]. Therefore, with declining working memory, older adults are affected by increased task complexity, which will result in greater comprehension error and inconsistency in decision making [29].

Current Research on Technology Designed for Older Adults. Older adults are very often depicted as weak, bumbling and indecisive [30]. General stereotypes of older adults reflect low levels of competence, not as capable as younger adults [31], and they are consistently grouped with disabled and developmentally retarded people [32]. Researchers tend to have the bias as well. Usability of technology has been extensively investigated for older adults [33]. The underlying assumption seems to be that usability is the major concern for older adults' acceptance of technology [34]. However, some prior studies found that improved usability was not enough to guarantee older adults' technology acceptance [35].

In the context of older adults' adoption of mobile technology, the research focus has also been usability issues. The problems revealed included small buttons and screen, complex menus and functions [36, 37]. The role of smartphones in ageing, i.e. its daily usage by older adults, remains largely unexplored. As for wearable devices, the leading industry players (e.g. Microsoft, Samsung) continue flocking to a saturated market filled with devices gathering reams of largely superficial information for young people whose health is not in question or at risk [38]. Given the limited number of wearable devices designed for older adults, there is lack of research to find out whether their requirements are addressed and their level of acceptance, as usually the wearable was created through a conventional process of brainstorming, conceptualizing, and prototyping [39]. There is a need to identify the real desired functions of older adults.

3 Methodology

The work described in this paper is informed by a case-based program of research within our on-going work with older adults living in community dwellings in Singapore. Many of them live alone, and are beneficiaries of community welfare organizations for their physical and social needs. The project is focused on understanding the adoption and appropriation of technology by older adults. In this paper we describe two studies that were put together to understand the needs and aspirations of older adults towards technology.

3.1   Recruitment of Participants

In order to maintain a more controlled environment for collecting data, instead of random household or street sampling, we contacted Lion Befrienders Service Association (LBSA)[1] to seek their collaboration. It is worth noting that LBSA's SACs are commonly located at the void decks of selected 1-room (35 to 45 m^2) rental blocks. Older adults living in these blocks tended to have lower income.

Recruitment guidelines were provided to the person-in-charge to ensure that participants were qualified for the interview and focus group respectively, and their participation was voluntary. For the in-depth interviews, all the participants were recipients of iPhones in a corporate social responsibility program known as "Silverline"[2]. For the focus groups, we targeted to recruit older adults that were active and able to express themselves clearly.

3.2   Data Collection

The interviews and focus groups were both semi-structured, covering topics of attitude towards ageing, ageing-related issues, as well as perceptions of technology in ageing. They were conducted in participants' preferred languages (i.e. Mandarin, English and Malay). A audio recorder was used to record the interviews and discussions.

---

[1] LBSA is a voluntary welfare organization founded in 1995 to provide friendship and care for older adults to age in place with community participation, enabling them to enjoy enriching and meaningful lives.

[2] To reduce isolation and open their world to new experiences, Singtel, a local telecommunication company, initiated the project calling for the donation of used iPhones and chargers to needy older adults.

Observation notes were made to record participants' body languages, expressions and patterns of interaction.

Interviews. Face-to-face interviews, ranging between 1–2 h, were conducted with 10 iPhone recipients from 8th to 19th November 2013. For this group of participants, smartphone was used as an example of technology for discussing its impact on ageing. Photos were taken sporadically during the interviews as the researchers felt the need to capture certain aspects such as photos taken in the iPhone. The average age of the interviewees was 74.8 years old, and 6 of them are female.

Focus Groups. In March 2015, follow-up focus groups were carried out with 26 older adults in one of LBSA's SACs. The 26 participants were divided into 4 groups: Group 1 (11 participants) and Group 2 (8 participants) were conducted in Mandarin; Group 3 (4 participants) and Group 4 (3 participants) were conducted in Malay.

For these 4 groups, wearable devices were used as examples of mobile technology for discussion. To ensure a better understanding, before the start of each session, presentation slides and a short video on wearable devices were played, and two samples of wearable devices, i.e. Pebble Watch and Mio Alpha 2, were passed around for the participants to try out. Pebble Watch is a smart watch that can communicate with smartphones for displaying caller ID, text messages, calendar alerts etc. [40], and Mio Alpha 2 features functions such as heart rate sensor and speed accelerometer [41].

3.3　Data Analysis

The audio records were transcribed and translated into English (as needed) immediately after each visit. The 14 transcripts were coded in 3 stages: open coding, axial coding and selective coding [42]: Open coding was used to code each line of all the transcripts; next, similar concepts were grouped into categories and axial coding was used to explore the relations between the categories; in the last stage of selective coding, the categories were re-examined and synthesized into a series of related concepts.

A code book was developed to include code definition and their hierarchies. Using the code book, 2 coders started coding separately and then the files were merged together in NVivo. The inter-coder reliability was satisfactory (Cohen's kappa = 0.75). In total, 1,544 responses were coded and categorized for the interview transcripts, and 931 for the focus group transcripts.

4　Findings and Discussion

This section presents results of analysis. Respondents were shown as R# for the interviewees and G#R# for the focus group participants. The face-to-face interviews gathered more in-depth data, while the focus groups collected broader views on the discussed topics.

4.1 Attitudes Towards Ageing

The respondents tended to have different attitudes towards ageing. Some were positive with satisfaction of their current life, believing that there was nothing to be afraid of and trying to keep themselves happy everyday (e.g. R1, R3 and R9). One respondent (R4) expressed his enjoyment as a senior citizen, as he could sense more care and respect from others: *"I think they respect this [thumping his walking stick]...Bus drivers are very good to old people... VIP treatment."*

However, it is worth noting that respondents (e.g. R2, R5) showed pessimistic attitudes towards life, focusing on the negative impacts of ageing, e.g. unable to work, closer to death. As shown in the literature, the age people feel of themselves could be an important phenomenological variable which determines whether they take into account their aging attitudes when evaluating their own lives [43].

These articulated attitudes towards ageing may also influence attitudes towards technology. Although it was not our original intention in our research to draw the links between attitudes towards ageing and attitudes towards technology, this link, if any, is important to understand. With positive attitudes, the level of technological efficacy may be higher and consequentially, the desire to learn and use technology. On the other hand, a negative outlook on ageing can influence attitudes in other areas of life, including attitudes and intentions to use technology.

4.2 Ageing-Related Issues

Four major ageing-related issues emerged from our analysis: health problems, financial difficulties, loneliness, and security concerns.

All of the participants mentioned about the health problems they were facing, such as heart disease, high blood pressure, high cholesterol and asthma. Some of them raised issues such as the inconveniences (e.g. R3, R5) and concerns over falling (e.g. G4R3, G4R1) caused by their physical declines.

Although such needs are opportunities for technological interventions (for instance, applications on the smartphone can be designed to send alerts to caregivers or health workers when necessary), technology must also consider the impacts on their health issues from technology use while studying how older adults interact with technology to come up with relevant design implications and improve technological accessibility.

Nearly all of the participants expressed concerns about financial issues, either explicitly or implicitly. Some of them (e.g. R2, G3R1) worried about not having enough money to spend, while the rest used the words "expensive", "cheap", "save" frequently during the interviews (e.g. R5, R9).

The points raised under this theme involve understanding the social structure in which technology is made accessible to older adults. Many community organizations serving the needs of older adults are often caught up with what they perceive to be bread and butter needs, like improving the infrastructure and living environments of older adults, providing food and other supplies, and technology is regarded as a nice to have, but not an essential solution. The other pragmatic consideration for many of such organizations is that technology can be expensive, and there are always concerns about the sustainability of technological solutions especially when donations and funding are already limited. This implies that improving accessibility to technology for older adults must be a concerted effort with the involvement of stakeholders in the caregiving value chain. Design accessible interfaces and technology are crucial, but the impacts are limited on their own.

Loneliness is another issue shared among the majority of the participants, as they were living alone and their children and relatives seldom came to visit them (e.g. R2, R7, and G4R1). As one participant (R2) shared, loneliness is a fundamental reality that comes with ageing: *"I feel very lonely at home. Who can I talk to?... If I go down, I will also sit there quietly...They (my relatives) don't care about me. We seldom meet."*

The immediate implication is that technology may be used as a way to connect to others and meet such social needs. In our interviews participants have also articulated their habits of using smartphones to connect to social network sites such as Facebook (e.g. R1), and using it to play games (e.g. R5, R8). However, there may also be the implication that using technology for such means can also further augment loneliness.

Three interviewees (R4, R7 and R10) and one of the focus group participants (G4R3) raised security issue and potential risks for living alone: "If you stay alone, the others won't know what happen to you...One of my neighbors passed away without anyone knowing." (R10).

The findings of this and other studies have led to the development of our concept of UbiCuts in the research center which can function like a life-logging device to capture images in the environment of the wearer. It is not the intention of this paper to focus on the utility and impacts of the solution, but it is an example of how understanding the needs of older adults can help inform the design of technological solutions for this group. There are many other innovations that have been designed with the aim of addressing this problem, such as those aimed at actively monitoring the motions and behaviors of older adults in their homes. For example, Ghasemzadeh et al. [44] developed body sensor networks worn by older adults at multiple joint positions to recognize their movements; Klack et al. [45] invented sensitive floor with sensor units installed under floor tiles to detect falls.

4.3   Perceptions of Technology in Ageing

Participants of the interviews and focus groups shared their perceptions of smartphones and wearable devices respectively, covering their attitudes, adoption and expectations.

Perceptions of Smartphones in Ageing. Six of the interviewees thought that smart-phones were not meant to be used by older adults, but it is interesting to note that all of them considered themselves as exceptions as they were not really old (e.g. R1): *"For me it's easy, but for the old people I would say... (shaking head), as it's quite hard to use."* Nevertheless, the majority (7) of them still felt that older adults can learn to use smartphones (e.g. R3, R4).

Still the reflections should be understood in the context that these participants have already been exposed to the smartphone for at least a year, and received basic training in using it before they were given a smartphone. The 'others and me' distinction in terms of technological efficacy is interesting, and leads to more research questions which we hope to address in future work: what factors other than exposure contribute to higher levels of technological efficacy? Will greater use result in "use-effects" – in the sense that using a technology more will persuade themselves that technology has a role in ageing?

The most frequently mentioned barriers to the adoption of smartphones are listed in Table 1. They are mainly objective factors which the older adults cannot try to control or avoid, such as high price of smartphone, declined mental and physical abilities. The subjective factor is the lack of skill or knowledge to use smartphones, which can be overcome by learning and practicing. These barriers provide practical clues in terms of designing programs and services to improve the accessibility of smartphones for older adults.

As for the role of smartphones in ageing, 8 interviewees mentioned they were playful and enjoyable, which could help them to eliminate their boredom and even became part of their lives (e.g. R1, R5, and R7): *"[It has become] part of my life. Because I stay at home, I [have] nothing to do. I play games [to] pass my time." (R1)*.

Half of the interviewees also mentioned that using iPhone also provided a chance for them to learn new things, to exercise their brains, hands and even legs (e.g. R1, R2). In addition to meeting their entertainment needs, their informational needs are satisfied which also connects to their desire to connect with the rest of the society, as captured in the following reflection: *"It keeps me young, keep me connected with young people. There is this saying: You are as young or old as you think. So it is all in here [pointing to his head]. I keep myself alert." (R3)*.

Perceptions of Wearable Devices in Ageing. Smartphones have been around for some years now, so even though it may not have been adopted much by older adults in our research, there is prior exposure to it. In order to understand how older adults perceive "new" technology, we went on to conduct focus groups on wearable technology. Only 2 out of the 26 focus group participants had seen or heard about wearable devices with limited knowledge of their functions and usage. The rest did not even know that such technology was available before the briefing. Nevertheless, 11 of them showed interest in the devices and willingness to adopt it in their daily lives (e.g. G2R1, G2R4, and G4R1), as articulated by one participant: *"Yes, it's best if I can wear it. It will tell me if my blood pressure goes up or down… I want to buy something like this." (G2R1)*.

Table 1. Barriers to the adoption of smartphones

Barrier	No. of interviewees	References across transcripts	Example
Lack of skill or knowledge	9	99 (41.25 %)	"I don't know how to use this… I'm not familiar with it." (R5)
Financial issue	8	41 (17.08 %)	"Because it's very expensive…I'm concerned about the money." (R4)
Declined mental ability	6	38 (15.83 %)	"Sometimes I will forget… When I want to pick up the phone, I will forget which button to press." (R8)
Declined physical ability	6	24 (10.00 %)	"I can't see clearly if the words are too small." (R2)

Table 2. Desired functions of wearable devices

Function	No. of participants	References across transcripts	Example
Health monitoring	8	27 (27 %)	"I hope there's a watch, most importantly it needs to tell us about our blood pressure, whether it's high or low." (G2R1)
Safety alert	3	28 (28 %)	"If we have such device, we can wear it when we are out. If there's anything we can press a button and let people know where we are." (G1R8)
Physical support and protection	4	20 (20 %)	"Improve our physical strength, leg strength, support my waist." (G1R8) "Able to protect from sunrays. Help us to see things clearly." (G2R4)
Navigation	2	7 (7 %)	"I'm quite 'blur'. I always alight at the wrong stops when taking bus." (G1R3)
Communication	2	4 (4 %)	"With these devices we can update our children where we are going. If anything happens, they will know." (G4R1)

According to the collected responses, the desired functions of wearable devices can be summarized into 5 categories (Table 2). Meeting navigational needs is notable with participants expressing challenges in understanding changes to the transport system with information being too complex for them. These responses provide practical implications for wearable innovations for older adults, but also reflect their aspirations for the technology.

5   Conclusion

Drawing on our on-going research with older adults, we report findings in this paper on salient issues in ageing and discuss their implications for the design, attitudes and intentions to use technology. We also explore realities of technology use in ageing, highlighting both the barriers and aspirations of older adults for technological interventions.

Acknowledgement. This research is supported by the National Research Foundation, Prime Minister's Office, Singapore under its International Research Centers in Singapore Funding Initiative and administered by the Interactive Digital Media Program Office.

References

1. Mitzner, T.L., et al.: Older adults talk technology: technology usage and attitudes. Comput. Hum. Behav. **26**, 1710–1721 (2010)
2. Czaja, S.J., Lee, C.: The impact of aging on access to technology. Univ. Access Inf. Soc. **5** (4), 341–349 (2007)
3. McConatha, J.T., et al.: Turkish and U.S. attitudes toward aging. Educ. Gerontol. **30**, 169–183 (2004)
4. Lasher, K.P., Faulkender, P.J.: Measurement of aging anxiety: development of the anxiety about aging scale. Int. J. Aging Hum. Dev. **37**(4), 247–259 (1993)
5. Bodine, C.: Aging well: the use of assistive technology to enhance the lives of elders. In: Stephanidis, C. (ed.) HCI 2007. LNCS, vol. 4554, pp. 861–867. Springer, Heidelberg (2007)
6. Charness, N., Boot, W.R.: Aging and information technology use: potential and barriers. Curr. Dir. Psychol. Sci. **18**(5), 253–258 (2009)
7. Bean, C.: Meeting the challenge: training an aging population to use computers. Southeast. Libr. **51**(3), 17–26 (2003)
8. Karakas, S.: Digit span changes from puberty to old age under different levels of education. Dev. Neuropsychol. **22**(2), 423–453 (2002)
9. Gao, Q., Sato, H., Rau, P.-L.P., Asano, Y.: Design effective navigation tools for older web users. In: Jacko, J.A. (ed.) HCI 2007. LNCS, vol. 4550, pp. 765–773. Springer, Heidelberg (2007)
10. Li, H., et al.: Designing effective web forms for older web users. Educ. Gerontol. **38**(4), 271–284 (2012)
11. Killeen, C.: Loneliness: an epidemic in modern society. J. Adv. Nurs. **28**(4), 762–770 (1998)
12. Luo, Y., Waite, L.J.: Loneliness and mortality among older adults in China. J. Gerontol. Ser. B: Psychol. Sci. Soc. Sci. **69**(4), 633–645 (2014)
13. Heylen, L.: The older, the lonelier? risk factors for social loneliness in old age. Ageing Soc. **30**, 1177–1196 (2010)
14. Chen, Y., Hicks, A., While, A.E.: Loneliness and social support of older people in China: a systematic literature review. Health Soc. Care Community **22**(2), 113–123 (2014)
15. Diggs, J.: Activity theory of aging. In: Loue, S., Sajatovic, M. (eds.) Encyclopedia of Ageing and Publich Health, pp. 79–81. Springer, Boston (2008)
16. Chou, K.L., Chi, I., Chow, N.W.S.: Sources of income and depression in elderly Hong Kong Chinese: mediating and moderating effects of social support and financial strain. Aging Ment. Health **8**(3), 212–221 (2004)
17. Litwin, H., Sapir, E.V.: Perceived income adequacy among older adults in 12 countries: findings from the survey of health. Ageing Retire. Eur. Gerontol. **49**(3), 397–406 (2009)
18. Stoller, M.A., Stoller, E.P.: Perceived income adequacy among elderly retirees. J. Appl. Gerontol. **22**, 230–251 (2003)
19. Aldrige, E.: Digital Inclusion and Older People. Age Concern, Enfield (2004)
20. Nahm, E.S., Resnick, B.: Homebound older adults' experience with the internet and e-mail. Comput. Nurs. **19**, 257–263 (2001)
21. Miskelly, F.G.: Assistive technology in elderly care. Age Ageing **30**, 455–458 (2001)
22. Hill, R., Beynon-Davies, P., Williams, M.D.: Older people and internet engagement: acknowledging social moderators of internet adoption, access and use. Inf. Technol. People **21**, 244–266 (2008)
23. Ridings, C.M. Gefen, D.: Virtual community attraction: why people hang out online. J. Comput.-Mediat. Commun. **10**(1) (2004)

24. Leist, A.K.: Social media use of older adults: a mini-review. Gerontology **59**(4), 378–384 (2013)
25. Dickinson, A., Gregor, P.: Computer use has no demonstrated impact on the well-being of older adults. Int. J. Hum.-Comput. Stud. **64**, 744–753 (2006)
26. Kobayashi, M., Hiyama, A., Miura, T., Asakawa, C., Hirose, M., Ifukube, T.: Elderly user evaluation of mobile touchscreen interactions. In: Campos, P., Graham, N., Jorge, J., Nunes, N., Palanque, P., Winckler, M. (eds.) INTERACT 2011, Part I. LNCS, vol. 6946, pp. 83–99. Springer, Heidelberg (2011)
27. Bruner, J.S., Goodnow, J.J., Austin, G.A.: A Study of Thinking. Wiley, New York (1956)
28. Salthouse, T.A.: Why do adult age differences increase with task complexity? Dev. Psychol. **28**(5), 905–918 (1992)
29. Finucane, M.L., et al.: Task complexity and older adults' decision-making competence. Psychol. Aging **20**(1), 71–84 (2005)
30. Day, T. Bias against the elderly creates a negative view of aging (2010)
31. Cuddy, A.J., Fiske, S.T.: Doddering, but dear: process, content, and function in stereotyping of elderly people. In: Nelson, T.D. (ed.) Ageism, pp. 3–26. The MIT Press, Cambridge (2002)
32. Blaine, B.E.: Understanding the Psychology of Diversity, 2nd edn. SAGE Publications, Thousand Oaks (2013)
33. Chen, K., Chan, A.H.S.: A review of technology acceptance by older adults. Gerontechnology **10**(1), 1–12 (2011)
34. Yi, M.Y., Hwang, Y.: Predicting the use of web-based information systems: self-efficacy, enjoyment, learning goal orientation, and the technology acceptance model. Int. J. Hum Comput Stud. **59**(4), 431–449 (2003)
35. Guritnob, R.S., Siringoringo, H.: Perceived usefulness, ease of use, and attitude towards online shopping usefulness towards online airlines ticket purchase. Procedia – Soc. Behav. Sci. **81**, 212–216 (2013)
36. Kurniawan, S., Mahmud, M., Nugroho, Y.: A study of the use of mobile phones by older persons. In: Computer Human Interaction, Montreal, Canada (2006)
37. Mann, W.C., et al.: Use of cell phones by elders with impairments: overall appraisal, satisfaction, and suggestions. Technol. Disabil. **16**(1), 49–57 (2004)
38. Herz, J.C.: Wearables are totally failing to people who need them most. Wired (2014). http://www.wired.com/2014/11/where-fitness-trackers-fail/
39. Angelini, L., et al.: Human factors considerations in the design of wearable devices. In: ACM Conference on Pervasive and Ubiquitous Computing Adjunct Publication (2013)
40. Clarke, T.: Sync with the Pebble Watch. J. Prop. Manag. **78**(3), 49 (2013)
41. MIO. Mio Alpha 2: Heart Rate Watch + Activity Tracker, 1 February 2016. http://www.mioglobal.com/Mio-ALPHA-2-Heart-Rate-Sport-Watch/Product.aspx
42. Flick, U.: The Sage Qualitative Research Kit. SAGE Publications, Los Angeles (2007)
43. Mock, S.E., Eibach, R.P.: Aging attitudes moderate the effect of subjective age on psychological well-being: evidence from a 10-year longitudinal study. Psychol. Aging **26**(4), 979–986 (2011)
44. Ghasemzadeh, H., Loseu, V., Jafari, R.: Structural action recognition in body sensor networks: distributed classification based on string matching. IEEE Trans. Inf. Technol. Biomed. **14**(2), 425–435 (2010)
45. Klack, L., Möllering, C., Ziefle, M., Schmitz-Rode, T.: Future care floor: a sensitive floor for movement monitoring and fall detection in home environments. In: Lin, J.C., Nikita, K.S. (eds.) MobiHealth 2010. LNICS, SITE, vol. 55, pp. 211–218. Springer, Heidelberg (2011)

Aging, Mobility and Driving

Immersive Virtual Reality Simulation as a Tool for Aging and Driving Research

Christopher R. Bennett, Richard R. Corey, Uro Giudice, and Nicholas A. Giudice[✉]

School of Computing and Information Science, The University of Maine, Orono, ME, USA
nicholas.giudice@maine.edu

Abstract. The aging process is associated with changes to many tasks of daily life for older adults, e.g. driving. This is particularly challenging in rural areas where public transportation is often non-existent. The current study explored how age affects driving ability through use of an immersive virtual reality driving simulator. Participants were required to respond to typical driving events: stopping at an intersection, controlling vehicle speed, and avoiding objects in the road. Results showed that older adult performance was consistently lower than the younger adult group for each driving event, and matched those of real-world accident data. Post-study survey data suggested that all participants were able to easily interact with the driving simulator. Results also demonstrate the efficacy of immersive virtual reality as an effective research tool. Findings from this research will influence the development of compensatory augmentations, or navigational aids, and enrich our understanding of driving and age-related concerns.

Keywords: Spatial cognition · Aging · Gerontechnology · Human computer interaction · Virtual reality

1 Introduction

Driving is an important means of navigation for older adults who want to maintain their health and independence [1, 2]. However, the aging process often leads to cognitive and physical changes that can have profound effects on driving behavior, such as magnified safety concerns, increased risk of getting lost, and greater self-doubt for older drivers. It is estimated that there will be more than 71 million adults over the age of 65 by the year 2030 [3]. Addressing the dearth of research on spatial aging and driving, as is the goal of the current study, is vital to the safety and well-being of older adults, who represent the fastest growing demographic in the country.

There are several driving concerns specifically known to be issues for older drivers. This research addresses four key areas of concern, including: breaking at intersections, drifting out of lanes, avoiding obstacles, and maintaining proper speed [4]. The Insurance Institute for Highway Safety has found that older drivers (65+ years) are over-represented in collisions involving these problem areas [4]. The current work was motivated by two major goals. The first was to better understand challenges for older drivers that ultimately effect their safety and independence. This was assessed by evaluating error performance and reaction times for the four areas of concern for older

© Springer International Publishing Switzerland 2016
J. Zhou and G. Salvendy (Eds.): ITAP 2016, Part II, LNCS 9755, pp. 377–385, 2016.
DOI: 10.1007/978-3-319-39949-2_36

drivers. The second was to extend current VR research to evaluate the efficacy of using immersive virtual reality simulations as a tool supporting this program of research.

The virtual reality simulation used here differs from previous investigations by utilizing a head mounted display (HMD). Most previous work studying spatial aging and driving research has employed static displays incorporating desktop monitors and CAVE systems (see [5] for review on different VR approaches). These approaches do well at providing the experimental control and safety that VR affords, but often require high computational demands and are less realistic than HMD-based immersive simulations. Unless these traditional systems include a 360 degree field of view (requiring many monitors/projectors, significant space and cost, and computationally intensive hardware/software) they lack the immersion that an HMD provides. The advantage of HMDs is that they couple visual updating with head movement, similar to the experience of real world driving, thus providing a more realistic interface for use in driving research. Modern HMDs are compact and are becoming more and more cost effective as the virtual reality industry moves into the commercial gaming/entertainment sector. Within the past few years, the enthusiasm surrounding VR technology has skyrocketed and has significantly benefitted from strong corporate interests (e.g., the 2 billion dollar purchase of Oculus by Facebook). Competition between new and existing VR companies is leading to sharp increases in the advancements of VR hardware while continuing to reduce the cost of the constituent technology. Increased testing of its efficacy as a research tool with various demographics (such as older adults) and reduced cost will improve availability and favorability with researchers. This is important given the lack of research that currently exists using immersive VR to study aging and driving.

The results from this work will also provide important foundational knowledge to guide future development of what we have termed compensatory augmentations. These augmentations will incorporate simulated information to enhance normal decreases in sensory and cognitive abilities that occur across the lifespan, thereby supporting safer and more efficient navigation. For example, enlarging or highlighting a sign as a driver approaches can compensate for reduced age-related processing speed by allowing the driver to notice important information more quickly, thus providing them with more time to react. We postulate that drawing a driver's attention to important signage and information cues will help with improving driving events, such as breaking at intersections and avoiding obstacles, as is tested in this research.

2   Virtual Reality Simulation Experiment

2.1   Equipment

This study investigates a novel use of VR as a research tool by evaluating the driving safety of older adult populations. VR motion sickness is a concern for younger adults and is further exacerbated with age [6]; thus, we designed our system to help alleviate simulation sickness through careful matching of real and virtual visual expectations, choice of textures/models, and superior clarity/refresh rate of the display. We used a Sensics, Inc., Z-Sight 60° FOV HMD that provides dual OLED 1280 × 1024 resolution displays to render the virtual environments [7]. This unit provides clear graphics and a wide field of view. The selection of textures/models for the environment was established through pilot testing that evaluated and compared various parameters known to potentially cause nausea and negative VR side effects. We used these pilot results as a guide in our design decisions to use lower polygon models with simplified textures during rendering. These models/textures both improved the frame rate of the simulation as well as reduced the visual strain that is often associated with the rendering of complex textures, especially those that move in peripheral vision. The virtual environment designed and implemented in this experiment was developed with Unity 3D, employing the Easy Roads 3D package to create the course. The Unity Car platform was used for the physics engine. The driving simulator was constructed in-house using the driver's seat from a Ford Crown Victoria and the steering wheel and pedals from a disassembled Playseat racing seat. The low platform and roll-cage style stabilization bars were designed for safety given the intended use of the driving simulator with an older adult population. Figure 1 shows the driving simulator used for this research.

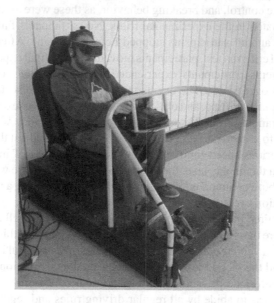

Fig. 1. Photo of participant using the VEMI driving simulator

2.2 Participants

Thirty-two participants completed the study, evenly split between two age groups. The older adult age group consisted of sixteen people (7 female), ages 60–82 (M = 69.4, SD = 6.2). The minimum age was set at 60 years, as research suggests that this is when the largest age-related effects on spatial abilities begin to manifest (see [8, 9] for reviews). The younger adult age group included sixteen people (8 female), ages 18–34 (M = 21.9, SD = 3.6). Prior to starting the experiment, the older adult group completed the Montreal Cognitive Assessment, a common instrument in aging research for assessing cognitive impairment (all participants scored equal to or greater than 26, indicating no abnormal cognitive impairment) [10]. The research was approved by the University of Maine's local ethics committee and written informed consent was obtained from all participants.

2.3 Procedure

Participants began the experiment with a 5 min practice phase. During this period, they practiced on a simplified course where they could adjust to both the driving simulator and the virtual reality experience. Upon completion of practice, a criterion test was given to assure that participants were comfortable with the entire system. For this test, they had to maintain a speed between 10 and 15 mph while weaving back and forth between 6 cones, which were placed a set distance apart in the middle of the virtual road. They then observed a stop sign after passing all traffic cones. The criterion test was designed to assess the participant's ability to use the driving simulator while managing acceleration, speed, vehicle control, and breaking behavior, as these were all factors of interest subsequently evaluated in the experimental trials. No participants failed this criterion (no cones were hit and all participants stopped before the sign). After completing the practice session and criterion test, participants moved on to the final experimental course.

The driving events participants experienced during the final course are known hazards for drivers over 65 [4]. The events tested included: intersection surveillance, speed maintenance, lane drifting, and obstacle avoidance. The course contained multiple speed limit zones ranging from 25 to 65 mph. Speed maintenance was defined as the participants ability to properly accelerate/decelerate in order to adjust their speed as they encountered the various speed limit signs. Two different types of intersections were incorporated within the final course: those with stop signs and those with traffic signalization, which are both common intersection types. Figure 2 shows a simulator screenshot of an intersection event.

The course required participants to drive through a town, as well as operate on the highway. There were two situations requiring obstacle avoidance within the final course: the first was to pass a vehicle controlled by pre-programmed artificial intelligence while on the highway, and the second was to go around a small construction area in the road. Participants were informed prior to beginning the final course that during this phase, their primary goal was to abide by all regular driving rules and regulations as well as adhering to any posted information.

Data was continuously collected throughout the trial, logging parameters about the participant's behavior and vehicle status (at 100 ms intervals). To assure consistency, all participants completed the same course and experienced the same events. Results were then evaluated based on direct comparisons of event performance and reaction times between the older and younger groups.

3   Results

Data collected during the experimental driving course included status parameters of the vehicle, such as current lane, speed, direction, and driving event completion. Lane drifting

Fig. 2. A simulator screen shot of an intersection event (4-way stop)

(LD) was defined as approximately 25 % of the vehicle width leaving the intended lane and entering the oncoming lane. Drifting out of the correct lane was a particular problem for the older adults who averaged 3.25 LD per person. By contrast, younger adults averaged only 0.81 LD per person. Comparison of these means yields a significant difference between the two age groups, $t(30) = 2.74$, $p = 0.01$, with older adults LD performance being 4 times worse than that of younger adults. Indeed, this decreased performance is indicative of a general lack of attentional focus maintained by the older adults as they drove in the simulation. A higher number of lane drifts increases the chance for an out of lane collision with an oncoming vehicle, as has been shown from real world data [4].

Analysis was conducted for each driving event with success rates determined by: properly stopping at an intersection, passing obstacles without collision, and correctly observing posted speed limits. When we separated success rates out by the individual events, we found that the older adult group achieved only a 56 % success rate for correct intersection behavior, compared to the 82 % success rate found with the younger adult group, $t(30) = 2.83$, $p < 0.01$. This result indicates that only 44 % of older adults properly stopped before the white line at the intersections. Reaction times for older adults were also 15 % slower than the younger adults for breaking at intersections. The slower reaction time for older drivers represents the difference between stopping in time at an intersection versus crossing the line or even hitting a car in front of them.

Accurate speed limit maintenance, defined as making a change in acceleration or deceleration towards the correct posted speed, for the older adult group was also surprisingly low at 48 %, while performance was at 80 % for the younger adult group, $t(30) = 3.94$, $p < 0.01$. When evaluating reaction times for initiating this change in speed towards the correct limit, older driver's reaction times were 85 % slower than their younger counterparts. Given the already reduced reaction times shown in the intersection data, in-proper speed maintenance can further reduce time to react for other driving events, such as obstacle avoidance.

Analysis of obstacle avoidance performance also showed the older adult group to be at a disadvantage compared to their younger peers, with an 81 % success rate compared to the 100 % success rate for the younger adult group, $t(30) = 2.42$, $p = 0.02$. This means that the older adult participants hit 19 % of the obstacles whereas the younger adults hit none. Reaction time data for obstacle avoidance also showed older adults to be at a disadvantage with 75 % slower times to react to the obstacles than younger adults. An important factor required for safe driving is the ability to perceive and react to the surrounding environment. Anything less than achieving 100 % for successful obstacle avoidance represents a red flag and indicates that this is a real problem that needs to be addressed.

The lower overall performance observed for the older adult drivers as compared to the younger driving group is consistent between each measure and can explain problems in real-world driving behavior. When we aggregate the data across the driving events, the older adult group averaged only a 62 % overall rate of success, while the younger adult group performed reliably better, with an 87 % overall rate of success, $t(30) = 5.40$, $p < 0.01$. These low success rates by the older adult group are concerning given the lack of any distractions during the experimental course that are often experienced during real-world driving (e.g., traffic, pedestrians, severe weather, etc.).

4   Conclusions and Future Work

This research set out to investigate known driving concerns, e.g., lane drifting and obstacle avoidance, for older adults through the use of immersive virtual reality simulation. The use of VR simulation for aging research affords benefits of experimental control and human safety that are difficult to obtain via real-world testing. These factors are particularly important for driving research where participants and experimenters may be exposed to greater risks in real-world settings. Customization of virtual worlds allows researchers to create and test limitless scenarios as well as eliminating the dangers associated with testing driving events.

Previous studies have shown the benefits of virtual reality technology using CAVEs and desktop systems [5] and the current work extends this effort to using immersive HMD-based simulations. The current results support the efficacy of this technology as a research tool, given that less than 15 % of participants in this study experienced any negative affects compared to upwards of 60 % in previous research [11]. We attribute this reduction of negative affects to the use of a high quality immersive display and careful a priori selection of the 3D environment content (models/textures). Post-study survey data indicated that the participants reported having a positive experience with the driving simulator and all expressed a desire to continue participation in future projects using our system.

Reaction time results from the current study compared well with other research addressing older adult driving performance using virtual reality. One such study, using three large televisions as monitors, found older adult's reaction time for breaking events to be about 16 % slower compared to performance by younger adults [12]. This is congruent with our finding of a 15 % slower reaction time for older drivers with our immersive HMD-based simulator. The same study also found that the reaction time for younger drivers was significantly faster than older drivers, but this difference between groups disappeared when the younger drivers were using cellphones [12]. The effects of slower reaction times have been shown to increase the frequency and severity of collisions in real world driving [13, 14]. Likewise, in the current work, slower reaction times led to lower success rates for driving events (e.g., failure to stop at an intersection or avoid an obstacle in the road). The lower performance here may explain the over-representation of older adults in real world collision data for the same problem areas.

The driving events tested in this research pose real world risks for older drivers who tend to be over-represented as a group for collisions related to lane drifting and intersection behavior [4]. Of note, this research lacked any distraction that could have captured or divided the driver's attention during the final course. In other words, even given an ideal driving scenario with no potential distractions, there were still significant age-related differences across multiple performance categories. In the real world, such ideal circumstances are rarely the case, suggesting that our data are likely a conservative estimate of the problem. When taking this into consideration, the low success rates of the older drivers are a serious issue and serve as a stark reminder of the real-world risks faced by this demographic that need to be further studied.

Future work will explore augmented reality solutions to improve the driving performance of older adults and specifically address the problem areas evaluated in the present study. Compensatory augmentations are aimed at enhancing pre-existing abilities that older adults still possess in order to compensate for the sensory and cognitive decline experienced through the aging process. These augmentations will help draw the driver's attention to navigation-critical information. For example, speed limit signs are important to identify, yet are usually spatially separated by a significant distance. Should a driver miss a sign, they would be unaware of that road's speed limit until they came across another sign. One solution, based on development of compensatory augmentations for driving, would use augmented reality to enhance the size and brightness of signs, as seen below in Fig. 3. This type of aid would help direct the user's attention to important driving-critical information and could be implemented in a number of ways (e.g., increased size, brightness, or via multisensory cuing such as vibration, visual, or audio cues) for various types of signage (speed, stop, yield, etc.). Other possible compensatory augmentations will deal with improving mental representations (cognitive maps) and spatial awareness through landmark identification. This sort of augmentation will keep the navigator informed of their position in relation to important landmarks around them, helping to provide a better grounding between their immediate perception and their cognitive map of the environment.

Fig. 3. An example of a possible compensatory augmentation. Left image has a normal size sign while the right image shows a sign that has been enlarged as the driver approaches.

During the development of these compensatory augmentations, consideration will also be given to common age-related diseases that may affect navigation. For example, Age Related Macular Degeneration (AMD) is known to reduce visual acuity and contrast as well as other eye conditions, such as glaucoma that can affect the peripheral visual field [15, 16]. These visual deficits could be compensated for via the presentation of additional visual information or with better identification of key environmental cues. Future work from our research group will focus on developing and evaluating these compensatory augmentations in a virtual setting before moving to real world testing. We postulate that successful virtual testing and subsequent implementation of compensatory augmentations will lead to an increase in safety and independence for older navigators during real-world driving.

Acknowledgments. We thank everyone at the VEMI lab for their assistance creating the driving simulator. We specifically thank Jonathan Cole for his development of the VR software used during this research. We acknowledge funding support for this project provided by a University of Maine Aging Research and Technology Seed Grant awarded to Dr. Nicholas Giudice and Dr. Richard Corey.

References

1. Mooney, J.: Driving status and out-of-home social activity levels: the case of older male veterans. GRC News **22**(3), 3 (2003)
2. World Health Organization: The Social Determinants of Health: The Solid Facts-Second Edition (2003)
3. United States Census Bureau: Census Data (2008). http://www.census.gov/population/projections/data/national/2008.html
4. Insurance Institute for Highway Safety: Highway Safety Research and Communications (2012). http://www.iihs.org/iihs/topics/t/older-drivers/fatalityfacts/older-people/2012#Trends

5. García-Betances, R.I., Arredondo Waldmeyer, M.T., Fico, G., Cabrera-Umpiérrez, M.F.: A succinct overview of virtual reality technology use in Alzheimer's disease. Front. Aging Neurosci. **7**, 80 (2015). doi:10.3389/fnagi.2015.00080
6. Brooks, J.O., Goodenough, R.R., Crisler, M.C., Klein, N.D., Alley, R.L., Koon, B.L., Wills, R.F.: Simulator sickness during driving simulation studies. Accid. Anal. Prev. **42**(3), 788–796 (2010)
7. Sensics, Inc. (2012). http://sensics.com/portfolio-posts/zsight/
8. Klencklen, G., Després, O., Dufour, A.: What do we know about aging and spatial cognition? Reviews and perspectives. Ageing Res. Rev. **11**(1), 123–135 (2012)
9. Moffat, S.D.: Aging and spatial navigation: what do we know and where do we go? Neuropsychol. Rev. **19**(4), 478–489 (2009)
10. Nasreddine, Z.S., Phillips, N.A., Bédirian, V., Charbonneau, S., Whitehead, V., Collin, I., Cummings, J.L., Chertkow, H.: The Montreal Cognitive Assessment (MoCA): a brief screening tool for mild cognitive impairment. J. Am. Geriatr. Soc. **53**, 695–699 (2005)
11. Keshavarz, B., Riecke, B.E., Hettinger, L.J., Campos, J.L.: Vection and visually induced motion sickness: how are they related? Front. Psychol. **6**, 472 (2015)
12. Strayer, D.L., Drew, F.A.: Profiles in driver distraction: effects of cell phone conversations on younger and older drivers. Hum. Factors: J. Hum. Factors Ergon. Soc. **46**(4), 640–649 (2004)
13. Brown, T.L., Lee, J.D., McGehee, D.V.: Human performance models and rear-end collision avoidance algorithms. Hum. Factors **43**, 462–482 (2001)
14. Lee, J.D., Vaven, B., Haake, S., Brown, T.L.: Speech-based interaction with in-vehicle computers: the effects of speech-based e-mail on drivers' attention to the roadway. Hum. Factors **43**, 631–640 (2001)
15. Jager, R.D., Mieler, W.F., Miller, J.W.: Age-related macular degeneration. N. Engl. J. Med. **358**(24), 2606–2617 (2008)
16. Tan, O., Li, G., Lu, A.T.H., Varma, R., Huang, D., Advanced Imaging for Glaucoma Study Group: Mapping of macular substructures with optical coherence tomography for glaucoma diagnosis. Ophthalmology **115**(6), 949–956 (2008)

Ensuring the Safety and Accessibility of Transportation for an Aging Population

Walter R. Boot[✉], Kimberly Barajas, Ainsley Mitchum, Cary Stothart,
and Neil Charness

Department of Psychology, Florida State University, Tallahassee, FL, USA
{boot,barajas,mitchum,stothart,charness}@psy.fsu.edu

Abstract. As drivers and pedestrians, older adults face greater risk for serious injury and death resulting from a crash. Part of this increased risk can be attributed to increased fragility with age, but increased risk is also due in part to a mismatch between the demands of the driving/pedestrian task and the perceptual, cognitive, and motor abilities of the aging road user. This paper presents a broad overview of the approaches that have been taken to reduce the crash risk of aging road users by either changing the vehicle and roadway environment or changing the road user (i.e., strategy training/cognitive training). A summary of the work conducted by the Aging Driver and Pedestrian Safety Lab (ADAPtS Lab) investigating the efficacy of roadway modifications to reduce crash risk is presented. Further, we provide a brief review of how technologies on the horizon (i.e., autonomous and semi-autonomous vehicles) might impact the safety of aging road users. These technologies will likely result in the solution to some problems while introducing new problems that warrant additional human factors studies involving participants of all ages and levels of driving skill. The promises and challenges of roadway modifications, driver education and training, and automation as solutions are compared and contrasted.

Keywords: Older adults · Driver · Pedestrian · Crash · Mobility · Independence

1 Introduction

The Importance of Mobility. Transportation has been identified as an Instrumental Activity of Daily Living (IADL). It is difficult to live independently without some means to leave one's own home to shop and keep appointments (e.g., physician visits), and a lack of transportation also limits opportunities to engage in social and recreational activities. It is important to explore ways to enhance transportation opportunities throughout the lifespan. In the United States and many other nations, the automobile is the most popular and preferred form of transportation (other than perhaps walking short distances). Yet, as we age a variety of physical and cognitive changes make the driving task more difficult, sometimes resulting in the cessation of driving altogether. While driving cessation may reduce the crash risk of older adults experiencing age-related driving difficulties later in life, it is associated with its own risks. Driving cessation has been linked to higher levels of depression, isolation, and poorer health (for review, see [1]). There is strong reason to believe that multiple benefits to

© Springer International Publishing Switzerland 2016
J. Zhou and G. Salvendy (Eds.): ITAP 2016, Part II, LNCS 9755, pp. 386–394, 2016.
DOI: 10.1007/978-3-319-39949-2_37

wellbeing and health are possible when efforts are made to ensure that older adults have access to safe transportation options.

Aging Road User Safety. Unfortunately, a variety of physical and cognitive changes occur that put aging road users (drivers, pedestrians, cyclists) at greater risk compared to their younger counterparts. One of the major factors contributing to this increased risk is increased fragility. As we age our bodies become more susceptible to damage from crash forces. A crash that injures a 20-year-old driver might kill a 90-year-old driver due to an increased risk of injury and bone fracture, and decreased ability to recover from crash injuries. Some have argued that this is the primary factor behind the increased risk of aging road users (rather than excess crash involvement [2]). However, we also know that age is associated with perceptual changes (e.g., decreased visual acuity, increased susceptibility to glare), cognitive changes (e.g., decreased visual processing speed, slower response time, decreased memory and spatial ability), and physical changes (e.g., decreased muscle strength and range of motion). These age-related changes put aging road users at greater risk for being involved in a crash and make the driving task more challenging and less comfortable (for review, see [3]). Changes in fragility and ability not only influence the safety of aging drivers, but of other aging road users as well. For example, Fig. 1 depicts pedestrian fatality rates in the United States as a function of age. There is an elevated risk for aging pedestrians, especially older men.

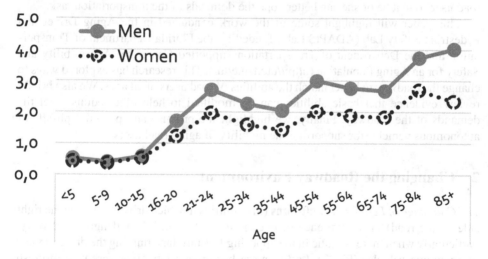

Fig. 1. Pedestrian fatality rate per 100,000 in the population as a function of age and gender (NHTSA, 2012 data).

Safe and Accessible Transportation for an Aging Population. A variety of solutions have been explored to decrease the crash risk and increase the comfort of aging road users. One fruitful approach to reducing driver risk has been the introduction of safety features to protect vehicle occupants such as crumple zones and airbag systems. Safety features that decrease the impact of crash forces have the potential to differentially benefit older drivers and passengers who are more susceptible to these forces. This is consistent with a general trend for a decrease in the fatality risk of older drivers relative to younger drivers over the past few decades as automobiles have become safer [4].

With respect to age-related changes to perceptual, cognitive, and motor abilities, the problem can be framed in terms of a classic person-environment fit model. Each individual brings to a transportation task (e.g., making a left-turn as a driver, crossing the roadway as a pedestrian, reading and understanding a bus schedule) certain ability levels (e.g., visual acuity and reasoning ability). Each transportation task requires minimum ability levels for accurate, safe, and comfortable task performance. For example, driving requires adequate vision to detect road hazards and adequate visuospatial skills to estimate safe gaps in traffic when turning. When the abilities of the individual match or exceed the demands of the transportation task, the task can be performed safely and comfortably. However, when a mismatch occurs between the demands of the task and the abilities of the road user, safety and comfort are compromised. Unfortunately, as a result of age-related changes, there is a greater opportunity for a mismatch between the demands of the transportation task and the abilities of the aging road user. Ensuring safe and accessible transportation for an aging population requires, in part, strategies to address this mismatch and bring the demands of the transportation task and the abilities of the aging road user back into alignment. Two general strategies are available to address this mismatch; (1) change the demands of the transportation task to better match the abilities of the aging road user, and (2) change the abilities and strategies of the aging road user so that he or she can better cope the demands of the transportation task.

This paper will highlight some of the work conducted in the Aging Driver and Pedestrian Safety Lab (ADAPtS Lab), funded by the Florida Department of Transportation and the Department of Transportation supported Center for Accessibility and Safety for an Aging Population (http://utc.fsu.edu/). This research has explored ways to change the roadway to better match the abilities of road users of all ages. We also briefly review evidence that basic abilities can be modified to help older adults meet the demands of the roadway. Finally, we highlight the promise and potential pitfalls of autonomous vehicles for supporting the mobility of aging road users.

2   Changing the Roadway Environment

The Challenge of Left-Turns. Left-turns (in countries in which drivers drive on the right side of the road) in the presence of oncoming traffic can be challenging and risky, particularly when there is traffic in the opposing left-turn lane limiting the driver's view of oncoming vehicles (Fig. 2). Left-turn crashes are a relatively severe type of crash since oncoming vehicles are typically moving fast when they strike turning vehicles. This type of crash is also particularly common and severe for older drivers [4–6], which may partly be explained by age-related declines in spatial abilities [7, 8]. Misjudging either the speed of an oncoming vehicle or its distance can result in the left-turning driver entering a gap that is too small, resulting in a crash.

Fig. 2. Negative offset (above) and minimal offset (below) left-turn lanes tested in a driving simulator study in the ADAPtS Lab. Note in the panel below, the white car to the left of the opposing left-turn lane is visible, while in the negative offset configuration it would not be seen.

To help support left-turning older drivers, one potential solution is to shift opposing left-turn lanes to the right, allowing a better view of oncoming traffic (compare top and bottom panels of Fig. 2). This allows left-turning drivers more time to estimate the speed and distance of oncoming traffic. The ADAPtS Lab has used a driving simulator to investigate whether this change might benefit older drivers [9]. Younger (ages 21 to 35; N = 31), Middle-Aged (ages 50 to 64; N = 20), and Older (ages 65 and older; N = 22) drivers were asked to make a left turn in the presence of oncoming traffic. Our measure of safety was how close the nearest oncoming vehicle was when the participants' vehicle entered the oncoming stream of traffic. Larger distances (more clearance) indicate a safer decision. In general, when drivers had a better view of oncoming traffic (minimal lane offset condition), drivers entered the intersection when the nearest vehicle was 40 feet further compared to when the opposing left-turn lane blocked more of the view of oncoming traffic (negative offset condition). This effect did not vary as a function of age, meaning that a roadway change intended to benefit older drivers benefited drivers of all ages. Changing the demands of the driving task (allowing more information to be extracted about the speed and distance of oncoming traffic) allowed for greater alignment between the demands of the roadway task and the abilities of aging road users, increasing safety.

The Challenges of Night Driving. Driving at night can be particularly challenging for older adults for a number of reasons. These include changes to the eye that result in less light reaching the retina, increased susceptibility to glare, and more time needed to dark adapt compared to younger adults [10]. These issues cause some older adults to avoid night driving altogether. Improving the visibility of signs and lane markings at night is one potential solution to increase the safety and comfort of older drivers in nighttime driving situations. The ADAPtS Lab has investigated this issue with respect to symbolic warning signs (e.g., Stop Ahead, Yield Ahead, Signal Ahead). Younger (N = 22), Middle-Aged (N = 14), and Older (N = 25) drivers were asked to identify signs in a field study by driving towards them at night, using either low or high beam settings [11].

The critical manipulation was whether the sign sheeting was standard material, or whether the sheeting was fluorescent. Fluorescent sheeting reflects back more light to the driver. A clear effect of age was observed, such that older drivers needed to be closer to the sign to identify it correctly. However, drivers of all ages benefited when the sign featured fluorescent sheeting under low beam conditions (signs could be identified about 40 feet further away compared to standard sheeting; Fig. 3). As with the left-turn study, a change to the driving task that can benefit older drivers appeared to help drivers of all ages. In fact, signs with fluorescent backing were as visible under low beam conditions as standard signs under high beam conditions. Manipulations that increase sign and lane marking visibility can partly compensate for the fact that, under low light conditions, less light reaches the retina of the older eye.

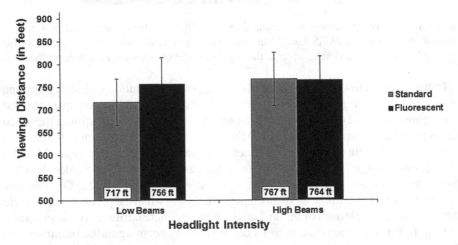

Fig. 3. Minimum distance at which signs could be correctly identified, as a function of headlight setting and sign sheeting material.

Accounting for Age-Related Slowing. One of the most common findings in the literature on aging is that older adults need more time to process and respond to information [12, 13]. This has implications for various calculations related to intersection design and signal timing. For example, yellow light duration is partly based on an estimate of perception-reaction time (PRT) that assumes that one second is enough time for most drivers to perceive and react to a signal change. In a simulator study, we examined how long it would take younger and older drivers to perceive and react to signal changes from green to yellow [9]. This sample consisted of 27 younger and 25 older drivers. However, before we conducted the study, we also modeled the task of detecting and responding to a yellow signal using GOMS (Goals, Operators, Methods, and Selections Rules) modeling, with this model accounting for age-related perceptual and cognitive changes [14]. GOMS modeling predicted that older adults needed 767 ms more time to begin braking in response to a yellow signal. This was strikingly consistent with observed results in the simulator study, with older adults taking 803 ms longer to respond. Given the large difference in measured response times to yellow signals between younger and older adults, results suggest that there may be benefits to adjusting estimates of PRT to better account for age-related slowing.

The three examples presented here suggest that the roadway can be changed in ways to improve the safety and comfort of aging road users. This reduces the mismatch between the aging road users' abilities and the demands of the transportation task. Next, we turn to two alternative approaches to reduce this mismatch.

3   Changing the Road User's Abilities

Another approach to increasing safety and comfort is to enhance the aging road user's abilities. There have been numerous investigations into whether or not various cognitive training programs can boost perceptual and cognitive abilities and reduce or reverse age-related cognitive decline. Some of these studies have examined outcomes related to aging road user comfort and safety (e.g., [15, 16]). While positive effects can be found in the literature, these effects are controversial [17]. A recent consensus statement signed by over 70 scientists concluded that there exist no compelling evidence that brain training programs can meaningfully improve the performance of important everyday tasks such as driving [18]. Not long after this statement was released, a counter-consensus statement was put forward, signed by over 120 scientists and practitioners, suggesting that some brain training programs are effective [19]. Given the uncertain efficacy of brain training programs at this point, they are difficult to recommend as a solution to improving the safety and accessibly of transportation for an aging population. Further, there has been no work examining the comparative effectiveness of brain training programs and other potentially beneficial programs to reduce crash risk (e.g., driver education and strategy training, on-road training).

It should be noted that crash reduction programs targeting the driving task itself often produce little observable benefit with respect to crash risk. Older driver education programs that teach strategies for avoiding risky driving situations (driving at night and during heavy traffic, making left-turns) can increase driver awareness of risk and change behaviors, but may not result in a reduction in crash rate [20, 21]. Educational programs alone may not result in reduced crash risk, but similar programs in combination with on-road training may reduce unsafe driving maneuvers [22, 23]. Results are generally consistent with the idea that specific unsafe driving situations and risky maneuvers should be targeted in order to improve aging road user safety and comfort. This strategy is consistent with theories of learning and skill acquisition that posit that the largest performance gains obtained are through practice on the task one wants to observe improvement on (near transfer).

4   The Role of Autonomous Vehicles

In the case of driving, a third general strategy to reduce the mismatch between the abilities of the aging road user and the demands of the roadway is to offload some or most of the driving task to the vehicle itself (semi-autonomous and autonomous vehicles, [24]). The potential for this strategy to increase the safety and mobility of older adults and individuals with disabilities is large. However, automation is rarely a panacea and important issues need to be considered with respect to how best to design autonomous vehicle systems, taking into account the abilities, attitudes, and preferences of aging road users, and how best to design training programs to teach drivers of all ages to use autonomous functions (see [25, 26] for designing systems and training for older adults).

No automation system is perfect, and as with any automated system in some situations a human will need to intervene [27]. Issues such as driver complacency, skill degradation, and loss of situational awareness need to be considered. Will drivers be ready to quickly regain control of the vehicle should autonomous functions fail? Will younger and older drivers be equally able to do so, given age-related changes in attention, executive control, and other age-related changes? If not, the differential risk of older drivers may persist. Other important issues to consider are factors that influence technology adoption (see [28] for factors related to the adoption of information and communications technology as an example). There is often a digital divide, with older adults adopting newer technology at a much slower pace compared to younger adults. The same is likely to be true of autonomous and semi-autonomous vehicles. Issues that influence adoption of autonomous vehicle technology (trust, perceived usefulness, perceived ease of use, price) need to be considered in order to ensure that the potential benefits of autonomous vehicles are available to drivers of all ages. There is likely to be a great deal of research into these issues (safety and usability of systems, factors influencing adoption) in the near future.

5 Conclusion and Discussion

Here we have outlined a number of approaches to help ensure the safety and mobility of the aging population. This is a critical issue as transportation is vital to independent living. Our work in the ADAPtS Lab has demonstrated clearly that the roadway environment can be changed to help accommodate age-related perceptual and cognitive changes. Left-turns become safer when drivers can extract more information about oncoming vehicles. Nighttime navigation can become easier with more visible signs. Older drivers may benefit from longer yellow light durations to account for age-related slowing. Changes such as these can help support aging drivers. However, it is also important to consider transportation more broadly, and think about additional countermeasures that specifically benefit aging pedestrians and cyclists [29, 30]. Accessible public transportation deserves attention as well. These are all important aspects of designing what the American Association of Retired Persons calls "Age Friendly Communities." Other options are to boost the abilities of the aging road user, though this topic is controversial (particularly the effect of brain training programs on driving comfort and safety). Even if these programs are found to be beneficial, they depend upon individuals investing time, effort, and often money to complete them (compared to roadway changes that may benefit all individuals with little investment from the individual). Finally, it is likely that autonomous and semi-autonomous vehicles in the near future will play a role in reducing aging road user risk. However, as outlined previously, a number of important issues need to be addressed before this can be proposed as a complete solution to age-related risk. Moving forward it is likely that changes to the roadway, changes to the vehicle, and driver training and education all will play some role in minimizing the risk of aging road users by bringing into alignment the abilities of the aging road user and the demands of various transportation tasks.

6 Disclaimer

The opinions, findings, and conclusions expressed in this publication are those of the authors and not necessarily those of the State of Florida Department of Transportation or the U. S. Department of Transportation.

Acknowledgments. The ADAPtS Lab is funded by the Florida Department of Transportation, and the Department of Transportation supported Center for Accessibility and Safety for an Aging Population.

References

1. Chihuri, S., Mielenz, T.J., DiMaggio, C.J., Betz, M.E., DiGuiseppi, C., Jones, V.C., Li, G.: Driving cessation and health outcomes in older adults. J. Am. Geriatr. Soc. (2016, Epub ahead of print)
2. Li, G., Braver, E.R., Chen, L.H.: Fragility versus excessive crash involvement as determinants of high death rates per vehicle-mile of travel among older drivers. Accid. Anal. Prev. **35**(2), 227–235 (2003)
3. Boot, W.R., Stothart, C., Charness, N.: Improving the safety of aging road users: a mini-review. Gerontology **60**(1), 90–96 (2014)
4. ADOT. Report No: AZ-SP-903. A study of the relationship between left-turn accidents and driver age in Arizona. Arizona Department of Transportation (1996)
5. Preusser, D.F., Williams, A.F., Ferguson, S.A., Ulmer, R.G., Weinstein, H.B.: Fatal crash risk for older drivers at intersections. Accid. Anal. Prev. **30**, 151–159 (1998)
6. Yan, X., Radwan, E., Guo, D.: Effects of major-road vehicle speed and driver age and gender on left-turn gap acceptance. Accid. Anal. Prev. **39**, 843–852 (2007)
7. Anderson, G.J., Enriquez, A.: Aging and the detection of observer and moving object collisions. Psychol. Aging **21**(1), 74–85 (2006)
8. Scialfa, C.T., Guzy, L.T., Leibowitz, H.W., Garvey, P.M., Tyrrell, R.A.: Age differences in estimating vehicle velocity. Psychol. Aging **6**(1), 60–66 (1991)
9. Boot, W.R., Charness, N., Fox, M., Mitchum, A., Lupton, H., Rebekah, L.: Final report: aging road user, bicyclist, and pedestrian safety: effective bicycling signs and preventing left-turn crashes. Technical report BDK83 977-15. Florida Department of Transportation (2013)
10. Owsley, C.: Aging and vision. Vis. Res. **51**(13), 1610–1622 (2011)
11. Charness, N., Mitchum, A., Champion, M., Cowing, B., Stothart, C.: Aging drivers and pedestrians. Technical report BDK83 977-09. Florida Department of Transportation (2011)
12. Birren, J.E., Fisher, L.M.: Aging and speed of behavior: possible consequences for psychological functioning. Annu. Rev. Psychol. **46**, 329–353 (1995)
13. Salthouse, T.A.: The processing-speed theory of adult age differences in cognition. Psychol. Rev. **103**(3), 403–428 (1996)

14. Jastrzembski, T.S., Charness, N.: The model human processor and the older adult: parameter estimation and validation within a mobile phone task. J. Exp. Psychol.: Appl. 13(4), 224–248 (2007)
15. Ball, K., Edwards, J.D., Ross, L.A., McGwin Jr., G.: Cognitive training decreases motor vehicle collision involvement among older drivers. J. Am. Geriatr. Soc. 58, 2107–2113 (2010)
16. Edwards, J.D., Myers, C., Ross, L.A., Roenker, D.L., Cissell, G.M., McLaughlin, A.M., Ball, K.K.: The longitudinal impact of cognitive speed of processing training on driving mobility. Gerontologist 49(4), 485–494 (2009)
17. Boot, W.R., Kramer, A.F.: The brain-games conundrum: does cognitive training really sharpen the mind? Cerebrum, pp. 1–15, November 2014
18. A Consensus on the Brain Training Industry from the Scientific Community, Max Planck Institute for Human Development and Stanford Center on Longevity (2016). http://longevity3.stanford.edu/blog/2014/10/15/the-consensus-on-the-brain-training-industry-from-the-scientific-community/
19. Cognitive Training Data (2016). http://www.cognitivetrainingdata.org/
20. Janke, M.K.: Mature driver improvement program in California. In: Transportation Research Record 1438, TRB, National Research Council, Washington, D.C., pp. 77–83 (1994)
21. Owsley, C., McGwin, G., Phillips, J.M., McNeal, S.F., Stalvey, B.T.: Impact of an educational program on the safety of high-risk, visually impaired, older drivers. Am. J. Prev. Med. 26(3), 222–229 (2004)
22. Bédard, M.: The combination of two training approaches to improve older adults' driving safety. Traffic Inj. Prev. 9(1), 70–76 (2008)
23. Marottoli, R.A., Van Ness, P.H., Araujo, K.L., Iannone, L.P., Acampora, D., Charpentier, P., Peduzzi, P.: A randomized trial of an education program to enhance older driver performance. J. Gerontol. Ser. A: Biol. Sci. Med. Sci. 62(10), 1113–1119 (2007)
24. Reimer, B.: Driver assistance systems and the transition to automated vehicles: a path to increase older adult safety and mobility? Pub. Policy Aging Rep. 24(1), 27–31 (2014)
25. Czaja, S.J., Sharit, J.: Designing Training and Instructional Programs for Older Adults. CRC Press, Boca Raton (2012)
26. Fisk, A.D., Rogers, W.A., Charness, N., Czaja, S.J., Sharit, J.: Designing for Older Adults: Principles and Creative Human Factors Approaches, 2nd edn. CRC Press, Boca Raton (2009)
27. Parasuraman, R., Wickens, C.D.: Humans: still vital after all these years of automation. Hum. Factors: J. Hum. Factors Ergon. Soc. 50(3), 511–520 (2008)
28. Czaja, S.J., Charness, N., Fisk, A.D., Hertzog, C., Nair, S.N., Rogers, W.A., Sharit, J.: Factors predicting the use of technology: findings from the Center for Research and Education on Aging and Technology Enhancement (CREATE). Psychol. Aging 21(2), 333–352 (2006)
29. Boot, W.R., Charness, N., Roque, N., Barajas, K., Dirghalli, J., Mitchum, A.: The flashing right turn signal with pedestrian indication: human factors studies to understand the potential of a new signal to increase awareness of and attention to crossing pedestrian. Technical report BDV30-977-13. Florida Department of Transportation (2015)
30. Charness, N., Boot, W.R., Mitchum, A., Stothart, C., Lupton, H.: Final report: aging driver and pedestrian safety: parking lot hazards study. Technical report BDK83 977-12. Florida Department of Transportation (2012)

Rethinking Public Transport Services for the Elderly Through a Transgenerational Design Approach

Roberta Grimaldi[1,2], Antonio Opromolla[1,2], Giovanni Andrea Parente[1],
Eliseo Sciarretta[1(✉)], and Valentina Volpi[1,2]

[1] Link Campus University, Rome, Italy
{r.grimaldi,a.opromolla,g.parente,
e.sciarretta,v.volpi}@unilink.it
[2] ISIA Roma Design, Rome, Italy

Abstract. In discussing the city suitability to people's needs, generally a special attention has been given to people with special needs, e.g. the elderly. In this sense, most of the research about accessible cities has focused on the architectural design of public spaces, aiming at ensuring the access to urban places through the removal of architectural barriers. However, as technologies have been diffusing in many different city services, it also should be given attention to the constraints derived from this unavoidable change affecting the elderly life. The focus is on the potential of the technologies for improving the elderly city experience. In this paper the authors, starting from the principles of the transgenerational design, focus on how the technologies applied to the public transportation services could improve citizen experience and promote really inclusive mobility services.

Keywords: Transgenerational design · Public transport service · Elderly · Redesign · Technology adoption

1 Introduction

The connection between city development and technologies has been largely discussed in the scientific literature about the so-called smart city [1–3]. Beyond the definition of a theoretical framework of the city, technology has effectively permeated different sectors of the urban environment. In several cases, the implementation of interactive systems has been really enhancing the spaces and the services of public interest and has been producing information about citizens and city that can be usefully reused to improve their quality of life [4, 5].

The delivery of smart services and real time information can lead to a real breakthrough and improvement in the way people live and experience their cities, but most of the smart cities initiatives do not already properly consider the citizen's needs. However, in order to be really effective, city services have to take into account all the different kinds of needs and limitations that people may have, according to a human-centered approach. So, the use of the technologies should be consistent and suitable for the users experience and their physical and cognitive features. Nowadays many different technologies have been showing their potential benefits among different categories of

© Springer International Publishing Switzerland 2016
J. Zhou and G. Salvendy (Eds.): ITAP 2016, Part II, LNCS 9755, pp. 395–406, 2016.
DOI: 10.1007/978-3-319-39949-2_38

adopters [6]. In such a complex and rapidly evolving context of various interactive systems, a particular attention should be given to older people, as they often need support in using technological systems and need more effort and time in becoming confident with the required know-how [7]. However, beyond their potential reluctance, older people actually are nearly forced to use different kind of technological systems, as they often are the only or the more advantageous mean for accessing certain services and information [7, 8]. So, the elderly needs have to be considered and evaluated in the design research about smart services.

The academic literature has been largely debating about the elderly user experience and level of acceptance and adoption of information technology within the home context, e.g. IT health systems, assisted living technology, ambient intelligence, sensors, etc. [9–12]. On the contrary, few studies have focused on the adoption and use by older people of technology situated in the open urban space. Moreover, the research on the needs and requirements of aged population outside the domestic context mainly has concerned the planning of physical public places [13, 14], and the role of the Public Administrations in taking into account the elderly needs (e.g. in planning the transport sector) [15, 16]. In this regard, Gilhooly et al. [17] analysed the difficulties of older people during their experience in public spaces (e.g. difficulty in carrying heavy loads, running late, behaviour of some passengers, etc.).

On this basis, the analysis and evaluation of the influence of technology on the older people urban experience has to be integrated.

So, in this paper, the authors will focus on the study of the interaction modes between older adults and some of the enhanced services offered by the smart city, in order to safeguard the inclusion of older adults, as long as, mainly in the industrialized countries, the population continues to age and the rate of the elderly on the total number of people is expected to increase [18]. In detail, in this paper, the authors intend to focus on the analysis of mobility services, as they are a relevant element of the cities that enables the use of other public spaces. Moreover, it is a sector extremely digitized and, at the same time, necessary to the life of citizens, elderly included [19, 20]. In this sense, the design of accessible and usable interactive systems relating to the transport services might prevent the social isolation of the elderly. So, in the next section, the authors present the work related to elderly needs in public transport services. In the third section they present the approach adopted in reflecting about a truly inclusive design of mobility services, while in the fourth section the different steps of the service journey, from the trip planning to the effective use of public transportation means, are described and then discussed in the fifth section. Finally, in the conclusion, the authors focus on the general principles to be considered in designing public transport services and on the future work.

2   Related Work

Many studies about public transport requirements for people with special needs mostly focus on the hindrances caused by the physical environment in accessing to different city services, as the presence of architectural barriers [21–23]. In this regard, most of the problems are caused by the lack of information about the physical barriers present at the stations or along the way [24]. Regarding more in general the elderly needs, Bekiaris et al. [19] observed that it is very important to provide additional information, such as: coming buses with platforms to facilitate the access in the transport mean, presence of staircases on the path, information about reduced rates for pensioned or disabled people. On the contrary, little attention has been given to user sensory impairments, such as the difficulty to see and to listen acoustic notices on board and within the stations or at the bus shelter.

In general, by considering the presence of different kind of obstacles, the necessity of an inclusive design approach emerges. In this regard, Bogren et al. [25] highlight the importance of the active involvement of the elderly in designing solutions that favor the accessibility in the public transport. The accessible technology is a key component that has to be adequately considered into the service design process, as it greatly influences the user experience and sets different challenges in respect of the peculiar features of the involved subjects [20, 22]. In effect, older people are one of the main groups to which heavy cognitive efforts are required in the adoption of modern information technology [26]. So a good design of the interaction between the elderly and the digital devices should primarily understand some human aspects of the user experience: the devices daily routine, the problem-solving skills, the interaction preferences, etc. In this perspective, Subasi et al. [27] focus their attention on the many factors that positively influence the online tickets purchase experience of the older users. The elderly see benefits both in real life ticketing services and web ticketing services. The preference for the first interaction mode depends on the reluctance of the elderly at changing their habits, but clear benefits perceived into the experience of online ticketing might induce them to use also the second one. In detail, the online ticket purchase is perceived allowing timesaving and ease and convenient purchases. Regarding the whole user experience, the use of portable devices, especially PDA and smartphone, seems to positively influence the access to mobility information.

Due to the differences among older people needs and the variables among the technological interactive systems, the design of the elderly user experience in the public transports has been proving to be fragmentary, more focused on single aspects, as physical barriers, or on single step of the whole journey. Despite that, in using public transportation service, there are some needs in common among elderly and even very different social groups. For example, Grotenhuis et al. [28] show how there were for the elderly and younger people some common needs regarding various types of information (e.g. including interchanges with other means of transport, remaining travel time, etc.), although the elderly have more need of information than younger people, especially in the pre-trip, to save physical effort.

In conclusion, in order to achieve a comfortable experience for elderly in using the public transport services even a focus on the influence that technology may have on the whole journey is needed. Moreover, it should be oriented towards an integrated and inclusive service design approach.

3   The Role of Transgenerational Design in Rethinking Public Transport Service for the Elderly

In order to improve the citizen experience and promoting really inclusive mobility services, in this paper the authors have been inspired by the transgenerational design approach to re-think the public transport services. In detail, the transgenerational design aims to propose solutions suitable for everyone, regardless of age or ability, by designing products and environments according to the simultaneous accommodation of the requirements of the widest possible range of people who would use them, from the young to the older people, from the able bodied to the disabled people [29].

The transgenerational design has emerged in the 1980s as the result of the public's growing awareness of the increasing aging of population and of the arising of the disability rights movement. This approach was developed by Pirkl and Babic, starting from the idea that the accommodation to the widest spectrum of human needs is a pivotal responsibility of the designers [30]. In this sense, the transgenerational design aims to create or reimagine products, services, and places for ensuring safety, comfort, accessibility, and ease of use to the end user, allowing at the same time a convenience and a good design. All products and services should be designed to fit the changing sensory and physical needs, through designs that do not stigmatize, but rather maintain and reinforce everyone's dignity and self-respect. Indeed, one of the transgenerational design challenge is to emphasize beauty while actively avoiding the sterile and clinical solutions. So, in summary, the transgenerational design "accommodates rather than discriminates, sympathizes rather than stigmatizes, and innovates rather than replicates" [31].

Then, the authors of this paper refer to this approach because of its focus on the way humans actually use and live things, spaces, and services. In fact, this design process is value oriented [32], rather than aimed at merely adapting interactive systems to principles, standards, and dimensions. Furthermore, in this paper the transgenerational design approach has to be intended as inclusive of the traditional web accessibility and usability design principles [33]. In fact, these concepts complete the transgenerational approach in respect to the interactive systems, as technology is by now integrated in several types of service touchpoints. In this regard, in this paper the authors analyse how technological systems intervene into the different steps of public transportation services and affect the whole user service experience. The focus of the study is on the elderly, even if the authors try to maintain an inclusive point of view. In effect, although the World Health Organization suggests that "most developed world countries have accepted the chronological age of 65 years as a definition of "elderly" or older person" [34], this is a simplification. As Nielsen states [35], people do not change all their behaviours on their 65th birthday; instead the human aging process starts when people turn 20. Designing for elderly is challenging because there are several skills that decline with age: vision, dexterity and motor skills, memory and cognition, hearing. These conditions can occur either separately or jointly. Still, these problems, typical of the elderly, can also be experienced by other people as a permanent or temporary issue. Disabled people can be young and have one or more of these problems, tourists with luggage or parents with strollers can have mobility issues, sunny conditions can give rise to vision problems, and so on. In this sense, the transgenerational approach results a valid solution to adequately meet the widest range of user needs and abilities.

4 Analysis of the Interactive Systems in the Public Transport Service User Journey

In analyzing the possible influences of technologies on the whole elderly user experience with the public transport service, the authors need to focus on one specific case, in order to refer to an effective touchpoints ecosystem. Because of practical needs, they choose the one of Rome. The resulting analysis should not lead to any value judgment about the specific provided service. It deals with the potential user journey related to the use of the public transport service, split into its main stages, each one characterized by specific functionalities and technologies: (1) planning of the trip; (2) ticket purchase; (3) access to real time information; (4) ticket validation; (5) ride.

1. *Trip Planning.* This first stage consists in getting information and data useful to plan the movements within the city. In Rome, the activities related to this phase are performed both through digital applications and non-digital tools. A lot of web and mobile applications belong to the first category. They provide users some basic parameters and features, useful to plan the trip between two different places of the city. Among the provided parameters: the choice of the starting address and the destination address (in order to identify the way to go), the choice among the most favorite means of transportation (e.g. only buses, bus and underground, etc.), the propensity for walking (e.g. high, medium, low), the time shift (e.g. setting the departure time or time of arrival), the possible integration with other means of transportation (car sharing, bike sharing, private means). The final user can access to these features both in the home environment (e.g. through a desktop application) and in the city environment (e.g. through a mobile application). Some of them are designed with an attention to the needs of specific users, in particular the visually impaired. Concerning the use of non-digital tools, different solutions are provided: the bus stop signage that show the route of the single transport line, the city geo-referenced map with the main transport lines, etc.
2. *Ticket Purchase.* This stage consists in getting the ticket good for a ride on the public transport services by paying a fee to purchase it. There are different sales channels, also depending on the ticket type (i.e. paper ticket, e-ticket, pass, and touristic ticket). In general, the interaction between the user and the ticket purchasing system can be set entirely offline (through physical channels) or online (through digital ones), or it can be set partly offline and partly online. In detail, the user can purchase all the ticket types at the carrier ticket offices or at the other authorized sales points and agencies (e.g. tourist agencies, news-stands, tobacco shops, etc.), by paying by cash or other accepted payment instruments (e.g. credit card). The latter can cause troubles especially for non-expert users. Automatic ticket vending machines are another physical sale channel that requires an in-person interaction. In this case difficulties may occur because of the poor and not standardized interface of the system and the lack of the assistance by a human operator. These machines are generally set at the

entrance of the subway, near the turnstiles, at the main bus terminals and at other strategic sites, that may be crowded and cluttered places, where the user may be in a hurry. Moreover, even in this case the user can use different payment instruments, e.g. credit card (contact or contactless) or cash. Conversely, the customer can purchase an e-ticket (a single ticket or a personal pass) through the smartphone by accessing to a mobile app for paying and obtaining a digital item that stores the ticket information, such as a QR Code or a code redeemable through NFC technology. The customer can also load e-tickets on a rechargeable card (passes or touristic cards). In this case, the tickets can be purchased online on the carrier website or at the carrier ticket office and loaded on the user's card, that can be required at one of the carrier ticket office or on the carrier website and then collected at the carrier ticket office or received by mail. The passes can be topped up also at the ATM or on the website of the affiliated bank or at one of the affiliated point of sale. The online purchase may require the user to do different steps: selecting the desired product, selecting the desired collection method, filling different personal information, paying (by using different payment instruments), receiving confirmation about the transaction, and inserting the required digits composing the personal code on the card. Eventually, the paper ticket can be purchased on buses and on other surface public transport means at the ticket issuing machines available on board.

3. *Access to real time information*. This stage consists in getting information and data for the journey that is going to begin. In the city of Rome, these activities are mainly performed through digital tools. The single transport means are monitored through satellite systems and the related data are used to give the final user real time information about the state of the public transport, accessible through web and mobile apps. The main information the user can access to are: the arrival time of the single transport mean by digitizing the number or the name of the bus stop, or the number of the bus line; the access to the favorite bus lines and stops (by add them to bookmarks); the access to real time general news, always related to the service status (e.g. crashes, strikes, etc.). The same real time data are also used for the digital bus stop signage that shows the list of the buses that are arriving and for each of them by how many minutes it arrives and the number of stops before it arrives. Some added tools for the real time information to the city users particularly focus on the possible delays and problems of the mobility of Rome, such as one Twitter account and an Instant Messaging service through the WhatsApp platform.

4. *Ticket Validation*. This stage consists in validating the ticket on the appropriate machine. There are different validation systems, depending on the ticket support type. In the city of Rome the validity of the ticket is essentially based on time (starting from the moment of ticket validation). In certain cases there are constrictions concerning the period of use, e.g. the current month. The validated ticket entitles the user to access to all the public transport services provided by the carrier and by the affiliated transport companies within all the city of Rome (i.e. bus, trolleybus, tram, railroad train, and subway train). The ticket has to be validated any time the user boards a public mean of transport, both to begin and continue the trip. In some metro stations ticket validation is also needed to open the exit turnstiles. In general, to validate paper tickets, the user has to insert them into the validator integrated into

the metro turnstiles or located on board on buses, trolleybus, and trams, or located at the train stations. The validator stamps the date and expiration time on it, making it valid for the use, and returns it to the customer. The user has to insert the ticket according to a precise pre-defined direction. To validate tickets and pass loaded on contactless smartcards the user has to tap it on one of the contactless smart card readers available on board of surface public transport means, at railroad train stations or integrated into the metro turnstiles. The area where to place the ticket is in general demarcated by different shapes and colors on the validator surface. A similar technology is adopted for the validation of e-ticket through the mobile app provided by the carrier, since it uses the NFC technology. However, to travel on the subway and validate the e-ticket by smartphone, the user has to access the mobile app provided by the carrier and select a purchased e-ticket to make the mobile app generating a QR Code. Then the user has to approach this code displayed on his/her smartphone to the optical reader placed on the subway turnstiles to validate the e-ticket. Otherwise, if the user owns a NFC-enabled smartphone, once generated the QR Code, he/she has to place the smartphone near to the reader integrated into the turnstile to validate the e-ticket. Lastly, to travel on the surface public transport means and validate the e-ticket by smartphone, before boarding the mean the user has to access the mobile app provided by the carrier and select a purchased e-ticket to make the mobile app valid for the time allowed by the purchased ticket, starting from that moment. In any case, the user may be asked by a ticket inspector of the carrier to show the validated ticket.

5. *Ride.* At this stage the user is on board. If the journey variables do not change, the user requires to know only a few more details, mostly: at which stop the vehicle currently is (to know when he/she has to get off), how long it will take to get to the destination, which connections are available. Instead, if anything changes, the user needs to recalculate the route and maybe choose other options. In both cases, these needs have already been discussed in the previous stages, i.e. "access to real time information" and "trip planning". However, there is a major difference regarding the environmental conditions: the user is no longer at home, or at least standing firmly on the ground; now he/she is on a vehicle, moving towards the destination. Decisions must be taken within seconds, and this makes some tools (e.g. paper maps, or slow loading websites) less efficient. To overcome these problem, at this stage other tools that let users access real time information are often available: led displays showing the next stop name, descriptive acoustic messages, screens that supply a set of useful tips. Generally, these tools are always non-interactive, but provide the user with effective and quick information.

5 Reformulating the Public Transport Service According to the Transgenerational Design Approach

In this section the authors reformulate the stages described in the previous paragraph, trying to give some indications that meet the needs of a larger part of city users. As in the previous section, the focus is not on the whole user experience, but only on the user interaction with the ICT related to the service. In fact, the authors sustain that a wider number of people categories has been increasingly assimilating the idea that technologies may support several types of activities (including the use of the public transport services). Concerning the digital devices, both personal (e.g. smartphones and tablets) and non-personal ones (e.g. digital signage and interactive kiosks), it is important to consider during all the stages of the traveller's journey the accessibility issues related to the possible hearing, mobility, visual, and physical impairments and the usability requirements related to the interactive systems. In effect, a good design of the user interfaces of interactive systems gives the elderly a greater control of their daily activities, making them more active and consequently more willing to opt for new habits [23]. Following, the authors detail the discussed stages, indicating some specific elements that could be implemented or changed in order to improve the public transportation service, according to the transgenerational design approach.

1. *Trip Planning*. At this stage, the users need to know all the different travel options, by choosing the public transport means that most meet their desires. For this reason, the authors propose to improve the structure of the different applications helping the user to do the right choice. In the previous paragraph the authors showed the presence of different travel options (e.g. the propensity for walking, the time shift, the duration of the ride, etc.). Here, in addition, they propose the implementation of more options helping users to identify their better travel solution. A possible proposal is the possibility to choose a public transport means with specific characteristics (e.g. the presence of wheelchair ramps). Another fundamental aspect of the service is the personalization of the experience, as it helps the user to stay focused on his/her objective. In detail, the user, after the identification of the route to follow, should receive only the information he/she needs during his/her specific journey, omitting the data that are not useful for him/her. An example is the use of maps that only put in evidence the elements the user needs most, providing him/her a support for the orientation.

2. *Ticket Purchase*. For this stage the authors propose to consistently design the whole ticket purchase through the different channels. By this way the digital interaction (e.g. the graphical interfaces, the navigation path, etc.) and the physical one (e.g. the design of the automatic vending machines, etc.), should be rethought seamless by facilitating the transition from online and offline or avoiding it when useless. For this reason, the authors suggest that this process should be characterized by a clear explanation of the process steps and by a wealth of information. In doing that, also specific people categories, as elderly, that need more information during and after the purchasing process (e.g. price comparison, travel opportunities, final report, etc.) [27], are encouraged to use these services. Specific improvements are necessary for the automatic vending machines and the mobile app. On the one hand, the first should provide multi-sensory aids and feedbacks (e.g. acoustic messages and selective lighting) to facilitate the interaction for all the users, filling a gap both of abilities and competences. Moreover, the context of use of the vending machines should be chosen or specifically designed to avoid confusing and noisy situations, as well as crowded environments, in order to allow all the users to accomplish the ticket purchasing process with serenity and concentration. On the other hand, the interaction with the smartphone and the mobile app may probably require a familiarity with

these kinds of systems by the user, so it could be useful to provide at the first use an app walkthrough to explain functionalities or just some intuitive hints that appear during the use of the app. Regarding the ticket, there are some practical advantages to prefer the rechargeable card rather than the paper ticket, as the former is: robust, replaceable, easy to validate, reusable. Furthermore, the rechargeable card, as unique material support, enables the users to focus only on a single, recognizable item, avoiding confusion.

3. *Access to real time information*. During this stage it is important to reduce the gap of information that could bring, not only the user to make wrong choices, but also to be irritated, frustrated, and nervous, mainly while exploring little-known spaces. This element is particularly true for the elderly, who feel anxiety when they are in new places or in unfamiliar situations [22]. So, in these cases the user should not only be sure that the path he/she is following is the right one, but also that he/she is receiving real time information and services only related to the route he/she has to do. In fact, it could be useful that the system automatically changes on the basis of the stages of the journey. A push-oriented approach facilitates this kind of interaction between the user and the needed information; the use of personal devices (e.g. smartphone, tablet, etc.) allows for better personalizing the experience. An example: when the user is waiting for the bus, he/she can receive information, not only related to the time arrival, but also to the characteristics of the mean (e.g. crowding, spaces and services on board, presence of wheelchair ramps, etc.). At the same time, the use of digital screens on board could be very useful by giving people detailed information (e.g. time of arrival at the different stops).

4. *Ticket Validation*. The validation of the e-tickets, both through smartphones and contactless smart cards, requires the use of technological systems that may be less known by the elderly. However, even if paper tickets are more used, the possession of the e-tickets could be over time more useful for the elderly. This kind of ticket can be more immediate, making the validation process faster and efficient. In fact, it requires a lower cognitive effort concerning the needed position of the ticket for the validation operations, since the user has only to place the ticket near the contactless reader. Anyway, a good communication of these operations, for example by realizing tutorials, is necessary. Regarding that, if nowadays the elderly are more ready to validate e-tickets through a smart card (since it is a more immediate tool), they are probably less ready to validate them through the smartphone that could be more complex in the mode of operation. The authors sustain that to allow the elderly to familiarize with an e-ticket on the smartphone some elements are required, for example the possibility to visualize the ticket in a version that resembles the paper ticket. Letting the elderly familiarize with these technologies is important for the future adoption of digital services. Moreover, the reproduction of the behaviour of other people that already use these services can be really helpful. Finally, also the product design and the user interfaces of the validators are important elements to consider. For example, the "affordance" of the contactless validator is important, as the user needs to understand where to exactly place the ticket.

5. *Ride*. As stated above, the main problem at the ride stage is represented by the changing surrounding conditions. In fact, the vehicles are on the move and so the

users might easily miss their stop if not properly addressed. As the authors said, personal tools such as smartphones can help them, thanks to localization services and other additional features, but users should not exclusively rely on those, since they could stop working right in time of need, due to lack of data connection, low battery or overuse. For this reason, as stated, it is important that users can count on other tools, which have to be reliable, sharable, designed on purpose to satisfy user needs whenever occur. For example, acoustic messages could inform about the following stop with proper anticipation, so that users can have time enough to figure out it is the right stop, prepare and get off, even if they are inattentive, slow or squeezed in a crowded vehicle. On board screens are nowadays scarcely used to offer information and they end up being mainly advertising spaces. Instead, they could be used to provide real time information about the localization of the vehicle (so that the user can always know where he/she is) and about surrounding activities and points of interest.

6   Conclusion

In this paper the authors have dealt with the re-design of a public transport service according to the transgenerational design approach, focusing on technological issues. In fact, the increasing presence of innovative technologies, e.g. ICTs, in the public services leads to consider the effective access required to them by all the people categories. In general, the principles that orient the design of digital applications according to the transgenerational design approach are: minimizing the effort for each task, accommodating rather than discriminating, using multiple service solutions, personalizing the experience, designing a seamless experience, clearly explaining all the steps of the process, reducing the gaps of information. Furthermore, to facilitate the technology adoption also by the elderly a good communication that points out the advantages and the benefits of these solutions is needed. This is a key point to consider, since it really induces the change in the older adult's habits.

However, in order to allow a real inclusion it is necessary to redesign all the human experience, also improving the other elements of the public transport service (e.g. the spaces, the products, etc.) that may still present hindrances for the older part of the population. For example, an important element to take into account is the signage of the urban spaces, and especially that of the spaces related to the public transportation. In this paper the authors mostly focus on the influence of technologies on the whole experience, postponing this analysis to a large-scale design process with the users. In effect, in redesigning the overall human experience, it is necessary to understand the people needs, especially the elderly ones, really engaging them in the design process. So, in the future work the authors are going to apply the human-centered design methodologies in order to identify how people act in the urban environment and what solutions better meet their needs and desires.

References

1. Anthopoulos, L.G.: Understanding the smart city domain: a literature review. In: Bolivar, M.P. (ed.) Transforming City Governments for Successful Smart Cities. Public Administration and Information Technology Series: New York, vol. 8, pp. 9–21. Springer International Publishing, New York (2015)
2. Cocchia, A.: Smart and digital city: a systematic literature review. In: Dameri, R.P., Rosenthal-Sabroux, C. (eds.) Smart City: How to Create Public and Economic Value with High Technology in Urban Space. Progress in IS Series, pp. 13–43. Springer International Publishing, New York (2014)
3. Schaffers, H., Komninos, N., Pallot, M., Trousse, B., Nilsson, M., Oliveira, A.: Smart cities and the future internet: towards cooperation frameworks for open innovation. In: Domingue, J., et al. (eds.) The Future Internet. LNCS, vol. 6656, pp. 431–446. Springer, Heidelberg (2011)
4. Anttiroiko, A., Valkama, P., Bailey, S.J.: Smart cities in the new service economy: building platforms for smart services. AI Soc. 29(3), 323–334 (2014)
5. Kitchin, R.: The real-time city? Big data and smart urbanism. GeoJournal 79(1), 1–14 (2014)
6. Rogers, E.M.: Diffusion of innovations. Simon and Schuster, New York (2010)
7. Hernandez-Encuentra, E., Pousada, M., Gómez-Zúñiga, B.: ICT and older people: beyond usability. Educ. Gerontol. 35(3), 226–245 (2009)
8. Hanson, V.L.: Influencing technology adoption by older adults. Interact. Comput. 22(6), 502–509 (2010)
9. Magnusson, L., Hanson, E., Borg, M.: A literature review study of information and communication technology as a support for frail older people living at home and their family carers. Technol. Disabil. 16(4), 223–235 (2004)
10. Milligan, C.: There's No Place Like Home: Place and Care in an Ageing Society. Ashgate Publishing Ltd., Farnham (2012)
11. Blaschke, C.M., Freddolino, P.P., Mullen, E.E.: Ageing and technology: a review of the research literature. Br. J. Soc. Work 39(4), 641–656 (2009)
12. Augusto, J.C., Nakashima, H., Aghajan, H.: Ambient intelligence and smart environments: a state of the art. In: Nakashima, H., Aghajan, H., Augusto, J.C. (eds.) Handbook of Ambient Intelligence and Smart Environments, pp. 3–31. Springer, US (2010)
13. Acebillo, J.: UrbAging: designing urban space for an ageing society. In: NFP 54, SNF, Bern (2009)
14. LoukaitouSideris, A., LevyStorms, L., Brozen, M.: Placemaking for an Aging Population: Guidelines for Senior-Friendly Parks. UCLA Lewis Center for Regional Policy Studies, Los Angeles (2014)
15. Williams, K.: Spatial planning, urban form and sustainable transport: an introduction. In: Williams, K. (ed.) Spatial Planning, Urban Form and Sustainable Transport, pp. 1–13. Ashgate Publishing Ltd., Aldershot (2005)
16. Vigoda, E.: From responsiveness to collaboration: Governance, citizens, and the next generation of public administration. Pub. Adm. Rev. 62(5), 527–540 (2002)
17. Gilhooly, M., Hamilton, K., O'Neill, M., Gow, J., Webster, N., Pike, F.: Transport and ageing: extending quality of life via public and private transport. In: ESRC Research Findings from the Growing Older Programme 16. Economic and Social Research Council Swindon, Wiltshire (2003)
18. Eurostat: Eurostat Regional Yearbook 2014. Publications Office of the European Union, Luxembourg (2014)

19. Bekiaris, E., Panou, M., Mousadakou, A.: Elderly and disabled travelers needs in infomobility services. In: Stephanidis, C. (ed.) HCI 2007. LNCS, vol. 4554, pp. 853–860. Springer, Heidelberg (2007)
20. Fischer, G., Sullivan J.F.: Human-centered public transportation systems for persons with cognitive disabilities. In: Proceedings of the Seventh Participatory Design Conference, Malmö, Sweden, June 23–25, pp. 194–198 (2002)
21. Tranter, R.T., Slater, R., Vaughan, N.: Barriers to mobility: physically disabled and frail elderly people in their local outdoor environment. Int. J. Rehabil. Res. 14(4), 303–312 (1991)
22. Phillips, J., Walford, N., Hockey, A., Foreman, N., Lewis, M.: Older people and outdoor environments: pedestrian anxieties and barriers in the use of familiar and unfamiliar spaces. Geoforum 47, 113–124 (2013)
23. Hanson, J.: The Inclusive City, What Active Ageing Might Mean for Urban Design, pp. 143–145. University College, London (2002)
24. Parker, C.J., May, A., Mitchell, V., Burrows, A.: Capturing volunteered information for inclusive service design: potential benefits and challenges. Des. J. 16(2), 197–218 (2013)
25. Bogren, L., Fallman, D., Henje, C.: User-centered inclusive design: making public transport accessible. In: International Conference on Inclusive Design–Royal College of Art, London, UK (2009)
26. Sayago, S., Sloan, D., Blat, J.: Everyday use of computer-mediated communication tools and its evolution over time: an ethnographical study with older people. Interact. Comput. 23(5), 543–554 (2011)
27. Subasi, Ö., Leitner, M., Hoeller, N., Geven, A., Tscheligi, M.: Designing accessible experiences for older users: user requirement analysis for a railway ticketing portal. Univ. Access Inf. Soc. 10(4), 391–402 (2011)
28. Grotenhuis, J.W., Wiegmans, B.W., Rietveld, P.: The desired quality of integrated multimodal travel information in public transport: customer needs for time and effort savings. Transp. Policy 14(1), 27–38 (2007)
29. Pirkl, J.J.: Transgenerational Design: Products for an Aging Population. Van Nostrand Reinhold Company, New York (1994)
30. Pirkl, J.J., Babic, A.L.: Guidelines and Strategies for Designing Transgenerational Products: A Resource Manual for Industrial Design Professionals. Copley Publishing, Acton, Massachusetts (1988)
31. Home of Transgenerational Design Matters. http://www.transgenerational.org/
32. Cagan, J., Craig, M.V.: Creating Breakthrough Products: Innovation from Product Planning to Program Approval. FT Press, NJ (2002)
33. Rogers, W.A., Fisk, A.D.: Toward a psychological science of advanced technology design for older adults. J. Gerontol. Ser. B: Psychol. Sci. Soc. Sci. 65(6), 645–653 (2010)
34. World Health Organization, http://www.who.int
35. Pernice, K., Estes, J., Nielsen, J.: Senior Citizens (Ages 65 and older) on the Web. Nielsen Norman Group (2013)

Transportation Accessibility Assessment of Critical Emergency Facilities: Aging Population-Focused Case Studies in Florida

Ayberk Kocatepe[1], Eren Erman Ozguven[1(✉)], Hidayet Ozel[1],
Mark W. Horner[2], and Ren Moses[1]

[1] Department of Civil and Environmental Engineering,
Florida A&M-Florida State University College of Engineering, Tallahassee, FL, USA
eozguven@fsu.edu
[2] Department of Geography, Florida State University, Tallahassee, FL, USA

Abstract. Over the last two decades, the task of providing transportation accessibility for aging people has been a growing concern as that population is rapidly expanding. From this standpoint, serious challenges arise when we consider ensuring aging people's transportation-based accessibility to critical emergency facilities such as hurricane shelters. An efficient strategy to address this problem involves using Geographical Information Systems (GIS)-based tools in order to evaluate the available transportation network in conjunction with the spatial distribution of aging people, and critical emergency facilities, plus regional traffic characteristics. This study develops a Geographical Information Systems (GIS)-based methodology to measure and assess the transportation accessibility of these critical facilities through a diverse set of case study applications in the State of Florida. Within this evaluation, spatially detailed county-based accessibility scores are calculated with respect to designated hurricane shelters (both regular and special needs shelters) using both static and dynamic travel times between population block groups and critical facilities. Because aging of the Baby Boom generation (people born between 1946 and 1964) is expected to produce a 79 % increase in the number of people over the age of 65 in the next two decades, the proposed methodology and case studies can inform transportation agencies' efforts to develop efficient aging-focused transportation and accessibility plans.

Keywords: Transportation accessibility · Aging populations · Geographic information systems

1 Introduction

Due to the recently expanding aging population in the U.S., providing transportation accessibility for aging people has become a growing concern. As such, aging people's transportation accessibility to critical emergency facilities such as hurricane shelters represents a serious challenge. This challenge is exacerbated by their cognitive, physical, mental, emotional and health limitations that can affect their driving and route finding skills, especially in the aftermath of extreme events such as hurricanes. This problem

© Springer International Publishing Switzerland 2016
J. Zhou and G. Salvendy (Eds.): ITAP 2016, Part II, LNCS 9755, pp. 407–416, 2016.
DOI: 10.1007/978-3-319-39949-2_39

becomes even more complex for the State of Florida, which is ranked as second highest nationally for having 17.34 % of the population being 65 years or older [1]. One strategy to address these challenges involves the use of GIS-based tools. These tools can be used to assess the performance of the transportation network in conjunction with the spatial distributions of aging people (65+) and critical emergency facilities.

Transportation accessibility has been studied with a focus on different facilities in the literature; from urban and commercial facilities such as grocery stores and parks, to hospitals and assisted living facilities. Among these studies, accessibility to urban parks for the general populations has been studied in [2, 3] whereas sports centers, schools and older population-oriented markets were investigated in order to assess their accessibility to the public in [4]. GIS has also been used extensively in order to measure the accessibility of universities [5], health facilities [6], multi-modal facilities [7], and supermarkets [8, 9]. Several researchers have recognized the need of studying accessibility with respect to aging populations. In [10], the accessibility of libraries, parks and hospitals was assessed for both pedestrians and drivers in Florida based on the spatial structure of social, professional, and business opportunities. In another study, the accessibility of nursing facilities was studied in the aftermath of the Los Angeles Northridge Earthquake in [11]. Several previous studies analyzed the mobility and transportation needs of the aging population [12–16]. Please see [7] for a more detailed review on the transportation accessibility of aging populations to the multi-modal facilities, and see [17] for a more detailed discussion on the emergency accessibility and mobility needs of aging populations. To the authors' knowledge, there are no studies that focus on the transportation accessibility of emergency shelters with a focus on aging populations, and that use dynamic travel times to estimate potential accessibility.

This study utilizes a Geographical Information Systems (GIS)-based methodology, first developed in [7], to measure and assess the transportation accessibility of critical emergency facilities such as shelters through a diverse set of case study applications in the State of Florida. Within this evaluation, spatially detailed county-based accessibility scores are calculated with respect to designated hurricane shelters (regular shelters as well as special needs shelters –SPNS- are included) using both static and dynamic travel times between population block groups and critical facilities. This is followed by a small scale case study application presented for the Panama City area, using Bay County of Florida. This application focuses on the accessibility of critical facilities such as airports, bus stations and shelters that can be critical in the aftermath of an extreme event such as a hurricane. Because aging of the Baby Boom generation is expected to produce a 79 % increase in the number of people over the age of 65 in the next two decades, the proposed methodology can inform transportation agencies' efforts to develop efficient aging-focused transportation and accessibility strategies.

2   Methodology

This sections describes the steps of our GIS-based methodology (Please refer to [7] for more detail). The first step focuses on the spatial distributions of aging populations living in the State of Florida using available resources such as U.S. Census [1] (Fig. 1). As of

2010, the State of Florida consists of 3,259,602 people over 65 years (approximately 17.33 % of the total population), which makes about one in every six Floridian 65 years and older. Following this evaluation, the following data components are determined (Fig. 2): (a) origins (the geometric centroids of the U.S. Census population block groups), (b) destinations (the critical emergency facility locations including the American Red Cross (ARC)-approved regular and special needs (SPNS) shelters), and (c) the roadway network of Florida, with 127,343 arcs and 53,333 nodes, based on the Florida Standard Urban Transportation Model Structure (FSUTMS) of the Florida Department of Transportation (FDOT) [18]. Locations of the ARC-approved regular and SPNS shelters are obtained from the 2014 Florida Statewide Emergency Shelter Plan [19].

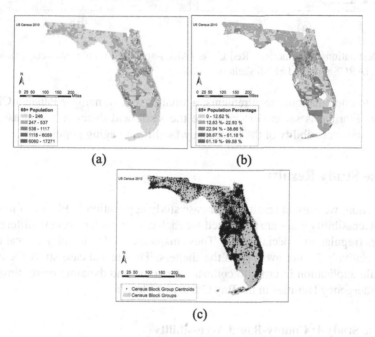

Fig. 1. Population demographics of Florida (a) 65+ population, (b) 65+ population percentage, (c) Population block group centroids (origins)

Between each population block group centroid and the closest facility of interest, identified by ArcGIS, the least cost path is determined. That is, each origin-destination (O-D) pair is assigned a travel cost in terms of different values: (a) roadway distance in miles, (b) free flow travel time in minutes, which represents the uncongested traffic conditions, (c) static congested travel time in minutes, and (d) dynamic congested travel time in minutes, which incorporates the effects of queues and delays (this is only performed for the second case study). Using the first three cost figures, emergency shelter transportation accessibility scores for each population block group are calculated for the whole State of Florida. Using these scores, aging population-weighted average accessibility scores of counties to ARC-approved regular and SPNS shelters are calculated. Since it would be almost impossible to obtain the dynamic travel times for the whole

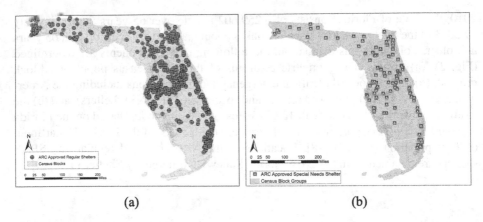

(a)   (b)

Fig. 2. Destinations (a) American Red Cross (ARC)-approved regular shelters, (b) American Red Cross (ARC)-approved SPNS shelters

state due to computational requirements, a smaller region, namely Panama City, Bay County of Florida, is selected to compare the static and dynamic traffic assignment results for the accessibility of the emergency facilities to aging populations.

3   Case Study Results

In this section, we present results of our case study application in Florida. First, aging-focused accessibility maps are illustrated for each county with respect to different types of shelters (regular and special needs). These maps are used to identify critical counties that are relatively further away from the shelters. The second case study focuses on a small scale application in order to compare the static and dynamic travel times to the critical emergency facilities in the Bay County of Florida.

3.1   Case Study 1: County-Based Accessibility

Population block group based accessibility measures are used to calculate the weighted average travel costs for each county in Florida, as described extensively per the methodology in [7]. Results are used to compare and rank the counties to point how accessible the counties are. Equation (1) is performed for each type of shelter with the different travel cost types. The weighted county accessibility formula, derived in [7], is as follows:

$$County\ weighted\ average\ travel\ cost = \frac{\sum_{i=1}^{n}\left(cost_i * Pop_{65-i}\right)}{\sum_{i=1}^{n}\left(Pop_{65-i}\right)} \tag{1}$$

where $cost_i$ is the travel cost (distance or time) at population block group "i" to the closest shelter, and Pop_{65-i} is the 65+ population living in the population block group "i". Results are presented in Fig. 3 visually where those counties that have the least accessibility are shown as red. Instead of presenting numerical scores for each county, the five most and least accessible counties to the shelters are shown in Table 1. We note that this case study only includes the static congested travel times due to the excessive computational requirements while assigning the traffic dynamically on the whole Florida roadway network. Dynamic traffic assignment results are presented in the second case study with a small scale application. Figure 3 and Table 1 show that Miami-Dade and Escambia counties stand out as the most accessible counties to the ARC-approved regular shelters although the accessibility of Miami-Dade decreases when congestion is experienced on the network. The five least accessible counties to the ARC-approved regular shelters are Monroe, Franklin, Collier, Lee and Gulf counties (Note that these counties are home to more than 50,000 aging people). Upgrading the locally planned shelters with respect to ARC standards will definitely improve the accessibility for these counties. On the other hand, Monroe County and Franklin County, with the overall lowest accessibility scores, are the least accessible counties to ARC-approved SPNS shelters whereas Miami-Dade County, the most urban county in Florida, stands out as the most accessible county. Repurposing regular shelters in order to serve the aging as well as special needs populations could be a viable option to increase the transportation accessibility for Monroe and Franklin Counties.

3.2   Case Study 2: Bay County of Florida

The focus area considered in this case study includes one of the largest cities of District 3, namely Panama City, which is located in Bay County. In addition to focusing on the accessibility of shelters, this case study also includes the emergency transportation accessibility of the Northwest Florida Beaches International Airport and the Greyhound bus station located in the Downtown Panama City. Based on the evaluation of the available data, Fig. 4 shows the major roadways and the aging population by block group as well as the locations of the airport, Greyhound bus station, the SPNS emergency shelter, and the only regular shelter outside the affected region. Note that the shaded parts of the maps of Fig. 4a and b show the highest concentration of the total aging populations and aging people living independently, respectively. Please note that the only special needs (SPNS) shelter and airport (Northwest Florida Beaches International Airport) available are located to the far north of the Downtown Panama City, which makes it important to assess the emergency accessibility of these facilities with respect to aging populations living in the downtown Panama City. Due to space limitations, only aging people living independently are considered for this case study (the aging living independently population block group centroids are shown as green dots in Fig. 4). For the purposes of this paper, airport and bus station accessibility scenarios are designed based on non-emergency traffic conditions, and do not consider the closure of any roadway and/or bridge. On the other hand, regular shelter and SPNS shelter scenarios focus on the emergency evacuation of the aging population living independently in Panama City, with closures of the north-bound bridges as well as including the background traffic during the evacuation.

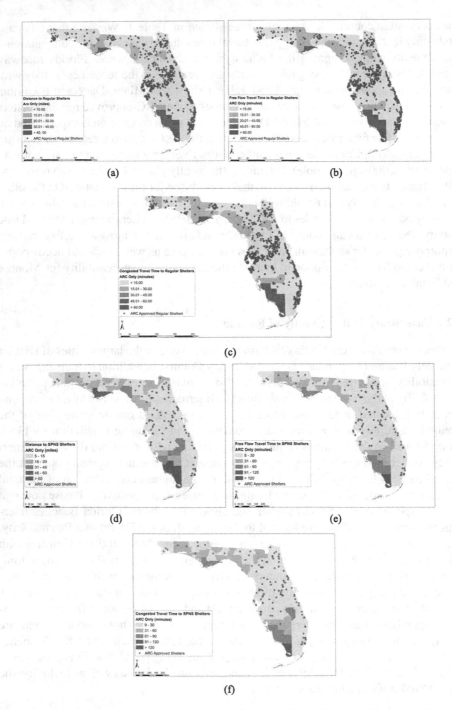

Fig. 3. Aging population-based county accessibility maps for distance, free flow and static congested travel times: (a, b, c) ARC-approved regular shelters, (d, e, f) ARC-approved special needs shelters

Table 1. Aging population-based accessibility of Florida Counties with respect to ARC-approved regular shelters and ARC-approved SPNS shelters.

	FLORIDA COUNTIES					
	FIVE MOST ACCESSIBLE			FIVE LEAST ACCESSIBLE		
ACCESSIBILITY	Weighted Average Distance (miles)	Weighted Average Free Flow Travel Time (minutes)	Weighted Average Static Congested Travel Time (minutes)	Weighted Average Distance (miles)	Weighted Average Free Flow Travel Time (minutes)	Weighted Average Static Congested Travel Time (minutes)
REGULAR SHELTERS	Escambia	Escambia	Escambia	Monroe	Monroe	Monroe
	Miami-Dade	Miami-Dade	Broward	Franklin	Franklin	Franklin
	Seminole	Seminole	Seminole	Collier	Collier	Collier
	Broward	Broward	Orange	Lee	Lee	Lee
	Orange	Orange	Miami-Dade	Gulf	Gulf	Gulf
SPNS SHELTERS	Seminole	Miami-Dade	Miami-Dade	Monroe	Monroe	Monroe
	Miami-Dade	Seminole	Alachua	Collier	Franklin	Franklin
	Alachua	Alachua	Hernando	Franklin	Collier	Collier
	Hernando	Duval	Osceola	Gulf	Gulf	Gulf
	Volusia	Hernando	St.Lucie	Lee	Lee	Lee

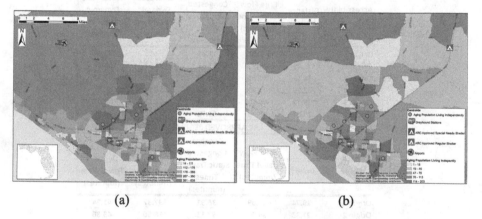

(a)   (b)

Fig. 4. GIS-based representation of Panama City/Bay County with the destinations (airport, bus station and SPNS shelter) and origins (population block group centroids for aging people living independently) (a) Total aging populations, (b) Aging people living independently

Overall results can be seen in Table 2 with different cost measures: distance, free flow travel time, static congested travel time, and dynamic congested travel times. From an emergency management perspective, it is critical to observe the best and worst case scenarios during the entire evacuation period, presented by two different dynamic congested travel times in Table 2 (calculated based on different evacuation start times). Table 2 indicates that accessibility to the regular shelter, airport and SPNS shelter, in terms of travel time, can increase upto 5, 9 and 17 min more for the selected origins, respectively. This is due to the delays and queues experienced on the transportation network, which cannot be measured by static but dynamic traffic assignment. Travel times also increase when the evacuation starts during the peak hours (presented by the worst case dynamic travel times). This may indicate the need to avoid the peak hours for evacuation purposes, since the transportation accessibility gets relatively reduced.

Table 2. Aging population-based accessibility of 6 Panama City origins with respect to airport, Greyhound bus station, ARC-approved regular shelters, and ARC-approved SPNS shelter.

	AIRPORT				GREYHOUND BUS STATION			
Accessibility	Distance (miles)	Free Flow Travel Time (minutes)	Average Congested Static Travel Times (minutes)	Average Congested Dynamic Travel Time (minutes)	Distance (miles)	Free Flow Travel Time (minutes)	Average Congested Static Travel Times (minutes)	Average Congested Dynamic Travel Time (minutes)
Origin 1	27.26	41.39	48.63	49.73	6.24	10.10	11.32	11.76
Origin 2	19.79	28.48	35.13	36.56	1.77	3.01	3.37	3.75
Origin 3	18.76	27.13	34.57	35.72	3.54	6.06	6.69	7.21
Origin 4	19.36	32.66	35.70	40.83	3.58	5.88	6.57	8.24
Origin 5	19.86	34.59	35.79	41.57	4.55	7.49	8.24	9.06
Origin 6	18.32	33.08	33.55	40.87	8.63	13.79	14.37	14.43

	ARC APPROVED SPECIAL NEEDS SHELTER				
Accessibility	Distance (miles)	Free Flow Travel Time (minutes)	Average Congested Static Travel Times (minutes)	Best Case Dynamic Travel Time (minutes)	Worst Case Dynamic Travel Time (minutes)
Origin 1	31.27	47.91	51.88	52.33	55.84
Origin 2	33.49	49.37	53.52	53.57	58.46
Origin 3	34.09	50.61	55.22	57.02	67.31
Origin 4	32.20	47.60	49.42	52.57	57.90
Origin 5	29.72	44.50	45.26	48.11	52.41
Origin 6	25.57	38.90	39.78	43.00	44.50

	ARC APPROVED REGULAR SHELTER				
Accessibility	Distance (miles)	Free Flow Travel Time (minutes)	Average Congested Static Travel Times (minutes)	Best Case Dynamic Travel Time (minutes)	Worst Case Dynamic Travel Time (minutes)
Origin 1	19.74	32.09	36.91	37.32	41.24
Origin 2	21.33	34.29	37.13	38.56	43.86
Origin 3	22.62	37.44	40.54	42.01	52.71
Origin 4	20.11	32.45	35.14	37.56	43.3
Origin 5	17.94	29.3	31.73	33.1	37.81
Origin 6	14.4	24.43	26.45	29.49	28.4

4   Conclusions and Future Work

This study measures and assesses the transportation accessibility of critical emergency facilities through a set of spatial population characteristics and detail travel costs. Different travel cost measures (distance, free flow travel time, and static and dynamic congested travel times) are used to evaluate the accessibility of the counties with respect to these critical emergency facilities such as shelters. Worst and best accessible counties are ranked and presented in tabular format as well as visually with GIS-based maps. Following this, a small-scale emergency transportation accessibility analysis is presented via a case study application developed for Bay County of Florida. This analysis demonstrates the applicability of transportation planning and simulation models for assessing the emergency accessibility provided to aging populations due to extreme events such as hurricanes. The results of this study can be implemented by agencies and stakeholders to help increase the mobility of the aging populations by better planning of future critical facility locations, and by improving knowledge of the emergency and non-emergency transportation accessibility of counties in Florida.

This study currently focuses only on the travel time on roadways; however, waiting and dwelling times can also be critical, and should be added to the travel time costs while calculating the accessibility scores. In future work, this study can be extended to other critical facilities such as hospitals and the local shelters that do not meet the standards of the American Red Cross [20] as well as other vulnerable populations including mobile home residents and seasonal populations. In order to fully support emergency evacuation plans and policies, additional hypothetical scenarios can be developed based on changing the modeling parameters such as the demand loading time, the departure window, and considering different transit alternatives.

Acknowledgments. This project was supported by United States Department of Transportation grant DTRT13-G-UTC42, and administered by the Center for Accessibility and Safety for an Aging Population (ASAP) at the Florida State University (FSU), Florida A&M University (FAMU), and University of North Florida (UNF). We also thank the Florida Department of Transportation for providing the roadway data. The opinions, results, and findings expressed in this manuscript are those of the authors and do not necessarily represent the views of the United States Department of Transportation, The Florida Department of Transportation, The Center for Accessibility and Safety for an Aging Population, the Florida State University, the Florida A&M University, or the University of North Florida.

References

1. US Census Bureau Website: http://www.census.gov
2. Omer, I.: Evaluating accessibility using house-level data: a spatial equity perspective. Comput. Environ. Urban Syst. **30**, 254–274 (2006)
3. Chang, H.S., Liao, C.H.: Exploring an integrated method for measuring the relative spatial equity in public facilities in the context of urban parks. Cities **28**, 361–371 (2011)
4. Tsou, K.W., Hung, Y.T., Chang, Y.L.: An accessibility-based integrated measure of relative spatial equity in urban public facilities. Cities **22**, 424–435 (2005)
5. Yao, X., Thill, J.C.: How far is too far? - a statistical approach to context-contingent proximity modeling. Trans. GIS **9**, 157–178 (2005)
6. Islam, M.S., Aktar, S.: Measuring physical accessibility to health facilities-a case study on Khulna City. World health & population **12**, 33–41 (2011)
7. Ozel, H., Ozguven, E.E., Kocatepe, A., Horner, M.W.: An aging population-focused accessibility assessment of multi-modal facilities, in Florida, In: 95th Transportation Research Board Conference, Washington, D.C. (2016)
8. Widener, M.J., Steven, F., Tijins, N., Horner, M.W.: Using urban commuting data to calculate a spatiotemporal accessibility measure for food environment studies. Health Place **21**, 1–9 (2013)

9. Widener, M.J., Steven, F., Tijins, N., Horner, M.W.: Spatiotemporal accessibility to supermarkets using public transit: an interaction potential approach in Cincinnati, Ohio. Transp. Res. Board **42**, 72–83 (2014). Board 93rd Annual Meeting Compendium of Papers
10. Horner, M.W., Duncan, M., Wood, B., Valdez-Torres, J., Stansbury, C.: Do aging populations have differential accessibility to activities? Analyzing the spatial structure of social, professional, and business opportunities. Travel Behav. Soc. **2**, 182–191 (2015)
11. Saliba, D., Buchanan, J., Kington, R.S.: Function and response of nursing facilities during community disaster. Am. J. Public Health **94**, 1436–1441 (2004)
12. Metz, D.H.: Mobility of older people and their quality of life. Transp. Policy **7**, 149–152 (2000)
13. Rosenbloom S.: The Mobility Needs of Older Americans: Implications for Transportation Reauthorization, The Brookings Institution Series on Transportation Reform, pp. 1–20 (2003).   http://www.brookings.edu/~/media/research/files/reports/2003/7/transportation-rosenbloom/20030807_rosenbloom.pdf
14. Paez, A., Mercado, R.G., Farber, S., Morency, C., Roorda, M.: Accessibility to health care facilities in montreal island: an application of relative accessibility indicators from the perspective of senior and non-senior residents. Int. J. Health Geograph. **9**, 52 (2010)
15. Love, D., Lindquist, P.: The geographical accessibility of hospitals to the aged: a geographic information systems analysis within illinois. Health Serv. Res. **29**, 629–651 (1995)
16. Mowen, A., Orsega-Smith, E., Payne, L., Ainsworth, B., Godbey, G.: The role of park proximity and social support in shaping park visitation, physical activity, and perceived health among older adults. J. Phys. Act. Health **4**, 167–179 (2007)
17. Ozguven, E.E., Horner, M.W., Kocatepe, A., Marcelin, J.M., Abdelrazig, Y., Sando, T., Moses, R.: Metadata-based needs assessment for emergency transportation operations with a focus on an aging population: a case study in Florida. Transp. Rev. **36**, 383–412 (2015). http://www.tandfonline.com/doi/full/10.1080/01441647.2015.1082516. Published online (2015)
18. Florida Transportation Modeling Website (2016). http://www.fsutmsonline.net/
19. Florida Geographic Data Library (2016). http://www.fgdl.org/metadataexplorer/explorer.jsp
20. Florida Division of Emergency Management: Florida Statewide Emergency Shelter Plan (2016). http://www.floridadisaster.org/Response/engineers/SESPlans/2014SESPlan/documents/0%20-%202014-SESP-Complete%20Document%20FINAL.pdf

The Flashing Right Turn Signal with Pedestrian Indication: A Human Factors Study to Assess Driver Comprehension

Nelson A. Roque[✉], Walter R. Boot, Neil Charness, Kimberly Barajas,
Jared Dirghalli, and Ainsley Mitchum

Department of Psychology, Florida State University, Tallahassee, FL, USA
{roque,boot,charness,barajas,
dirghalli,mitchum}@psy.fsu.edu

Abstract. Given the increased fatality risk of older pedestrians, and the large and growing older adult population in the United States and around the world, many countermeasures to ensure aging pedestrian safety have been explored (e.g., different types of crosswalk markings). The present study sought to investigate the potential of an experimental countermeasure, the flashing pedestrian indicator (FPI). This signal, intended for right-turning drivers, alternates between a yellow arrow and a pedestrian symbol when a pedestrian calls for a walk phase at a signalized intersection. The purpose of this signal is to cue right-turning drivers to the potential presence of a pedestrian, encourage scanning to the right for crossing pedestrians, and promote driver yielding behaviors. We conducted a study to gauge the comprehension of drivers who were naïve to the signal to explore if the FPI's intended message was understood. Participants were presented with scenarios depicting the FPI and other signal states and were asked the meaning of the observed signal (open-ended and multiple choice questions). Comprehension was tested across a range of age groups: younger (21–35 years), middle-aged (50–64), and older adult (65+) drivers. While in general the signal was understood, some participants were confused regarding the meaning of the FPI in certain situations. Potential positive effects of the FPI need to be weighed against potential confusion before any further recommendations can be made regarding the FPI as a potential countermeasure to assist with pedestrian crashes.

Keywords: Pedestrian safety · Transportation safety · Traffic signals · Older adults

1 Disclaimer

The opinions, findings and conclusions expressed in this publication are those of the authors and not necessarily those of the State of Florida Department of Transportation or the U. S. Department of Transportation.

© Springer International Publishing Switzerland 2016
J. Zhou and G. Salvendy (Eds.): ITAP 2016, Part II, LNCS 9755, pp. 417–427, 2016.
DOI: 10.1007/978-3-319-39949-2_40

2 Introduction

Pedestrian Crash Risk. According to data from the National Highway Traffic Safety Administration (NHTSA), in 2012, pedestrians represented 14 % of all traffic fatalities in the United States, an increase from 11 % in 2003 [1]. Unfortunately, older pedestrians are at greater risk compared to their younger counterparts. Nationally, the fatality rate of individuals aged 75 to 84 was 2.70 fatalities per 100,000 in the population in 2012, compared to a rate of 1.51 across all age groups. Fatality rates were especially elevated for male pedestrians 85 years of age or older (4.02). Increased risk is likely due to greater fragility (a crash that might injure a younger pedestrian may kill an older pedestrian) and slower walking speeds that increase exposure risk [2, 3]. Additionally, fear of falling may cause older pedestrians to both move more slowly and to attend to the ground rather than traffic around them while crossing [4]. Attempts to protect pedestrians from crashes by alerting drivers to their potential presence, as a result, are likely to differentially benefit older pedestrians (in addition to making the roadway safer for pedestrians of all ages).

Why Do Pedestrian Crashes Occur? A fundamental aspect of visual processing is that we can fail to notice seemingly obvious objects and events (such as a pedestrian entering the roadway) if we are not actively looking for them. This likely contributes in part to pedestrian crashes. The classic example is the experiment Simons and Chabris conducted in which participants were asked to watch a video depicting two teams of basketball players, one wearing white and the other wearing black [5]. Participants were asked to count the number of times the players dressed in white passed the ball. During this short video, a gorilla walked through the group of players, pounded its chest, and walked away, being fully visible for 5 s of the 75-second-long video. Surprisingly, 50 % of participants failed to notice this unusual event despite it being easily observed by anyone asked to look for the gorilla. Of particular note is that instances of "inattentional blindness" have been observed in observers who directly fixated the unexpected event with their eyes, suggesting the problem in this particular case is often not one of looking (scanning), but seeing. Inattentional blindness has been proposed as a contributing cause in crashes and is consistent with numerous reports of drivers reporting not having seen pedestrians before a crash. If observers can fail to notice extremely salient and unusual events, they can also fail to notice pedestrians. By alerting drivers that they should expect pedestrians, these instances of inattentional blindness will likely be reduced. Scanning, however, may play an important independent role. A driver turning right may be biased to scan left for vehicles [6], and insufficient scanning to the right puts pedestrians crossing to the right at risk of being struck while crossing. Countermeasures that encourage scanning for pedestrians and the expectation that pedestrians may be present are likely to decrease instances in which drivers fail to yield to an unnoticed pedestrian.

A Proposed Solution. The Flashing Turn Signal Head with Pedestrian Indication (which we will abbreviate as Flashing Pedestrian Indicator, or FPI) has been one proposed solution to reduce pedestrian crashes at signalized intersections. The FPI alternates between a yellow arrow and pedestrian symbol (Fig. 1). Consider a right-turning driver. If the pedestrian button is pressed for the conflicting crosswalk (to the right), the Walk pedestrian signal would activate, and instead of a green arrow (in cases of a dedicated right-turn lane) or in addition to a circular green (in cases of a shared through/right-turn lane) the driver would see the FPI. This signal has two potential benefits. First, it may increase the awareness of pedestrians crossing or planning to cross, and second, it might encourage scanning to the right for pedestrians in and around the roadway. Based on the attention literature, this type of flashing/onsetting signal is one of the best methods to attract attention to a message [e.g., 7], and arrows have been found to reflexively orient attention in the direction they point [e.g., 8–11]. Thus there is reason to believe that this new signal may be effective.

Fig. 1. The flashing turn signal head with pedestrian indication (FPI)

However, as with any new traffic control device, it is important to understand whether drivers of all ages comprehend the meaning it is intended to convey (right turns are permissible but a pedestrian may be present, yield if appropriate). If this message is not conveyed, at best the countermeasure may not have its intended effect, and at worst drivers may misinterpret it in such a way that pedestrian risk is increased. For example, in a previous studies, some participants interpreted a solid yellow arrow as meaning "hurry up and turn" before the signal turns red [12]. If the yellow arrow component of the proposed signal results in a rush to complete a turn, pedestrian risk might be increased rather than decreased. In the subsequently reported study younger, middle-aged, and older drivers' comprehension of the FPI was examined.

3   Method

This experiment presented participants who had never seen the FPI previously with the FPI and other signal states and asked them for the meaning of the presented signal.

Participants. We collected open-ended responses, and then multiple-choice responses, from a total of 15 younger (21 to 35 years, $M = 23.4$, $SD = 1.9$), 15 middle-aged (50 to 64 years, $M = 58.9$, $SD = 4.1$), and 15 older (65 and above years, $M = 72.9$, $SD = 7.3$) participants who were recruited from the Tallahassee, FL area. All were licensed drivers. None of the participants had participated in previous studies in our laboratory involving a similar signal: the Flashing Yellow Arrow (FYA).

Materials. A survey was programmed to be run online (exclusively in Mozilla Firefox – http://cognitivetask.com/fyp) using HTML, CSS, PHP, and JQuery. The survey consisted of six sections: (1) informed consent; (2) open response questions related to signal states while turning right; (3) open response questions related to signal states while driving straight; (4) multiple choice questions related to each signal while turning right; (5) a section asking participants for their opinion of the signal after being informed about its meaning; (6) a section containing demographic questions and questions related to driving habits. All stimuli (1000 pixels × 564 pixels) were prepared in Google Sketchup, and signal states were added in Microsoft Paint (see Fig. 2 for an example).

Fig. 2. Example stimulus, in this case depicting the FPI in its arrow phase

Images depicted an intersection from the point of view of a driver in the far right lane. This intersection had two through lanes and one dedicated left-turn lane in each direction. Since the right lane was not a dedicated right-turn lane, when the FPI was active the signal also depicted a circular green for traffic proceeding forward through the intersection. An arrow above the signal mast pointed to the four headed signal furthest to the right to ensure participants knew which signal to which they were expected to respond. For the creation of the Flashing Pedestrian Indicator animated GIFs, GifMaker.Me (http://gifmaker.me) was used, with a delay of 500 ms between frames. Timing was derived from videos of the FPI provided by the Florida Department of Transportation.

Procedure. Those that agreed to the consent form continued on to the full survey while those that did not agree were thanked for their time. For the second section, participants were asked to interpret the meaning of each signal for a right-turning driver. Responses were collected via a text box underneath the image of the signal. Participants were asked to be as detailed as possible. The third section was essentially the same as the second, except that participants were asked to interpret the meaning of the signal for a driver going straight rather than turning right. In the fourth section, participants were asked again to interpret the meaning of the each presented signal state for a right-turning driver, but were given multiple options and were asked to check each option that applied. Options were based on information from the 2014 Florida Driver's Handbook and also discussions with FDOT regarding the intended meaning of the FPI. The options available were: (1) Come to a complete stop at the marked stop line or before moving into the cross-walk or intersection; (2) Go - but only if the intersection is clear; (3) A driver should prepare to yield to a pedestrian (if present); (4) A pedestrian is likely present; (5) A right turning driver should scan to the right for pedestrians; (6) Stop if you can safely do so, The light will soon be red; (7) A right turn is allowed. These options were randomly shuffled to control for response-order effects. For sections two through four presented above, signals were presented in the order of: (1) Green; (2) Yellow; (3) Red; (4) FPI. In the fifth section, an animation of the FPI was shown below a block of text explaining the signal. Below that, participants were asked to give their opinion of the signal, including any concerns they may have. The final section of the survey asked participants both demographic questions and questions related to their current driving habits (i.e. weekly driving distance, and frequency).

4 Results

Due to space limitations, we focus on open-ended and multiple choice response data. First, we explored the answers to open ended-questions in which participants were asked to provide the meaning of different signals. We begin with the scenario of primary interest: the meaning of the FPI for right-turning drivers. Two coders scored the answer of each participant for whether any part of the answer corresponded to the following categories: (1) the driver has right-of-way; (2) a pedestrian has right-of way; (3) a right turn is allowed; (4) a pedestrian is likely present; (5) the driver should scan or watch for pedestrian; (6) the driver should yield to a pedestrian if present; (7) the driver should slow or be cautious. In making the judgment of whether or not a driver thought a pedestrian might likely be present, we used any mention of a pedestrian as indicating awareness of potential pedestrians. Reported data represent an average of the percentage of participants providing an answer that fell within one of the previously mentioned categories across the two raters. Figure 3 depicts these results, in contrast to responses made when only the green circular of the signal above the right turn lane was active.

Encouragingly, over 90 % of participants interpreted the signal as relating to a pedestrian likely being present. Close to half (48 %) provided answers indicating that the driver should yield to pedestrians present. Fifty-four percent of participants indicated that they should scan for, slow, or be cautious in the presence of pedestrians. Few participants misinterpreted the FPI to mean that the driver had right-of-way. The two participants who made this response stated the meaning as "that you have the right away, but be safe about

the   right   turn   lane   was   active.

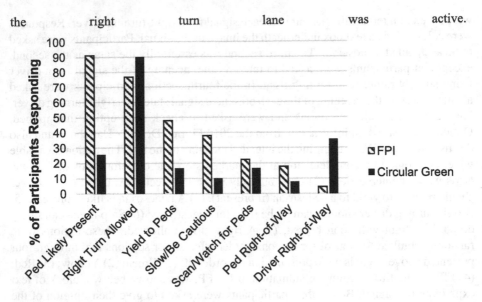

Fig. 3. Responses for drivers asked to provide the meaning of the signal for a driver turning right. Percentage of participants whose open-ended answers fell into each response category when the signal depicted the FPI (white with black bars) vs. only a circular green. (Color figure online)

pedestrian walking" and "to watch out for pedestrians even if it is my right of way." Both responses clearly indicate an awareness of potential pedestrians present and a need to be cautious. We also examined whether the distribution of responses was similar for younger, middle-aged, and older drivers and found this to be the case (Fig. 4).

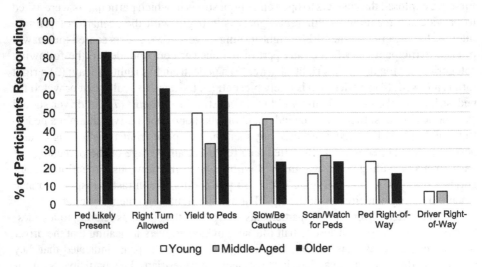

Fig. 4. Responses to the FPI for drivers turning right as a function of age

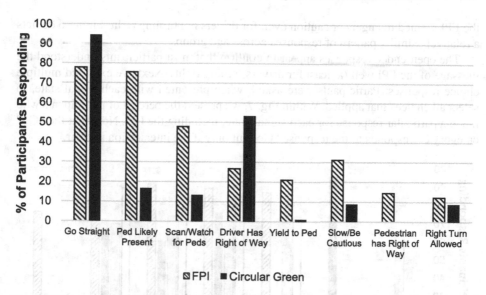

Fig. 5. Responses for drivers going straight. Proportion of participants whose open-ended answers fell into each response category when the signal depicted the FPI (white with black bars) vs. only a circular green. (Color figure online)

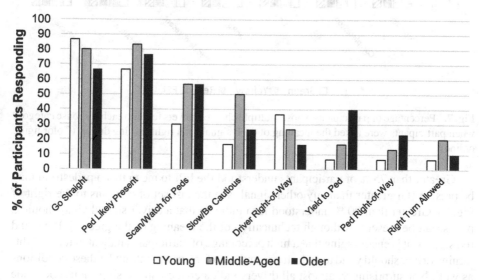

Fig. 6. Responses to the FPI for drivers going straight as a function of age

However, when presenting drivers with the same scenario, and asking the participant the meaning of the scenario for a driver going straight through the intersection, participants sometimes misinterpreted the signal as though the FPI applied to them as well (that they too needed to watch for pedestrians). Figure 5 depicts interpretation of the FPI and the circular green state for drivers going straight through the intersection. In general, the FPI seemed to engender caution even for drivers not turning right. Figure 6 depicts a relatively similar pattern of responses across age groups.

The open-ended responses appear to confirm that most participants understood the message of the FPI well (at least for drivers turning right). Next, we explored multiple choice responses. Participants were asked, when presented with each signal state, to select all choices that applied. Within Fig. 7, we present the percent of participants who made a particular response for each signal state, including the FPI. Note that the "Go" category corresponds to the response "Go, but only if the intersection is clear."

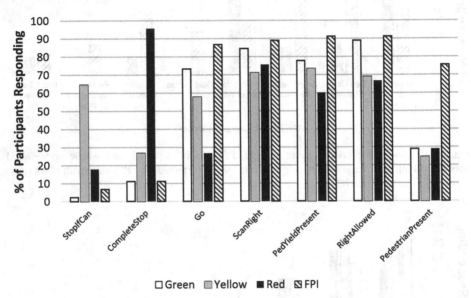

Fig. 7. Percentage of participants whose multiple choice answers fell into each response category when participants were asked the meaning of each signal for a right-turning driver. (Color figure online)

Greater than 75 % of participants understood the FPI to mean that a pedestrian may be present (far greater than any other signal; see the last set of columns to the right of Fig. 7). Greater than 90 % understood it to indicate that a driver should yield should a pedestrian be present. Although technically not the meaning of the green, yellow, and red signals, it is encouraging that a high percentage of participants indicated that a right-turning driver should yield to pedestrians and scan for participants under these conditions as well. Not surprisingly, almost all drivers indicated a complete stop should be made at the stop bar for a red signal. For a yellow signal, a mixture or responses were made, reflective of the fact that a yellow signal can mean different things depending on the context (stop if you can do so, or go if there is enough time to complete the turn). In addition to the message that a potential pedestrian was present, that they should yield if necessary, and that they should scan to the right, participants also understood that they could make a right turn in the presence of the FPI (go and right-turn allowed responses). Responses to the FPI were similar across age groups (Fig. 8).

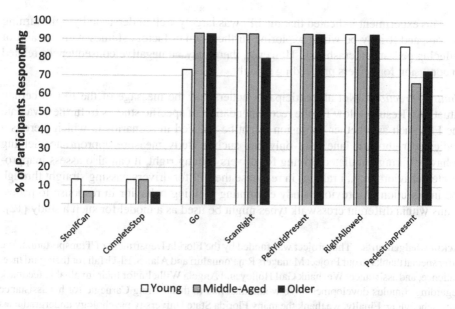

Fig. 8. Percentage of participants whose multiple-choice answers fell into each response category when participants were asked the meaning of the FPI for a turning driver as a function of age.

5   Conclusion and Discussion

The FPI was developed to reduce crashes by alerting drivers to the presence of pedestrians and encourage scanning to the right, potentially reducing instances of inattentional blindness-related crashes. When participants were asked to imagine they were a right turning driver, the FPI largely conveyed its intended meaning: in both open-response and multiple-choice formats, most participants understood that it meant pedestrians may be present, and most indicated that they should either be cautious, scan, or yield to potential pedestrians in the roadway while turning right. In the multiple choice portion of the experiment, 75 % of participants understood the signal as meaning that a pedestrian may be present, and over 90 % of participants responded that they should yield to potential pedestrians in the roadway. Comprehension was roughly similar across age groups.

When participants were asked to imagine they were driving straight the message received was mixed, with roughly 50 % of participants responding that they should scan for pedestrians. Drivers turning right, not drivers proceeding straight, should be on alert for crossing pedestrians in response to the FPI. Our study featured a scenario without a dedicated right-turn lane. Thus the FPI featured both a green circular, and the alternating yellow arrow/pedestrian figure at the same time. This mixing of signals for different drivers (those going straight, those turning) may be a contributing factor to the observed confusion. One can speculate that this confusion might be less likely to occur at intersections with a dedicated right turn lane since the FPI would only appear in the signal over the right-turn lane (without the green circular signal).

This experiment indicated that the FPI was largely well understood by right-turning drivers, and it may be worth exploring further human factors studies with the aim of reducing pedestrian crash risk. However, there may be negative consequences related to confusion for drivers proceeding straight.

Future Directions. Not all participants understood the message of the FPI in certain situations. Results allow for the recommendation of specific studies to further evaluate the FPI, such as whether confusion might be reduced in scenarios in which there is a dedicated right-turn lane. Not only can such a study measure appropriate yielding behavior during simulated driving for drivers turning right, it can also assess inappropriate behaviors (e.g., braking) in response the FPI for drivers passing straight through the intersection. A previous study examining yielding behavior in response to pedestrians within different crosswalk types might be used as a model for such a study [12].

Acknowledgements. This project was funded by the Florida Department of Transportation. We offer special thanks to our Project Managers Raj Ponnaluri and Alan S. El-Urfali for their guidance, patience, and assistance. We thank Gail Holley and Angela Wilhelm for their invaluable feedback regarding stimulus development. We would also like to thank Craig Carnegie for his assistance with scheduling. Finally, we thank the many Florida State University psychology undergraduates who worked on this project. We are also extremely grateful to all the Florida residents who participated in this research.

References

1. National Highway Transportation Safety Administration (NHTSA): Traffic safety facts 2012 data: Pedestrians. DOT HS 81 1 888 (2014)
2. Charness, N., Boot, W.R., Mitchum, A., Stothart, C., Lupton, H.: Final report: aging driver and pedestrian safety: parking lot hazards study. Technical report BDK83-977-12, Department of Transportation, Florida (2012)
3. Langlois, J.A., Keyl, P.M., Guralnik, J.M., Foley, D.J., Marottoli, R.A., Wallace, R.B.: Characteristics of older pedestrians who have difficulty crossing the street. Am. J. Public Health **87**(3), 393–397 (1997)
4. Avineri, E., Shinar, D., Susilo, Y.O.: Pedestrians' behaviour in cross walks: the effects of fear of falling and age. Accid. Anal. Prev. **44**(1), 30–34 (2012)
5. Simons, D.J., Chabris, C.F.: Gorillas in our midst: sustained inattentional blindness for dynamic events. Perception **28**(9), 1059–1074 (1999)
6. Summala, H., Pasanen, E., Räsänen, M., Sievänen, J.: Bicycle accidents and drivers' visual search at left and right turns. Accid. Anal. Prev. **28**(2), 147–153 (1996)
7. Yantis, S.: Stimulus-driven attentional capture. Curr. Dir. Psychol. Sci. **2**(5), 156–161 (1993)
8. Galfano, G., Dalmaso, M., Marzoli, D., Pavan, G., Coricelli, C., Castelli, L.: Eye gaze cannot be ignored (but neither can arrows). Q. J. Exp. Psychol. **65**(10), 1895–1910 (2012)
9. Kuhn, G., Kingstone, A.: Look away! eyes and arrows engage oculomotor responses automatically. Atten. Percept. Psychophys. **71**(2), 314–327 (2009)
10. Ristic, J., Friesen, C.K., Kingstone, A.: Are eyes special? It depends on how you look at it. Psychon. Bull. Rev. **9**(3), 507–513 (2002)

11. Tipples, J.: Eye gaze is not unique: automatic orienting in response to uninformative arrows. Psychon. Bull. Rev. **9**(2), 314–318 (2002)

12. Boot, W.R., Charness, N., Mitchum, A., Landbeck, R., Stothart, C.: Final report: aging road user studies of intersection safety. Technical report BDV30-977-13, Department of Transportation, Florida (2014)

Challenges of Older Drivers' Adoption of Advanced Driver Assistance Systems and Autonomous Vehicles

Dustin Souders[(⊠)] and Neil Charness

Florida State University, Tallahassee, USA
{Souders,Charness}@psy.fsu.edu

Abstract. The personal vehicle is increasingly the preferred mode of travel for aging adults. There are greater numbers of older drivers on the roads driving more miles than ever before, and it is important to be aware of declines that might affect them. Existing technology adoption frameworks are reviewed and relevant issues surrounding older adults' adoption of advanced driver assistance systems and/or autonomous vehicles are discussed. A secondary analysis is performed on recently collected Floridian survey data that over-sampled older adults (age 55+ yr). Exploratory factor scores are calculated based on survey responses and the predictive effects of age, gender, annual household income, ease of new technology use, and providing information relating to the technologies are examined. Results are discussed in terms of how best to increase older adults' familiarity with and trust of these transportation technologies in order to help ensure their adoption and safe usage.

Keywords: Older adults · Technology adoption · Advanced driver assistance systems · Autonomous vehicles

1 Disclaimer

The opinions, findings, and conclusions expressed in this publication are those of the authors and not necessarily those of the State of Florida Department of Transportation or the U. S. Department of Transportation.

2 Introduction

2.1 Population Aging and the Aging Driver

Older drivers are driving more miles on average than ever before, with drivers aged 75–79 years have driven 60 % more miles than their predecessors (1995–96 cohort versus 2008 cohort) and 51 % more miles for drivers 81 and older [1]. There are currently increased levels of licensure and driving by older adults (OAs) [2], and with Baby Boomers aging, it is projected that one in five Americans will be over the age of 65 in 2030 [3]. With greater numbers of older drivers driving more miles than ever before, it is important to be aware of age-related declines in sensory, cognitive, and psychomotor

© Springer International Publishing Switzerland 2016
J. Zhou and G. Salvendy (Eds.): ITAP 2016, Part II, LNCS 9755, pp. 428–440, 2016.
DOI: 10.1007/978-3-319-39949-2_41

abilities that might affect older drivers on the road. It has been shown both experimentally and through literature review that OAs take 1.7–2.0 times longer than their younger counterparts for elementary information processing operations [4]. For more in-depth review of how age-related declines affect the driving task, please refer to the following sources [5–10].

Older drivers tend to keep away from driving situations they perceive as difficult, and drive less overall (e.g., [11]), though as stated earlier, they are beginning to drive more miles, later in life than previous cohorts [1]. Some older drivers choose to self-regulate their driving to avoid situations they find stressful (e.g., heavy traffic), or situations in which these deficits are more pronounced (e.g., driving at night, or in poor weather conditions), and might even cease driving while they are still relatively safe drivers (for a complete literature review and framework of self-regulation in driving by OAs, see [12]). In-vehicle telematics systems (e.g., GPS, collision warning systems) are generally perceived as beneficial among OAs, especially older women, in increasing confidence in driving [13], and might help them avoid the deleterious effects related to driving cessation (e.g., [14]).

3 Older Adults and Technology Adoption

OAs differ from the general population in physical and cognitive capabilities as described earlier, and commonly have less familiarity with new technologies than younger adults [15–17]. It has been shown that OAs are aware of technological benefits though, and are willing to try new, useful technologies [18]. OAs are attracted to technologies they find useful and that provide clear benefits to their current lifestyle, and they are generally reluctant if they cannot foresee possible advantages (e.g., [19]). Czaja et al. [17] surveyed 1,204 participants and found that general technology use was predicted by age, education, race, fluid and crystallized intelligence, computer self-efficacy, and computer anxiety, with greater technology use generally found in younger, more highly educated individuals. Importantly, the relationship between age and technology use was mediated by cognitive abilities, computer self-efficacy, and computer anxiety. Due to a lack of proper assessment of OAs' needs, this large demographic group with considerable spending power is underserved by industry [16, 20, 21].

3.1 Models of Technology Adoption

Technology Acceptance Model and Its Offshoots. The Technology Acceptance Model (TAM; [22]) was developed as an empirical framework to explain user acceptance and adoption of information technology, and has been proven to be quite robust in explaining the adoption patterns of many different types of information systems in different contexts [23–25]. TAM consists of two main factors: Perceived usefulness (PU; i.e., the belief that use of a new technology will help or enhance a person's job performance) and perceived ease of use (PEOU; i.e., the belief that use of a new technology will be relatively free of effort). Other influencing factors have been added to TAM in subsequent work. Venkatesh and Davis' [25] TAM2 included seven external variables that influenced users' PU and PEOU (i.e., voluntariness, experience, subjective norm, image, job relevance, output quality, and result demonstrability). Another variation of TAM is the Unified Theory of Acceptance and Use of Technology (UTAUT; [26]), that poses three direct determinants of behavioral intent to use a technology: performance expectancy, effort expectancy, and social influence. Trust was added to TAM by researchers in e-commerce [27] and e-government [28] due to the risk/uncertainty inherent in web-based environments. Experience with technology and its effects have also been discussed in the TAM literature, with increasing experience shifting personal judgments away from social information or norms, and toward personal preference and attitudes [25, 29]. Experience moderates behavioral intent (BI) to use a technology such that effort expectancy is stronger in early stages of experience, and facilitating conditions becoming stronger in later stages [26].

UTAUT Extension to Advanced Driver Assistance Systems. Adell [30] let 38 drivers trial a system that alerted the driver when (1) the car was too close to the vehicle ahead of it, (2) when positive relative speed suggested an impending collision, (3) speed was too high considering road geometry, and (4) also when the car was exceeding the speed limit. The study defined driver support system acceptance as, "the degree to which an individual intends to use a system and, when available, to incorporate the system in his/her driving" (p. 482). Findings showed support for UTAUT in the area of driver support systems, but with low explanatory power. These results showed the importance of social influence for behavioral intent, but not effort expectancy. This lead the author to stress that UTAUT constructs be measured in the context of driver support systems with special attention given to performance expectancy. The author further suggested that more extensive studies with more targeted experimental design be conducted with larger sample sizes.

TAM Extension to Autonomous Vehicles. Choi and Ji [31] developed a model based on TAM explaining early intent to use an autonomous vehicle (AV) that demonstrated that PU and trust were necessary precursors to the intention to use an AV, with a very weak effect of PEOU on behavioral intent to use AV. They discerned three constructs that positively influenced the individual's trust in AV: (1) System Transparency (i.e., degree to which users can predict and understand the operating of AV), (2) Technical Competence (i.e., degree of user perception on the performance of AV), (3) Situation Management (i.e., user's belief that he or she can recover control in a situation whenever desired), which in turn alleviated their level of perceived risk. They further proposed that users with an external locus of control might take a more passive role with an automated system [32], making it easier for them to rely on automated driving system [33].

UTAUT Extension to Automated Road Transport Systems. Madigan et al. [34] investigated user acceptance of automated road transport systems (ARTS) involved with the European CityMobil2 project through the UTAUT model. ARTS are highly automated vehicles that run at low speeds on dedicated, demonstrated routes (i.e., predetermined demonstrated path, not based on active mapping) meant to complement and feed in to the main public transport network in areas of low or dispersed demand [35]. Prior survey work [36] found that travelers' decision to use motorized public transportation hinged the quality of the weather, illumination, on-board comfort, and distance travelled on foot, with a preference for cybernetic transport systems (i.e., ARTS, portrayed by system descriptions and in operation around the surveyed city) that increased with age. Madigan et al. [34] assessed user acceptance of ARTS vehicles being used in two different European cities (La Rochelle in France and Lausanne in Switzerland) as part of the CityMobil2 project using the UTAUT framework, and found that performance expectancy, effort expectancy, and social influence were pre-dictors of behavioral intentions to use ARTS, with performance expectancy having the strongest impact. The authors further suggested that future studies should gauge on-board comfort, as hedonic motivation has been shown to be an important deter-minant of behavioral intention in consumer-based contexts [37]. The authors also suggested that actual interaction with ARTS rather than the system descriptions used by Delle Site et al. [36] lead to age not having a significant impact on UTAUT variables.

Automation Acceptance Model. The Automation Acceptance Model (AAM; [38]) is an augmentation of TAM that stresses the importance of trust and task-technology compatibility in order to account for automation use's dynamic and multi-level nature. AAM additionally emphasizes that actual system use (i.e., experience with the automated system) feeds back into the user's perceptions of compatibility, trust, PU, PEOU, and behavioral intention to use automation. Trust formation through experience and task-technology compatibility are expanded upon below and then discussed in the context of using Advanced Driver Assistance Systems (ADAS) or AV to enhance OAs' mobility.

Trust in the Technology. Trust is social in nature and is largely based on our inter-personal relationships with other humans. A framework discerning the similarities and differences between human-human and human-automation (decision support systems, to be specific) trust can be found in Madhavan and Wiegmann [39]. Broadly, this framework states that humans naturally tend to react socially to seemingly intelligent machines, deferring to them as advisors, as decision support systems rigorously following well-designed schema to make their decisions. This deference is fragile though, and prone to break down due to the system's rigidity, as they lack human adaptability. Attitudes relating to trust in automation play an important role in user reliance and acceptance [40, 41], and indeed, users show more reliance on automation they trust [42–44].

After reviewing the trust literature, Lee and See [40] described the basis of trust as comprising three dimensions: Purpose (i.e., degree to which the automation being used as intended by the designer), Process (i.e., how the automation functions in the situation to fulfill the user's needs), and Performance (i.e., past or present operation of the automation including reliability, predictability, and ability). These three dimensions are judged by the user on the system's surface features (i.e., aesthetics, feel, information structure; [45–47]) and depth features (i.e., the automation's performance, observ-ability, controllability; [40]). These dimensions should lead to properly calibrated levels of trust being placed in the automation based on its capabilities. Over-trust can lead to misuse (i.e., using the automation in situations where it is not appropriate to) and complacency (discussed later in the Task-Technology Compatibility section), while under-trust can lead to disuse (i.e., not using the automation when it is capable of helping; [48]). Lee and See [40] stress that automation should be designed to be technically capable of performing a prescribed task (i.e., trustworthy), but also be operationally unintimidating and easily understood (i.e., trustable). Hoff and Bashir's [49] dissection of factors that influence trust formation in automation use resulted in a three-layered model that accounts for unique characteristics belonging to the user (dispositional trust), situation (situational trust), and the dynamic effects of experience (learned trust), and aligns well with AAM.

Task-Technology Compatibility. It has been shown that adding task-technology fit model constructs into TAM helps predictions of use [50]. Compatibility consists of the degree of fit between the human, technology, task to-be-performed, and the situation [51]. This involves an older driver and their potentially age-compromised faculties, the particular device or devices that might complement them, and the level of assistance called for in the situation (e.g., providing warnings to draw the driver's attention to unheeded hazards or some form of automated take-over if the driver does not respond to these hazards in time).

In the automation literature, high levels of automation (LOAs) have been shown to lead to complacency, degraded situational awareness, de-skilling, and mode confusion (e.g., [48]), and conversely, low LOAs can lead to poor performance when the system's demands exceed the operator's capacity [52]. With this in mind, the appropriate LOA and type of ADAS to maximize task-technology compatibility for OAs can be discussed. It has been suggested that fully automating a process should be limited to situations where the user fails to respond, or cannot respond fast enough [53]. An example of when automated takeover of this nature might occur would be when an older driver (1) does not notice a sudden stop by the vehicle they are following, or (2) does not or cannot react fast enough to this sudden stop. In the first case, a forward collision warning system might call attention to an unheeded deceleration by the car in front of them and allow the older driver to react appropriately, and hence might not require further intervention or takeover of the driving task. But in the second case, an older driver's reaction time to this surprise deceleration of the car in front of them might not be sufficient, and an automatic braking system might help them avoid a rear-end collision. Interestingly, it has been shown that both methods can be effective, but drivers are actually more accepting of collision warnings than automatic braking which overrides their control, even if it performs better than they could [54].

3.2 Important Considerations for OA Technology Adoption

Facilitators and Determinants of OA Technology Adoption. Lee and Coughlin [55] conducted a review of the technology acceptance literature and posited ten facilitators and determinants of OAs' technology adoption, which show some overlap with TAM and UTAUT (bolded items are novel contributions of [55] that are particular to OAs):

- Value: perception of usefulness and potential benefit (analogous to PU from TAM)
- Usability: perception that technology is easy to use, user-friendly (analogous to PEOU from TAM)
- **Affordability**: perception of potential cost savings

- **Accessibility**: knowledge of the technology's existence and its availability in the market place
- Technical support: Availability of quality professional assistance throughout use (analogous to facilitating conditions from UTAUT)
- Social support: support from family, friends, and peers (analogous to social influence from UTAUT)
- **Emotion**: perception of emotional and psychological benefits
- Independence: perception of social visibility, or how a technology makes them look to others (analogous to image from UTAUT)
- **Experience**: relevance with their prior experiences and interactions
- **Confidence**: empowerment without anxiety or intimidation

OA Adoption of ADAS and/or AV. In the case of using ADAS or AV to help OAs maintain their mobility, Lee and Coughlin's [55] accessibility, independence, and confidence are of particular interest. Accessibility is important in that an OA needs to know that the ADAS or AV technology exists and that it is capable of helping them safely maintain their personal mobility in order for them to be urged to adopt it, and it must be within their price range. Many of these technologies are included on luxury brand vehicles, which might be too expensive for an older driver thinking of giving up their keys. Many older adults equate the personal vehicle as vital to their well-being and independence (e.g., [56]), and these technologies may help them maintain that sense of independence so long as they avoid stigmatization, as it has been shown to drive OAs away from adoption [57, 58]. Finally, in terms of confidence, these technologies have the best chance of being used properly if their adoption is discretionary, rather than mandatory (i.e., forced to do so in order to maintain licensure), as under mandatory or forced use an individual might delay, obstruct, underutilize or sabotage a system [59].

As fully autonomous vehicles are not available in the short term, and their time of arrival is questioned by experts in the area, Ghazizadeh and colleagues' [38] insistence on task-technology compatibility is nicely informed by Eby and colleagues' [60] review of in-vehicle technologies and their potential to help older drivers extend the amount of time they are able to drive safely. Eby et al. [60] emphasize the importance of training and/or education on the operation of the particular system to maximize these systems' effectiveness and safe usage.

4 Methods

As part of an FDOT contract aimed at assessing attitudes towards AV in older Floridians, Duncan et al. [61] collected survey data. This survey included questions on familiarity with, general opinion of, and willingness to use particular ADAS systems that had not yet been examined, as the report was commissioned for, and largely dealt with AV. Hence, secondary analyses were conducted on the data set regarding OAs' attitudes and acceptance of not only autonomous vehicles, but ADAS as well. Data were collected by mailing out surveys using voter registration lists, and over-sampled older adults (age 55+) in order to gain a better idea of this age group's knowledge and preferences related to AV and ADAS. Respondents either completed and mailed back their surveys, or completed the survey online. In total, 5,000 surveys were mailed out in two waves, and 459 total responses were received, for a response rate of 9.18 %, which was consistent with other mail-out survey response rates. Before being mailed, half of the survey packets were randomly selected to include an additional informational insert describing AV and different ADAS systems. This lead to 188 of survey respondents receiving this extra information (271 did not receive this informational insert). This was done to examine the effects of a basic level of AV and ADAS education on respondents' attitudes toward these technologies. After controlling for age and income level, these groups were not found to differ on willingness to use AV ($F(1, 392) = 2.96$, $p = .09$), and were combined for the following analyses.

5   Results

5.1   Exploratory Factor Analysis of AV Survey

A principal components exploratory factor analysis with varimax rotation was conducted on 51 survey items concerning familiarity with, general opinion of, and willingness to use AV and select ADAS systems (Cruise Control, Lane Departure Warning, Blind Spot Monitor, Active Lane Centering, Automatic Braking, Adaptive Cruise Control, and Self-Parking Systems), comfort of yourself or having a loved one riding in AV, AV-related concerns and benefits (e.g., concern with AV driving as well as human drivers, benefits of less traffic congestion with AV), questions of pricing of AV, and interest in different ownership models (privately-owned, shared-ownership, autonomous public transit, AV for hire). Principal components was used to identify and compute composite scores for factors underlying survey respondents' attitudes towards AV and ADAS. This resulted in 10 unique factors that explained 70.4 % of the variance.

5.2   Regression Analyses of Factors

Multiple linear regressions were calculated to assess potential predictors (age, gender, annual income, education level, and ease of new technology use) of each factor from the exploratory factor analysis. Age was measured in years; gender was self-reported as 0 = female, 1 = male; annual income was self-reported by selecting one of six levels: under \$25k, \$25k–49,999, \$50k–74,999, \$75k–99,999, \$100k–150k, or more than \$150k; ease of new technology use was self-reported on a 5-point Likert scale ranging from 1 = 'strongly disagree new technology is easy to use' to 5 = 'strongly agree new technology is easy to use'; and received info was dummy coded as 0 = did not receive informational insert and 1 = received informational insert. See Table 1 for the results of these regressions. Significant predictors are elaborated on below.

Factor 1: General AV Attitudes and Willingness. Table 1 shows that those reporting higher levels of ease of new technology use, and to a lesser extent those who received an information sheet, were generally more accepting of automated driving technology (both AV and self-parking systems) for themselves and others, were more interested in different models of AV ownership, and looked forward more to potential benefits like fewer crashes, reduced crash severity, and more enjoyable travel.

Table 1. Regression results. Non-significant predictors withheld. $^\wedge$ = p < .10, * = p < .05, ** = p < .01, *** = p < .001

	$F_{(5, 325)}$	p	R^2	Age	Ease of New Technology Use	Received Information?	Income	Gender
F1: General AV Attitudes & Willingness to Use AV	4.91	<.001	0.07		$\beta = .22^{***}$	$\beta = .095^\wedge$		
F2: Benefits of AV	3.23	<.01	0.047		$\beta = .20^{**}$			
F3: AV Concerns	4.37	<.01	0.063		$\beta = -.15^*$	$\beta = -.12^*$	$\beta = -.096^\wedge$	$\beta = -.09^\wedge$
F4: ADAS Familiarity	15.31	<.001	0.19		$\beta = .27^{***}$		$\beta = .14^{**}$	$\beta = .25^{***}$
F5: ADAS General Opinion	1.07	0.38	0.016					
F6: Willingness to Use ADAS	6.01	<.001	0.085	$\beta = .25^{***}$	$\beta = .13^*$	$\beta = -.094^\wedge$	$\beta = .13^*$	
F7: High Cost AV	0.57	0.72	0.009					
F8: Cruise Control Attitudes	4.22	<.01	0.061		$\beta = .13^*$			$\beta = .12^*$
F9: Different AV Ownership Models	2.88	<.05	0.042		$\beta = .11^\wedge$			$\beta = .14^*$
F10: Willingness to Use ACC	1.19	0.32	0.018					

Factor 2: Benefits of AV. Those reporting higher levels of ease of new technology use were generally more prone to think the introduction of AV would lead to benefits such as fewer crashes with reduced severity, less traffic congestion, shorter travel time, better fuel economy, more enjoyable travel, as well as enhanced mobility for those unable to drive and improved pedestrian safety.

Factor 3: Concerns of AV. Those reporting higher levels of ease of new technology use, who received an information sheet, and to a lesser extent those reporting higher income levels, reported less concern about issues involving AV deployment such as safety consequences, legal liability in a crash, vehicle security, data privacy, sharing the road, safely interacting with AV, as well as learning to use AV.

Factor 4: ADAS Familiarity. Greater comfort using new technology, greater household income, and being male were associated with greater familiarity with ADAS systems.

Factor 6: Willingness to Use ADAS. Higher age, levels of comfort using new technology and reported income were associated with greater willingness to use ADAS, while curiously those who had received an informational sheet expressed lower willingness to use ADAS.

Factor 8: Cruise Control Familiarity, Opinion, and Willingness to Use. Greater comfort with new technology use and being male were associated with higher levels of familiarity, opinion, and willingness to use cruise control.

Factor 9: Different AV Owner/Ridership Models. Men were more willing to use different AV owner/ridership models such as shared-ownership, AV public transportation, and/or AV for hire.

6 Discussion

It is clear that TAM's PU and PEOU maintain their importance in the case of OA adoption of AV and/or ADAS. Adell [30], despite being under-powered and evaluating a mix of systems combined as one, provides a good first step and informs future studies of ADAS acceptance about the importance of social influence, effort expectancy, and tailoring measures to the driving task. Madigan and colleagues' [32] study on acceptance of ARTS highlighted comfort's role in the consumer acceptance domain, as well as the necessity for some sort of actual interaction with the technology. Choi and Ji [31] showed strong effects for PU in relation to personal AV adoption, but weaker effects for PEOU. This weaker effect of PEOU might be true for their younger sample, but might not remain true for an older sample. Here within an older sample, self-reported ratings of their ease of new technology use were found to be a significant predictor for factors relating to increased general comfort with and willingness to use AV (F1), greater expectation of AV related benefits (F2), reduced AV concerns (F3), increased familiarity with ADAS (F4), and greater willingness to use ADAS (F6), and was marginally associated with more passive modes of AV (F9).

The importance of trust in automation adoption is highlighted by AAM [39], and Choi and Ji [31] show that this extends to AV. Choi and Ji [31] stress that a user's trust in an AV is predicated on its level of predictability and easy comprehension of its function (system transparency), an acceptable level of performance perceived by the user (technical competence), and finally, the perception that they can intervene if they find it necessary (situation management). Appreciation for trust's dynamic process of formation during adoption of automation, and its many levels and sublevels during use of automation elaborated by Hoff and Bashir [49] provide frameworks to accurately assess trust throughout these processes.

It is apparent based on the literature that trust is a major component of adopting automation, and that this trust is dynamic in nature (e.g., [38]). Many technology adoption studies assessing ADAS systems (e.g., [30]), are cross-sectional in nature, and hence are unable to account for how trust in a system may change with repeated use and/or successful incorporation of the technology into the individual's lifestyle. Furthermore, as Hoff and Bashir's [49] layers of trust suggest, cross-sectional studies dealing with trust at the very least might only be assessing the individual's dispositional trust, or an under-informed trust that may grow with repeated successful usage, if given the chance. Future studies should account for this by incorporating more dynamic measurements of trust into a longitudinal design.

The exploratory factors calculated based on the Floridian AV survey need to be replicated by other similar studies, but make sense in light of AV and ADAS adoption by aging drivers. Interestingly, receiving the informational sheet significantly lowered AV concerns (F3), and was marginally associated with more positive attitudes towards AV (F1), but was associated with lower willingness to use ADAS (F6). Of particular interest is age positively predicting willingness to use ADAS (F6), and provides support for Eby and colleagues' [60] "optimistic yes" to the question of whether ADAS could help older drivers drive more safely, later in life.

One area of interest for future research is investigating the effects of different levels of training on a particular ADAS's acceptance by an older driver. As was seen in the secondary analysis of the survey data, the informational sheet did not affect respondents' willingness to use AV, but it did impact more global views of AV, as shown by the first factor. Eby et al. [60] stressed that some ADAS (e.g., adaptive cruise control) needed to be paired with driver training in order to be recommended for OAs' use. Training can take a variety of forms, from written manuals or instructions to informational videos or hands-on tutorials. Assessing which one of these is most quick and effective in accurately calibrating OAs' trust in a given system would be valuable for advancing the field.

Acknowledgements. This research was funded in part by the Florida Department of Transportation, Contract BVD30 977-11 Enhanced mobility for aging populations using automated vehicles http://www.dot.state.fl.us/research-center/Completed_Proj/Summary_PL/FDOT-BDV3 0-977-11-rpt.pdf.

References

1. Insurance Institute for Highway Safety: Decline in crash risk spurs better outlook for older drivers. Status report, vol. 50, no. 2 (2015). http://www.iihs.org/iihs/sr/statusreport/article/50/2/2
2. Sivak, M., Schoettle, B.: Recent changes in the age composition of drivers in 15 countries. Report No. UMTRI-2011-43, University of Michigan Transportation Research Institute, Ann Arbor, MI (2011)
3. Colby, S.L., Ortman, J.M.: Projections of the size and composition of the U.S. population: 2014 to 2060. Current Population reports, pp. P25–1143. U.S. Census Bureau, Washington, DC (2015)
4. Jastrzembski, T.S., Charness, N.: The model human processor and the older adult: parameter estimation and validation within a mobile phone task. J. Exp. Psychol.-Appl. **13**, 224–248 (2007)
5. Marottoli, R.A., Richardson, E.D., Stowe, M.H., Miller, E.G., Brass, L.M., Cooney Jr., L. M., Tinetti, M.E.: Development of a test battery to identify older drivers at risk for self-reported adverse driving events. J. Am. Geriatr. Soi. **46**, 562–568 (1998)
6. Charlton, J., Koppel, S., O'Hare, M., Andrea, D., Smith, G., Khodr, B., Langford, J., Odell, M., Fildes, B.: Influence of chronic illness on crash involvement of motor vehicle drivers. Report No. 213. Monash University Accident Research Centre, Victoria, Australia (2004)
7. Anstey, K.J., Wood, J., Lord, S., Walker, J.G.: Cognitive, sensory and physical factors enabling driving safety in older adults. Clin. Psychol. Rev. **25**(1), 45–65 (2005)
8. Dobbs, B.M.: Medical conditions and driving: a review of the scientific literature (1960–2000). Report No. DOT HSW 809 690. US Department of Transportation, Washington, DC (2005)
9. Eby, D., Molnar, L., Kartje, P.: Maintaining Safe Mobility in an Aging Society. Taylor and Francis, London (2009)
10. Boot, W.R., Stothart, C., Charness, N.: Improving the safety of aging road users: a mini-review. Gerontology **60**(1), 90–96 (2014)
11. West, C.G., Gildengorin, G., Haegerstrom-Portnoy, G., Lott, L.A., Schneck, M.E., Brabyn, J.A.: Vision and driving self-restriction in older adults. J. Am. Geriatr. Soi. **51**(10), 1348–1355 (2003)
12. Molnar, L.J., Eby, D.W., Zhang, L., Zanier, N., St. Louis, R.M., Kostyniuk, L.P.: Self-regulation of driving by older adults: a synthesis of the literature and framework for future research. AAA Foundation for Traffic Safety Website (2015). https://www.aaafoundation.org/self-regulation-driving-older-adults-longroad-study-0

13. Hutchinson, T.E., Massachusetts Institute of Technology. Department of Civil and Environmental Engineering: Driving confidence and in-vehicle telematics: a study of technology adoption patterns of the 50+ driving population, 98, [6] (2004). http://dspace.mit.edu/handle/1721.1/29389

14. Chihuri, S., Mielenz, T.J., DiMaggio, C.J., Betz, M.E., DiGuiseppi, C., Jones, V.C., Li, G.: Driving Cessation and Health Outcomes in Older Adults. AAA Foundation for Traffic Safety, Washington, DC (2015)

15. Brown, S., Venkatesh, V.: Model of adoption of technology in households: a baseline model test and extension incorporating household life cycle. MIS Q. **29**(3), 399–426 (2005). doi:10.2307/25148690

16. Carrigan, M., Szmigin, I.: In pursuit of youth: what's wrong with the older market (1999). doi:10.1108/02634509910285637

17. Czaja, S.J., Charness, N., Fisk, A.D., Hertzog, C., Nair, S.N., Rogers, W.A., Sharit, J.: Factors predicting the use of technology: findings from the Center for Research and Education on Aging and Technology Enhancement (CREATE). Psychol. Aging **21**, 333–352 (2006). doi:10.1037/0882-7974.21.2.33

18. Demiris, G., Rantz, M., Aud, M., Marek, K., Tyrer, H., Skubic, M., Hussam, A.: Older adults' attitudes towards and perceptions of "smart home" technologies: a pilot study. Med. Inform. Internet Med. **29**(2), 87–94 (2004). doi:10.1080/14639230410001684387

19. Melenhorst, A.-S., Rogers, W.A., Caylor, E.C.: The use of communication technologies by older adults: exploring the benefits from the user's perspective. In: Proceedings of the Human Factors and Ergonomics Society 45th Annual Meeting (2001). doi:10.1177/154193120104500305

20. Hopkins, C.D., Roster, C.A., Wood, C.M.: Making the transition to retirement: appraisals, post-transition lifestyle, and changes in consumption patterns. J. Consum. Mark. **23**(2), 87–99 (2006). doi:10.1108/07363760610655023

21. Niemelä-Nyrhinen, J.: Baby boom consumers and technology: shooting down stereotypes. J. Consum. Mark. **24**(5), 305–312 (2007). doi:10.1108/07363760710773120

22. Davis, F.D.: Perceived usefulness, perceived ease of use and user acceptance of information technology. MIS Q. **13**, 319–339 (1989)

23. Davis, F.D., Venkatesh, V.: A critical assessment of potential measurement biases in the technology acceptance model: three experiments. Int. J. Hum.-Comput. Stud. **45**(1), 19–45 (1996)

24. Davis, F.D., Bagozzi, R.P., Warshaw, P.R.: User acceptance of computer technology: a comparison of two theoretical models. Manag. Sci. **35**(8), 982–1003 (1989)

25. Venkatesh, V., Davis, F.D.: A theoretical extension of the technology acceptance model: four longitudinal field studies. Manag. Sci. **46**(2), 186–204 (2000)

26. Venkatesh, V., Morris, M.G., Davis, G.B., Davis, F.D.: User acceptance of information technology: toward a unified view. Inf. Manag. **27**(3), 425–478 (2003)

27. Pavlou, P.A.: Consumer acceptance of electronic commerce: integrating trust and risk with the technology acceptance model. Int. J. Electron. Commer. **7**(3), 101–134 (2003)

28. Carter, L., Bélanger, F.: The utilization of e-government services: citizen trust, innovation and acceptance factors. Inf. Syst. J. **15**(1), 5–25 (2005)

29. Karahanna, E., Straub, D.W., Chervany, N.L.: Information technology adoption across time: a cross-sectional comparison of pre-adoption and post-adoption beliefs. MIS Q. **23**(2), 183–213 (1999)

30. Adell, E.: Acceptance of driver support systems. In: Proceedings of the European Conference on Human Centred Design for Intelligent Transport Systems, Berlin, Germany, pp. 475–486 (2010)

31. Choi, J.K., Ji, Y.G.: Investigating the importance of trust on adopting an autonomous vehicle. Int. J. Hum.-Comput. Interact. **31**(10), 692–702 (2015)
32. Stanton, N.A., Young, M.S.: Driver behaviour with adaptive cruise control. Ergonomics **48**, 1294–1313 (2005)
33. Rudin-Brown, C., Ian Noy, Y.: Investigation of behavioral adaptation to lane departure warnings. Transp. Res. Rec. **1803**, 30–37 (2002)
34. Madigan, R., Louw, T., Dziennus, M., Graindorge, T., Ortega, E., Graindorge, M., Merat, N.: Acceptance of automated road transport systems (ARTS): an adaptation of the UTAUT model. In: Proceedings of 6th Transport Research Arena, Warsaw, Poland (2015)
35. Alessandrini, A., Campagna, A., Delle Site, P., Filippi, F., Persia, L.: Automated vehicles and the rethinking of mobility and cities. Transp. Res. Procedia **5**, 145–160 (2015)
36. Delle Site, P., Filippi, G., Giustiniani, G.: Users' preferences towards innovative and conventional public transport. Procedia-Soc. Behav. Sci. **20**, 906–915 (2011)
37. Venkatesh, V., Thong, J.Y.L., Xu, X.: Consumer acceptance and use of information technology: extending the unified theory of acceptance and use of technology. MIS Q. **36**(1), 157–178 (2012)
38. Ghazizadeh, M., Lee, J.D., Boyle, L.N.: Extending the technology acceptance model to assess automation. Cogn. Technol. Work **14**(1), 39–49 (2012)
39. Madhavan, P., Wiegmann, D.A.: Similarities and differences between human–human and human–automation trust: an integrative review. Theor. Issues Ergon. Sci. **8**(4), 277–301 (2007)
40. Lee, J.D., See, K.A.: Trust in automation: designing for appropriate reliance. Hum. Factors **46**(1), 50 (2004)
41. Muir, B.M.: Trust between humans and machines, and the design of decision aids. Int. J. Man-Mach. Stud. **27**(5–6), 527–539 (1987)
42. Lee, J.D., Moray, N.: Trust, control strategies and allocation of function in human-machine systems. Ergonomics **35**(10), 1243–1270 (1992)
43. Lee, J.D., Moray, N.: Trust, self-confidence, and operators' adaptation to automation. Int. J. Hum.-Comput. Stud. **40**(1), 153 (1994)
44. Parasuraman, R., Sheridan, T.B., Wickens, C.D.: Situation awareness, mental workload, and trust in automation: viable, empirically supported cognitive engineering constructs. J. Cogn. Eng. Decis. Mak. **2**(2), 140–160 (2008)
45. Kim, J., Moon, J.Y.: Designing towards emotional usability in customer interfaces—trustworthiness of cyber-banking system interfaces. Interact. Comput. **10**(1), 1–29 (1998)
46. Fogg, B.J., Marshall, J., Laraki, O., Osipovich, A., Varma, C., Fang, N., Paul, J., Rangnekar, A., Shon, J., Swani, P.: What makes web sites credible? A report on a large quantitative study. In: Proceedings of the SIGCHI Conference on Human Factors Computing Systems, pp. 295–299 (2001)
47. Karvonen, K., Parkkinen, J.: Signs of trust: a semiotic study of trust formation in the web. In: Smith, M.J., Salvendy, G., Harris, D., Koubek, R.J. (eds.) First International Conference on Universal Access in Human-Computer Interaction, Erlbaum, Mahwah, vol. 1, pp. 1076–1080 (2001)
48. Parasuraman, R., Riley, V.: Humans and automation: use, misuse, disuse, abuse. Hum. Factors **39**(2), 230–253 (1997)
49. Hoff, K.A., Bashir, M.: Trust in automation integrating empirical evidence on factors that influence trust. Hum. Factors **57**(3), 407–434 (2015)
50. Dishaw, M.T., Strong, D.M.: Extending the technology acceptance model with task-technology fit constructs. Inf. Manag. **36**(1), 9–21 (1999)
51. Karahanna, E., Agarwal, R., Angst, C.M.: Reconceptualizing compatibility beliefs in technology acceptance research. MIS Q. **30**(4), 781–804 (2006)

52. Parasuraman, R., Sheridan, T.B., Wickens, C.D.: A model for types and levels of human interaction with automation. IEEE Trans. Syst. Man Cybern. Part A: Syst. Hum. **30**(3), 286–297 (2000)
53. Moray, N., Inagaki, T., Itoh, M.: Adaptive automation, trust, and self-confidence in fault management of time-critical tasks. J. Exp. Psychol.-Appl. **6**(1), 44 (2000)
54. Inagaki, T., Itoh, M., Nagai, Y.: Support by warning or by action: which is appropriate under mismatches between driver intent and traffic conditions? IEICE Trans. Fundam. Electron. Commun. Comput. Sci. **90**(11), 2540 (2007)
55. Lee, C., Coughlin, J.F.: PERSPECTIVE: older adults' adoption of technology: an integrated approach to identifying determinants and barriers. J. Prod. Innov. Manag. (2014). doi:10.1111/jpim.12176
56. Hassan, H., King, M., Watt, K.: The perspectives of older drivers on the impact of feedback on their driving behaviours: a qualitative study. Transp. Res. Part F: Traffic Psychol. Behav. **28**, 25–39 (2015)
57. Demiris, G., Rantz, M., Aud, M., Marek, K., Tyrer, H., Skubic, M., Hussam, A.: Older adults' attitudes towards and perceptions of "smart home" technologies: a pilot study. Med. Inform. Internet Med. **29**(2), 87–94 (2004). doi:10.1080/14639230410001684387
58. Kang, H.G., Mahoney, D.F., Hoenig, H., Hirth, V.A., Bonato, P., Hajjar, I., Lipsitz, L.A.: In situ monitoring of health in older adults: technologies and issues. J. Am. Geriatr. Soc. (2010). doi:10.1111/j.1532-5415.2010.02959.x
59. Leonard-Barton, D.: Implementation characteristics of organizational innovations: limits and opportunities for management strategies. Commun. Res. **15**(5), 603–631 (1988)
60. Eby, D.W., Molnar, L.J., Zhang, L., St. Louis, R.M., Zanier, N., Kostyniuk, L.P.: Keeping older adults driving safely: a research synthesis of advanced in-vehicle technologies. AAA Foundation for Traffic Safety Website (2015). https://www.aaafoundation.org/keeping-older-adults-driving-safely-research-synthesis-advanced-vehicle-technologies-longroad-study
61. Duncan, M., Charness, N., Chapin, T., Horner, M., Stevens, L., Richard, A., Souders, D.J., Crute, J., Riemondy, A., Morgan, D.: Enhanced mobility for aging populations using automated vehicles. Florida Department of Transportation Website (2015). http://www.dot.state.fl.us/research-center/Completed_Proj/Summary_PL/FDOT-BDV30-977-11-rpt.pdf

Age Effects on Inattentional Blindness: Implications for Driving

Cary Stothart[1]([⊠]), Walter Boot[1], Daniel Simons[2], Neil Charness[1], and Timothy Wright[3]

[1] Florida State University, Tallahassee, USA
{stothart,boot,charness}@psy.fsu.edu
[2] University of Illinois at Urbana-Champaign, Champaign, USA
dsimons@illinois.edu
[3] University of Massachusetts Amherst, Amherst, USA
wright@umass.edu

Abstract. We may fail to notice things in our environment because our attention is directed somewhere else, a phenomenon called inattentional blindness. Our susceptibility to inattentional blindness increases as we age. We explored three potential moderators of the age and inattentional blindness relationship: (1) the spatial proximity of the unexpected object to our focus of attention; (2) the match between the features of the unexpected object and those we have prioritized—our attention set; and (3) the salience of the unexpected object. Using a large sample of participants, we found no evidence that any of these moderate the effect that age has on inattentional blindness; the effect of age is robust. We discuss the implications for older drivers.

Keywords: Aging · Attention · Inattentional blindness · Attentional breadth · Attention set · Salience

1 Introduction

We may fail to notice an object or event in our environment because our attention is directed elsewhere—a phenomenon called inattentional blindness [1, 2]. Even very consequential events such as a pedestrian walking in front of our car or a car merging into our lane may go unnoticed when our attention is directed elsewhere. In fact, we may miss something in front of us even if we're looking directly at it [3]; visual fixation does not guarantee detection.

We are less likely to notice an unexpected object as we age. When counting the number of ball passes made by a team of players in white shirts while ignoring the passes made by a team in black shirts, 60 % of younger participants, but only 10 % of older participants, noticed when a woman in a gorilla suit walked through the game [4]. And, when visually tracking white shapes while ignoring black ones, every 10 years of age predicted a 1.3-fold increase in the probability of missing a gray cross that traversed the display [5].

What moderates this age effect? One moderator that has been explored is spatial proximity; we are more likely to notice something the closer it appears to our focus of

© Springer International Publishing Switzerland 2016
J. Zhou and G. Salvendy (Eds.): ITAP 2016, Part II, LNCS 9755, pp. 441–448, 2016.
DOI: 10.1007/978-3-319-39949-2_42

attention [6, 7]. Given that our breadth of attention declines with age [8], are older adults exceptionally more likely to miss unexpected objects that appear away from their focus of attention? A large online study found no evidence of this: When tracking moving objects on a screen, the effect of age did not depend on how far away from an attended line the unexpected object appeared (see Fig. 1) [5].

Another possible moderator is attention set—the features we prioritize [9]. We're more likely to notice something when it matches our attention set. For example, attending blue makes blue things more noticeable. Attention sets also help us ignore irrelevant objects. If we're attending white while ignoring black, we're more likely to notice white things, but less likely to notice black things. Given that our working memory capacity—something that helps us ignore irrelevant information—declines as we age [10], older adults may be less able to maintain an attention set than younger adults. Only one study has so far explored this [11]. When tracking black shapes while ignoring white ones, the difference in noticing between white and black unexpected objects was 63 % for older participants, but only 25 % for younger participants. Despite these differences, the interaction between age and attention set was not significant. Further exploration is warranted, however, as the sample size used in the study was relatively small (∼20 per cell).

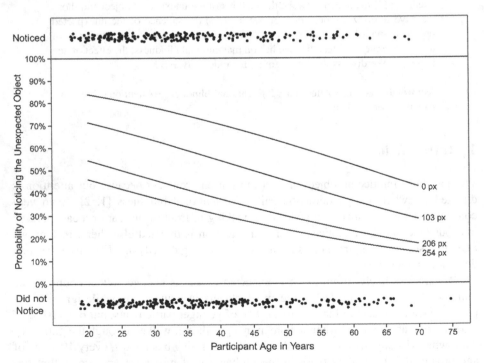

Fig. 1. The probability of noticing the unexpected object as a function of age and distance from the focus of attention. Originally appeared in Stothart et al. [5]. By Cary Stothart, Walter Boot, and Daniel Simons. Available under creative commons attribution 3.0 unported (http://creativecommons.org/licenses/by/3.0).

In an exploratory analysis, we assessed the interaction between attention set and age using a larger sample of participants. We also explored the interaction between age and spatial proximity using an unexpected object that appeared at a distance further away from the farthest distance used in Stothart et al. [5]. Finally, we explored a novel interaction: age by salience. We are less likely to notice salient unexpected objects than ones that match our attention set [9]. Given that our vision deteriorates with age [12], would older adults be exceptionally less likely to notice a distinctive unexpected object than one that matches their attention set?

In order to rapidly recruit our sample and collect data from a population more diverse than the typical undergraduate one, we crowdsourced data collection online using Amazon Mechanical Turk. Using a large sample also allowed us to use age as a continuous variable.

2   Method

The experiment took place online and participants completed it using their personal computers. The experiment was programmed in JavaScript, PHP, and HTML/CSS.

2.1   Participants

The analysis included data from 618 participants who were recruited and tested on Amazon Mechanical Turk (425 females, Mean Age = 33.74, *SD* = 11.30, Median Age = 30, *Min* = 18, *Max* = 71; Fig. 2 shows the age distribution). All participants lived in the United States, had normal or corrected-to-normal vision, were not color blind, passed an attention check test, and had not participated in a previous inattentional blindness experiment.

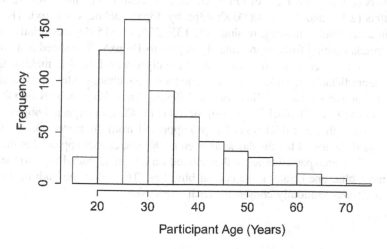

Fig. 2. Age distribution of the sample

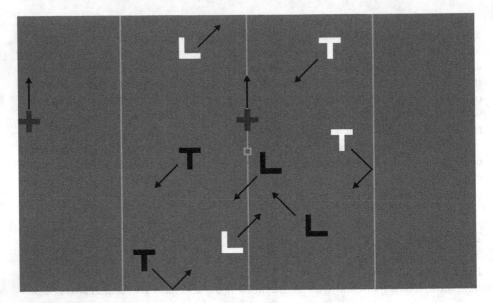

Fig. 3. The inattentional blindness task. The unexpected object was either a red, black, or white cross, and it could appear either on the attended line or away from it. Both paths are shown in the figure. (Color figure online)

2.2 Inattentional Blindness Task

Figure 3 shows the inattentional blindness task. Participants viewed a gray (#777777) 900px by 546px display that featured three vertical blue lines that spanned it (#0000FF; thickness = 2px). One line was positioned in the center of the display and the two others were positioned on opposite sides of the center line at a distance of 250px. In each of the three, 15-second-long trials, participants counted the number of times 4 white letters (2 L's and 2 T's; #FFFFFF) crossed the central blue line while ignoring 4 black letters (2 L's and 2 T's; #000000; 43px by 43px; thickness = 11px). The letters moved in a randomly-chosen direction (45, 135, 225, or 315 degrees relative to vertical) at speeds ranging from approximately 90px/s to 180px/s. The speed and direction of each letter changed randomly and independently every 1 to 4 s, making the trajectories unpredictable. Each letter was assigned a unique change interval, meaning that the letters changed speeds and directions at different times. Five seconds into the third trial, a white (#FFFFFF), black (#000000), or red (#FF0000) unexpected object (a 43px by 43px cross with a line thickness of 11px) appeared from the bottom of the display, moved toward the top of the display at a speed of 90px/s, and disappeared at the top of the display. The unexpected object either moved on a vertical path 157px to the left of the left-most blue line or along the central blue line. The color and path of the unexpected object was randomly chosen for each participant.

2.3 Procedure

Participants first completed the inattentional blindness task. They were then asked if they noticed the unexpected object. Regardless of their answer, they were asked if the unexpected object was moving, what direction it was moving in, what shape it was, and what color it was. Participants then answered a number of questions about their computer and demographics. Finally, they completed an attention check task where they chose the middle number in a list of numbers and entered it on the next screen.

3 Results

Participants were coded as having noticed the unexpected object if they reported noticing it and correctly answered one of the questions about its features. Using this scheme, 55 %, [95 % confidence interval: 51 %, 59 %] of participants noticed the unexpected object. We report the results using age as both a continuous and categorical variable.

3.1 Age as a Continuous Variable

Replicating previous experiments, older participants were less likely to notice the unexpected object, $B = -0.02$, $SE = 0.01$, $Odds\ Ratio = 0.98$, 95 % CI [0.97, 0.99], $p = .005$.

Attention Set. Replicating previous studies, the attention set participants adopted predicted noticing: Whereas 69 % [62 %, 75 %] of participants noticed the unexpected object when it matched attended items (the white letters; $n = 215$), only 17 % [12 %, 22 %] of participants noticed it when it matched ignored items (the black letters; $n = 200$), $B = 2.41$, $SE = 0.24$, $Odds\ Ratio = 11.18$, 95 % CI [7.05, 18.15], $p < .001$. This effect, however, was not moderated by age, $B = 0.01$, $SE = 0.02$, $Odds\ Ratio = 1.01$, 95 % CI [0.97, 1.06], $p = .650$.

Salience. The unexpected object was slightly more noticeable when it had a distinctive color (red; 78 % [72 %, 83 %], $n = 203$) than when it shared the same color with attended items (white; 69 % [62 %, 75 %], $n = 215$), $B = 0.46$, $SE = 0.22$, $Odds\ Ratio = 1.59$, 95 % CI [1.03, 2.48], $p = .039$. Age did not moderate this effect, $B = 0.01$, $SE = 0.02$, $Odds\ Ratio = 1.01$, 95 % CI [0.98, 1.05], $p = .469$.

Spatial Proximity. Noticing depended on whether or not the unexpected object appeared near the focus of attention: 62 % [57 %, 68 %] of participants noticed it when it appeared near the focus of attention ($n = 307$) and 48 % [42 %, 53 %] of participants noticed it when it appeared away from the focus of attention ($n = 311$), $B = 0.60$, $SE = 0.16$, $Odds\ Ratio = 1.81$, 95 % CI [1.32, 2.50], $p < .001$. This effect was also not moderated by age, $B = 0.01$, $SE = 0.02$, $Odds\ Ratio = 1.01$, 95 % CI [0.98, 1.04], $p = .411$.

Table 1. Noticing as a function of age group

Factor	Younger adults	Older adults	Y, O n
Attention set (Tracking White)			
White unexpected object	77 % [64 %, 87 %]	65 % [52 %, 76 %]	49, 60
Black unexpected object	18 % [10 %, 31 %]	7 % [3 %, 19 %]	50, 51
Spatial proximity			
Near	67 % [57 %, 77 %]	57 % [46 %, 68 %]	83, 82
Far	53 % [42 %, 65 %]	36 % [27 %, 47 %]	73, 80
Salience			
Salient unexpected object	84 % [72 %, 92 %]	65 % [51 %, 77 %]	57, 51
Set-matching unexpected object	77 % [64 %, 87 %]	65 % [52 %, 76 %]	49, 60

3.2   Age as a Categorical Predictor

Table 1 shows the noticing rates for each moderator. The youngest 25 % of participants were coded as younger adults ($n = 156$, Mean Age = 22.64, $SD = 2.03$, Median = 23, $Min = 18$, $Max = 25$) and the oldest 25 % of participants were coded as older adults ($n = 162$, Mean Age = 49.72, $SD = 8.19$, Median = 49, $Min = 39$, $Max = 71$). Participants between the ages of 25 and 39 were excluded from the analysis. Using this coding scheme, 61 % [53 %, 68 %] of younger participants and 47 % [39 %, 55 %] of older participants noticed the unexpected object, $B = 0.57$, $SE = 0.22$, *Odds Ratio* = 1.76, 95 % CI [1.13, 2.76], $p = .013$.

Attention Set. The difference between white and black unexpected objects was 58 % for older participants and 59 % for younger participants. This difference was not significant, $B = 0.33$, $SE = 0.77$, *Odds Ratio* = 1.39, 95 % CI [0.31, 6.79], $p = .672$.

Salience. The difference between salient and attention-set-matching unexpected objects was 0 % for older participants and 7 % for younger participants. This was also not significant, $B = 0.45$, $SE = 0.64$, *Odds Ratio* = 1.56, 95 % CI [0.45, 5.54], $p = .484$.

Spatial Proximity. The difference between near and far unexpected objects was 21 % for older participants and 14 % for younger participants. This difference was not significant, B 0.27, $SE = 0.46$, *Odds Ratio* = 1.31, 95 % CI [0.53, 3.24], $p = .564$.

4   Discussion

We are less likely to notice unexpected objects the more we age. And, we are more likely to notice unexpected objects the closer they are to our focus of attention and when they match the features we prioritize—our attention set. Although we replicated these three effects, we found that the effect of age on inattentional blindness is pretty robust—it does not depend on either the color of the unexpected object or its spatial proximity to the focus of attention. Furthermore, the pattern of results did not change depending on if we used age as a categorical or continuous predictor.

We found this despite using a much larger sample than ones previously used—the benefit of this being greater power to detect an effect and more confidence about the effect sizes. Although we collected our data online using Amazon Mechanical Turk, we replicated three in-lab findings. Additionally, Mechanical Turk has been validated on a number of other measures, including behavioral [13] and clinical ones [14]. Given this, it's unlikely that our results depended on the use of an online sample.

The topic of inattentional blindness is very relevant to driver safety; we can't respond to something on the road if we don't notice it. Indeed, "looked-but-failed-to-see" accidents—where a driver looks at, but fails to notice something on the road—may account for 69 % to 80 % of intersection crashes [15] and inattentional blindness is likely the cause of many of these. Therefore, the factors that predict inattentional blindness can likely be used to reduce traffic accidents [16]. For example, the attention set we adopt can substantially change our chances of getting into an accident. When looking for a yellow road sign, 36 % of participants collided with motorcycle when it was blue, but only 7 % of participants collided with it when it was yellow. As most drivers likely adopt an attention set for "car," making other roadway objects look similar to cars (e.g., motorcycles) may reduce collisions [16].

Although we know that age predicts inattentional blindness, there are likely additional individual differences that can tell us which older adults are more likely to get into a crash. One candidate is working memory capacity. In younger adults, working memory capacity may only predict noticing in specific contexts [17, 18] and for certain subsets of people [19]. However, it may predict overall noticing in older adults [20]. Indeed, studies finding lower inattentional blindness rates among those with higher working memory capacities tend to use samples with larger variabilities in age [21, 22]. Therefore, age's moderating effects on working memory capacity should be explored further.

In summary, the effect of age on inattentional blindness is robust to both attention set and spatial proximity to the focus of attention. In order to reduce roadway accidents, future research should explore additional factors that may moderate the age and inattentional blindness relationship.

References

1. Mack, A., Rock, I.: Inattentional Blindness. MIT Press, Cambridge, MA (1998)
2. Simons, D.J., Chabris, C.F.: Gorillas in our midst: sustained inattentional blindness for dynamic events. Perception **28**(9), 1059–1074 (1999)
3. Koivisto, M., Hyona, J., Revonsuo, A.: The effects of eye movements, spatial attention, and stimulus features on inattentional blindness. Vis. Res. **44**(27), 3211–3221 (2004). doi:10. 1016/j.visres.2004.07.026
4. Graham, E.R., Burke, D.M.: Aging increases inattentional blindness to gorillas in our midst. Psychol. Aging **26**(1), 162–166 (2011). doi:10.1037/a0020647
5. Stothart, C., Boot, W.R., Simons, D.J.: Using mechanical turk to assess the effects of age and spatial proximity on inattentional blindness. Collabra **1**(1), 1–7 (2015). doi:10.1525/collabra. 26

6. Newby, E., Rock, I.: Inattentional blindness as a function of proximity to the focus of attention. Perception **27**(9), 1025–1040 (1998)
7. Most, S.B., Simons, D.J., Scholl, B.J., Chabris, C.F.: Sustained inattentional blindness: the role of location in the detection of unexpected dynamic events. Psyche, 6(14) (2000). http://psycnet.apa.org/psycinfo/2001-03402-001
8. Ball, K.K., Beard, B.L., Roenker, D.L., Miller, R.L., Griggs, D.S.: Age and visual search: expanding the useful field of view. J. Opt. Soc. Am. A **5**(12), 2210–2219 (1988). doi:10.1364/JOSAA.5.002210
9. Most, S.B., Scholl, B.J., Clifford, E.R., Simons, D.J.: What you see is what you set: sustained inattentional blindness and the capture of awareness. Psychol. Rev. **112**(1), 217–242 (2005). doi:10.1037/0033-295X.112.1.217
10. Hertzog, C., Dixon, R.A., Hultsch, D.F., MacDonald, S.W.: Latent change models of adult cognition: are changes in processing speed and working memory associated with changes in episodic memory? Psychol. Aging **18**(4), 755–769 (2003). doi:10.1037/0882-7974.18.4.755
11. Horwood, S., Beanland, V.: Inattentional blindness in older adults: effects of attentional set and to-be-ignored distractors. Attention Percept. Psychophys. (2016). doi:10.3758/s13414-015-1057-4
12. Boot, W.R., Stothart, C., Charness, N.: Improving the safety of aging road users: a mini-review. Gerontology **60**(1), 90–96 (2013). doi:10.1159/000354212
13. Crump, M.J.C., McDonnell, J.V., Gureckis, T.M.: Evaluating amazon's mechanical turk as a tool for experimental behavioral research. PLoS ONE **8**(3), e57410 (2013). doi:10.1371/journal.pone.0057410
14. Shapiro, D.N., Chandler, J., Mueller, P.A.: Using mechanical turk to study clinical populations. Clin. Psychol. Sci. **1**(2), 213–220 (2013). doi:10.1177/2167702612469015
15. Cairney, P., Catchpole, J.: Patterns of perceptual failure at intersections of arterial roads and local streets. In: Gale, A.G. (ed.) Vision in Vehicles VI. Elsevier, Amsterdam (2015)
16. Most, S.B., Astur, R.S.: Feature-based attentional set as a cause of traffic accidents. Vis. Cogn. **15**(2), 125–132 (2007). doi:10.1080/13506280600959316
17. Kreitz, C., Furley, P., Memmert, D., Simons, D.J.: Inattentional blindness and individual differences in cognitive abilities. PLoS ONE **10**(8), e0134675 (2015). doi:10.1371/journal.pone.0134675
18. Beanland, V., & Chan, E. H. C. (2016). The relationship between sustained inattentional blindness and working memory capacity. Atten. Percept. Psychophysics, 1–10. doi:10.3758/s13414-015-1027-x
19. Seegmiller, J.K., Watson, J.M., Strayer, D.L.: Individual differences in susceptibility to inattentional blindness. J. Exp. Psychol. Learn. Mem. Cogn. **37**, 785–791 (2011). doi:10.1037/a0022474
20. O'Shea, D.M., Fieo, R.A.: Individual differences in fluid intelligence predicts inattentional blindness in a sample of older adults: a preliminary study. Psychol. Res. **79**, 570–578 (2015). doi:10.1007/s00426-014-0594-0
21. Hannon, E.M., Richards, A.: Is inattentional blindness related to individual differences in visual working memory capacity or executive control functioning? Perception **39**(3), 309–319 (2010)
22. Richards, A., Hannon, E.M., Derakshan, N.: Predicting and manipulating the incidence of inattentional blindness. Psychol. Res. **74**(6), 513–523 (2010)

Author Index

Printed in the United States
By Bookmasters